Around the world

in

65 years

Biku Ghosh

ISBN: 978-1-8381917-0-2

Dedication

To the future generation with sincere hope, they can enjoy the splendour of this world I have been so lucky to witness, and they try to protect nature in its diversity and address the injustices and sufferings of the fellow human being.

During my recent community volunteering, I have been spending time with an 83-year-old engineer with severe dementia who I learnt used to travel abroad a lot. He loved looking at the world maps and pictures of places. He could remember nothing but only had glimpses of memory hearing the names of places or seeing them on the map or in pictures.
He would say, 'I think I have been there.'

Soon as I began writing this book, memories flooded back with astonishing detail. I want to hold on to them and share it with the future generation.

'Memory is like fiction.'
— Haruki Murakami

Contents

It was all planned 2020

Part one: Early adventures 1955 – 1981

Learn to ride a running train if you want to travel. India. 1955. - Let's go to Darjeeling. India. 1964. - Enough of college routine - we are leaving. Nalanda. India 1965. - What about Kathmandu? Nepal. 1967. - The first taste of the real mountains. India. 1968. - Golden triangle mostly without a ticket. India. 1969. - Travels in South India. 1969. - First ascent and naming a peak in the Himalayas. India. 1971. - Attending the birth of a nation. Bangladesh. 1971. - Expedition to the 2nd highest mountain in India, Kamet. India. 1973. - A brief stint in the UK. 1974-77. – Ireland. 1976. - Hitchhiking in Europe (and almost thrown out of a train). 1977. - One day in Kabul. Afghanistan. 1977. - Burying dead cows after a super cyclone. Andhra. India. 1977.

Part two: Family and work travels, adventures and volunteering 1982 – 2013

Back to the UK. 1982-2020. - Italy. 1982. - Learning to ski from the children. Austria.1985. - Donegal, Ireland. 1986. - In search of rhino on elephant back. India 1991. - Bhutan. 1991. - John O'Groats. Scotland. 1993. - Cyprus. 1995. - Wales. 1997-2012. - Ailwee cave and the Ring of Kerry, Ireland. 1998. - Starting a health link in Ethiopia. 1999-2002. - New York, Boston, Salem, Las Vegas, Grand Canyon, New Orleans. The USA. 2001. - Cornwall, England. 2003. - Toronto, Montreal, Quebec, Rocky Train, Jasper, Spirit Island, Lake Louise. Canada. 2004. - Why not climb Ben Nevis? Scotland. 2005. – Climbing Kilimanjaro, Ngorongoro and Serengeti. Tanzania. 2006. - Sorrento, Mt Vesuvius, Pompeii, Amalfi, Syracuse, Catania and Mt Etna. 2007. - Everest Base camp. Nepal. 2008. - Washington DC, New Year's Ball drop in New York 2008-9. - Defeated in the Atlas Mountains. Morocco. 2010. - Health link grows in Ethiopia 2003 -12. - Prague, Czech Republic. 2010. - In search of a tiger. Sundarban India. 2011. - Climbing Stok Kangri 6153m. India. 2011. - Gibraltar. 2012. - On to the other side of the globe -Griffith, Uluru, Kings Canyon. Australia 2012 – 13. - Hawaii 2013.

My world stopped March 2013

Part 3: Retirement work, volunteering, adventure and travel 2013 – 2017
Pages 174- 365

Sharing the grief of the loss of a child. July 2013. - Scuba diving in Great Barrier Reef 2013. - NSW coast and Broken Hill 2013. - Broken jaw capital of the world, Darwin, Litchfield and Kakadu. Northern Territory. 2014. - Skydiving and white-water rafting, Queenstown. Milford Sound. New Zealand. 2014. - Kangaroo Island, Australia. 2014. - Chile, Galapagos, Peru - Machu Picchu. 2014. - Ajanta and Ellora caves, India. 2015. - World cup cricket final, Melbourne, Australia. 2015. - China, Tibet – Everest Base camp, Vietnam, Cambodia. 2015. - Murida's story. Back to Ethiopia. 2015. - Iceland. 2015-16. - Giant's Causeway, Northern Ireland. 2016. - Bolivia – volunteering in Penas, Tarija and Sucre province; Desert Mountain and Uyuni Salt Flat. 2016. - Iguassu Falls - Brazil /Argentina. 2016. - Paraguay 2016. Rio, Amazon forest. Brazil 2016. - Buenos Aires, Patagonia and Land's end Ushuaia - Argentina 2016. - A voyage to Antarctica 2016. - Aurora in Tromso, Norway. 2016-17. - With the young Reef Doctors. Madagascar. 2017. - Volunteering in Tanzania. 2017. - Finally meeting the tigers. Bandhavgarh. India. 2017. - Volunteering in Kerala. India 2017. - Denali Park and Singing to a grizzly in Brook's Falls. Alaska. 2017. - Almina Castle slave trade. Ghana. 2017.

My brain hurts - it's a bleed   Nov / Dec 2017

Part 4: Volunteering, adventure and travel 2017 – 2020
Pages 3 6 8 - 5 0 6

Volunteering in Rajasthan. India. 2018. - Moscow, Murmansk, Leningrad. Russia. July 2018. - Giving away a proxy daughter in a wedding on the North Pole. 2018. - Game Park, Cape Town and Hermanus. South Africa. 2018. - Volunteering in The Gambia 2018. - Volunteering in Sierra Leone. 2018. - Cuba, Costa Rica. Jamaica. 2019. - Brunei, Borneo, Tasmania. 2019. - Volunteering in Sierra Leone. 2019. - Uzbekistan, Kyrgyzstan. 2019. - Volunteering and adventure in Mongolia. 2019. - Travels in Europe: Germany, Sweden, Denmark, Finland, Estonia, Poland, Slovakia, Hungary. 2019. - Genocide museum Kigali. Volunteering in Kigali. With the Gorillas in the mist. Rwanda 2019. - Fall colours in Canada. 2019. - Death of a humanitarian. Sierra Leone. 2019. – Dubai. UAE. 2020. - Sleeping in an igloo under the Aurora Greenland Feb/ March. 2020.

It was all planned

March 2020

It was all planned.

Following my return from Greenland, I was returning to Sierra Leone in the last week of March, and then to Peru in mid-June, also for volunteering, followed by a tour of the Nazca Lines, Rainbow Mountain and the Easter Island. Everything booked and confirmed. I was also hoping to arrange a trip in between these, to Japan in May, to enjoy Sakura, the Cherry Blossom festival. And maybe a tour then to Jordan, Israel, Palestine and Egypt in the autumn.

But the world stopped. Covid-19 came.

Part one

Early adventures 1955 -1981

Learn to ride a running train if you want to travel

1955 Joteram, West Bengal, India

No one was looking for us - two eight-year-old boys, walking to the railway station only a kilometre from our village through muddy rice fields. We had done this few times already. Getting to the station before the passenger train arrived was important.

From our rooftop, we had watched with wonder trains speeding along. We had wandered close to the railway line at every opportunity – sensing the adventurous sensation of venturing away to a world beyond our imagination.

We were even lucky one day to climb up the engine room of a goods train with nineteen bogies when it had stopped by a level crossing. Men in the engine room were kind to let us two boys come up. We had looked in awe at one of them stoking the massive fire inside its boiler with coal. Few minutes being up there was enough to make us hungry to find what was beyond our daily routine, only if we could travel on these trains.

Only a few weeks back, my father had bought the first radio in our village. Neighbours and friends had gathered around every day listening to the voices coming out of this special box. We heard exotic names of faraway places such as Delhi, Bombay and Madras. My elder brothers talked about London and Paris they had heard on the radio and read in their history books, all in distant countries thousands of miles away.

No one had told us, but we agreed amongst us, Mantu and I, learning to get on and off a running train was a must before we grew up and travel to these places. The train stopped in the village station for only thirty seconds. In busy times often there was not enough time to board unless you knew how to jump in while it had already started.

Our small station did not have any platform. Soon we heard at a distance roaring of the steam engine. The hissing giant arrived, puffing away an impressive deal of smoke and pulling five passenger carriages. Both of us got ready, standing apart so we could hop into separate coaches as the train slowed. The trick was to run by the side of the slowing train and jump to its stairs before it stopped.

Both of us got on to the slowing train, this time with no problem. As the train stopped, we got inside the compartment to let passengers get off. Soon the station master waved his green flag, and the guard blew his whistle. We got ready down the steps to get off once the train started moving. Only now reverse the steps of getting into it. Mantu, as he ran, trying to keep his balance after jumping off, almost fell over today.

On the way back home, we agreed that we needed more practice.

Next day I was engrossed reading Ramayana on our roof when someone came up and said, 'Mantu had fallen from a tree. His bones were sticking out. They have taken him to the hospital.'

Mantu was the best tree climber of all the boys in the village, even the older ones. I thought he would be all right soon. But when he came back from the hospital two weeks later with a big plaster, I could sense he was different. He never climbed trees again, and there was no question of jumping into and from the running trains any more.

I knew then when I grow up; I would have to make my plans around the world, mostly on my own.

Let's go to Darjeeling

1963 December India

A new life in college was fun. It did not take long to make friends in the hostel.
Only after a few months, I suggested we should do something adventurous. 'Let's go to Darjeeling' I said.

It was going to be five of us, all recent friends. Living in the plains of West Bengal, we had no idea what it would be like in Darjeeling in December. We knew it was around the mountains so it will be colder than in Calcutta now in the mid 20°C. Each of us took a full sleeve jumper and a cotton wrapper. It was the first time any of us were travelling overnight by train and as a grownup. Soon the excitement of buying snacks and tea from the vendors wore out. We fell asleep. We reached Siliguri on the foothills in the early afternoon.

Toy train We changed from meter gauge train to 'Toy train'. The puffing steam engine pulled four coaches and after only a few miles, stopped at Sukna to take a breath and water before the real ascent began. We looked with awe through clouds at the blue mountain ranges on the north.
Soon the train moved through jungles. Nepalese passengers said it was not uncommon for a train to stop when elephant herds crossed the track. There were also tigers in these jungles, but you never saw them. The train passed through tea gardens crafted out on the hillside like shelves full of herbs and leaves. It stopped every station taking its breath and have water. View of the distant mountains and the deep valley in fading lights of the afternoon sun kept us speechless.

After Tindharia station in front was the impressive jagged rock-faced hills, Eagle's Craig. Here, with one driver standing on the side of the moving engine, the train started zigzag reverse through the rock face. The train stopped for water near Pagla Jhora (mad torrent). Now only a small waterfall, but during monsoon, it swelled up and often washed away the railway line.

Arriving at Kurseong station 1483m, the train drove straight through a market. Stalls split itself to allow the train to pass through and then again went back to as it was. Colourful Tibetan flags and scriptures in white on rocks marked the Buddhist shrines around the track. By the time we reached Ghoom 2258m, unbelievably, clouds were floating well below us. Most people left the train here. Even inside the compartment, we were now cold. Outside, soon was only black lumps of hills.

Darjeeling 2042m

We reached Darjeeling at 9 pm. All the shops were closed. December in Darjeeling was not the tourist season. We were lucky to find a small restaurant for food before it shut. They said there were no hotels open at this time of the year. We wandered around the deserted town, looking for a place for an overnight stay. Shivering with bitter cold, we found an area which looked like a weekend open market area. There was a closed shed on stilt. Five of us huddled together under it to keep warm.

Exhausted after travelling over 24hrs, we fell asleep, only to wake up when someone prodded us with a baton and shouted in Nepalese. A policeman was doing his last round and had found a few suspicious characters under the hut.

He took pity on us. Some stupid college boys from Calcutta on a whim had come to Darjeeling in the winter. We followed him as he knocked on doors of several hotels, with no answer. After a while, a bleary-eyed young man opened his door.

In Nepalese, he explained to the policeman his hotel was closed. But his ears pricked up as he heard us talking in Bengali. It turned out he was from Calcutta and was spending two months in his hotel for some repair works. He was glad to receive a few fellow Bengalis in this desolate place. We thanked the policemen from our heart and rushed inside.

We woke up to bright sunlight. After breakfast and coffee together, the junior hotel manager offered to show us around Darjeeling. At the famous mall, we gathered around the clock-tower before a stroll.

We looked with reverence at the ice-covered Kanchenjunga 8586m in front in all its glory. Walking across the mall, in every gap between the trees, we stopped sneaking at those peaks. Layers and layers of tea gardens lay below us. At another end of the mall stood the Himalayan Mountaineering Institute. We walked inside timidly along by the galleries of photos from famous Himalayan expeditions - and above all, pictures of Tenzing Norgay and Edmund Hillary. How could anyone dare to climb those peaks, I could not imagine.

After two lovely days in Darjeeling, our friend suggested as the weather was clear, we should go to Tiger Hill. He arranged a jeep for us and telephoned the only tourist lodge there was fortunately still accepting guests.

Initial travel from Darjeeling to Ghoom by car zigzagging up narrow mountain road was exhilarating, but soon became scary as we were climbing up a very steep narrow road. In less than two hours, we reached the lodge, the only place to stay on the Tiger Hill.

Tiger Hill – the best sunrise in the world

It was already getting dark and freezing cold. We were glad for the woollen rugs our Darjeeling friend had lent us. Even with the cold, I could not but step outside looking up in the sky at thousands and thousands of brilliant stars and the clearest ever Milky Way I have seen in my life. Inside the small lodge, we huddled around a fireplace with burning logs.

The hotel keeper woke us with hot cups of coffee before 4 am. We left by our jeep to the top of the hill. It was bitterly cold and harsh wind took our breath away. We were grateful to get inside a glass observatory for the view. It was still dark. Most of the stars were shining. The stars soon started fading slowly. At a distance, below us, were the rolling hills of Eastern Himalayas, all still clumped together in the dark. We were absorbed watching panorama of the eastern hills becoming easier
to separate from each other. I had a tap on my shoulder by our driver asking to turn back and look at the opposite direction. We turned to the west.

There, the first golden rays of the sun had transformed the peak of Kanchenjunga into a magical beauty. Peaks of Makalu and even the dark peak of Everest was visible and looked magnificent bathing in the first rays of the sun.

We turned to find that the sun was yet to rise on the east above the hills. We kept turning back to the west and then to the east to soak in the elegance of this sunrise. Soon the sun rose slowly above the hills, hundred shades of yellow, orange, pink and purple, clashing with each other to cover the eastern hills. Peaks in the west became brighter and brighter and imposing.

On the south, Kurseong town lay on lower hills, and beyond we could see the silvery strips of Teesta and Mahananda Rivers meandering down. We were all speechless for a long time. Later in my life, I had travelled all around the world. I had seen many sunrises, never better than one from the Tiger Hill.

Enough of college routine - we are leaving

1965 January Nalanda India

By the end of the first year at college, with monotonous routine, Naru and I were bored to the point of becoming boring ourselves.

The initial sense of fun being away from families and being 'independent' had now worn off. Fed up to our teeth, we decided to leave college and home. Monthly allowance from our parents had arrived in the last few days. We left for good with that money in our pockets.

We had not agreed upon where we were going but arrived in the evening at the busy Howrah station. Trains went from here in all directions to the rest of India. Like many, we knew of fascinating stories of Nalanda University, the oldest university in the world, its ancient sites excavated less than fifty years back. We bought one-way tickets to Nalanda. In the packed train with no place to sit, like many others, we sat on the floor.

Soon we were starving. Almost a third of our money had already gone into buying the tickets! In Burdwan junction station, we bought a few bananas and samosas. Nearly a third of our money had already gone into buying the tickets! Banana and a couple of samosas would never be enough for the two hungry eighteen-year-olds. A lady on a bench next to where we sat on the floor, opened boxes of food for her family. We were eternally grateful when she offered us some puris with dry aloo gobi.

We had fallen sleep on the floor and woke up with lots of noises. The train had reached Kiul Junction. We changed there and later got off at Rajgir. It was already dusk and in early January, freezing. With all our spare clothes on, we slept on the benches by the ticket counter. Next morning a brief bus ride took us to the ancient sites of Nalanda.

Nalanda was the first university in the world, founded in 5th Century BC. Buddha had visited Nalanda in his lifetime. At its peak, in 7th century AD, Nalanda University had 10,000 students and 2000 teachers. We were mesmerised by this ancient place where the university had lasted almost continually from 5th century BC until its destruction in 1202 by the Turkish invader, Bakhtiyar Khilji. It attracted scholars from as distant as China, Korea, Japan, Tibet, Mongolia, Turkey, Sri Lanka, Central and South-East Asia. Xuanzang, a famous historian of the time from China, visited Nalanda in 637 AD and again in 642 AD. He studied under the guidance of the ancient scholar Shilabhadra. He returned to China with Buddhist texts and relics and translated the manuscripts, thus bringing Buddhism to China.

We spent four days in Nalanda, immersed in its history and ancient sites. At the end of each day, we had our dinner of cheap dahl and roti at the local shop. We stayed up until the shop closed. Then we slept huddled outside the door under a tin roof. Nalanda in early January was bitterly cold.

We knew we did not have enough money to stay, even in the cheapest of the hotel nearby. By the end of four rough nights, we were exhausted from lack of proper sleep and any decent food. When we had discussed leaving home and college life, we had not thought about what we will do next for the rest of the days and months! And where would the money come from? We counted the money we had leftover. Just enough to buy return tickets to Calcutta, if we skipped all food. Nothing more, not even a visit to Rajgir, famous for its ancient Buddhist and Jain temples.

After being away for almost a week, we agreed to return to our boring hostel lives.

What about Kathmandu?

1967 December Nepal

'What about Kathmandu?' I asked Sanku.

We were waiting near our hostel to get on a bus to go to Calcutta Maidan to see a football match. He looked only slightly surprised, but promptly agreed. Paying our hostel and canteen dues for the previous month could wait. We did not have much money between us, but might just be enough. We returned to our hostel and hurriedly put warm clothes in our side bags. In early December we knew it would be cold - very cold.

The night train left Howrah station for Raxaul, at the border and gateway to Nepal. The 16 hours express train arrived only two hours late. By then, the last bus for Birgunj on the other side of the border in Nepal had left. We slept on the benches in the station.

Next morning, we got up to find puddles on the street after a rain in the night. The bus for Birgunj left soon. Within an hour, we reached the India-Nepal border. Loaded trucks crowded the place. We got out of the bus and walked through a gate to step into our first country outside India and soon arrived at Birgunj 3 km away. From this bustling Nepalese town, we took another bus for Kathmandu.

Last night's rain had cleaned up the surrounding air of its dust. Greens of the foothills stood out sharp and clear. The road narrowed, and we drove through several hairpin bends, crossing open hillsides with places where a drop over a thousand meters waited for a single mistake by our driver. Rice fields terraced side of the hills. Our rickety bus rattled tortuously upwards for nearly four hours before it stopped on a plateau. We all got out.

Daman - a glorious view of the Himalayan giant peaks
The bitterly cold wind hit us immediately. But we were speechless with the panorama of the majestic Himalayan peaks rising above the clouds, stretching over the horizon from left to right. Standing on top of this foothill in Daman at 2400m, glimpses of these distant peaks made them seem unreal.

A Nepalese man tried to name the mountains. Of all the fourteen summits above 8000m in the world, you could see ten of them from this spot. He pointed out Everest, Annapurna, Manasulu, Ganesh Himal,

Langtang, Dorje Lakpa, Gaurishankar, Cho Oyu and others.

Mesmerised, we could not take our eyes off the glorious view until the driver's assistant hurried us back into the bus. We sat in silence with the picture still in our minds, which would remain with me for the rest of my life.

Kathmandu 1400m

Kathmandu valley was below us. The bus drove down through dangerous roads for two and a half hours before reaching Kathmandu in the late afternoon. We needed to find a place to stay overnight. After asking at the shops, most closing down by then, we found a cheap place to stay away from the bus stand. By the time we reached there, the cold wind was making us miserable.

Luckily, in winter, the place was empty. The lady running the site asked us in Nepalese if we had eaten. We could understand most of what she said as Nepalese was close to Hindi. When we said we had nothing since the morning, she kindly offered us her home-cooked food for a minimal price. Boiled rice, dahl and then freshly cooked warm Momo. This popular dish of Nepal, a dumpling filled with meat and vegetables, with achar, a spicy tomato pickle, brought tears of joys in our tired eyes.

Next morning, we visited the Pashupatinath temple outside the city. Dating back to 400 BC, it was one of the four most important shrines of Hindu religion in the whole of the Indian subcontinent. According to legend, Shiva and Parvati came to Kathmandu Valley and impressed by the beauty of the valley, they transformed themselves into deer and lived in the forest. Lord Shiva was known as Pashupatinath, Lord of all animals.

This impressive complex with a pagoda-style main temple had over five hundred temples on the banks of Bagmati River. In one of its four entrances stood a colossal bronze statue of Nandi bull. Bagmati River was only a shallow stream with several cremations going on its bank. Next to the river and by the shrines were many Sadhus, Hindu religious men, covered in ashes with knotted hair.

We returned to the town centre, and after a cheap but hearty lunch, we visited the famous Durbar Square. We passed by Kumari Chowk, home of Nepal's living goddess, a young girl in her early teens. The inner complex of Durbar Square was the site of the Old Royal Palaces with fountains, old statues and courtyards of religious sites. In the outer part of the square stood many pagoda-style temples with delicately carved wooden facades. Most of these buildings were from the 16th-century, but the history of this site dated to the 3rd century AD.

Following day, we went to the impressive Boudhanath Stupa outside Kathmandu, one of the holiest Buddhist sites in Kathmandu. This 36m tall stupa, built on an octagonal base, was surrounded by many prayer wheels and images of Buddhist deities. Largest in the world, it had a giant dome on top of huge steps shaped like mandalas. Buddhist monks and pilgrims prayed, many prostrated by the stupa.

Back at Kathmandu, we walked to the impressive Swayambhunath Stupa, a holy site for Buddhists and Hindus. We strolled up its 365 steep steps. From trees on the side, monkeys tried to snatch food from the tourists. A golden spire crowned the stupa, with painted Buddha's eyes and eyebrows. Buddha's eyes looked in all four directions. Above each pair of eyes was another eye, the third eye of wisdom. There was no nose between the eyes but only drawing of the number one in Nepali alphabet, signifying the single way to enlightenment was through the Buddhist path.

Surrounding the stupa were many Buddhist shrines and prayer wheels, temples with statues of Hindu deities, and Shiva lingams. Hindu temples by this important Buddhist stupa showed the intermingling of Hinduism and Buddhism in the religious trends of Nepal.

On our return journey, the bus stopped only briefly in Daman. We rushed out to enjoy the magnificent panorama of the Himalayan peaks once again.

The first taste of the real mountains

April 1968 Garhwal Himalayas India

It had been my addiction, waiting to read the weekly Sport and Pastime magazine. A half-page advertisement there caught my eye. 'Basic Mountaineering course' at Nehru Institute of Mountaineering in Uttarkashi. The four week's course was starting in the third week of April for 300 rupees - a lot of money. After qualifying next year, as a medical intern, I would make only half of that in a month. But I could not get learning to climb mountains out of my head. Lofty peaks of Himalayas I had seen from Darjeeling, and on the way to Kathmandu, filled my dreams.

Over the weekend, I visited my parents and timidly mentioned this to them. Of course, I did not mention my fourth-year final exams will be only three weeks after I return. We were from a lower-middle-class family. I knew my parents had only been just about managing with expenses for bringing up seven children. To my surprise, my father agreed, he had never said no to me. My mother only asked if it was safe.

After a long train journey from Howrah, I arrived in Haridwar. The mighty Ganges, River Ganga, left foothills of the Himalayas here to start its 2400km journey towards the Bay of Bengal. Rishikesh by bus was only 20 km away and less crowded. River Ganga came here out of the mountain gorges in a torrent. Like others, I held on to a metal chain by the river to take a mini wash in the freezing water.

From there, a 170km bus journey took me to Uttarkashi following the side of mountain streams, now in outbursts from the melting snow in April.

Uttarkashi 1158m

By the time we arrived at Uttarkashi, the sun was setting over the hills. At Nehru Mountaineering Institute, I registered and was glad to go inside a dormitory in biting cold. A dinner of soup, rice, dahl and vegetable curry was served on aluminium mugs and plates. They told us it was our duty to keep them clean, as those will be for our personal use for the four weeks of the course.

After dinner, I was ready to go to sleep but was intrigued with talks from the other participants. Of the thirty in the group apart from myself, there were only three other private members. Rest of the team consisted of either Indian Infantry or Border Security Force. After a humiliating loss at Indo-China Border war of 1962, Indian authorities had realised the importance of its border forces to have mountaineering training to fight in the Himalaya.

Wake up call at 5 am with hot coffee poured in my mug started the day. We lined up to collect our kits. I had never seen a sleeping bag and felt high that a new adventurous life was beginning for me. Soon they said we would be a going for a short trek, and everyone must carry daily a minimum of 30kg. With all my gear and water, it was probably more than that. After collecting our packed lunches, we started our hike.

Going up and up on a hill with 30kg on my back was not something I was expecting. When we stopped for a break after almost forty minutes, I was out of breath. I thought to myself, what am I doing here? I was fit - I played sports regularly and could run around the football field 10-12 times to warm up with no problem. But this was something else. Surprisingly, after only a five minutes stop, I was ready again for the trek. After five hours of hike, we returned to the institute and enjoyed a hot mug of soup.

Trek to Gangotri

We left early next morning for Gangotri 94km away. Compared to the trek up the hill day before, walking through gentle slopes by the side of the river with beautiful views was a relatively straightforward walk. But even with a brief lunch break by the river where we washed our plates and cups after, by the time we reached Gangnani, 48km distance, we were all exhausted.

Here we learned to put up our tents, then helped with either the cooking, cleaning or general sorting out of equipment. For the first time, I saw apple trees, now full of small unripe fruits. In my three-person tent, shared between four, I got to know my tent mates for the next few weeks. Two of them were from the Border Force, and the other from the army. All three had families in the plains, and this was also their first encounter in the mountains. They gave me a special reverence calling me 'Doctor Saab' although I was still a medical student, and helped me a lot in the next three weeks when the trek got tough.

Next day we travelled through a steeper path for 28km to tiny Harsil village 2396m. Red-cheeked children ran around by the only small shop selling tea and snacks. The following morning after a leisurely breakfast we left for Gangotri 3415m only 18km away. We stopped several times on the way to enjoy River Ganga curving through and creating beautiful gorges in the rock.

At Gangotri, a renowned Hindu pilgrim site, most walked to pay their respect at the temple. From there, I walked with two others up to a cave where a Sadhu lived throughout the year, even in the harsh winter. He happily received the fruits which we brought with us. He said he had found peace and harmony with nature here after living for several years and wished us all the best with our ambitions. Our spirits lifted further when the thick cloud in the sky cleared to reveal at a distance the famous Bhagirathi peaks.

We packed our tents and set out early next morning for a 14 km trek to Bhojbasa 3775m. By now, carrying 30kg, even at this altitude on the rugged hike had become a routine. The journey became most enjoyable with an unobstructed view of the impressive and impossible looking Shivling Peak 6543m in full view and the Bhagirathi peaks 6454m at a distance.

Shivling   Bhagirathi Peaks

We, the aspiring novice mountaineers, talked amongst ourselves thinking of any route to the top of Shivling. We looked from all angles but did not see any! Our trainers said both British and German climbers had declared there was "no feasible route" on this mountain because of its steepness and threat of falling seracs.

Later in Bhojbasa and on next morning, we spent hours learning rock climbing attached to ropes. Now we were feeling like real mountaineers! While learning about 3 points climbing, making the best of any foothold or handhold and belaying was interesting, chimney climbing was exhausting. Abseiling was fun though.

Gomukh

After lunch, we trekked to Gomukh 4023m, only 4 km distance. As soon as we arrived, snow started falling. Being on the snow and ice for the first time in life was supposed to be a great experience. But we were all miserable, cold and wet. With frozen fingers, we somehow erected our tents and were glad when they offered hot soup from the kitchen tent. By 7 pm we were happily tucked in our sleeping bags, now in a two man's tent used by three.

In a bright morning, we walked over to the end of the glacier to have a look at 'Gomukh', beginning of the holy Ganga River. Lord Shiva had received the river in his matted locks (glacier?) at Gangotri. King Bhagirath prayed to Lord Shiva for the salvation of souls of his 60,000 sons. Shiva obliged and requested Goddess Ganga to release her water. This mythological story elevated the status of River Ganga to cleanse one's soul. Gomukh translated as the mouth of a cow; prime reason cow was sacred to Hindus.

Firm believers in the team tried to tell us, 'Look from this angle or that. It exactly looks like the mouth of a cow.'

I could not see any real resemblance, but it was spectacularly beautiful. As the day was about getting used to the altitude and drying out our damp clothes with light training, few wanted permission to immerse in the sacred water. I only washed my face in the icy glacial water, and immediately decided against a dip. Religion was never my thing - suffering for its cause was not on.

Clouds gathered again in the afternoon, which seemed to be the usual pattern. Soon snowing started. We were now better prepared and had fun, like children, we threw snowballs at each other. After dinner, we rubbed our mugs and plates with snow to clean and were in our sleeping bags by 7 pm.

Trekking up next morning on the glacier, we were awestruck by the crevasses of various sizes and depths. Later they lowered us down into an abyss. Inside the blue walls of ice, it was a world beyond imagination. For the rest of the day, we learned ice crafts - how to cut steps on steep slopes, fix ropes with ice pitons and to cross large crevasses with rope ladders. Now we were feeling like proper mountaineer ready for a decent climb!

Trail next day to Tapovan was the most challenging so far. We climbed over glacial moraine, stepping carefully on scree slopes and traversing the glacier. We rushed across steep avalanche-prone areas after survival training in case we faced one sweeping us. Trekking through a combination of hard ice and slippery boulders was tricky. So far we have been climbing in the terminal moraine next to Akash Ganga, Ganga in the sky, which flew vertically down a rock face. Avoiding occasional rock falls from above, three men attached to a rope, we crossed Akash Ganga. After a quick break, a steep climb towards Tapovan 4407m. Everyone was by then exhausted and glad to pitch tents. The afternoon was luckily free of cloud and snow. Views from the campsite of the Shivling peak and the peaks of Meru and Sumeru were magnificent. On the other side, the Bhagirathi peaks were as beautiful as ever.

The first ascent of a mountain peak

In mess tent, they announced tomorrow we would attempt to climb an unnamed peak. We would leave around 4 am to avoid falling loose rocks with the warming morning sun. By 6 pm we returned to our tent all excited. In cramped space inside, we got our climbing gears ready. It was -15°C when unfortunately I had to get out for a toilet in the middle of the night. With all the excitement, I could not get back to sleep.

Before 4 am, we were all geared up and shivering in our borrowed mountain clothes. Soon, six of us in each group started the climb following our group leader, only one with a head torch. Our concentration was on following his trail of light at this high altitude. After almost two hours, it got lighter. During a break there, the trainer said at this rate, in another three hours we should be at the top. Although we could not see the peak from there, this energised us enormously. We started again. Just before 9 am, we reached the top of an unnamed peak. Our trainer took out his altimeter. We were at 5267m! We congratulated each other and spent a long time soaking in the magical view of the world below and front.

Going down over ice and loose rock was more than challenging, but we were high on spirits. Then easy descent from Tapovan to Bhojbasa with only a brief stop at Gomukh. We chatted all the way excitedly and even at night in the tent we could not stop. After two more days of trekking, we returned to warm Uttarkashi. Next day we returned our gears and the winter-proof clothes.

Entire experience reached its zenith in the afternoon. With others, I received a certificate of completion of the mountaineering course. Brigadier Gyan Singh, Leader of the first-ever successful All Indian expedition team climbing the Everest, pinned a commemorative medal of an ice axe on my chest.

The Golden triangle mostly without a ticket

(only caught once!)

March 1969 Rajasthan, Agra and Delhi India.

I was never good at table tennis. Yes, I loved to play. We played till late in the night in the common room. A letter came to the students' union inviting teams for an All India Inter Medical College Table Tennis tournament in Delhi. None from our college was interested, all busy with the finals coming in 4 months. Only five of us, all close friends, were ready to go. Sanku had won college championship, and Alfaz had reached the semi-final - legitimate grounds to represent our college. But for the rest of us, Balak. Kanu and I were keen, but not good.

Sanku, Balak and I travelled to Rajasthan and Agra before the tournament. Alfaz and Kanu had family commitments and planned to join us in Delhi before the competition.

Three of us left with only one side bag between us with the documents from our college for the event and a few underpants, no extra clothing. We wore a pair of jeans which did not need washing for days. Sanku and I had dark shirts, Balak, a white top to look savvy. Other two agreed to bring the TT rackets and our sportswear with them.

Between us, we had very little money. No way could we afford the full ticket fare for the 1500km journey to Jaipur, our first destination. We decided to try as much as possible going without tickets. The train left Howrah before midnight, teeming with people. We were glad we had bought tickets for up to the next stop, as within twenty minutes a ticket collector appeared. After he left, we discussed whether we should try to buy a ticket at the next stop or not. But when the train arrived at Burdwan, the place was quiet. No sign of authority anywhere. We took a chance going without to save money.

After a long nap, sitting and half lying on the floor, we woke up to sounds of vendors. We bought tea and debated about spending money buying a few bananas for breakfast.

In the late morning, the train slowed down and entered Mughal Sarai junction station. Even before the train had stopped, several ticket collectors with the railway police got into the train. Special Magistrate checkers caught us without a ticket. They ignored our plea and put us in a police cell on one platform. Through metal bars on the window, we watched our train slowly leaving the station. In a dark cell, apart from us, there were fifteen other people. Half an hour later, two railway policemen opened the door and marched us to an office where a ticket inspector had just opened his tiffin box.

We pleaded our innocence in broken Hindi and Bengali interspersed with some English words. He looked at us with pity and asked what our job was. We said we were students at the Calcutta Medical College. He laughed with disbelief. But luckily the certificate from our college about the tournament seemed to satisfy him. By then, he had also finished his tiffin. He asked us to pay five rupees each towards fine for travelling without a ticket. Police then escorted us outside the station.

Once outside, we checked the time for the next train to Jaipur, which was due a few hours later in the evening. After all the excitement of the day, by now, we were famished. Outside the station, we found a jhupri selling roti and tarka dahl for next to nothing. We sat down under a tree and counted all the money we had left.

Not much. We agreed we did not have enough money to pay for the full fare to Jaipur and then return via Delhi. Only two choices - go back to Calcutta, which we discarded quickly. Another option was to be cleverer going without a ticket.

We bought a ticket for each of us for the next junction station, knowing that the train will arrive there around midnight. Most likely there would be no ticket collectors in late night. From then on we waited for the train to slow down before any junction station before jumping off the train. Then we walked casually by the railway line to get to the platform to catch the same train. The tactics worked. By late morning we got off the slowing train before it reached Jaipur station and walked into the city through a level crossing.

Jaipur   The Pink City of Jaipur, was amazing with geometrically designed boulevards and beautiful pink buildings and ornate arches. Jantar Mantar, the largest human-made sundial in the world, built two centuries back, was most impressive. Even modern scientists cannot fault its accuracy.

Late in the day, we arrived outside Hawa Mahal, the Windy Palace. Magnificent Pink Palace looked stunning in the glowing lights of the late afternoon sun. Now tired and hungry, we had a strategy meeting. We agreed with the money we had left; we could only spend one rupee per day for the three of us towards food if we want to see more of Rajasthan. We had already decided we would spend the nights outside the shop arches as it was still warm in the evening. After some chapatti, dahl and a banana each, we were ready to go to sleep. But unfortunately, in Jaipur, shops didn't close until after ten in the evenings! Then we slept soundly on the floor outside a shop. Luckily the shop didn't open till after nine in the morning.

In the morning we walked to the railway station washroom. There we had a shower, and with no towels, we just put on our clothes on our wet bodies to dry.

Arriving at Jaipur Palace, we were amazed at the grandeur of architecture, majestic windows and turrets. An unbelievable lavishness of the Kings who built this place combining Mughal, British and Rajasthani architecture. We sneered at the luxury of a massive 800 Gallons silver yarns brought along by a King from England. Only so he could wash every day in Ganges water stored in it! It was incredible seeing the vast courtyard marked as a giant chessboard. Actual soldiers, knights and elephants took part in the game, watched by the King from his balcony!

From the city, we took a bus to Amer Fort. Public bus fare, fortunately, was next to nothing. This red stone and marble fort set on a hillside by the Maotha lake was imposing. From the gate, many took an elephant ride up the windy path. We plodded along on foot. The palace was laid out on four levels, Diwan-e-Aam, Diwan-e-Khas, Sheesh Mahal, and Sukh Niwas (happy palace) - the life of a King at the expense of so many!

Pushkar   Back in Jaipur, we waited for the shops to close for our sleep. Early the next morning a four hours bus took us to the ancient city of Pushkar, bordering the Thar Desert. The town was on the Pushkar Lake, a sacred Hindu site with 52 ghats where pilgrims bathe. After a lengthy bus journey in the desert heat, we were drenched and took a dip with our clothes on, more for a chance to clean ourselves than for spiritual reasons.

Peacocks wandered the area, India's national bird we saw for the first time. Amongst hundreds of temples in Pushkar, most revered was the Brahma Mandir, dedicated to the god of creation. The temple walls were inlaid with silver coins. Pilgrims threw coins at the temple. We wished we ould collect some to boost our budget. Sleeping outside a shop front here was rather cold from the desert chill. Next day a bus took us to the hilltop Hindu temple of Savitri, first wife of Brahma. From there we enjoyed the sweeping views of the Thar Desert valley.

Chittorgarh Fort   Next morning, after another dip in the Pushkar Lake, we took a bus to the famous Chittorgarh Fort. By the time we reached, after a roadside tyre puncture, it was already late afternoon. We wandered around the town below the fort, rising sharply above us on the only hill in the plains of a vast valley. Built over a thousand years back by the legendary Maurya Empire, it was one of the largest forts in India. Against the setting sun, it looked exceptional.

After a steep spiral ascent of over 1 km from the plains, the next day, we arrived at the impressive limestone main gate. Chittorgarh had seven massive stone gates in succession, with secure fortifications for defence.

As we wandered inside this fort, standing 180m from the ground, we tried to remember its history of undergoing many sieges over centuries. This fort boasted of water bodies fed by natural rainfall catchment with combined storage to meet the water needs of an army of 50,000 for four years. In 1303, Alauddin Khalji, Sultan from Delhi led an army and captured Chittore after an eight-month-long siege and ordered the massacre of 30,000 Hindus.

According to legends, all this was to capture Padmini, Ratnasimha's beautiful queen. Padmini and many other women saved themselves by committing suicide by Jauhar, throwing themselves to a funeral pyre. Next, we visited there the temple of Meera Bai, most famous female Hindu spiritual songwriter, whose compositions are still popular.

Udaipur   In an overcrowded local train next day to Udaipur, we got away without a ticket like most of the passengers on the train. This beautiful city of lakes with a backdrop of mountains and its historical palaces was beyond expectation. A few centuries back five major contiguous lakes were artificially created, to provide water supply to the newly formed capital of Mewar Empire. Beautiful white marble Lake Palace in Lake Pichola was glowing with the rays of the setting sun.

Next day we took a ferry to Lake Palace. Its walls were made of black and white marbles and adorned in the past by semi-precious stones. Successive rulers used this palace as their summer resort. We heard rumours the place would soon be turned into a tourist hotel. After another full day in Udaipur, we left Rajasthan for Agra as the table tennis tournament was only a few days away.

After a shower in the morning in the railway washroom, we washed our only shirts with running water and then rinsed by hand. Sanku and I were glad we were wearing dark shirts. But Balak's white cotton shirt, after days of grime, looked like pigeon drippings on a white wall. It looked even worse once it dried up. Our unwashed blue jeans were not only comfortable but were easily hiding the dirt.

We had planned to take a train to Agra in the early evening to avoid ticket inspection issues. By boarding time, Balak was missing. We searched inside and outside and then looked in the park by the station. There he was. Lying prostrate on a bench and snoring happily. We woke him up and only got to our train just in time. By now we had almost perfected our low or no cost train travelling routine. With ticket only for the next station, we snoozed happily seated on the floor of a crowded third-class compartment.

One thing about travelling in Indian trains in the night was there were always families with home-cooked food. The kind lady on the bench next to where we were sitting on the floor, smiled at us. We instantly knew we were in luck. She offered us puri and aloo, most welcome as we had not eaten anything except a banana each the whole day. Balak soon fell sleep under a bench while the two of us nodded off on the floor.

We woke up with all the hustle as the train slowed down, entering Agra junction. We quickly got ready and with practised ease got off the moving train well before it reached the platform.

Agra Who has not heard about Agra from their history book? But being there, now we were very disappointed to find how dirty the city was. We walked from the town to the historic Agra Fort, the residence of Mughal Emperors with the most impressive architecture inside. Intricate white and red marble engravings, some like beautiful lace curtains, were beyond belief. It was touching looking at Taj Mahal at a distance on the banks of Jamuna from the window in the room where Shah Jahan spent the last months of his life under house arrest.

By late afternoon we reached outside the gates of Taj Mahal. Sanku and I wanted to go inside straightway while Balak wanted to have a look at the souvenir shops to buy something for his girlfriend back in Calcutta. He was the only one amongst us who could boast a girlfriend!

Once inside, the magical beauty of Taj Mahal was mesmerising. Its white marble was glowing in the late afternoon sun. We sat quietly on a marble bench, just enjoying the experience.

A desperate cry for help from Balak by the main gate broke our reverie. A policeman was escorting him. Apparently, as he wandered around shops, he was caught by the police suspecting him to be a pickpocket! His dirty white shirt and uncertain movement had added to the suspicion. Once apprehended, he had tried to convince the policeman in his broken Hindi he was a medical student. Not believing this dirty, smelly boy, police had asked him to name the medicine for the treatment of gout. The policeman knew about this through his personal suffering. Our friend had shouted out the pharmacological name of the drug for gout, which had sounded nothing like the drug the policeman used.

Just as they were bundling him into a police van, he had remembered to tell them he had two friends waiting inside the gates of Taj Mahal. The police asked us to confirm his story. We showed him our medical college letter, and he was released.

Three of us walked to the mausoleum of Mumtaz Begum lying next to her beloved husband, Shah Jahan. Its beautifully carved marble inside, originally inlaid with precious jewels, was later looted by the British invaders.

With the pink evening clouds, the palace turned itself into a fairy castle. Soon, Taj Mahal took on a faint golden yellow glow from the full moon in the sky above. The palace of love became genuinely magical. We spent spellbound until it was time for the site to close.

Delhi   A crowded passenger night train to Delhi helped us travelling without tickets. In the morning, we arrived at the doctor's residence of the All India Institute of Medical Sciences. Two senior colleagues from our medical college now worked there and had agreed for us to stay with them when we had written earlier. First, they took us to the canteen, and after over a week we gulped into proper food, paid by them. After showing us to their room, looking at our dirty clothes, they lent us some clean shirts and trousers. Then they left for the day for their duties. Three of us took turns in having a proper shower and washed our clothes with soap and let them hang to dry outside.

Suddenly complete exhaustion took over, and we decided to have a nap. I slept on the floor while the other two slept in the two single beds in the room.

I was woken up suddenly from my deep sleep with the voice of Balak saying, 'Oh no. No. No.'
At first, I thought he was talking in his sleep. But soon I woke up to find he was sitting on his bed, shamefaced.

Apparently, with the comfort of a proper bed after so many rough days and nights, he has wet himself. Luckily, it was very sunny outside. While he washed his clothes and bed sheet, we carried the mattress out to dry.

Later in the evening, we walked to Chandni Chowk in Old Delhi. This three-centuries-old busy market with its old street and bazaars reminded us of parts of old Calcutta. We passed through smells of attar at Dariba Kalan markets selling gold, silver and pearl jewellery; varieties of spices and beautifully embroidered clothes made of silks, satin, cotton and muslin. Later we walked to the Old Delhi Railway station where our two friends from Calcutta were arriving. After travelling almost 1500 km, they arrived only two hours late.

The tournament was starting in two days. We left the next day to see the famous Red Fort also built by Shah Jahan. While our two new arrivals marvelled at this three centuries old red marble stone fort, we said we had seen better in Rajasthan, to make them jealous.

Then we visited Qutub Minar. This 83m tall, beautiful Minar built in the 13th century took our breath away. We were delighted to climb its spiral staircase to the top floor and have a glorious view of Old Delhi. In the wide, well-planned roads of New Delhi, the traffic was awful. Soon we visited the Parliament House, built only over thirty years back, the seat of the largest democracy in the world.

It was time to get ready for the tournament. Over 200 participants from all over India, attended. I, with three others from our college, was knocked out in the first round - not surprising. We cheered Sanku for two more rounds before he too lost to the eventual champion.

We returned to Calcutta paying full fare courtesy of our two late-arriving friends. In a crowded third-class compartment of a passenger train, we spent sitting or sleeping on the floor for the 36 hours' journey.

Travels in South India

August 1969

Final exams were over. I was now a doctor! There were still a few weeks before starting my pre-registration job. I planned to travel southern part of India, to the southern tip of India, Kanyakumari, 2400 km from Calcutta.

Howrah to Madras, 1700Km distance was only 32 hours by train. Shouts of 'Chai, Chai' woke me up at Vizianagram in the morning. After a cup of tea and a loaf of bread, half asleep I watched our train getting into Vishakapatnam, known as Vizag popular for its beautiful beaches.

The train slowed down to a red signal next to a village. I noticed big red mounds of something outside most of the cottages, almost as high as these huts themselves. I asked a local passenger who explained they were red chillies being dried in the sun by the families. I gulped and tried to imagine what the food would be like from now on.

After another 15 hours, we arrived at Madras Central, only two and a half hours late, two hours before the sunrise. I slept on a bench until hundreds of people came rushing and shouting to board their morning trains.

Madras   This city was not that much different from Calcutta, a mixture of crowded streets with people hanging out from overloaded buses, rickshaws and occasional taxis. After a leisurely breakfast of Idli and Sambar, I walked a few kilometres to the Portuguese built 16th century San Thome Church. I rested inside, looking at the beautifully painted glass windows with Bible stories.

It was scorching, but luckily soon it rained a bit. Next, I went to the Kapaleeshwarar temple, a large 12th century Shiva temple complex, built in typical Dravidian architectural style. I could not take my eyes off from its massive 37m Gopuram, gateway tower with stucco religious figures representing religious stories.

By the time I returned in central Madras, it was dark. A meal of Dosa, Sambar, vegetable curry, yoghurt and spicy chutney served on a banana leaf was not only big enough to fill my stomach but cost next to nothing. Madras, close to the equator and near the coast, was hot in the night. I slept the night happily on a bench in a park.

Marina Beach next morning was only a 5km walk. The train from Howrah had followed the Eastern Coast of India and came within a few miles from the sea. But this was the first time in my life I was by the sea. The vast Indian Ocean, with its gentle waves and warm water, was inviting. It did not take me long to leave my small backpack and clothes by the shore to jump into the water. I did not have a towel and did not need one either as the scorching sun dried me up immediately. I washed up my only spare shirt and trousers in the sea. Left on the sand, they dried within minutes. Apart from a quick break for a cheap lunch, I kept walking and diving back in the water. This 7km long beach was the 2nd longest in the world.

I stayed in an open place for the night and fell sleep with the sounds of the crashing waves. I got up early before the sky was light and sat down, watching the most beautiful sunrise over the Indian Ocean. After a few more dips in the sea, I walked back to Madras by late morning.

Mahabalipuram Shore Temple   Next day I arrived at Mahabalipuram, 56 km by bus. This shore temple complex was built in the coastline of Bay of Bengal in the 8th century. Early explorers like Marco Polo and later European merchants called the site Seven Pagodas because of its style.

Built with blocks of granite, these temples seen today were part of a more massive complex, much of which remained submerged in the sea. I spent most of the day at this beautiful site numb with admiration.

Pondicherry   In the afternoon, I took a bus along the coast to Pondicherry, 100km distance. This small enclave on the eastern coast had changed hands among the French, British, Portuguese and Dutch colonists several times between the 17th and 19th century. It remained a French Colony until 1954, seven years after the independence of India. Growing up, like all Bengali, I had heard of this place associated with Sri Aurobindo Ghose. This revolutionary believed, at the beginning of the 20th century, that only way to free India from the British yoke was for people to embark upon a total revolution. He espoused approach for an armed rebellion, also to organise the masses for non-cooperation and passive resistance against foreign rule - a decade before Gandhi returned to India from South Africa to start his passive resistance movement.

Pondicherry was striking because of its cleanliness compared to what I was used in the rest of India. Sri Aurobindo Ashram by the seashore offered free food to visitors. I was grateful. After sleeping at a park, I got up early to catch another glimpse of the magical sunrise on the Bay of Bengal. Later I walked to Arulmigu Manakula Temple, a stone-built Hindu temple for Lord Ganesha. At the gate, an elephant was giving blessings to anyone who was giving it food and money. The animal cleverly gave the money to its keeper before eating the food. Then gave the nod with its trunk to the visitor. I returned to the Ashram in time to have a free, hearty lunch. Then I strolled by the seashore most of the afternoon before another free meal. Later, I got into a night bus for the ancient city of Madurai 300km away.

Madurai   I slept soundly until the bus reached Madurai city on the banks of Vaigai River. From a distance, I could see many colourful gopurams dominating the skyline, lit by the early morning sun. Madurai's history dated back to 300BC. Pilgrims from all around the world came to pay a visit to Meenakshi Amman Temple.

This Dravidian-style temple was dedicated to Meenakshi, a form of Parvati, and her consort, Sundareshwar, a form of Shiva. Meenakshi meant 'fish-eyed'. Along with many other temple towns of South India, this temple complex with its riches of gold, silver and precious jewellery was looted and destroyed in the early 14th century by the Delhi Sultanate army.

The current temple was rebuilt in the 16th century. The shrines spread over 14 acres inside three walled enclosures. Each of these had four gateways, outer tower growing larger and reaching higher to the corresponding inner one. It had 14 gopurams up to 50m high, each a multi-storeyed structure, covered with sculptures painted in bright hues. Four tallest gopurams on the outer walls alone depicted nearly 4,000 mythological stories. Temple complex here also housed temples of Lakshmi, Krishna, Brahma, Saraswati and other Vedic and Puranic deities – mind-blowing.

Only Hindus were allowed inside the temple. I have been a non-believer since age eight. But I looked like a Hindu and had no problem getting in. Inside the shrine, adorned with jewellery and fresh garlands, a green stone image of Meenakshi stood in a bent-leg posture.

(Almost) dying for a meat curry   So far, I had been happily gorging on very cheap or free south Indian vegetarian food. It was hot and spicy, but you could cool it down with plain yoghurt served with most meals. But I have had no meat or fish for over a week! I had not come across shops selling anything but vegetarian food either. Walking outside the walls of Meenakshi Temple, in a narrow street, I came across a small shop selling meat curry! I was in heaven. Sitting inside the dour place, I waited for my heavenly food to arrive, plain rice and meat curry. Once the food arrived, I put a bit of meat curry with rice in my mouth, and I almost died. It was extra extra hot and spicy! Almost choking, I drank a lot of water. Too hot to handle! But I had already paid, and it was meat, there was no question of giving up. With tears rolling down my face, somehow, I finished everything.

Rameswaram   Next day I took a 175 km train to Rameswaram Island, between peninsular India and Sri Lanka. The train crossed over the open sea on a long railway bridge. Sea waves crushed from both sides. Half an hour later, we reached Rameswaram at the eastern edge of the island. Ramanathaswamy Temple was dedicated to god Shiva, one of the four holiest Hindu sacred sites in India. According to the legend of Ramayana, Rameswaram is where Rama built Rama Sethu, a bridge across the sea to Lanka to rescue Sita from Ravana. After slaying Ravana, Rama returned here and offered his repentance prayer to Lord Siva to absolve his sins he had committed by killings in the war.

Rama wanted to have a large lingam (phallus symbol) to worship Shiva. He asked Hanuman, the monkey general, to bring a lingam from Kailash in the Himalayas. Hanuman was late arriving, and Rama's wife Sita built a small lingam out of sand from the seashore. There are now two lingams inside the sanctum - one made by Sita from sand and the one brought by Hanuman from Kailash known as Vishwalingam.

A famous festival was due at this temple in two days. Rameswaram was already buzzing with devotees. I stayed for a few days to enjoy the atmosphere. During free meals at the temple, I came across a Bengali family travelling around south India. This family, with a teenager boy and a girl of eight, took a liking to me, a young doctor from the same state. More so, as I was the only person, they could speak Bengali to since they left Calcutta. Next few days, I wandered the beautiful pillared corridors, carved with original compositions. Including the inner halls, the total length of these passages was over 1175m, longest in the world. It was peaceful and relaxing, even if you are not religious.

Thirukalyanam festival annually marked the marriage ceremony of Siva and Parvati. Cultural programmes and processions were held daily, along with the recitation of Vedas. Hundreds of devotees after taking a cleansing bath in the sea spent the day in the temple. Women sat in rows making garlands for the festival, while men helped with cleaning, cooking and carrying. I enjoyed the free meals with thousands of people sitting in a row on the pillared corridors.

One day I slipped out from there to the eastern tip of the island to Dhanushkodi, a harbour and a pilgrimage centre. I had read in the newspaper, in December 1964 a cyclone had washed away the site, claiming over 2,000 lives. I stood on the shore, remembering I was only 200km from Sri Lanka.

Festival would go on for three weeks. By the third day, I had enough of religious festivals, and I left for Kanyakumari.

Kanyakumari   The train arrived in the late afternoon at Kanya Kumari, 320 km distance. I followed a small crowd taking positions on the rocks by the seashore to watch a gorgeous sunset over the Indian Ocean. Next dawn, I got up early to watch the beautiful sunrise on the sea from the very spot. I don't believe there are many other places in the world where you can watch both sunrise and sunset on the sea, so magnificent, from the same spot.

The small ornate temple here, with thousands of years' history, was dedicated to Kanya Kumari. Women prayed for marriage to this virgin goddess, sister of Krishna. According to the legend, she was going to marry Shiva, who failed to show up on the wedding day, probably fallen sleep somewhere after drinking bhang. Rice and other grains meant for the wedding feast remained uncooked and unused. The story goes the uncooked grains turned into stones as time went by. Same small stones looking like rice grains were on the shore now.

During the colonial period, the British called the place Cape Comorin. After India's independence, it reverted to its original name.

Later, I took a short bumpy ferry to a small rocky island where a century back, the famous Bengali philosopher Swami Vivekananda prayed and attained his enlightenment. A memorial including a meditation hall was being built here in his honour about 2500 km away from Bengal. I felt proud to have been born in Bengal.

Vivekananda Rock

Back on the mainland, I sat mesmerised, watching the sunset on the ocean again. Next morning, after watching the magical sunrise once more, I left for Trivandrum. The usual three and a half-hour bus journey took much longer; we had a flat tyre in the middle of nowhere.

Trivandrum   This capital of Kerala state on the west coast of India, had a history as a trading post of spices, sandalwood and ivory back to 1000 BC. The famous temple of Lord Padmanabha in Trivandrum was noted in the literature from 500 BC.

Padmanabha reclined on serpent Anantha in the large sanctum sanctorum. The snake had five hoods facing inwards, as if in contemplation. Padmanabha's right hand rested over a Shiva lingam. Lakshmi, Goddess of Prosperity and Bhudevi, Goddess of Earth, two consorts of Vishnu were by his side. Lord Brahma emerged in a lotus (Padma) coming out of Lord's navel. Hence the name, 'Padmanabha'. After ascending the Mandapam, only parts of the deity is visible through each of the three doors.

A local bus took me to the stunning Kovalam beach only 8km away. This partly secluded beach with its partially black sand, on the Indian Ocean, was most welcome after the intense heat. I plunged into it several times, swimming in the gentle waves. Soon it was the time for another stunning sunset on the sea.

From Trivandrum, I took a night train to Cochin 200km distance.

Cochin   As usual, I had fallen sleep on this almost empty train but woke feeling cold and wet. Rain and wind came through the open window. By the time we arrived in Cochin, the rain had stopped. Black clouds in the sky, but everything felt fresh after the oppressive heat for the last few days.

Cochin, a major port city on the south-west Malabar Coast of India, was known as the Queen of the Arabian Sea. An important spice trading centre from the 14th century, networking with the Arab merchants.

Busy, crowded Cochin had a famous attraction I wanted to see. I visited the coast to see the Chinese fishing nets, a stationary lift net. Each was at least 10m high with an outstretched net suspended over the sea. Large stones suspended from the ropes provided counterweights at another end. This way of fishing is unusual in India and almost unique to the area. Chinese explorers probably introduced them in the 14th century. Some interpret the city name as 'Co-chin', meaning 'like China.'

I wandered around the city, and then after days of vegetable curry, thoroughly enjoyed fish and prawn curry with coconut. As I was coming out after my meal, I came across the Bengali family I met in Rameswaram. It turned out they were going on a boat ride the next day on the backwaters of Cochin. I had heard about these rides but did not have money to hire a boat. They insisted I come with them as they were paying for a whole boat, anyway.

It was fascinating cruising in a small boat through narrow rivers and lakes, lined up with coconut trees in the inner parts of beautiful Kerala. We stopped for lunch in a local village watching children diving into the water. The family insisted on paying. After the busy city of Cochin, this captivating landscape and lush greenery, with occasional views of the hills at a distance, were serene and most refreshing.

When we returned in the afternoon, the inky sky was threatening rain. The famous monsoon of the Malabar Coast had arrived. It was time for me to get back to Calcutta to start my first job as a doctor. After saying my heartfelt thanks to the family, I went to the railway station.

As I got into my Train to Howrah via Madras, the sky opened up. I settled down for sleep for my two-and- an a-half-day return journey of over 2200km.

First ascent and naming a peak in the Himalayas

1971 India

A short advertisement in the newspaper sports section caught my eye. A mountaineering club from Asansol, a regional town in West Bengal, was looking for a doctor to join an expedition team in the Garhwal Himalayas. I sent a postcard the same day, explaining I was a doctor and also a trained mountaineer. Reply postcard came back after a week. A team member came to Calcutta in two weeks, and we met.

The four weeks expedition, in late September, was to explore the Tharkot range in Garhwal and try to climb Tharkot and any other unclimbed peaks there. Between my jobs in the hospital, it suited me well.

The expedition team consisted of six members, including me. A postcard from Asansol team asked my shoe sizes as they would rent our mountaineering gears, clothes and boots from the Mountaineering Institute. I started collecting medical supplies from the friendly wards and the pharmaceutical representatives.

Two days after Durga Puja, our team of five arrived in Asansol Station with a small group of volunteers helping to load luggage into the train. The sixth member had already left to get our equipment from the Mountaineering Institute and will join us on our trek. For the 24 hour journey in the packed train, while young children asked us many questions, others looked in awe. They also took turns to make sure we had decent seats to rest and shared their food. While my colleagues talked to them about the expedition, I slept most of the way.

The train arrived late at Kathgodam in the evening. We slept on the station benches. Next morning, we loaded our paraphernalia on the roof of a rickety bus for Bageshwar at 185 km distance. This ancient town stood at 1000m on the confluence of the Sarju and Gomati Rivers. We waited there for our other team member to arrive with our gears.

There we visited the 7th- century Bagnath temple. One of our team members, Mansoor, had brought a shooting rifle with him, hoping to shoot mountain goats to provide fresh meat on the trek. He went to the district office to get his licence registered. Other colleague arrived later with all the rented gear he had managed. We decided it might be better and cheaper if we tried to find the high altitude porters at our next stop, Khati village. We bought some of our essentials here, which may not be available further up the road.

After four hours bus journey, we arrived at Khati 2262m by lunchtime. After a lot of bartering, we hired twelve porters. Five had previous experience of expeditions, and seven others would carry loads and manage four horses carrying our packs. We bought more local provisions from the only village store. We then distributed our rented gears to the team. That night we crammed ourselves in a small room at the back of the same store. I slept on top of my unrolled rented sleeping bag.

Following breakfast, we left for Jatoli, a 7 km trek following the Pinder River. On the steep, narrow mountain path, we crossed several waterfalls, substantial after a late monsoon rain. Our laden horses, and we negotiated with care several areas of recent landslides. When we reached Jatoli 2500m in the early afternoon, black clouds were covering the sky. In this small and only village in the valley, they kindly gave us shelter in a small room. Soon we had our first snowfall of the expedition.

While we rested, Mansoor left with two young villagers to find any mountain goat in the light snowfall. Soon sounds of gunfire reverberated with its echo in the mountain. An hour later, they returned with a large animal. That evening we had a grand feast with the villagers and chatted for the whole evening.

In another few weeks, most would go down to Khati for the winter to return in late April. We also heard because of early snow this year, Tharkot peak may not be achievable anymore this season.

Bright sunshine in the morning with a magnificent view of the Tharkot range. The trek was challenging climbing up and down the mountain and then through thick alpine forest to reach Sunderdunga 3200m. After five hours' hike, we stopped for lunch in the woods and discussed our strategy for the next part of our expedition. From what we had seen, it looked like because of the early heavy snowfall, climbing in the Tharkot range would not be possible with the equipment and the manpower we had.

Heavy snow fell again before we could get going. Our porters said horses would not go any further beyond the river, anyway. Reluctantly, we pitched our tents for the night in the middle of the jungle. We had already heard about leopards in this forest. It was scary to get out of the tent to relieve oneself in the night.

Next morning, we saw a few animal footprints next to a tent! Shortly we reached Sunderdunga River. We bade goodbye to our horses and two porters. One of our expedition team carefully crossed the river with a rope tied around his waist. On the other side, he secured the line to a large boulder. Then, one by one, we crossed the river holding on to the rope. One porter, while crossing, slipped on a rock underneath and got carried down the powerful stream for almost 20m. We ran either side of the water to help him, luckily the heavy pack he was carrying on his back got stuck on a rock. We pulled him to shore, wholly soaked and shaking like a leaf.

After a brief rest, we slowly climbed a steep ridge of about 600m and then traversed a slope of 1000m. We stopped for lunch there, before trekking for another two hours to reach the site of our base camp at Sukhram 3960m. Between two large rocks, we set our tents. Peaks in the Tharkot range looked gorgeous. While we settled down for hot soup, Mansoor left with a porter in search of fresh meat. A few hours later they returned and said although they spotted a herd of mountain goats, it was too far away to shoot and retrieve. It snowed all evening and in the night. Several times we got up to push our sagging tent roof of snow.

Next day we left in two teams, three expedition members and two experienced porters in each, to find suitable routes. The first team trekked the known path for Tharkot, while the other to seek another course. In the afternoon, we sat inside our mess tent and discussed the options. One of the porters and I took off our boots to find the socks were wet from our leaky rented mountain boots. We dried them by the stove fire. We all agreed Tharkot peak was out of the question, especially after the radio forecast of the weather for the next few days. The second team had seen an impressive-looking peak on the range which we might try. According to the map, it was so far unclimbed. We all agreed to try this mountain.

We left early the next morning. After about five hours' climb, we found a suitable place to establish our next camp at 4600m. It was sunny in the afternoon for a change. While enjoying the sunshine and beautiful views all around, we dried our clothes on the rocks. I dried my leaky boots by the fire. Next morning, we left again in two teams to find our possible route for the next camp. One team member was feeling a bit of altitude sickness and stayed back. In the steady sunshine climbing in fresh snow was invigorating. We returned after a few hours just before it started snowing. We agreed we needed to establish another higher camp before we can attempt the peak, we have set our goals.

By lunchtime the next day, we established our camp two at 5050m. The afternoon was relaxing in the sunshine and sorting out gears for the summit attempt. The porter with leaky boots had early signs of frostbite in three toes. I gave him the best treatment I could at this altitude, emphasising he needed to go down as soon as possible. Two team members were not feeling strong enough for any further climb up. Mansoor also did not want to go any higher. Our summit team was going to be Pranesh, Manoj and I, plus two high altitude porters. After dinner, we were in our sleeping bags by 6 pm.

Before 4 am, pitch dark outside and the temperature of -12°C with our full gear and head torch on, we set out for the peak, attached in two ropes. Pranesh and a porter in one. Manoj and I with the other porter in the second. For the first couple of hours, we made grounds quickly in the frozen snow.

Sun rose in all its glory against the backdrop of the snow-covered mountains. All five of us felt strong and invigorated with the golden rays on our back. We continued climbing. But now the snow was melting. In areas where we suspected of a covered crevasse, we prodded hard with our ice axes. Soon climbing became hard and slow, especially in the soft snow, now almost knee-deep in places. By midday, with the sun glaring, we could see the last 200m of climb separating us from the peak. After removing outer jackets, we prodded slowly upwards with the snow now in places almost waist-deep.

On top of a 5816m unclimbed peak

By 2 pm on 15th October, all five of us reached the summit. We hugged each other and then planted the Indian flag and our mountaineering club flag on the top. As it was Durga Puja festival season, we named this unnamed 5816m peak Durgakote. View from the top all-around was awe-inspiring. We could not take our eyes off for a long time at the distant mountains, now below us. After about half an hour on the top, we made our way down.

Going downhill, snow was now waist-deep in most places. Suddenly there was a jerk on the rope. Manoj, in front of me, had fallen in a crevasse! Between the porter and me we held on to the rope and shouted for help. Our other two climbers arrived soon. With their help, we pulled him out of the crevasse. He looked shell-shocked and amused at the same time. We carried on.

After almost fourteen hours of climb and excitement, we were utterly exhausted. From a distance, we could see the lights in our tents. Arriving by our tent, we could not wait to get inside the warmth and enjoy hot drinks our friends had made. Outside the tent, we took off our crampons. While the rest of my friends took their boots off and rushed inside, I kept struggling to take mine off. Soon I realised my leaky boots have got plastered inside against my wet socks, which had now turned into ice. One quick-thinking porter poured all the hot drinks over my frozen boots. After a bit of a struggle, I got them off and got inside the tent. But there was no more hot drink! I slowly removed my socks and was glad that luckily my toes had not suffered frostbite. Unfortunately, the toes of our porter looked worse than the day before.

We packed in the early morning sunshine. The porter with frostbite put his boots on his uninjured foot and wrapped up the other with warm clothing. Two porters, alternating, carried him on their backs. We shared their packs between us.

Going down was easy. We were in high spirits. Almost halfway down, I found a large ice slope. While others trundled slowly down over the snow, I decided to glissade down the icefield. It was brilliant fun going down at speed for a few minutes. But soon I saw the icefield down below was ending over a rocky field! I shoved my ice axe repeatedly into the ice with all my force, but could not stop. Only about

10m above a boulder, I managed to break the downward slide with a mighty thrust with my ice axe. I realised how lucky I was, but the exhilaration of this only brought a broad grin onto my face.

By late afternoon we reached by the Sunderdunga River. The river crossing was like before, holding on to a rope. One porter, tied to a line, carried our frostbitten friend to the other side. We camped outside the forest for the night. At dawn, two porters left for Jatoli to get the horses. Before leaving, they said there were leopard footprints outside.

I kept checking up on the frostbitten toes of our friend. They looked shrivelled and darker than before. After packing the gears, while most of the team moved on, a porter and I waited with our injured friend. Soon the horses arrived. We loaded him and the rest of our gears on the animals and walked beside them.

I talked with my fellow climber porter about lives in their villages. It sounded very tough maintaining their agriculture around the area. Also, the place had no facilities for health and proper education. Many people were now moving to towns to earn their livings. In about four hours, we reached Jatoli. Villagers had joined our team celebrating with joyful noises and singing.

But before I could join them, a man came and asked if I would go to see his mother and a child in his village. They were too sick to travel. I left at once with a small pack of usual medicines, only to realise later his place was another two hours away over the hills. I returned late in the evening after my house call. By then, some of my friends had already gone to sleep. But two were waiting for me with the food.

I woke up after a sound sleep in the night, feeling very hungry. Looking for my breakfast, I came outside. There was a big gathering of people. Patients had come from the surrounding villages to be seen by a doctor! First, I arranged for our frostbitten friend's transfer on horseback to the hospital in the next town.

While the rest of the team packed, I ran my impromptu clinic and gave whatever medicine I had to the villagers.

On our return to Bageshwar, I checked my friend at its only hospital. A doctor there said, very likely they would have to amputate his toes. But he looked in good spirit and thanked me for coming over to check upon him.

Attending the birth of a nation

1971 Bangladesh   Just after Diwali, three weeks after return from the mountains, I heard one of our chest surgeons was looking for volunteers for an Indian Red Cross mission to East Bengal. Newspapers and radio had been busy broadcasting the struggle in East Bengal (I could never call the country East Pakistan) by Mujahedeen freedom fighters against the Pakistani army. Millions of refugees from East Bengal had already flooded West Bengal, fleeing from the torture and killings by the Pakistani military. My friend Kanu and I were the only ones who dared enough to join the Red Cross in the middle of an ongoing war. No question about telling our families. We knew they would immediately try to stop us.

Five days later three of us, an experienced surgeon and two surgical trainees, left Calcutta in an ambulance flying Red Cross flag and with boldly painted Indian Red Cross sign.

All together three ambulances from Calcutta drove together to the India-East Bengal border 75km away. After an hour we came to a military station with many armed vehicles. While the seniors went inside to talk, we got out and wandered. Army vehicles there had soldiers in smart uniforms with impressive automatic rifles. One car had a massive cannon covered with tarpaulin. None from the army spoke to us, but only smiled when we asked anything. After about an hour, our surgeon came out of the office, followed by soldiers carrying boxes, our medical supplies.

Two Indian army vehicles in the front and a few following, three Red Cross vehicles moved on. By the roadside were hundreds of makeshift houses. Several kilometres before the border, we saw thousands of men, women and children coming from the border. Tired and weary men walked with tin suitcases, some with rolled-up mattresses on their shoulders. Women carried their babies while holding the hands of young children. They let us drive without even looking up. Soon, we passed several large refugee camps made up of new tents. Children in ragged clothes ran around outside.

We stopped at Bongaon border. The Indian army was everywhere. In a mess tent, later we attended a meeting with the entire team of medics, army officers of the Eastern Command and two civilians. I learnt with awe and envy that these two civilians, barely older than me, represented Mukti Bahini, the freedom fighters of Bangladesh Liberation War. One of them was the Commander of Jessore Division. They said the Pakistani army in their attempt to suppress people's aspiration for liberation was brutally slaughtering many in their villages and towns and were burning the houses. There were many injured who would benefit from the help of medical units, especially as all hospitals in the country were now under military control.

Liberation fighters suggested three Red Cross ambulances should try to cover three different sections. That way we would help a significant number of population within the East Bengal Border. They insisted we call their country Bangladesh from now on, a request which we honoured.

Next morning our vehicle passed the border heavily fortified on the Indian side, but none on the other side. One liberation fighter joined us. Two other cars escorted us with people in civilian clothes carrying guns. They did not look Bengali or civilians, and none even spoke Bengali. We knew they came from the Indian army in disguise. India had not yet officially declared war against the Pakistani military.

We drove through deserted road for several kilometres before stopping at a place where a sizeable crowd had gathered. We got out to find a man, tied against a tree by ropes, begging for his life in tears. This man was allegedly an agent of the Pakistani army and was caught by his fellow villagers. They had called the freedom fighters.

In front of us, swift justice took place. After confirming the story from a few more villagers, one freedom fighter took out his sten gun and showered the man with volleys of shots. I could not breathe. My heart had already stopped. I wanted to shut my eyes but only kept staring at the man being killed right in front of me. To add to my horror, this person, although shot by at least twenty bullets, did not die instantly. He remained alive for more than a few minutes with his body slumped but still faintly crying for help. Finally, his head drooped, and his crying stopped. My heart now started beating out of my chest.

We moved on, all of us sitting in complete silence. After a few kilometres, we stopped at a deserted village health centre next to the road. This would be our field station. Even before we set up, a lot of injured and sick people came from almost nowhere, villagers from the surrounding areas, including several children. Some had suffered burn injuries. There were a few liberation fighters with superficial bullet wounds. Patients with common illnesses also came as they had no treatment available for months. By the time we finished in our makeshift hospital for the day, it was late in the evening.

We got up early the next day to attend to a big queue of patients with similar problems as the day before. We finished by early evening.

Next morning we started our clinic, but soon we learnt in a village 4 km away, the Pakistani army had killed and injured many. Our ambulance rushed there following two liberation fighters on motorbikes. Few houses were burning. Several dead women and children lay by their homes, a few killed by a bayonet, while others were shot. I retched, but my stomach felt empty. Kanu threw up next to a ditch.

I wanted to sit down there clutching my head, but an old man lay with bayonet injury to his abdomen, in shock but still alive. We put him in the ambulance along with others injured. The freedom fighter who was keeping an eye from outskirts of the village rushed back. He told us to leave the place immediately. The Pakistani army has been spotted not very far away, beyond the fields in the next village. In our field hospital, under local anaesthesia, we opened up the abdomen of the man with bayonet injury, belly full of blood. But luckily he had only a major bleeding vessel supplying the intestine damaged. We controlled this without too much difficulty. It took us the rest of the day to patch up the rest of the injured.

Following day, there were not as many patients in our clinic, possibly people too scared to come out with the oppressing army not so far away. We finished by late morning and were glad to hear some villagers have brought chickens for us. They started cooking chicken curry and rice. After having chapati with molasses and occasional bananas for the last few days, this sounded heavenly. We sat outside under a mango tree talking to the villagers, as our lunch cooked on an open fire.

But soon a liberation fighter came on a motorcycle and said we must leave at once. They have spotted the Pakistani army moving with Howitzer guns. These cannons had a range of 25-30 km. As the border was almost 40km away, we must leave immediately. But the chicken curry was almost ready and smelt delicious. Kanu and I argued with our senior surgeon, if the Howitzer had a range of 30km, it did not matter if we left immediately or after having our lunch. Our insistence paid off. Hurriedly we put as much of our medical supplies back in our ambulance. Then we had the most delicious chicken curry and rice.

We left immediately after and in less than an hour reached the border. This time we found many Indian army vehicles going towards where we had just come from, into Bangladesh.

Expedition to the second-highest mountain
in India – Kamet 7757m

1973 Garhwal Himalaya. India   A redirected letter from the Asansol Mountaineering Club reached me in March. By now I was busy working as a doctor in a village health centre. I opened it eagerly to find they were planning an expedition of a grand scale to Kamet, the second-highest mountain in India - a five-week campaign in September. Immediately I sent a letter to the authority requesting my leave. A month later, I took time off to go to Asansol. Local members were busy there collecting donations of various items for the expedition and raising money. There was a buzz in the club with such a big undertaking in the Himalaya. I started collecting medical supplies.

In early September an enormous crowd, including the press, gathered at the train station to see us off. There were seven of us as climbers. Manoj, Pranesh, Mansoor and I had been on Durgakote only two years back. Mountaineering Federation rules said as a doctor of a high altitude expedition; I could not attempt the summit, only go up to the last camp. After 1300 km train journey, in Dehradun, four Sherpas from Darjeeling joined us.

Early morning, a 300km bus journey, followed the River Alakananda, with stops at Devprayag, where Alakananda met with Bhagirathi and then at Rudraprayag, at the confluence with the Mandakini. We reached Joshimath 1875m in the dark.

We spent a day there, checking and supplementing our provisions and for a visit to the district office for a permit, as our journey and the expedition was close to the Tibet border. Joshimath had one of the four great monasteries of India, established by Shri Shankaracharya in the 8th century AD.

The bus drove for 80km to Ghamsali 3500m, where we stopped for two days to hire our porters. Mansoor had a unique idea. He bought all the eggs available in this village, hundreds of them. He had them hard- boiled for us to carry on our trip. In the cold, eggs lasted for weeks. We had boiled eggs daily from then on. Mansoor had brought a movie camera for filming the expedition. It did not require permits but was heavy and needed an extra porter to carry. From Ghamsali we started our trek with six laden donkeys, eleven climbers and ten Dhotia porters.

After the crowded train and bus journeys, walking in the mountains was most refreshing. Our trail passed through woods before we came to the spectacular Niti gorge. After crossing a log bridge over the Maoli River, we reached Niti 3600m, the last tiny village before the gateway to proper mountains. Here we hired six more porters and then carried on through a stony track zigzagging upwards. On the opposite hill, a few mountain goats grazed. Mansoor regretted not bringing his gun. After two hours, we reached the desolate valley of Goting on the edge of Tibet. In falling sunlight, we set our camp just before it started snowing.

We knew the trek to establish our base camp beyond Raikana Glacier would be lengthy. We left early in a cold but clear morning. Soon we reached a torrent from Raikana glacier meeting Dhaoli River. Horses with their packs crossed easily. But we had to pass carefully. The porter carrying the movie camera slipped over a rock, but another porter next to him held on to him in time.

Base camp 4648m   Breasting up from the river into the glacier moraine, we could spot the site of our base camp at a distance. We continued laboriously through glacial drift of boulders and rocks. In the late afternoon, we arrived at a suitable place to pitch our base camp. It took us an hour to level the grounds between the rocks to set up our tents. Soon we settled in mess tent to discuss our plans. Mansoor tuned the radio into daily local weather forecast by the meteorological station. Next few days' weather forecast was calm with heavy snowfall forecast after that for a few days. From our tents, we heard distant rumblings of avalanches.

Camp One 5029m   In the bright morning, the horses returned to Niti. We looked in awe at a distance, the most impressive peak of Kamet and the snowy peaks of the high mountains between Garhwal and Tibet. On our south, top of Nandadevi 7816m became briefly visible. Then we trekked through the moraine. After about four hours of hard work, we found a place to camp where the glacier turned northwards. There was no place for a mess tent there on the moraine above the glacier, only for the smaller tents. The area had very little sunshine, even though the sky was blue, as Bidhan Parvat cast its shadow. After helping us to set up our tents, most of the porters went down to bring up more supplies. We settled ourselves, resting for remaining part of the day. Fascinating being on the rocks just above this vast glacier as avalanches came down with mighty roars from the steep mountain slope on the other side. Luckily, no avalanches on our side of the glacier.

Trudging through knee-deep snow over glacial rocks next day was hard. Pranesh cursed the people who came to the railway station to bid us good luck with such fanfare.

'Where are they now? Enjoying their day, strolling around for Puja marketing, while we struggle here,' he remarked. We all smiled but agreed.

Camp Two 5670m   Until then, at the junction with East Kamet glacier, Raikana glacier was mostly covered in deep snow. But now walking was considerably easier over its undulating hard icy surface. After a few hours, we found an ideal place for our camp two at 5670m with a beautiful view of the Mana Peak ahead. Avalanches regularly crashed down on the other side of the almost 1km wide glacier.

East Kamet glacier

Above us, the East Kamet glacier narrowed into a massive gorge. Next day we stayed in camp two to acclimatise. After a leisurely breakfast, we trekked to explore upwards by the canyon to find a suitable way up. Outside the tent, I found going hard. Only after 100m, I was utterly exhausted. While others moved on, I had to sit on a rock for a while before returning to the camp. Altitude sickness had hit me!

After dinner, I checked everyone's blood pressure, including mine. Manoj, hoping to be on the summit team, had a very high blood pressure of nearly two hundred. I told him if it remained high at the next camp, he must not go higher to avoid the risk of brain and lung oedema. My blood pressure was normal. I was already feeling better after the gentle strolls around the camp for the rest of the day. Soon the sun passed behind Kamet, and the ice wall of Mana peak turned dark. By 6 pm, we crawled into our sleeping bags.

We set early next day crunching over still frosted snow. After about 1 km, we found the almost hidden steep couloir we knew we had to go up through to establish our next camp. In the last few days, the single copy of 'Kamet Conquered' by Frank Smythe had done its round. When Smythe's team did the first successful climb of Kamet in early June, this gully was covered with snow. But in mid-September, it was filled only with boulders and loose rocks. Hard work, but it was gratifying climbing up with careful steps on the loose rocks and unstable boulders. After almost two hours of strenuous climb, we reached the top of the gully and sat to rest.

East Kamet Glacier was now below us along with snowfields and icefalls from Mana Peak with regular avalanches. We were above 6100m, but feeling surprisingly good. Soon we got up and slowly traversed a large sloping icefield with seracs in another hour. In a suitable place on the icefield, we set up our advanced camp.

Advanced camp 6280m   Some porters returned to camp two to bring up more supplies. Almost as soon as we had pitched our tents, it snowed heavily. That night everyone had a nasty headache. I distributed pain killers liberally.

It was cloudy all of the next day. After midday, the wind picked up, and it snowed heavily. Freezing and blizzard condition forced us into our tents for the rest of the day. In the evening, we managed to get the meteorological forecast. Outlook for the next few days was better with light wind and snow. I checked everyone's blood pressure, including mine. Everyone had reasonable blood pressure, except our old friend Manoj. His was still very high. We agreed on summit party without him, Pranesh and Anil with four Sherpas.

Most of the porters next morning were in poor shape with altitude sickness. We sent them down with our disappointed friend Manoj to camp two to recover. Rest of us trudged in deep snow, avoiding hidden crevasses. We soon reached the very steep rock and ice wall separating us from Meade's col. Our final camp/camps would be above it. Some of us helped to fix ropes on this challenging near-vertical 450m wall. Others ferried in supplies for the camps above and moved our advanced campsite closer to the ice wall.

Next morning was cloudless. For the first time, majestic Mana peak in all its glory was in front. Kamet was not visible from here. Spirit of the team matched the weather. We all helped the summit party with their loads to the wall with fixed ropes. We wished them all the luck and bade goodbye. After a while, they reached the top part of the wall. We then helped them to pull up from above the heavier loads with rope.

On the slopes of Eastern Abigamin 6350m   Once they were out of sight, our friend Mansoor returned to his tent. One young high altitude porter and I roped up and climbed up the slopes of Eastern Abigamin. We were not planning on climbing to the top but wanted to go as far as possible. On the slopes, at a distance in the north, the plains of Tibet were below us. We carried on upwards for about three hours before we took out our snack packs. We looked towards the Kamet route and could see the Mead's col, just above the level of us. We estimated we were at above 6350m. From this distance, we tried to spot our summit team. My fellow climber said he had seen some dots moving. I did not see anyone. We knew without another camp, climb up to the top of Eastern Abigamin 7,355m was not possible. Although tantalisingly close at just over 1000m. I was not supposed to attempt a summit climb, anyway! After enjoying the views for a little longer, reluctantly we trekked down.

Kamet and East Abigamin

Next day we got up late, tidied up the campsite and spent the day in leisure looking towards the summit route - a calm day. We tried to imagine our friends toiling up to the summit. Even with a binocular, we could not see their course. Snow flurries came in the afternoon, and we retreated inside our tents. Following morning after breakfast, we packed our stuff. Mansoor kept an eye with the binocular over the ice wall for our returning summit party, ready with his movie camera.

Around mid-morning, he shouted out he had spotted them. Soon with flasks of hot drinks, we trudged to the wall. All six of them came down after a while, slowly and wearily. We greeted them with cheers and hugged them. But they were too exhausted to celebrate yet. Refreshed with hot drinks, they told us Pranesh and two Sherpas had made it to the top on 20th September. Others had returned from halfway to the summit because of the challenging condition. After taking movies of the summit team, we returned to the camp. The summit team needed rest. While they lunched and rested, we packed the tents and got ready to descend.

In high spirit, we started our descent. Soon we reached the couloir. Large unstable rocks we traversed coming up, were now covered with slippery ice. We moved down wearily. On one boulder, suddenly my left foot slipped on ice and got trapped between three unstable rocks. The boulders moved towards each other and started tightening around my boot. All happened within a split second. I tried to take my foot out from between these rocks. Just at the last second, before the gap between the boulders almost closed, I managed to squeeze out my foot. I sat on a boulder for a few minutes and tried to imagine what might have happened if my foot got stuck between those massive stones, over a ton in weight - no chance of escape. Soon, I joined the descending party ahead of me who did not even know what almost happened to me.

Two days before the Durga Puja festival, we arrived at Asansol station. A massive crowd with the local and national press was there to welcome us back as heroes.

A brief stint in the UK

1974 -77

A letter came from London with approval for higher surgical training. The first thing that came to my head was it would allow me the opportunity of travelling in Europe.

I got my passport and then visa, in the next few months. I exchanged rupees for only three pounds the UK authorities allowed for an Indian to bring along. I wrote to a classmate already in England to meet me at the airport and lend me some money. He replied within four weeks and agreed. I borrowed money from my friend Sanku's mother for the airfare and sent a telegram to my friend in England with flight details. My other friend Baburam bought a second-hand woollen coat for me. Over thirty people, my family and friends, came to see me off at Dumdum airport in Calcutta.

On my first ever flight, the excitement heightened as we took off and the lights of Calcutta were below. Next, when I awoke from my slumber, fascinating Alps Mountain range was under us. An hour later, the plane circled for some time over a dense cloud before an announcement came. Because of thick fog around London, they were diverting the flight to Preston in north-west England.

After a long journey by coach from Preston through dreary weather, we arrived in Heathrow only six hours late. Luckily, my friend was still waiting. My first ever ride on an underground train took us to Kings Cross. My friend kindly bought a train ticket to Doncaster and lent me the promised money. Three pounds in my pocket would not have been enough. I woke up just a few minutes before the train arrived in Doncaster. It was dark and raining. Shivering in my soaked woollen coat, I arrived at my hospital. This was supposed to be an Indian summer in England this autumn!

It took some getting used to my first few months in England. Food tasted of nothing. It was always raining and cold. I felt miserable with no sign of the sun in the sky for weeks. I could speak and understand English, I thought, but following the accent of the Yorkshire mining community was a definite challenge. But after hearing so much before about the 'stiff' English attitude, I found most people, friendly and down to earth.

In the next few months, the excitement of working in an unfamiliar environment and getting ready for the specialist exam took over my life. Soon I had to go to Edinburgh for my exam. In a town charity shop, I bought a smart-looking side bag. At Glasgow station, there was over an hour for my connecting train to Edinburgh. I walked outside the station. A large procession with colourful banners came by. As I was watching this rally with interest, three enormous men ran towards me.

One of them pushed me, saying 'Are you taking a piss?'

I had no clue why they were so upset. Before I got almost beaten up, an older man came running from the procession and stopped them. He pointed to my shoulder bag, written 'Celtic' in bold letters. Until then, I had no idea that word could have any other connection than with the famous football club. He asked me to go inside the station. He explained this was a Protestant parade. People can get very upset with any Irish connection such as Celtic.

I liked Edinburgh. A small city with a lovely castle on the hill. Luckily, the weather was good. Walking over the cobbled streets around old-style buildings in the evening before my exam helped to take some pressure off my mind. Exam results the next day made me like the city even more.

In the first two years, my jobs took me to a few cities, mostly in Yorkshire mining towns. Drinking in the pub eight to ten pints in the evening was the common pastime for most, not my scene. Moving to Hull, I found it slightly different, being mainly a fishing port. I wanted so much to go out in one of the fishing boats and watch them catching fish. But ships always left late in the night and came back mid-morning, not suitable for my work.

My next job was in Eastbourne, on the south coast of England. It was mid-summer and sunny. The sea here was just about warm enough to swim as long as you took the courage to plunge after sunbathing for a while. Walking along the path close to the white cliffs with beautiful sea views at Beachy Head was a cherished pastime. But almost once a month someone jumped from here to take his or her life.

One weekend I took myself to see the prehistoric monuments at Stonehenge. Mesmerised, I walked around this Neolithic site of the stone circle. I could not even begin to imagine what ingenuity humankind had so many thousands of years back to build this.

Heavy work schedule, looking for and then changing jobs every six months, and getting my final fellowship exam out of the way, allowed very little spare time. I managed a long weekend off to go to London for the first time. Like most tourists, I visited Big Ben and Parliament House by the River Thames; Trafalgar Square; Tower Bridge and the Tower of London and watched the ceremonial changing of guards at Buckingham Palace. But my fondest memory was going to watch a drama in a London theatre.

In the late evening, I was travelling by underground train. My coach was empty, except for me. In one station, two young guys got in and sat opposite me.

One of them showed me a knife in his jacket pocket and said with a laugh, 'We are going to rob you now'.

I held my nerve to smile at them and said, 'Go ahead then. But it won't be worth as I only have two pounds in spare changes.' I took them out of my pocket and held out in my open palm.

They sneered at me and got off at the next station. I kept hold of the thirty pounds in my other pocket.

Next day I visited the Natural History Museum, with mesmerising building architecture and its vast collection. Then to the British Museum and the British Library. In this expansive museum, display of monuments from all around the world was a definite reminder of plunders of the British Colonial era. Still, one cannot but get immersed in history and its splendour.

Ireland

August 1976 When my girlfriend invited me to come to Ireland with her, I jumped at the opportunity. After a long train journey from the south of England to Holyhead in North Wales, we got onto a massive ferry just before midnight. Fortunately, in midsummer, the Irish Sea was quiet. Our ferry arrived in Dun Laoghaire port as the morning broke out. Getting off our bus in the Dublin city centre, first, we grabbed some hearty Irish breakfast.

Historical GPO, General Post Office, was nearby. I looked with admiration at the site. During Easter Rising of 1916 against British colonialism, it served as headquarters of the liberation leaders. As a tribute to the Rising, there was a statue depicting the death of the mythical Irish hero Cuchulainn. Later we walked across the town to O'Connell Bridge over River Liffey. Ha'Penny Bridge, the oldest bridge of the city, stood at a distance. After crossing the bridge, we walked inside Trinity College campus, most prestigious Irish university. Soon we walked into Grafton Street, a famous shopping area. Buskers played music every ten meters.

Next morning we took a train to Tullamore, in the centre of Ireland. After lunch at a family-friendly Italian restaurant, we walked nearby to the new landmark of the town - a traffic light! Cars were dangerously getting each other's way, confused with the changing colours of the lights. My girlfriend's village was only 8km away. We started walking. Soon a car stopped. The driver recognised her and gave us a lift.

A wonderful Irish farming family welcomed me in their house. I was curious about the bricks they used to keep the fire going. I learnt it was called 'Bog'. I told them in Indian villages; people often use dried cow-dung cakes for lighting a fire.

Next day, after watching milking of the cows, I walked to the nearby bogland and tried my hand on with bog digging. Hearty welcome of the family made me feel almost homesick.

We took a bus to Galway on the west coast and drove through villages and towns, with interesting names such as Lisdoonvarna, made famous in old Irish song.

Before entering a small B&B, my girlfriend took out a ring from a finger in her right hand and put it on her left ring finger. She said in this profoundly catholic country; they would frown upon an unmarried girl sharing room with a man. They may even refuse us. I smiled. Later in the afternoon, we walked by Galway bay, with a dark cloud above, it did not look beckoning.

On a sunny morning, a bus took us to beautiful Connemara 80km away. Within low mountains, grasslands and forests, we walked until we came over a tiny hill overlooking the serene surroundings. We relaxed there, but soon two wild ponies came sniffing at us, wondering at the rare visitors to their place.

A short flight on a twelve-seater plane the next day took us to the Aran Islands. Three small islands, Inishmore, Inisheer and Innisman in the Atlantic waters almost huddled each other. In our B&B in Inishmore, the largest of the three islands, my girlfriend kept the ring on her left ring finger. In good weather, we visited the ancient forts of O'Brien's castle on the cliff top, ruins of Bronze Age and Iron Age forts. Before we left the islands, my girlfriend bought me an Aran sweater, renowned for its warmth.

From Galway, we went by bus down south to County Clare to the Cliffs of Moher. In clear weather, we walked dangerously close to the cliff edge. These scenic cliffs ran for 14 km, rising almost 214m above the Atlantic at its highest - stunning.

Soon it was time to get back to our work. I genuinely hoped one day I would return to this lovely country to explore more.

Hitchhiking in Europe

March-August 1977

I have been nearly three years in the UK. I had planned to come for a maximum of three years before returning to India. My two goals were to get the specialist qualification and experience and then travel as much as around Europe as possible during that time. I had achieved the first object. Now was the time for my most important goal.

To prepare for my travels in non-English-speaking countries, I took evening classes in French and German. Unfortunately, these two languages were geometrically opposite and did not work for me. I took membership of the Youth Hostel International. In London I queued for hours for my European Union visa, covering Belgium, Luxembourg, The Netherlands, Germany, Italy and France. I would have to get permits for others from the neighbouring countries.

By the end of March 1977, I packed my small backpack, with some warm clothes, and left for my overland tour of Europe.

Brugge Belgium   I took a bus to the port city of Felixstowe and then got into a massive car ferry to Zeebrugge. I slept until we arrived at the port and found a solo driver going to Brugge, who agreed to give a lift.

I had read about Venice but never known about Brugge. I spent two days, often late in the evening, walking and enjoying this beautiful city with its network of canals. Burg square, the city centre, was charming with the ornate 14th-century City Hall, busy Market square, 13th-century Belltower and chiming 47-bell carillon.

Antwerp Belgium   In the late afternoon, standing by the major road, I got a ride to Antwerp, 90 km away. On arrival, the driver treated me for a coffee and highly recommended the Rubens Museum and the Diamond Quarter.

Next morning I wandered around Grote Markt, a central square in this medieval city on River Scheldt, surrounded by the beautiful architecture of Flemish Renaissance. After coffee and Belgian chocolates, I visited the centuries-old Diamond District with hundreds of diamond traders, cutters and polishers. Over the last 500 years, this place has seen transactions of hundreds of billion dollars' worth of diamonds. Inside the World Diamond Centre, large cut and rare uncut diamonds dazzled.

Later, I visited the 17th-century Rubens House with artworks of famous Flemish Baroque painter Peter Paul Rubens. I am not an art expert by any means, but I loved his painting of Massacre of the

Innocents and the picture of Saint Sebastian.

I spent the next day at the Middelheim Park with open-air sculptures of immense beauty. 'Running Girl' and 'Two Pregnant Women' within its vast gardens were stunning.

In the night, at the Youth Hostel, I talked to fellow travellers. Most, men and women from all around the world were mainly hitchhiking. There was even an 18-year girl by herself, on her year break from studies. She had hitched rides from western France, including with some truck drivers. I learnt a few tricks of hitchhiking. Best time to get a ride was in the morning, not in the afternoon. It was always better to wait with your destination placard on the smaller roads at least a 100m before the motorway. That way, the driver had time to stop and pick you up.

Keukenhof The Netherlands   I held out a poster next morning saying Amsterdam, although I was hoping to go to the nearby town of Keukenhof, the most extensive flower garden in the world. Soon a driver stopped and let me in. When I explained I was hoping to go to Keukenhof, it turned out he lived nearby in Lisse, not very far.

In early April, Keukenhof was a fantastic showcase for millions of Tulips, Daffodils and Hyacinths. Walking amongst rows of beautiful flowers, I could easily imagine how in the 16th-century price of Tulip bulbs were higher than of Gold. It created the 'Tulip Mania', the first economic bubble.

While talking to a couple in the coffee shop, I found they were returning to Amsterdam and were happy to take me.

Amsterdam   The couple kindly dropped me off by the Youth Hostel near the centre of the city. It was full, but the other Youth Hostel was only 2 km away. I walked by the illuminated streets of this lovely city of intricate canals to find my overnight stay.

Like anyone else, I have read with fascination about the famous artist Van Gogh. I could not wait to get inside this recently opened museum in a modern building. I have heard so much about his Sunflowers painting. But in reality, standing in front of this painting took my breath away. I did not know before there were several versions of this famous painting - I loved them all.

Amongst Van Gogh's other works, I could not move away from his 'A pair of shoes', 'Almond blossom', 'Irises' and then his self-portrait. For the first time, I watched there and enjoyed the collections of his famous contemporary masters such as Claude Monet, Pissarro and Gauguin.

After spending most of the day there, my route back to Youth Hostel took me through the Redlight District of Amsterdam, known for its nightlife. This side of life never attracted me. I just walked by the lighted glass doors with women with inviting eyes.

Next day was at Rijksmuseum, Dutch National Museum. The beauty of Rembrandt's paintings was exceptional. Night Watch and Anatomy Lesson of Dr Tulp was beyond belief.

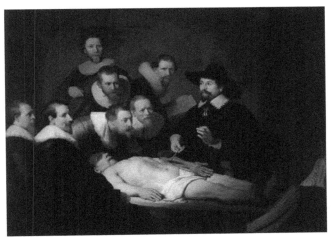

I walked the galleries in wonder through hundreds of other beautiful compositions. I especially loved the Milkmaid painting by Vermeer and also paintings by Frans Hals. Slowly I am turning into an art lover!

After several hours there, I visited the Anne Frank House by the canal. I had to hold back my tears walking in this family home of Anne Frank, now a museum. This young teenager wrote her diary over two years while her Jewish family spent in hiding during the Nazis' occupation of the Netherlands. They took Anne and her family to Auschwitz and then to Bergen Belsen Concentration camp. She died of Typhus with her mother, just a few weeks before the camp was liberated. Her father was freed and returned to find her hidden diary and published it.

Bicycles were everywhere in Amsterdam. You could hire one for a cheap price for the day. Next day I hired a bike and rode to De Gooyer Windmill only a few kilometres distance. This 26.6m tall windmill was the highest in the Netherlands. When I visited, they were restoring the mill after recent storm damage. It was still a beautiful example of engineering, built three centuries back. Then back to Amsterdam and cycling around until nighttime.

Bremen West Germany   Next day it took three changeovers of hitchhikes before I got to Bremen in West Germany on my way to Hamburg and then to Berlin. I arrived there in the evening and checked into its only Youth Hostel. And then I had dinner by the lovely market square, next to the beautifully illuminated 600 years old town hall.

Hamburg   It did not take long to find a ride to Hamburg 130km away. I was not interested in spending time in Hamburg, but Berlin was another 300 km distance. I explored this northern German city on river Elba, including its beautiful city hall, rebuilt since WWII. I couldn't imagine this busy modern city completely destroyed during the war.

Early next morning I walked to the road, joining the autobahn going east. I was expecting a long wait, but a car pulled by within fifteen minutes. When I asked if he was going to Berlin or to somewhere on the way, he said Berlin. On the autobahn, it took us just over an hour to reach the border check post with East Germany. Despite all the things I had heard about communist state bureaucracy, guards at the border were pleasant. One of them even smiled at me, checking my Indian passport before handing it back.

East German corridor to Berlin   We now travelled through autobahn with the sign 'Transit' posted in places. Journey through the transit corridor to Berlin should have taken three hours at the most. But after an hour's drive, the driver left the autobahn and drove to a side road. He then went around a few roundabouts before returning to the autobahn. He did the same again at the next exit road before returning to the autobahn. I was curious and slightly concerned. On these transit corridors, other nationals coming to East Germany must stay on the autobahn and could only use designated service stops. At the third exit, after going through two roundabouts, he took a side road and stopped next to a house.

He got out and indicated for me to follow. He knocked at the door. An old lady came out and gave him a big hug. The driver gave her a bag of presents he had with him. She invited us inside and offered us a light lunch, followed by a lovely homemade cake and coffee. It turned out the man had not seen his auntie in East Germany for over a decade. On his way for an assignment in West Berlin, he wanted to meet up with her after a long time. After saying goodbye to the kind lady, we left for Berlin and arrived in the late afternoon.

West Berlin   The friendly driver waited outside for me until I checked at the Youth Hostel in West German section of West Berlin to make sure there was a place for me. I came out after registering to say 'Danke Sehr'.

Next morning, I walked to the historic Brandenburg Gate with the infamous Berlin Wall behind separating West and East Berlin. Here a decade earlier President Kennedy had given his 'Ich Bin Berliner' speech in front of a large West Berlin crowd showing American support for West Germany.

Later I walked to the Victory Column in Tiergarten. Built after victory in the Prussian war, 67m tall column with its winged statue of a goddess of war, Victoria, looked down at the city. It was not possible on the day to climb up its stairs.

Next, I walked by the Reichstag Building by the river and the Berlin Wall. This impressive building was the monument of the power of Imperial Germany. Although once used as Reichstag for the Weimar Republic, it became infamous as the symbol of Nazi Germany until a fire destroyed it in 1933. Visit inside was not allowed.

I loved wandering along the broad empty boulevards of West Berlin, occasionally taking the spacious subway. Although on the whole people were friendly, there was a feeling of tension everywhere, maybe because of the heightening of the cold war.

Checkpoint Charlie   Following day I walked to the cold war famous Checkpoint Charlie near Friedrichstrasse subway. Very strict looking American soldiers examined my passport, and sternly asked why I was going to East Berlin. I answered only for a visit. They took my passport inside another cabin and after a while returned it stamped and gave back with a stern face. Then I crossed about 50m before coming to the East German side of the gate. Here East German soldiers were friendlier and after seeing my Indian Passport said 'Indisch' with a faint smile.

East Germany Once in East Berlin, it didn't take long to find the youth hostel. Facilities there were basic but much cheaper than in the west. After wandering around the streets, I found a cafe for lunch. Not much choice, but the price was very low.

I knew about German Playwright Brecht. In the early evening, I visited a beautiful theatre building where his famous play 'Life of Galileo' was being played. The theatre was almost full, but I managed a standing seat for cheap at the back. Although my understanding of the German language was sparse, I had read the play in translation. I enjoyed the theme and the beautiful orchestral music played with it.

Following morning was at the famous Pergamon Museum with its vast collection of antiquities from all over the world, especially from Greece and Egypt. By afternoon I came out and visited nearby Humboldt University, regarded as the preeminent university in the world for natural sciences. Also famous for ground-breaking discovery in physics by Albert Einstein. In the evening, I strolled with hundreds of people in the massive Marx-Engels-Platz, used for colourful state ceremonies.

Next day was another stroll on the streets of East Berlin. Contrary to what I had heard, it was easy to make a simple conversation with locals in my sparse German. Although I walked in the areas with an unimpeded view of the infamous wall, I decided not to bring up the issue with anyone I talked. Travelling by underground in East Berlin was not much different to that in the West, but here the coaches were old- style. By the famous Alexanderplatz were ruins of several old buildings destroyed by WWII bombings, the city now rebuilt around these.

I returned to West Berlin the next day through Check Point Charlie. East German soldiers amused me by wishing me 'Good Bye' in broken English. But American Soldiers at the other end received me with stern faces as before.

From Berlin, I wanted to go to the University City of Heidelberg. I knew it wouldn't be possible to hitch a ride there directly from Berlin. Instead, I waited on the road by Checkpoint Bravo in the morning, holding a sign for Frankfurt. Soon a couple picked me up for 550km journey to Frankfurt. I slept in the back most of the way. They stopped at a designated service station for a break and treated me with a cup of coffee and a slice of delicious Bienenstich, Bee Sting Cake. After almost six hours, we reached Frankfurt. I had no interest in Frankfurt, and it did not take long to find a lift to Heidelberg only 90km distance.

Heidelberg   I wanted to visit Heidelberg because it was the college town of West Germany, with the oldest university in Europe. Reverend Martin Luther's disputation at Heidelberg in the 16th century made a lasting change in Christianity. University here was the centre of democratic **thinking during** the Weimar Republic **in** the early 20th century. Unfortunately, the Nobel Prize winner physicist Philipp Lenard, later Chief of Aryan Physics under the Nazi regime, was once head of the physical institute there too.

Goethe wrote *'I saw Heidelberg on a perfectly clear morning, with a pleasant air both cool and invigorating. The city, just so, with the totality of its ambience, is, one might say, something ideal.'*

I could not agree more. Views from the ruins of an old castle in forested hills over River Neckar, old bridge, old town and with the easy-going atmosphere at the university, was incredible. I spent an extra day here, sampling many Black Forest Gateau.

Getting a ride on was easy on the autobahn, as long as you stood at the right place. Within half an hour, I got a lift to Munich 350km away.

Munich

Munich was the most beautiful German cities I had visited so far. This Bavarian city definitely had something more than its impressive architecture and many fantastic museums. People were lively and offered warmth to its visitors.

At Deutsches Museum Verkehrszentrum, a fantastic museum of transport, I spent some time learning about the inventions contributed by the Germans. Later I visited the Bavarian National Museum. It had an extensive collection, but unfortunately, there were only a few translations into English.

Late afternoon, I paid a visit to the Munich Olympic stadium with the memory of the 1972 Olympics, infamous terrorist attack, still fresh. Then I remembered it was the venue, only two years back, where Germany won World Cup Football Final beating Holland. Franz Beckenbauer and Johan Cruyff played here!

Next day was at the spectacular Deutsches Museum, one of the world's largest science museums. In its endless floors, it seemed to cover everything in the history of science. I had intended to spend only the morning here but ended up spending the entire day. It was still not enough.

Getting drunk in the beer hall

Munich's famous Oktoberfest was still a few months away. First time I arrived in the UK, I had tried lager. But it had tasted like fever mixture we had in India. Since then, I did not drink. But I wanted to see the famous Munich beerhalls. I arrived there in the early evening only for the atmosphere and possibly have some cold drinks. Once inside Hofbräuhaus München, the most famous beer hall in Munich, I was stunned by its size and the number of people. It could easily hold a thousand.

While I was looking around, people I had never met invited me to their table. Before I could say anything, they ordered a round of beer for all. Beer arrived, not a pint like in the UK, but a litre each. I drank it slowly. Before I had finished, another person ordered another round. I struggled to finish the second litre, but for politeness's sake, I ordered another round for the table. After three litres of beer, I was truly drunk. I returned to my youth hostel swaying all the way and happily singing Bengali song loudly.

I got up late with a massive hangover and spent the day strolling Munich streets and sorting out my visas for the rest of my travels.

Vienna Austria (embarrassed for my outfit)

Fellow travellers in Munich advised me it may not be easy to find a ride by car to Vienna from Munich because of the nature of the road. I took a train for this 350km journey, settling by a window seat for the few idle hours. Between nodding off to sleep, I watched the beautiful scenery running past the windows of hills, rivers and creeks.

As I arrived in Vienna in the evening, it started raining. After drying myself in the youth hostel, I walked through the nearly empty streets of the beautiful city to a small restaurant and then tucked into famous Viennese cuisine, the schnitzels!

They said at the youth hostel if I left early the next morning, entrance to the Hofburg Palace and the morning practice session at the famous Spanish Riding School was free.

Hofburg palace complex was a reminder of Imperial grandeur, a legacy of mighty Habsburg monarchy and their home for over six centuries. Before exploring the palace complex, I watched the Lipizzaner stallions performing elegant equine ballet, their riders showing off some of their expertise and finesse for almost an hour. Then I visited the elegant Imperial Chapel, where Vienna Boys' Choir sings Sunday Mass. I wanted very much to see a performance at the world-famous Vienna State Opera and was lucky to get a standing ticket for the next evening performance of Romeo and Juliet.

I took a tram next day to the terminus and then a walk up the hills to Kahlenberg, in the Vienna Woods. In bright sunny day view from there of Vienna below and the snow-capped Schneeberg Mountain was stunning.

I returned early to my hostel to have a shower before the evening performance. During my travel, I had with me only two pairs of jeans and three shirts. I washed and dried them at the youth hostel wherever I stayed. I chose a clean pair of jeans and a dark shirt for the evening.

Feeling smart, I arrived early at the State Opera and walked inside. It was one of the most elegant halls and staircases I had ever seen. While I was admiring its beauty by myself, other people started coming in.

I have never been so embarrassed in my life for my outfit. All the women arrived in their beautiful long black evening dresses followed by men in their tailored evening suits. I wanted to hide somewhere. Luckily, soon, the bell rang. I hurried to my standing place inside and immersed in the performance.

Yugoslavia (at a village wedding)   On the seven-hour, 500km train journey to Belgrade from Vienna, I met a group of Yugoslav seasonal workers, men and women, returning home for a wedding after their stint of work in Austria. They insisted on sharing their foods with me. When they heard I had no fixed travel plan, they invited me to their village for the wedding ceremony. I gratefully accepted. From Belgrade, we took a bus to their place and arrived in the late evening. Family of one of the fellow travellers let me stay with them for free and also offered some soup and bread. I slept heavily that night.

Next morning after a hearty breakfast, two children of the family, a twelve-year-old boy and a six-year-old girl took me around their village. Everywhere they welcomed me as an honoured guest and almost as a treasure. This was the first time any of them met an Indian. One family invited me for a sumptuous lunch and another for dinner that night. Next day I was one of the honoured guests of the bride's family at the church wedding and the grand reception afterwards. They roasted several hogs on an open fire, turning them around. Although bitter taste, I drank with everyone else the Rakija (I learnt later it contained 65% alcohol!) to celebrate. Several girls danced with me. Next day was quieter, but there was still more of hog roast, Rakija and dancing. All of this went for two more days. After that, reluctantly, I had to say goodbye to all and took a bus for Belgrade.

Belgrade   Belgrade stood at the confluence of Danube and Sava Rivers. I took a boat tour with a beautiful view of the city in the daytime. Then, I spent the evening in Skardarlija, the Bohemian street, drinking coffee and eating Baklava. But after spending a wonderful time in the village, the city felt crowded with people and cars. Buildings appeared like functional housing blocks. In this big city, people everywhere were friendly and welcoming. But two days here was enough for me.

Bulgaria (almost thrown off a train)   To go to Sophia, a 330km journey, it took much longer by train than by bus. But it was almost half the price. Before getting on the train, I saw people buying food and drinks at the station. They said there was no catering on this journey. Just in time, I bought some supplies for the next ten hours.

For the first couple of hours, the scenery outside of the Balkan Mountains was pleasant viewing. But soon the weather changed with light snow. I fell asleep. When I woke up, an hour before reaching Sofia, I tried unsuccessfully to strike conversations with some Bulgarians who had embarked at the last station. Light snow flurry fell outside when we arrived in Sophia around 9 pm. Only a few people were around, and the trams were almost empty. It took me a while to find the youth hostel.

Sofia   The weather did not improve the next morning. Only occasionally, through a gap in the cloud, I could see the Vitosha Mountain at a distance. I visited Aleksandr Nevsky Cathedral in the morning before going to the nearby Archaeological Museum. For at least 9000 years, the human had inhabited Sofia. In the museum were some delightful treasures of Thracian and Roman artefacts, including a priceless gold burial mask thought to be from the 4th Century BC.

It was still drizzling in the afternoon. I entered a coffee shop and tried striking conversation with the locals but found them not keen to speak to foreigners, almost suspicious of them. It was a setback, especially after coming from Yugoslavia. I walked across the city, full of socialist era functional housing blocks. The theme of almost unfriendly people continued during the rest of my stay in Sofia.

Next day was clear. I walked to the beautiful park, Borisova Gradina, in the centre of the city. From here I could see, at a distance, the Eagles' Bridge, *Orlov most,* over the Perlovska River. I walked by four statues of Eagles on the bridge, to a lovely square for lunch.

From Bulgaria, my train left for Bucharest in Romania, a ten-hour journey, in the early evening. I soon settled down to sleep in an almost empty compartment. I woke up when one of the ticket collectors poked me in my chest. I showed him my ticket. But he talked for a few seconds to another rail official with him.

Then they started shouting 'Americano' with all the hatred in their eyes and pulled me off the seat. They started dragging me to the door and tried to throw me off the running train. I was terrified but kept my cool enough to bring out my Indian passport and showed it to them repeating over and over 'Indisch. Indisch. Not Americano'.

They let me go. I dropped to my seat, sweating profusely.

Romania

Soon the train crossed into Romania and stopped at a small station, and the two men got out. I stayed awake for the rest of the journey to Bucharest. Outside the station, I found a coffee shop and ordered a large cup of coffee and a big breakfast.

Bucharest (at the table of the feast) At the youth hostel, I took a hot shower to get rid of my last night's memory. Situated on the banks of Dambovita River, with its elegant architecture and sophistication of its elite, Bucharest once earned the nickname Micul Paris, Little Paris. But now, French-designed Art Nouveau architecture and grand municipal buildings were mixed with utilitarian multistorey living quarters.

In the afternoon, I visited the famous bookshop Carturesti Carusel in Old Town. In gorgeous galleried space was a fantastic range of books, stationery, vinyl records and a coffee shop. After a hearty dinner there of Sarmale, cabbage Rolls filled with pork and vegetables, and Papanasi, cheese doughnuts, I made it an early night to catch up on my sleep.

I had heard of the world-famous sculptor Constantin Brancusi and was keen to see his works. Following day I walked to Targu Jiu Central Park by a river to the ensemble of the most outstanding works of the 20th-century outdoor sculpture. On the way, two teenagers followed, walking on either side of me. I stiffened but wanted to show I was relaxed and walked slowly. In their broken English, they wanted to know if I was an American. I said no; I was an Indian. But they were not interested in my nationality. They only wanted to buy off me the pair of Levi jeans I was wearing and showed some Leu notes for that. It took me some time to convince them I was not interested; they walked with me a little more trying before giving up.

At the park, I watched The Gate of Kiss, a symbol of eternal love that defies death. Underneath, young couples kissed each other passionately.

Nearby was The Endless Column, a 30m high sculpture representing the concept of infinity and infinite sacrifice of the Romanian soldiers. It stacked 15 rhomboidal modules, with a half-unit at the top and bottom. Incomplete top and the base units were to express the concept of the infinite.

In the empty field was the famous Table of Silence, comprising a circular stone table with 12 stone stools. One stool for each month of the year; their hourglass shapes stood for the passage of time. I sat on one seat and reflected on my travels. I remembered it was Easter Sunday, and in the UK, people were opening their chocolate Easter Eggs.

Shortly, a man walked from the other side of the park. He sat opposite me and put the side bag he was carrying on the table.

He said 'Bună ziua', to which I replied with the same words.

Then he took out a bottle of wine and two small glasses from his bag. He poured the wine for us before taking out a few beautifully painted eggs. We raised a glass to each other before reluctantly breaking the coloured shells of the boiled eggs. At that moment, the Table of Silence became the Table of Feast for us.

We sat silently afterwards for a long time until he left saying 'Goodbye'.

I stood up and said 'Pa! Ceau!'

After a while, I walked through a bridge to the small island in the middle of the Jiu River with sculptures of various famous artists from all over the world. On my walk to the youth hostel, few teenagers again accosted me, desperately wanting my Levi Jeans. I managed to shrug them off.

Istanbul Turkey (move away from the junkies!)   I wanted to travel to Hungary, Poland and Russia, but I had to give up on those countries. A fixed amount of money one had to exchange and spend daily as a foreigner to these Eastern blocs was beyond me. Instead, I travelled to Turkey. The train from Bucharest for Istanbul ran for a while through Bulgaria. I kept my Indian passport ready with a nervous grin.

Istanbul in the early evening was warm and made me feel at home. In the youth hostel of my four-bed dormitory room, two beds were empty. I put my backpack on one. Two roommates, from two different countries, greeted me. After a usual chat, one of them left for his dinner.

Lying on my bed, I was thinking of doing the same. Then I watched my roommate was nicking stuff from the other roommate's bag. When he found I had seen him, he just grinned and put them back. From then on, I held on to my backpack all the time, even going for my shower and then to dinner.

I dined with lightly spiced rice with eggplant and tender lamb, reminding me of northern India. Walking back in my room, I found the two roommates were now helping each other in injecting Heroin in their forearms. I left the hostel immediately and booked myself in a cheap hotel.

I had read so much about Istanbul, also formerly known as Byzantium or Constantinople. This transcontinental city straddled over Bosporus strait separating Europe and Asia. Even on the European side, there was a feeling of the Orient. Colourful shops were full of merchandise one would easily find in a bazaar in Old Delhi. But the difference was in the aroma from the coffee shops mixed with smoking from Nargile, known as Hookahs and cigarettes.

Sultanahmet Park had two of the great monuments of the world. 14th century Hagia Sophia, originally built as a cathedral, the largest human-made building in the world for over a thousand years. Its massive 30m wide dome stood 55m tall. Fascinating mosaics on its walls, including the famous 13th-century Deesis Mosaic, was a pioneer of Renaissance.

Walking in silence, I could hardly believe the engineering marvel of its time. Later I walked to the smaller Blue Mosque at the other end of the park. This 17th-century mosque with its dome and tall minarets also looked magnificent. Inside, its twenty thousand handmade intricate ceramic tiles of sapphire hue gave this mesmeric place its name.

I didn't sleep well that night. Four cups of unfiltered Turkish coffee was not a good idea.

Next morning, I walked over the recently completed Bosphorus Bridge, one of the three suspension bridges in Istanbul connecting Europe and Asia. I stood with a glint in my face, straddling Europe and Asia in the middle of the 1500m bridge. At the south side on the Asian continent, I found a shop serving Black tea and Balik-Ekmek, delicious fish sandwich.

Later at the 18th-century Cagaloglu Hamami, the largest bathhouse in Istanbul, I relaxed in a lovely bath at the end of the day. After a hearty dinner of Doner Kebab and Avya tatlisi, I slept well that night.

Greece   The express bus next day to Thessaloniki at 500km distance had a brief stop at the old town of Kavala in northern Greece on the bay. I regretted not allowing myself time in this 3rd century BC city with its five-hundred-year-old aqueduct and archaeological sites.

We reached Thessaloniki at the northwest corner of the Aegean Sea in the evening. From this 315 BC Macedonian city, was a panoramic view of venerated Mount Olympus. I spent most of the day on its seashore with a splendid view of the Ottoman White tower. In the evening, after spending a while in the opulent

Aristototelous Square, I walked to Ladadika, a busy shopping area. I filled myself with delightfully cooked, freshly caught whole fish, yoghurt and salad.

Athens   It did not take long to find a driver stopping and picking me up for Athens 500 km away. But after about three hours, he stopped at Larissa and explained this was as far as he would go. I got out to find an attractive small city surrounded by mountains and greenery. After spending almost an hour there, I found another driver going all the way to Athens. He said there were several youth hostels in this vast metropolis. Fortunately, he was from Athens and kindly took me to one in the centre of the city.

     Athens was crowded. Cars were driving like mad. But in the evening, my spirits lifted at the sight of the Acropolis on the hill at a distance.

     I left early for the Acropolis, the 2500-year-old citadel on a hill above Athens. After walking through the complex of many ruined ancient buildings, I came by Parthenon. I stood silent amongst the partly ruined majestic columns of the most famous monument of Ancient Greece, democracy and human civilisation.

     Exceptional skills of the workers who built this marble wonder so long ago were unbelievable. Even the smaller number of surviving sculptures in the place was breathtaking. I could only rage at the thought of the plunder in the recent era of more remarkable sculptures from Parthenon for display in other European museums. I spent the entire day wandering around the beautiful Metopes. Gyganomachy, the mythical battle between the Olympian gods and the Giants above the main gate, was stunning. So were the marble sculptures of the Parthenon frieze, fifty sets of statues, and the pediments, damaged like many of the marble pillars. After being thoroughly immersed in ancient history for the day, I returned numb to my hostel.

Next day was at the National Archaeological Museum. An awe-inspiring collection of Prehistoric Antiquities dating back to 1050 BC. Artefacts here brought to life the history of Rome, Greece, Egypt and the Neolithic age.

In the evening in a roadside café, I had Souvlaki with fries, tzatziki, and pita bread, with the majestic view of the Parthenon against the evening sky.

Olympia   The local bus via Pyrgos arrived in Olympia at 300km distance. Being on this historic site was magical. Unbelievable to think this place held the Olympic Games every four years from 8th century BC to 4th century AD.

Through a crypt, I entered the stadium and sat in silence for a long time on one of the broken stone seats. Then I walked around the stadium slowly, trying to imagine the special events 2000 years back with thousands in the crowd cheering.

Vast ruins of the 3000-year-old Zeus temple lay within an archaeological site of temples and buildings. Nearby Olympia Museum held extensive collections of priceless artefacts, including statues once decorated in the temples.

Ferry to Italy (brunch before wasn't a good idea!)   By midday, I settled on the ship's deck with other travellers. The first hour of the voyage went well, exchanging experiences of Greece. But once on the Ionian Sea, waves got more substantial. Most were seasick. I deeply regretted having that big brunch, all of which I threw up in the toilet. Like many, I lied on the floor inside, my gut-wrenching with every rolling wave. I wanted the eighteen-hour journey to end. I fell to sleep. Later I woke to find people rushing to deck. We were approaching Italy. With a nasty headache, I limbered up and watched our ship entering the port of Bari on the Adriatic Sea in the early morning.

My initial plan was to travel to Rome soon after I got off the ferry. But I was miserable and could not contemplate a 375 km bus journey. Youth hostel in Bari was crowded, but I only wanted a place to lie down.

Rome   Next morning I was still not right. I took a train to Rome instead of trying my luck on the road. After arriving in the afternoon, the first thing for me was to find the nearest youth hostel and rest.

In the evening, feeling better, I walked in Rome, the city of seven hills. Narrow cobblestone streets opened into Trevi Square with the famous Trevi Fountain; the marvellous 19 BC fountain stood 26m tall, with beautiful statues of Baroque design. After walking around enjoying its beauty from all angles, like everyone else, I threw a coin with my right hand over my left shoulder, hoping to come back to Rome one day. Soon I walked to the Spanish Steps, linking French Trinità dei Monti church to Spanish square below with its fountain, Fontana della Barcaccia. Popular with the locals and tourists alike.

While sitting over the steps and enjoying the atmosphere, I came across a group of young men and women of my age and started chatting to them in my sparse Italian. A girl and a boy amongst them could speak and understand English. Soon they asked me to join them as they were off to a place for dancing. I knew I was a terrible dancer but still joined for fun. After an hour of fun at the disco, I headed back to my hostel. Traffic was light in the late evening, but I realised why Italian drivers are so famous all over the world for their crazy driving.

Next morning, I visited the Palatine Hill, the centre of historical Seven Hills of Rome. According to mythology, in a cave here a she-wolf raised Romulus and Remus. It was unimaginable walking around this colossal ruins of architectures, first built by the Roman Emperor Augustus in 27 BC and subsequently by many other emperors. Nearby was the Roman Forum. Amongst its ruins and historic buildings, I came across a place which used to be a bustling marketplace. I tried to imagine this place in its heyday thronging with people of all walks of life, especially the people who had to earn their livings with hard work. I stood in silence at the venue for public speeches, wandering how much freedom of expression was there in those days for the people not in power?

Then I walked to the famous Colosseum. An iconic symbol of the Roman Empire and one of the New Seven Wonders of the world, next to busy roads. This 2000 years old masterpiece was now in a ruinous state after fire, earthquakes and through the stealing of its stones but still one of the most magnificent amphitheatres built anywhere in the world.

Its many tiers were divided into sections by curved passages and low walls, subdivided by steps and aisles. Sitting on its stone steps in one of its many galleries, I tried to imagine being there with 80,000 spectators cheering the mighty gladiators.

After spending many hours at the Colosseum, I wandered along the crazy atmosphere of the streets of Rome.

Vatican City The Vatican, just over 100 acres in size, became an independent state following a treaty signed by Mussolini and Pope Pius XII. At the entrance entry through the grand St. Peter's Square, an Obelisk, brought from Egypt, stood next. Colourful Swiss guards stood outside St. Peter's Basilica, erected over the tomb of St Peter the Apostle.

Once inside the Basilica, I was immediately drawn to Michelangelo's sculpture of La Pieta. Most beautiful human-made creation I had ever seen or imagined. Looking at this display of Virgin Mary holding the dead body of Christ after his crucifixion, her utter sadness and devastation, yet graceful acceptance, and

Christ depicted almost in peaceful slumber; I almost forgot it was carved out of stone - what a genius!

Vast yet magnificent basilica, the centre of the Catholic world, had its dome designed by Michelangelo. Everything was in such proportion it was easy to forget that from floor to the top of the dome was over 120m.

Soon I was in the greatest art galleries in the world. I walked through a gallery of statues, including Sleeping Ariadne; Belvedere Torso; artefacts from Ancient Egypt including papyruses; animal mummies, and reproductions of the Book of the Dead. Paintings from Leonardo da Vinci, Bellini, Titian and Caravaggio, filled other rooms.

Next was the exceptional Raphael room. By now, my head was almost reeling with ethereal art. I sat on the spiral staircase inside quietly for a few minutes.

My mind exploded as I entered the glorious Sistine Chapel, the papal chapel with arch windows and flattened barrel vault roof. Frescoed hangings in silver and gold by Raphael, decorated the walls and arched windows. But I could not stop focussing all my contemplation towards its ceiling with a series of Michelangelo's frescoes; venerated God's Creation of the World, God's Relationship with Mankind and Mankind's fall from God's Grace. Reluctantly, I had to leave the chapel soon because of the number of spectators coming in behind us.

My mind and heart still full with the exquisite beauty of art, I climbed up hundreds of steps to the top of the dome, the last section through a very narrow spiral staircase. There, I stood next to the giant statues of the apostles and lazed at the spectacular view of the Vatican City and the St Peters square.

Florence   Others at the hostel told me it might not be easy to find a ride to Florence. I took a chance, and luckily soon found a couple going all the way to Florence, the birthplace of Renaissance art. After leaving busy Rome, a journey through the picturesque Tuscany was most refreshing.

From the youth hostel, I walked over the bridge on River Arno to Piazzale Michelangelo over the hill. In the empty square stood a beautiful large bronze cast of David looking down at Florence. In the setting sun, Florence looked like an artist's palette.

Uffizi Gallery is the best art museum in the world. It displayed collections crammed in many halls and corridors, so many that one could easily spend a full day watching the assemblage on only one of its walls. Medieval, pre-Raphaelite and Renaissance art of geniuses such as Botticelli, Donatello, Raphael, Leonardo da Vinci and Michelangelo stood heaped on one other - breathtaking.

In its hallways were exquisite marble statues, almost stacked on each other. Any museum anywhere in the world would be proud to have only one of them. An art lover could easily spend days here, enthralled in its collections.

Birth of Venus – Botticelli

Florence cathedral

After a full day there, my head still full of grace and style, I walked to Piazza della Republica, the city square. After coffee there, in the early evening, I strolled by the beautiful domed cathedral of the city, Santa Maria del Fiore with nearby Giotto's bell tower.

Academia Gallery offered viewing of the acclaimed statue of David by Michelangelo, as well as his many unfinished figures of the Slaves. At Museo Galileo, I watched Galileo's unique artefacts, including his telescopes and the lens with which he discovered the Galilean moons. It also exhibited the Arab celestial globe, the oldest in the world. In its many rooms on several floors, were beautiful displays of scientific progress from the 15th to 19th century.

Colossal palace Palazzo Pitti by the river, in its Palatine Gallery, had hundreds of paintings by influential artists such as Raphael, Titian, Perugino, Rubens - also, by Artemisia Lomi, a female artist, now considered as one of the most talented painters of that era since Caravaggio.

Self- portrait as a female martyr - Artemisia Gentileschi

Pisa   Next day a short hitchhike to Pisa only 80 km away. My only reason to come to this old city was to see the renowned Leaning Tower of Pisa.

The amazingly beautiful clock tower looked in pristine condition, but visibly leaning over four degrees to one side. It has been leaning soon after built in the 12th century because of an unstable foundation. Its height from the ground on the low side was 55.86m and 56.67m on the high side. In the 16th century, Galileo Galilei had dropped two cannonballs of different masses from the tower to show their descent speed was independent of their mass. We could only go up the first two floors of its seven storeys, because of the conservation need.

After a visit to the beautiful cathedral next to it, in a nearby restaurant, I made sure to have a lunch of spaghetti Bolognese. I was in Bolognia after all.

Venice   A five-hour train journey reached Venice in the early evening. This floating city was gleaming with city lights reflecting in its canals, indeed the city of Romance. Soon I was strolling around narrow streets, occasionally crossing over canals in this dreamy place. No cars or any other traffic. Couples, old and young, ambled holding hands, a few standing by the ornate bridges and passionately kissing. Did I feel a shiver - was it the breeze from the canal or a bout of loneliness?

I woke from a deep sleep with the wake-up call of the gondoliers' 'Ooooeeeee' in the morning. Then I roamed this elegant city on the Adriatic Sea, on a group of small islands separated by canals and linked by hundreds of bridges. Refugees from nearby Roman towns and countryside originally settled Venice, fleeing waves of Germanic and Hun onslaughts almost two thousand years back. Buildings of refined Rococo designs now crowded the city centre.

Soon I was at the attractive Piazza San Marco. After nearly an hour taking in its sights, I sat in a coffee shop by the square. Over a cup of coffee and mouth-watering seafood Cicchetti, I remembered Venice was repeatedly devastated in the 14th, 16th and 17th century by plague, the Black Death.

Away from the square in the afternoon, I found a Gondola stop on one of the smaller canals. Price was cheaper in the afternoon than it would be in the evening for the romantic couples. Although alone on the Gondola, I did not have to pay extra as it was not a busy time. Soon we were travelling gently between the old buildings, under narrow bridges and by the small waterfront restaurants. It was the most relaxing one hour before we moored on the broader part of the canal. I got out and looked towards the open sea at a distance and Venice, once an important trading place between the Byzantine Empire and the Muslim world.

With the sun setting over the horizon, the entire city and its waterways took a light pink colour and looked otherworldly.

Later, I treated myself to a decent dinner of the Venetian version of enticing moules mariniere. Next day, I walked through narrow backstreets, with several small churches and Basilicas with priceless paintings of Bellini, Tiepolo and Titian. Rialto Bridge over the Grand Canal looked the most ornate and beautiful bridge in Venice. After standing by it for a while there, I walked to St Marco's Square to relax. Before the sunset, there was a lot of cloud in the sky. The whole spectacle again became magical in fuchsia pink

Milan (The Last Supper by Leonardo)   I arrived by train to Milan, the city of modern fashion. But my only reason to go to Milan was to visit the nearby Santa Maria della Grazie, thirty minutes bus ride from the station.

I wanted to see Leonardo da Vinci's 'Last supper' painting and arrived by a quiet convent with this revered composition in the end wall of a refectory dining hall. I stood in silence in front of the towering 15th-century mural, the best-known works of Christian art. Flanked by his twelve apostles, Jesus has just declared that one of them will betray him. The painting showed the reaction of each disciple to the news, capturing twelve individuals amid querying, gesticulating, or displaying various shades of horror, anger and disbelief - amazing.

From Milan, I left for Zermatt by train, only six hours' ride and tantalising close to the Alps.

Zermatt. Switzerland   Crossing Italian Alps into Swiss Alps was breathtaking. But soon it started snowing heavily. Zermatt was miserable. I was glad to get inside my youth hostel. I wanted to see the most known Alpine mountain, Matterhorn. The famous peak and the town, both derived their names from the alpine meadows or 'matten' in German and was only a few kilometres apart.

Next morning snowfall was only a flurry with thick clouds. No chance of seeing the high mountains of the Pennine Alps surrounding this place! Hoping to find a break in the weather, I took the ski lift. After 700m ascent, Zermatt below was invisible in the snow.

At the top, most people got out with their ski poles and left prodding over the fresh snow. By now the sky was lighter, and snow had stopped. I waited at the top station by myself for over two hours to get a view of the Matterhorn. Several ski lifts came and went, I was shivering but stay put. Then, for only for five minutes, the cloud cleared away. In front appeared the zagged peak of Matterhorn. Clouds came back, and it started snowing heavily.

Down in Zermatt, after a warming bowl of Swiss barley soup, I visited the Matterhorn Museum. Along with dramatic pictures of Matterhorn and recent climbs, it told the story of its first ascent. Only three of the seven climbers survived the descent.

In worse weather the next day, I took a train to Geneva.

Geneva   I arrived on a sunny day in Geneva. At the foot of Alps, on the shore of Lake Geneva, the city looked stunning. In the cold evening, I walked around the banks of the largest lake in Switzerland. Geneva sparkled all around me. Jet d'Eau in the lake, tallest water fountain in the world, unfortunately, was closed for maintenance.

Following morning, I walked by the United Nations Buildings and the International Red Cross opposite the park. I watched from a distance the World Health Organisation complex and thought about the contribution the nations can do for each other, only if they pulled together.

Later, I strolled by the promenades and across the Rhone River into the expensive shopping and banking area. I gaped at the prices of wristwatches and pieces of jewellery displayed in windows on Rue de Rive and Rue du Rhone. Later I treated myself to some inexpensive but delightful Swiss chocolate instead.

Geneva was too expensive for me. I would have liked to have taken a boat tour on the largest Lake Geneva at the foot of the Alps. Instead, I walked to the Town Hall, founding places of the League of Nations and the Red Cross. Later, I wandered into the Plainpalais, a large outdoor flea market, selling antiques, curios and cheaper chocolates.

In the afternoon I took a 3 hour's train journey to Zurich.

Zurich (caught in a boyfriend/girlfriend plot)   On the train, I met another backpacker, a girl of my age. She had been to Paris, mostly hitchhiking, now going home to Zurich. We exchanged our experiences on the road. When she learnt I had no fixed plan in Zurich, she invited me to her place. I was surprised but did not hesitate to accept the offer. I was already running short of money.

We arrived in Zurich, the largest city in Switzerland, in the early evening. In her one-bedroom flat, she cooked a simple dinner. I slept later on the sofa in the living room.

Over breakfast, she elaborated her cunning plan. Before she left for her backpacking tour, she had a big row with her long-term boyfriend. She wanted me to accompany her when she meets him today to make him jealous. There was a fair in one of the many parks in Zurich. He was working there in a stall. Two of us walked side by side, nonchalantly eating bars of chocolate, to his stall. He came running over to her and gave her an enormous hug and a long kiss. They talked in German for a while. Then only, he said hello to me, still holding her close. The plan had worked!

They invited me to join for dinner in a restaurant, and the boyfriend would pay. I soon left the couple to make up their lost time, to explore the city.

Zurich, with its mountain, blue lake, two rivers and many parks, brought city life and idyllic nature very close together. This financial capital of Switzerland, glittering with high-end shops and fancy chocolates, had been settled permanently for over 2,000 years.

After a relaxing day in the city, in the evening they treated me to a lovely dinner of cheese fondue, rosti and chocolate fondue. In the morning, the boyfriend cooked breakfast for the three of us and then gave me a lift to the main road for my onward journey.

Luxemburg   It was easy to find a ride to Luxembourg, the wealthiest country in the world. This smallest country in Europe with less than half a million population in the evening looked opulent with many historic buildings. Its streets looked deserted. I found a restaurant close to my hostel and had a bowl of Bouneschlupp, thick meat and vegetable soup, expensive but very tasty.

By lunchtime the next day, I realised there was nothing for me to explore here in this rich city.

Belgium Brussels   Soon I got a ride to Brussels. We stopped at a service station for coffee, and the driver kindly paid. In three and a half hours, we reached Brussels, capital of the European Union.

Large Town square, known as Grand Place or Grote Markt, was surrounded by opulent buildings. Every other shop sold the most delicious chocolate I have ever tasted. After enjoying coffee and chocolate, I strolled to the small bronze statue of a naked boy urinating in a basin, Manneken Pis. This 17th-century statue is the best-known symbol of Brussels showing their sense of humour.

Next day I visited the Atomium, the landmark 102m tall structure built during the World Expo in 1958. Large stainless steel spheres formed the shape of an iron crystal magnified 165 billion times! I did not go up. Instead, I lied on the grass, gazing at this fascinating construction.

Back to the UK

Around the service station, I managed to find a friendly truck driver going to Ostend. It turned out he was going back to England to a place near London and agreed to take me.

My original plan was to spend a maximum of three years in the UK. After I had visited Western and Eastern Europe, now I wanted to go to France, Spain, Portugal, before crossing over to North Africa. Then to continue overland to reach Egypt to see its ancient treasures. From there to Mecca and Medina, the most important Islamic pilgrimage site. Afterwards overland via Iraq, Iran and Afghanistan to India. As an Indian, I had to exclude Pakistan as the two countries have fought only recently.

But I learnt as a non-Muslim I would not be allowed in Mecca or Medina, my only reason to travel to Saudi Arabia. Also, a war had broken between Egypt and Libya. Another was looming between Iraq and Iran. Extremely disappointed, I changed my plan. I would travel to France and Spain before flying back to India.

Paris France   My girlfriend came to see me off at Dover Ferry. But at the last minute, she decided to join me in coming to Paris.

After a ferry crossing, and then a train journey, we arrived in Gare du Nord. Trying to find our way to the youth hostel, I found most French people avoided speaking in English to English speakers. My sparse French and my girlfriend's high school French got us to the place.

We strolled on the busy boulevard to Arc de Triomphe, a glorious gate built in honour of those who fought and died for France in Revolutionary and Napoleonic Wars. Soon we settled ourselves down for a cup of coffee and chocolate croissants in one of the many cafes by Champs de Elisse sitting outside and enjoying the flow of life.

Early next morning we queued to get into Louvre. After going through its extensive grounds, soon we were inside the largest art museum in the world. We felt lost into its vast number of rooms displaying antiquities from Assyria, Egypt, Greece and everywhere in the world. The entrance hall had the most beautiful statue of Venus de Milo, and the 2000-year-old statue of Aphrodite, Greek goddess of love and beauty. We explored rooms full of Egyptian antiquities from Nile civilisation, Ptolemaic, Byzantine, Roman and Greek periods.

Then we dream-walked through displays of rare and beautiful creations. We gaped at a 7000 BC statue in plaster and reed from a Neolithic archaeological site in Jordan, 800 century BC Human-headed winged bull from Assyria, 190 BC Greek marble statue of Winged Victory and the sombre 15th statue of Tomb of Phillipe Pot, amongst so many others.

Head reeling with beauty, we entered the galleries of the masters, Raphael, Van Dyck, Delacroix, Caravaggio, and so many others. Caravaggio's Death of the Virgin illustrated a brutal view of the religious theme, magical in its work of light and shadow on the canvas.

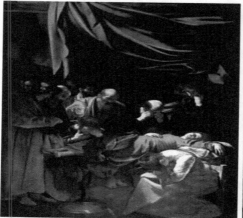 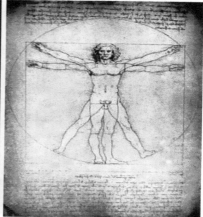

Heads still spinning, we entered the room of Leonardo da Vinci paintings. There was an enormous crowd by his most famous painting. We walked across to his other masterpieces. I stopped, stunned by his portrayal of Vitruvian Man, a painting blending mathematics and art in the study of proportions of the human body. So anatomically correct yet a masterpiece in artistry.

Soon we came to the world-renowned, enigmatic painting, Mona Lisa. We watched in silence before being asked to move on. We came back there again to bury ourselves in its incredible mystic beauty.

But unfortunately, closing time came too soon, and we had to leave.

In the evening we walked to the beautifully lit iconic Eiffel Tower 324m, the tallest human-made structure until 1930. We walked the steps to the second level, open to visitors. But even from the second level, the view of Paris in the evening was enchanting.

Next morning I said goodbye to my girlfriend at the rail station. Knowing her sense of directions, I made sure she did not end up taking a train going in the opposite direction.

Crossing over River Seine, I arrived by the celebrated Notre-Dame Cathedral. Even from a distance, the place with two towers, one larger than the other, looked majestic. Like many, I had read Victor Hugo's The

Hunchback of Notre-Dame and could not wait to get inside. Only over a decade back, the place celebrated its 800th anniversary. Inside walls and arches dazzled with stained glass windows.

After spending several hours at the place, I walked across the River Seine. Pleasure boats sailed under its many bridges. Couples walked around holding hands. I felt a pang, was I missing my girlfriend already?

Next day I took a 25km bus to the Palace of Versailles. Most of the day, I spent promenading its vast yet beautiful gardens and many rooms in the Palace. I could not stop thinking of the generations of Emperors living in such luxury and extending the palace over the centuries, while most of the population lived in destitution - justifiably resulting in the French Revolution.

Champagne District   Outside the Paris suburb, I stood by the motorway going east. I wanted to visit the Champagne district. I do not drink, but this drink of celebration fascinated me. As luck will have it, the driver who gave me a ride, was a wine trader, returning home after two years in England.

He was going to a village 20km west of Reims. On our 130km journey, he gave me a beginner's tutorial on Champagne. There were three main Champagne districts in the region. Only wine produced in this region can be called Champagne, something to do with the amount of chalk in the soil. He said only a handful of villages has Grand Crus ratings, a percentile rating based on their location and quality of grapes. Theirs produces received the highest price.

Champagne was a blend of up to three grape varieties. Pruning, vineyard yield, pressing, and maturation time had strict rules. A National Institute regulated the quality. My head was still bubbling with all this when I saw by roadside acres and acres of vineyards. I asked if I could go to one of the Crus villages. He dropped me next to a tiny village.

I saw people working in the vineyards and asked if I could go there. They waved me on to the field. In mid- July, the vines were full of beautiful round grapes. I learnt from one man it will be another seven to eight weeks before they will be ready for harvesting. He picked up a handful of grapes for me to taste. Lovely, but still sour.

After spending an hour there, I walked to the only restaurant in the village. Delightful Soupe a l'oignon, a traditional soup made of onions and beef stock, served with croutons and melted cheese on top. I asked if I could see any place they pressed wine by treading on. They showed me outside a huge wooden bowl, which they traditionally climbed barefoot to make red wines.

A villager working at Moet & Chandon wine cellar gave me a ride. The place was massive.

Soon a free tour started. They guided us through the process of winemaking, bottling and then storing to age. We explored only a small section of the 28 km underground cellars - staggering. At the end of the tour, we all had a large glass of Champagne - delightful.

I spent the night in a youth hostel in Reims. Then I hitched ride west towards Paris and then again towards the west close to the border with the Basque Country in Spain.

Angouleme I stopped at Angouleme as it was already close to evening, and my destination to Hendaye on the border was still 300 km. Ramparts from Roman times surrounded this town on the riverbank with many beautiful small gardens around. For my dinner, they served duck meat and liver with foie gras with a free bottle of red wine. Together it tasted good. Am I turning into a wine lover? Next morning, I got up late with a bit of a hangover. From the small bottle of red wine? Surely not.

A ride from Angouleme to Hendaye, a French border town, via Bordeaux, took over nine hours, although only 300km distance. I had to wait outside Bordeaux for a long time before somebody picked me up to Hendaye.

I arrived at a small railway station in Hendaye, empty in the late evening. The last train for the day to San Sebastian had left only 15 minutes earlier. By now, I was very, very hungry. With my 'hangover' in the

morning, I had escaped breakfast. Later on the road, I only had cups of coffee. I found a small restaurant near the station. It was closing, but the waitress took pity after having a look at me. She said nothing from the menu was available, but she could get some seafood chowder. It was the first time I had sampled chowder. It tasted heavenly, not only because I was famished. I slept on a bench in the park by the railway station to catch the first train.

San Sebastian Spain Next morning an hour's train to San Sebastian, on the Bay of Biscay. I could easily see why they called it mini Paris in Basque style. I relaxed and swam the rest of the day on its beautiful seashore in the warm sunshine.

After watching a gorgeous sunset on the Atlantic, I walked to lively Parte Vieja. It would be packed in a few weeks during September Basque festival. Thousands gather then to celebrate Basque culture, singing and dance contest, poetry reading, many old games and contests, including stone lifting and cider tasting to go with all. I was sorry it was over a month away. I filled myself with Pintxos, Basque answer to Spanish Tapas.

Next day I visited the nearby museum. Its displays showed evidence of the human presence around here dated from 24,000 - 22,000 BC. Carved stone used as knives to cut animal skin and other artefacts proved the settlers here were hunters and Homo sapiens.

After a delightful lunch in a seaside restaurant of Gilda Pintxo - pinkish anchovies, chillies and a freshly pitted olive which looked like a lollipop, I took a train to Bilbao.

Bilbao The sun was setting on the Atlantic as I reached Bilbao, the biggest city in Basque Country, which was busier than San Sebastian. Fishing boats crowded its harbour. I wandered to Casco Viejo, the seven streets, the original medieval site. Narrow roads were full of colourful taverns offering mouth-watering plates of seafood and varieties of drinks, including ciders and Kalimotxo. I had a dish of Bilbao's famous Txangurros, beautifully cooked crunchy spider crabs - heavenly.

I went to the docks in the morning, where boats had just returned with their plentiful catch of varieties of fishes. I thought about asking one of the fishermen if I could accompany them when they sail next time to the sea. I knew the waves in Atlantic would be very strong. My memory of seasickness on the passenger ferry from Greece to Italy came back, and I chickened out.

In France, I had found people were friendly and always helpful. They also did not mind speaking English once they realise you are not English. But in this Basque Country, where the Spanish Revolution started in the 1930s and then brutally squashed, people were vibrant, jolly and always welcoming visitors with open arms.

After wandering around the port for a while, I had a lovely lunch of Kokotxas, Basque speciality of fleshy cheeks of cod served in a sauce of garlic, white wine and olive oil thickened with flour.

Then, I waited by the roadside for a ride to Segovia, 300 km distance. After a while, a driver pulled by. He was going to Madrid and asked why I wanted to stop in Segovia. I explained I wanted to see the famous Roman aqueduct.

Segovia After checking in at the hostel, I walked with the backdrop of the beautiful Roman architecture, to a restaurant where they served Cochinillo Asado, the speciality dish of Segovia, best not only in the Castilla region but in the whole of Spain.

They found me a table close to the open kitchen where chefs were preparing dishes. From several roasting suckling pigs on large skewers, soon one was taken out. The chef cut the meat with a dinner plate instead of a knife! A bit of a show-off. But the meat was so tenderly cooked, it did not need a knife.

My plate arrived, complete head of a pig with large cheeks - the whole thing melted in my mouth like butter - luscious. I finished every bit and heartily thanked everyone.

The famous Roman Aqueduct, most extensive of its kind, stood proudly intact in Segovia. This 1st-century engineering wonder brought water to the old city from a river in the mountain. In places, it reached a height of 28.5m. Both single and double arches, in total almost 70, stood supported by pillars.

Later, I visited the Alcázar of Segovia, the fortress. High above on a rock above the confluence of two rivers, shaped like the bow of a ship, it looked like a fairy tale place. No wonder Walt Disney copied this in Cinderella Castle. In the late afternoon, I got a 70 km ride to Madrid.

Madrid Although I reached Madrid around sunset, it took me a couple more hours to find a place in one of the youth hostels, all full of tourists.

Next day I visited the world-famous Prado museum. There were displays of hundreds of beautiful paintings of great masters such as Velazquez, El Greco and Bosch. But for me, exhibitions of the most famous Spanish romantic painter, Francisco Goya were exceptional. 18th-19th centuries artist Goya was known, both as the last of the Old Masters and the pioneer of the moderns. Exquisite colourful and vibrant works were easy to relate to for someone like me with no artistic background

Colossus Goya

Late afternoon at Puerta del Sol, the city's thriving spot, the centre of all the Roads in Spain, I tucked into baguette stuffed with deep-fried, battered squid.

Next day, a Sunday, I visited the large open-air market. Music bands played next to food stalls. After happily mingling with the crowd, I saw some people eating prawns from paper cones. Soon I bought a cone full of lightly cooked prawns in saltwater served with a wedge of lemon - simple food at its best. Without feeling guilty, I went back for more later.

In the afternoon I went to the Las Ventas bullring. Initially, I was excited. Several matadors, elegantly dressed and riding on padded horses, entered to cheers from the packed arena. They paraded the stage and raised their caps to the 'presidente' and then to the crowd accompanied by band music.

Then they let out one of the many bulls from its caged enclosure when two picadors, each armed with a lance, entered the place. Riding on heavily padded blindfolded horses, they went by the bull running towards them. Each of them stabbed on the bull's neck, leading to the animal's first loss of blood. Picadors left the place, and the matador entered the arena alone on foot, waving muleta, a red cloth encouraging the bull to come towards him. Then he planted two decorated barbed sticks in the bull's shoulders. He left the place to cheers from the crowd.

By now the beast was bleeding heavily and moving slowly, weakened by blood loss. Finally, the matador re-entered the ring alone with his muleta in one hand and a sword in the other. After several passes, making the bleeding bull further weak, audience shouting 'jole', he stabbed the animal between its shoulders, puncturing the animal's heart and killing it. The dead animal was then pulled out by some ponies around the ring triumphantly before taking it outside.

It was horrible to watch, especially when one realises the bull had no chance. There would be more bulls to come to 'fight' the 'brave' matadors. But I could not watch this cruel sport anymore and left the place halfway.

Before getting onto the train for Barcelona, I bought coffee with yummy Calamari sandwiches for the 500km trip.

Barcelona   The capital city of Catalonia, had suffered a lot under ruthless General Franco until his death only a few years back. Walking in this beautiful city in the evening, one could easily sense an air of newly earned freedom. Almost a party atmosphere everywhere.

In the morning I arrived at its beautiful beachside. Swimming in the warm Mediterranean Sea was refreshing after all my travels - reminded me of South India. I spent most of the day there, tucking myself with ice creams, alternating with croquettes of shellfish and cheese.

I would have loved to see a football match of world-famous Barcelona Football club at Camp Nou to watch players like Johan Cruyff play, but the season was yet to start.

Instead, in the evening, in a small theatre, I watched the famous Flamenco dancing. Recitals, accompanied by guitar beautifully followed the emotional intensity, proud carriage, expressive use of the arms and rhythmic stamping of the feet - breathtaking and exotic.

Late next morning I walked to Barri Gotic, the Gothic Quarter in the old city with quaint narrow cobblestone streets. Many buildings here dated back to the Roman settlement of the place including the picturesque Gothic Church. Most remarkable place next was the work of Antoni Gaudi, the magnificent unfinished church Sagrada Familia. Of its many spires, some were built after Gaudi's death, and there were some yet to be made. Spires of ascending orders in height represented the apostles, Mary and Jesus. Its interior was equally spellbinding. Art Nouveau movement started here a century ago. Catalan legacy of this was visible throughout Barcelona.

Ruins of Roman and Medieval walls and colourful Magic Mountain of Montjuïc by Palau National in the evening looked charming. Later I walked to Boqueria, one of the many food markets in Barcelona. After passing by many zestful shops, I noticed a stall with the most colourful paella. I sat outside, eating paella and watching people happily walking by.

It was not difficult to get a ride next morning to Toulouse 250km distance through spectacular Pyrenees Mountains. After waiting there for an hour, I managed a 200km ride to Bordeaux, known for its speciality drink. From Bordeaux, I got a night train to Brest, another 500km away and ten hours' journey.

I slept until arriving in Brest in Brittany in the early morning. Brest in a sheltered bay at the western tip of the peninsula, occupying slopes of hills, looked beautiful in the morning sunshine.

I had the entire day to spare before my night ferry to England. I walked over Pont de Recouvrance, a massive drawbridge 64m high over the Penfield River. Brest had been part of many naval wars. Massive bombings during the WWII by allied air force over occupying German submarine base destroyed most of the city's old architecture. I strolled by remaining oldest monument in the city, the Tanguy Tower. Soon I found a creperie and had melt in the mouth buckwheat crepes stuffed with ham, egg and cheese.

People in Bretonne were different compared to the French people I met elsewhere. More traditional, family-oriented, firm believers in Christianity, reminding me of the Irish. Celtics in Ireland, of course, came from around here a few centuries back.

After more crepe, this time with honey and strawberry, I took the night ferry to Plymouth in the south-west of England. I slept most of the 14 hours on the floor. Luckily the English Channel crossing was not bumpy.

I said my last goodbye to my girlfriend, not knowing that our love will pull us together again. With my rucksack as the only check-in luggage, I boarded my plane to Delhi via Kabul, three years since my arrival in the UK.

A day in Kabul Afghanistan

1977 September   My flight arrived in Kabul before dawn, and the connecting flight to New Delhi was in the evening. Airport was only 5 km from the city. I followed the crowd to get a bus to the city.

High in a narrow valley between Hindukush Mountains, Kabul stood at 1790m, beautiful in the early morning sunshine. The city was in a strategic location along the trade routes of South and Central Asia for 3,500 years. Because of its position, over the centuries many foreign powers had invaded the country. Afghans were known to be fearless fighters, yet friendly towards visitors.

Kabul in 1977

Kabul River ran through the heart of the city, dividing its main bazaars, situated around narrow, bendy streets. Relaxed atmosphere, reminding me of the markets in north India. I sat in a roadside tea shop, taking my time over Kahwah, a combination of green tea, cardamom pods, cinnamon bark and saffron strands with freshly fried crunchy sambosas.

It was easy to chat with the locals as they could understand my Hindi a bit. A couple was taking a late morning tea break. The husband worked in an airlines office, and the wife was a lecturer in the nearby university. Both spoke excellent English and Hindi. I saw younger women going to university, most wearing miniskirts and chatting happily. Different from what I had seen women wearing in Istanbul recently, where they wore more reserved clothes. The couple explained that only older women wore traditional Firaq partug trousers, with a long Kamis shirt with a belt. Only a very few wore a burqa.

Afghan women were eligible to vote in 1919, a year after in the UK and a year before in the USA. Purdah had been abolished. Only a decade ago, the constitution had secured equal rights for the women. Men mostly wore traditional clothes, although a small number chose European style suits and neckties. The couple talked excitedly about a very successful rock concert in Kabul they attended, only two years back.

Nearby was 16th-century Eid Gah Mosque inside the Gardens of Babur, built by the emperor commemorating his invasion of India and to glorify Islam. After a lovely late lunch of Qabli pulao, a pulao with lamb, I headed back to the airport in the afternoon.

Arriving in New Delhi in the evening, I found someone had gone through my rucksack, my only check-in luggage. I had coins for my brothers from every country I had visited. All were gone with other items from inside the bag.

Burying dead cows after a super cyclone

1977 November Andhra Pradesh. India

We all heard the terrible news on the radio overnight. A super cyclone had hit Andhra Pradesh with 250km/hr wind. Tidal sea wave from the Bay of Bengal had gone inland for over 16 km, destroying everything in its path.

For the next few days, it was headline news in all the newspapers. As more report came in, we learnt over 10,000 people had been killed, and hundreds of villages wiped out. Krishna River delta was the worst affected areas. A 6m high storm surge had hit the region. The newspapers were full of heart- wrenching pictures of bloated bodies floating in the waters and of mass pyres.

I grew up with flooding in the nearby Damodar River every few years. I had seen my father arranging relief for the affected villagers. He organised shelter for them on our school grounds, running the mass kitchen and vaccinating them against cholera. Later, while in college, I had organised similar efforts for river floods in other parts of our district, with my younger brothers and friends helping. But this was massive. Still, we wanted to do something. It did not take long for me to find seven junior doctors and dentists to form a party to go to Andhra and offer our help.

We collected medical supplies as much as we could. Eight of us got on a train from Howrah station to Vijayawada in Andhra. On the train, the first thing I did was to inoculate everyone as soon as we left the station - enough time to get over the after-effects of vaccination on the 20 hours long journey.

We arrived Vijaywada twelve days after the cyclone. The station was full of various national and international relief agencies and the army. We visited the district magistrate office in the town teeming with people. One official said if we wanted to help, we could go to Vuyyuru 30 km away.

The tidal wave had washed away the railway line between Vijaywada and Vuyyuru. No bus service was running. We managed a ride on an empty relief truck going there. Closer to Vuyyuru, the road became terrible. Frequently we got off so the car could move over the washed-out broken road. All along the way, carcasses of uprooted giant tamarind trees and telegraph poles pockmarked an otherwise eerily peaceful landscape of flooded agricultural fields. Surprisingly, many coconut palms had withstood the storm.

Vuyyuru was swarming with relief workers and army personnel. Hundreds of bedraggled villagers with children filled several relief camps. Government with support from International and larger relief organisations were now running a full-fledged relief operation. An official explained very little we could do to help as a medical team. He suggested, however, if we wanted to help, we could go to the washed-out villages and help with burying carcasses of the dead animals. They were becoming health hazards. He said not only well over ten thousand people had died, but over a hundred thousand livestock were also killed.

We talked amongst ourselves and quickly agreed we were there to help in any way possible. Dead animals rotting around will be a significant health risk when, eventually, people returned to their villages.

Local shops have opened up their supplies and were cooking rice for the victims. Looks on the faces of the people who had lost everything, despite being alive, told the actual story. From a few villagers outside the relief camps, we heard many had seen their mothers, sisters and husbands washed away before their eyes. They had seen their children swept away, and their houses collapse. Some were swept away themselves by the wave for several kilometres.

We bought a few shovels, a tarpaulin and other essentials such as rice, onions and chillies from the local shops. We knew there would be no safe drinking water and bought a few jerrycans. Then we spent the night in the deserted railway station. We agreed to have only one meal a day, in the evening, to save time and our provision.

Early next morning, we got drinking water from a tap in the town and left on foot for the villages suggested by the officials. The stench of decomposing animal bodies and rotting flesh consumed our 8 km journey. Village after the village was razed to the ground. A few of us sobbed when we spotted a rotting human body in a small pond behind uprooted trees.

We found two villages close to each other and set a camp next to an uprooted tree, only a tarpaulin roof for shelter. There were dozens of dead animals. Many lay between the ruined huts, others on the field. We set out to work immediately. Four of us dug a mass grave outside the village. Others carried the corpses there. It was hard work under the scorching sun of south India. But we carried on. After working the entire day and then cleaning ourselves in the slimy water in a pond, we boiled our rice. With chilly and onion, it went down well. Rest of the evening, we sang choruses.

We had set ourselves a routine. In five days we cleared both villages of the dead animals. We were all in a wonderful spirit, but at the end of five days there, we had run out of provisions, more importantly of drinking water. We decided to return.

Part two

Family and work travels, adventures and volunteering 1982 – 2013

We had said a final goodbye to each other in 1977, but the power of love brought us together. My girlfriend came over to India in 1980. We got married in a small non-religious simple ceremony in my village with close relatives and friends. Her brother visited from Ireland. We went to Darjeeling for our honeymoon. View of the Kanchenjunga and the Sunrise at Tiger Hill was even more breathtaking with my wife by my side.

1981 Ireland

Only a few months after our first daughter was born in Kolkata, we realised for many reasons it would be more than a struggle to live as a family in India. We returned to Ireland at the end of November to my wife's family, with only allowed five pounds for each of three of us. With borrowed suit and tie from my father-in-law, I tried unsuccessfully for a job in Ireland for a few weeks.

1982- 1996 Isle of Wight England

Luckily, soon I secured a job without interviews, first for six weeks in the north-west of England and then another for three months in the country's south in the Isle of Wight. Three months of the job there carried on for fourteen years on this lovely Island.

We loved this small island with the children growing up. Beautiful Freshwater Bay beaches were our regular weekend place to relax. Hill-walking with our dog, Digger in the winter evening under bright stars with a torch, trampling over dried brambles bushes, was our favourite evening pastime. We called it our star walk.

We also visited Carisbrooke Castle occasionally. In this pre-Roman motte-and-bailey castle, famous in English history, Charles I was imprisoned before his execution in 1649.

But our favourite time was outside, by the moats surrounding the castle. Our girls loved rolling down them on their back, with Digger running after.

Visits to The Needles at Alum Bay for a chair lift down to the shore by its multi-coloured sand cliffs, was always a favourite to bring our friends and visitors.

1982 Italy   We took a family holiday with our baby daughter to Italy, which I had enjoyed so much and had found to be the most child-friendly.

We visited the usual sites of Rome for a few days before going to Assisi in Umbria on our way to Venice. Situated amid rolling hills, Assisi is best known as the birthplace of St. Francis, Italy's patron saint, also remembered as a lover of nature. St. Francis was buried in the Basilica of San Francesco next to a friary. There was a beautiful fresco of Lorenzetti's at the church depicting the Crucifixion, Deposition from the Cross and then the Entombment of Christ.

After spending two beautiful days in this Umbrian town, we went to Venice. With my wife by my side, the beautiful city indeed became a romantic city.

1985 Kitzbuhel Austria   Although I have been to the mountains a few times, there was no scope of skiing on the Himalayan slopes. My wife and I needed a holiday. We chose Kitzbuhel with our two daughters, three and a half years old and the other who would be 2 yrs soon. Between Hohenenkamm and Kitzbuhel Horn mountains, it was Europe's best-known winter sports resort and held the annual World Cup ski races and downhill races on its Strief slope.

We arrived on a sunny afternoon with heavy snow on the ground. Our girls loved sploshing around the soft snow in their new snow boots. In the town, we went to a ski shop and arranged for a beginner ski instruction class for my wife for the next few days and hired skis for all of us. I would spend time with the children on the low slope.

The girls on their skis, even with no ski poles, quickly picked up the sport. With their centre of gravity close to the ground, they had no fear of falling. Whereas, I found it challenging to stay upright most of the time and kept falling over with my daughters laughing at me. My wife did not have a grand time learning to ski either.

We celebrated our youngest daughter's second birthday in the evening with a beautiful chocolate cake made in the hotel.

Salzburg   Following day, we took a day trip to Salzburg. The bus drove through beautiful snowy mountains to Salzburg 80km away. We wanted to visit this place so famously associated with Mozart and the film 'Sound of Music', I am ashamed to say I had seen a few times.

Nestled in the foothills of the Alps, Salzburg had the perfect blend of history and culture, being home to Mozart, an ancient fortress, and several of Sound of Music sites. Salzburg means 'salt fortress', and for thousands of years, salt was mined from around this place, making it an important trading city. We roamed through its baroque architecture overlooked by massive Hohensalzburg Fortress before walking by the birthplace of Mozart, now a museum, in the heart of the city.

Lunch was at the Residentplatz square, bordered by Salzburg Cathedral and the Sound of Music film famous fountain. Even though we were full, we could not resist Sacher torte, a beautiful chocolate dessert. Soon it was time to return to Kitzbuhel.

Next few days in Kitzbuhel, we spent all day having fun learning how to ski from our children. We were still falling over and were being laughed at by the younger ones.

1986 Ireland Donegal   One of the best thing about travelling in Ireland was that within only a few hours' drive you could be in any part of the country. We drove to Donegal, in the northwest between the ranges of low mountains, the most picturesque part of the country.

We came by the roadside to a Neolithic site known as Kilclooney More Portal tomb, from 3000 BC. On a rough moorland, enormous roof stones on two portal stones rested on its two chambers.

Soon we drove by a long empty beach on the Atlantic before walking down to a long stretch of pristine golden sand. Beautiful untouched beach, at least 4 km long, in the middle of summer, did not have a single person except us. Our girls went on creating a long line of their footprints on the untouched sand as we watched.

In search of endangered Rhino in the foothills of Himalayas

1991 Jaldapara India   The girls were growing up quickly. I wanted to take them to see wildlife in their natural environment. Three of us took a trip to India to see the Indian greater one-horned Rhinos, found only in the Terai at the Himalayan foothills. This magnificent beast was on the list of extinction risk animals, only two thousand remaining in the wild.

They loved the toy train from Siliguri, then pony rides on the mall and dressing up as tea picker girls in Darjeeling. Later, we took a 3 hours car journey from Siliguri to Jaldapara National Park through the jungles. They were excited to hear wild elephant sometimes crossed these roads, but luckily we did not come across any. But they loved when we stopped to let a group of spotted deer cross the road.

Tourist lodge in Jaldapara was on a wooden platform. They told us not to get out of the place after dark. Leopards and rarely, tigers roam the park. Next morning we had a ride on the back of an elephant in the jungle in search of Rhinos. There were only around seventy-five of Rhinos in this national park. For the first couple of hours, the only exciting thing apart from the ride itself was seeing a group of Gaurs, Indian Bison, munching in the thick vegetation. The girls loved when the elephant stood on a snake, a Cobra, crushing it to death.

Later in the afternoon, the girls watched with delight the Mahut, and his helpers washing the elephants in a stream.

Next morning before going out for another elephant ride, we saw a rescued cute orphan Tiger cub in a cage, then we spotted two more Rhinos on our elephant ride in the day.

1991 Bhutan

We drove next day to Jaigaon, India's border with Bhutan. Through an impressive Bhutan Gate separating two countries, we soon came to picturesque Phuentsholing in Bhutan.

Crocodile Sanctuary there was just outside the town. Home to marshy, enormous crocodiles and gharials. Amo Chhu centre bred these endangered species and then released them into nature once old enough. When we arrived, several crocodiles were lying still with their jaws open, as if made of stone. Soon someone threw pieces of meat at them. Their quick reflex to get at the meat startled us all. We bought some meat, and the girls threw them at the crocodiles - good fun.

From there, we visited the Buddhist temple in the town. The girls loved turning on the prayer wheels outside the temple with Om Mani Padme Hum written in Newari language. I would have liked to have gone to Thimpu, another 4 hour's drive to see the renowned cliff-side Tiger's Nest monastery. But it would have been an extra couple of days in Bhutan. My daughters wanted to get back in time for their first-ever Diwali, the festival of light, in our village in India.

1993 John O'Groats Scotland

An opportunity came for two weeks of summer locum work in Wick, in the North-East corner of Scotland. Wick town straddled River Wick by the Bay. A busy fishing town, a former Viking settlement, had three harbours, all protected by breakwaters from the regular blast of North Sea wind.

The mysterious-looking ruins of 16th-century Castle Sinclair Girnigoe nearby had a dramatic history of the seizure by the Cromwellian army. But now, looked magnificent on high, rugged cliffs over the swirling North Sea.

On my day off, I hired a taxi to visit John O'Groat, 'Journey's End' in the UK.

We stopped a few times to enjoy the gorgeous plants in bloom in the surrounding moors against a background of brackish cliffs. Purple coloured Thistles, Scotland's national flower, along with sea buckthorn, juniper, mint, hawthorn, bog myrtle flourished on wetlands and marshes.

From Canisbay village we drove 4 km to the landmark 'Journey's End' signpost at John 'o' Groats. The legend was 'o' Groats referred to John's charge of one groat charge for his ferry to Orkney. After walking around there for a while, we went 25km west to Dunnet Head, geographically the most northerly point of mainland Britain. A stunning yet dangerous coastal path, full of heather, with steep ascents.

After an hour and a half of exhilarating hike along weather-worn sandstone cliffs, we returned to Canisbay. I was hungry, and Scotland's national dish haggis in a village restaurant was most welcome.

1995 Larnaca. Cyprus

An invitation came to a conference in Larnaca in Cyprus for two days. Larnaca in the southern part of the country was called Greek Cyprus, only culturally Greek, not a part of Greece as often misunderstood. From Larnaca, we drove to nearby salt lake with thousands of flamingos. In the evening, a swim in the warm water of the Mediterranean Sea was most refreshing.

Both days the conference finished early. On the first afternoon, we visited the Neolithic settlement of Choirokoitia, occupied from 7th to the 4th millennium B.C., an important prehistoric site in the eastern Mediterranean.

There, and on the way, several old water wells stood by the landscape, many centuries old and some oldest in the world.

Later we dined at a Greek restaurant. Men and women danced Sousta, opposite each other with elements of courtship and eroticism with Cypriot song. Dinner was warm meze of traditional Koupepia, made of grape leaves stuffed with rice, minced beef, fresh herbs and other seasoning and then cooked in a tomato sauce. Then, followed Muhallabia, light milk pudding with a hint of rose water -wonderful.

Next afternoon we visited Nicosia, capital of Cyprus, 36km away. We explored on foot this only divided capital in the world, separated by a green borderline. After delightful Cypriot coffee at Ledra Street, we drove to the western part of the country with a gorgeous view of Troodos mountain range at sunset.

Next morning before my afternoon flight, I spent a while on parasailing a few times. It was fun, but it will be more interesting from the top of the mountain.

1997 -2012 Wales

After spending well over a decade in the lovely Isle of Wight, we moved to Abergavenny with my next job, the one until my retirement. This old medieval town known as a Gateway to Wales stood by the River Usk, surrounded by mountains which lead to the Brecon Beacons National Park. Sugar Loaf, Blorenge and the Black Mountains provided marvellous places for my hillwalking, although walking on Hatterall Ridge, Pen y Fan and Corn Du were more challenging. Some areas nearby which I had taken my visiting family and friends to visit remains in memory.

Blaenavon - pioneering in the industrial revolution   Sitting beyond Blorenge Mountain, this small Welsh town probably changed the world forever through its contribution to the Industrial Revolution in the 18th century. Surrounded by hills rich in coal, limestone and iron ore – the fuel of Industrial Revolution, in 1789 Blaenavon Ironworks was the first to harness the power of steam to blowing air into its blast furnaces. A century later it was here world's steel industry was transformed by inventing a method to remove phosphorus from iron ore. This place once became the most important producers of iron in the world.

Next to it were refurbished workers' cottages giving a fascinating insight into the social history of industrial Britain. Nearby was the Big Pit Colliery, now the only showcase mine in Wales open for experiencing underground.

Hay on Wye - the book town This tiny town on the bank of River Wye and north of Black Mountains, is well known for annual Hay on Wye literary festival, attracting around 80,000 visitors over ten days at the end of May. Visitors hear from and mingle with big literary names from all over the world.

But I preferred Hay when it was not crowded. This place of only 1500 people has two dozen bookshops, selling specialist and second-hand books. Every other shop in its two narrow streets is a bookshop. Outside an 11th century ruined castle, with the oldest Norman tower in Wales, in open ground are shelves of books. One can choose from and then pay the meagre amount in an 'honesty box'.

The bookish town began its history when in 1961 a Richard Booth opened the town's first second-hand bookshop, soon to be followed by others. In 1977 the same Richard had a publicity stunt. He declared Hay-on-Wye an 'independent kingdom' with himself as its monarch and a National Anthem written by a British folk musician.

Bookshelves on the streets, books in the castle, every other shop a small or large old bookstore, Hay-on-Wye, my most favourite town on the Welsh / English border.

Symonds Yat England   This fabulous spot, sitting over the ruins of an Iron Age fort, was another favourite place to visit and relax. In the forest of Dean, a few kilometres from the Welsh border town of Monmouth, and before the picturesque Ross-on-Wye town, Symonds Yat is a favoured place for many. But it is never crowded.

152m Symonds Yat Rock overlooks a stunning gorge through which the River Wye meanders, curving itself in the shape of a ring. Archaeologists had traced here evidence of human habitation dating back to 12,000 years. But to me, like many, the attraction of this place is the gorgeous view.

Birdwatchers from all over the country come here, to watch pairs of Peregrine Falcons, nesting annually within sight from the rock. One can also spot flying Buzzards, Sparrowhawks, Ospreys, Kestrels and rarely Tawny owls. Down by the river, there is canoeing and kayaking. And there are lovely trails in the Forest of Dean linking to the River Wye and even some rock climbing on its sandstone cliffs - no better place to unwind.

Hereford England   Another favourite place of mine, was Hereford, a cathedral city lying on the River Wye, only a few miles over the Welsh border. But most interesting here is the cathedral. Outside stands a statue of the famous local composer Elgar, standing by his bicycle. From this imposing 8th-century cathedral, I usually drifted soon to the attached museum. On display, there is *Mappa Mundi*, an original copy of *Magna Carta* and the *Chained Library*.

Mappa Mundi, drawn on a single sheet of calfskin, is the largest surviving medieval map of the world. It depicts Jerusalem as the centre of the world. It shows how scholars over 700 years back imagined the world. Over a thousand drawings and inscriptions superimposed on to continents and over 400 cities, it sketches the history of humankind as the marvels of the natural world - a gem. Around are many other esteemed maps made centuries back in many countries.

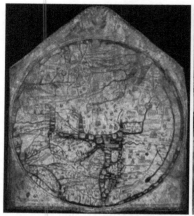 

Mappa Mundi   Chained Library

The museum here also holds one of the only four known original copies of the Magna Carta documents issued in 1217. Great Charter of Liberties or Magna Carta is one of the most famous testimonies in history. This script was the foundation of English common law and from its interpretation grew the right of individual freedom, habeas corpus. It said *'No free man shall be arrested, imprisoned, dispossessed, outlawed, exiled or in any way victimised, or attacked except by the lawful judgement of his peers or by the law of the land.'*

Other attraction there was the Chained Library. It held over two hundred manuscripts, the earliest 'Hereford Gospels' dating from the eighth century, and over one thousand rare printed books from the previous centuries. These hand-transcribed and bound volumes on religion and law were irreplaceable, precious assets. Librarians here solved the problem of theft by chaining the books to the shelves. Books now remain here chained to the four-hundred-year-old bookshelves where one can read them.

1998 Ailwee cave and Ring of Kerry Ireland

Four of us drove to Burren in County Clare, its eerie landscape dominated by glaciated Karst formed from the dissolution of soluble rocks in a moon-like vista. Bedrocks dissolved over centuries had created here many sinkholes, sinking streams, caves and springs. Inside Ailwee cave, one km passage leads into the heart of the mountain.

An underground river slowly flows to the west into a waterfall. Large stalactites and stalagmites looked like pictures from science fiction, some of them over 8,000 years old. The guide warned and then turned off all lights for a minute. In total darkness, we stood silently listening to the gentle sound of the stream flowing by us - unearthly.

From there we went to the cliffs of Maher. Our girls loved the adventure of walking by the sheer cliffs over the Atlantic. After spending a few hours there, half an hour drive down the coast to the gorgeous beach of Spanish Point, named after a Spanish Armada crashed there in the late 17th century. Three of us enjoyed swimming in the gentle Atlantic waves while our oldest daughter engrossed herself in exploring every rock pool.

Later we drove to Dingle, westernmost points of mainland Ireland. As the sun was going down, we walked enchanted amongst the changing colours in the wild landscapes of the deserted Dingle beach.

Ring of Kerry Next morning we drove the 'Ring of Kerry' in an anticlockwise direction. After Milltown, we passed by falls and narrow rivers through Killorglin and Glenbeigh before stopping at Cahersiveen in one of its seafood restaurants, overlooking a harbour. Then drive again through the craggy landscapes and jagged hills on our left and the rugged seashore on our right with frequent stops to take in the immense allure of the panorama.

After a while, we left the shore and drove inland and came to Molls gap - a panoramic viewpoint over the fields and the mountains dotted with red sandstone rocks. It was also a place for riding horses on the trails. The girls wanted to ride. My wife, a reluctant adventurer, also decided to give it a try. We got on our ponies, my wife on the most benign-looking one at the back with a big nervous smile. We gently strolled on horseback.

Suddenly we heard a scream and noticed that my wife's pony had gone into a canter, then into a gallop, passing us by quickly. Her hands were up in the air; both legs were dangling away from the horse. Her crash helmet was covering her face, and she was screaming. Soon the animal and she disappeared into the forest. The pony owner quickly got onto a horse and left in her direction.

After about half an hour they returned, both of them walking by the horses. She declared the animal wanted to kill her by throwing off its back. The pony owner said she must have let the rein go loose and kicked the animal on its belly with her heels. We soon drove to Killarney, all of us alive!

Start of a Health Link in Ethiopia

1999 -2001 Ethiopia

A UK based charity was looking for volunteers to train doctors in Ethiopia in 1999. I immediately responded to go to Gondar in northern Ethiopia. Six weeks before the date, the programme got cancelled because of a border conflict with Eritrea. An alternative was for a similar programme in Dilla, in the south in early 2000 - I agreed.

March 2000   In Addis, a surgeon from Dilla met me with a pickup truck. We then picked up a retired UK gynaecologist from the hotel. A UK anaesthetist and the co-ordinator had already gone to Dilla.

After the sprawling city of Addis, we drove south for over an hour before a brief stop in Mojo. When I left Wales, it was snowing. The temperature here hovered around 40°C! Soon we took the road towards Kenya. Our truck drove on the side of the road, on sand, ditches and rock. The main road was being rebuilt and unusable. Creating a sandstorm, we arrived in the late afternoon by Lake Ziway, less than halfway in our 290km journey.

So far the landscape had been arid, with only a few acacia trees and massive termite mounds. Now it changed to green with many trees and bushes. I saw for the first time fields of Teff, a type of grass. From its grain, they made injera, like a non-sweet pancake, the Ethiopian staple food. By lakeside, farmers sold melons and onions. Not the picture of Ethiopia I had imagined. TV at home always showed the country in the desert ravaged by famine. Lake Langano on our left was the only lake in Ethiopia with no bilharziasis, and popular for swimming. On our right, the sun went down by two other lakes, Lake Abidjatta and Lake Shalla.

Aberra said in Ethiopia, people used their first name, and their fathers' name becomes their surnames. Dr Aberra Gobeze was known as Dr Aberra.

After Mojo, for nearly 200 km journey, we did not see a single brick-built house, except rare banks or restaurants in tiny towns. Others were all mud houses - tin roof for the rich and eucalyptus tree branches for the rest. By 7 pm we reached Awassa, by Lake Awassa. Another 90 km to travel. From then on, the road bordered on dangerous. The driver had to negotiate all the cracks and bumps in the dark. We reached Dilla after 10 pm.

Accommodation in a lodge was a room next to a noisy bar. Too late to get any food, but drinks would be available for another hour! I was starving after only an omelette on an entire day. Too tired, I retired. At least it had a clean bed but no mosquito nets or any toilet. I applied a lot of insect-repellent and fell to sleep immediately.

Next morning, with two colleagues who had arrived earlier, we visited the new Health Sciences College. It trained Health Officers, Nurses and Laboratory Technicians. An orthopaedic surgeon from my hospital arrived in the evening looking shattered.

In the college, we trained for five days eight junior doctors, from distant parts of the Sothern Nations, Nationalities and People's Region (SNNPR). Some travelling over thirty-six hours. In this vast region of 14 million people, there were only 12 hospitals, many without a doctor. There were 34 health centres (HC), each run by a Health Officer (HO). HOs had three years of training, mostly in public health and some clinical medicine.

After the course finished, I requested to visit some of these HCs where most people in the country received their health care. For the most, hospitals were at a far distance, sometimes over 150 km away. Aberra kindly took me the next day to two HCs. In Gedeo district of nearly 2 million people, there were only six HCs.

Yirgacheffe HC was only 30 km from Dilla and Chelelektu HC another 20 km from there, but terrible road all the way. Despite leaving early, we got to Yirgacheffe just before midday as the HC was closing. Only one HO, one nurse, one midwife and a pharmacist, served the town and villages around, a population of about 110,000. Staff were delighted to see us and asked for training and essential equipment. Facilities in this place, one of the oldest HC in the region, were in a dire state.

Soon we left for Chelelektu and reached there after 3 pm. Staffing in this HC was similar, but the facilities here were virtually non-existent. Helen, a newly qualified 22 yrs old HO, was only two years older than my oldest daughter. She sobbed, seeing us there.

After training, they had posted her in this place, far away from her family and friends. She was responsible for the health care of nearly 100,000 people with virtually no resources. She had met no one from outside the area for over six months! I promised we would meet again soon.

Next day I visited Dilla Hospital, the only hospital for 2 million people. The hospital worked for emergency only between 9 am and 3-30 pm and only on weekdays. Aberra was the only surgeon. There was one gynaecologist, four junior doctors and fourteen nurses. No blood bank and hardly any essential equipment. There were regular issues with oxygen supplies. With irregular running water supply, the whole hospital looked dirty.

I met a man waiting outside the female outpatient. I asked through one doctor what he was doing there. With shocking disbelief, I heard their story. Two weeks back, his 20-year-old wife had gone into labour with their first child. Traditional village birth attendant after a few hours had told them to take her to the local HC, 10 km away. Villagers had carried her there on a homemade stretcher. After having only one look, they had said she needed to go to Dilla Hospital immediately.

Within an hour, they were lucky to find a ride on the back of a truck going to Dilla, 60 km distance in the evening. By this time, she looked terrible. Doctors at Dilla told them she needed an emergency operation to save her life. She had ruptured her uterus inside. But they could not do the procedure in Dilla as there was no blood bank. They advised going to Yirgalem Hospital, another 50 km distance. With a ride on the back of another truck, they had reached the Norwegian charity supported Yirgalem Hospital. She

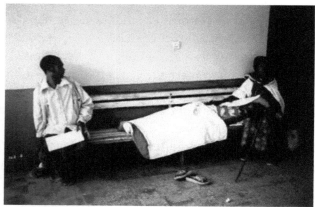

had an operation there immediately. The baby was dead. But he was grateful they had saved his wife's life. They had learnt she could no longer have children as she needed a hysterectomy to save her life. She was discharged a week later. Now two weeks since surgery they had come to Dilla, for removing stitches and a check-up.

I was shocked. But he told the whole story calmly, without any grudge against anyone or the system. Just grateful his wife was alive. I learnt rupture uterus was very common, and one of the prevalent causes of death in pregnancy in the country.

I returned to the UK, knowing just one visit to Ethiopia was never going to be good enough.

In the next few months, I discussed with my colleagues at my hospital in various specialities. There were several challenges in Ethiopia. I had realised training of medical and nursing staff alone would not work if their workplace did not have essential equipment and supplies. The first challenge was to provide some essentials to Dilla hospital. Without oxygen supplies and surgical equipment, no emergency surgery, including many caesarean sections, was possible. A blood transfusion service was badly needed. The hospital laboratory had staff but no reagents even to check blood sugar.

We formed a team of a paediatrician, anaesthetists, two laboratory specialists and the two surgeons, including myself and the other orthopaedic surgeon who had visited there.

Over the next sixteen years, I was lucky to have travelled to Ethiopia for over thirty times. Mostly in its southern region, usually for around two weeks each time. I am proud they called me an Ethiopian, Dr Biku.

November 2000 We returned to Dilla in November when the temperature was cooler.We had collected over the last few months, many essential supplies and surgical instruments. Ethiopian airlines allowed 40 kg check-in luggage and 10 kg for carry-on luggage. We agreed to have all our belongings in the carry-on luggage to take as much as material to Ethiopia as possible.

Aberra met us in Addis with a minibus provided by the college. Addis at an altitude of 2300m had a chill in the air now. Beautiful purple Jacarandas were making a magnificent spectacle against the mountains surrounding the city.

Before our 360 km journey, I insisted on everyone having a light breakfast in a place outside the airport. We filled our minibus with bottles of drinking water and bananas for the journey. The road after Mojo was still in poor shape. But in a big team, fed and watered, listening to the healthcare background and history of Ethiopia from Aberra, it was a pleasant journey.

After about 50 km outside Mojo, our car stopped. Driver asked us to get out and have a look outside. There was a crack in the soil many meters deep, running across both sides of the road. The gap on the road had been filled up with stones to make it passable. The rift had separated a roadside house in two halves. We learnt it was not uncommon to see cracks in the earth like this in the Rift Valley.

We arrived in Dilla before 9 pm. This time the kitchen in a different lodge had some food ready whenever we got there.

Next day, Sunday, after breakfast, we saw outside many people going to church. Women in their white clothes, men in their best outfits with white scarves. Beautiful children were walking, holding their hands - a wonderful scene. We followed the crowd and were soon outside a small village church. After asking permission, we went inside. Soon the entire congregation of over two hundred people sang together - most touching experience.

In Ethiopia, just over half the population were Christian, majority Orthodox and a growing number of Protestants. Other half were Muslims. Despite all the issues over the world in the last two decades between these two religions, in Ethiopia, both communities lived in harmony. There had not been a single incidence of trouble.

In the next five days, our medical team ran a refresher skills training course for HOs from all six of the HCs in the district. Helen attended with a big smile on her face. The laboratory team trained laboratory science students.

One lunchtime we visited the enormous college library- shelves full of books. To our surprise, we found there were several old edition books of plastic surgery, cardiothoracic surgery and so on, but not a single book on essential medicine or surgery. I asked the college head what these books were doing here.

Even in Addis, they don't do these kinds of specialised surgery. He said these were donations from an American charity. They had sent a container full of books like these. The college had not refused the contributions, so as not to upset the Americans!

Before the end of the week, we signed an MOU, with the health science college for supporting the training of health workers at all levels.

On Friday morning, we had left the lodge early to follow our schedule when the place was quiet as ever. We returned after an exciting week of sharing knowledge and experience, feeling happy. As we walked towards our lodge, the area was swarming with people. We heard with amusement; a new beer company was treating people to a meal and beers in the hotel in the evening.

As we walked through the gate, we found one room was full of raw chunks of meat and some spices. We looked forward to a lovely free barbeque later. After a shower, we left for a walk in the streets. We returned after an hour, feeling hungry to find the place was even more crowded as if the entire town had descended there.

To our horror, we saw people were eating raw chunks of meat, dipping into spices - there was no barbeque! They explained raw meat was still a delicacy in Ethiopia. If we did not like big chunks, we might have the minced version - Kitfo, everyone's favourite. All of us politely declined and left to find some pasta in the town.

We returned later and danced late in the night with free beers.

Most woke up with a hangover. After 20 km drive, we reached Wonago. From there we walked on a dirt track through between villages and forests to the ancient Tuttofella Megalithic site. A dense cluster of hundreds of basalt Stelae lay in the area, measuring from 0.5m to 6m in height. Many had fallen on the ground -poorly preserved site. Archaeologists had found here human remains buried in different layers, with household utensils in each tomb in various periods from 10th - 13th century AD.

In the next few days, we signed an MOU also with the Regional Health Department, to support training and providing resources to the hospitals and HCs in the region.
We returned to Wales, all of us keen to develop a regular health link.

Back in the UK, the support from everyone around the hospital was tremendous. We did not realise how many items they threw away in the NHS every week - some just out of date or someone had decided not to use them anymore. Soon my office was overfilling with materials. Hospital staff, from all parts, brought up items which they thought could be of help, to take to Ethiopia next time. The response was overwhelming. It became my regular job sifting through things which could be of actual use in Ethiopia.

During my last two visits to Ethiopia, I had experienced in the hospital and in HCs, many boxes donated by various charities clogging up their storerooms - of no practical use there, like the cardiothoracic surgery books in the library. No wonder Ethiopia was known as the 'Graveyard of Charities'!

March 2001   A smaller team of eight travelled using all our luggage allowances. This time we spent a day with each of the six HCs we had identified to support. We donated essential items and organised skills training for the staff. We sat down with the team, and the local community leaders for detail needs assessment. Common issues for the local people were lack of essential facilities and cleanliness. Often people came from a far distance for help, only to be told HC did not have necessary items to deal with the problem. Then they were advised going to the hospital, far away, a total waste of time. Most locals did not have confidence in the HC and its staff. Also, they said the place was always dirty. HC staff wanted more training and equipment. They badly needed oxygen supply, delivery beds and instruments. We agreed with the community leaders and HC staff to address these issues through our link best we could.

David Beckham in a Tukul!   We had seen Tukuls, huts on the roadside and in villages. One afternoon on our way back from an HC, I asked the driver if it would be possible to visit one of these. As we stopped, children came shouting happily 'Firingi, Firingi'.

Over the fields, we came outside a Tukul, walls made of mud and the roof with eucalyptus branches. A young mother stood by the door with a baby on her lap. Two small children hung by her. The driver asked her in Amharic. She nodded and smiled at us. Tukul had an outer wall. Within this, they kept the animals. Inside another wall, lived her family of eight, husband, his parents plus her widowed sister. It was very dark inside except for a corner where there was an open fire for cooking. No wonder so many children end up with burns in villages in Ethiopia!

I asked permission to take some pictures inside. She nodded. I took a few photos with a flash. To

my surprise, on one wall, was hanging a picture of David Beckham! We all laughed. We learnt her husband is a mad football fan! After spending a while inside, we said 'Amasheganalu', thank you in Ethiopian. We got another lovely smile from her. On the way to the car, her children, amongst others, came holding our hands, smiling all the way. And then they said 'Amasheganalu' to us.

At Dilla Hospital, we talked about the significant issue of oxygen and the need for a blood bank. Aberra volunteered to work nights without pay to do emergency operations if we could resolve these. He mentioned the Norwegian charity had donated oxygen concentrators in Yirgalem. In our hospital, we never think of where the oxygen supply came from. Patients living at home with severe respiratory problems in the UK used oxygen concentrators. I added this to our shopping list for the next time.

On my return, the phone call to an Oxygen Concentrator manufacturing company luckily got me to their boss. She agreed to donate several demonstration models of the older type they were upgrading. Fundraising events like Celidih & Curry, raffles for prizes, donations by staff, some running marathon to raise funds, helped to support our link.

November 2001   During the visit in November, we brought over and donated oxygen concentrators to

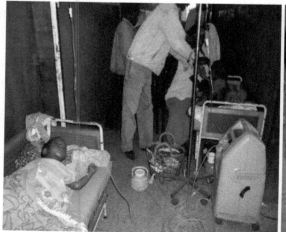
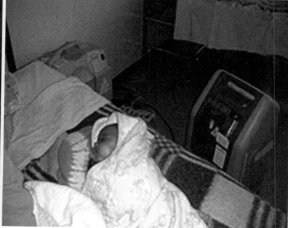

Dilla Hospital and one to each of the six HCs. We bought delivery beds for the HCs from Addis. Our laboratory team helped to start a blood bank in Dilla. Its operation theatre had now more instruments than ever. With Aberra on call at night, Dilla was now working 24 hrs a day for emergencies. We extended skills training course for the HOs and other health workers from the HCs in all of the SNNPR region.

During my previous visits, I had heard people mentioning an ancient cave beyond the forests from Dilla College. But when I asked if we could go there to have a look, they had said it was in a dangerous place to go. Rumour was of a ferocious tribe living nearby. Anybody from outside venturing there risked their balls cut off!

After a lot of persuasions, we persuaded two security guards from the college to come with us with their guns. From the college, we descended into a thick forest which ran for miles. After walking more than an hour, we were in the sandbank of dry Hanshi Malcho River, a sacred river used for ritual ceremonies. It was boiling in the mid-day heat.

Soon we came across a few fallen, large rocks of some ancient caves. Rock walls had many engravings of animals like which we had seen in our history books. Even the security guards relaxed and left their guns on the floor to explore this fascinating prehistoric archaeological site. We laughed on the way back. Lucky not to have met those ferocious tribes.

But a few days later, I could see why the locals feared them. A group of ten tall tribesmen, decorated body covered only with a loincloth, holding spears marched in town. They bought salt and tef. Everyone stood as far away from the group as they could, looking with reverence.

In Yirgacheffe, we had seen most houses had one or two coffee bushes on their grounds. There were acres of coffee bushes on the hill slopes. Olive-like seeds of coffee turned from green to red before they were harvested and dried in the open in the sun. Low hills of Yirgacheffe produced the best quality coffee in the world. But its farmers did not get enough support and publicity compared to the big corporations in Brazil or Columbia.

Coffee originated in the Simien Mountains in the north of Ethiopia. Legend says goat herders noticed animals became energetic after eating the berries from a particular bush. Herders then made hot drinks with these berries to find it had kept them up and fresh all night.

A village elder invited us to his Tukul. Traditionally all first-time visitors in Ethiopia are treated to a coffee ceremony in the house. At the door, they lay Eucalyptus branches to keep the dust away. We sat in a circle on low stools around an open fire. An elderly lady dressed in white robes, roasted dried coffee beans on a hot plate. The aroma was intoxicating. Then she grounded the roasted beans on a traditional wooden grinder before putting the powder in boiling water in a small black terracotta pot.

While waiting, we all got served popcorns, totally unexpected! Next, the lady poured thick black coffee for us in tiny teacups. It was bitter and thick, sticking to my palate. While I was thinking to myself all this fuss just for a tiny cup of drink, she poured more water into the same pot. Once boiled, we got a second

Coffee ceremony at Wondogenet health centre

round, less thick but still very, very strong. Soon she put more water into the pot, and we had the third round. This time a bit lighter, but stronger than any coffee I had tasted in Italy. After these three rounds of coffee, I did not sleep for three nights!

During some of our trips, our return flights left in Addis in the early morning. We stayed overnight in Addis after our long journey back from the south.

On one of those trips after checking into our hotel after dinner, everyone else retired to bed. I left by myself for a walk outside around 10 pm. Most shops were closed. Streets were quiet. As I was approaching my hotel, only about 50m away, two men walked beside me. They offered 'Magazine', 'Girls' and so on. Getting closer and almost pressing against my sides.

I sternly said no and started walking towards the hotel. I felt one of them trying to put his hand in my pocket. I swiftly turned around and punched him in the face. Both moved away quickly. I walked straight back to my room in the hotel.

Fifteen minutes later, a phone call came from the reception asking me to go down; the police were waiting for me. Down at the reception, police had two men in handcuffs. They enquired if these were the men who were bothering me. The hotel security guard had seen the incidence from the gate and called police immediately. I looked at the faces of these two in handcuffs. When I was approached in dim light, everything happened quickly. Police might have apprehended the usual suspects. I could not confirm if these were the men. I did not want any innocent man to go behind bars. Police let them go with a warning.

New York, Boston, Salem, Las Vegas,

Grand Canyon, New Orleans USA

2001 New York   My wife and I strolled in midtown Manhattan craning our necks to look at the sky between the high rising skyscrapers. At famous Times Square, was a big gathering and hilarity around Naked Cowboy, a street performer, with a guitar strategically placed to cover up his nudity! Nearby were Broadway theatres. In London, we were regular theatregoers. Luckily we got two tickets for the next evening's show of the famous musical Chicago.

In the evening from the 86th floor of Empire State Building, the city lights, surrounded on most sides by darkness from water, was spectacular. At a distance, stood tall the ornate Chrysler building and on another side the twin towers of World Trade centre.

A boat ride next day took us to a small island with the iconic Statue of Liberty. We hovered around the base of the tall copper structure with an inscription by Emma Lazarus.

> "Give me your tired, your poor, your huddled masses yearning to breathe free, the wretched refuse of your teeming shore. Send these, the homeless, tempest-tost to me. I lift my lamp beside the golden door!"
>
> --Poet Emma Lazarus (inscribed at Ellis Island)

Our ferry took us next to the Ellis Island Immigration Museum. Between 1892 to 1954, this place processed 12 million immigrants in pursuit of the American Dream. The processing station had a series of unthinkable medical and mental inspections procedures. Collections of clothing, household accessories, documents and many photographs told poignant stories of human dreams and sufferings.

In the evening we arrived at the Broadway theatre for the show 'Chicago'. We immersed ourselves with dramatic music and dancing of Roxy, Velma, and Billy Flynn, singing and dancing to sensational songs like 'All that Jazz', 'Funny Honey', and others. We got out after 11 pm, dizzy with the song and dances.

We were used to travelling on London underground, even after midnight. But last evening, only around 9 pm, we had felt uneasy on the subway. Maybe it was only us or the ill reputation! We took a taxi, very cheap in New York.

Central Park, next to Fifth Avenue, was a breathing space for New Yorkers amidst its concrete jungle. After living in the countryside, an hour in this park was enough. We walked nearby to a house, previously a small hospital, where my wife's mother was born. After grabbing some coffee and tasty bagels nearby, we took the subway to Brooklyn Bridge. It was fantastic walking this 2 km suspension bridge, a masterpiece of 19th-century engineering with a dramatic view of Manhattan from the Brooklyn side over the East River.

Soon we left for a view of the United Nations building. I stood outside this place with flags of every country flying high, a place supposed to be for co-operation and friendship between all nations in the world. I

100

reflected upon how this institution had failed repeatedly against aggression by superpowers and vetos by a handful of superpowers had repeatedly rejected resolutions condemning blatant injustices around the world.

Boston   Boston by bus was only four and half hour journey. Arriving in the evening, we dined with clam chowder and Boston cream pie. Next day via Boston Common, we reached The Boston Tea Party Museum. It had displays from protests by the American Colonists against the British government in 1773, including one of the two tea chests from the original revolt.

Later we took a bus to the Harvard University campus outside Boston. In summer, it was not busy, but still, many students and professors ambled the compound. We sat for coffee outside the campus, buzzing with young people having animated discussions. It reminded me of my college days in Calcutta.

Back in Boston, we walked solemnly by the State Street, previously known as King Street, the site of the infamous Boston Massacre where British Soldiers clubbed many to death, a significant landmark in the history of the American Revolution.

Next day we took a guided tour to Concord and Lexington, 100 km away. There in the Minute Man National Historical Park visitor centre first they showed us a short film 'Road to Revolution' - an introduction to the Lexington-Concord events and a comprehensive account of first military engagements of American Revolutionary War against the colonists at North Bridge. We then walked over the reconstructed North Bridge and to *Minute Man* statue and the Obelisk, country's first memorial to its war casualties. Our bus then drove through 'Battle Road Trail' in the forest between Lexington and Concord, area of combat with the British troops.

Salem New England   We wanted to spend at least a day in a small town in New England. Only 25 km outside Boston, Salem was a natural choice, the place of infamous Salem Witch trials in 1692, beautifully portrayed in The Crucible, by Arthur Miller. This small port town was the former site of an American Indian village, at the mouth of Naumkeag River. After cities full of skyscrapers, I loved the timber-framed houses with steep roofs in Salem.

Salem Witch museum visit was first on our list. Three young girls, Abigail, Betty and their friends were playing with a mirror and egg when accused of witchcraft. Salem witch trial resulted in the execution by hanging of 19 people from such false accusations.

In the late afternoon, we visited the attractive but quiet Salem Harbor. From here, American ships had sailed to China, Southeast Asia and Zanzibar at the end of the 18th century for trade.

For dinner, we visited a small seafood restaurant by our lodge. We sat around a large metal grill heated on a wood fire with many other customers. Fantastic grilled oysters with garlic sherry butter and king crab legs with cherry pepper. I ended up eating a lot of oysters for one evening.

We would have liked to stay in Salem longer but had to catch our flight the next morning from Boston for Vegas.

Las Vegas   I had no real enthusiasm for this city of casinos, strip club and cabarets. But for our next destination, Grand Canyon, we needed our connecting flight from here. On the journey from the airport, Las Vegas looked like a dream castle in the middle of the sands. We checked into Flamingo Hotel, at the end of Strip, famous for its connection with 60s' singers like Dean Martin and Frank Sinatra. One of the oldest hotels in Vegas, its ground floor was full of casinos of all kinds. It was sweltering outside, and we stayed in our air-conditioned room eating ice creams till the evening.

The temperature dropped in the evening with some cool breeze from the desert. The strip was now full of activities and vibrant with lights from the surrounding hotels. We strolled with the crowd. Soon we were by a free show outside the Treasure Island Hotel and Casino, showing black-bearded pirates fighting the crew on a ship. Then we walked to the Bellagio Hotel with a fantastic fountain outside. Inside its glitzy hotel corridor, crowds gathered around several casinos.

I did not expect to adore Vegas, but on the way back had a quiet smile to myself for its quirky, expensive tackiness.

Grand Canyon   Our twelve-seater plane took off from Vegas in the morning. After vast barren desert land, it entered the Grand Canyon range. I could not take eyes off from this magical spectacle. In another fifteen minutes, they announced we were going to fly over the famous Hoover Dam. This massive dam over Colorado River was the largest in the country when built 70 years back. Over one hundred people died during its construction.

We flew over the snaking mighty Colorado River between the canyons, receiving its various sized tributaries from impressive multi-coloured gorges. Native American Hualapai and Havasupai tribes had been living in this area for centuries.

Immediately after checking in, we caught a free shuttle bus to the viewpoint over the south rim. Standing at a promontory, at an elevation of over 2000m, the gorgeous spectacle of the Grand Canyon continued forever in front. North rim on the other side was almost a mile away. Copper-coloured Colorado River ran approximately 1500m below us. No wonder there were at least four climate zones from the rim to the river shore. After some quick lunch, we returned to watch the magical sunset over the canyon. Layers of rocks changed colour every minute as the sun went down - an unforgettable experience of a lifetime. We returned to our lodge, after dark, mesmerised in this natural wonder.

Before Sunrise we were back at the rim. Magic of the light, this time played against the canyons in a different tone. There was an option for a hike down to the river and canoeing. I decided against, seeing that my wife would have been unable to join me for this challenging trail down and up. Instead, we spent by the south rim and then returning for another unforgettable sunset over the canyons.

Next morning reluctantly we left Grand Canyon. After three hours waiting in the sterile Phoenix airport, I got into our flight to New Orleans.

New Orleans   Our hotel was in the French Quarter of this lively city. We wandered its narrow streets between the beautiful houses of French and Creole architectural styles. Coloured beads hung from them and the surrounding trees and shops. By the time we came out after having some coffee and delightful beignets, in the early evening, the streets were buzzing with tourists like us. We followed the crowd to the famous Bourbon Street. Bars, cafe restaurants and night clubs filled this famous street and its adjacent alleyways. Only eight in the evening, but the place was packed. Like most, we purchased some coloured beads and tried to imagine how the city might be like during the Mardi Grass festival, another month away. At dinner in a jazz bar, listening to Dixieland music, we tucked into tasty dishes of Gumbo, made of okra, onions, green pepper with crawfish and shrimp. It was late. We had been travelling for most of the day. But in the festive atmosphere, we hung around the streets well after midnight.

On the mighty Mississippi River sailed many steamboats and ships for tours. Sitting by this massive river, I reflected on how it had been a powerful musical inspiration for generations. I remembered how this river once also played a significant role in the slave trade. Most of the New Orleans proper was below the mean water level of this great river and the nearby Lake Pontchartrain. Many natural and human-made levees only just about protected the city from being flooded at any moment.

Rest of the day, we spent by the Jackson Square and its tranquil park, walking streets lined by shotgun houses, Creole cottages with intricate wrought-iron balconies. Families rested on rocking chairs with wind chimes hanging over them. Later, we drifted back to Bourbon Street.

Next day we took a tour to the Oak Alley plantation heritage site, named after the 300-year-old alley of oaks leading to a mansion house. The owner was known as 'King of Sugar' - the wealthiest men in the south at the time. This vast plantation had on display a most elaborate mansion as well as nearby crowded slave quarters. Its most noted slave, worth thousands of dollars in the slave market, was listed as 'Antoine, 38, Creole Negro gardener.' The place filled me with anger at the injustice by fellow human over another.

Old slave quarters

On our last day in New Orleans, my wife decided to stay in the city, just relaxing. I took a tour to the Honey Island Swamp. After leaving the city suburbs, were many dilapidated looking trailer-parks, full of derelict looking people with their children. I had seen Gypsy travellers in Europe, but these were ordinary Americans in poverty, a familiar scene in many places. The bus soon came by Lake Pontchartrain, one of the largest bodies of water in the country. We drove over an incredible 39 km long parallel pair of spans, bisecting the wilderness of the lake, longest bridge over water in the world.

Soon we were at the Honey Island and got into an open boat. We gently sailed over a pristine river swamp. From the crooked cypress trees, mosses hanged out everywhere, giving the place a mystical feel. Tales of sightings of Honey Island Monster, Big Foot, made this place even more otherworldly. The smell of wild azaleas and other plants was hypnotising. We were strictly told not to touch the crystal clear water. Soon we understood why. We spotted several giant alligators, some sunning by the fallen trees with their mouth open, others gently swimming by. The crew said to be careful when we came near the low tree branches there were snakes in them. Sometimes they fell into the craft! Large turtles gently swam by, and a few nervous, wild, muddy pigs grazed on the shore. Great blue herons waited patiently to catch fish -birds of all kind in this place, bird watcher's paradise. Before we realised, three hours had passed by in the swamp - time to return.

While waiting for our bus, I had the tastiest ever plate of boiled crawfish, shrimps and maze.

Cornwall. UK

2003 Bude   From Wales, we drove to Bude in Cornwall with miles of white sands beaches. Rocky outcrops ideal for rock-pooling bordered the Crooklets beach. Our oldest daughter immersed herself in searching from one rock pool to another for the tiny sea creatures. Soon our younger daughter found paddleboards and the two of us had fun bodyboarding. After a while, my wife bravely gave it a go and promptly turned herself over with the first wave. She came out from less than knee-deep water, convinced she almost drowned. By the evening, we drove to Boscastle for the night, only half an hour away.

Boscastle   In the evening with old street lamps, this tiny place on the quay sat in a theatre of quaint

stone-built thatched and white-washed cottages was the ideal place to relax.

The unconventional Witchcraft Museum here offered an intriguing view of witchcraft and occult culture from all around the world. Its collection included from crystal balls and broomsticks to paraphernalia used for divination and spells, the 'cunning woman' surrounded by a multitude of herbs and divination tools, ritual chalices and swords. Over 2000 objects related to witch trials, Wicca religion, Satanism, Freemasonry and Alchemy. An enchanting place.

Only 15 minutes' drive away stood the ruins of spectacular Tintagel Castle built half on the mainland and half on a jagged headland into Cornish sea. Its history dated back to the late Roman period. But the site was more famously associated with King Arthur's grave, an inventive lie of the medieval monks to raise money. Narrow footbridge to the island was rewarded with the view and ruins steeped in legend and mystery.

Later, we took the scenic route to Penzance with a spectacular view of the setting sun over Atlantic.

Land's end   From Penzance in the morning, we headed towards renowned Land's end, most south-westerly point of Cornwall and England. Arriving there, we were initially disappointed to find this famous landmark sat close to a hotel and was within a private property. National Trust, however, owned the cliffs. Walking over the cliffs made of igneous rock, became more enjoyable as the Atlantic waves battered below.

After spending over an hour, we headed to Porthcurno, 6km away. We had a ticket at the Minack Theatre for the afternoon show we did not want to miss.

Minack Theatre   We arrived there with time to amaze at the spectacle of this Cornwall's world-famous open-air theatre, carved into granite cliff. Overlooking the dazzling panorama of Porthcurno Bay, was a unique place to watch a Shakespearean drama.

Walking down the rocky steps set in glorious gardens, with ice cream cones in our hands, we sat perched on the cliffs high above the Atlantic Ocean. Then, we immersed ourselves in 'A Midsummer night's Dream' for the next couple of hours.

Toronto, Montreal, Quebeck, Rocky Train, Jasper, Spirit Island & Lake Louise Canada

2004 Toronto   Toronto was only a whistle-stop for us on the way to the famous Niagara Falls, 125km distance. This renowned waterfalls, disappointingly, was surrounded by tall casinos and hotels. Even then, Niagara, straddling the Canadian and USA border, with over 50m vertical drop was breathtaking. Boat cruise on aptly named Maid of the Mist carried us right under the rapids. Luckily the crew had offered everyone waterproof ponchos. Under the vast amount of water falling next to us in a thick mist, with the noise of the rapid, we had a broad grin.

In Toronto, despite its many skyscrapers, one could not avoid a glimpse of the soaring CN Tower from anywhere. I had booked a ticket for the two of us for dinner in its restaurant, as a surprise.

Arriving by this world-famous tower, she was thrilled. Our revolving restaurant was 340m above the ground. View of Toronto and Lake Ontario was stunning. After dinner, we walked down to the transparent glass floor. Few people tiptoed over it while some lied down like a cross and pretended to have acrophobia. In the stadium, next door to the tower, a baseball game was going on. From the glass-floor, it appeared right under us.

Montreal   Well known through its hosting of a very successful Olympics in 1976, Montreal was an obvious choice in our Canadian itinerary. Maybe because it rained intermittently, I found this city rather dull. Even its trams looked dated and always crammed.

But Old Montreal, with its cobbled streets and the architecture, had a certain charm. In the evening at a restaurant, we noticed many people were eating a strange-looking dish called Poutine, famous here. We ordered the same. It turned out to be a large plate of chunky chips soaked with thick gravy and crumbled cheese on top, unusual and very filling.

Weather was better the next morning. A tramcar took us to Mount Royal, a volcanic hill in the city with the vast Royal Park overlooking Downtown Montreal. Saint Joseph's Oratory there, was famous for its connection with Brother Andre, renowned as a miracle healer in 19th century. Its basilica had a wall covered with thousands of crutches from the reportedly healed here!

Quebec   After arriving by bus in Quebec, we walked through the city and fell in love with this place. Almost like a small town in France. A delightful old town within gated walls, only one in North America, with classical architecture in narrow cobbled streets, had quaint shops bustling with people. Most spoke French. Dufferin Terrace had a magnificent view of the river below. Name Kebec came from the word meaning 'where the river narrows' as Saint Lawrence River narrowed to the promontory of Quebec.

From this beautiful promenade, we walked up to the ruins of Saint Louis Forts and Châteaux. By the evening we walked along busy Rue Saint-Jean, to find a restaurant. We indulged in delicious French onion soup and crispy, savoury crepes followed by mouth-watering Maple taffy. After a hearty dinner, we lazed on streets late into the night, with a magnificent view of the Château Frontenac, towering over at a distance.

Next day, we happily rambled the old city, stopping to take in the sights at Beautiful Basilica-Cathedral Notre-Dame de Québec. After a long ice cream stop by the river, we walked its shore aimlessly. Day went by without us noticing. Our flight was early the morning, but we did not return to our hotel until midnight.

Vancouver The seven-hour flight, because of three hours' time difference, arrived in Vancouver in the afternoon. Vancouver Island separated the city from the mighty Pacific Ocean. Against the backdrop of high mountains, on the shores of blue water, Vancouver looked magnificent.

From our downtown hotel, we walked to the waterfront and then to Chinatown. The most ethnically diverse city we had come across. Many did not speak English or French at all. Surprisingly, shops sold Marijuana and hard drugs being offered in the streets almost openly.

Next day, massive Stanley Park, waterfront with a backdrop of the mountain range, was the ideal place to recuperate. After a thoroughly refreshing day, we returned to downtown by the uninterrupted waterfront path, the famous Seawall.

In the evening we walked to a popular restaurant. I spoiled myself with luscious seafood chowder and fresh salmon steak. My wife skipped the starter and indulged in a yummy-looking chocolate dessert after her main course.

Very happy, both of us were returning to our hotel, my wife most animated I had seen for a long time. Maybe the Canadian wine was talking. Walking on marble steps close to our hotel, she suddenly slipped and banged her head and face on the steps. I checked she had not suffered a head injury, although she was bruised and groggy. I stayed up all night doing head injury check-up every so often to make sure we did not need to go to a hospital.

Rocky Mountain train Next morning she was fine, but the bruise on her face looked worse. We walked to the nearby rail station for the Rocky Mountain train. I had to ignore the looks from several fellow passengers, silently accusing me of being one of those wives-beaters!

On the train, we had silver level service in a coach with full glass-dome windows and outdoor viewing area. After the city, we moved through beautiful valleys before crossing the impressive Fraser River. Soon we came to the Hell's Gate and went through a canyon where the river narrowed to less than 40m. Fraser River dashed fast between rugged cliffs on both sides. Before long, they called us for a delicious lunch in the dining car.

Soon we settled down for glorious views of pristine lakes and peaks of the Canadian Rockies, including a glimpse of majestic Mount Robson. Soon it became dark. But with the clear sky, enormous lakes glistened in the moonlight. Mountain peaks looked mystical. I don't remember falling asleep but woke up to the noise of people getting ready to get off the train at Jasper.

Jasper   At Jasper, my wife, decided to rest in this rustic hill town by herself. I left for hiking a trail on the mountain. After a bus ride to upper Jasper Sky tram terminal, a 1000m ride on the sky tram. From there, the 8 km return hike on the Indian ridge to Whistler Peak was fabulous with the views of the snow-capped peaks and blue lakes in between. The last half an hour of the trail was demanding. Loose rocks fell thousands of meters down the hill. View from Whistler Peak at 2,184m was thrilling. In the evening, we exchanged our stories in a petite restaurant serving delicious grills.

Lake Maligne and Spirit Island   Our bus drove 45km through thick forest, breathtaking waterfalls and canyons with early morning sunshine pouring over to Lake Maligne at 1500m. In bright sunlight, Lake Maligne sparkled with crystal clear blue water, enhanced by the still shadows of beautiful peaks on its shore.

A small boat cruised the azure water of this vast lake with sloping glaciers on its shore. After about half an hour, we turned a corner to another part of the lake. We got off to a deserted shore amongst wild trees and fallen leaves. A small boat cruised the azure water of this vast lake with sloping glaciers on its shore. After about half an hour, we turned a corner to another part of the lake. We got off to a deserted shore amongst wild trees and fallen leaves. In front was the most beautiful sight in the world. Spirit Island, with the backdrop of Lake Maligne and snow peaks, took my breath away. A narrow isthmus connected the tiny island with tall conifers to the shore - an unforgettable mystical beauty.

Columbia Icefield was only two hours away. I had been on Himalayan glaciers. But here you did not need mountaineering experience and a long trek to get to the largest icefield in the Rocky Mountains. Six massive glaciers, including Athabasca and Columbia glacier, fed into the icefield. We reached the icefield on giant Ice Explorer buses from the park gate in less than half an hour.

My wife slipped as she got off from the bus. The guide was close by to hold her and break the fall. Soon, with no crampons, everyone was learning to balance on the hard ice, repeatedly falling and having fun for an hour.

Lake Louise   We came to our hotel, magnificent Fairmont Chateau on the shores of Lake Louise as the evening was setting in. Most beautiful place to relax for two nights. While my wife retired to a long hot bath, I left for a gentle walk by this world-famous lake with street lamps on the shore. From a distance, our palatial hotel against the lake looked like a fairy castle. Later, dining by the window, we ate silently, enjoying the vista.

There were boating, canoeing activities on the water and horse riding on the mountain trail. But we just wandered the banks of this moraine lake with emerald green water for the day.

Following day, on our way to Calgary for departure from Canada, we stopped in Banff. We only had a few hours in this pretty hillside station. Banff was more substantial than Jasper in size and population. It looked a bit too much developed and full of tourists lacking the rustic feel and remoteness of Jasper.

Why not climb Ben Nevis? Scotland

2005

Glasgow city centre pleasantly surprised me, contrary to its reputation. A thriving modern city, with many 19th-century buildings and upmarket shopping areas in Buchanan Street and Princess Square. My sister-in-law lived in Bearsden, affluent north of Glasgow. Going to them for overnight stay via rundown residential areas of Possilpark, where levels of unemployment and drug abuse were highest in the country, however, was an eye-opener.

Leaving Glasgow, in an hour we reached Loch Lomond, the largest lake between the lowlands of Central Scotland and the Highlands. We drove along the lake and then through the Scottish Glens amidst the beautiful Highland scenery for another hour before reaching Glencoe. Between the shores of Loch Leven and mouth of the famous Glen, Glencoe was charming. No wonder it attracted so many visitors exploring its valleys. We spent a while walking in the Glen silently. Visitor centre pictures gently reminded this was the site of one of the most treacherous massacres in British History - the Massacre of Glencoe in the 17th century.

After driving along the shores of the lake on our left and highland hills on our right, we reached Fort William. Old garrison town, by Loch Linnhe, once was the site of a wooden fort in 17th century. Base for English troops to keep local clans under control after the British Civil Wars.

Ben Nevis   As we walked by the waterfront with a gorgeous view of Ben Nevis, my wife, chose the moment to throw me a personal challenge. 'You claim to be a mountaineer. Why not try to climb this peak tomorrow?' she said casually.

I looked at Ben Nevis 1345m, the highest peak in the British Isles. It was summer, but still, I knew from my previous experience that with no preparation, taking on a mountain of this proportion could not be easy. I did not even have a proper pair of trekking shoes! But I took up the challenge. The first thing was to go to an outdoor equipment store to buy a pair of decent walking shoes and a windcheater.

Next morning, I took the popular ascent route. I was out of breath after only an hour of trek. It was not the most arduous route in any mountaineering sense. But over the last two decades, with 80+ hours of on-call and only an occasional game of cricket on some weekends had not helped my physical fitness. But I carried on, never considering giving up. Soon the view of Fort Williams and the Loch below reinvigorated me. From there, I climbed slowly through a steep path full of loose rocks. I was grateful that it was not raining and tried to imagine how the route might be in its notorious winters.

With no warning, clouds came in. I could see only less than 5m in front. There was no route marking, only to follow the chatter of climbers ahead. I walked wearily over the slates of broken rocks for about an hour.

Suddenly I was on the summit. I stood at the highest point marked with a built cairn, on top of which was an Ordnance Survey trig point. Unfortunately, with the low misty cloud, the view was still only of a few meters around. But after nearly four hours, I had finally done it. I looked with awe at the north face with buttresses and impressive ridges and tried to picture the route in winter.

As the weather closed in, after only twenty minutes at the top, I started my descent. After the tricky first half an hour through loose rocks with little visibility, I was below the cloud. From there, it took me another one and a half hour to get down to the starting point. But by this time, my knees were killing me.

My wife was near the visitor centre. She only said 'Well done', then treated me to a most welcome cup of coffee. My knees were in agony; I could hardly stand. I needed to find a chemist for strong painkillers. It took the next three days before the pain got better, but I had a satisfying grin on my face for the entire time.

My wife drove the next morning to Loch Ness an hour away. Vast deep lake with its black water, well known for dubious sightings of Loch Ness monster, looked very peaceful with Urquhart Castle on its shore. Like most people, we got out and tried to be the first to photograph this mythical beast.

After spending a while at nearby Loch Ness centre surrounded by gift shops of all imagination related to the monster, we treated ourselves to a dish of grilled fresh fish and chips before our journey down to Oban 150km distance.

By the time we reached Oban, it was raining and dark. I was glad to stretch my aching knees properly, lying flat on the bed.

Ferry next morning to the Isle of Mull was in excellent weather. Second largest of the Hebrides, Isle of Mull, was just off the west coast of Scotland. We spent two nights in this small quiet island exploring its beauty along its diverse coastline. Our hotel was in Tobermory, home to Mull's Single Malt Whisky distillery, but neither of us was keen on whisky.

For the next two days, we drove aimlessly in this idyllic island, taking in its caves, locally known as a broch, of ten thousand years history of human inhabitation. My knees were quietening down. Each hilltop we passed, I was now trying to figure out the best route to get to the top. After leaving our car by the roadside, we walked down an iron ladder on the side of a cliff to access the stony beach. Burg peninsula was a most stunning Hebridean hinterland, with its steep precipitous bluffs, grassy lowlands now colourful with summer flowers. The famous 50-million-year-old fossil tree was several kilometres walk away. We decided against.

After an entirely refreshing few days in Scotland back to Wales, to our daily routine.

Why not climb Ben Nevis? Scotland

2005

Glasgow city centre pleasantly surprised me, contrary to its reputation. A thriving modern city, with many 19th-century buildings and upmarket shopping areas in Buchanan Street and Princess Square. My sister-in-law lived in Bearsden, affluent north of Glasgow. Going to them for overnight stay via rundown residential areas of Possilpark, where levels of unemployment and drug abuse were highest in the country, however, was an eye-opener.

Leaving Glasgow, in an hour we reached Loch Lomond, the largest lake between the lowlands of Central Scotland and the Highlands. We drove along the lake and then through the Scottish Glens amidst the beautiful Highland scenery for another hour before reaching Glencoe. Between the shores of Loch Leven and mouth of the famous Glen, Glencoe was charming. No wonder it attracted so many visitors exploring its valleys. We spent a while walking in the Glen silently. Visitor centre pictures gently reminded this was the site of one of the most treacherous massacres in British History - the Massacre of Glencoe in the 17th century.

After driving along the shores of the lake on our left and highland hills on our right, we reached Fort William. Old garrison town, by Loch Linnhe, once was the site of a wooden fort in 17th century. Base for English troops to keep local clans under control after the British Civil Wars.

Ben Nevis   As we walked by the waterfront with a gorgeous view of Ben Nevis, my wife, chose the moment to throw me a personal challenge. 'You claim to be a mountaineer. Why not try to climb this peak tomorrow?' she said casually.

I looked at Ben Nevis 1345m, the highest peak in the British Isles. It was summer, but still, I knew from my previous experience that with no preparation, taking on a mountain of this proportion could not be easy. I did not even have a proper pair of trekking shoes! But I took up the challenge. The first thing was to go to an outdoor equipment store to buy a pair of decent walking shoes and a windcheater.

Next morning, I took the popular ascent route. I was out of breath after only an hour of trek. It was not the most arduous route in any mountaineering sense. But over the last two decades, with 80+ hours of on-call and only an occasional game of cricket on some weekends had not helped my physical fitness. But I carried on, never considering giving up. Soon the view of Fort Williams and the Loch below reinvigorated me. From there, I climbed slowly through a steep path full of loose rocks. I was grateful that it was not raining and tried to imagine how the route might be in its notorious winters.

With no warning, clouds came in. I could see only less than 5m in front. There was no route marking, only to follow the chatter of climbers ahead. I walked wearily over the slates of broken rocks for about an hour.

Suddenly I was on the summit. I stood at the highest point marked with a built cairn, on top of which was an Ordnance Survey trig point. Unfortunately, with the low misty cloud, the view was still only of a few meters around. But after nearly four hours, I had finally done it. I looked with awe at the north face with buttresses and impressive ridges and tried to picture the route in winter.

As the weather closed in, after only twenty minutes at the top, I started my descent. After the tricky first half an hour through loose rocks with little visibility, I was below the cloud. From there, it took me another one and a half hour to get down to the starting point. But by this time, my knees were killing me.

My wife was near the visitor centre. She only said 'Well done', then treated me to a most welcome cup of coffee. My knees were in agony; I could hardly stand. I needed to find a chemist for strong painkillers. It took the next three days before the pain got better, but I had a satisfying grin on my face for the entire time.

My wife drove the next morning to Loch Ness an hour away. Vast deep lake with its black water, well known for dubious sightings of Loch Ness monster, looked very peaceful with Urquhart Castle on its shore. Like most people, we got out and tried to be the first to photograph this mythical beast.

After spending a while at nearby Loch Ness centre surrounded by gift shops of all imagination related to the monster, we treated ourselves to a dish of grilled fresh fish and chips before our journey down to Oban 150km distance.

By the time we reached Oban, it was raining and dark. I was glad to stretch my aching knees properly, lying flat on the bed.

Ferry next morning to the Isle of Mull was in excellent weather. Second largest of the Hebrides, Isle of Mull, was just off the west coast of Scotland. We spent two nights in this small quiet island exploring its beauty along its diverse coastline. Our hotel was in Tobermory, home to Mull's Single Malt Whisky distillery, but neither of us was keen on whisky.

For the next two days, we drove aimlessly in this idyllic island, taking in its caves, locally known as a broch, of ten thousand years history of human inhabitation. My knees were quietening down. Each hilltop we passed, I was now trying to figure out the best route to get to the top. After leaving our car by the roadside, we walked down an iron ladder on the side of a cliff to access the stony beach. Burg peninsula was a most stunning Hebridean hinterland, with its steep precipitous bluffs, grassy lowlands now colourful with summer flowers. The famous 50-million-year-old fossil tree was several kilometres walk away. We decided against.

After an entirely refreshing few days in Scotland back to Wales, to our daily routine.

Kilimanjaro, Ngorongoro and Serengeti

2006

From my mountains days, I had dreamt of a trek to Everest Base camp. Before my 40th birthday - it did not happen. Work and family took over. Before my 50th – the same story. Next year, I would be sixty!

But now I had to choose between the Everest Base Camp and climbing Kilimanjaro, another of my dream. News about the rapidly melting glacier on Kilimanjaro decided for me. I would climb the highest free-standing peak in the world first.

Once I made my decision, I started going to the gym and trekking the hills of the Brecon Beacons range on my off evenings and weekend with a heavy backpack. I knew it would not be easy. But after walking on average of 40km up and down wet Welsh hills most weeks, I was as much ready as possible at 59 yrs of age for this dare. As I was taking on a serious challenge, I also started fundraising for Breast Cancer Charity, my speciality, through this.

At Nairobi airport, twelve members for the trek met up for the first time. Most were in mid-twenties to mid-forties, only two of us were in our fifties. Our cramped minibuses left Nairobi at dawn and drove by miles and miles of slums in its suburb and then through villages. After almost three hours, we reached the border with Tanzania at Namanga and got off the bus to stretch our legs.

After another hour, we stopped near the Masai village of Tinga Tinga for a buffet lunch on a field. Bypassing Arusha, with sightings of Giraffes, Ostriches, Impalas and Dik-Diks by the roadside, we arrived later at Moshi bush.

Mt Kilimanjaro 5895m　　Next morning, we drove to Machame Gate on the boundaries of the Kilimanjaro National Park. After the usual formalities, we met our four high altitude guides. A multitude of porters would carry our tents and gears, and we had two cooks. We had only to take our backpack with water (with iodine) and our essentials for the trek.

After a brief introduction, we left for a gentle trek uphill through lush, dense rainforest. Mosses hung from the trees covered in mists. We walked amidst sounds of many exotic birds while black and white colobus monkeys watched us from the branches in this wet forest. After four hours of trek, we reached Big Tree campsite 2800m. They put our two men tents in a semicircle with the big mesh tent and the portable shower/toilet tents at one end.

My tent partner was in his early fifties. We both snored, competing against each other through the night. An early morning call by a porter with a bowl of warm water to wash our face and having a cup of tea became a welcome routine for the rest of the trek. At breakfast, we heard funny stories of snoring from all the tents. Soon we got out of the rainforest into lighter vegetation and had the first invigorating view of Mount Kibo, highest of the three volcanic cones of Kilimanjaro.

After seven hours' trek, we reached 3050m. Some were already having altitude sickness when we reached Shira One campsite.

During dinner in the mess tent, our lead guide Felix reiterated few rules. He said - 'from now on, you must go Pole, Pole', meaning slowly, slowly. Then he told us the story of a top-class rugby player from Wales, very fit and additionally prepared for this climb. His girlfriend was working in Arusha as a voluntary teacher. He laughed when she joined him for the challenge. During the trek, every morning, he set off quickly and waited at the destination camp. Laughing and sniggering, as weary climbers arrived there.

At the last camp, when trekking started before midnight, they could not find him anywhere. The guides were worried the stupid man had set off on his own for the peak. But on the way to the summit and back, he was to be seen nowhere. The girlfriend struggled but slowly made to the top. Worried, the team got off the mountain and then found the 'super fit' rugby player waiting in the lodge. Apparently, at the last camp, he had suffered severe altitude sickness and could not even move a few steps before feeling breathless. Embarrassed, he had gone off the mountain on his own before the team started climbing up!

Felix repeated 'Pole, Pole' to us with a broad smile on his face.

We had a choice next day - either to take a five-hour acclimatisation trek via Shira cathedral or a relatively more straightforward three hours' hike via Shira Plateau to Shira Cave at 3840m. I wanted to get as much acclimatisation as possible. The climb was rather steep, but by Cathedral peak at 3895m, the view around was incredible, especially the unforgettable views of the Mt. Meru, floating above the clouds.

Next morning was a six-hour trek across the rest of the Shira Plateau, a relic of a gigantic volcano and oldest of the three volcanos. Most memorable was having our packed lunch, sitting by the edge of a volcanic crater before reaching the next campsite at Shira two 3900m.

Felix said from now on; we would walk for a maximum of 40 minutes before taking a five minutes' break. He repeated that 4 litres of water every day on the route was a must if we want to avoid altitude sickness from dehydration. His novel idea was a toilet break at every third stop. Boys would go behind one set of rocks and the girls behind another. We should check each other's pee to make sure it was coming out clear and not yellowish, suggesting dehydration. In that case, drink more water.

Next day was eight hours' challenging trek on high moorland with a very changed landscape. We traversed the southwest side of Kilimanjaro, passing underneath the Lava Tower, reaching a height of 4400m. Then we followed the mountaineering code of 'walk high, sleep low', going down to our next campsite at Barranco Hut at 3900m.

The sight of Giant Lobelias, reaching over 3-4 meters, made us forget all the hardship. We camped by a deep ravine. In fading daylight, we could see our next day's challenge, the sheer rock face of Barranco wall. Looked impossible at first sight, but that was for tomorrow. I was feeling fit. While they prepared dinner, I walked up with my head torch towards the wall, only to introduce myself to this rock face.

By the time we gathered at the dinner table, most were knackered. The mood changed when the guides brought in a large birthday cake for me. They had carried this up from the town. Everyone sang Happy Birthday for my 59th birthday.

Next morning, we walked down to ford a stream before taking on the vertical 257m tall Barranco Wall. It did not require technical rock climbing but was at least a class 4 scramble in places, requiring the use of all four limbs. My previous mountaineering experience paid off. I climbed relatively smoothly and occasionally lent my hand to fellow climbers in challenging sections.

Over the ridge, we had 15 minutes break and the first close views of Mount Kibo with its glaciers. We soon carried on across Karanga valley, negotiating slippery wet rocks, to our high altitude campsite at 4270m. After a late lunch, was an optional trek to visit the first signs of ice. I knew it would help acclimatisation and enjoyed the additional hike without my backpack. Soon the clouds came in. It became tricky getting back to the campsite, but luckily we had our headlamps. At the camp, several members were now feeling the altitude sickness and were throwing up. But apart from a mild headache, I felt good.

Starting early, we set off for a hard uphill slog, climbing over 600m in the first two hours. After a brief break, we continued to take on Barafu Ridge, almost 45-degree climb in places. After nearly 4 hours' trek, we reached our last campsite at 4870m, just after midday. Our tents were not yet ready. After a drink of hot chocolate, I left my backpack and walked by myself over the scree slopes on the summit route. View of Mount Meru and few other peaks rising above the clouds but distinctly below us was exhilarating.

Back at the camp, our guides said we would leave for summit push at 11 pm. Soon as the tent was ready, I retired. Unable to sleep for a while with the excitement, I nodded off. A porter woke me up at 5-30pm and asked to come for a light supper and our final equipment check. The temperature would be around -20°C. We had to pack our bags, including sleeping bags and air mattresses before we leave the tent. Porters will take them down while we attempt the ascent. Two members of the team were feeling unwell and would not go up.

Soon we were back to our sleeping bags. I could not sleep and was packing my stuff by 10 pm. By 10-45 pm, wearing five layers of clothing and still shivering in the -10°C temperature, sheltering from the wind inside mess tent, I was ready and excited.

It was a clear night as we started our climb with head torches. Our group had regulated to 40 minutes' climb and 5 minutes rest schedule. Unable to see beyond 2m, treacherous and challenging rocks in front, I gathered all my willpower to carry on. After about six hours of strenuous and breathless climb, the sky was lightening. On our way up, we could see the porters were bringing down a few climbers from other teams holding them from both sides. They looked desperately ill with altitude sickness. Two more members of our team also gave up at this point. Soon I realised my water tube was frozen. I had no choice but to continue my climb with no water! After another hour of struggle, we reached Stella Point at 5750m.

The scene behind us of the rising sun over the jagged peaks of Mount Kenya lifted our spirit tremendously. Then, walking over the thick ice at -20°C, I stood spellbound by the rim of the massive volcanic crater of Kilimanjaro, filled with ice and snow.

Still over one hour's climb to Uhuru Peak! Trek along the crater rim was a relatively gentle up and down after the steep climb to Stella Point. Exhausted, but I carried on slowly and steadily. Summit was now within reach. I kept going, although with no water.

After about 45 minutes, the most spectacular Kilimanjaro's glaciers were on our left. I could not resist going down into them. Incredible to see such a massive glacier so close to the Equator in Africa! It had been shrinking at 2.5% each year in the last two decades, but still looked massive. After spending about half an hour on glacier field, the guide hurried me for the next half an hour's climb to Uhuru Peak.

Trekking over the bumpy rocks, I could see the sign at the summit with people at a distance. My pace picked up. Once on the Uhuru peak 5895m, Uhuru meaning freedom in Swahili, I had my Charity Challenge photo taken. View of the equatorial plains of Africa below us through the cloud was captivating. I could not get enough of it. But the guide said it was dangerous to remain at that altitude for long. After only fifteen minutes on the top of Kili, we started our descent. Yes, I can now call it Kili, a privilege only granted to people who had climbed to the top!

Approximately 50,000 people attempt Kilimanjaro every year. On average, 70% climbed to the top, depending on the routes taken. Longer the trek, more is the chance of success, with better acclimatisation on this seriously high altitude mountain. Every year, they evacuate 1000 climbers from the mountain because of high-altitude sickness, and with about ten deaths.

The descent was supposed to be easier. But by now, fatigue added by dehydration was taking its toll. The sun was scorching above. At last, I was getting an occasional trickle of water from my almost frozen water tube. By the time we returned to the Stella point, it was 11 am. I had climbed for nearly twelve hours. But there were still several hours of arduous and dangerous descent ahead. From the rim of the crater, the steep climb down through loose rocks was treacherous at every step to avoid falling and injuring myself. After about two hours of struggle, we reached the site of our overnight camp, now deserted. We stopped for a break. I was happy my water tube was now almost defrosted.

Revived with water, we walked down to the Mweka camp. Over 1020 metres of ascent, then 2390 metres of descent in seventeen hours of walking! But I had done it and was very happy. After a hearty dinner at the camp, the Swahili porters and our guides put on a traditional dance. Soon most of us joined in dancing around the victory campfire.

Next morning, we walked through the lovely rainforest before the presentation of our certificates at the office. Here we said goodbye and thank you to our excellent guides, hardworking porters and the kitchen staff.

Ngorongoro Crater

I had decided to treat myself to visit a couple of nature reserves before I returned after climbing Kili. First on my list was Ngorongoro, the largest volcanic caldera in the world, 20km wide and 600m deep. Its wildlife included all the Big Five and, and if lucky, spotting the endangered black rhino.

Going down in this vast Crater, on our tarpaulin-covered Land Rover, was immediately rewarded. A pride of a lion was resting after their feast the night before. Five lionesses lay on their backs, with all four legs in the air and their full belly sticking out. Cubs happily played around. A single male lion with a darkish mane relaxed by himself a few meters away from the girls.

We stopped to take pictures. Even in midmorning, it was sweltering in the open plains. Soon the male lion yawned and gently walked towards our car. The guide said not to panic and stay still. King of the beasts came until he found the shade under our car. He decided to take a nap there. We could not move

for almost twenty minutes. Some of the lionesses came to check the place up. His Majesty's reverie was broken only when another vehicle came and stopped behind us. He gently got up, yawned and then moved away towards his harem.

In the varied landscape of grassland, lakes and swamps, we came across all the Big Five except the leopards. A large flock of flamingos rested in an almost dry salt lake in the centre of the park. By Lake Magadi, we came across a herd of elephants with their cubs, having fun in the water.

On the other side of the lake were several hippopotamuses. I would have loved to have gone to the site of 3.6 million years old human footprint in this crater, but it was not in the itinerary.

After a fantastic day amongst wild animals, we came up to the crater rim and got off the car to stretch our legs. From a distance of about 20m, I spotted four tall Masai men dressed in red robes and carrying spears, walking towards us. Awed by this fearless Masais, whom even the lions fear, I asked the guide if it was OK to take photographs. By this time they were no further than 5m away.

One of them shouted out in a thick Yankee accent 'Go on Mann, take a photo if you want' with a broad smile on his face.

Serengeti National Park

I stayed overnight at a lodge by Serengeti. On our dawn safari, we stopped to watch a group of lionesses chasing a hippo running back towards a pool.

It was near the end of the annual migration, but there were still thousands and thousands of wildebeests nursing their babies. Interspersed amongst them were thousands of big fat zebras. There were several giraffes, kudus, Thomson's gazelle and dik-diks and bat-eared foxes. As we were returning for our breakfast, the guide spotted a leopard on a tree. We stopped. A few minutes later, the animal got off the tree and gently ambled past us to the jungle. Soon after we came across a leopard tortoise by the bush, its shell was coloured as we have seen on the leopard earlier.

Soon there was a hush from our guide. He had spotted two black rhinos grazing. We approached slowly and got a close-up view of these magical beasts. Our car next drove to another part of the park. Then we came by a mother cheetah with three of her babies by a bush. During our afternoon/evening safari, we saw more lions with their playful cubs.

On the way, we came by a big herd of Buffalos. And there were lions everywhere there. By now we had seen enough lions, over thirty, on the day! We stopped by the side of a large waterhole before dusk. A large herd of elephants happily played in the mud. At night over dinner, we could hear cries of animals not very far from us - possibly a lion killing a fat zebra or a wildebeest.

I returned to the UK a very happy man. Became happier when I realised my charity challenge had raised over six and a half thousand pounds for the Breast cancer Charity.

Sorrento, Mt Vesuvius, Pompeii, Amalfi, Syracuse, Catania and Mt Etna Italy

2007 Sorrento Naples looked gloomy and almost seedy. We stayed in. We took a train the next morning to Sorrento. After crossing the unattractive Naples suburb, a beautiful countryside separated the sea and the mighty Mt Vesuvius. Then through a succession of tunnels, we were in Sorrento.

I fell in love with this idyllic town above the shores of Bay of Naples, made better with a perfect sea view from our balcony with blossoming bougainvillaea.

Lazily, we walked across alleyways. Children played football on the path, and mothers stood by doors gossiping with their neighbours. Lunch was in Piazza Tasso in the open with an ocean view. Time went by with a relaxed Italian way of life all around.

We walked hand in hand, eating delicious gelatos. At dinner in the same place, my wife talked about Byron, Keats, Dickens, Ibsen and Goethe. They also loved this place of 2000 years of history for their holiday. I just loved its pace.

A tour operator shop advertised tandem scuba diving for beginners. I wanted to have a go. My wife was not interested but was happy to spend the day on her own.

First-time scuba diving Long way down at the jetty, I met up with my scuba instructor. After putting on my dive suit, I had 20 minutes safety lesson. How to adjust your mask and get rid of water from it under the water and so on. Soon a small boat took us about half a mile outside the harbour.

After safety instructions once more, we put on our fins and the heavy tanks on our back. Next, we jumped into the sea with the regulators in our mouth. I was mesmerized at the weightless feel as we swam gently. Gradually we dived deeper and colourful batches of fishes swam by us and with us. There was some beautiful coral, too - hypnotizing. Time passed by. Still engrossed, I swam until I saw my instructor making signs of going up. Back in the boat, I realised thirty minutes had gone by - the best thirty minutes of my life. I promised myself to do it again soon.

My wife had come down to the pier to meet me. Myself still babbling, we booked for a day tour to the island of Capri the next day.

From our boat to Capri, Mt Vesuvius stood over the bay at a distance. After half an hour, the small island with a rugged coastline dotted by expensive yachts was in front. From the grand marina, we took a funicular going up. We left past many elegant villas and in front, the stunning Anacapri on the slopes of Mt Solero.

We arrived by the main square of Capri, the Piazza Umberto. By a quaint clock tower, we found a colourful open-air shop where we stopped for coffee served with biscotti. From the square, we walked to the Gardens of Augustus, built only in the last century. From this botanical garden was a 180-degree panoramic view of Capri including Mount Solero, bay of Marina Piccola and Faraglioni rocks rising from the sea. After having a delicious but expensive lunch there, we returned to the main square.

The atmosphere was most congenial, with clusters of tourists and locals ambling around expensive shops and cafes. Soon it was time to go down to catch our return ferry. We regretted not allowing another day to spend here to visit Anacapri and its famous Blue Grotto.

Herculaneum   Next day the Circumvesuviana train took us to Ercolano in 45 minutes. From there we walked to Herculaneum, destroyed and buried under volcanic ash at the same time as Pompeii, in 79 AD. Herculaneum, although smaller than Pompeii, was a wealthier town of the Roman elite. Pyroclastic material covering Herculaneum carbonized and preserved wooden objects like beds and doors and also food and papyrus.

We walked by the several excavated grand houses and the Central Thermae, bathhouses, with lavish coloured marble cladding and beautiful frescos on the walls. Villa of the Papyri, most magnificent retreat by the seaside of Julius Caesar's father-in-law, even now in its ruin, looked grand with a fresco of Theseus on the wall. We loved Herculaneum.

Mt Vesuvius   A public bus took us through Mt Vesuvius National Park to Mt Vesuvius 22km away and stopped below the ticket office at 1,050m. From there we walked a gentle trailhead for the crater with a stunning view of the Naples Bay, Campanian Plain and ruins of Pompeii below us.

Vesuvius 1281m is still an active volcano, although its last eruption was in 1944. Its incredible crater (Gran Cono) with a diameter of 700m, a circumference of 12 km and 200m deep, funnily reminded me of an empty cone of tubri, like one of the fireworks in Diwali festival.

Pompeii   Our bus arrived at Pompeii the next morning. It was scorching hot. We started a four-hour self- guided tour from the Porta Marina by an impressive gate of the ancient town walls. The ruined city looked massive.

By the old market place, known as the forum, were ruins of 2000 years old Temple of Apollo. Many classic columns surrounded this sacred area, with a podium in its centre. Next, we came to the earliest known Basilica of the Roman world, a large, rectangular room with five entrances from the forum. This most important public buildings in Pompeii served as a law court and was the place for business and financial deals.

After a brief stop for gelato, we continued to the Mercury temple, Tempio de Vespasiano, with its perfectly preserved alter and then to the impressive Tempio de Giove, the temple of Jupiter. Nearby was Macellum, one of the focal points of the ancient city, its enormous market square.

By the forum, we found a small but busy cafeteria for lunch and cold drinks. Next, we followed the crowd

121

into the House of the Faun, one of the largest and most impressive private residences in the place. We followed others into the most famous brothel in the ruined city, Lupanare, with many intact erotic paintings on its walls. Nearby was Terme Stabiane, a large thermal bath with an impressive gymnasium.

We then walked into the massive 2nd-century-BC Teatro Grande, a vast 5000-seat theatre. The place now holds a summer season of classical theatre every year.

We rested there on the stone seats of the theatre. Afterwards, we continued to a wooded area outside the Amphitheatre of Pompeii. There we entered through a tunnel inside a vast complex, the oldest surviving Roman amphitheatre.

We realised we had not seen the burnt figures of the people buried under the lava so far. After asking for directions, we realised we had gone past this building on our way. We returned there to see several figures preserved as they were at the time of the eruption almost two thousand years back.

Overwhelmed and exhausted, we returned to Sorrento.

Amalfi Coast Early next morning we left for a scenic bus tour along the Amalfi Coast. Our first stop after an hour was at the pretty town of Positano. Colourful houses looked incredibly beautiful on the slopes of Montepertuso. We had about an hour to spend there. We walked down and down its steep, narrow streets lined with boutiques and cafes to the pebbled beach. After grabbing some coffee there, my wife bought the heaviest traditional pasta maker from a local shop. Coming up the slope for hundreds of meters with the heavy bag dragging me down tested my fitness.

Soon, with the beautiful landscapes and sea views on our right, our coach continued to the peaceful town of Ravello. We stopped to visit the beautiful Villa Cimbrone and Villa Rufolo and their colourful terraced gardens against the backdrop of the natural beauties of the coast. This resort town, 365m above the Tyrrhenian Sea, now holds summer music festival and had been named the City of Music.

Amalfi stood at the foot of Monte Cerreto, surrounded by spectacular cliffs and coastal backdrop. In the 9th -12th century, Amalfi was the seat of a powerful maritime republic. Sant'Andrea cathedral at the town centre, with its striped Byzantine facade, survives from this era.

We walked up through steep staircases to this charming cathedral overlooking Piazza Duomo. A wooden 13th-century Crucifix and another crucifix, made of mother-of-pearl, brought from the Holy Land adorned inside of the building.

Nearby Choistro del Paradiso, was a burial ground for the noble families of Amalfi. Its white columns and pointed arches, similar to those found in the courts of the palaces in the Middle East, reflected Arab influence on Amalfi.

In Piazza del Duomo, we sat for a late lunch. While enjoying the ambience of the place, we ate scialatielli ai frutti di mare, a seafood speciality dish of Amalfi with fresh pasta. Soon it was time to return.

The flight from Naples to Catania arrived after midday. Then, a bus to Syracuse for another 50km distance. I wanted to come to Sicily to see Mt Etna, but while we were there, I also wanted to see the birthplace of the pre-eminent mathematician Archimedes in Syracuse.

Syracuse Sicily   This 2500 years old city, in the southeast corner of Sicily by the Ionian Sea, was an independent Greek colony at the time of the birth of Archimedes around 287 BC. In the late afternoon, we strolled to the marina with a great view of the Castello Maniace, a citadel, against the setting sun.

Most charming for me on the streets of this Sicilian city was an abundance of shops selling varieties of sweets. Not only chocolate sweets but like which I had not seen since leaving West Bengal! Although it was close to dinnertime, we had to stop and try some.

At dinner by Piazza Pancali, we sat with a view of the ruins of the ancient Greek Temple of Apollo. I had for my first-course pasta with sardines, and mahi-mahi, a lovely fish dish, for my main. My wife didn't have the starter, but after the mains, she had a delicious-looking almond pastry cannoli. But I was already too full by then!

Next morning, we visited the Necropolis of Grotticelli, attributed as the 'Tomb of Archimedes', but now known to be of Roman origin dating two hundred years after Archimedes' death. Both of us recalled our physics days, learning the Archimedes' principle - 'when a body is immersed in a fluid, it experiences an apparent loss in weight that is equal to the weight of the fluid displaced by the submerged part of the body.' An idea which came to this genius when getting into a bath!

We did not see his tomb but learnt about Roman philosopher Cicero, a great follower of Archimedes, claimed to have found his grave carved with an illustration of his other famous mathematical proof, a sphere and a cylinder of the same height and diameter.

Later we visited the ruins of the Greek Theatre, one of the largest ever built by the ancient Greeks. It had 67 rows, divided into nine sections with eight aisles. Nearby were the stone quarries, also used as prisons in ancient times. One of its vast quarries was the Ear of Dionysius. The name comes from its similarity in shape to the human ear. Our voice echoed here over a dozen times.

Then we watched from a distance the crowded Fountain of Arethusa before settling ourselves for another sumptuous Sicilian dinner.

Catania Sicily Catania, an ancient port city on Sicily's east coast, lay at the foot of Mt. Etna. View of this active volcano from anywhere in the town was incredible. We wandered around the city's broad central square, Piazza del Duomo, next to the massive Catania Cathedral. Soon we found the fish market, surrounded by seafood restaurants. From a street food stall, I had yummy arancino alla norma, fried rice balls with eggplant, tomato sauce and ricotta cheese.

My wife chose cassatelle, filled with ricotta and covered with almond paste and almond cookies. Sitting by the strange-looking statue of Fontana del Elefante, in the main square, we savoured our lunch.

Later we rambled happily on the streets of this lovely city, one of Italy's most important cultural, artistic and political centre in the Renaissance period. I was even happier to find sweetshops selling non-chocolate sweets there in every corner. I could have blissfully spent days in this gastronomic city of Sicily.

Mt Etna 3350m   For our guided tour to the volcanic mountain, Mt Etna, we proceeded through small Sicilian mountain villages and many vineyards. The guide said because of the fertile nature of the lava flowing through these places; this was one of the finest wine-growing region in the whole of Italy. Side of this mountain had the most dramatic contrast of black lava and green vegetation. We moved through areas of recent lava flows and then through centuries-old pristine woodland. Soon we stopped by Alcantara Gorges. Mountain river flew between basaltic rocks and the Ionian coastline below looked breathtaking.

Later we arrived at Rifugio Sapienza 2500m, a small chalet. By then, it was chilly and windy. Gloomy clouds came in. None of us had more than our summer clothes! Funivia, a cable car could take us to another 500m up before hiking another 500m to a crater rim.

We decided against further adventure. Instead, after finding a shop selling hot drinks nearby, we explored the area. Nearby was Valle Del Bove, Valley of the Ox, a huge Caldera formed after the collapse of several ancient craters. Nearby were other old volcanic craters and a field of a lava flow still warm to touch.

Next by car, we went to a lava tube. Kitted with helmets and headlights, we walked inside. Lava, as it flew, had created a solid layer around remaining liquid inside. We entered Grotta Tre Livelli in the upper level of the cave. After descending on a ladder for a few meters and then by a few more steps, we reached the main passage, Galleria a valle. Its galleries stretched over 1100m. It was eerie, to say the least, inside the tunnel and we walked a few hundred meters in near darkness. Sharp lava floor dug into our shoes. Soon we gave up and returned to our car.

On our way down, we stopped by a place where the lava flow had partly buried a house only a few years back.

By the evening, the cloud lifted. During our dinner in the plaza, in the background, we could see Mt Etna glowing with its eruption.

Everest Base Camp Nepal

2008

Returning from Kili, my desire to go to the Everest Base Camp had multiplied. In spare times, I intensified my hill walks around the Brecon Hills. Finally, it would happen in April 2008.

Arriving in Kathmandu, I met the rest of the group, nine trekkers and three Sherpas. Most 20-35yrs. I was the oldest at 61yrs. Kathmandu, after forty years, I found overcrowded. In the next two days after a quick kit check, we visited the usual sites in Kathmandu.

Next morning we gathered at the crowded domestic airport for our flight to Lukla. Our team had booked all the seats in this 12 seater plane. After Kathmandu valley, amongst the Himalayan peaks, our sherpas pointed out the twin peaks of religious tales, Gauri Shankar.

Before landing at Lukla, our small plane hovered around a soaring cliff. Then suddenly the aircraft headed straight into a gap in the crag, and the plane circled to slow down inside stone walls. One of the most dangerous airports in the world! From outside the airport, we watched a plane taking off. After only less than 100m of taxiing on a short runway, the plane just dropped off in the air from the end of the cliff. Scary, but that will be for another day when we return!

While we relaxed in Lukla having our lunch, Sherpas distributed camping equipment and baggage to Ghopkyos, a mixed breed of cows and yaks. Only means of transportation from now was on foot, no cars in this region. Then a delightful five-hour trek on Khumbu Himalayas, with a superb view of Kusum-Kangru peak at a distance, we arrived at our night stay in a village house in Phakding 2652m, by the Dudh-Koshi River.

Next morning after crossing over a suspension bridge, we continued our steady trek. In isolated villages, children played with makeshift seesaws and waved at us with their puffy red cheeks and shy smiles. At Benkar village, we turned the prayer wheels at the Buddhist temple for good luck. Soon we crossed another long suspension bridge over Bhote Koshi River, taking turns with lines of Ghopkyos and porters carrying heavy loads. Next to Monjo village, we rested while our Sherpas sorted out permits at the Sagarmatha National Park entrance.

From there we descended to the Jorsalle village, the last hamlet before Namche Bazar - a brief lunch break.

Further down, we walked by large stones covered with Buddhist prayers, Om Mani Padme Hum. We then trailed by the banks of Imjatse River. At a distance, we could see a very high suspension bridge we will be crossing. With amazing views on bright daylight of distant tall snow peaks and colourful rhododendrons everywhere, we quickly handled the uphill walk to the bridge from the riverbed. Crossing the spectacular high suspension bridge on wooden planks held together by steel wires was hair-raising. Memories of Indiana Jones films came into mind.

There was a hush from our Sherpas after reaching the other side of the river. They pointed to the north. Floating clouds had cleared. For a brief few minutes, we had a view of Mt Everest.

Namche Bazar 3440m and Khumjung 3790m   The trek now was a steep uphill. We all struggled. I caught an irritating hacking cough which lasted me through the rest of the tour. It was like a smoker's cough, except it lasted all day, and I am a non-smoker. After about two hours, we came out of the bush path and could see the colourful houses of Namche Bazar. Our campsite, however, was another half an hour away. The 13km trek had taken over six hours; all of us were exhausted but happy to have been through our first uphill challenge.

Most of the Sherpas came from this town of fewer than four hundred families. We had three nights here to acclimatise. Our Sherpas organised supplies, high altitude porters, Yaks, and took the time to visit their families.

Next day was an optional trek to Khumjung village over the hill. From Namche valley, we reached Khumjung after three hours steep trek over the mountain. This tiny village had a high school built through a charity set up by Edmund Hillary, the first person with Tenzing Norgay to set foot on the peaks of Mt Everest. There was a statue of him there. Our sherpas said, around here, they revered Hilary more than Tenzing, the Nepalese hero because Hillary's charity was doing much development works for the local people.

Other attraction in Khumjung was the only purported head of a Yeti in its monastery. In a small sanctuary, we paid our respects to the resident monks. Then they allowed us to see the specimen, head of an animal, possibly a bear, inside a locked box. It was over 240 years old. Villagers held it in high respect as a good luck charm. We all silently hoped for our luck over the next few days.

Going down to Namche took an hour. We were all happy with our acclimatisation day, only to be disheartened to hear the school children from Namche made this journey daily to Khumjung!

Next morning, we walked half an hour to a hotel outside Namche. From there, the most amazing views of Mt Everest and other snow-capped giant peaks lifted our spirits. Rest of the day was to ourselves. For my hacking cough, sherpas called it Khumbu cough, so far, I had tried throat lozenges and cough syrup with no avail. Sherpas advised rubbing Tiger Balm on my chest. It was soothing but made no difference to the cough.

After sorting out my gears, I walked amongst the houses away from the tourist shops. Most houses were stone-built. In broken Hindi, I conversed with the locals. They invited me to one of their homes and offered traditional spiced sweet tea. Outside the house, a man was laboriously chiselling out stone blocks from large slabs. I asked what a day's hard work would be worth.

He said he would be lucky to make a dollar a day. But with a smile, he joined us for a glass of tea and asked me about India.

Above Namche Bazar, we trekked through a winding trail with enchanting views of Nuptse, Lhotse, Ama Dablam, occasional sightings of Mt Everest and a close-up view of Tharmaserkhu. On the narrow track, we often stopped to give way to yaks making their way from or coming back to Namche. We gaped to see men carrying uphill on their back, wood planks for building, easily over 120kg in weight.

All of us, including our porters, stopped at Shanasa for a break. Nepal's national bird, beautifully coloured Danphe pheasants, were found here. We only saw one at a distant tree for a brief time before it flew away.

Next, we descended to the banks of Imjatse River at Phungitenga 3250m and then crossed the river on a rickety bridge. From the river bed, we trekked strenuously uphill. We took several breaks, taking pictures of many varieties of blooming rhododendrons on mountainside and prayer stones covered with dried leaves and flowers. After nearly three hours from the riverbed, we saw from a distance a big Gompa. We knew we were reaching Thyangboche, our overnight campsite, 10km from Namche.

Thyangboche 3876m   Thyangboche looked an ideal place to relax in the afternoon sunshine. Most beautiful place to have a campsite with the largest Monastery in Khumbu region at one end, and the highest in the world bakery and coffee shop at the other. From our camp, we gazed at the panoramic view of Everest, Nuptse and Lhotse. Tenzing Norgay was born in Thani village nearby and was at this monastery in his young age to be a monk. We walked to the monastery and watched young trainee monks learning their prayers from the wise ones, probably dreaming like Tenzing of climbing those majestic peaks one day! Soon I was at the bakery and ordering coffee with a chocolate cake. Unbelievable at 3876m!

Next morning a descent through a forest of junipers and blossoming rhododendrons until we came out to an open space at Deboche 3650m. Again another breathtaking view of the Everest and Ama Dablam. We walked past many scripted prayer stones before coming to a narrow bridge over the gorge of river Imja-Tse. Trekking mostly uphill from there, we arrived at the gate of an old monastery in Pangboche village. Sherpas and other trekkers visited inside the Gompa to give their offerings, while I chatted with the local villagers.

We walked downhill before taking a short but arduous climb to Shomare village and had our lunch there with a close-up view of Ama Dablam. After an hour of further trekking, we left the path to the north face of Ama Dablam and continued further north. After a brief stop by a prayer stone, we continued to Imjatse valley beneath the majestic peaks of Ama Dablam, Nuptse and Lhotse.

Dingboche 4401m A beautiful jumble of fields surrounded Dingboche, our next campsite. Stone walls protected barley and potato fields from the icy wind. With small shepherd huts, it looked enchanting. Even after the 12km walk at this altitude, I was in excellent spirit. Soon I walked into the hamlet of 150 inhabitants, in its only chai shop for a glass of Nepalese tea and a chat with the locals. In the late afternoon, under cloud cover, it was freezing. They offered me something I never had before, spiced tea with a lump of butter. It was magical and made me feel warm from inside immediately.

Next day we had an acclimatisation climb to the top of nearby Nangkartshang 5083m. After leaving the village, we crossed a river and yak pasture before our ascent. A strenuous trail all the way. After three and a half hours of struggle, we were at the peak of Nangkartshang. Makalu, Ama Dablam, Taboche, Island peak, Cholatse and Lobuche stood gloriously in front. We had climbed almost 700m - bone-tired but thrilled.

After a gruelling descent, I returned to my friendly Chai shop for another glass of spicy butter tea. After the high climb, we slept low. Nothing better for acclimatisation.

Trek next day to Lobuche 4928m was only 8km. After two hours we crossed a wooden bridge over the river of the Khumbu glacier to reach Dugla, another hamlet for a relaxing lunch by the river, originating from the glacier of our destination.

Everest memorial stone

Next section of the trail had several memorials on boulders of climbers who had died attempting Everest. We stood solemnly for a while before continuing as the weather closed in.

Gorakshep 5288m We had trekked 8km without too much difficulty. It was only mid-afternoon. But the flurry of snow drove us to our hut in Gorakshep, a stone hut dormitory with bunk beds.

Gorakshep

Next day half of the team left early for their trek to Kalapathar. Although I had been feeling fit except for my Khumbu cough, I had decided to keep all my energy to get to the Everest Base Camp. I did not want to risk this after coming so close.

Our group, after breakfast, started acclimatising trek over a moraine path. Views on the route of icy glacial ponds and walking through icebergs of lower Khumbu Glacier was stunning. Sitting on an enormous stone in the bright sunlight, I dozed and soaked in the incredible surroundings. Trekkers from Kalapathar returned in the evening looking shattered. But soon they were buzzing with talks about the unobstructed views of the Everest from there.

Next morning was our final trek for the Everest Base Camp was only 5km. But this was so far the most difficult of the entire trip. We trekked up and down within broken Khumbu glacier. The glacier looked dirty with loose rocks covering the ice. Larger stones and scree were pushed away to the side by the glacier. There were several narrow crevasses to negotiate. But our efforts were compensated, as we walked amongst the magnificent seracs and alluring ice ponds. In some places in the late morning sunshine, the glacier was melting. Forming springs and then dropping several meters to create ice ponds - captivating.

Also, the glorious view of the Khumbu icefall kept me going in this challenging terrain.

Everest Base Camp 5357m   By the time I reached the Everest Base Camp, it was already early afternoon. Clouds were pulling in. But I stood there enchanted amongst many tents and looking at the infamous icefall above. Broken seracs and numerous crevasses on the Khumbu Glacier made the glacier route above looked impossible. I regretted not to have booked for a trek where you could go to the Camp one above the glacier.

Rest of my team, except one young sherpa, had already left. Reluctantly, I, with my Sherpa, left the site, last of the group. By now, my Khumbu cough was worse. Soon we turned on our headlamps. The sherpa lead, walking through rocks and ice on the glacier- hard work. After a couple of hours, eventually, we left the glacier and came to its moraine bank.

Here, as I relaxed, my front foot slipped on a rock. At the last millisecond, I broke my fall through my walking pole, stopping me from crashing my head on the stone. The sherpa, in front, looked back at the sound. He came and took over my backpack. I drank some water and wearily continued on the loose rocks. Fifteen minutes before we reached the camp, a porter came out with a most welcome flask of hot chocolates.

Our trek next day back was up to Thyangboche, where I again indulged in coffee and lovely chocolate cake in the bakery. We arrived at Namche the following day where we said goodbye to many of our porters and our cook. After a relaxing day in town, we headed down for Lukla, about six hours trek, all in a cheerful mood despite my persisting cough.

While we stopped briefly near Jorsalle village, a young woman carrying a child on her back went past us quickly. The child seemed in some distress. I asked the porters to find out what was wrong with the baby. One porter ran after them. Soon he caught up and brought them back to us, explaining to her there was a doctor on the team.

The 2-year-old baby had burnt his hand on an open fire in the house last evening. The mother had travelled from her village, several kilometres from here, first thing in the morning, leaving two other children at home. She was taking her son to the only health centre in the area, close to Lukla, another two hours walk. I attended the child and gave the necessary treatment.

Luckily; although there were large blisters, it was superficial burn and should heal with simple treatment. His mother was pleased, but the boy was upset with me, even after I gave him a bar of chocolate!

On our way before Lukla, I spotted the health centre near our track. I walked there with a sherpa to find out the facilities. The place was closed for the day. If we were not there, the mother with the baby would have made this long journey for nothing! It appeared to be the typical fate of all in this region who needed even primary healthcare.

After our overnight stay in Lukla, the flight the next morning was even more terrifying than we had imagined. After only a brief run, our small plane just fell off the rock face and floated for a while in the air, adjusting to the prevailing wind, before flying towards Kathmandu.

Returning from Khumbu, the crowded Kathmandu looked even less appealing.
In the evening, we were treated to a celebratory dinner at the Rum Doodle restaurant, its name deriving from the book by W E Bowman 'The Ascent of Rum Doodle'. This parody of serious mountaineering tells the story of an imaginary 40,000ft Rum Doodle Peak climb.

The restaurant had signatures of all the greatest mountaineers who have scaled Mt Everest including Edmund Hillary, Reinhold Messner, Ang Rita Sherpa and Rob Hall. Sadly, Tenzing Norgay had died before they reopened the place. A picture of him was there instead. There were also cards and signatures on the walls from the mountaineers who had climbed high peaks in Khumbu valley, but they only allowed high altitude trekkers to the Everest Base camp to add their cards on the wall.

We all signed a card to hang on the wall, my writing in it said *'To the Base camp and back. Coughed all the way'!*

Washinton DC and New Year's Eve Times Square
Ball Drop in New York

USA 2009/10   Our older daughter was doing marine biology research in Washington DC, a city we have not visited. We arrived after Boxing Day.

First, was a visit to the acclaimed White House on Pennsylvania Avenue. Standing outside, we talked about recently elected President Obama and hopes of people in the country and the rest of the world for the future. We then walked to the National Mall. Washington Monument, 152m stone obelisk, tallest in the world, stood circled by American flags in the vast memorial park. Three of us sat on its steps for a while.

Lincoln Memorial at the other end of the mall, built like a Greek temple, contained a large seated sculpture of Abraham Lincoln. Visitors stood in front of an inscription of his renowned Gettysburg Address. We stood by the Reflection pool and remembered in this place in 1963, a hundred thousand people listened to Martin Luther King Jr.'s ' *I Have a Dream'* speech. A dream still unfilled for so many.

Later we visited the Capitol Building with a massive dome and pillars, home of world's 2nd largest democracy. Eleven of the twenty Smithsonian Institution museums were are at the National Mall. We visited the National Museum of American History. It displayed 'Taking America to Lunch', a celebration of the history of American lunch boxes! Large original Star-Spangled Banner, the garrison flag that flew during the Battle of Baltimore, drew a large crowd.

Next day we paid a visit to the Arlington National Cemetery across Potomac River – a national cemetery for the dead from nation's conflicts beginning with Civil War till this day. How many had given their lives needlessly?

New year's eve at Times Square   It was only three and a half-hour bus to New York. After checking in our hotel in an alley by the Times Square, we walked to the site of the famous Ball Drop due at midnight. It was only 4 pm, but already the area was crowded. We decided to come back soon.

We returned to Times Square before 6 pm. A flurry of snow and the temperature was around -5°C.

Revellers packed the place within tight security. Festivities formally started with the 20 second '6 hours to Go' countdown followed by raising of the ball at 6:00 p.m. Twelve students from New York City high schools switched on the lights of the massive 550kg Waterford Crystal ball. The cast of a Broadway show took the stage to everyone's applaud. In slushy weather, we stayed with an even louder scream from the crowd until the countdown said 5 hours to go.

We left to catch some dinner at a nearby busy restaurant. We returned before ten for the countdown - 2hours to go. Fever pitch atmosphere now with live music performance. But the temperature with the wind had dropped to below -10°C! Too cold for my wife. She decided to return to the hotel. I accompanied her and then returned by myself to the square just after eleven. The atmosphere was mad now.

Counting began at 11.59:00 pm, everyone chanting. At midnight the lighted ball dropped down a flagpole. Confetti and balloons came flying down from nowhere. Lots of kissing all around. Some now took out their colourful 2009 glasses and tossed hats marked 'Happy New Year' into the crowd.

After 15-20 minutes there, I left the place for our hotel room where my wife had watched the Ball Drop on TV in warm comfort.

Defeated in the Atlas Mountains

2010 January Morocco

I was feeling smug after climbing Kilimanjaro and the Everest Base Camp in the last two years. I wanted to add Mt Toubkal 4167m in the Atlas Mountains, the highest peak in North Africa to my triumphs.

Atlas Mountains Range stretches over 2500km through Morocco, Algeria and Tunisia, separating the Mediterranean and Atlantic coastline from the Sahara Desert. It had several peaks over 4000m, Mt Toubkal the highest. In summer, climbing this peak was simple 2-3 days trekking. Instead, I took the difficult winter challenge.

From Marrakech, we left for Imlil by minibus through enchanting villages in middle Atlas and then drive uphill to High Atlas through windy road. Traditional houses, standing precariously against the rock, looked stunning. After three hours', we arrived in Imlil village 1740m.

After a cup of refreshing mint tea and slices of almond pastry, I walked in the village. A group of children returning from their school followed me. I asked to see their school books. Proudly they showed their home works, including English. We had fun speaking English. Suddenly it became cloudy and windy. Before I reached my lodge, it was spitting with cold rain.

Next morning, the rain had stopped, but black clouds hung over us. It was very windy. The guide said the weather forecast for the next few days on the mountain was not good. But all in our group were seasoned trekkers and were prepared for the challenge of the mountain in the winter.

We left after a breakfast of bread dipped in oil and honey with olives. We trekked, leaving the fields and walnut trees behind and followed the Mizane valley passing by the Muslim pilgrimage shrine of Sidi Chamarouch. We walked steadily up scree path, now covered with snow in most areas. The weather was looking ominous with layers of snow falling. We carried on carefully on a treacherous path.

The temperature quickly plummeted. A snowstorm hit us hard, and we were glad to see our shelter within 50m. We struggled to open the door of Toubkal Refuge at 3209m against the blistering wind. After 12 km trek in the worsening weather, we are glad to be inside. Many frustrated climbers crowded the place.

Toubkal refuge, 'Les Mouflons' was named after a local breed of deer (Mouflon). We stayed in one of its seven dormitories. While having hot drinks, we heard stories from many disheartened climbers of their failed attempt on the day and the day before to win Toubkal.

It was still a few hours before the evening. Fully kitted out in my winter gear, I walked outside by myself. Visibility in the blizzard was between 5-10m. I braved kicking through deep fresh snow, zig-zagging up the U-shaped breach in the mountain wall behind the hut slope towards the col. No one else was outside. For a while, I felt great about this solo adventure. I trudged for about half an hour through knee-deep snow in a windstorm, tricky in places because of the slippery stone slabs underneath. I reached the bottom of the col. Walking up the steep 30m col was precarious, and I just about managed to get to its top without fall.

From there, I tried to look above at our summit route, although there was no question of being stupid enough to attempt it now. Visibility was now only 2-3m, and it was getting dark. With only a few minor falls descending on the col, chilled to the bone, I walked back to the hut. Our guides said the next day's weather forecast was even worse. We had to decide on whether to stay on and attempt a climb, hoping the weather improves. Or leave after breakfast to Imlil. We all agreed to defer our decision until the next morning.

While I was chatting with the fellow hikers, around 10 pm, three climbers returned after making it to the top. They looked utter wrecks. One of them was a young French ski instructor in the Alps. Other two were seasoned Royal Marines. We heard the condition was dangerously treacherous to the top. One marine had got into serious difficulty. Luckily two others were there to help him.

Next morning the weather was worse. Everyone from the hut was going down, two marines taking the lead. Only the French ski instructor trudged up the mountain on his own. He would try to bag another peak. Going down, struggling against the gale on slippery rocks was challenging. After four hours, we reached Imlil. Soon we left for Marrakech, arriving there in the afternoon, disappointed, but alive.

Marrakech   I loved Marrakech. This densely packed, walled medieval city with mazelike alleys with thriving souks selling traditional textiles, pottery and jewellery, was most charming. I strolled in world-famous Jemaa el-Fnaa square, packed with stalls and snake charmers. I found a restaurant

there. Sitting on its balcony, I had a mouth-watering Tagine chicken while watching the lively square below.

Next day I walked across Marrakesh by its ramparts. This 12th-century orange-red clay and chalk wall stretched for 19 km around the city with 20 gates and 200 towers. I strolled enchanted for hours in the honeycomb of alleyways and bought myself a Tagine pot to take back home, which over the years became a talking point for my family and friends over my Moroccan cooking. Then I indulged again on a lunch of Tagine with typical Moroccan salad.

Fully sated, I walked lazily by the square to the red stone Koutoubia Mosque with its 77m minaret. Sadly, it was time to leave for the airport.

At the airport, there was a hush amongst our local guides. They had just heard from their head office. The frozen body of the French man was found earlier in the day, not very far from the col.

I left Morocco defeated by nature and mournful for the young adventurer.

Health link becomes stronger

Ethiopia 2003 – 2014

In July 2003, I visited Gondar for doing some training. From Addis, we flew north over rugged mountains before going over massive Lake Tana, source of the Nile. Gondar at 2133m, home of many emperors since the 12th century, was invaded by Italy in the last century. The city, with ruins of royal castles, was in decay and suffering neglect.

During the training programme, I stayed outside the hospital. In the evenings a boy of about 15-16 years of age came by with his friends. In between kicking a football against the wall, they loved talking about Chelsea Football club which he and his friends supported.

One evening this boy invited me to their house for a coffee ceremony. He lived with his mother, a cleaner in the hospital and his 10-year-old sister in a small hut. His father had died of malaria a few years back. They welcomed me in a traditional coffee ceremony. Only the boy could speak a few words of English, and I could say only a few words of Amharic.

The 10-year-old girl had the most fantastic football dribbling skill with a piece of wrapped up cloth! We had a wonderful evening. This poor family's kindness and hospitality touched me deeply.

Simien Mountains   After the programme, I left for a drive to the Simien Mountains with a colleague from the hospital. We drove on a rough road through tiny villages for about three hours before reaching the small town of Debark. There we stopped for our lunch of injera and doro wot.

My colleague left to get our passes for the National Park. I bought water and snacks for the next part of our journey while smiling children surrounded me shouting 'Firingi, Firingi.'
The road got tricky. But the view of the jagged cliffs, pristine alpine valleys and plateaus were spellbinding. After about two hours, we stopped at Kossoye viewpoint for a gorgeous panoramic view of the Simien. Down below on a plateau, we spotted a group of rare Walya Ibex, looking magnificent with their long curved horns. From the small lodge in the park, we walked to a cliff edge to enjoy the majestic sunset over the Simien.

Dashen Peak 4550m, the highest in Ethiopia, was standing tall over other stunning crests in sumptuous sunset colours. Soon it got very dark, and at 3300m in the winter was freezing cold. We retired for the night in our hut only with an oil lamp. Next morning we got up in time to enjoy the sunrise on the Simien. Walking back to our car, we came across a group of Gelada Baboons, known as Bleeding Heart Baboon, because of the heart-shaped mark on their chests, warming themselves in the morning sunlight.

Arbaminch   Our next training programme was in Arbaminch, in the south-west of the country, 500 km journey from Addis. At Arbaminch, as we were checking in our hotel, loudspeakers started Azan from a nearby mosque. Soon, not to be outdone by the Muslims, even louder prayer call came from a nearby church. We laughed at this over dinner. But the cacophony from both started again at five in the morning, sounding louder at dawn. Over breakfast, we agreed that to work for the next five days; we needed decent sleep. Our local organiser shifted us to a guest house above a hill where the sound from the town did not reach.

On our rest day, we drove to Nechisar National Park, separating Lake Chamo from Lake Abaya. In this national park, we saw zebras, dik-dik and bush pigs. Troops of baboons watched us from nearby trees. Lake Abaya was much larger, 60 km long and 20 km wide, with no crocodile. People fished for Nile Perch there. In sharp contrast, the smaller Lake Chamo was full of crocodiles and hippos. On our boat ride, large Nile crocs swam by us and many more basked on the grassland. Several families of hippos occupied another part of the lake.

In the late afternoon, we sat in our guest house garden, enjoying our drinks with a view of the lakes separated by the forest. Outside, a baboon mother sat with her baby inside the garden. Our food arrived. Happily chatting, we had not noticed a large male baboon had come from another side. He quickly jumped to our table and grabbed some food before running away. We laughed and moved inside for our meal.

Non-doctor Emergency Surgeons   Our training programme in SNNPR region, was now in its fifth year. Training had been extended to include all the HOs and all the midwives from this region. Many came travelling for two days to attend the programme.

On the first morning of training in Arbaminch, one HO came to me and said, 'Hello Dr Biku. Do you remember me?'

His face looked familiar. I said 'I remember your face but remind me.'

His name was Wodajo. He attended our second training programme in Awassa. When I asked what he was doing these days, he replied he was working in a remote hospital close to the Sudan border. He said his hospital had no doctor, only another health officer. He then said, to my surprise, he was doing caesarean sections and laparotomies for emergencies.

When I asked where he learnt to do these operations, he replied 'you taught us some skills and gave us confidence. I used them plus improvised. Next hospital with a surgeon is more than 150km away on a poor road. Patients would not survive if I sent them there.'

This got me and Aberra thinking. If with only with basic skills training, this was possible, how many more lives could be saved with a structured training programme for the HOs in the rural hospitals? Fortunately, we managed to arrange a meeting in Addis with the Health Ministry on our way back in ten days through Aberra's contacts and our link's reputation.

Back in Addis, we had an all-day meeting arranged by the health ministry. They invited WHO Ethiopian representative, British Embassy and the surgeons from Addis University. I, with Aberra, outlined our idea for formalised training of the HOs, to save lives in rural hospitals. While all other present agreed, the surgeons from Addis said these HOs are not doctors. They could not agree to such a programme. The health ministry asked politely but sternly which of them would like to be posted in a rural hospital. They backed out immediately. I had never come across before the forming of a National task force within a day. But it happened there by the end of the day! In the next two years, a formal three-year MSc programme, Integrated Emergency Surgery and Obstetrics, IESO, training the HOs started in the country, led by Dr Yifru, one of our link coordinators in Awassa.

Motorbike ambulances   One of the constant theme from the village communities over the last five years had been about access. A seriously ill patient needed to be carried on homemade stretchers, sometimes from 20km distance. And if the patient then needed a transfer to hospital, often another 100km or more, the only option was to try their luck on the back of a truck, if any was going that way.

We found a UK based company which produced in South Africa a vehicle called Motorbike Ambulance. These motorbikes had a sidecar which could be reclined for a patient to lie down if needed. It seemed to be an ideal solution, especially as they were light, sturdy and could easily negotiate rough roads.

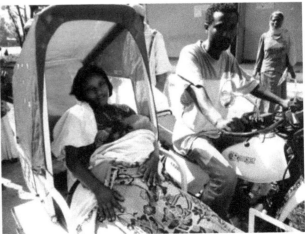

Redoubling our fundraising effort, within a year we ordered four motorbike ambulances to be delivered to Ethiopia. We insisted that the driver must be from HC staff, so he could be contacted at all hours - an instant success. Stories of women with difficulties in labour brought to HC for assisted delivery or transferred to hospital successfully, lives of mothers and babies saved, were repeated everywhere. By the next three years, we provided a dozen of these three-wheel ambulances to different HCs in the region.

Alaba   We returned in Alaba for three days in Alaba for continuing our training of the health workers there and providing them with more essential supplies for the HC and the hospital. The area, known after Halaba people, had a Muslim population of almost 95%. But the Muslim and Christian community lived in harmony.

Alaba community had one unique feature. Their Tukuls were painted depicting daily actions or elements of nature in organic colours. Although dilapidated, they looked pretty. Also, Alba was scorching hot, compared to other parts of the south we had worked. To counter this, Halaba men wore an elongated top hat. It not only gave an elegant look but kept their head cool.

We donated several vital pieces of equipment to the HC, and the newly opened hospital, built through money raised by a local Christian in this mostly Muslim population.

After the continuing training programme there we went to a remote health centre. From the main road, even in the dry weather, it took us an hour and a half to get there. We tried to imagine transferring a sick patient from there. As we arrived there with our donation of a motorbike ambulance, scores of people stood by the roadside, the women welcoming us chanting with ululation.

During the customary coffee ceremony, they gifted each of us with an Alaba hat. We wore them proudly.

Over the years, routinely, we brought lots of medical supplies from the UK. We loaded them on the roof of a minibus in Addis for the 300km journey to the south. We had noticed every 30-40 km, one or two police stood by the roadside. They waved the driver to stop, check his licenses and make sure there were no illegal items like Chaat. They were never looking for money, but a nuisance, especially on a lengthy drive. Soon we adopted a plan of having one of the UK team sitting by the driver on the passenger seat. He/ she waved as soon as they spotted any police at a distance. Most of the time, the police seeing a 'Firingi' on the car, waved the vehicle to go through, mainly because they were not keen to speak English to a foreigner.

On one such journey, after many hours on the road, I had fallen asleep inside the car. I woke up when the door of the minibus was opened. A policeman had entered. On the passenger seat, our colleague had fallen asleep. Police had asked the driver to stop. It was in the middle of nowhere.

As soon as the young policeman entered the minibus, he shouted, 'Oh hello! It is you, Dr Biku!'

It turned out before he joined the police, he had met us a few years back while we were donating equipment and training at the HC near his village. After a chat with us, he told the driver to look after us properly.

Our health link's most successful area had been our midwifery team regularly training the midwives in the HCs and the hospitals. Hundreds of midwives were trained in antenatal, delivery care and care of the newborn. They also trained the midwifery trainers in the college.

Within ten years, our link's midwifery team trained over two thousand midwives and their trainers as well as the health care assistants in the region.

Bicycles   One problem faced by these health care workers was that they had to travel on foot to deliver care, sometimes walking many kilometres a day from one village to another.

During the next few visits, our link bought almost 300 bicycles from Addis and donated to the local community health posts. Again, this went down very well with the community. Only occasional funny stories we heard were of some of these girls falling off their bikes while learning to ride them!

Peter, our haematology specialist, who set up the blood bank in Dilla Hospital, developed cancer. After completing his surgery and chemotherapy, he returned to Ethiopia for training again. Unfortunately, he passed away within the same year. One of his dying wishes was to have his ashes buried in Dilla.

In our next trip, we carried his ashes and scattered outside a village he had loved, remembering him in a solemn ceremony.

Czech Republic Prague

October 2010

We took a long weekend trip to Prague, in the Czech Republic, the former kingdom of Bohemia and cultural centre. Nicknamed 'City of a Hundred Spires', bisected by the Vltava River, Prague was beautiful.

We strolled across the 600 year's old Charles Bridge from Old Town to Lesser Quarter over the Vltava. Fifteen statues of Catholic Saints stood on the bridge. Statue of The Crucifix and Calvary was interesting. A recently added bronze tablet had an explanatory text in Czech, English and Hebrew. The Hebrew text from 1696 on the crucifix was added after a local Jewish leader was accused of blasphemy. His punishment was to raise funds to purchase the gold-plated letters. An inscription around the head of the statue said, 'Holy, Holy, Holy, the Lord of Hosts' - a symbolic humiliation and degradation of Prague Jews in medieval Europe.

We returned to our hotel soon to get ready for a special dinner. Searching for things to do in Prague, I had come across this unusual restaurant in the city. Restaurace Peklo, meaning 'Hell' in Czech, in a 12th- century cave, had a great review and sounded inviting. I wanted to treat my wife to an unforgettable romantic dinner in an atmosphere once favoured by King Charles IV. The place was always in demand and needed booking in advance.

Our cab took us to Strahov Hill area outside an old monastery. The area looked deserted. Following the signs, we passed through a tunnel and entered a high cave. A waiter took us to our table. My wife smiled when the waiter gave her a single rose. The interior was like a medieval wine cellar with candles everywhere. During reservation, I had booked their famous 12-course dinner.

After drinks, the waiter brought one after another four courses of appetisers. Creamy pumpkin soup; octopus with chorizo; grilled squid with red pepper; eggplant parmigiana; grilled tiger prawns with ginger, garlic and coriander coulis and a variety of home-made sausages. With many types of bread, onion chutney, fig jam and seasonal fruits laid on the table.

Every item was delicious. They asked if we wanted a few minutes before the main courses. Both of us said yes please, at least 15 minutes.

Main courses included deer goulash, yellowfin tuna, roasted baby chicken, rib eye beef entrecote, crispy slow roast duck, red cabbage with apples and all kinds of roasted vegetables. Although each was in petite quantity, by now, we were stuffed and asked to give us at least twenty minutes. We walked inside this atmospheric cave. The restaurant could easily hold a hundred customers, and on the weekend, it was full.

We returned slowly for our three-course desserts of bublanina and pryanik, followed by an assortment of ice creams. At the end of two and a half-hour meal, we were bursting at the seam, but very happy. Czech 'hell' was most definitely heavenly.

Outside, we walked, trying to help digest the enormous dinner. View of the Prague Castle at a distance over the river was incredible.

Next morning my wife wanted to have a lie-in for the morning. After agreeing to meet up for lunch by the medieval Astronomical Clock in the Old Town Square, I left for a wander around the city.

After visiting the Jewish Quarter, I took a packed tram for Prague Castle. I stood surrounded. I could sense something happening around me but could not quite figure out what. At the next stop, some people around me got off quickly. Something inside me made me check my pocket. I realised for the first time in my life I have been pickpocketed. Credit cards and the travel money was gone. I got off and took a cab to my hotel. From the reception, I called my wife to come down and pay the taxi driver. By the time I finished making expensive calls from my room to credit card companies, we were in no mood to go out for lunch.

In the evening, to make the most of our holiday, we walked on Charles Bridge. Then had dinner in the Old Town Square by the Astronomical Clock, giving an hourly show to a big crowd. My wife clutched on to her handbag, all the time.

Following morning, we visited the Prague Castle, the largest ancient castle in the world according to the Guinness Book of Records. It had a Gothic cathedral, monastery, several palaces, and defence towers with colourful changing of the guards and museums dedicated to Czech history. After spending the entire morning there, we returned to the airport.

In search of the Royal Bengal Tiger in Sundarban

Sundarban India January 2011

I had seen many wild animals, including the Big 5. But I was yet to see the most majestic of all, the tiger. Living in West Bengal, I had grown up with the stories of the most ferocious and the finest of all animals - Royal Bengal Tiger of Sundarban.

A college mate of my nephew in India was a top forest ranger in Sundarban National Park. My nephew arranged a tour of this famous delta with him.

My nephew and I arrived at Rai Dighi, by Mani River, the gateway for Sundarban and met our forest ranger friend. The unmarried ranger was glad to have company after living alone in the Sundarban reserves. We got into a motor launch full of villagers from isolated islands on the delta who had come for their weekly shopping.

Best of Sundarban was its mangrove in the delta, formed by the confluence of Ganges, Brahmaputra and Meghna Rivers in the Bay of Bengal. It spans from Hooghly River in West Bengal in India to Baleswar River in Bangladesh. This almost 10,000 sq.km alive delta region was among the largest in the world. Most think the name Sundarban came from Bengali word 'Sundar' meaning beautiful. But the name arrived from an abundance of Sundari trees in its jungle. Apart from the famous Royal Bengal Tigers, its densely covered forests had a variety of birds like Minivet, black-hooded Oriole, Mangrove Whistler, grey-headed fishing Eagle, brown fish Owl and Ospreys. Soon the river got more expansive, and we entered the delta in high tide.

The Indian side of Sundarbans measured around 4000 sq.km comprising 102 islands - Fifty-four inhabited and 48 forested, crisscrossed by innumerable river tributaries. I recalled stories of our childhood, how Arakanese and Portuguese pirates once infested this area. After two hours, our launch stopped next to a long narrow jetty by Damkal village, where our Ranger friend had his living quarters. He left with my nephew to have a quick wash from a pump well. I spent the time talking to the villagers. Even in this place, not far from the mainland, there was a tiger attack in the last few months. After a lovely lunch cooked by our forester's maid, we left on a small motorboat to continue deeper into Sundarban, the world's largest estuarine forest.

We sailed past small islands now floating in high tide. Children played by the water. Small fishermen's boats were returning after the morning's catch. In one island villages we passed by, only a few weeks back, they had called the forester's team. A tiger had entered a house and had stayed put. With strict conservation rules, no one was allowed to harm a tiger, even inside one's own home. Villagers had summoned the foresters who went with large nets. After surrounding the house with the nets, our friend had shot the tiger with a tranquillizer dart. After capturing, the tiger was released by an uninhabited island.

Soon we passed a small island with impenetrable forest. The boatmen said only the day before; they had seen a tiger swimming towards the island when they were going back to Damkal.

After another hour, we entered the mighty Matla River. Our boat crossed the river and came by Kalash Camp, where our forester friend had official business to sort out. We got off to stretch our legs and talked to the foresters stationed there. We heard now, in the winter, it was breeding grounds of olive ridley turtles that arrive in high numbers on its beach for nesting. Visitors were allowed to the beach only with armed forest guards. Royal Bengal Tigers come here to drink freshwater pond by the camp.

We left the place, now in low tide. Ebbing waters revealed nature alive on glistening mudflats and exposed tangle of mangroves roots. All the islands looked similar in this vast expanse of water. I asked the boatmen how they navigated to find distant islands on this estuary. They said it was more straightforward in the night. They follow directions by the position of the stars. But they did not like sailing in nights when an attack from a swimming tiger was not uncommon.

By fading sunlight, we arrived at Bonnie Camp, close to the Bay of Bengal, our overnight stay. High 3-4m walls, with metal fences on top, surrounded the large campsite. Below the wall was muddy banks of rivulet separating the camp from the thick jungle. As we entered through a high metal gate, local foresters came and whispered to our ranger friend. Only an hour back, a tiger was outside the walls. There were cries from deer. We walked by the place and climbed a ladder inside the wall. In front was the half-eaten bloody remains of two deer and large tiger footprints. They said the tiger would return sometime to finish his meal, maybe tonight or tomorrow.

After a cup of tea and freshly made snacks, we walked to the watchtower, 16m high, the highest lookout in Sundarban. From the top, we could see far into the surrounding forest, so thick if a tiger was roaming, there was no way we could spot it. A freshwater pond lay outside the wall where often the tigers came to drink - we had no luck.

At dinner, the foresters told us stories of recent attacks on nearby islands. Locals believed Bonbibi, goddess of the forest, protects the wood-cutters, honey-collectors and fishermen on their hazardous missions in the jungle. Here the saying was, 'the tiger is always watching you.' With the lurking fear of the Royal Bengal Tiger nearby, an eerie feeling lasted all around. It was a moonlit night. We returned to the watchtower to enjoy the beauty of the jungle crisscrossed with shiny rivulets and creeks.

Very early next morning, we got into a small fishermen's boat. Apart from the three of us, there were only three other boaters, one of them a cook. It was still low tide. After leaving the camp gate, we had to go through a small creek between the muddy banks. The sailor in front put his fingers on his mouth and asked us to be quiet. Soon we found out why. On the mudbank was fresh tiger footprints and blood. They said it must have been an early morning kill. Fiddler crabs were extending their cherry-red claws out of mud tunnels. Mudskipper fishes climbed stilt roots of mangroves on their flipper-like fins. But we wanted to get out of that area as soon as possible.

In the main river, fishermen waited in their boats by the creeks, waiting for the tide to come in before going to the inner part of the jungle. Their hazardous missions were to collect honey, catch fish and prawns or to collect woods.

In Sundarban, tigers kill up to fifty people every year. Apart from praying Bonbibi, locals, both Hindus and Muslims, pray to the tiger god Dakshin Roy for their safe passage. We heard it was not unusual for a tiger to jump from mud bank on to boats and take a man away back to the jungle with one leap. Our sailor friend narrated a similar story which happened to one of their relatives only six months ago.

Because tigers usually attack the neck from behind, fishermen invented masks made to look like faces to wear on the back of their heads. It worked only for a brief time. But the tigers quickly got smart of it, and the attack continued. Patrolling officials often wear stiff pads rising to the back of the neck. We wished we had some for ourselves now. We did not see a tiger, but its presence was strong.

Soon we left the islands with exposed mangrove roots and were into the last section of the Matla River opening into the Indian Ocean. The land was not visible in any direction. Now, with the tide coming in, our small boat looked vulnerable. But our cook calmly called us under the arched roof of boat for our late lunch. I don't know how, but in that brief time, he had made Bengali luchi and fish curry of small fishes I had seen him catching earlier. It was the tastiest dish I had for a long time and remains in my memory.

As the wind picked up, it was time to get back. Now waves were rolling our small boat. Several saltwater crocodiles and turtles swam on the river with high salinity. We learnt there were several varieties of fishes, turtles, Ganges dolphins and even snakes in the river. By mudbanks were eels, starfish, king crabs, prawns and tree frogs. Then we were lucky to see the most beautiful sunset on the Matla River.

It soon got dark quickly. But the moon came up. Three hours later, with expert navigation by our boatmen, we arrived at Bonnie Camp. We had a last look from the watchtower at the allure of the forest in the moonlight.

Next morning our motorboat came to pick us up. I was sad to leave this beautiful place on earth. We did not see a tiger, but Sundarban was truly Sundar.

Climbing Stok Kangri 6153m,
the highest peak in Ladakh

August 2011 Ladakh India

I wanted to climb another high peak before I was too old. I have so far not been to the Western Himalayas. I chose Stok Kangri 6153m, the highest peak in Ladakh.

At a pre-expedition weekend, our team of eight climbers had a full day of hiking the north ridge of Tryfan 917m in the Snowdon range in Wales - at least a classic Grade 2 scramble.

Three weeks later, we flew via Delhi to Leigh in Ladakh – the first day was at leisure. Acclimatising in this lovely hill city at 3524m, reminded me of Kathmandu in the late 60s.

Next day was to the 11th-century monastery in Alchi, oldest in the region by the Indus River. Inside, a large image of Maitreya was flanked by Avalokiteshwara and Manjushree. The library had 108 ancient volumes of Buddha's teachings. Two teenage monks read under oil lamps, oblivious of us.

We heard a funny story. Earlier, one of our group commented on the long-drop toilet there. The guide said only a few weeks back, a tourist from Delhi had gone to use the facilities. She had with her one of those fancy mobile phones, still novel in India. During her time there, suddenly the phone had rung. Trying to answer, she had dropped the mobile 5m down on the bowl of faeces. She had come out of the place, the phone still ringing below, offering money to people to get the phone out of the pot - no one had volunteered!

We had a pit stop at the Magnetic Hill, where Ladakhis believed once existed a road that led people to heaven. Those who rightly deserved were pulled to the path directly while those who didn't deserve could never make it there. The guide said the Indian Air Force planes divert their route to avoid magnetic interference on them. We only got pulled away by its mystic beauty.

Next day we drove 40km to Khardung La pass 5359m, close to the Pakistan and China border, one of the highest motorable pass in the world, only five meters lower than Everest Base camp. The road was with multiple hairpin bends and sheer drops - no wonder Khardung La pass features on many a die-hard cyclist's bucket list.

From Khardung La, I could just about make out the distant peaks of the Himalayas beyond Nubra and Shyok Valleys of Ladakh. A few of our team were feeling unwell at this altitude. After an hour there, we drove back. On the way back, we saw a group of cyclists coming up, and we raised our hats to them - a superb day of acclimatisation.

Later at Leh, we tried out the portable hyperbaric Gamow bag, an inflatable pressure bag, large enough to accommodate a person. Once the affected person with high altitude pulmonary or cerebral oedema inside, it was sealed and inflated with a foot pump and oxygen was provided from a cylinder - something new.

Next morning we stopped by Thiksey Monastery outside Leh. Its twelve-storey complex, largest Gompa in central Ladakh, had a 15m tall statue of Maitreya, covering two stories of the building.

Soon we started our trek at Shang - easy three hours' hike with several river crossings, with an abundance of birdlife. Then we camped by the Sumdo gorge 3,800m. A hill next to it looked inviting. With still hours of daylight left, I walked up there with some team members.

Next day we headed up the valley by the river, crossing a few villages. After about six hours' trek, we reached a beautiful campsite at Shang Phu 4,365m. Several animals grazed by a cattle pen. I talked to two shy shepherd boys. They said, in here, they had to be careful as wolves often came out in the night and attacked their cattle.

Our trek the next day was challenging. First, we climbed up for over six hours, crossing many spurs and minor passes, before reaching the high point on Shang La 4,960m. We then descended to Tokpo River for lunch. We continued contouring around the spurs and over a 4,550m pass to Gangpoche 4,435m, our next campsite, utterly exhausted.

Next day was a steady climb to reach Matho La pass 4,965m. The first sight of Stok Kangri at a distance immediately lifted our spirit. After walking along the ridge, we had a splendid view of Saltoro Kangri 7742m in the Karakoram Range. Soon we descended to a river before coming up to a lovely wild valley.

Smankarmo 4,380m was the most picturesque place to camp after 7 hours of trek.

Next day the trek to Stok Kangri Base camp 4,980m took only over two hours. A meltwater stream flew by the campsite on a grassy area. In the afternoon, I walked above the camp for views of the Rimo peaks, next to Siachen Glacier in East Karakoram. I felt as fit as I hoped to be for this challenge.

An acclimatisation hike next day to 5,400m with a chance to scope out the route. After climbing the moraine above our camp for about two hours, we were on the glacier. With crampons on, we trekked over a few small crevasses. Our ascent steepened as we scaled onto Kamet's south face to the previous site of the last camp before the summit. After a brief rest there, we descended to our base camp.

Next day was rest day and time for the last preparations for the summit. With makeshift wickets from stones, a flat piece of wood for a bat and a tennis ball, I arranged a cricket match. Our expedition team played against the Sherpas and the porters at an altitude just under 5000m - we crushed them.

With our head torch on at 3 am, we left for the summit climb. Exciting but freezing and exposed to the prevailing wind. On the moraine, one of the team members could not move any further and returned to the camp. We continued steadily to the old campsite as the sun was just rising. After a brief stop there, I roped up with my sherpa friend and kept scrambling up the steep south ridge. The view of the icy mountains bathed in early sunrays below and behind was breathtaking. In the last hundred meters before the summit, the route was worse than we faced on Tryphan, except we were now at almost 6100m altitude! Soon I could see the prayer flags on the summit. My pace picked up.

Soon I was standing on the peak at 6135m. It felt unreal. I hugged my Sherpa friend.

At a distance, we could see the Karakorum Range. The sherpa pointed out K2. On our way down, he said his younger brother died there in 2008 trying to rescue climbers who got trapped in an avalanche during descent. Upon my return, I read up the story of these tragic eleven deaths on K2, including the heroic effort made by his brother.

We slowly descended to our camp before the evening, 14 hrs trek at high altitude, exhausted. But I have done it!

We trekked down the next day for over six hours through a dramatic canyon with spectacular red sandstone formations. Blue sheep, not sky blue but only a blue tinge, scampered across the steep rock faces.

During the trek, I had many chats with my friend, Sherpa Pasang. In his mid-forties, he was already finding the expedition work hard. But he had to take care of his two adolescent sons and wife. He was thinking of setting up a small shop in Kathmandu. We kept in touch through email over the next few years. But since the massive 2015 earthquake in Nepal, I did not hear from him anymore.

Gibraltar

2012 March   Retirement from the NHS was coming up. There was a job opportunity at a major hospital in Gibraltar afterwards. Gibraltar is a British Overseas Territory with a population of just over thirty thousand and an area of only 6.7 sq.km.

Gibraltar airport was unique. Our plane dived over the sea and came to a stop at a small piece of land. The airport had barrier gates with cars waiting at both ends. As soon as the plane stopped, they opened the gates. Public traffic streamed through the runway until the next flight!

Soon I realised how small the country was. You could walk from one end to the other on an afternoon stroll. Claustrophobic, not a place I could live for a few years.

Rock of Gibraltar, is known as the symbol of strength and resilience all over the world because it resisted thirteen Spanish sieges during the 18th century. This prominent landmark was visible from anywhere on this small settlement. A monolithic limestone promontory, at the southwestern tip of Europe on the Iberian Peninsula, was worth a hike.

Initially, the trail was easy. After hiking up the rocky south-eastern end of the Rock with the Mediterranean Sea as the backdrop, I passed the Jewish cemetery. The higher part of the hike became steep. I was not interested in stopping at the WWII tunnels. In the upper section of the rock, Barbary Macaque monkeys hung around, looking for food from the walkers.

At the highest point of Gibraltar at 426m, s day, the view across the Strait of Gibraltar was stunning. I could even make out the mountain range in Morocco at a distance.

After spending time enjoying the view, I walked to the Mediterranean Steps to go down. I went past St. Michael's Cave, a network of limestone caves within the upper rock nature reserve, unfortunately, closed to the visitor on the day.

I arrived in time for my return flight. I regretted not having time to visit the Gorham's sea cave complex, on the eastern side of the Rock, known as one of the last known habitations of Neanderthals in Europe.

On the other side of the globe

Australia 2012-14

After my NHS retirement, I found a job in Australia, an opportunity to travel that part of the world. But I needed to pass an English language test! Even though I have been working and teaching in the UK for over three decades!

I wanted a job outside the major cities. I got an offer from Griffith in New South Wales, a small town 500km west from Sydney. In an informal online interview, they asked me what I could bring to their hospital. I asked if they had a cricket team. When they said no, I replied there would be a hospital cricket team in my first year there. After passing the English test, I had to make a brief trip to Melbourne to the College of Surgeons, only to prove I existed. My long-expected divorce finally official, it was an ideal time to move to the other side of the globe.

Griffith From Sydney, a small regional plane flew over the Blue Mountains to Griffith. It was springtime in October there. Griffith Hospital served a population of some coming from up to 250km distance. Most impressive for me was, this town of 20,000 had three proper sports stadium with floodlights, packed over the weekend.

Outside the city, fields were full of oranges. Griffith Spring Fest of Citrus sculptures went for a week at the end of October. Fun citrus fruit sculptures decorated the town's parks. Extensive vineyards and many famous wineries surrounded Griffith in Riverina, known as the fruit bowl of Australia.

In the evenings by the golf course near the airport, I saw my first kangaroos. As the dusk fell, these amazing animals came out in herds to ravage the grass on the lawn, females with babies in their pouches, a wonderful sight.

In long spring evenings, I drove outside the town. I could go for tens of kilometres without seeing another vehicle on the road or any settlement. But there were always kangaroos by the bush and occasional groups of shy emus on the field. My colleagues said by the dusk suicidal kangaroos waited by the roadside. At the sight of light from an oncoming vehicle, they try to cross the road at the last second, causing significant damage to cars and their death.

I heard a funny story from a colleague. Next hospital to ours was at Wagga Wagga, 180 km distance.

He was returning in an early evening from there. In an empty road, he was following a solitary car about 200m ahead. He noticed the vehicle in front swerved and stopped just before hitting a tree.

Our colleague stopped his car and walked to check. He found the driver was dazed but not injured. The car's windscreen was shattered. A kangaroo was sitting on the passenger seat. Carefully he opened the passenger door, and the animal hopped away. He called the ambulance. It arrived more than an hour later with its headlights broken. The ambulance was delayed because another suicidal kangaroo had hit it!

Like most, I had heard about issues with the indigenous population of Australia, known as Aboriginals. They now consisted of less than 4% of residents of the country. I had heard the painful history of 'Stolen Generations' which lasted until the late 1960s. Australian government agencies and the church missions had removed children of the Aboriginals from their families. Around Griffith, there were several isolated Aboriginal settlements. There was a Government establishment for training Aboriginal Community Health workers in Griffith. Soon I got involved in the training of them in essential emergency surgical care in distant locations and made several friends amongst them.

As it was summertime in Australia, in the first two months, I organised a hospital cricket team. We were feeling cocky after beating the town's police team but then got thrashed by the aboriginal health workers' side. In between the innings, kangaroos came into the field to munch grasses.

Over my off weekends, I took off to Cocoparra National Park, only half an hour drive. In this empty place, it was great to unwind on wooden benches amongst western grey kangaroos, red kangaroos and sometimes wallabies. Trees were alive with varieties of parrots, warblers and cockatoos. It was fabulous walking in its dramatic craggy hills. Walking over the fallen dry tree trunks, I was always conscious of the deadly poisonous snakes of Australia. Luckily, I never came across one. The trail to Jacks Creek was gorgeous with orchids, daisies, wattles and tea-trees in dazzling colours.

Occasionally emus, possums, pangolins wondered in the park. Driving in the park, one had to be careful of wombats. These short, stubby animals weighed like a stone. If bumped against, it could do a lot of damage to the car. One day I was relaxing on a bench while a giant Iguana slowly came towards me, eyeing me with its enormous eyes. At the last moment, it stopped and hurried up a tree.

Small Griffith airport had a flying club. Something I had dreamt for years. Now I could not resist enrolling for flying lessons. In a four-seater Jabiru, my young instructor took me through safety checks. Then we took off from the runway. Once in the air, he let me control the direction and altitude - always keep the horizon as our tilt.

In the next few lessons, I learnt to taxi the Jabiru from the hangar to the runway and back. Of course, the instructor took off the plane into the air, where I learnt to control before landed back by him.

Uluru and Kata Tjuta   On my first Christmas day in Australia, I was on call but free for a week after. I booked a tour to Uluru, Australia's iconic natural landmark.

From Alice Spring airport, we drove through an arid landscape to reach our resort near Uluru in the evening. After checking in, they took us out for an open-air barbeque in a field. Moon was up in the sky. I had my first view of Uluru, standing alone proudly in the bright moonlight and my first Australian barbeque.

Next morning we were at Uluru, a sacred sandstone monolith of great cultural significance for the Anangu people, traditional inhabitants of the place. We walked around its base and then to the Mutitjulu waterhole, one of the few permanent water sources around Uluru. Sitting in the shade, we listened to the ancient stories from our guide, how Kuniya, the python woman and Liru, the poisonous snake man, created Uluru. A few wallabies wandered among the tall grasses and river red gum trees. The guide showed how

Aboriginals found bush foods like tjantu - bush tomatoes, ili - figs and arnguli -bush plums, even in the deserts.

Next, our bus drove around this mountain while the guide pointed out the sacred caves, still used by the Anangu people. One of them restricted for men and another for women only. This was a truly special place.

In the afternoon, we had a tour to Kata Tjuta, a land of dozens of picturesque sandstone monoliths, in a wild and craggy landscape. There we had a captivating walk into the Walpa Gorge within its sheer walls. At a distance, wallabies hopped around sandstone domes.

Soon our guide rounded us up to go to the viewing area a few kilometres away for the sunset over Kata Tjuta - gorgeous change of fading light over this landscape of ancient red stone hills.

We rose at 4 am for a drive to a camel stable. After a welcome cup of coffee, guides helped us to get up on single hump dromedary camels.

Now the sky in the east was getting lighter as we rode through stunning dunes for a few kilometres. Soon came the spectacular sunrise behind Uluru. The red monolith changed its colour every few minutes - mesmerising.

After the ride back, they treated us with billy tea, beer bread with quandong jam.

There were almost half a million camels in Australia. Colonists introduced the camels in the country by the late 19th century, mainly for transport in the arid central and Western Australia. Since then, the camel population had exploded. Most of them became feral, causing significant damage to the local environment and cultural sites. Now a culling programme has been introduced in the country. Australia was currently the world's largest exporter of live camel and camel meat to the Middle East!

After lunch, we drove for four hours to a Glamping tent site outside the Kings Canyon National Park.

Kings Canyon   Arriving next morning at Kings Canyon, we walked over the five hundred steep steps for the rim. Once at the top at 100m, I could see the immensity of the canyon walls, deep valleys, crevices and sandstone domes in all its glory. Soon we were on the spellbinding Rim Walk. In this 6 km circuit, we squeezed through Priscilla's Crack, a very narrow gap between the massive twin rocks, made famous by the classic Australian movie Priscilla, Queen of the Desert.

Next, we walked to the lookout point at the edge of the rim to view the sandstone rock formations known as the Lost City – an indescribable 360-degree view.

Then we descended 200 steps down a gorge known as the Garden of Eden. The beauty of this rock pool of clear water, surrounded by lush greenery, within the dry canyon was mind-blowing. I sat there for several minutes, numbed with the allure of this corner of the world.

Soon we took the stairs back up to the south side of the canyon. By this time, it was boiling, and we walked down the narrow steps to the car park.

We then left for Alice Springs 320km distance for our overnight stay. Next morning, I visited the Aboriginal Australia Cultural Centre. It had a lovely collection of a contemporary selection of Aboriginal art from all over the country, most enchanting dot paintings in stunning colours of the land and animals.

A man beautifully played the didgeridoo. He allowed me to try. I managed to make only some bizarre noises!

New year's eve fireworks Sydney   Back at Sydney in the early evening, from my hotel by the Sydney Harbour, I strolled with a lovely view of the Opera House on one side and the Harbour Bridge on the other. Next day I walked to the Opera House, with a distinctive sail-like design. After walking around the nearby Royal Botanic Garden for a while, I returned to the Opera House. I sat on its stairs with a snack lunch and tried to imagine Paul Robeson in 1960, climbing the scaffolding here and singing 'Ol' Man River' to the construction workers as they ate their lunch.

I did not have time to climb the Harbour Bridge, tallest steel arch bridge in the world. I needed to get back to my hotel to get ready for the New Year's Eve fireworks later.

Blues Point was a brief walk on the other side of the bridge. Having already booked in advance, I arrived there just after 7 pm. I was glad to have arrived early and lucky to have the best spot with the view of the Bridge and the Opera House over the harbour. The place was filling up quickly. Pleasure boats with jolly folks sailed by.

Excitement built up as it got closer to midnight. Then there were the world-famous midnight fireworks, choreographed to music. As the crowd cheered welcoming the New Year, swirls of colours in magenta, yellow, purple and red from the bridge illuminated Opera House and the city skyline. The enchanting light show carried on for several minutes after midnight into the New Year. As impressed as I was with the light show, the orderly crowd also impressed me with no drunkenness and litters in such a lively evening.

In search of Koalas Narrandera NSW

January 2013

Narrandera Aboriginal health workers' group invited me to go on a Saturday morning to do some training and promoting Breast Cancer awareness to the local women. This reserve, on the banks of Murrumbidgee River, was only 90 km from Griffith. Indigenous Wiradjuri people were all but destroyed by the European settlement, through diseases brought by and clashes with the settlers. In this township of 5000, almost 10% were Aboriginals or Tores Strait Islanders, higher than the national average of under 4%.

After our training session finished in the afternoon, one local health worker asked if I wanted to see koalas in the forest nearby. So far, in Australia, I have not seen koalas. I immediately agreed. She took me in her car to the National Park on the riverbank.

Koalas, the national icon though it was, like indigenous people, could not survive the advance of the Europeans into its domain. By the turn of the 19th century, most koala populations were annihilated through destruction of natural habitat, accidental poisoning, and shooting. In Narrandera district, between 1900 and 1972, there was not a single Koala. First koalas were reintroduced here in 1972.

The reserve here hugged the Murrumbidgee River with a surplus of red gum and eucalyptus trees. Red Gum leaves provided an ideal diet for the koalas. We drove around and then walked in search of the koalas. After a while, we spotted only two of them sleeping in the top branches. These marsupials slept almost 18 hours a day. In the wintertime, some even walked into the town!

The local community had taken the Reserve and its inhabitants to heart. In May every year, supervised by the National Parks and Wildlife Service, annual koala count takes place here. Town folks, young and old, spread quietly throughout the reserve. Once sighted, they mark the koala's location with a ribbon, and the sightings are then tallied. Although there were no formal picnic areas, people then roll out their picnic blankets and enjoy packed lunch. Despite flood and fire during the past three decades, 200 healthy koalas now colonised this park.

I knew I had to come back another time to see more of these cuddly animals. A few weeks later, in one afternoon, I was lucky to see several of them, including a few mothers with their babies.

Evonne Goolagong Cawley tribute

On my return journey, I took a detour via Barellan. During the centenary celebrations in 2009, Barellan erected 'Big Tennis Racquet' as a tribute to the former local indigenous and Australian tennis player, Evonne Goolagong Cawley, a world-leading tennis player in the 70s. The display was 20:1 scale model of Evonne's battered wooden signature racquet.

Honolulu, Maui and Big Island Hawaii

February 2013

Australian Healthcare system had the best allowance for professional development. Along with four weeks of leave, registration fees, airfares and hotel expenses, they reimbursed for any national or international conferences. I registered for two symposiums in Hawaii, one in Honolulu and other in the following week in Maui.

Honolulu   Just before landing after 8200km flight from Sydney over the Pacific Ocean to Oahu, we looked out of our windows at the infamous Pearl Harbour.

My hotel in Honolulu, the venue of my first conference, was next to the famous Waikiki beach. I got over my jet lag next day by spending time on the iconic crescent beach beyond palm trees. Watching surfers and bodyboarders having fun in the gentle waves of warm water only made me jealous as I could not surf. I swam instead.

I had the next day all to myself and hired a car. We drove east, leaving behind skyscrapers and the sprawling city of Honolulu into lush valleys. After going through Koolau Mountain Range, it was a different world. The turquoise sea shimmered at a distance. At Diamond Head dormant volcanic cone, I walked up steps to the rim. The place was more aptly known in Hawaiian as Le' ahi as the ridgeline resembled the shape of the dorsal fin of a Tuna.

We drove further east on the Windward coast until we came to the beautiful Makapu'u beach at the eastern point of the island. The nearby trail led to a lighthouse. But I just wandered around with a view of Manana Island, also known as the Rabbit Island. It looked like a giant rabbit's head popping out of the sea - tranquil and stunning natural beauty.

Afterwards, we drove northwest to the nearby Kualoa Ranch with a dramatic backdrop, made famous in the Jurassic Park film. After a brief stop there, we went to the northernmost tip of the island, to Oahu's North Shore, the best surf spots in the world. Luckily, Junior World Surfing competition was taking place on the day.

With a takeaway lunch, I watched with envy surfers tackling dangerous-looking gigantic waves. I had always wanted to surf and wished I was younger to learn. But now my gut wrenched watching surfers in front tackling giant waves easily over 10m high, known as barrels. I was thrilled and jealous at the same time.

After most of the afternoon watching the spectacle, we left for the Sunset Beach and arrived there in time to watch a magnificent sunset on the Pacific.

The two-day conference ended on the second afternoon with a Luau around sunset. Sumptuous dinner of as much as you can eat. On the open stage, lively music and spirited cultural performances. Beautiful Hawaiian women in vibrant grass skirts and colourful garlands around their hair and neck danced the Hula of Hawaii and Greater Polynesia. Male dancers followed dancing ancient warrior stories through Hula including some fire dance.

Captivated watching the dance, I filled myself unashamedly with Poi, pounded taro root; shredded Kalua Pig cooked in an underground oven; Laulau, steamed meat wrapped in taro leaves and Haupia and delicious coconut pudding.

Hula dancer's intricate hand motions reminded me of Indian Kathakali dance. Hand movements in Hula signify aspects of nature. Like swaying of a tree in the breeze, an ocean wave, or a feeling and emotion. Dance culminated in exciting fire-knife dance - most enchanting evening.

Maui   By Hawaiian Airlines flight the next day I went to Maui for my second conference starting the day after. After checking in my hotel on the shorelines of Kahului, I headed for the nearby beach. While swimming in the shallow warm water, I watched two humpback whales only about 200m away. They were breaching by leaping into the air and then slapping the water with their fins. Luckily, I was in the best season for watching the whales in Hawaii. I sat on the sand, watching these giants in and out of the water until it got dark.

Next day immediately after the conference, I returned to the beach. Paddling in shallow water eating coconut ice cream, I watched more whales and their calves. On the second evening after the conference, they treated us to another Hula, telling different ancient Polynesian stories through dance and music.

I had only one free day in Maui. I had to choose between going on a hiking trail to the famous volcanic Haleakala National Park with its scenic waterfalls or to a whale-watching boat tour. I decided on whale watching.

A small boat took off on a bright sunny day. Within half an hour, we came across a pod of whales. The first sign of them coming out of the water were their blows, exhaling air. The crew educated us on Maui's whales, federally protected creatures. On average, adults come up to breathe every 15 minutes, while the babies need to surface every 5 minutes. Whales breached around us, creating enormous splashes, just to be show-offs. We saw a few of them tail slapping repeatedly and doing pectoral slaps. They lay on their sides on the water surface and then lifted their fins into the air, before slapping, creating a loud smack.

All these movements were to make loud noises, to communicate across long distances. In their spy hops, they rose vertically up with their head, curious to find what was happening above the water. Then they arched their massive tail flukes up into the air, and then slowly and gently dived into the deep. Crew said this was a whale's way of saying 'Aloha'. We won't see them for a while.

Whales did not eat in these waters and lived off their body fat. Humpbacks hunt and feed during the summer months in the icy waters of Alaska shore before migrating to Hawaii to give birth and mate. Creatures playing in front were about 13 metres long and weighed nearly 40 tons. Calves were born weighing in at around 1300 kg. They grew at a rate of 90 kg every day, drinking as much as 600 litres of milk daily to help prepare for the trip towards the colder waters.

I flew back to Oahu the next day and walked around Waikiki beach. Full of surfers and bodyboarders, but unfortunately no barrels or whales.

Big Island   Before dawn, I flew to Big Island for an all-day tour. The car took us to Waipio Valley lookout with the backdrop of sheer cliffs dropping into the sparkling blue Pacific. Next, we arrived at the towering 135m Akaka Falls. Afterwards, we carried on to our next stop, Rainbow Falls, a beautiful 24m waterfall with a giant banyan tree next to it.

Soon we were by the 182m long Nahuku, also known as Thurston Lava Tube, formed hundreds of years ago. Lava caves like this were formed when a river of flowing lava gradually builds solid walls and a ceiling around it. Then, as the lava flow stopped and the last of it passed downhill, it formed a tunnel. Nahuku's ceiling height in places was around 6m. After strolling the lighted trail, our guide took us to a section utterly dark with an uneven floor. With his flashlight, he showed us solidified drips and waves of once- liquid lava and the beautiful shapes and colours of minerals leeching from the rock. We came out of the tunnel to a tropical rainforest.

Our car moved then towards the Kilauea Visitor Centre, on Crater Rim. Before coming to the visitor centre, we asked to stop the car as we saw steam coming out of the ground in many places next to our path. We got out and watched in delight mixed with unease, steam vents coming out at regular intervals. By the roadside were molten lava from previous eruptions. Soon we were at the rim of Kilauea.

Kilauea at 1247m was a shield volcano, wide with shallow sloping sides, most active of the five volcanoes that together formed the island of Hawaii. At about 600,000 years old, erupting continuously since 1983, Kilauea is still relatively young for a Hawaiian volcano.

After spending a while at the visitor centre, I took a short hike around the crater rim. Steam slowly spewed out from the crater. The trail over cracks and holes, loose rock, and thin lava crust was tricky but thrilling. Summit caldera had a lava lake, Halema'uma'u, said to be the home of Hawaiian volcano goddess.

Soon it was time to go back. We drove to Punalu'u Black Sand Beach. Black sands of this beach were created when the lava reached the ocean and exploded as it cooled. Green sea turtles frequented the beach.

Returning to Waikiki in the night, I slept till midmorning, getting up in time to catch my long flight to Sydney.

My world stopped

March 2013

There was a one day conference related to my speciality in Banbury, near Perth in Western Australia. I wanted to visit the WACA cricket stadium in Perth, famous as a fast bowler's Mecca. Also, in Banbury, there was an opportunity to swim with the wild dolphins in the sea.

I would be back in time to Griffith before my first daughter coming to visit me. Both of us were eagerly looking forward to this. I had bought her business class tickets for the long flight. A day earlier she rang to say they had upgraded her to first-class!
From Perth, I took a train to Bunbury, three hour's journey.

In the middle of the night, a phone call woke me up.

My first daughter has suddenly passed away in London. She was not yet 32 years old.

My world stopped.

Part 3

Retirement work, volunteering, adventure and travel
2013 – 2017

Sharing the grief of the loss of a child

July 2013 Lake Cargelligo NSW Australia.

The ambulance rang to say to be on standby. They were bringing an injured child from Lake Cargelligo. At the hospital, our team got ready immediately. The ambulance called again to say the patient had a cardiac arrest on the route, but they had resuscitated him and should be at the hospital within 15 minutes.

We took him straight to the operating table. The 14-year-old boy had stabbed himself in the stomach, tearing his vena cava, a major vessel in the abdomen. Despite our try, he died on the operating table forty- five minutes later.

I went outside to speak to the family and give my condolences. I said very sorry; we could not save the child.'

They thanked us in tears. The child's mother was not there. We heard more about the incident. This young boy's close associate, 17 years old cousin, had committed suicide by hanging himself only six weeks back. This boy had an argument with his mother before going to bed. His mother had got up at around 4 am, probably because of motherly intuition, to find him covered in blood and barely conscious. She had immediately called the ambulance. But at winter dawn, in kangaroo infested road, it took almost two hours for the ambulance to reach him.

I had driven to the tiny settlement of Lake Cargelligo only a few weeks before this incident, just to explore the area. The two-hour drive through the empty roads with vast fields of grazing kangaroos and emus was very relaxing. About 135 km outside Griffith, it was by a small lake fed by the Lachlan River. Once a prosperous mining town for gold, silver, copper, lead and zinc, in mid-morning, the town was almost empty.

I heard from my friends in the Griffith Aboriginal Health Workers group that in this town, and Murrin Bridge on the other side of the river were large reserve settlements of Wiradjuri people. I resolved to organise basic emergency skills training for local health workers there one day.

Two months later, I returned to Lake Cargelligo for the training schedule and a breast awareness programme for the local women. A female Aboriginal Health Worker accompanied me from Griffith. On our journey, she told stories about growing up as an indigenous woman. Although she was now a graduate, it was a struggle all the way. Even in the second decade of the 21st century, subtle and overt discrimination was rife. High unemployment, alcohol abuse, mental health issues and suicide rates were high amongst the community.

At the end of the programme, while I was talking to the attendees, a woman came up to me. She said, 'Doctor, thank you very much for trying to save my son.'

She then gave me a hug and silently; we both shed tears.

Scuba diving in the Great Barrier Reef

2013 November Cairns

Great Barrier Reef, a gem in the Seven Wonders of the World, had always fascinated me. Who wasn't? It took some effort to get over my mental shutdown before planning the visit.

Great Barrier Reef in the Coral Sea, off the coast of Queensland, is the world's largest coral reef system. Over 3000 reefs and 900 islands stretched over an area of 344,400 sq.km, visible from the outer space, the world's biggest single structure made of living organisms.

At Cairns, I booked a scuba diving cruise. The ship sailed by several small islands and sandbars, before arriving by a small island before anchoring about 200m from its shore. The majority were there for snorkelling. Soon by the steps on one side of this enormous ship, they jumped into shallow open water.

About forty of us were for scuba diving. Half of the group, certified divers, left for diving on their own. Beginners, after putting on our wet suits, fins, buoyancy control device, our masks and breathing apparatuses in our hands, sat in two rows near the steps for safety instructions. We learned hand signals, how to clear our masks, how to equalise pressure in our ears and emergency ascents. One instructor for a group of five.

One instructor strapped my weight belt, almost a tenth of my weight. Next, I put on my BCD buoyancy control device and got connected to an oxygen cylinder. Holding the breathing apparatus in the mouth and mask on, we stepped into the water, less than 2m in depth. We practised buoyancy in shallow water and learning to float using only our fins, not using our hands as we did for swimming.

After twenty minutes, we got on board for another briefing. Most of us were having a problem clearing the masks of water. We learned the technique of how to get rid of it. Inhale deeply through the mouth, then press the top ridge of your mask to your forehead while opening the bottom seal and blow hard through the nose - easy.

Confident, we left by two dive boats to the other side of the ship. Five of us jumped into the water with our instructor. We slowly went down in the water, holding on to the ship's anchor rope. Every few meters, the instructor stopped and checked on us. We all signalled ok with our hands. Soon we were at the bottom of the sea at about 12m. I was feeling good except for a mild ache in my ears. There we left the anchor rope and gently dived over the beautiful coral. Our instructor got busy taking pictures of us.

But soon I had a lot of water inside my mask. I tried all the techniques I learnt but without success. It was getting difficult to breathe. I used my not OK/Problem sign by touching my chest and pointing to my mask. But the instructor and the other divers were busy taking pictures and did not see me. After almost a minute, my mask was practically full of water. I had no choice but to make an emergency ascent by myself.

I came up straight out of the water. I took my mask off and took a few gulps of air. I realised the current had taken me away from the ship, hovering at least 50m distance. Luckily, I was a reasonable swimmer. I swam against the current with all my strength before reaching the side of the craft. A crew spotted me and quickly lowered a set of steps. Wearily, with my heavy cylinder on my back, I got up. He helped me to take off my tank and other gears and then offered me a drink.

As we had still an hour before the ship sailed back, I gently snorkelled in the shallow water.

Back in the marina in the afternoon, immediately, I found another tour company offering scuba diving the next day in two separate locations. I booked without hesitation.

Our catamaran next day took us offshore at high speed for about an hour. During this, a marine biologist showed slides about the reef ecosystem. Little animals called coral polyps, like tiny inverted jellyfish, excrete calcium to form limestone skeleton on which they lived, called a coral reef. Soft corals have light feathery tentacles, whereas hard corals have six smooth ones. While soft coral did not create a reef, they played a vital role in the coral reef ecosystem. Their branches provided a safe and rich habitat for fish, prawns and other sea creatures. Often, these marine animals camouflaged having the identical colour pattern to the soft coral in which they lived. Soft coral produced chemicals to make them distasteful to avoid being eaten by fish, snails and crustaceans. They also had spiky spicules which functioned like thorns on a rose bush.

We moored about 100m from a small sandbar, the famous Michaelmas Cay. In our dive suits and carrying the rest of our diving gears, we got into beach-buggy shuttles. About 25m outside the dune, we jumped off the buggy and walked in the shallow water.

A sand cay is a low sandy island found on the surface of coral reefs, created when sediment drifting on ocean currents descends on the same reef, piling atop one another to form an island.

Stunning Michaelmas Cay was also a protected nature reserve, an important nesting habitat for migrating birds. Most of the cay was out of bounds marked by a fence. Hundreds of various sea birds, nested with their newborn chicks. Eggshells and seashells lined its shore.

After a while in this picture postcard-perfect cay, many left for snorkelling around the spectacular fringing reef teeming with colourful marine life. The group of us on our introductory dive had our usual safety checklist and instructions. We geared up fully and started our dive with a skills practice session walking in the shallows. It was a simpler and easier way. By the time we came to a vertical drop into the ocean, we were ready.

We dived into the magical underwater world. I moved along with shoals of fish with an extravaganza of colours. Strikingly bright coloured soft coral, gently moved their jelly-like parts with the current as if to wave at us. They could easily be mistaken for plants. Hard coral was larger and less colourful, looking almost like rocks on the sea bed.

While diving by, I accidentally touched a coral. To my amusement, it closed like the pages of a book. We dived deeper. Colours were now sensational. With arresting colourful markings, Angelfishes nibbled at the coral. Then there were spectacular butterflyfish, clownfish, and Nemo, to name a few. Time stood still until the instructor signed with his hand. It was time to go up. Slowly we came up and then swam to the cay.

Our beach-buggy took us back to the catamaran. During the lunch break, we had another briefing from our marine biologist. Coral reproduced in two ways: asexually and sexually. Some coral divided to form new individuals, known as asexual reproduction. Sexual reproduction took place as mass spawning. Polyps, either male or female, or both release millions of eggs and sperm. Eggs and sperm float to the surface. Fertilised eggs that escaped predation by animals hatch into larvae and drifts with plankton. Tiny per cent that survives settle on the reef, to begin new coral colonies. Over several nights each year, around the full moon in November, Great Barrier Reef 'explodes' as coral spawn in a mass synchronised event like no other.

After lunch, there was an option for going back to the cay to relax and snorkel. Or to go to another site for deeper scuba diving at around 20m. I chose to dive.

Our buggy took us further out to an area known as the ribbon reefs running parallel to the Continental Shelf. Just 2km beyond the outer edge of these reefs, the seafloor drops away to over 500m deep. Here at the very outer edge, ocean waters surrounding these unique ribbon reefs were clear and pure. Clearwater from the deep ocean washing over these outer barriers helped promote prolific growth of coral and supported a spectacular marine life.

We jumped out of our boat and dived deep in this world of never-ending beauty. We dived deeper and deeper, negotiating carefully amongst these living rock like beauty. We floated through billowing clouds of neon-coloured damselfish. The reef vibrated with hues, stripes, and shimmering of a myriad of fishes.

Butterflyfish, parrotfish, angelfish and elegant nudibranchs danced before our eyes and the coral gardens beckoned us to explore further. Entranced, I watched as a clownfish snuggled into the embrace of a sea anemone. Immense shoals of fish of unimaginable beauty swam by. Some came nibbling at me, trying to wake me up from a reverie.

I don't know how it was possible, but fortunate to be at this mesmerising underwater wonder; tears stemmed from my eyes. I could not stop thinking of my daughter, who was a marine biologist.

The instructor pointed to look towards the seafloor, a Wobbegong, a bottom-dwelling shark of just over 1m length, camouflaged on sea bed next to a hard coral.

Time passed by until he signed for us to go up. On our ascent, a giant turtle gently swam by us to say goodbye. The instructor said we have been to a depth of about 20m.

Back on the catamaran, I sat in silence, my mind going over and over about what I have been lucky to witness. I hoped we would protect and conserve this fragile beauty for the generations of the world to cherish.

They do not advise flying in commercial airlines at high altitude for 24 hours after multiple dives. I had a full day to spend in Cairns. At the marina information centre, I booked a scenic seaplane flight over the reef in the afternoon.

At the appointed hour, I was the only passenger on a six-seater Cessna. I explained to the pilot I had taken a few flying lessons on a Jabiru. After taking off with Cairns below us, we flew above the Great Barrier Reef and let me take some control.

At an altitude of 300m above the turquoise waters, we flew over the Middle Cay and the famous Koala Reef and then over the Green Island, a small Sand Cay covered with emerald green rainforest and surrounded by an azure-coloured ocean.

After about half an hour enjoying the splendour of wonder of the world from the sky, we turned back.

In the evening, in a restaurant by the marina, I treated myself to a hearty dinner of seafood platter with the largest lobster I have ever seen.

New South Wales coast and Broken Hill

November 2013

I had promised myself one day I would treat my two closest friends, Sanku and Baburam, to a holiday abroad. I arranged for them, with Sanku's wife Ruby, to come over to Australia in early November. I drove 570km to collect them in Sydney.

From Sydney, we drove through the coastal road towards Narooma 350 km away. Near our shared accommodation by the coast, I took them out for a takeaway dinner of beer-battered prawns and chips. They had tasted nothing like this and were over the moon, or maybe they were just too tired! Soon they retired to bed.

I booked an afternoon boat tour to the Montague Island, only 10 km away in the Tasman Sea. On the ship, there was a commotion. The crew called out - whales ahead. My friends got very excited, but the whales were too far to have a decent viewing.

Montague Island   Soon we approached the rocky Montague Island. Hundreds of penguins and seabirds paddled in the water. After watching their playful display for a while, we docked on a precarious wharf. Nearby, a few seals enjoyed the late afternoon sun on rocks. After climbing the steep winding staircase to the impressive granite lighthouse, from its balcony, we enjoyed the sunset over the east coast of NSW.

It was getting dark now. The guide said to find a seat on the viewing platform near the jetty and keep quiet -no flash, please. One by one, Little penguins climbed up the rocks from the sea. Then they hobbled past us to their nesting place above us. This small uninhabited island, with no predators, had over 10,000 Little penguins. We watched until all the penguins came ashore. Soon we quietly boarded our boat.

Sanku loved driving and had an international licence. After getting used to the automatic and speed control, he loved driving on the empty highway to Canberra, a change from chaotic traffic in Kolkata. We shared our drive from then on.

After a lunch stop in Canberra by a lake opposite the National Library, we proceeded to Griffith, another 375 km with occasional stops to watch emus and fleeing kangaroos on the vast fields.

They loved the easy, relaxed way of Australian life in the modest Griffith town. We drove to Cocoparra National Park and also half a day in a winery near Griffith observing wine production and storage, followed by sampling.

Two days later we left for Mildura, 430 km distance. We drove past vast vineyards on the side before we came by the banks of Murrumbidgee River. We were meeting there, a friend of mine from Ethiopia days for lunch. Later we left for Broken Hill, another 300 km. Bringing food was banned between the states in Australia with a 10,000 dollars fine. It intrigued and annoyed my friends when I asked them to dump fresh bananas before crossing the borders. They hurriedly gobbled them up rather than throwing them away!

Broken Hill   Broken Hill, 'The Silver City', was forged out of a hill that was almost pure silver, lead and zinc. This mining town sat on the edge of the desert at the central-western end of NSW.

The small township of Silverton was 26 km north-west of Broken Hill. It sprung up after the discovery of rich deposits of silver in the late 19th century. After finding of a more productive silver-lead-zinc ore near Broken Hill, it became a ghost town with a population of less than fifty, mainly connected to tourism. Several famous artists lived here, maintaining their galleries because of the surrounding desert landscape.

We stopped at the old Silverton Hotel, the only place to eat and drink, amongst the deserted colonial buildings. The hotel had featured in several cinematic productions such as The Adventures of Priscilla, Queen of the Desert and The Flying Doctors. Memorabilia from these cinemas decorated its walls where we had our coffee.

Nearby was the Mad Max 2 museum. I was not a fanatic about Mad Max. But the museum's extensive collection of photographs, life-size characters in full costumes, original and replica vehicles including two Interceptor's were most charming. It was fascinating to hear the museum was the product of the passion of one man, Adrian Bennett. After seeing the film in his hometown in Northern England, he had moved halfway across the world to build this museum.

Later we passed by the disused 19th-century Daydream Mine on our way to the Living Desert State Park.

Living Desert Sculptures   On a hilltop, stood 12 sandstone sculptures by the artists from around the world, each with a story to tell. I stood in awe before the statues of Motherhood, symbolising the connection between the mother and the child. The graceful sculpture of The Bride illustrated the figure of a reclining woman with her face and breasts facing the sun, her hands raised in greeting, with Emu, kangaroo and the Southern Cross symbols represented on her body. The Horse, by a Georgian artist, paid tribute to these beautiful creatures, reminding Stalin ordered the slaughter of all Georgian horses. A sculptor described Angels of the Sun and the Moon as a device to measure time and light. Its eastern face reflected the moon, and the western front reflected the sun. Each season brought about changes in the statue because of the shadows that flit across. The Moon Goddess represented a legend of a Wiljaali woman who stole the moon and placed it in a bag.

Then there was the Bajo el Sol Jaguar, the most famous sculpture. Light and shadow reflected on the stone, changing the colours of the sculpture as the sun went down, a rendering of the duality of day and night - fascinating.

Bajo el Sol Jaguar

Sunset from the sculpture hill, with the desert in front and all around, was the most beautiful sunsets, one can experience in the Australian Outback. Light reflected all over the outback plains. Colours changed from soft pink to dark violet, from golden orange to scarlet red as we stood in silence.

Soon it got dark and cold and time to get back to our hotel.

We went to the world-famous Air Ambulance station the next day. This charity provided retrieval service for seriously ill and critically injured by helicopter and aeroplanes in vast and remote regions of Australia. They also offered flying hospital service by highly experienced aeromedical teams with their fixed-wing planes. In smaller towns and settlements without safe birthing facilities, they brought pregnant women to hospitals in bigger towns. Expectant mothers lodged there with one family member from a few weeks before delivery until a week after the birth.

Next morning we left for Griffith at 730 km distance. Sanku did the bulk of the driving on an almost empty road with many dead kangaroos lying by its side with a lunch stop at the small township of Ivanhoe, named after a historical fiction. Then evening approaching we had to be careful to avoid the suicidal kangaroos waiting by the road!

Broken Jaw Capital of the world Darwin, Litchfield and Kakadu Northern Territory

January 2014

'Broken jaw capital of the world' - Darwin, the northernmost city of Australia, held a world record, with around 350 cases per year. About 17 per 10,000 population! A symposium on 'Violence and trauma' there picked my interest.

Darwin   Colleagues had warned about safety in Darwin, especially around Mitchell Street. But I needed somewhere to eat. Mitchell Street was full of pubs and restaurants and teeming with people. After a decent dinner, on my way back, I came across many intoxicated people. Soon I was reminded why it earned the reputation as 'Broken jaw breaking capital' of the world. I watched in dismay how simple banter was turning into arguments and then fights between the aboriginal and white Aussie youths. It was only 8 pm!

Aboriginal Social workers from different parts of Northern Territory took part in the symposium. They elaborated on how alcohol had devastated most of Darwin and Alice Springs's indigenous community. Before the invaders arrived, local people infrequently used only mild alcoholic drinks made from a variety of plants. Their use, however, was strictly controlled. Aboriginal words for 'alcohol' meant 'dangerous', 'bad' or 'poisonous'.

Alcohol use changed significantly after the white people arrived. Invaders paid the indigenous labourers in alcohol or tobacco if paying at all. In the early 1800s, a favourite spectator sport of the white people in Sydney was to ply aboriginal men with alcohol and encourage them to fight each other - often to the death. Domestic violence, fire injuries, falls and drownings, road and industrial accidents were now rife. Now almost 70% of police time involved tackling alcohol-related crime. Unemployment, depression and suicide rates amongst indigenous people were very high.

Interestingly, although Darwin was a major trauma centre, it had no neurosurgery provision. They flew patients to Adelaide, over 2600km distance for such treatment!

Northern Territory

I took a two-day tour of the region with an indigenous travel company. Our guide narrated the history and culture of this region, where over a quarter of the population was indigenous. 1976 Aboriginal Land Rights Act provided the basis upon which Aboriginal people in the Northern Territory could claim rights to land-based on their traditional occupation. Pride in Aboriginal culture and heritage was slowly returning in many parts of the country.

Litchfield National Park   About one and a half-hour after leaving Darwin, we entered Litchfield National Park and stopped by the Finniss River crossing, well known from the recent killer croc films. Until the late 70s, the river was heavily polluted because of uranium mining at nearby Rum jungle. But now it was a popular spot for catching highly prized Barramundi fish.

Then we drove to iconic Wangi falls, the largest in Litchfield, plunging out of dry rocks into a crystal clear blue pool. Wangi Falls was a special place for indigenous women of the area to bathe, swim and enjoy. Men who wandered near had to look away, not staring at the falls or the pool. They believed if any men looked that way, a beautiful woman appeared nearby and enticed them towards the water and eventually, their death.

We walked towards the pool through lush rainforest with wandering wallabies and surprised lizards towards the water. There were two barricades in the river flowing down from the pool. The guide explained between May and December; park authorities closed the plunge pool for swimming. Saltwater crocodiles occasionally came upstream. They assured us before opening the pool to the public in the tourist season; authorities net the crocs and then take them by helicopter to release in the sea. In the dry season, the river from the pool did not have enough water for the crocs to swim up from the sea.

I swam in the pool, watching out for stray saltie! Most refreshing on a hot day.

At the marvellous site of Termite mounds, we strolled through these intriguing structures, up to 100 years old. On dry river bed were hundreds of magnetic mounds up to 3m high, each like a giant magnetic compass. Their thin edges pointed north-south like the needle of a compass and the broad backs east-west, minimising their exposure to the sun, keeping the mounds cool all day long for the termites inside. Nearby were the large cathedral termite mounds - tallest of them over 4m.

Magnetic mounds   Cathedral mounds

We had our lunch in the middle of rainforest near the Woolaning spring - a lovely dish of freshly cooked wild-caught barramundi. Nearby was a one-teacher school for the students from transition to grade six. The population of the community was between 5 and 20 people at any one time. A school enrolment varied year to year depending on who was living in the area at the time.

After crossing the Reynolds River Track and two creeks, we arrived at heritage-listed Blyth Homestead. This tiny, rough-hewn homestead, built in 1928, a reminder of rugged solitude of pioneer life in days of working cattle, vegetables and tin mining.

We drove next to the famous Florence Falls, looking stunning from the plateau-top. I walked down over a hundred stairs to the clear, blue waters of Florence's stone-walled gorge and plunge pool.

Same story about crocs here. But I swam happily. After about half an hour in the refreshing water, it was time to move on.

We drove through Marrakai track in the ford by Adelaide River, renowned for its high concentration of saltwater crocodiles. Only the week before, a croc had eaten a man nearby. After crossing the river, we stopped by a billabong to view an abundance of varieties of herons, storks, cormorants, egrets, kingfishers, spoonbills and many other birds - a paradise for birdwatchers.

Emus, kangaroos and wallabies lazed in the dryland against the backdrop of setting sun along our track. We came across massive cattle stations. Unfortunately, there were also several large mining sites on the way, completely destroying the natural habitats of this place.

We stayed at the Wildman Wilderness Lodge for the night. After a delicious meal of kangaroo meat, I slept well after a long but enriching day.

Kakadu National Park

Home Billabong   Well before sunrise, we left for a cruise on the wetlands of Home Billabong. A naturally occurring water pocket fed by the rising waters of Mary River. At the end of the monsoon season, it becomes secluded with lower water levels. As the sun came up, we glided between overhanging mangroves, paperbark, pandanus and water lilies amongst reeds in the water.

Giant salties, measuring over 5m, and smaller freshwater crocs rested on the shore, waiting to warm up in the sun. Some gently swam by. Only a few months back, nearby, a teenager was eaten while swimming with his friends. We heard legends about largest of the resident, over 5m meter saltie, named Big Boy.

On the shore was an enchanting bounty of birdlife, both local and visiting - Jabirus, white-bellied Sea Eagles, Magpie Geese, Whistling Ducks, Ibis, Egrets and many more.

Ubirr

From there, we arrived at Ubirr. There, first, we met our guides, who were also the traditional Aboriginal owner of the northern Kakadu National Park. Only with their blessing, we could visit this world-renowned rock art site, one of the world's most significant concentrations of rock art. In many rock caves and walls were paintings, some 20,000 years old, the longest historical records for any group of people on the earth.

Aboriginal word for rock art was gunbim. These artworks provided a fascinating history of Aboriginal life for thousands of years, showing close personal relationship Bininj and Mungguy people shared with their land and spiritual heritage.

Aboriginals painted rock art for several reasons. Art had been an expression of their cultural identity and connection to the country. Act of painting was more important than painting itself. As a result, the older images were sometimes covered by the younger ones. Rock art is still very relevant to the aboriginal people. Most of the old paintings were red, from haematite and these lasted the longest - a mind-blowing look back in human history.

Numbed, we drove to a picnic site by the East Alligator River. Sitting in the shade of large paperbark trees, we had Top End's famous barramundi for lunch. We then cruised along the East Alligator River in the pristine wilderness of world heritage landscape. The guide provided insight into their culture and local mythology. Afterwards, we disembarked on the Arnhem Land side of the river. There in the jungle, we practised spear throwing and boomerang. My spear throwing was better than my boomerang!

Bowali Visitor Centre   At the Bowali Visitor Centre, we learnt more about the vast lands of Kakadu and how they were now jointly managed by their Traditional Owners and Australian Government. A young woman in her early twenties was our guide there. She took us in the jungle and showed us bush survival skills, including how to dodge crocs while going swimming or collecting water. Back at the visitor centre, with about six of us sitting in a semicircle around, she demonstrated weaving baskets from the reeds. Then she asked us if we had questions for her.

I asked if she had any chance to get education living here and did she feel isolated in this remoteness. She answered calmly she went to a boarding school in Darwin to complete her secondary education. She did not enjoy the experience there at all. When someone else asked why she calmly replied it was because of subtle and overt racial discrimination.

Then she elaborated her father was chief of the tribe here and respected by everybody around. She proudly said as his only child; she will become chief one day here when he becomes too old. She had a 2-year-old son and was very happy in this place. I then asked about alcohol-related problem in the area. She proudly said her father had banned alcohol in his tribe. No one drinks unless they go to town. She added this was the same in many other tribal areas regarding alcohol. At the end of half an hour we spend with this young lady, I was most impressed with her calm demeanour and intelligence.

I had no doubt one day she will be a great leader of her tribe there.

Queenstown - Sky diving / white water rafting & Milford Sound   New Zealand

2014 July Queenstown
Australia and New Zealand Surgeons annual conference was taking place in Queenstown. I enrolled. Queenstown in South Island of New Zealand sitting on the shores of Lake Wakatipu, set against the dramatic Southern Alps was renowned as the adventure capital of the world.

Conference dinner in the last evening was in a restaurant high above the town. Gondola ride nearby was closed in the night. Opposite me sat two vegetarians. Our first course arrived, a lovely bowl of soup, followed by delicious crayfish and salad with prosciutto ham. I looked at the plates of my vegetarian colleagues. They had only boiled potato, a lump of cheese and lettuce. We joked about their meagre serving. Soon we saw on the next table mains were being served. Non-vegetarians had sizeable portions of lamb with all the trimmings, while for the vegetarians only plate full of boiled veg and more cheese.

One colleague suggested we leave to find something better in town. Two of us joined the two vegetarians and shared a taxi. The driver advised the famous burger place in the town and dropped us next to Fergburger. Even at late winter night, a lengthy line to get inside. My two colleagues ordered vegetarian burgers, and we ordered beef burgers. It was the most delicious burger I had evertasted.

Sky diving   Next morning, I came across a tour operator offering tandem skydiving. I was immediately interested. I thought for a minute if I should ask my only daughter, but then realised she would say no. But if I did not take this opportunity now, it would never happen. If I died, there was nothing for me to think about after, anyway. And it was a tandem dive, and the tandem master has got a family and all that. Options were of a dive from 15,000 ft., 12,000 ft. or 9,000 ft. I chose the 12,000 ft option in the afternoon.
Motto in NZONE dive was **'Embrace the fear. Be brave. Even if you are not, pretend to be, no one can tell.'**

I had a free morning. I took the Skyline Gondola to its upper terminal on Dob's peak. View of the town below surrounded by pristine lakes was stunning. A sign showed the direction to a treehouse for zip lining, something I had never done.

Soon they fitted me with a zipping harness and helmet and then I was flying through the treetops on two breathtaking zip lines with a spectacular view of the lake. It was interesting, but I was looking forward to the afternoon's adventure.

Later a bus took us outside the town to the skydiving centre by a private airstrip. After watching a video of the adventure, one in our group of seven dropped out. After a safety briefing, my tandem master helped me to gear up and briefed me again. In the back of a small plane, with its door open, we sat in a circle. Each next to his/her tandem master. Soon we were high above the Wakatipu basin, with a bird's-eye view of dramatic mountains and lakes.

After the plane reached the altitude, each tandem master nodded to us and fastened themselves to their jumpers. I was third in line for the dive. First, a photographer jumped out of the plane. I watched two other divers jumping out and disappearing from view to who knows where. Then I was by the open door, and my tandem master gave me a nod. I jumped out with my arms and legs horizontal, flying like a bird.

Absolutely weightless, I was flying with the gorgeous lakes and the icy mountain peaks well below me. I could not stop smiling. I could have stayed there forever. Now I knew how birds felt flying. After almost 40 seconds of this ecstasy, free-falling at about 200km/hr, suddenly there was a jerk, and I was pulled up higher. The tandem master had opened the parachute.

We glided down slowly, floating in the air for another five minutes over magnificent lakes and mountains before we were close to the ground. I used the skills I had learned in getting to the ground without breaking my legs. From my hotel, I telephoned my daughter. A grin stayed on my face for the next few days.

Canyon rafting   Adrenalin still flowing high, next morning, I took the challenge of white-water rafting on Queenstown's famous Shotover River. We drove through a narrow dirt road hugging the canyon's sheer cliffs, with dramatic views over the river we would raft. At the rafting base, we got fitted in our gear and had a safety briefing.

After cruising over peaceful waters for a short while, we headed towards the exhilarating rapids of the lower canyon. Soon our raft was tackling grade four to five rapids through the canyon. In the narrow rapids often we turned a corner, coming right next to jagged rocks. While we paddled furiously, the guide calmly steered us out into the middle. In the clear water, we could see our craft going over submerged rocks. The guide said they designed the raft for cruising even over only 10 cm depth of water.

We tackled six grade 3-5 rapids, named like Aftershock, Squeeze, Toilet, and Pinball. Soon we moved through the darkness of the 170m Oxenbridge Tunnel and then shot the Cascade Rapid to complete the challenge. Getting off the raft, soaked despite our waterproofs gears, we took deep breaths and greeted each other.

Paragliding   My thrill-seeking continued in the afternoon. I had jealously watched before gliders past our house in Wales next to the Blorenge Mountain. Now I booked a tandem paragliding.

At Coronet Peak, a popular skiing area, outside Queenstown, I had my gear and briefing from my tandem master. Chairlifts took us over the snow near the launch point on the icy slope. From there, my tandem carrying the parachute on his back, we climbed up, treading heavy snow for another 100m to Rocky Gully, the highest take-off area. While my tandem started preparing the parachute by laying it on the snow and sorting out the ropes, I enjoyed the magnificent view of the surrounding snow peaks from the altitude of about 1700m.

Soon we were ready. Harnessed in front of my tandem connected to the chute, I ran down the slope for a few meters. Then we were flying in the open sky. From almost 1100m vertical, we flew with the wind taking us higher above the summits, with a gorgeous view of Lake Wakatipu and Lake Hayes.

After a few minutes, my tandem asked me to take control. I made some slow turns in the air. Then he took over and did some spins and rapid turns to add to the thrill. After about 20 minutes of fun in the air, we slowly descended on the other side of the mountain. I had accomplished another of my dreams.

Following day started with a breath-taking journey along the shores of Lake Wakatipu. We often stopped to take pictures on this New Zealand's most famous scenic road journey - spectacular views around each bend.

After passing through the sleepy village of Glenorchy at the end of the lake, we drove through awe-inspiring Mt Aspiring World Heritage Park. Middle Earth came to life here in Tolkien's book. Soon we literally arrived in Paradise, aptly named because of its beauty with the glacial lakes, ancient forests and neck stretching peaks of Lord of the Rings film trilogy as the backdrop. All of us got off to capture the memory of paradise in our cameras.

We then boarded into our jet boat on Dart River, Te Awa Wakatipu. The guide explained about the area's rich history and countless Maori legends. In a while, we reached the spot where the Dart glacier melted to become the river. Mount Aspiring on the background in the middle of winter looked extremely challenging. No wonder Edmund Hillary used this area for practice before attempting Mt Everest.

On our return, we got off in a forest. Walking amongst the ancient beech trees for a while, we remembered pictures from the Lord of the Rings films. Later on the river, our crew made several 360 spins in this Grade 2-3 rapid, just to show off!

Milford Sound   It took only thirty-five minutes flight to Milford next day. After taking off, our small plane flew over the vast shiny blue lakes before entering the dramatic alpine scenery of icy mountains, glacier and gorges - winter wilderness at its best. Soon, with the sensational Milford Sound in front, we touched down into its small airport.

It was after lunchtime. In winter, with limited daylight, high mountains were letting in very little sunlight into the valley. Everything was covered in snow, and the fiord land was freezing. I would have liked to have trekked the famous Milford Track, but now in winter, avalanches were frequent, and the trail was closed. Fortunately, my lodge was next to the sound. In front of me was the majestic Mitre Peak, casting its shadow on the waters. I walked around in awe on the nearby coastal path until it got dark and snowed.

Next day, I took a cruise on the sound. Milford Sound was a fiord in the southwest of New Zealand's South Island. Its history dated back over 1,000 years. Maori people travelled there to fish and hunt around the inlet and collect pounamu, the precious green stone. European settlers did not explore Milford Sound by boat, not realising that inside its narrow entrance from the Tasman Sea was such a beautiful region.

Our cruise went into the fiord under towering Mitre Peak 1692m and other peaks with almost vertical rocks. We cruised under many mighty waterfalls with glacial water falling on top of us. Lady Bowen Falls at 162m, the tallest of them was well over three times the height of Niagara but the second-highest waterfall in the sound, Stirling Falls 151m, was more beautiful.

Then we cruised through this narrow inlet of less than 2km width for about 15km to the open Tasman Sea at Dale Point. A pod of dolphins swam gracefully in the turbulent sea. Nearby, on the rocks, many seals basked in the sunshine. On our return, we stopped under the mystical Four Sisters waterfalls. Four identically sized waterfalls lined up along the mountainside. Our boat came right under one of its falls. The crew gave us empty glasses to have a drink straight from it. It was the purest & best water in the world! According to the myth, water from Four Sisters made one look ten years younger. I don't know how I looked but felt much younger.

In the afternoon, our return flight to Queenstown took a brief detour after leaving Milford Sound. The pilot announced to look below at Sutherland Falls. At 580m, the tallest waterfall in New Zealand, now partly frozen in winter, looked sensational.

Kangaroo Island

August 2014

My resignation letter was already submitted. My only daughter was expecting twins - I would be returning to the UK. Only nine weeks before that date, one of my submissions got accepted for presentations in Adelaide. A lot of training expenses were still left to be used.

Adelaide with Victorian-style houses interspersed with high-rise buildings and tram cars was relaxing. I would have enjoyed the city more if I was a wine connoisseur.

Kangaroo Island After coming so far down to the south, I could not miss out on the nearby Kangaroo Island. From Adelaide, a scenic coach trip through Fleurieu Peninsula with vineyards and wineries took me to Cape Jervis. A ferry from there brought us to Pennenshaw on the north coast of Kangaroo Island.

Our first stop was at Rob's Shearing. Rob, a real Aussie character and his dogs skilfully mustered sheep herd and demonstrated sheep shearing. He allowed us a go. Like others, I failed miserably.

Before our lunch at Emu Ridge Distillery, we watched the production of eucalyptus oil from Narrow Leaf Mallee tree, abundant here. We then stopped by an area which locals use as their post office. There were many old freezes, micro-ovens and other furniture, individually marked for the postman to make deliveries. Kangaroo Island, with over 4000 sq.km in size and only 4000 population, was too sparse for the postman to make individual deliveries!

Next, we arrived in the south was Seal Bay, home of the endangered Australian sea lions – the third largest breeding colony in Australia. The park ranger said we should maintain a distance of 10m from the animals. Only ten people were allowed at any time. Against the backdrop of the turquoise ocean and golden sands, we walked towards the colony. Seal pups played. Mothers rested with suckling babies, and some just basked in the sun. Kangaroo Island had over 1000 sea lions. While we were taking pictures, one pup came out of the water straight to me. I stopped immediately. The pup sniffed my shoes and hobbled towards the dune, looking for his mother. He frequently stopped, bleating like a sheep, calling out for his mother. He was too young yet to have learnt the 10m rule!

Nearby Little Sahara was an area of spectacular white dunes. From the top of the dunes, there was an opportunity for sandboarding. I gave it a miss. By now, the sun was setting spectacularly against the Tasman Sea. We then headed for Pennenshaw. Before reaching our boarding place, we stopped by a jetty. He asked us to go down there and wait quietly. An old man came with two buckets full of fish. Even before he started throwing the fish in the sea, dozens of pelicans flew in and walked around him like house pets in anticipation. This man had been feeding the pelicans from his catch for over 15 years. It was a lovely scene of human connecting with nature.

During our dinner, the guide narrated Kangaroo Island, also known as Karta (Island of the Dead), was Australia's third-largest island. The native population of Aboriginals of the area disappeared from the record when after last glacial period, the place became an island with rising sea levels. Sealers and whalers settled here intermittently in the early 19th century. British explorer Flinders named the place 'Kangaroo Island' because of an abundance of the endemic subspecies of the western grey kangaroo.

From the car park at Stokes Bay, on the north coast, we walked through a labyrinth of volcanic rocks and caves as the sky was getting light. Suddenly in front of us was the vista of sunrise in all its glory. A giant pool surrounded by rocks protected the beach from the pounding surf - sumptuous. On our return to the car park, we walked to the nearby Bush Garden with hundreds of native flowers and plants, including seasonal native orchids. Nearby in a rocky field, kangaroos were up early and grazing.

After breakfast at Raptor Domain, we watched a display of rescued 'In-Flight' Birds of Prey like Wedge-tailed Eagles, Sea Eagles and Owls, being rehabilitated before going back into the wild. They allowed me to have an Eagle fly in and rest upon my gloved hand - it was heavy!

Next stop was at the Kangaroo Island Wildlife sanctuary. A fun place for families with a chance to hand-

feed kangaroos, hold koalas, see Penguins play and let giant reptiles slither over our body.

We proceeded to a forest with rows of Eucalyptus trees. Koala families went on sleeping in most of them. Within a half an hour of walk, I spotted nearly fifty koalas. Some mothers slept while their babies clutched on. Koalas were not a native of this island. As a result, in recent years a programme of sterilisation of koalas had started.

In the 1920s, 18 koalas were introduced from Victoria in response to a countrywide decline in koala numbers following hunting for the fur trade - one of the earliest conservation attempts in Australia through relocation. By 2001 there were around 27,000 koalas.

By the car park, in an enormous field, numerous kangaroos grazed. Two roos started a boxing match, just for us.

Flinders Chase National Park, on the north-western part of the island, since its creation in 1919, has become a sanctuary for endangered species. Including those introduced from the mainland such as koalas and platypuses. There we walked to a rocky riverside, known to be the best place in Australia to see the enigmatic platypus. But even after half an hour, we had no luck.

Then we drove to the coastline before reaching a truly remarkable place known as the Remarkable Rocks. Five hundred million years of rain, wind, and waves pounding granite boulders had created this signature landmark – a wonder of natural sculptures.

Golden orange lichen covered many of the rocks, contrasting against black mica, bluish quartz, and pinkish feldspar granite - visual magic.

After an hour there, we drove further west through the coastal road before arriving outside the beautiful stone-built Cape du Couedic lighthouse. We walked past the tower, then down many steep steps to the rocky shore. On the rocks were sunbathing many New Zealand fur seals. New Zealand fur seals are native to Australia, despite their name. Smaller compared to what we saw in Seal Bay, still very cute with their long noses. Because of hunting by early settlers for their fur, New Zealand fur seal was endangered. But now, fortunately, this island was home to a population of almost 100,000 of them.

On our return path, after watching the fur seals, we stopped in silence at the Kangaroo Island's most impressive and unusual natural landmarks, the Admirals Arch. Thousands of years of erosion had created this distinctive rock bridge. Stalactites dangling from the rocky ceiling of this former cave, with crashing waves of the Tasman Sea beyond, gave it an extra dimension. We sat for some time watching this nature's mesmerising creation. Fur seals played behind us on the rock.

Admiral's Arch

Chile, Galapagos, Peru.

September 2014

Galapagos was one place I wanted to visit more than anywhere else. And there was also a personal connection.

I had only a month left before I departed Australia. With over three weeks' accrued annual leave left, I arranged for a trip to the Galapagos Islands in September. And as I was going to that part of the world, I also wanted to see Machu Picchu.

Santiago, Chile   Arriving in Santiago from Sydney around mid-day, soon I left to explore the city.

In Palacio de La Moneda, the residence of the President of the Republic of Chile, a changing of the guard ceremony was going on. I remembered they bombed this palace during a military coup in 1973. Democratic president Salvador Allende committed suicide inside. Walls here still had preserved bullet marks.

I stood by the public square, Plaza de la Ciudadania, constructed next the palace to celebrate the bicentenary of Chile's independence in 2010. I recalled the dictatorship of Pinochet. He assumed power in Chile following the USA backed coup overthrowing the democratically elected socialist government and ended the civilian rule. His regime resulted in executions of over 3000 people, the internment of many, many thousands, and forced disappearance of at least three thousand. On his 60th birthday, Pinochet launched Operation Condor, a campaign of political repression and state terror.

In the evening I walked to Barrio Bellavista, lying between the Mapocho River and San Cristobal Hill, known as Santiago's bohemian quarter, with its boutiques, modern galleries, restaurants and bars. It was packed. Nearby was Noble laureate poet Pablo Neruda's house but closed in the evening. I enjoyed a hearty dinner of Chilean Completo and coffee.

Andes from Santiago

Next morning I had a brief city tour. First stop was at Plaza de Armas, the main square of Santiago with beautiful architecture, including the stunning Post Office and the museum. Then to the highest point of Santiago at 630m Huelen Hill, a remnant of 15 million-year-old volcano with a superb view of Santiago below and Andes Mountains at a distance. The traffic in Santiago was choking up. I did not want to miss my afternoon outward flight and arrived at the airport just in time.

Quito, Ecuador   Quito, capital of Ecuador, was only my overnight stop. Hotel booked was near the city centre, over 30 km from the airport, not smart! Quito at 2850m was an enormous city sprawled on the slopes of many hills. By the time I arrived at my hotel, I had only time for dinner, and then I had to leave for the airport in the early morning!

Galapagos Islands

My flight arrived in Isla Baltra, a small flat island near the centre of Galapagos, 300km from Quito. This was one of the only two airports connecting Galapagos Islands with the mainland. The other was at   San Christabel Island. Galapagos guides took us to a ship. After sailing a short distance, we anchored by Mosquera Island. A paddleboat took us to its rocky shore for a wet landing. A colony of vast sea lions completely ignored us. Brown pelicans nesting nearby only cast a cursory glance towards the visitors.

The small ship for my Galapagos cruise had a comfortable cabin and a sundeck. For ten passengers, there was one naturalist, two National Park Rangers with their photo albums, five crews and a cook. I learnt a lot from them about Galapagos in the next few days.

Everyone knows of this archipelago of volcanic islands, for its connection with Charles Darwin's observation, contributing to his theory of Evolution by Natural Selection. Galapagos archipelago comprises 7,880 sq.km of land spread over 45,000 sq.km of the ocean with eighteen main islands, three smaller islands, and many rocks and islets. The archipelago is on the tectonic Nazca Plate, which is moving east/southeast at a rate of about 6.4 cm per year. Its landmass was declared a national park in 1959, the centenary year of publication of The Origin of Species. Three decades later, the surrounding 70,000 sq.km of the ocean became a marine reserve. Sitting at the sundeck, as we watched the sunset, frigate birds flew above and occasionally dived to catch fishes next to us.

Isabela Island   Our guides woke us up at dawn for an early breakfast. Our ship had already anchored by Isabela. Only 1 million years old, Isabela was one of the youngest islands on the western edge of the archipelago near the Galapagos hotspot. From the pier, we drove for 10 km on a dirt road between barren lava flows and endemic vegetation. Then we hiked uphill along an enormous caldera and beautiful landscapes across the terrain of Sierra Negra volcano, a merger of 6 shield volcanoes - Alcedo, Cerro Azul, Darwin, Ecuador, Sierra Negra, and Wolf, formed Isabela. All but Ecuador were still active, making it one of the most volcanically active places on the earth. Our trail curved uphill on a relatively gentle slope through fern-covered trees. Vegetation got drier and drier as we walked up.

Then we were on the edge of a rim of 9.5 km diameter and 100m deep caldera, the second-largest crater in the world. We hiked along the rim at 1100m for a while with a beautiful view of the island below.

Next, we visited The Wall of Tears, tragic human history in Galapagos. In the late 1940s, this place was a penal colony. They made prisoners collect heavy, sharp lava rocks by hand from around the island. To build a wall which had no purpose in the middle of nowhere, except to make them suffer and thus loss of lives of thousands of prisoners!

Wall of Tears

Outside town of Puerto Villamil, was the Arnaldo Tupiza tortoise breeding centre. Isabela is home to more wild tortoises than all the other islands in Galapagos. Isabela's large size and notable topography created barriers for the slow-moving tortoises. These creatures were unable to cross the lava flows and other obstacles, which resulted in the development of several tortoise sub-species.

Inaugurated in 1995, in response to a major fire on southern Isabela that threatened tortoise habitat, the centre now housed 69 breeding adults, including endangered tortoises from Cerro Azul and Sierra Negra. They raised approximately 250 young every year and released them in the wild at five years of age. Today, tortoises roam free in the calderas of the volcanoes of Isabela. Visiting these wonderful creatures reminded me of Lonesome George of Pinta Island. In his last years, known as the rarest creature in the world, George served as an important symbol for conservation efforts in the Galapagos Islands. It had prompted my older daughter to come here for volunteering a few years back. It upset both her and me when George died in 2012.

Isabella had a resident population of around 1700, who had settled before Galapagos was declared a national park. In these islands, human-introduced goats which multiplied to over 100,000 destroying natural habitat.

But with a superb effort, the National park Service and the Charles Darwin Foundation had eradicated them by 2007. Since then, the vegetation is recovering remarkably.

During our short break by the Puerto Villamil Pier, sea lions came off the sea and slept on a bench next to me as penguins raced each other in the water. Soon we headed south for a short sail towards the group of islets known as Las Tintoreras.

Las Tintoreras Soon we headed south for a short sail towards the group of islets known as Las Tintoreras. Carefully, we got off from our boat there onto an outcrop of lava rocks for our first real taste of the Galapagos Islands' biodiversity. Endangered Galapagos penguins came up from the water and hobbled past us to their nests, feeding their chicks. Galapagos sea lions and marine iguanas bathed in the sun.

In the trail, there was a narrow channel of crystal clear seawater about 3m wide between the two arms of lava. At the bottom of the water, were asleep tintoreras, just over 1m long white-tipped sharks, animal these islets named after.

Two turtles swam quickly past us before more sharks swam by.

Back on our boat, as the sun was setting, we sailed by large colonies of magnificent blue-footed boobies, settling for the night on the rocky shore.

My daughter with blue-footed boobies

Back in our ship, we had a lovely evening of learning more about these islands from our naturalist. While we slept, our cruise sailed on to another part of the island. This became a routine for the few nights on the ship.

Rabida Island   We wet landed onto the only permitted site of Rabida Island, also known as a red island. Lava rich in iron oxide and magnesium, 0.7-1.5 million years back, poured out of scoria cones. That, when exposed and rusted, gave the island its astounding, unearthly reddish colour. This unpopulated island was less than five sq.km in size. On dark red sand beaches, rested a horde of snoring sea lions. I sat on the sand to enjoy the scenery and their company.

A baby sea lion came out of the water and started noisily suckling his mother lying next to me. Nearby, brown pelicans wandered by their nests in scrubby bushes. Only a short distance from the colony of females and babies was the beach master, a big male. This enormous male kept an eye on his harem of about 30 females for any potential rivals coming up. Our guides warned us to steer clear of these males, who could attack.

Later we walked up a trail up into the forest of Palo Santo trees through scrubby bushes and cacti before reaching the highest point of the island at 350m. Landscapes with small craters, cliffs and red beaches were stunning. From the clifftop, we saw a few turtles swimming in the sea below. There were many flamingos in a small lagoon at the back of the island. This small island was a bird-watchers delight. Some of the rarest species were in abundance, including all of Darwin's nine varieties of finches, flycatchers and Galapagos hawks.

After coming down from the trail, we spent more time on the beach with sea lions around us.

Chinese Hat   For the last hour of our sailing, as the frigate birds kept us company, we had noticed this interesting looking small volcanic landmark getting closer. Chinese Hat, Sombrero Chino in Spanish, looked like an old- fashioned Chinaman's hat. Our guides asked to be careful, near our wet landing place, was a large colony of sea lions. Their beach master still in the water, popping his head in and out to keep an eye.

We carefully walked past the sandy area to the lava field. Sitting by a lava cactus, we watched the sea lion group in silence. An Oystercatcher flew in and rested on another cactus tree. Lava lizards moved in out of the cracks.

Soon in front was a mini-battle. A smaller male sea lion came ashore from behind the resting group. But even before he could get close to them, the larger beach master jumped out of the water and chased him away promptly. We had hoped to snorkel on this beach. The guides advised against, sensing the mood of the big boss.

Santiago Island   We wet landed for snorkelling on the shores of Santiago Island, opposite Chinese Hat. Here also were many sea lions, resting and nourishing their babies while bright coloured Sally Lightfoot crabs scuttled around nervously over lava rocks. Sally Lightfoot Crabs, native to Galapagos, fed on a varied diet that included sea lion placenta and ticks on the Marine Iguanas! After exploring this bay of lava rocks between the sea lion colonies, I snorkelled amongst a group of sea lions having fun in the water. No sooner than   I had entered the water, a baby sea lion came nibbling my toes playfully. This fun carried on for the next half an hour while we snorkelled. There was only one sighting of a white-tipped shark, but we saw a few turtles. It was getting dark, and it was time to get back to our ship.

Santiago Island, also known as James Island, at 585 sq.km, was the fourth largest island in Galapagos. In this island, Darwin had stayed the longest. Here he first noticed the differences between the tortoises from different islands, which had different shapes and sizes. Darwin also mentioned in Voyage of the Beagle of thousands of land iguanas on this island. He wrote, 'I cannot give a more forcible proof of their numbers, than by stating that when we were left at James Island, we could not for some time find a spot free from their burrows on which to pitch our single tent.'

But now land iguanas have completely disappeared because of introduced species; especially goats, pigs and rodents, although recently they have been eradicated. Santiago was also the site of the first introduction of black rats in the late 1600s. Today black rat was present on at least 33 islands and islets in the archipelago. Each of these introduced species had wreaked havoc on flora and fauna of Galapagos. Restoration of vegetation is rapidly occurring now. But now there is a problem with introduced plant species, held in check by the goats in the past.

Puerto Egas   Overnight the ship had sailed hundreds of miles west and then to the north side of Santiago Island before anchoring by Puerto Egas. Its long lava shoreline with eroded rock formations housed an array of wildlife. Marine iguanas with wide-set eyes, spiky dorsal scales and salt-crusted heads were basking in the sun. Sally Lightfoot crabs busied themselves picking off ticks and algae from the iguana's dry skin. Crabs moved nervously around as there were varieties of birdlife including herons, hawks, oystercatchers, finches and doves perched nearby looking for a grab.

Our trail came to a sea channel between the lava rocks where Galapagos fur seals were sunbathing. While watching them, two more came up from the water and climbed clumsily up the cliff to claim a spot in the sun. Soon a turtle floated into the clear blue water. The guide pointed to a dark brown, almost black, Galapagos hawk keeping an eye for suitable prey, the world's rarest raptors with a population of only 150 breeding pairs. Galapagos hawk had a unique breeding system known as cooperative polyandry. Males were entirely monogamous, but females could mate with up to seven males throughout the nesting period. These males helped to raise the chicks, usually three in a clutch, by taking turns incubating eggs and feeding the hatchlings. In front of us, an unsuspecting lava lizard got picked up by the bird before it flew away.

Playa Espumilla   Hundreds and hundreds of marine iguanas covered this rocky beach along with their friends, Sally Lightfoot crabs. In some places, there were so many they looked like loose rocks. They seemed impervious to human presence. So many that we had to watch our step, not to tread on one.

Marine Iguana was the only lizard that had adapted to eat a marine diet. It can hold its breath for an hour while it forages for algae at depths of up to 20m. In front of us, many came back from the sea after foraging, sneezing out the salt crust from their noses.

Carefully, through these marine iguanas, we continued to the most idyllic volcanic beach - flamingo and sea turtle nesting sites. From there our guide took us for an inland hiking trail past a dry lagoon. Galapagos hawks circled overhead.

Before returning to our boat from there, I requested the guide to let me be alone there for a few minutes. They did not allow visitors to be alone on the islands without a guide for obvious reasons. I explained to her that my deceased daughter had spent several weeks volunteering for conservation work on these islands. I wanted a few minutes alone to think of her. The guide left me alone, reminding me not to be too long. With tears flooding, I stood there thinking of my daughter, amongst this awe-inspiring nature, she was so keen to help preserve.

Later, we sailed past Buccaneer Cove, colours of setting sun played magic against the towering cliffs. On the coppery red sand beach, hundreds of seabirds perched, getting ready for the night.

Volcanoes at the west end of the archipelago were younger and taller, with well-developed calderas, and mostly composed of tholeiitic basalt. Those in the east were shorter, older, without calderas and had more diverse composition. Ages of the islands, from west to east, were 0.05 million years for Fernandina in the far west and 3.2 million years for easternmost San Cristobal. Our ship had sailed in the night north of Santiago Island and then southeast to the North Seymour Island.

North Seymour Island   This less than two sq.km island was an important nesting site for the marine birds. North Seymour was a tectonic uplift, a result of earth's crust uplifting from below sea level. This had created the island cliffs to drop dramatically into the ocean. We wet landed where a giant manta ray was swimming by. Once he swam away, we walked up a stiff path past many marine iguanas, sea lions and swallow-tailed gulls. The ground above was strewn with Palo Santo, sandalwood with a strong aroma and grey saltbush among white-splashed rocks.

Suddenly our guide in front stopped and signalled to be quiet, and pointed to a bush. In front was an iconic land iguana, with bright yellow with white, black and brown blotches, about 1.5m long. He stood on his powerful hind legs with sharp claws on its toes, looking at us with his large eyes on a short head with a blunt nose. We stood in silence. After a while, the mini dragon lost interest in us and disappeared in the bush, leaving us mesmerised.

Next, we tiptoed by the nesting area of frigate birds, the largest colony in the archipelago. Darwin called them 'condor of the oceans'. They had the largest wingspan to body weight ratio of any bird in the world and could spend days in the ocean. Males were all black with a large red throat pouch which they inflated time to time, emitting a shrill noise before an acrobatic aerial display in front of the larger female. Female had a white breast and shoulder, and a blue eye-ring. Several of them already had white chicks. Others waited by their nests of a few twigs in the low shrubbery next to their single eggs.

Nearby, in the open nesting grounds, were blue-footed Boobies. Female rested on the ground showing least interest, while the male started courting dance. He lifted his feet in succession, strutting himself in front of the female, whistling and honking to catch attention. It was great fun to watch and record on video. But during our twenty minutes there, I did not see a single female showing the slightest of interest!

On the other side on the shore, we were lucky to see a small flock of the largest of Galapagos bird, Waved Albatross. They walked from their nest most inelegantly with their large wingspan of 2.5m. But once in the air, they soared magnificently.

Sadly, it was soon time to go back to our boat for a return trip via Baltra.

Machu Picchu Peru

Machu Picchu, the 15th century Inca Citadel in the sacred valley, one of new Seven Wonders of the World, can be reached in three different ways.

The easiest way, a train ride to the bottom of the mountain and then a cable car to the top. The site itself, with its steep steps, was still not for the fainthearted. The second option was the classic Inca trail. Four days and three nights trek, though impressive ancient ruins, beginning outside the town of Ollantaytambo. Only 200 tourist permits per day and was sold out months in advance. The third option which I chose was Lares Trek, which did not require permits. After my knee surgery a year back, I had been practising with a knee brace on the rocks in Cocoparra National Park near Griffith.

Lares Trek   This trek benefited from an authentic Andean cultural experience in Lares Valley. Home to several traditional Andean communities that have changed little in the last 500 years.

I arrived in Cusco 3399m from Quito in the evening. The hotel was next to the old colonial town square. Next day I wandered around vibrant Plaza de Armas square before going inside Cusco Cathedral, built in the

late 16th century. There was an interesting 18th-century copy-painting of Leonardo's The Last Supper by Marcos Zapata. This one curiously depicted Jesus and twelve apostles gathered around a table preparing to dine on a guinea pig, a local delicacy!

We left the next morning, through twisted mountain roads towards the sacred valley of the Incas. After traversing through stunning Andean mountain range for several hours, we reached Pisac, a colourful market town in the heart of the sacred valley. Giggling school children were walking miles to their school, women in their colourful wide skirts with colourful capes and men in their intricate ponchos - a unique world. We drove to Hualcapunku pass 4,400m, with a magnificent view of snow-capped Ausangate 6,370m, highest mountain in Cusco region.

Then, following a mountain river on our side, we hiked on a rocky path for three hours. Occasional llamas checked us out. We stopped by a cave 20m above our track. Our guide said it was where locals left their dead bodies. With permission, one by one, we walked up. Inside the narrow cave decorated with colourful ribbons were many mummified bodies.

Nearby we stopped for coffee and visited a local weaver busy in her vibrant craft. Later we camped for our first night by a river in the tiny Andean village of Huaca Wasi 3600m. Night came quickly on the mountain.

We settled down for a dinner of tasty papa a la Huancaina, potatoes in a spicy cheese sauce. On our way, we had passed many potato fields on the mountainside, with rows of llamas passing by, carrying sacks of potatoes down the valley to the market. The guide said here they grew almost a hundred varieties of potatoes.

We were only five trekkers in the group. Other four were in their late twenties. Of the French couple, the woman was an architect and the man an accountant. Of the German couple, the woman was a medic and the man a physiotherapist. Our guide was in his mid-twenties. From our guide, we learnt the people in the province were mainly indigenous of Quechua descent. Most spoke Quechua, only less than a third spoke Spanish.

Since Spanish conquest four centuries back, all the people in the Andes have been nominally Roman Catholic, the religion of the conquistador. Quechuas still held on to their traditional faith of Pachamama, particularly belief in Mother Earth, an ever-present and independent deity with self-sufficient and creative power to sustain life on this earth. Four cosmological Quechua principles were Water, Earth, Sun, and Moon. Our young guide in his spare time studied Pachamama philosophy and hoped one day to become a full-time priest. Sitting in that Andean mountain village and reflecting on the damage we are doing to our planet, I could not but admire his philosophy.

It had rained heavily in the night. It was soggy and cold on our campsite. Our German friends were feeling under the weather with the altitude and went down. Soon the sun was out, and we started our ascent. Trek now was more demanding, but the magnificent mountain views and sights of the curious alpacas on the rocks kept us amused. The last section of trekking was getting more challenging, although Abray Ipsay 4,400m, the highest pass on the trek was in sight. We were stopping every half an hour for breaks—me taking longer. A lady from the village was going up next to us with her pony, hoping we would hire a ride.

200m below the pass, my knee in brace finally pushed me to accept the ride. Although the ride gave my poor knee a rest, it was most uncomfortable going up with the beast swaggering on the rocky path. As we reached the highest point of the pass, I got off and paid the lady. No way would I go down on a saddle on the steep downward path!

View from the pass in front of snow-capped mountains and Ipsaycocha Lake in front made me forget everything else everything else.

Usually, steep descent through screes was fun, but I had to be extra careful going down with my knee brace. We stopped for a late lunch by the lake. Llamas and alpacas grazed alongside Andean Ibis and Andean geese. Soon we made a relatively easy descent to our camp at Patacancha 3,700m, a village renowned for its traditional weaving. Shops were closed. But women and children wandered by in their colourful garments. Hearty dinner of Peruvian chicken soup was most welcome after a hard day trek.

Trek next day was through Patacancha valley with a brief stop at Willoq village. It gave us more sight into the Andean community. It was refreshing to hear and see in recent days, people here were meeting the visitors as their equals in their lively and cordial manner. We walked past Pumamarca ruins, a hillside fortress built on a steep slope that once guarded the entrance to the fertile Sacred Valley. Our car was waiting there.

Ollantaytambo We drove past lush pastoral landscape of ancient farms to arrive at the archaeological remains of Ollantaytambo by Patakancha River, one of the oldest and most significant ruins in the Sacred Valley. Originally built for religious purposes, during Spanish invasion it served as a stronghold for the leader of Inca resistance. Here was the lesser-known Wall of six Monoliths, standing approximately 11m wide and 4m high. They created this incredible piece of Incan ingenuity out of pink granite. Stones, weighing between 50 and 100 tons each, were mined from Chachiqata quarry, on the other side of the 300m deep valley, across Rio Vilcanota and then dragged 4km to this site. This mammoth effort in 15th century dumb-founded even my engineer friend. Littered around Temple Hill were even larger blocks called 'Tired Stones', named so after the local belief they were too tired to reach their final destination within the complex.

In the colourful town of Ollantaytambo by the river, we stopped for a late lunch/early dinner. While they were getting ready sorting out our meal, in the garden, three of us played with the local children, age's two to ten. I showed them with a lot of hilarity, steal the handkerchief game, an Indian traditional game and the French couple showed them a version of la barbichette. Next to us in the cages were many plump guinea pigs, but for our meal disappointingly they served chicken!

Machu Picchu

From there, we took the last train to Aguas Calientes, the station below Machu Picchu. National park bus next morning took us up to Machu Picchu. Machu Picchu at 2430m was over 900m lower than Cusco. However, drop from this hill was sharp, falling a breathtaking 600m to the River Urubamba directly below.

Once we left the entrance gate, after going up the slopes and then turning a corner, in front stood the breathtaking 15th-century Inca citadel - Machu Pichu with its polished dry stone walls and Huayna Picchu on the background. Soon we walked down rather steep steps to explore this wonder. Our two French friends left to climb up Huayna Picchu. Permits for this was even limited than a visit to Machu Picchu itself. My braced knee was now glad that I had not got one in advance.

The guide and I explored the area, and I learnt a lot. Machu Picchu was divided into the urban and agricultural sector, and an upper town and a lower town. Temples were in the upper town, warehouses in the lower. Adapted to the mountains, they arranged about 200 buildings on expansive parallel terraces around an east-west central square. Built in the 15th century, the place was used only for 80 years before being abandoned. There is a debate whether it followed the Spanish conquest in other parts of the Inca Empire or because most of its inhabitants died from smallpox introduced by the travellers as the conquistadors arrived. The site remained unexplored until 1911 when American historian Hiram Bigham travelled the area looking for the old Inca capital. A villager, Melchor Arteaga, led him to this marvel in ruins.

Temple of the Sun here was like the Sun temple we had seen in Ollantaytambo. Sun temple was orientated to winter and summer solstice. It had three windows, the largest one facing to the north and two facing the east. Within the temple stood a smooth stone platform, used as an altar. A 'Serpent's Door' opened onto a series of pools, and a striking view of Huayna Picchu.

In its heyday, about 750 people lived there, mostly as support staff. Farming, mainly corn and potatoes, were done in its hundreds of human-made terraces built to ensure proper drainage and soil fertility -a work of remarkable engineering.

Up the steps near the top was Intihuatana stone, a ritual sacrificial stone. Sitting on the terrace nearby, I tried to imagine the lives here five centuries back. Nearby was a dangerous looking a precipice below the stone wall with an enchanted view of the snow-covered peaks at a distance and the sweeping green rocky valley along a river beyond Machu Picchu and its ruins.

After a while, the French couple returned. Apparently, the steps of Huayna Picchu were even steeper. The trail was crowded but had a gorgeous view from there.

Our guide explained the technique of stoneworks in this massive complex. Buildings throughout the Inca Empire did not use any mortar. They cut the stones precisely and wedged them closely together using a technique known as ashlar. We could not even insert a credit card between the rocks. Aside from the obvious aesthetic benefits of this building style, there were engineering advantages. Peru is a seismically unstable country. When an earthquake occurred, stones in Inca buildings danced, bouncing through tremors and then falling back into place.

I asked our French engineer friend if one wanted to build now a structure like this on the top of a mountain here, with all the modern equipment and facilities available and money no object, how long it would take. She answered she could not even think of how this could be achieved.

After a full day visiting this amazing city of the Incas, we took a train from Aguas Calientes to Cusco.

Cusco   In the morning, we visited the sacred Qoricancha Temple of the Sun God, once the most important and holy temple in the Inca Empire. When the Spanish arrived in Cusco, they destroyed most of the temple. They built the massive Santo Domingo Church on the foundations, preserving only a small part of this

indigenous beauty.

Now within the opulent church building, only part of its walls was preserved. Its name roughly translated to 'Walls of Gold'. Spaniards arriving in Cusco found its every wall covered with a layer of gold. There were deities everywhere to celebrate different gods, such as a silver depiction of Moon Goddess. Animal figures made entirely from gold filled the gardens. Spaniards had never seen so much gold in one place before. They sent most of these to King of Spain as a 'thank you' for allowing expeditions to South America. Several major earthquakes over the centuries severely damaged the church. But the Inca stone walls, built out of huge, tightly interlocking blocks of stone, still stand because of their sophisticated masonry.

Next, we drove to the holy site of Q'enqo, meaning labyrinth, carved out of a gigantic monolith. This temple stretched across a hillside, carved out with many tunnels and chambers underneath. Sacrifices and mummification took place here in the subterranean chamber, once covered in gold.

At the ancient sites of Tambomachay and Puca Pucara, amongst the ruins were aqueducts, canals and waterfalls flowing with water even after 500 years of abandonment. The proximity of Tambomachay to the ruins of a military garrison of Puca Pucara suggested it may have been the quarters for the military elite, including a bathhouse. Puca Pucara played an important role in defence of Cusco and the Inca Empire.

We left for the fortress of Sacsayhuaman. It extended over an area of over 30,000,000 sq.meters between the hills. Walls of Sacsayhuaman were built with giant stones up to 5m high and 2.5m wide, with watchtowers on zigzag walls. This exceptional architectural work of the Incas took seven decades and 20,000 men to construct. Two tunnels underneath this fortress, the longer tunnel without an exit found so far. I came out of the shorter tunnel outside.

Local women in their colourful Andean outfit were sharing coffee, taking a break from selling souvenirs. Through our guide, I asked how far they had travelled to come here. Some had come only 4-5 km, while others from nearly eight km. Their husbands made these crafts at home between their agricultural works. Children helped after they came home from school.

The guide left looking for others in our group. One woman vendor understood and spoke a bit of English, a lot better than my Spanish. She said on a good day they made about 40,000 sucre, less than two dollars. She asked me about my job. When I said I was a doctor, some of them asked advice for themselves and their children. One of them, in her late pregnancy with her first baby, had a terrible headache all morning. Luckily, I had paracetamol with me. I gave it to her. I also gave some paracetamol to another lady to take home, whose ten-year-old son was having a high fever.

They shared coffee and churro, a delightful fluffy pastry, with me, laughing and joking - a wonderful end to my travel in Peru.

Ellora and Ajanta caves India

January 2015

I had travelled to many parts of India, but not to Ellora and Ajanta, the two most significant architectural heritage sites - about time.

In Mumbai, I stayed with my niece for one night. I had no interest in Mumbai, a vast metropolis famous for Bollywood movies. Travel from the airport to their house through heavy traffic and crowded roads settled the issue. After a day of catching up and enjoying home food, I took a night sleeper bus to Aurangabad at 300 km distance. On a hilly upland terrain in Deccan hills, Aurangabad, once the mighty capital of powerful Mughal Empire, was busier than Mumbai. Cars crawled the roads because of swerving scooters from all sides. It was mad.

Before catching my connecting bus to Ellora, 30 km away, I had my brunch. This Muslim predominated area was a delight for non- vegetarian gourmet. I had naan bread served with khaliya, a slow-cooked spicy mutton curry, hot but delicious.

My budget hotel, appropriately named Hotel Kailas, was next to the Ellora caves. In the nearby truckers' place, I had my dinner of chapatis and very spicy dahl. I chatted with the only waiter cum cashier. He could not finish school when his father became ill as he needed a job. Now, from only a waiter, owner trusted him to manage the cash after only six months, he proudly stated. He earned almost two dollars a day, more than his father managed after working on the fields.

Ellora   I walked to the entrance before the busloads of visitors came. Ellora was the largest rock-cut monastery-temple cave complexes in the world. Jain, Buddhist and Hindu caves here dated from 7th to 11th century AD. About one hundred caves were excavated from the cliffs in Charanandri Hills. Only a third was open to the public. There were 5 Jain, 12 Buddhist and 17 Hindu caves: each group of caves, epitomising divinity and mythologies prevalent of the respective religion.

Five Jain caves, excavated in the 9th century, belonged to the Diagambara sect. Their monastic practice was of neither possessing nor wearing any clothes. Caves here had pillared verandas, symmetric mandapa for worship and depiction of twenty-four Jinas - spirituals who had gained liberation from the endless cycle of rebirths.

These temple caves also included carvings of gods and goddesses, Yaksa and Yaksi (male and female nature deity) and human devotees from Jain mythology of 1st millennium. On the hill, over 500 steps was a Jain temple dated 1234 Ad. A tall rock-carved image of Lord Parshvanath stood flanked by Dharendra and Padmavati.

In the Hindu cave complexes, built between the 7th and 11th century, was Kailash Temple, dedicated to Lord Shiva, the largest single monolithic rock excavation in the world. This chariot shaped monument was carved with a gateway, an assembly hall, a main multi-storey temple surrounded by an integrated space for gatherings, an inner sanctum where the Lord lived and a spire. Shaped like Mount Kailash, all of this was carved from one rock! Sculptures of gods, goddesses and mythologies found in Shaktism and Vaishnavism adorned its walls. Large sections of the wall showed stories from two major Hindu epics, Ramayana and Mahabharata. Within the complex were shrines carved from the same rock dedicated to many Vedic and non-Vedic gods and goddesses.

Kailash temple, a freestanding, multi-level temple complex covered an area twice the size of Parthenon in Athens. Approximately 200,000 tonnes of stone was excavated to build this - mind-boggling.
Amongst other Hindu caves was Dhumar Lena, one of the earliest excavations in Ellora. This temple centred around 'Vale Ganga', a natural waterfall integrated into the monument. It falls over Lord Shiva's brow during the monsoon season. Rameshwar Lena cave depicted Parvati and Shiva at leisure, Parvati's wedding to Shiva and the dancing Shiva. In another cave was a carving of Surya, the sun in its ceiling.

Walking between the caves was boiling. But once inside a cave, it was a different world. After grabbing a cold drink, I walked to the Buddhist caves.

Eleven out of twelve Buddhist caves comprised Viharas, monasteries with prayer halls. Large, multi-storeyed buildings, carved into the mountain face, included living quarters, kitchens and other rooms. Monastery caves had shrines, including carvings of Buddha and Buddhist saints. Striking amongst the Buddhist caves stood a worship hall named Vishwakarma cave, built around 650 AD. Also known as the 'Carpenter's Cave', because the rocks had a finish giving the appearance of wooden beams. Beyond its multi-storeyed entry was a cathedral-like stupa hall, a prayer house. A 4.5m statue of Buddha seated in a preaching pose in the heart of the cave.

Caves important to three main religions of India built here close to one another illustrated the religious harmony existing in ancient India. Coming out of the complex, I reflected that this place, while displaying unique artistic expression and technological ingenuity in the 1st millennium, also showed the spirit of tolerance that was so distinctive of ancient India.

How much of that spirit we needed now.

Ajanta Early morning the bus arrived in Ajanta as the place was opening. The site was smaller than Ellora, with approximately thirty caves within the rocky walls of a U-shaped gorge of the Wagur River. Several waterfalls in the canyon were now dry in January.

Buddhist caves in Ajanta were dated from 2nd century BC to about 480 AD. They served as monsoon retreats for monks, and a resting site for merchants and pilgrims in ancient India. Many of the excavated thirty caves were monasteries, while others were prayer halls featuring Buddha in praying or teaching postures. Chinese Buddhist travellers to India in the medieval period had recorded Ajanta Caves in their memoirs. Ajanta remained covered by jungle until accidentally found in the early 19th century by a British colonial officer on a tiger hunting party.

Ajanta caves are the finest surviving examples of ancient Indian art with expressive paintings presenting emotions through gesture, pose and form. These caves were built in two distinct periods. First during the 2nd century BC to the 1st century Ad, and the others several centuries later. Ajanta caves had the most elaborate carved facades, with relief sculptures on entablature and decorative carving and paintings on the walls and ceilings. Some of these artworks were in a fair state of preservation, but most were damaged.

Scenes depicted were mostly didactic, devotional, and ornamental. Paintings included stories of Buddha's former lives as a Bodhisattva, the life of Gautama Buddha, and his veneration. Two most famous individual painted images at Ajanta were two over-life-size figures of protective Bodhisattvas, Padmapani and Vajrapani on either side in the first cave.

The second cave is best known for its feminine focus, showing many noble and powerful women in prominent roles in society. A 5th-century fresco in a cave showed children at a school. Those in the front rows were paying attention to the teacher, while those in the back distracted and acting up - nothing has changed!

Depictions in the caves through carvings and paintings weaved in the norms of the early 1st-millennium Indian culture and society. Themes were diverse - a shipwreck; a princess applying makeup; lovers in scenes of dalliance; and a wine-drinking scene of a couple with the woman and man amorously seated. Ajanta paintings also gave valuable insight into the socio-economic state in ancient India. Particularly to Indian interactions with foreign cultures. Pictures of many foreigners illustrated the cosmopolitan character of Buddhism, which opened its way to men of all races, Greek, Persian, Pahlava and Huns.

Ajanta cave arts are a window into the culture, society and religiosity of India shining a light on the life here around one thousand years back. An inscription here read '*a memorial on the mountain that will endure for as long as the moon and the sun continue*'.

Sitting on a step by a cave in this extraordinary place, I genuinely hoped so.

World Cup Cricket Final Melbourne Australia

March 2015

I dreamed of watching the world cup cricket final in Melbourne Stadium with 100,000 people. Even though I was back in the UK, soon as tickets were for sale online, I purchased three. Two to treat my closest friends.

Alfaz and I left London and met up with Sanku from Kolkata at Tullamarine Airport.

In my previous visit to Melbourne, I did not get to explore the city. Three of us strolled around Melbourne by Yarra River. We wandered by the riverbank in bright sunshine, eating ice cream, before going to the National Gallery of Victoria, Australia's oldest and largest public museum. Brilliant collections of Chinese art, Australian indigenous art and artefacts, colonial and contemporary Australian art. Collections of old masters like Cezanne, Constable, Van Dyck and Dali picked great interest for Sanku, himself an artist.

In the evening, we watched on a giant screen TV the semi-final between India and Australia. Unfortunately, India lost badly.

Next day, a tram to St Kilda beach 6 km south, a sandy beach full of sunbathers and joggers. Swimmers and windsurfers played in warm seawater. We settled in a restaurant and gorged ourselves to a lovely seafood lunch.

On Saturday, the day before the final, we arrived at busy Flinders Street Station. We sat eating ice cream at Federation Square by Princes Bridge, watching the spectacles of street shows nearby. Then we walked by the riverbank, to have a glimpse of the famous Rod Laver tennis arena. From there, at a distance, we could see the famous MCG, Melbourne Cricket Ground. Already, the day before the final, many cricket related fun activities were going on.

Final was due to start at 2 pm. But we wanted to get there well before, to enjoy the atmosphere. By ten in the morning, Federation Square was already full of people. We joined a procession of people going to MCG only 1 km away. Lot more fun and interactive sports on the way, from face painting in Aussie or Kiwi colours to mini-competitions of bowling and batting. Slowly we made our way to the massive stadium, outside already filled with people.

MCG as a shrine is to Melbourne what the Opera House is to Sydney, the Eiffel Tower to Paris. It was the birthplace of Test cricket in 1877 and one-day international cricket in 1971. The main stadium for 1956 Olympic Games, it attracted up to 100,000 fans during the annual Australian Rule Football League Grand Final.

Around the stadium, we walked amongst thousands of spectators, buzzing with excitement. People in yellow Aussie colour tee-shirts and banners were everywhere, interspersed with some black and white Kiwi colours. In places were also people in blue Indian tee-shirts holding tri-coloured Indian flags and banners, although sadly India was already out. Making our way through this festival of colours and merriment, we frequently stopped before the statues of giants of Australian cricket like Donald Bradman, Keith Miller, Dennis Lillee and Shane Warne. There were also statues of great Australian rule football players and athletes we did not recognise.

At midday, they allowed us into the stadium. We rushed in with thousands through one of its many gates. From inside, the place looked massive and even more impressive. Famous sports museum in the grounds with thousands of its memorabilia was closed. We found some snack lunch to settle down in our seats, well before the game was due to start. By one-thirty, the stadium was full. Supporters of two teams began chanting.

At two pm, an indigenous Australian lady in bright-coloured clothes entered the stadium. She welcomed everyone to her homeland. Soon it was time for the festivities on the ground. Adults and children paraded with banners of all participating fourteen nations. Then umpires and the captains of both teams, Michael Clark and Brendon McCullum entered the grounds for the toss amongst deafening cheering sounds from all around. New Zealand won the toss and elected to bat.

The match started. Crowds cheered between each delivery. But in the fifth ball of the first over, the left-hand bowler Mitchell Starc bowled Brendon McCullum with a beautiful inswinger. An eerie silence all over the ground for a few seconds before loud cheers from the Aussie crowd. We knew the game was over. After all the build-up, it was anticlimax from then on. New Zealand struggled and was all out for meagre 183 in 45 overs. Australia reached the score easily in 33 overs, losing only three wickets.

The ground now burst with songs and chants and fireworks in the background. After the presentation was over, we left the stadium. Despite a massive world record crowd of over 93,000, not a single litter anywhere inside or outside the stadium. A lot of merriment, but not a single incidence of an alcohol-related nuisance, before or after the game - most impressive.

Next morning, we arrived at the airport for Sanku's flight to Kolkata. Our flight was much later. Earlier Alfaz had surprised me by saying although he had been to Australia before, he had never seen a kangaroo! In a hired car, we drove for only fifteen minutes to the Woodland National Park. My friend had his first sight of eastern grey kangaroos in dozens, including some mothers with their babies in their pouches – a big smile came on his face.

China, Tibet, Everest Base camp, Vietnam, Cambodia

September 2015

I have admired China's independence struggle, fighting three colonial powers only a few decades back and its progress in the lives of its millions in the country since.

China

Arriving in Beijing in the evening, I strolled looking for somewhere to eat. To my delight, nearby about two dozen street food stalls sold exotic looking foods - hand-pulled noodle soup, grilled fish, dumplings, hot pot or grill of varieties of meat, steamed or fried noodles, fried rice and steamed vegetables. My attention drew to the fried scorpion, crickets, spiders, bullfrog and other smaller creatures. People on the way home from work were

queuing up. Along with fried noodle and grilled fish, I bought a stick of fried crickets. The crunchy insects were not bad at all!

Great Wall of China

Great Wall of China, most well-known of the Seven Wonders of the World, was my first destination. Mutianyu section of the Great Wall was 70km outside the city centre. After spotless clean roads with orderly heavy traffic past high-rise apartment blocks, the countryside had many factories, the principal cause of Beijing's environmental pollution apart from its number of cars.

The Great Wall of China has so far been the most impressive architectural feats in human history. This series of fortification started as early as 7th century BC and completed by Ming dynasty in the mid-17th century. The entire wall, with all its branches, measured 21,196 km.

The Great wall measured almost 8m high and 5m wide. Both sides of the wall had crenellated parapet for soldiers to fire arrows at the enemy. Here on an ascending mountain ridge were 23 watchtowers spaced at about 100m. It was steep. The wall had some branches which ended up with watchtowers on hill ridges. Most in our group stopped at tower 6, only three of us climbed higher with the guide.

The climb got steeper, but the panoramic view of the wall against the hills and forest was captivating. With still three more watchtowers to go in this 2.2 km walk, the couple in our group called it a day. It was only me, my guide and a lively group of Chinese young men and women. I joined them and chatted. Most could speak and understand English. They were in their first year in an Engineering college.

Now the walk became like a Grade 2 climb. In some places on steep steps, we needed to go on hands and knees to go up. After turning the corner next to a watchtower was a poster of Chairman Mao with his quotation. My college friends translated - 'If you don't get to the Great Wall, you're not a man.'

My new friends said education at all levels in China was free. I asked what they thought of Mao Zedong. The impression I got from this group of young Chinese and my guide was they revered him as a lovable great grandfather who made the liberation of the country possible and made the lives of millions of people better. They were happy to ignore some mistakes made during his era well before they were born.

Finally, we reached the topmost tower, tower 23. We could see the Great Wall stretching over the mountains to infinitude in both directions. An incredible sight. We took some photographs together, wondering and laughing if anyone from outer space could see us and was taking a photo. Soon we started going down carefully, in one dangerously steep section on all fours.

Beijing   Back in Beijing, I visited the Summer Palace and the imperial garden centred on Longevity Hill and Kunming Lake with small islands in its middle. By the lake, a 728m long corridor had its pillars, beams and ceilings decorated with paintings of famous places in China, scenes from mythology and folktales and landscapes along with flowers, birds, fish, and insects. Over 14,000 images, all different. After walking through this beautiful display, we exited by the Marble Boat - a beautiful stone made boat, not navigable, only as decoration.

We then took a ride in a colourful old-style boat across the lake with an impressive view of the opulent summer palace beyond the lake.

For the evening, I had booked The Legend of Kung Fu Show at the Red Theatre. After an acrobatic display, best kung fu practitioners from all across China narrated the story about a young boy who dreamed of becoming a Kung Fu master and reaching enlightenment. In his path of becoming a master, he faces many obstacles, both from this world and of his mind to overcome his fears - a captivating spectacle of martial arts by hugely talented performers.

Tiananmen Square   Tiananmen Square in bright morning sunshine looked massive. National parades were held here to celebrate milestones in the birth of the Republic of China. Walking in this colossal square, between the Forbidden City on one side and the Great Hall of the People, and the National Museum of China on the other, I came across the Monument of People's Heroes.

I stood by this ten-story obelisk, erected as a national monument of China to the martyrs of revolutionary struggle during the 19th and 20th centuries. I could not stop thinking of the pictures on TV of an unknown protester in this square, who stood in front of a column of tanks leaving Tiananmen Square on June 5, 1989. A day before this picture, the Chinese military had suppressed protests at this square, its Chinese name meant 'Gate of Heavenly Peace.' They had fired from tanks and rifles at demonstrators seeking democracy killing between two to three thousand and wounding many more. I stood in silence in memory of the martyrs who liberated the country and also of those who sought democracy.

Nearby was a big line to get into Mausoleum of Mao Zedong. I gave it a miss and instead went to the Great Hall of People, the place for legislative and ceremonial activities of the People's Republic of China. Designed to symbolise national unity and ethnic equality of the nation, Great Hall embodied the new Chinese character of time in its features, proportion and details and could hold ten thousand people. I stood there thinking of the role this place had played in this nation's history and would play in the future for the rest of the world.

Forbidden City   Across the top of Tiananmen Gate to the Forbidden City, was an enormous poster of Mao Zedong and the Chinese national flag. Forbidden City complex of nearly one thousand buildings was built between 1406 and 1420 by more than a million workers. After entering via the Gate with its large watchtower, we came into a large square, with meandering Inner Golden Water River, with five bridges.

Standing almost 30m above the square at one end was Hall of Supreme Harmony, once the ceremonial centre of imperial power, and the largest surviving wooden structure in China. The inner Court had several palaces. Centrally placed Palaces were residences of the emperor and his immediate family. Surrounding buildings were for the distant relatives and the imperial consorts.

Religion played an essential role throughout Ming and Qing dynasties. There were sites for Shamanist ceremony and native Taoist religion. Temples and shrines devoted to Tibetan Buddhism or Lamaism scattered the Inner Court. Interestingly Swastika sign of Hindu religion decorated some walls. To the north stood Jingshan Park, known as Prospect Hill, an artificial hill created from the soil excavated to build the moat around the tall walls.

Forbidden City was the culmination of the two-thousand-years of development of classical Chinese architecture, meticulously planned to reflect philosophical and religious principles. Above all, it symbolised the majesty of Imperial power. Yellow was the colour of Emperor, and all roofs in the Forbidden City had yellow glazed tiles except in the library at the Pavilion of Literary Profundity.

In 1860, during the Opium war fought by the Anglo-French forces on behalf of the drug traffickers with full blessings of British and French Government, foreign troops took control of the Forbidden City. They occupied it until the end of the war. In 1933, the Japanese invasion of China resulted in the looting of the national treasures in this place.

Saturated with history of imperial power and of foreign invasion, later in the day, we visited The Temple of Heaven, a complex of religious buildings in another part of Beijing. This temple, well known for its annual ceremony of prayer to Heaven for a good harvest, was also a shrine for newlyweds seeking eternal marital bliss. While we were there, a bride in her flowing wedding dress and a shy husband in a suit, came to pay their respects and for photographs.

Before returning to my hotel, we drove by the spectacular Birds Nest stadium, site of 2008 Olympics. One of the most successful recent Olympics.

In the evening was a dinner of Peking duck, a delicacy I had heard so much - luscious.

Tibet

Lhasa From Lhasa airport, the road to the city, followed Yarlung Tsangpo River, a tributary of great Brahmaputra River. Lhasa, 3656m in the centre of Tibetan Plateau, was surrounded by mountains rising to 5,500m. The guide said for many years, chemical and car-making plants opened around these suburbs, resulting in significant pollution. Only now this was changing.

Over an ornate bridge, we entered the city. With a mild headache, I wandered the streets for a while before settling in. My hotel even had a provision of Oxygen in the room if anyone wanted. I declined.

Next morning a visit to the Potala Palace 3700m, the extensive iconic complex visible from far. In its vast gardens, groups of locals and pilgrims danced and chanted to religious music coming out of loudspeakers.

Lobsang Gyatso, 5th Dalai Lama, who unified Tibet, moved his administration to Lhasa in 1642. Named after Mount Potalaka, the mythical abode of Bodhisattva Avalokitesvara, it had been the winter palace of Dalai Lama from 1649 to 1959. Thirteen storeys of buildings, containing over 1,000 rooms, 10,000 shrines and about 200,000 statues, soared 117m on top of the Red Hill.

It had two sections. The White Palace served as administrative area and along with courts of successive Dalai Lama, now had offices of the Tibetan government. The higher Red Palace was a religious section. A mecca for Buddhists around the world, it had ten thousand painted scrolls, hundreds of murals, and thousands of exquisite statues made from precious alloys and jewels. Inside were the tombs of eight Dalai Lamas and many shrines. Butter lamps lighted the hallways and monks stood in every area, ensuring the dignity of the place.

Its chapels were dedicated to the study of Buddhism and its advancement. Mausoleum of fifth Dalai Lama stood five stories high, laid with gold, diamonds, pearls, and other precious gems. Housed within this unique stone and wood structure were artefacts from Tibetan history, religion, and culture. Centuries-old statues of Buddha, murals, and antiques graced every area.

On top of the Red Palace was a unique view of the golden roof of the palace. Seven roofs made of gilded bronze, decorated with flower-and-bell-shaped spires, glittered magnificently. From the top, there was a marvellous view of Lhasa, below the floating clouds.

Lhasa had long been a beacon for both Tibetan and foreign Buddhists and had many ethnically and religiously distinct communities, including Kashmiri Muslims and Ladakh merchants.

Potala Palace was captured and looted many times. In 1904, a British force had entered, forcing the Dalai Lama to leave. Later, in 1959, China invaded the place, resulting in the current Dalai Lama's exile. In the mid-60s, during the Chinese Cultural Revolution, the palace suffered significant damage. But now it was a world heritage site.

Jokhang Monastery, in Barkhor Square, is considered by Tibetans as the most sacred and important temple in the country. Built in 652, among many images in the temple, was 7th century small wooden Buddha statue. During the Cultural Revolution, the Chinese had smashed the clay image. The temple complex had over 3,000 images of Buddha, other deities, manuscripts and other objects. On the rooftop, an iconic statue of a golden deer flanked a Dharma wheel. From this place over the centuries, Dalai Lama was selected.

Next day was at the Sera Monastery on Lhasa outskirts. Set against hilly terrain, the largest university monasteries in Tibet, the colleges here trained monks over a 20-year programme of philosophical knowledge.

Sitting on the steps of Avalokitesvara temple, I watched with intrigue in a small courtyard debate among trainee monks in the presence of their teachers. The discussion opened with an invocation to Buddhist Goddess Manjushri in a loud and high-pitched tone, punctuated with vigorous gestures. Each gesture had meaning. Debater presented his case, clapping loudly to stress power and decisiveness of his argument. Then he made circles with his hand around the defender's head, followed by loud screaming to unnerve the defender. Loud clapping and intense verbal exchanges followed for a while. The teacher acknowledged by bringing back of his right hand to his left palm when a question was answered correctly – a unique experience. In the large nunnery here, debating practices were similar.

A Buddhist shrine in the monastery had a long queue of parents with their babies. A monk anointed every child with the shoot from a burning lamp. Parents believed if anointed early, children do not become naughty growing up. I thought of bringing my twin toddler granddaughters as soon as possible.

We then drove through part of the Silk Road in beautiful roads and tunnels. Through the vast plateau, we went along the valley of the Kyi Chu River and then to its confluence with Yarlung Zangbo River with the majestic mountains at a distance. In early autumn, only a few had snow on their peaks. Farmers worked in large fields with machinery. Bored, magnificent yaks stood by unwanted.

As often, I was the solo traveller and had ample opportunity to talk to my Tibetan guide, and with her interpreting, with the driver. The guide was in her early thirties, her husband ran a small business in Lhasa, and they had no children. She was born in a village, not very far from the road we were taking, about 150km outside Lhasa. After finishing school, she had been to a college in a town in mainland China for her tourism training. The driver in his 60s had one son, who worked in an office near his hometown.

Soon we arrived at the massive 72km long Yamdrok Lake, one of the three largest sacred lakes in Tibet. By the lake, farmers used yaks for farming. I asked to stop when I saw several monks on its bank, a few of them enjoying a run with their robes flying in the air. This lake was home to the famous Samding Monastery, associated with Padmasambhava, the Second Buddha, who brought Buddhism to Tibet in 8th century Ad. The monastery, on a peninsula, jutted into the lake – the only Tibetan monastery, headed by a female re-incarnation.

We carried on by the lake before stopping on a pass. Then walked up a hill to a beautiful panorama of the highest Tibetan mountain at a distance against the turquoise lake.

My guide asked what kind of lunch I wanted. I said I would love to try local cuisine. She rang a relative. We stopped after a few kilometres. In a small village house, her auntie lived with her husband and their 15-year-old son. She was delighted to have an Indian guest in her house. She added a few more things to her already

home- cooked lunch. Soon the husband who worked for road maintenance came home. We had a family lunch talking. I loved the simple Tibetan food, rice and dahl as the main ingredient and some momo, a lovely dumpling with yak meat. We finished with Tibetan sweet tea - a fabulous experience.

By the time we arrived in Shigatse 3845m, nicknamed gateway to Everest, it was dark and cold. Shigatse hotel was delightful, with traditional Tibetan decorations and beautifully painted wooden beams. I don't take pictures of the hotels. But here I could not stop clicking my camera to capture some of its facades. I invited my guide and driver to join me for dinner.

We visited the Thashilhunpo Monastery briefly the next morning. The guide and the driver wanted to offer their prayers before the long journey ahead. The traditional seat of successive Panchen Lamas, the site was founded in 1447 by the 1st Dalai Lama and in its heyday had over 4000 monks and four Tantric colleges.

Soon we drove through Friendship Highway before taking a turn at Tingri town. Road surface now varied between tarmacs to gravel stretches with a stunning view all around. The zigzagging road through the mountain stopped at Gawu la Pass 5211m, one of the best spots in the world to enjoy a panoramic view of the Himalayan mountain range. The place was strewn with Tibetan Buddhist prayer flags, tied to almost every post and large rocks around.

I had my first sight of the north face of Everest and other peaks, Lhotse, Makalu, Cho Oyu and Shishapangma, all well above 8000m. I was ecstatic. Even at this altitude, the landscape was barren hills, not with snow and ice!

Through a hypnotising landscape, we drove for many more hours before reaching Rongbuk 5010m. We stopped by Rongbuk monastery, regularly mentioned in the diaries of early expeditions to Mt Everest in the 1920s and 1930s. It was a rare monastery in Tibet that housed Monks and Nuns together. To me, it was the best viewing deck of Mt. Everest in Tibet. I watched the majestic mountain under a clear sky for a long time in stunned silence. Magical lights from the setting sun reflected on its peak. Soon it got dark and with the wind picking up, freezing.

We then walked into the only guesthouse near the monastery. In its open kitchen cum reception, the lady owner offered us hot soup with a warm smile. Soon after throwing my stuff in my small bedroom, I joined rest of the boarders with my guide and the driver for a simple, hearty meal of tsampa, roasted barley, with steamed vegetable soup, followed by mugs of sweet tea.

The owner had been managing the place with her husband, a son and a daughter for many years. In the winter months, the guesthouse was usually empty when they go down to Tingri, where she was born.

By 9 pm, we all retired. I had to get up around midnight to go to the toilet on the other side of the courtyard. It was freezing. Moon was up in the clear sky. I could not resist staying outside for an enchanting view of the Everest in the moonlight.

Everest Base camp

After a breakfast of bread, yak butter and tea, we left for the base camp at 8km distance. From the car park, we walked through a mountain trail by the river flowing off the Eastern Rongbuk glacier for 2 km. And suddenly I was at the Everest base campsite on its northern route.

Everest from here in the morning sun looked unbelievable. Site of Camp One on the summit route was only a few kilometres up the mountain and did not appear very difficult. I so much wished that I could have gone up there. I tried to fantasise the northern route to its peak against the massive, beautiful mountain, through ice slopes and bare rocks. I tried to imagine if mountaineers were already there pitched up in their camps.

I felt fortunate to have visited both the Nepalese and the Tibetan Mt Everest base camps. After spending almost an hour there, sadly, it was time to leave.

I sat in silence, watching the vista through the car window. I must have nodded off when our driver stopped the car by the roadside. The guide motioned me to get out. On the side of the road, was an incredible sight - an imposing glacier was hanging between black rocks, right next to the road. We walked by a small stupa with prayer flags on a gentle rocky path to the bottom of the hanging glacier, only 20m above us. This glacier had originated at Mt Noijin Kansang 7197m and now hanging at its lower end, shining in the sunlight against the dark black stone gorge. We were at above 5000m – amazing!

During our dinner at Gyantse 4000m, we sat together and talked for a while. I asked what they thought of the Chinese coming and taking over Tibet. First, they corrected me, saying Tibet was an Autonomous Region, with its internal rules. Soon they opened up. They said there was no doubt the lives of people had improved. Even in the remotest village now there were schools and primary health care, free for all. But there were many destructions of religious sites in the 1960s during the so-called Cultural Revolution. Now there was more freedom of religious expression. Then they added despite all this; most Tibetans resent Chinese presence what they see as a takeover. Although there was autonomy, they felt like second-class citizens in their own home.

Next morning, we went to the 9th-century Palcho Monastery, the largest complex in Tibet. On a rugged hill, this monastery had gigantic paintings of Shakyamuni Buddha with two of his principal disciples, Maitreya and Manjushri on his side. The site was well known for the five centuries-old Gyantse festival, held in the fourth lunar month of the Tibetan Calendar. In 1904, British Soldiers attacked the town and the monastery. Bullet holes from this attack remain in the sanctuary to this day. Chinese ransacked this place again during the Cultural Revolution in the 60s.

We watched from the road the famous Gyantse Dzong, Gyantse Fortress, perched high above the town on a spur of grey-brown rock, one of the best-preserved dzong in Tibet. Gyantse was known as 'Hero City' because of the determined resistance of Tibetans against the far superior British Expeditionary forces to Tibet in 1903 and 1904. Chinese dynamited the walls again in 1967 during the Cultural Revolution. Now it has been restored.

I said goodbye to my Tibetan friends at Lhasa airport and left for Xian.

Xian   Xian from the aeroplane window looked cloudy. But as soon as I was out of the plane, I choked and realised it was thick pollution over the entire area. On the way to the city, in crowded streets, everyone wore face masks. Instead of my usual stroll in a new place, I stayed indoors for the evening to breathe.

Pollution was no better the next morning. On our way to the Terracotta Warrior Museum, several factories by roadside bellowed smoke.

Although Terracotta Warriors was the most famous visitor site, a skull found nearby was the oldest fossil of a Homo erectus ever found in northern Asia, dated 1.63 million years of age. Stone tools there dated before 2.1 million years, earliest known evidence of hominid outside of Africa.

Terracotta Army   Terracotta Army site was part of a much larger necropolis, ground-penetrating radar suggesting an area of 98 sq.km. This necropolis was constructed as a microcosm of the imperial palace of the first emperor. It comprised several offices, halls, stables and an imperial park around the tomb mound.

In three excavated pits, open to the public, were over 8000 soldiers, 130 chariots with 520 horses, and 150 cavalries.

The largest pit measured 230m by 62m. It had the main army of thousands of life-sized figures. In this massive site, all the soldiers and horses faced east in a rectangular array, each one armed with a long spear or dagger.

Behind the soldiers were horse-driven chariots. About every 3m, a wall fortified with wooden columns on brick floors separated the army into columns - rows of kneeling and standing archers, stood next to the chariots ready for war.

Smaller Pit two had cavalry and infantry units and chariots, representing a military guard. Pit three was the command post, with high-ranking officers and a war chariot. There was fire damage in some figures and some missed weapons, evidence of looting and subsequent burning of the site.

The museum had painstakingly restored the figures on display from the fragments. Figures varied in height and uniform according to their rank. Each of the thousands of soldiers had individual and different faces. Now only clay coloured, once all of them had coloured lacquer finish and unique facial features to give the figures a realistic feel. Excavation and restoration were still going on.

I returned to Pit one for another look. I stood in silence on the balcony overlooking this colossal display which had involved years of hard work by about 700,000 ordinary workers in 210-09 BC. Over 30,000 families were brought here only for this project, only to protect a powerful emperor in his afterlife! Recently outside this area, they found remains of 45 simple tombs of the workforce, who had died for this mammoth task.

A local farmer, Zhao Kangmin, who discovered the site in 1974, now worked at the museum and was around. I shook hands with him.

Xian City Walls Back in Xian, air pollution seemed marginally better, or maybe I was getting used to it. This ancient capital of China had one of the oldest and best-preserved 14 km city walls from the 14th century. Along the top of the wall, was a walkway with a moat, drawbridges, watchtowers and gate towers. We walked inside the fortification by an archery Tower, once providing security to one of the four gates of the wall.

Traditional Chinese folk dance   My evening was at the Tang Dynasty Palace to watch traditional Chinese folk dance with dinner. In the auditorium holding over 600 diners, after delicious courses of the meal, the dancing programme started.

First, was the ethnic minority folk dance. China had 56 ethnic minorities, each with a characteristic set of folk dances. Dancers in colourful costumes shared common themes of rivalry, jealously, love, forgiveness, marital bliss and communal bond. Soon followed the Court dance of Tang Dynasty, depicting tradition and style of classical Xian. Next, was Prince Qin's Cavalry dance celebrating the might and grandeur of the imperial army.

After the break, started the most popular Chinese folk dance, lion dance. In Chinese culture, lion symbolised power, wisdom and superiority. Two dancers performed in a lion costume- one in front was the head and front limb, other behind the back and hind legs. They finished to rapturous applause. Soon followed Dragon Dance which I enjoyed more because of its acrobatics. Writhing antics of the dragon required leaps by about 50 dancers animating to suggest undulating, swooping motions of an enormous creature - a captivating evening of culture.

Shanghai   At Xian airport, waiting for my flight, I met a Chinese couple in their sixties, both retired, the woman only recently. They were going to Shanghai for the first time for a holiday. The retired man worked in a factory. I learnt from him the pension he was having from his job and the government was more than adequate. He was more than happy with the way his country was going. He got agitated when I asked him his impression of the Cultural Revolution when he was in his youth. He curtly said in the history of any country; there will always be a period about which the future generation would look back and think they should have acted differently.

Time to get on board.

In Shanghai, I walked in the evening by Bund, a beautiful waterfront promenade lined with colonial-era buildings. Across Huangpu River was the much-photographed Pudong district's futuristic skyline with 632m Shanghai Tower and Oriental Pearl TV Tower with its pink spheres. The waterfront bustled with people of all ages, promenading with family and friends.

I returned via a small street lined with shops selling traditional Chinese festival goods: coloured lanterns, wind chimes and dragons made of paper and many other vibrant decorations.

A brief visit next morning to the impressive Shanghai Museum, designed in the shape of an ancient cooking vessel called 'ding'. The collection contained priceless Ancient Chinese sculpture, bronze, ceramics, coins and seals including one from Genghis Khan. It also had an extensive selection of ancient paintings, calligraphy and arts and crafts by Chinese minority groups. Carved lacquer furniture from Ming and Qing dynasties looked flamboyant and not that comfortable.

Shanghai's Old City was full of people in its warren of narrow alleys. Small shops sold antiques, jewellery and souvenirs. Noodle houses serving soup dumplings made me feel hungry. I sat down with my guide for lunch along with a crowd of children munching sesame-seed candy after finishing their lunch. On my guide's recommendation, I ordered a plate of savoury Tangyuan and enjoyed the ambience.

Only a small part of the Old City walls had survived with a small tower. After crossing over the zig-zagging bridge, we came to Ming Dynasty City God Temple, highly revered in Shanghai. This Taoist temple included nine palaces and enshrined three town gods. Cockfighting and open-air acrobatic performances were going on. People bought snacks watching the performances. I could not resist purchasing some steamed crab buns.

After passing by many temples, we came to the famous Yu Garden, a traditional Chinese Ming-style private garden, built in the 16th century. It had been ransacked and restored several times. Yu garden aimed to represent the world in miniature with its rivers, mountains and villages. It had six scenic areas with no geometric shapes. This unique garden in its design perfectly blended decorative halls, elaborate pavilions, glittering lotus pools, zigzag bridges, pagodas, archways, and rockeries.

In the garden stood the famed Jade rock, a large spiky 14m rock, built with thousands of tons of stone. We walked over the Jiu Qu Bridge, the Nine-Turn Bridge. Chinese believe the number nine symbolised auspiciousness and walking across this bridge brought good luck. In the centre was the Mid-Lake Pavilion Teahouse, the oldest teahouse in Shanghai offering a traditional tea ceremony. Kings, Queens and other dignitaries had visited the place over the years. I looked at the price and decided I was not VIP enough.

Instead, we visited Yuyuan Bazaar, outside Yu Garden. In this lively place, families crowded narrow lanes to buy daily supplies and modern handicrafts, festive goods and jewellery. I sat with my guide in a coffee shop. He said Shanghai was a major centre of higher education in China with fifty universities and colleges, including four of the most prestigious universities in China. He proudly said he went to one of them for his tourism degree.

I returned to the Bund in the evening. Walking amongst hundreds of families at leisure, I reflected on this massive country with almost a fifth of the world population. Through a small window of my visit, I found its people were overall happy. There were areas, like most countries, it could do better. China had decent healthcare, education and infrastructure. Everywhere was spotlessly clean. When I spoke to people about the excesses of the 60s and late 80s, I soon realised that these events were over 30 years or more back. China had moved on. I wondered how many people of the current generation in the west reflect on the excesses of their countries affecting other countries around the world in the 60s or even in the 90s!

Vietnam

September 2015

In the 1960s, in my youth, I had raged at the way France, and then the USA had systematically tried to destroy Vietnam, only because it wanted to be independent of colonial powers. I was appalled with the barbaric atrocity against humanity. Neighbouring Cambodia was caught up in this, resulting in even greater human tragedy. I wanted to visit these countries and meet its people.

Hanoi   From my accommodation in the Old quarters, I walked to the Hoan Kiem Lake and Ngoc Son Temple. The road was busy with hundreds of scooters. Small street blocks and alleys, with its traditional Vietnamese atmosphere, reminded me of some parts of old Kolkata in the 60s, except for the orderly traffic here.

In the middle of the busy city, Hoan Kiem Lake was a peaceful retreat. Ngoc Son Temple, a pagoda, sat in the centre of the lake. I sat by the lake enjoying the tranquil atmosphere until dark.

Later, in a tiny restaurant, I enjoyed delicious Bun Thang, rice Vermicelli with chicken and egg.

France colonised Vietnam from 1883 to 1945. Between 1940 and 1945, Japanese forces occupied Hanoi. Under Ho Chi Minh's leadership, Hanoi was liberated in 1945, briefly becoming the capital of the newly independent country, the Democratic Republic of Vietnam. The French returned and reoccupied the city in 1946. After nine years of fighting between the French and Viet Minh forces, culminating in the humiliating defeat of the French army at Dien Bien Phu, Hanoi became capital of an independent North Vietnam in 1954.

Ho Chin Min Mausoleum Complex   I was eagerly looking forward to visiting the Ho Chi Minh Mausoleum Complex. At large Ba Dinh Square, there were banners of the 70th-year celebration of the declaration of independent Vietnam. At one end of the square stood the Ho Chi Minh's Mausoleum, constructed in 1990 on his birth centenary. Each province contributed with their signature material to build the Mausoleum, expressing the country's love for the exceptional leader and indicating Vietnam's national unity.

Inside the Mausoleum, I stood in silence before Ho Chi Minh's famous quote *'Nothing is more precious than Freedom and Independence.'* The mausoleum held embalmed remains of Uncle Ho. Although when President Ho was alive, he had asked for a simple burial. He wanted cremation and then burial in three parts of Vietnam. The first part in the North, where he worked; the second in the Middle, his homeland and the last one in the South, where he started his journey to free Vietnam.

Ho Chi Minh, the most iconic national hero of Vietnam, was Prime Minister and then President of North Vietnam from 1945 to 1969. Under his lead, Vietnamese people succeeded in the resistance war against French colonialism and stood up against the aggression of the mighty USA.

At another end of the square stood the massive Presidential Palace, built in French colonial architectural style. After Vietnam achieved independence in 1954, Ho Chi Minh refused to live there. He said it was unsuitable for him to live in such luxury while people in the country were poor and starving. Instead, he lived in a small house in the garden which once belonged to an electrician. The palace was used for meeting state guests and for the Vietnamese children to come and visit their beloved Uncle Ho.

Uncle Ho was asked to replace the old and out-of-date furniture in the house. He refused by saying 'they are good and are gifts from my friends, nothing can be compared.'

President Ho later moved to a stilt house nearby, built in the design similar to homes in Northern mountainous areas, to remind him of arduous days preparing for the Revolution. This house had two floors. The lower one was the meeting area while the upper one had only a bedroom and a study with a bookshelf - simple and pure lifestyle. Walking around the place with trees from various sites of Vietnam and a small fish pond, my reverence for this great revolutionary was stronger than ever.

Ho Chi Minh's House

Nearby was One Pillar Pagoda, a unique piece of architecture, built in 1049 in the middle of a small square lake full of lotus. It harmoniously combined pagoda and a tower standing on one pillar, resembling a lotus blossoming from the pond.

Ho Chi Minh Museum was at the other end of the complex, dedicated to Ho's life, showing his upbringing and travel around the world to find support and to rescue the country from colonialism. I sat by the musical gift shop where a man played Dan Bau, a one-string instrument to beautiful music. He was kind enough to let me video record his song.

There I met an elderly couple sitting under the shade of a tree. Through my guide, I talked to them. The man was 82yrs old, and his wife was 75yrs. I learnt with fascination and reverence that the man, as a Vietcong, had fought against the USA until the country's liberation. He narrated his stories of building tunnels to survive Napalm bombings. In 1967, as a medical student, I had donated blood for Vietnamese Liberation fighters through the Indian Red Cross and felt proud when he agreed to let me have a photograph taken with him.

Temple of Literature   Later, I visited the Temple of Literature, the site of one of the oldest university in the world, established in 1010. This revered place had seen thousands of scholars graduate and now was a memorial to education and literature. Dedicated to Confucius, in various pavilions and halls, were statues and artefacts. One hundred stone stela of doctors (scholars) were carved in blue stone-turtles to honour the talent and encourage study - turtle being the symbol of longevity and wisdom. Stela depicted names and birthplaces of 1307 graduates and 82 triennial royal exams. With its many courtyards and halls, it was an excellent piece of history of learning in a serene environment.

Water Puppet Theatre show   The evening was at the world-famous Thang Long Water Puppet Theatre. The tradition of water puppet shows dated back to the 11th century. When rice paddy fields were flooded, the villagers made entertainment by standing in waist-deep water with the puppets. The performance started with a brilliant orchestra playing traditional music using drums, wooden bells, horns, bamboo flutes and cymbals.

In brief sketches, the puppets took us on a journey of the ancient village life, a celebration of rice harvest and dances of mythical creatures with humour. Operatic songs narrated the story, acted out by the puppets. I had experienced nothing like this - outstanding.

Ho Chi Minh City   Ho Chi Minh City, known previously as Saigon, was a busy metropolis, very unlike Hanoi and could easily have been one in the western world.

In October 2005, a rumour went around the 19th century Notre Dame Cathedral. Virgin Mary statue had shed tears! Although top clergy of the church could not confirm this, thousands flocked to see the icon for days.

Cu Chi Tunnel   I could not believe the famous Cu Chi tunnels were so close to the perimeters of Saigon, which was once teeming with US and South Vietnamese troops. Cu Chi tunnels were an immense network of connecting tunnels in Cu Chi district. They were part of a much more extensive intricate network of tunnels, once present in much of the country. Cu Chi tunnels were the location of several military campaigns during the Vietnam War, including the famous Tet offensive in 1968.

Arriving at Ben Dinh site, part of the 125 km preserved tunnels; I could not see any tunnel. The place looked like a field. Then guide lifted an area of grass, like a trapdoor, from the ground. I dropped inside a narrow opening and put the lid back. Although to accommodate tourists, now the tunnels were enlarged with lights inside, even now they were just high and wide enough to crawl. We explored parts of the tunnel with its recesses and corridors. Then, after giving us a warning, they switched off the light. We followed the guide with his head torch in the dark warren of narrow corridors, careful not to bang our heads, only for a minute - an incredible experience.

For the Viet Cong, life in tunnels was harsh. Food, water and even air to breathe were scarce. Most of the time, soldiers spent the day in the tunnels working or resting, out only at night to scavenge for supplies, tend their crops, or engage in battle. Sickness, especially malaria, was rampant. During the periods of massive bombing or American troop movement, they remained underground for many days at a time. Vietcong forces in their tunnels survived carpet bombing by B-52 bombers dropping 30-ton loads of high explosive, turning once lush jungles into a barren landscape. Inconceivably, Vietcong won the war and threw out the invading Americans.

Outside the tunnel, we saw displays of different booby traps Vietcongs used to protect the tunnel trap door entrances. Then in a small shop on bamboo stilt, we had a simple meal of rice with a dipping sauce, food that Vietcong fighters would have eaten. Nearby in the jungle was an enormous crater created by a B-52 bomb.

Exhibition House for Crimes of War and Aggression

(Exhibition house for the US and Puppet Crimes)

Visiting this museum was chilling, at the same time, heartbreaking account of recent human atrocity against the fellow human. Around the entrance was an extensive collection of captured or destroyed American rocket launchers, a Patton tank, F-5A fighter plane, Skyraider and Dragonfly attack bombers and even a daisy-cutter bomb weighing 6800kg. In one corner of the yard were several pieces of unexploded ordnance.

Once inside, there was a hush and sombre at the display of war atrocity through graphic photographs and artefacts. There was a powerful collection of 330 photos taken by 134 international journalists who worked throughout the Vietnam War.

A guillotine used by the French and South Vietnam soldiers until 1960 to execute prisoners was on display!

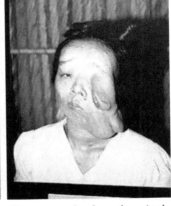

One area displayed effects on the population by Agent Orange and other chemical defoliants, and carpet bombing with Napalm and phosphorus bombs. A U.S. program, codenamed Operation Ranch Hand, sprayed over 20 million gallons herbicides including Agent Orange over Vietnam, Cambodia and Laos between 1961 and 1971. Agent Orange, deadly chemical dioxin, cause cancers and birth defects amongst the population. Effect of this continues almost forty years on.

Besides the massive environmental devastation and death of around 400,000 people, over half a million children had been born with severe congenital disabilities. Two million now have cancer or other illnesses. Claims by the hundreds of US veterans who also suffered exposure while dropping the bombs were settled in the US court. But claims by the Vietnam victims were dismissed. The museum had a few jars of severely deformed aborted human foetuses - the result of Agent Orange, bringing tears to most visitors.

Photographs there showed devastation by Napalm bombs, including the award-winning photos of a 1972 napalm attack. A single napalm bomb, generating a temperature over 1000°C, could destroy an area of up to 2000 sq.meter including its forest and human population. B-52 bombers dropped Napalm widely over Vietnam. The US dropped over eight million tons of bombs over Vietnam - three times the total bombing by all sides in WWII. Vietnam is only half the size of Texas.

Massacres　In the gallery of My Lai Massacre was stunned silence. In this most horrific incident of violence against unarmed civilians in the Vietnam War, a company of American soldiers brutally killed most of the people of My Lai village on March 16, 1968. They slaughtered 504 people, 182 women, 17 of them pregnant and 173 children, including 56 infants. Young girls and women were raped and mutilated before being killed. This brutality and the attempt of official cover-up fuelled anti-war sentiment and divided people in the USA over the Vietnam War.

Nearby was the gallery known as the sewer. In Thanh Phong village in 1969, a US SEAL team under the command of Bob Kerrey killed 20 civilians, including women and children. They stabbed an elderly grandfather who stepped out of the first thatched hut they encountered. With other photographs of the incident displayed was the sewer where the grandfather had hidden his three grandchildren. The US soldiers dragged them out of the sewer and stabbed two of them to death, one 8 yrs and the other 10 yrs old. Then they disembowelled the 6yr old.

Bob Kerrey was later awarded the Medal of Honour for heroism in combat and went on to serve as the Governor of Nebraska. In 1992, he was a nominee for the US Presidency and then served as US Senator until 2001. He only admitted to his crime in 2001 but was never punished.

My blood was boiling by the time I left the gallery.

Cambodia

October 2015

From Siem Reap airport, we drove to a group of Hindu temples built in the 10th century.

Preah Ko, the Sacred Bull, was the first temple built in the ancient and now defunct city of Hariharalaya by rulers of Khmer empire. Intricate carvings here included three-headed Nagas, the serpent, and a deity mounted on Kala, a ferocious monster associated with the destructive side of god Shiva. Bakong Temple Mountain was in the shape of a stepped pyramid, an example of early Khmer temple architecture. Bakong's striking similarity with Borobudur temple in Java suggested Borobudur served as a prototype of Bakong. Large statues of elephants stood as guardians at the corners of the pyramid, while lions guarded the stairways.

Prasat Krava dedicated to Vishnu had in its sanctuary a large bas-relief depicted Vishnu and Lakshmi. Four- armed Vishnu sat astride his vehicle Garuda, the legendary bird, holding the globe. Another depiction of an Eight-armed Vishnu showed him surmounted on a crocodile and surrounded by hundreds of tiny devotees and Lakshmi holding a lotus. In Lolei sandstone carvings had sky-god Indra mounted on an elephant, Airavata, surrounded by makaras, serpent-like monsters, and multi-headed snakes.

We arrived in Siem Reap in the evening, a small town with old colonial buildings and busy streets around a cluster of villages.

Angkor Wat Temple   Sky softened to a blue from dark over Angkor Wat on the shore of a wide moat. Floating golden clouds blushed against the outline of dark and enigmatic beauty. Sun rose behind the magnificent 12th century Temple City, and the sunlight gently caressed the lotus leaves in the moat in front - hypnotising.

Angkor Wat means City of Temples. This largest religious monument in the world was originally constructed as a Hindu temple. Breaking from Shiva tradition of previous kings, it was dedicated to Vishnu. Over the decades it was gradually transformed into a Buddhist shrine.

A long bridge over a 200m moat took us to the temple complex. Angkor Vat was built to embody Mount Meru, home of the gods. The central quincunx of towers symbolised the five peaks of the mountain.

Walls and moat represented the surrounding mountain ranges and the ocean. Within the 5km moat was a 3.6km long outer wall, with three rectangular galleries, each raised above the next. Gopuras stood at each of the cardinal points with towers. It's every side was with a library and a pond between the library and the temple itself. The temple stood at the centre with a pentagon of towers.

The temple was on a terrace made of three galleries, each level higher than the last, rising to a central tower. Inner walls had friezes with a series of large-scale scenes depicting episodes from Hindu epics, Ramayana and Mahabharata. In beautiful carvings, it showed the Battle in which Rama defeats Ravana and the Battle of Kurukshetra. On the eastern gallery was one of the most famous scenes, Churning of the Sea of Milk. The temple wall had around two thousand depictions of Apsara and Devata.

Stones of the walls were as smooth as polished marble and laid without mortar. Angkor Vat used up far greater amounts of stone than all the Egyptian pyramids combined and occupied an area significantly greater than modern-day Paris. Whereas the Egyptian pyramids used limestone quarried barely 0.5 km away, Angkor was built with sandstone quarried 40 km distance.

Being in this place of history and architectural beauty, I agreed with the description by the French naturalist Henri Mouhot who rediscovered this site in 1860. He wrote *'One of these temples, rival to that of Solomon, and erected by some ancient Michael Angelo - might take an honourable place beside our most beautiful buildings. It is grander than anything left to us by Greece or Rome.'*

Smiley Buddha Bayon   Built in the late 12th century as a state temple, Bayon stood at the centre of the old capital, Angkor Thom. Its upper terrace was home to the famous 'face towers' of Bayon. Each with four gigantic smiley Buddha. Anywhere I looked were numbers of serene and smiling stone faces on its towers. Temple complex here had over two hundred gigantic smiley Buddha faces, belonging to Bodhisattva of compassion, Avalokitesvara.

Walls of the gallery depicted historical events and scenes from everyday life of Angkor Khmer. It included a marching Khmer army with some Chinese soldiers. It also showed domestic scenes of Angkor houses, a market, open-air cooking, hunters, and women tending to children and even an invalid.

All of us were smiling like the Buddhas while leaving the site.

Vast Royal Square Phimeanakas was built in the 10th century, in the shape of a three-tier pyramid of a Hindu temple. Its tower was initially crowned with a golden pinnacle. Along with its five gopuras, there were two grand buildings on each side known as Khleangs, reception areas for visiting noblemen and ambassadors.

The ruined temple complex of Terrace of Elephants was an imposing 350m platform from which the King attended his victorious returning army and also used for public ceremonies. Decorations in its walls showed life-size garuda, lions and the famous parade of elephants with their mahouts.

The curious name of Terrace of Leper king referred to a statue of Leper King on the platform. Only a copy of the figure stood, showing the naked king in a seated position with his right knee raised. The theory was King Jayavarman VII was a leper. That is why he built many hospitals throughout his empire. Others thought the figure represented Kubera, the god of wealth, who was allegedly a leper.

The guide, our driver and I had our lunch in the pavilion under the trees by the moat overlooking the glorious Angkor Wat. On their recommendation, I had samlor machu trey, a sweet and sour soup with fish - delicious on a hot day. They said the country was only slowly recovering now after years of atrocities over decades from the 60s. Life expectancy has risen by almost 10yrs to 66yrs now. The long-neglected education system was slowly improving, albeit with many challenges. The guide told the story of a nearby village where the community found a place to build a primary school. It would have saved their children walking miles to their class. But when clearing out the area, they found hundreds of unexploded landmines surrounded the place. Both of them added, now with the increase in tourism, Cambodia was slowly turning a corner.

Ta Prohm   Ta Prohm, built in the late 12th century, was originally called Raja Vihara, royal monastery. Ta Prohm was in much the same condition in which it was found, unlike most temples around which were restored. Large trees growing out of the ruins and their bare roots embracing the temples were bewitching and mesmeric. No wonder it was one of the most popular and photographed of Angkor's temples. Although left untouched as a concession to picturesque appearance, much work was done to preserve the ruins with the help from the Archaeological Survey of India.

In Ta Prohm's garden, a group of about 20 musicians, most amputees, some blind and all scarred, sat under a tree and played traditional music. These musicians' lives mirrored the country's tragedy of over 3 million dead in three decades of a savage war, American bombing, Khmer Rouge reign of terror and civil conflict. Most still earned less than one dollar a day. Landmines laid since the 70s had resulted in over sixty thousand deaths and had a devastating impact on the people of Cambodia. The country had around sixty thousand amputees, the highest number in the world for any country.

These musicians supported over one hundred families in their community from their meagre earnings. We watched them sing in harmony, with their homemade crutches next to them. Blind ones holding on to their instruments tightly as the birds in the forest chirped - a unique testimony of human survival. We watched them sing in harmony, with their homemade crutches next to them. Blind ones holding on to their instruments tightly as the birds in the forest chirped - a unique testimony of human survival.

Floating Village Tonle Sap Lake   Tonle Sap, the great lake, is a seasonally inundated freshwater lake with an attached 120km long river connecting to the Mekong River. Its water volume fluctuates with the Mekong's, supplemented by monsoon rain. Our small boat sailed past communities in floating villages.

In stilt houses, women sat with their children, and small canoes sailed around selling everyday essentials. We sailed past a floating school. In classrooms lighted up by the morning sun, children sat listening to their teacher. A few ran along the corridor for fun, just as in anywhere else. Elsewhere children as old as ten sailed by themselves on small canoes.

Tonle Sap was home to large reptile populations, including nearly extinct Siamese crocodiles and many freshwater snakes. It had at least 149 species of fish; eleven globally threatened and six near threatened. Because of the Buddhist proscriptions against taking a life, Cambodians limited fishing to the amount necessary to support their families. Fishermen went to temple after fishing season for purification. When Tonle Sap flooded, surrounding areas become a prime breeding ground for fish. During this period, fishing was illegal, to prevent disruption of mating.

Our boat reached the confluence of the river with the lake - vast, as far as eyes could see. We returned after another half an hour in this enchanting place of human adapting to live in the middle of nature.

Murida's story Ethiopia

2015 November

At the end of the first long day of advanced skills training in emergency surgery and obstetrics, Murida Shamil approached me timidly. She was 28 years old and had travelled nearly a day and a half by public transport from her rural primary hospital near Somalia border to Awassa to attend this course.

'Dr Biku, I am sorry I have been late each time during breaks to return for the training, and you all had to wait.'

I said, 'No problem. What is the matter?'

'It's my husband's fault. Sorry. I have to breastfeed my 6-month-old daughter. He was supposed to bring the baby in between breaks. I have told him off,' she said.

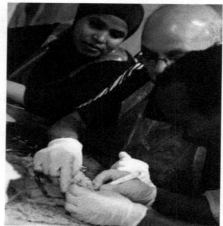

We were proud that after our initiation a Master's programme, non-doctor Integrated Emergency Surgical Officer, IESO, led by Professor Yifru, was rolled out in 2009. Since then it expanded to 11 universities. The first batch of graduates qualified in 2012/13. By the end of 2015, there was over 800 trained. With a hope to have one IESO available per 100,000 population throughout the country. Ethiopian Government had recently undertaken a massive hospital-building programme throughout the country. Many of these hospitals only had IESOs carrying out operations.

In our advanced skills training course, 24 IESOs attended most travelling long distances. Between them, they had already carried out about 5000 caesarean sections, operated over 500 ruptured uteruses, and done 1300 laparotomies for various other emergencies. Thus potentially saving over 6000 lives. Additionally, they had saved 5000 newborn lives in the past three years alone. Impact in the whole country now by these IESOs was breathtaking.

Murida graduated as an IESO three years back. Since then she had done 400 successful caesarean sections, dealt with 64 ruptured uteruses (with only one death), and done approximately 200 laparotomies. And she also managed to have her first baby daughter within that time!

All of us were all extremely impressed by the technical skills of these young IESOs during this course and knew that they would continue to save many thousands of lives in Ethiopia for years to come.

I always found the Ethiopians by nature very gentle, almost shy in the beginning, kind, always friendly and welcoming. More so in the rural parts of Ethiopia, where we did not speak any Amharic, nor did they understand English, never a barrier.

Ethiopia, with its history dating back to 10th century BC, is probably the only country in the world, which was never fully colonised by any foreign power. Italians occupied only its northern part for a while in the 1930s. Perhaps because of this, unlike in most colonised countries, corruption is still rare in Ethiopia. Of course, there are inefficiency and bureaucracy, but not bribing.

Ethiopians are proud of their history. Skeletons of Lucy, about 3.2 million years old, is the most well-known hominid discovery in the world. Discovery of a million years old stone tools at Kella in the west of the country shows a rich history of an ancient civilisation. Having lighter coloured skin, in between African and Arab complexion, and with African curly hair, Ethiopians look different from other African races. It was funny to hear some of our colleagues describing other nation people on the continent as 'those Africans'.

It had been a routine for us to take a stroll at night after dinner in the streets, empty by then of traffic and people. After a long day of work, the most refreshing way to unwind. During my last visit to Ethiopia, we finished our training programme in Awassa.

In the night, we walked towards Lake Awassa. Hardly anyone on the road. From a distance, we noticed a small family on the footpath under one lamppost. As we came near, we saw a mother with a baby fast asleep on the pavement. Next to them, a girl of 7-8 years of age was reading a book. As we stood beside, the mother woke up. We asked what the little girl was reading. The child gave me her notebook, her homework for English for the next day at school.

This hunger for knowledge of the young girl living on a footpath was the best lesson for me during my 16 years in the country.

Iceland

2015/16

My daughter gave me a thick woolly hat for Christmas. She knew I was going to Iceland in two days. Iceland fascinated me for its geography, winter tales and more than anything else with Aurora.

Keflavik International Airport was 50km from Reykjavik. By 5 pm, Reykjavik was already dark. Nothing planned for the evening, I took a walk to the seashore only 1km distance. Already -4°C and empty roads. The footpath, as I got closer to the shore, was icy and slippery. I came by Hofoi, the famous Reykjavik house of 1986 meeting between Gorbachev and Reagan, which subsequently ended the Cold War.

I crossed the main road with no traffic - a beautiful view of the city lights against the dark sea. I headed towards the railings by the shore. No streetlights.

And I slipped backwards on the ice, hitting my head on the pavement. I laid still on the ground for at least a full minute. The doctor in me told me that I was still conscious. My daughter's gift of the thick woolly hat might have saved my life. If I had banged my head without it and lost consciousness, no one would have found me here until the next morning. By then, I would have been a frozen corpse!

I returned to my hotel extremely carefully. First thing in the morning was to buy a pair of ice grips for my shoes.

Skogafoss waterfall

Drive the next day was through desolate wintry countryside to a massive waterfall. We walked cautiously on slippery rocks covered with ice. Partly frozen Seljalandsfoss waterfall looked wonderful cascading down steep cliffs. At the bottom, dreamless blue water before the waves had frozen over and stopped flowing. The main attraction, a walk behind its cascading water on a rocky path, was closed for winter.

We went up the icy steps for a view of spectacular Skogafoss waterfall with a 60m drop of frozen falls, one of Iceland's biggest. Trailhead at the top of the falls lead to several more waterfalls. Hikers walked past us to explore for the day trail to the beginning of Fimmvorouhals pass. The legend was one of the first settlers in Iceland, Prasi Porolfsson, hid a treasure chest behind one of these waterfalls. None of us dared enough to go looking for it in this hinterland.

Drive then towards the south coast. Icelandic horses stood in a desolate snowy field. Icelandic horses were a unique breed. Small but stout, long-lived and hardy. Icelandic law to stop interbreeding prevented horses from being imported into the country and exported animals could not return. We petted the horses for a while who seemed to enjoy the company in their solitude, then moved on.

Reynisfjara black volcano beach

Reynisfjara black volcano beach, 200km from Reykjavík, is the most stunning black sand beaches in the world. Lava flowing into the ocean had cooled instantly as it touched the water to create this. Deserted in the winter, a small group of us walked on the rugged wild beach of various sizes of shiny black pebbles and stones. Nearby an enormous natural pyramid made of basalt cliffs named Gardar looked like a staircase to the sky. We passed by this through a narrow section of beach to a mystic beauty. Two jagged rocks, known as Reynisdrangar, rose from the sea. A legend was these two rocks were two trolls. One night when they were trying to pull a drowning ship out of the sea, the sun rose. And, as in all Icelandic fairy tales, trolls were caught in the daylight and turned to stone. An enchanting hour in this place.

Kerio Crater   Iceland has hundreds of volcanoes with 30 of them active, most around the centre of the country. At Kerio volcanic crater, we trudged over the snow to its 50m rim. Kerio was one of the few volcanoes with an impressive caldera still intact in Iceland. Created following an eruption almost six thousand years back, it was 55m deep, 170m by 270m across. The guide said it was a crater lake in the summer. A few years ago, famous Icelandic singer Bjork sang here from a small boat. Thousands sat by the crater enthralled. We sat there on deep snow, trying to imagine the scene.

Kerio Crater

In the summertime

Geothermal power plant   Returning through frozen allure, we stopped at Hellisheidarvirkjun geothermal heat and power plant, largest in the country and second-largest in the world. On Hengill volcano, this power plant along with Nesjavellir power plant supplied the area around Reykjavik. Five geothermal heat and power plants provide over 85% of the energy supply for Iceland. The power plant used 500 kg/s of 180°C geothermal steam for electrical production, extracting energy from 30 wells, each around 2000- 3000m deep, then led through steam and mist separators before entering the turbines.

Hot-water pipes bringing heat supply to Reykjavik ran under the footpaths to keep them frost-free. Obviously, they did not have any hot water pipe running under the path by the sea where I had fallen last night! Large isolated farms stood by volcanic mountains having with their private mini geothermal plants for energy supply.

Aurora chase   Just before 11 pm, we left searching for Aurora, the Northern Lights. Aurora resulted from disturbances in the earth's magnetic field caused by the solar wind. It depended on solar activity and for apparent reasons better seen in Polar Regions.

Beyond the city and its lights, after about 30km, we reached the top of a hill. There, in minus 10°C we trudged on snow to an open field and waited, stamping our feet to stop them freezing. In the sky, with a moderate amount of cloud, suddenly there was a flicker of faint green. Everyone got excited. But soon clouds covered everything. We returned by our coach and had welcome drinks of hot chocolate. In the bitter cold, we ran around, danced and waited for another 45 minutes. But the cloud got thicker, and sadly we had to return.

Strokkur geyser   Drive next morning for 100km to Haukadalur, a geothermal field. From a distance, we could see water sprout shooting up in the air every few minutes by an icy mountain. Many steam vents and a small geyser was shooting up hot water a few meters in the air.

Then I stood by the famous Strokkur geyser, one of the two largest in Iceland. As I waited with few others around a large depressed spot, water on the surface of the saucer-shaped area bubbled. Suddenly, whoosh! A massive amount of boiling water shot up about 20m in the air for a few seconds. It quickly subsided as the wind took it away in a matter of seconds, leaving us covered with its hot spray. As the water column collapsed, everything went quiet. We waited around in anticipation. Suddenly, after three minutes, the geyser erupted, this time only about 15m high. But the next time, six minutes later, was massive and at least 35m high. I stood transfixed in this ecstasy.

Then I watched this spectacle for half an hour from the small cafe serving egg boiled in the hot spring nearby, with rye bread baked underground for 24 hours.

Gullfoss Waterfall   This was the most spectacular sight in the whole of Iceland so far. By partly frozen Hvita River, I walked up carefully a slippery path to the visitor point of this tiered frozen torrent. In front of me

wide frozen river abruptly turned into a broad curve. From there resembling a glacier, it cascaded three steps like a staircase and then plunged further in two more stages, 11m and 21m tall, finally into a crevice 32m deep. Hvita River ran in an outburst from there. A gigantic frozen waterfall of breathtaking beauty.

No wonder Iceland's most iconic waterfalls was lovingly called the Golden Falls. A local myth was 'Once upon a time, a farmer named Gygur lived nearby. He had plenty of gold and could not bear the thought of someone else possessed it after his lifetime. To prevent this, he placed the gold in a coffer and threw it into the waterfall.' Hence the name!

Thingvellir (Þingvellir)   Thingvellir is a rift valley which marked the crest of the Mid-Atlantic Ridge and the boundary between the North American and Eurasian tectonic plates. We drove carefully on an icy road to descend into a steep cliff and then into a valley. The face of this cliff we were looking at now was literally the edge of North America. After driving through the vast frozen valley, we ascended on the other side next to an ice-covered rocky wall, which was Eurasia.

Tectonic plates, for millenniums, had been moving apart approximately 2.5 cm/year. Because of this movement, the entire area was littered with ravines, ripped open by centuries of earthquakes. Iceland was the only place in the world where this rift was above sea-level.

Nowhere else one could see edges of both plates as clearly as in Þingvellir. Earthquakes continue every day in Þingvellir, although most were too minor to be felt. A major quake took place approximately every ten years. I felt a shudder, or was it a minor earthquake?

Continental shelf   Althing

Nowhere else one could see edges of both plates as clearly as in Þingvellir. Earthquakes continue every day in Þingvellir, although most were too minor to be felt. A major quake took place approximately every ten years. I felt a shudder, or was it a minor earthquake?

From the lower section of the road by the massive Almannagja canyon, we walked up the slippery road between lava boulders with a gorgeous view of the Silfra – the broadest and deepest fissures at the rim of the frozen Pingvallavatn Lake. Multiple springs fed Silfra fissure, during summer a popular place for snorkelling and diving. Hard to imagine now in the icy tableau. From the high viewpoint, at a distance within the desolate valley stood Althing – the national parliament of Iceland, established at the site in 930 AD. The oldest surviving legislature in the world is held in high esteem by all Icelanders and protected as a national shrine. Sessions were held at this location until 1798. Þingvellir translated as 'the fields of parliament'.

Aurora Chase (again) -   At night we drove further. Our guide said solar activity was low. We spent two hours in an open field with thick clouds. Snow started falling, and we returned.

Snaefellsnes   Jules Verne had set the start of his classic adventure 'Journey to the centre of the Earth' in this place. Apart from the intriguing name, its remoteness attracted me. Thick cloud covering the sky, we set for Snæfellsnes peninsula, 160km distance in the northwest. The guide said because of the weather no guarantee how much we can visit.

After Reykjavik, apart from an occasional farmhouse at a distance every few kilometres apart, it was just winter land of ice and snow on hilly terrain. Halfway stop at Borgarnes town on a peninsula on Borgarfjorour shore - a popular summer destination for nearby fjords, but now deserted. From its only one shop open by the road, we filled up our bags with chocolate bars and snacks.

From then we were on the Snaefellsnes National Park area. Surrounding beauty, even under the cloud, became otherworldly.

Budir   After an hour, we left the main road and drove down to Budir. A small cemetery and a black church stood alone against ice covering a lava field stretching out to a beautiful coastline of a partly frozen sea. Ice and snow partially covered holes in the lava field.

It was easy to imagine creatures from Icelandic fairy tales coming alive here in the dark. Budir was the place

where first inhabitants to Iceland had made their landing. The whole surrounding breathed mystery and intrigue.

Arnarstapi   Through a surreal, dreamy landscape, we arrived at Arnarstapi village and got off by an enormous stone sculpture of Barour Snaefellsas.

After walking under the statue, we walked carefully between iced lava caves to the seashore with a view of black rocks standing out from the sea looking like sleeping trolls. In the only shop in Barour, we lunched with an amazing view of the frozen coast. Nearby famous Barour cave was not accessible in the winter.

Driving further west, when we reached Saxholl volcanic crater area, light snow had started. Carefully we walked up the steps covered with ice about 100m to the crater rim. Even with the light snowfall, 360° view from the edge of the Snæfellsnes Peninsula was unbelievable. As the snowfall became heavy, we had to leave.

Back to my hotel in the evening, the situation did not improve. I knew there was no chance of seeing the Aurora on my last night in Iceland.

On the way to the airport, I stopped at the famous Blue Lagoon in Grindavik. In the middle of a snow-covered lava field, steam vented out in many places outside the geothermal spa. Water in a blue lagoon within in this natural field of lava came from filtered runoff of hot water from the geothermal power plant nearby.

It was almost surreal swimming in the lagoon. Immersed part of my body was having a hot bath, while my head was freezing with the outside temperature hovering below 0°C. Time to time, I had to dive in to warm my head. After a while, sitting by the pool, I lunched watching people having fun in the lagoon. Soon I returned in the milky blue water of the lagoon. Its colour was because of high silica content which formed white mud on the bottom. Many bathers rubbed the mud on themselves, believing it had some rejuvenating power.

After another half an hour in the steaming water, it was time to catch my transport to the airport 20km away.

Giant's Causeway   Northern Ireland

February 2016   I was invited to a Global health conference in Dublin. I added Giant's Causeway at the northern tip of the island, to my itinerary.

From Belfast Giant's Causeway was at 80km distance. Outside Belfast, we drove past massive Carrick Fergus Castle on the coastline. Then by Gobbins, a network of walkways and bridges hugging dramatic basalt cliff face and through tortuous and rugged coastline, we arrived at Glens of Antrim. Over the Irish Sea, we could see the Scottish shoreline. Inland, to the west, stood Slemish Mountain, remains of an extinct volcano. St Patrick, patron saint of Ireland, tended sheep as a young slave here.

We continued through craggy hills on a narrow road with gorse bushes blooming with vibrant yellow flowers. Nearby was a route to visit Game of Thrones famous Dark hedges - not interested. Carrick-a-Rede Rope Bridge, a 20m bridge 30m above the rocky channel of water connected mainland to the tiny island of Carrickarede. From there was a spectacular view of the Scottish coast, Rathlin Island and other unnamed islets against the Irish shoreline

Giant's Causeway   From the visitor centre, through a gently curved hill, I reached nature at its most primal. Around me were over 40,000 hexagonal shaped stepping stones, dating back to 60 million years. Result of an ancient volcanic fissure eruption, columns formed stepping stones that lead from the cliff foot and disappeared under the sea. Most columns were hexagonal, although a few had between four and eight sides. Tallest columns were 12m high. In places, the solidified lava in the cliffs was 28m thick. Subject to intense volcanic activity, highly fluid molten basalt had insinuated itself through the bed of chalks to form an extensive lava plateau. When this lava cooled, horizontal contraction fractured it. As it cooled further, like the drying mud, it left cracks with pillar-like structures, which then cracked further horizontally into these columns.

According to the legend, columns were the remains of a causeway built by the Irish giant Fionn MacCool, challenged to a fight by Scottish giant Benandonner. Fionn accepted the challenge and built the causeway across the North Channel of the Irish Sea so the two giants could meet. Seeing this formidable construction, Scottish giant had fled in terror!

Like many, I hopped and skipped on Honeycomb, where the pillars' hexagonal tops only showed above the surface. Then I walked around to see Giant's boot, a large stone resembling a boot, and a weathered reddish, short column, known as the Giant's eye. After walking by Chimney Stacks, Giant's Gate, and then Camel's Hump, I sat on a group of pillars at the sea edge, absorbed in this splendour of nature.

Bolivia–volunteering Salt desert and Uyuni tour

2016 June – August

At the end of April 16, I said my final goodbye to the UK NHS after 35 years. I wanted to continue working in developing countries as much as I could. South America was still a continent full of mystery to me. Bolivia, films showing as bandit country, held a certain charm. I found a local voluntary organisation there, now almost defunct since the American volunteers had stopped coming for the last few years. The USA got upset with Bolivia after they elected an indigenous Bolivian as their current president. A team in Tarija province was glad to have me offering my surgical services there for 6-7 weeks.

I tried learning Spanish, but not very well. Bolivian colleague assured they would have an English translator. My colleagues in two hospitals in Wales kindly collected many essential surgical supplies and useful instruments to take to Bolivia. Loaded with two cases full of supplies and my rucksack, partly filled with surgical materials, I left for South America.

La Paz   The 25-hour flight with one stop in Miami, arrived in La Paz airport 4062m - the highest international airport in the world. Soon I discovered one of my cases had not arrived. As I would stay in La Paz for two nights, they assured it would come in the next flight and would send to my hotel. From the airport, the taxi drove through spiral mountain road to La Paz city 3640m, in a bowl-like depression, set in a canyon of Choqueyapu River, surrounded by Altiplano high mountains. Overlooking the city was the triple-peaked Illimani 6438m, the second-highest mountain in Bolivia.

My taxi parked a few lanes before my hotel in Centro, downtown area. I walked up a narrow road with my rucksack and dragging one case. I was panting after suddenly arriving at this altitude, even with this small effort. A sign 'Brexit immigrants are welcome here' outside a hotel made me laugh. It was the day after they had declared Brexit election results.

The temperature dropped in the evening to -4°C. Next morning I spent at the centre of the city square by San Francisco Church, full of people in colourful costume gathered around musical and magic performances. I wandered around the busy market for a while. Later I saw from outside the Presidential Palace and the Metropolitan Cathedral. My lost luggage did not arrive.

Penas 3970m   Before coming to Bolivia, I had talked to an Italian Colleague in England about her experience of volunteering in La Paz. She had recommended a visit to an Italian mission in Penas, in the mountains. I had arranged to spend a few days in Penas before going to Tarija. In the afternoon, an Italian Padre came from Penas to collect me. We drove via the airport area, mostly slums, and then through beautiful Andean mountain range for 60 km. Penas, a small town of a mostly indigenous community in Andean mountains, was in a high valley with the privileged views of nearby Cordillera Real Mountains. The mission there supported several local schools teaching children in local crafts and computer skills, providing free meals, picnic and sport. They also offered limited medical help to the community whenever they could.

Both the Padres were keen mountaineers and took trekkers for 2-3 days to Cordillera mountains from time to time to boost the mission's income and for keeping up with their passion. We exchanged mountaineering stories. I was sorry I could not risk a trek on the high mountain, only a few days before my volunteering in the south.

I visited with them a 25yr old lady with three young children living in a hut in an isolated area. Recently she had lost her husband and had no means of support. The mission team was bringing them food every few days. Later I visited another remote place where a 51yr old lady had been paralysed from the waist down for almost seven years. Her son and daughter-in-law had been looking after her. When we arrived, they were moving her from the hut to a sunny area on a wheelbarrow. I was surprised she did not have a single sign of bedsore on her, even though she was being cared in such a primitive condition. In another village, we visited a 70yr old lady who had suffered a fractured femur a year back and still had difficulty walking. But she was the only one to care for her 20-year-old son with severe intellectual development issue. Life is not fair!

Next day, Sunday, was a festival day for the local community. School children from all around came to the mission for a day of fun, football games in mixed boys' and girls' teams and free food. By the church was a festival of dancing. Indigenous communities from far afield gathered for traditional singing and dancing in their colourful costumes - wonderful.

In the evening they invited us to a family in a village several kilometres away for dinner and to watch the Copa Americana football final. The family was the only one around with a satellite TV. With great excitement all around, the game finished at 11 pm. By this time, the temperature outside had dropped below -8°C. Car windscreen was frozen, and there was no heating. Continuing to stop to scrape the windscreen every so often, we returned to the mission through icy road. The padre, who was driving, was nonchalant.

Lake Titicaca   One of the Padre invited me to join on his visit to the churches near Lake Titicaca. We drove through gorgeous mountain scenery to Lake Titicaca. At 3812m this deep 8370 sq.km Andean lake, bordering Bolivia and Peru, was the largest lake in South America. From the shore, we walked through a rocky spur into the lake with a beautiful view all around.

Around us in the reeds were flying varieties of gulls, ibises, flamingos, egrets, black-crowned herons and ducks of all colours. Lake Titicaca had an abundance of endemic fishes to keep the birds interested. Nearby fishermen sailed on reed boats.

Soon we visited an old church where Padre had some business to attend. In the churchyard, volleyball was going on. They were happy for me to join. My highest altitude volleyball so far - we lost.

Later we walked to see a mission's project where they supported locals in building boats. They proudly showed me a catamaran they had made only from catalogue pictures with a minimum of equipment.

By the time we left after a terrific day, it was dark. Padre and I were starving by now. He stopped by any villages we passed looking for food. But all the shops in the evening were closed. Luckily we found by the roadside a food shop with its light still on. The shop was closing, but after seeing the padre; they served us fried fish, rice and potatoes - yum yum.

Qillqantiji cave   After day's work, the same padre took me to Qillqantiji cave in the Wirakoni hills with over 200 paintings of 100 BC to the post-colonial era. Its oldest paintings included two-headed birds and human figures of pre-Hispanic characters, whereas the newer images showed colonial churches and crosses. Only now this historic cave system was being protected by conservation efforts.

Tiwanaku   Another day, the other padre took me for a drive to the famous archaeological site of Tiwanaku. This four sq.km complex, built between 200BC and 110 AD, included many ancient monumental structures and megalithic blocks. The vast cross-shaped pyramidal structure of Akapana was most impressive. Kalasasaya temple composed of an enormous courtyard surrounded by high stone walls, once an observatory. It contained the monumental Gate of the Sun, carved from a single slab of stone.

A subterranean temple with red stone pillars had many carved heads, symbolising earlier practice of displaying severed heads of defeated enemies. Nearby was the ruined site of Pumapunku temple, meaning 'The Door of the Puma'.

Most of the place was previously looted, only some of its treasures were in its museum. Succeeding civilisations extending as far as Cuzco in Peru adopted innovations of pre-Incan Tiwanaku Empire, especially its techniques of irrigation in agriculture. Standing by the beautiful stone archway known as Gate of the Moon, I tried to imagine the advanced civilization who lived here over fifteen hundred years back.

After another day in Penas, I returned to La Paz. My lost luggage was still somewhere. Next morning I took a flight to Tarija.

Tarija   Arriving in Tarija, a provincial capital in southern Bolivia, a big reception party holding banners with my name surprised me. Twenty people, including local charity members, Health Ministry representative and Governor's wife, welcomed me with flowers. While other arriving passengers stood amazed, a man dressed in traditional costume played string music for me - overwhelming.

Travelling to my accommodation in one of the organiser's house, Tarija looked lovely with many parks and avenues, well organised and with less traffic, in stark contrast to the hustle of La Paz. In the evening we went to the town square for dinner. Even at nine in the winter evening, the place was full and lively with families, music, dancing and fashion shows.

The charity provided me with an interpreter, a big help for the rest of my stay.

At the regional hospital, provisions were basic but functional, with no shortage of surgical staff. They asked me to teach and train the residents. In this teaching hospital, they had not heard of the WHO safety checklist procedure before operations. I agreed with the Medical Director and Head of Surgery to help introduce this to their hospital.

One evening, I cooked chicken curry and rice for my host family, which went down very well. With my translator and Spanish PowerPoint, courtesy of Google Translate, I taught the residents in current concepts in surgery. I learnt residents in their four years of residency did not get paid. They worked about 80 hours per week, lived in bunk beds in a dormitory in the hospital and only got a free breakfast, lunch and dinner. But the dinner place closed by 6 pm! All of them depended on their parents plus bank loans for the training period. No wonder, after full training, most chose private practice.

After two days at this regional hospital, I had a meeting with the ministerial team from Tarija and Sucre provinces about the possibility of working in rural hospitals where I could be of more use. They were delighted and arranged for me to work in three rural hospitals in the region, one week or more in each place. I also agreed with them to introduce the WHO safety checklist in all their hospitals. Also, with their support, I had an hour on the local TV next evening on Breast Cancer Awareness, with a question-and-answer session at the end. Went very well, thanks to my interpreter.

Tarija with Spanish colonial-style buildings, churches and beautiful parks, was full of activities. Frequent festivals with bands marching streets and playing music. Very relaxed atmosphere and wonderful people. Tarija province, bordering Argentina, boasted South America's second-largest natural gas reserves. In this relatively affluent part of Bolivia, however, were many indigenous tribes who had not enjoyed the benefits of foreign investment in gas exploration. There were gross inequalities. Slowly changing since Evo Morales, an indigenous, became President a few years back and took the herculean task of rebalancing social inequality.

Before coming to Bolivia, I had arranged with another UK charity, donation of much-needed Pulse Oximeters for hospitals in this region. I learnt they had arrived in Bolivia but in the wrong city! My lost luggage was still to come!

On Sunday we drove for lunch out of town on a country farm, full of families and many musicians. After ordering our food, we walked to a lovely rock pool. Water was too cold in the winter to swim. By the time we came back, our lunch was ready. People here had a huge lunch and then a nap afterwards! Must try to introduce this back home.

Camargo Chuquisaca 2141m   One volunteer, my interpreter, and I left for Camargo in Sucre province. First, we drove through undulating barren mountains before descending to red hills and canyons. Embedded between the north-southerly mountain ridges, on the banks of Rio Chico, red rock mountains surrounded Camargo of 5000 population. Because of its soil, this area produced the best wine in the country and was well known for its fruit farms. The hospital served people coming from rural communities, some travelling most of a day to get there. With limited basic facilities and hardly any instruments or sutures for surgery - very little surgery was done. Most, including emergencies, were sent to Tarija about 3 hrs distance. Sucre was 5 hrs away.

Mayor and the town council welcomed us heartily. I learnt now most people had Government health insurance card allowing, free treatment. But because of the lack of resources in the hospital, they did not come except in a major emergency. Then they had to go to Tarija, anyway.

Authorities had already advertised on local radio, and through village councils and with many posters in the town that there will be surgical treatment carried out in the hospital for the week. We screened the patient's and got on with operations with the resources we had for the next few days. Staff in the hospital were excellent. The difficulty was operating on children without proper anaesthesia. But between the resident anaesthetist and I, operated on them with sedation and local anaesthesia. One parent holding the child's hand to give support. One evening after the day's work, the local staff asked me to arrange an hour of breast cancer awareness promotion. All the female staff, about thirty, attended. This became my routine in other hospitals I worked.

Following a request, one afternoon, I visited a small hospital at St Lucas. In this isolated community in high mountains between canyons, the hospital had only a final year resident as a surgeon. She was delighted to have someone medical after several months in complete isolation. She perked up even more when I gave her a few simple tips about managing routine hernias without requiring an expensive mesh. People could not afford mesh, and their insurances did not cover.

On our way back, we gave a ride to an old lady in her 60s. She was going to Tarija to do some seasonal work. She lived on her own and had a peach farm locally. Now, in out of seasons, she was going to Tarija to work. She hoped to get about 5 dollars a day, although she will spend about 4 dollars on her shared accommodation and food. Who said life was easy!

At the end of the week, Municipality officials thanked us with a bottle of their best local wine as a gift. Following my return to Tarija, I found my lost suitcase and also the Pulse Oximeters had finally arrived.

In the evening, I helped the young woman in the family and her boyfriend to cook my speciality, Peruvian chicken. Everyone loved it. I learnt in Bolivia with 95% of people being Catholic, contraception and abortion was banned - resulting in many unwanted pregnancies. There were many orphanages in the country. Multiple pregnancies amongst women were also common, explaining why so many young patients had gallstones.

Entre Rios Cochabamba   Next day, through the undulating mountain range and some very rough road we went to Entre Rios, the town between two rivers. The hospital had good facilities and very willing staff, but not much surgery happened. Final-year residents in surgery and anaesthesia came from Tarija only three days a week. Entre Rios had a population of around 5000, but the hospital served a sizeable remote area. These were key settlement areas of Quechuas, indigenous people who have inhabited this basin for millennia. Almost 80% of the population spoke Quechua. Even my translator needed a local translator.

In damp and cold dusk, with no floodlight, football was going on nearby. Late Sunday prayer in the Church by town square had a large gathering, including many teenagers.

Big welcome in the hospital grounds next morning with all the town officials and hospital staff with almost a hundred people. Delightfully dressed children handed me a gift of engraved leather hats.

263

Next few days, we worked hard and got as many patients had attended for surgery, operated. Lunch provided at the hospital with all the staff sitting together was always a joyful occasion – my precious memory for years to come. Working together, teaching and learning, we became a real team as if we had known each other for a long time. On our way back from work, freshly made street food Llaucha, a warm pizza-dough pastry filled with oozing cheese was irresistible and became our daily stop.

On one afternoon, the local Quechua people arranged for me to visit their community. Unfortunately, by the time we finished in the hospital, it was getting dark. We drove through jungles and a few river crossings to an isolated community of about ten houses. Villagers welcomed us with api, a purple maize drink with cinnamon and sugar accompanied by hot fried bunuelos, fritters. Beautiful children hung around us. Fabulous, but sadly, it was very dark by then. We had to return.

On Saturday, we left after breakfast. The mountain road back to Tarija would be closed by noon for blasting the rocks to make it wider. We just made through before the road was closed. We could hear the blasting noises behind us.

Yacuiba   Eight-hour car journey through mountain road to Yacuiba was often scary but breathtaking. We took a break by massive cactuses on the way with a beautiful view of undulating hills beyond. At only 3km from the Argentine border, Yacuiba of 80,000 population was a major commercial centre, close to profitable gas and oil industry. An army band played welcome songs, surprising us on our arrival at the hospital. A big welcome meeting with the hospital staff, town mayor, local officials and local MP followed by gifts of hat and poncho. After a tour of the hospital, I realised this place had 12 surgeons covering different specialities with appropriate anaesthetic support. More than in my last hospital in the NHS! I wondered, what was I doing here?

Soon talking to the local health officials, it became clear. Local surgeons were bringing up excuses they did not have enough keyhole surgery equipment in the hospital to do gallbladder surgery - hinting patients to go to their private hospitals. Gallstone diseases were common in young females. Many patients waited over four years to have any surgery and had suffered many complications. Local officials had not wanted to upset the surgeons in their only hospital. After an entire afternoon meeting with ministry, hospital director, local surgical team and myself, I was proud of my negotiating skill. They allowed us to go ahead with working in the hospital.

The ministry already had a list of waiting patients. I saw them in the evening and scheduled them for having age-old and tested standard open gall bladder surgery. Some of them had come from far, as the local health authority had announced my arrival well beforehand.

On my way to the hotel around 9 pm, they whisked me to the local TV station. Before I realised I was on live TV promoting Breast cancer awareness. Luckily by now, my interpreter and I had some practice. The one hour programme ran smoothly.

For the next few days my routine became an early morning start, operating till late afternoon, ward round, then a clinic to see the patients mostly with breast diseases and back to the hotel around 9 pm. One evening, I squeezed in a skills session on management of critically injured on the long corridor outside the OPD. About 60 turned up; some came from the rural health centres after travelling for 2 hours. Several asked if I could stay there longer to do more sessions like this.

Late next evening was a mouth-watering Argentine-style barbecue in the local MP's house with all the dignitaries. After many thank you speeches, they asked me to speak and give my recommendations as an outsider expert, why the local hospital did not work so well for the poor. Without holding back, I said they needed to enforce better work ethic on the local team who seemed to be only interested in their private clinics. Everyone agreed.

On my last morning, I finished operating by noon. We had to leave for the return eight-hour journey to Tarija. They surprised me with a big farewell and thank you party in the same long corridor.

A few of my patients, including some I had operated only the day before, had heard of this. They walked the corridors to everyone's surprise. Just to be there to thank me publicly. When they hugged me, tears flooded our eyes.

Back in Tarija, I stayed in a backpackers' hostel for the next few days. It was interesting meeting many young travellers, on route either to Argentina or Uyuni Salt plane.

The Governor of the province met me one day and wanted my recommendations on surgical care strategy for the hospitals in his region. After a frank discussion at length, I promised to send a short paper with my suggestions on my return, which I subsequently followed through.

Bermejo Governor's wife invited me to join her team, running a mobile health clinic in Bermejo. We drove for over 3 hours between beautiful mountain gorges to Bermejo. A shallow river full of fish separated the town from Argentina. Many people were walking back and forth, crossing the river to Argentina with their merchandise. Bridge over the river had half marked with Bolivian colours and another half with that of Argentina. We had lunch at a riverside place. They served a fried freshly caught huge whole fish. Most delicious.

Our mobile clinic site was in an agricultural field. Bermejo had extensive areas of sugarcane fields and factories. Thousands of migrant workers from as far as La Paz came for seasonal work. The mobile hospital was promoting disease prevention, vaccination, some medical and dental care, physiotherapy and psychological counselling. They also promoted the country's new free health insurance scheme to the rural population. I felt privileged to have gone there to help and watch such excellent work.

On our way back we visited an orphanage, sponsored by the charity. There were thirty children of age six months to sixteen years old. The carer teacher asked the older children to say a few words in English to me. They did it beautifully. The children then asked me to sing a nursery rhyme in English. I sang 'Twinkle, twinkle little star' as best I could. I noticed there were twin girls in the orphanage about two years old, almost the same age as my twin granddaughters. They wanted to come to me for a hug, making me miss my granddaughters.

My colleagues said the number of children in the orphanages was going up because of unwanted pregnancies. Women were expected back to work in the field within a day or two after giving birth, with their baby tied on their backs. It was not practical to earn their living working in the field while tending to children

I heard the saddest story I could imagine. Until only a few years back, if a mother gave birth to twins in the countryside, the father would take one of the weaker looking one outside and kill. It was not practical to have twins! Only in the last few years, the country had outlawed this practice. As a result, many of the twins were now ending up in orphanages.

Next day I took a taxi to Camargo Hospital with the surgical instruments and the pulse Oximeters. They almost cried with joy to see me back and profoundly grateful for all the material which nearly doubled their stock. In the evening, the central plaza in Tarija was even more fun place as it was the night before Bolivia day.

As Napoleon invaded Spain, an enormous vacuum of power and oversight in South America by the colonists permitted beginning of the independence movement in the continent. Simon Bolivar led struggles to liberate Colombia, Venezuela, Ecuador and Peru. The newly independent country between Peru, Brazil and Argentina was born in 1825 and named in honour of Simon Bolivar.

On Bolivia day, Tarija streets were full of colourful parades from schools, colleges, churches, police and many other organisations. Singing and dancing everywhere. On the side streets, groups of college students played the guitars to more modern music. Brilliant atmosphere.

But in the afternoon, the longest rally of the day tipped everything else - a protest march against unemployment. People of all ages marched banging their kitchen utensils to make incredible noises.

Sucre   I took a night bus to Sucre. Sucre remains the constitutional capital of Bolivia while La Paz is the de facto capital. Built during the colonial era, Sucre looked grand with beautiful vast plazas, streets organised in a grid, Andalusian architecture houses and churches in white.

Drive from the city centre to the hospital, took almost an hour. The hospital was one of the three serving 300,000 population - usual welcome meeting and donation of my items.

The medical director's secretary arrived in my clinic, and shyly asked if I could see her. It turned out this 30yr old lady had found a lump in her breast and had a few tests done. Local surgeons had warned it was likely cancer and advised an urgent operation in a private hospital. I checked her with all her reports, including a biopsy. There was no suggestion of any cancer. I reassured her. She started sobbing with relief. Usually, when I am in a clinic, I have a box of tissue for such a situation. But there was none here. I gave her my handkerchief to wipe her tears. She hugged me and left.

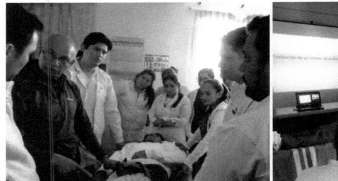 

In the next few days, I worked with the local surgeons in this reasonably well-equipped hospital with a keen surgical team. After day's work, I spent the evenings teaching residents, grateful as practical teaching was not common practice there.

Dinosaur footprints Cal Orck'o On a free afternoon, following suggestions from the residents, I visited a site outside the city with the most extensive collection of dinosaurs' footprints. During Mesozoic   Era, dinosaurs walked on the ocean shore here, leaving footprints on sediments. As the tectonic plates shifted, creating the Andes, the once flat beach where dinosaurs had set foot, rose to a near-vertical high limestone wall. A cement company, while drilling in the area, found thousands of footprints belonging to about 15 species of dinosaurs, including the T. Rex. Mining was halted. After excavation, the site became a conservation park.

It was an incredible place. Over 5,000 clear footprints on the wall of a hill, including the world's longest recorded baby T-Rex tracks, measuring 350m!

On my last working day in the hospital, as I was leaving about 5 pm to the building opposite to teach the residents, the medical director's secretary came up and said, 'I will see you tomorrow.'

I said 'no, it was my last day. I will leave Sucre early in the morning.'

She said nothing and left. Back at my hotel around 10 pm, I was packing my rucksack. The hotel reception phoned me - someone to see me. There, the same secretary was with a gift of three embroidered handkerchiefs which said in Spanish 'Thank you'. She had taken at least two changes of buses at this time of the night to come to my hotel, just to say thank you.

She gave me another hug, and now I needed a handkerchief.

Salt Desert

At Sucre bus station, I heard the local mineworkers had suddenly called a strike. All major roads were blocked. A minibus driver said he could take us through a mountain road to Potosi. It would take an extra one and a half hour instead of the usual three. The minibus drove through one-lane mountain road through villages. About 5km before we were to join the main road to Potosi, our car stopped behind a line of vehicles.

Even on this road was a blockade. Desperately, I tried an untested tactic. I walked up to the union people in the blockade with a stethoscope hanging around my neck, and my thank you certificate from the hospital. I explained to the man in charge with my poor Spanish that I had been working for the last few days at the hospital and was looking forward to going to Uyuni. They looked at me and my certificate. To my surprise, they lifted the blockade and let us all go. The privilege of being a voluntary doctor!

From Potosi, a shared taxi to Tupiza, another three hours' journey. The mining town of Potosi was at the foot of Cerro Rico Mountain, a major silver supply area for the Spanish empire. Now it mined mostly tin. The conical 1150m reddish-brown hill was honeycombed with underground working tunnels and mine dumps around.

Tupiza in the winter evening was deserted. On its streets stood many large, interesting and weird looking metal sculptures made from the parts of derelict cars. It was getting cold, and I settled in a dormitory for the night.

Early morning start for my four days and three nights Desert Mountain and Uyuni tour. No English-speaking guide. Luckily, two ladies in their 50s from Ecuador were my fellow passengers. Both of them well-travelled and one spoke good English. We stopped by Quebrada de Palala, 4200m high, an imposing red and pink rock formations. It's tall and thin rocks looked like giant needles. Next stop at El Sillar, eye-catching eroded rock formations. Also called Valle de la Luna, Valley of the Moon, because erosion here made the place look like a lunar landscape. Then we drove through dramatic Andean mountains and gorges with no sign of human habitation.

By a wetland, a large herd of llamas grazed. Two huts lay nearby on the mountain slopes. Only a few members of the family lived in these, looking after hundreds of domesticated lamas in the mountain. They made only 15 Bolivar, just over 2 US dollars, for each 1 kg of llama wool living in such harsh condition. Then, a brief stop at Nazarenito, once a gold mining village, now only a dozen derelict huts.

We continued through small settlements of Cerrillos, Polulos and Rio San Pablo. On the roadside, women sat with their children by their huts with home-made crafts, hoping for someone to buy. By the evening, we arrived at the foot of San Pablo de Lipez 4400m. Our driver said we had driven 350km on the day. After an early dinner, I retired to bed. Unfortunately, the toilet was outside the dormitory hut, and the temperature was -5°C!

We started very early the next day and arrived at San Antonio de Lipez, known as Pueblo Fantasma, the Ghost town. In the 16th century, this flourishing silver mining town had 150,000 inhabitants. It was abandoned many decades back when silver prices dropped in the world.

Although legend was its workers made a pact with the devil to give them a share of their wealth from mining. Miners did not keep their promise, which killed all the mine workers. Soon, the rest of the locals began to see ghosts, which triggered the abandonment of the town. We walked in the abandoned entrance to the mines, keeping an eye open for the ghosts!

From there, we drove by a lake of sulphur with a nasty smell in the air, like rotten eggs. After another few kilometres in front was a massive potassium lake with thousands of bright-coloured flamingos. On its shore lay large mounds of salt drying for collection. Surrounding mountains now were bursting in colour with their rich mineral contents.

We drove over a dried large salt lake, Laguna Morejon, before entering a gorge. From a distance, we could see a flooded basin surrounded by the volcanic mountains. At almost 4400m, Laguna Salada had natural pools. In the middle of the day, the outside temperature hovered around 0°C. Many swam in its lava pools. I walked between the rocks on the frozen salt lake, absorbed in its magnificence. A few wandering llamas took their daily salt supplements next to me.

Dali Desert and Stone Tree   We stopped at Dali desert, near the border between Bolivia and Chile. The landscape of this barren valley resembled Salvador Dali's painting 'Naked Woman in the Desert'. Amongst the rocks was the unique 'Stone Tree'. In the desert at 4660m, over the centuries, wind and sand had sculpted a large rock into a beautiful petrified tree. A human sculptor could not have done a better job!

Next stop was on a ridge into Laguna Verde, a magnificent green-turquoise coloured lagoon, sitting at the foot of the Licancabur volcano 5868m, straddling the border with Chile. Soon we made our way up to the geysers Sol de Manana. At 5000m, a geothermal area with intense volcanic activity. We walked among smoky, noisy geysers and boiling red and grey mud stew pots. The outside temperature was -3°C. But the boiling sulphur springs and steam pools kept us warm. A few old wells emitted pressurised steam up to 40m in the air - wonderful.

We drove on. On the way, a desert fox walked in from the hill to check us out.

After another 50 km, we reached the blood-red coloured Laguna Colorada. From the ridge, I walked to its shore with hundreds of flamingos. Some of these gracious birds pecked for algae and plankton while others rested on one leg. This lagoon was the main nesting area of three kinds of flamingos. Lake's colour resulted from the algae and plankton in its water, activated by sunlight and the wind, attracting the birds.

After almost travelling 320km on the day we stopped at our dormitory, Tayka del Desierto, in Siloli desert. In the background, were the untouched towering colourful mountains. At over 220km from Uyuni salt flat and 200km from San Pedro in the Atacama Desert in Chile, this was possibly the remotest hotel in the world. The temperature at night dropped to -15°C.

I had always loved the mountains, but they were in black and white. But here in the Andes, full of minerals, they looked as if they were in the middle of a Holi festival of colours in India. We continued our drive through Andean fauna, absorbed in the breathtaking beauty of Laguna Chiarkota, Laguna Hedionda and Laguna Chullunkani before reaching the massive Volcano Ollague 5868m. We passed by this mountain to stop at outlandish Turquiri lagoon. Fascinating rock formations, as if in a sculpture museum, had extraterrestrial looking green blobs of vegetation around their bases, sprinkled its shore. Known as Yareta, some of these plants were up to 3000 yrs old – unbelievable! But the next place, Laguna Negra, took my breath away. A black lava glacier flowed from a black mountain to form this small lake of ink-black colour. Even the few birds swimming there were charcoal coloured. Nearby, a volcano fumed gently.

In the afternoon, we arrived in San Cristobal village. This small dusty town of 350 people was once in a place 15km away. After discovering silver deposits under its ground, a Canadian mining company relocated the entire town and the church to this place brick by brick. We visited a primary school in there with jubilant children. The teacher was a volunteer from Italy. She was delighted to meet people from Europe. With her, all the children sang a beautiful song for us in the local traditional miners' language, a mixture of Quechua, Spanish and Aymara.

Train Cemetry, Cemetrio de Trenes　　Nearby was the eerie open-air train museum. Natural resources of Bolivia had attracted foreign interests for a long time. Just as now, with its largest deposit of lithium in the world and vast oil and natural gas reserves. In the late 19th century, British companies built a railway between La Paz, the local mines and the seaports of Chile, transforming the sleepy Uyuni town into a central transportation hub.

But in the 1940s, mining went into decline as prices fell and resources ran dry. With no economic incentive to continue, the railroad company abandoned the region. Now there were dozens of old steam engines and coaches, left to decay in the high altitude desert. Rusted out, stripped of their useful parts, some covered in graffiti, but it was a bizarre yet charming relic of an industry left behind.

274

Hotel Luna Salada   Our overnight stay was in Hotel Luna Salada, built of salt bricks on the edge of Uyuni salt flats. Its walls and chimney flutes were made from white salt, the floor from rock salt, even my bed headboard was made of salt. The place was designed and decorated in colourful Andean charm. No wonder this hotel was in the top ten list of unusual hotels in the world.

In a comfortable place after four days, after a hot shower, I settled down in its restaurant, sitting on salt blocks as chairs and tables. I filled myself with a big plate of picante de polo, spicy chicken with rice followed by chocolate para ti. Bolivians usually ate a large lunch and a small dinner. But I was hungry and had not eaten properly for the last few days, so I did not care.

Uyuni salt flats, Salar de Uyuni

After a solid six hour's sleep, with a ground temperature of -6°C, we left before dawn to watch the sunrise on Salar de Uyuni. After 40 minutes' drive through salt flat, we reached a small, rugged hill in the middle of nowhere, named Isla Incawasi, because it looked like a fish from a distance.

This fossilised coral hill was full of towering cacti, some of them one thousand years old. Soon the sun started rising on the horizon. Salt plain in front lightened up like a mirror to an amazing 360° view of the Salar. Most exotic and surreal view ever.

At 3668m elevation Uyuni salt flat extended to 10,582 sq. km, the world's largest salt flat. Fossils of coral and shells in the coral hill showed this was once an inland sea. During tectonic uplift of the Andes, this area became separated between the mountains to become a vast salt-water lake of over 150m depth. About forty thousand years back, following a major earthquake, one side of the mountain chain opened up, resulting in all the water from the lake draining back into the sea. Only the salt flat remained.

Soon the sun was up in the sky and time to return to our hotel for breakfast. I realised that I had used up all the memories in my sim cards. A French couple sitting opposite kindly gave me one of their spare sim cards, which I promised to replace soon we got to the town.

We returned to the salt flat. As far as one could see, there were polygonal patterns of a thick crust of salt extending to the horizon in all directions. The embossed hexagonal pattern looked like as if carved out of a factory. Because the whole plain was perfectly flat and white, it was fun playing with perspective in taking pictures there. Everyone used their imagination to take crazy photos. We played around the plain with our cameras for a while before it got scorching. Even with sunglasses, glare from the salt surface became too much.

Salar had over 10 billion tons of salt, and each year they harvested a portion. The salt crust was exceptionally rich in lithium and contained up to 70% of the world's known lithium reserves. We drove through many kilometres before we could see the low mountains on the horizon. Annual Dakar Rally started on the Salar from 2014. The guide said in its first year; two cars got lost here for hours, unable to locate the finishing point. We then drove to Dakar Monument, now a symbol of automobile lovers in Salar, with many salt carved sculptures.

Next, we stopped by the Ojos de Sal, Eyes of salt. Water bubbled up from subterranean rivers, full of algae, flowing under the edge of the Uyuni Salt Flat. Back on the salt flat, we sat on a salt bench by rows of salt mounts. Our driver brought out our packed lunch. We all added some salt from the ground to our lunch for tasting.

Back at Uyuni in the evening, I reflected on the last four unimaginable days within the high desert mountains and the salt flat I was lucky to have witnessed. Hidden in this remote part of the world was its beauty beyond the wildest dreams.

Santa Cruz   Morning flight was to Santa Cruz with a changeover in La Paz. The temperature in Uyuni airport was below 0°C and now in Santa Cruz boiling 35°C. After a cold shower, I put on a tee-shirt for the first time after several weeks and walked to the reverberating central square surrounded by colonial buildings and wide streets. I sat on a bench under the shade of a jacaranda tree, licking lovely ice cream next to people playing chess. Santa Cruz appeared more affluent than other places I had seen in Bolivia. Santa Cruz, on Pirai River, was Bolivia's commercial centre and received over 40% of foreign investments in the country. For the first time in Bolivia, I was also seeing obese people, not surprising with all the ice cream and cake shops around!

Eastern Andes Mountains range bisects Bolivia roughly from north to south. To the east of the mountain chain are lowland plains of Amazon Basin, and to the west, Altiplano of the highland plateau. Bolivia's climate varied drastically from one ecoregion to the other. From tropics in the eastern basin to polar climates in the western Andes.

After a gorgeous plate of Majadito, a risotto-style plate of duck, with Chicha, a sweet non-alcoholic drink made with corn and cinnamon, I hung around the plaza late in the evening with hundreds mulling around. I got up late next morning missing my breakfast and walked to the square for a brunch of freshly made Empanada de carne and coffee. A nationally famous singing group of Santa Cruz was coming today to sing in the park to celebrate the 15th anniversary of their most famous song. By lunchtime, the park filled up with hundreds of people. They sang their popular songs standing on the steps of the cathedral. Filming was going on, and everybody was dancing. A young lady whisked me away to dance in front of the camera!

Rest of the afternoon for me was doing more of nothing. In the evening in the plaza, the municipality gave a free concert to a packed audience. TV and cinema stars and famous musicians performed. Bolivians indeed enjoyed celebrating and having fun with any excuse.

There were many attractions in Santa Cruz city, but I just lazed around. There was an option to go jaguar spotting in the Amazon for 2-3 days, but sadly I did not have the time. I visited the Contemporary Art Museum with attractive massive paintings decorating its outside wall. Next to it, a film shooting for a TV soap opera was going on. I joined hundreds to watch and could not believe for one scene; they repeated 15 times to get it right - boring. Later I returned to the plaza, just enjoying the flow of life and the jovial atmosphere - my last day in Bolivia.

I thoroughly enjoyed my two months in Bolivia. Friendliness of the people there touched me deeply. They were extremely grateful for even the smallest thing you could do for them. Bolivians everywhere, in poor or rich cities, loved celebrations whenever and with whatever excuses and seemed happy despite so many struggles in their daily lives. With all the cautionary tales I had heard before coming to Bolivia, not for a single moment, I had felt unsafe anywhere. What a beautiful country!

From Viru Viru International Airport, I left Bolivia for Sao Paulo, Brazil, for my connecting flight to the Iguazu Falls.

Iguazu Falls

August 2016 Foz do Iguacu Brazil   I arrived at Foz du Iguacu in the evening. From the bus stop, I had no idea where my accommodation was. The place was empty. Fortunately, a kind girl, a 2ⁿᵈ year engineering student, took the trouble to walk me there over 200m away in the late evening, although very much out of her way.

Later, with some sandwiches and papa frita, in a corner shop, I watched the penalty shootout in Olympics final between Brazil and Germany. Brazil won to a loud cheer from all six of us.

Iguazu Falls   In the morning, I left for the famous Iguazu Falls on the Brazilian side. A park bus took us close to the falls. Soon I was standing against the barrier to a magnificent display of nature.

Iguazu Falls on the Iguazu River on the border of Argentina, with its 275 separate falls spanning 2.7km (Victoria falls - 1.7km), was the largest waterfall system in the world. Iguazu comprised two-step waterfalls, each step measuring between 35 to 40m. Many islands along its 2.7km width divided Iguazu into numerous waterfalls and cataracts, varying between 60 and 82m in height. I stood transfixed at the panorama. Several rainbows formed and disappeared by the rapids.

About half of the river's flow fell into a long and narrow chasm known as the Devils Throat, a canyon 90m wide and 80m deep. I carefully walked into a walkway to the lower part of the canyon. Standing so close to the massive flow of water falling next was an experience of a lifetime. But after only five minutes, I was completely soaked and had to come back.

A lift took me to within 5m of the upper section of Devils Throat. Standing safely on a balcony, I tried to imagine every second over 200,000 gallons of water flowed in this section alone.

Thoroughly soaked and hungry, I found an open-air cafe nearby with the gorgeous views of the falls. Many cute looking wild Quati (smaller version of Racoon) with their tails curled up were hanging around nearby. I got some Hamburger and chips with coffee. I put them down on an empty table and went to get some napkins. As I turned, a Quati came from nowhere, snatched my Hamburger and spilt my coffee on the chips! Not funny when you are so hungry and cold. I felt like, but I was not allowed, killing the wild animal in the National Park!

Iguazu Falls resembled a reversed letter J. Brazil- Argentina border ran through the Devil's Throat. On the right bank was Brazilian territory, home to 95% of Iguazu River basin but had just 20% of these falls. On the left side, jumps were in Argentina, which made up 80% of the falls. I planned to go to Argentina side to see this.

In the evening I found a fabulous Argentina/Brazil style barbecue restaurant. For about 8 dollars, you could eat as much as you like, and the amount of meat they served was impossible even for me to finish. Then there were so many kinds of sweets!

Iguazu Falls Argentina

Early morning at the border crossing formalities took less than ten minutes to go through. We stopped at the border town of Puerto Iguazu for breakfast. Shop's display cabinet had so many types of sweets that I could not take my eyes away. But I settled for some fresh empanadas and coffee and bought some sweets to carry as snacks for the day. Iguazu falls was another 18km.

From the middle of a forest, we got into a Rainforest Ecological train which took us to a trail where one could not miss the roars of the mighty falls. Soon we were in the middle of majestic falls. Through a track, with the gorgeous falls on our left, we arrived on the bank of Parana River. Long wooden bridges took us to a small island in the river. Over a walkway, soon I was standing directly over the falls of Devil's Throat. Vast Parana River every second disappeared here down the mighty fall. No wonder upon seeing Iguazu, Eleanor Roosevelt had exclaimed, 'Poor Niagara!'

I walked across other trails to elongated stretches of falls. Toucans with their colourful bills rested on the trees. Some places I stood right over the falls, in other I was standing right next to them. I had never seen so many rainbows in one place as was in front. Legend had it a deity planned to marry a beautiful woman named Naipi, who fled with her lover in a canoe. In a rage, deity sliced the river, creating the waterfalls and condemning the lovers to an eternal fall.

We came back to a cafe for lunch - capuchin monkeys were on the tree, and many Quati moved around the ground. Cautiously, I brought out my empanada and fruit juice and sat on a table. But unbelievably, an Argentinian monkey jumped from a tree behind me and took one of my Empanada away! You have to laugh sometime.

Before going back to the trails, I shared Mate with our guide, the driver, and a few of us. This national drink of Argentina is traditionally drunk in a social setting, such as family gatherings or with friends. Everyone drank from the same gourd containing the hot drink of infused leaves of mate and used the same metal straw known as bombilla. A lovely touch of community feeling, although the drink itself was very strong.

I returned to the trails to enjoy the marvels of the Iguacu Falls for the rest of the afternoon. I had walked over 10km on the day but still could not have enough of this place. Sadly, by late afternoon, we had to return.

In the evening, my gluttony brought me back to the same restaurant in Foz do Iguacu.

Itaipu Hydroelectric dam Paraguay

Fifteen kilometres from Iguacu stood Itaipu hydroelectric dam on the Parana River between Brazil and Paraguay. After border crossing to Paraguay, we stopped at the visitor centre for a short documentary. This hydroelectric power plant produced the most energy of any in the world. Built on binational cooperation between Brazil and Paraguay, it was one of seven modern engineering wonders of the world. Eight kilometres long Itaipu was four dams joined, 196m high, equivalent to a 65-story building.

An electric bus took us over the massive dam on lookout point with a panoramic view of floodgates. Only one was open with water bursting down to Parana River. On the other side was the 1400 sq.km reservoir. Since they built the dam, endemic species of freshwater basin got separated from species found below. Now there were two different ecoregions.

Itaipu provided 95% of electricity consumption in Paraguay and 25% of that in Brazil. At another end of the dam, our coach stopped where we had time for lunch by the reservoir.

On our return, we stopped at an eco-museum with stories of the dam's construction. Before it was built, around 10,000 families living by the Parana River were displaced. Now it employed 3,000 workers from these two nations and had social schemes of building schools and houses for poor families compensating its negative impact.

Rio de Janeiro Brazil

August 2016

Rio was busy, luckily not as much as it was a few days back when the Summer Olympics were going on. A lull in this beautiful and popular city with its 80 km of beaches, famous Corcovado and Sugarloaf Mountains. Luckily, my hotel was three blocks from the most famous Copacabana beach.

Arriving there, I headed straight to the Copacabana beach. No doubt one of the most beautiful beaches in the world. Thousands sunbathed, played football and volleyball or just lined up at kiosks for ice cream or snacks. Most vibrant and colourful ambience one could ever imagine. Only very few people were swimming on a sunny day. Water was cold. I spent the afternoon watching and dipping my toes in the water. I sauntered along the beach with views of Sugarloaf, Two Brothers and the table-topped Gavea Rock. Then a fantastic sunset as hundreds of lights illuminated the beach. Later I returned to a side street for Bolinhos de Bacalhau, fried cod cakes with cassava chips.

On next day's city tour, we passed by the impressive 18th century Carioca Aqueduct, Lapa arches, which now served as a bridge for tram route. Brief stop outside a large dilapidated warehouse where they made giant tableaus for the famous Rio Street carnival. Next, we went to the impressive Rio de Janeiro Cathedral. Built only three decades ago in a modern style based on Mayan style of Pyramids, it stood proud against the backdrop of Corcovado at a distance over the city.

Olympic Boulevard by the port area was a 1km walk between the Olympic rings and pyre. On the wall opposite shined the largest mural in the world. This legacy of the 2016 Olympics, depicted a Tajapo boy from Brazil, a Mursi woman from Ethiopia, a Kayin woman from Thailand, a Supi man from Northern Europe and a Huli man from Papua New Guinea. Representing humanity's common ancestors, indigenous people from America, Africa, Asia, Europe and Oceania. I tried to imagine the boulevard packed during the Olympics.

 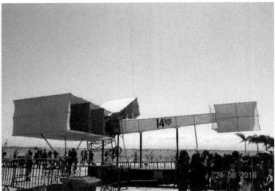

Outside by the seafront was a large display copy of the first aeroplane ever built. Santos-Dumont is a national hero in Brazil, where it is held that he preceded Wright Brothers. While Santos flew an aircraft in Paris in a public show on 23 October 1906, Wright Brothers claimed to have flown a plane privately before that date with no witness!

Museum of Tomorrow at the other end was built most imaginatively. The main exhibition was entirely digital, focusing on ideas rather than objects. Asking questions about where we come from, where we are and where we are heading. Displays ranged from origins of the planet to our possible futures. *'When people think of Future, it usually seems very far away. That's why we called the museum Tomorrow. It is closer. It depends on what we do today'* - it stated. Very interesting.

Next, to the old port and bars area were where famous Brazilian music and dance style Samba originated - brought by the former slave sailors who migrated from Bahia to Rio for a better life. Then a brief stop by the grandstand where they selected from many which of the shows could feature in their famous carnival parades. Sadly, many months away.

Maracana Stadium We circled around and then stopped by the main gate of the massive Maracana Stadium. This world-famous football stadium could once hold nearly 199,000 people and had been the venue of many football dreams. The stadium was used for the Summer Olympics and was now closed to prepare for the oncoming Para Olympics. Standing outside its gate with iconic statues of our football heroes, I had to make a video call to my brother in India, also a football fanatic.

At Copacabana beach in the evening, I stood by a volleyball game between the favela boys. After they finished a game, I persuaded them to let me play a few points with them. Good fun.

Sugarloaf Mountain   Beautiful beaches dotted between skylines everywhere I looked in the city's south. A scenic cable car took me to the breath-taking Sugarloaf Mountain. The gorgeous 396m granite and quartz peak jutted out, rising straight from the water's edge. Change of cable car at the promontory of Morro da Urca and then to Pao de Acucar. A short ascent from there and I was on top of Sugar Loaf. The 360° view of beautiful Rio below, Botafogo Bay at a distance and Mt Corcovado in its background - incredible landscape. While spending time at the top, I realised part of this near-vertical rock was a favourite place for urban rock climbing with over two hundred routes. I wished I was younger and had more time.

We then drove by one of many favelas on our way to Corcovado. From a distance, the colourful favela houses on the side of a hill looked picturesque, but their painful story belied their appearance. Significant disparities between rich and poor who lived in proximity was striking in Rio. Close to 1.5 million people, 25% of Rio's population lived in almost 1000 slums known as favelas, where 95% lived under the poverty level.

Corcovado   Our next destination was the most famous landmark of Rio, Corcovado. We drove through Tijuca, an urban forest. This 32 sq.km forest was the earliest example of human-made reclamation of land around a city. Following clearance and deforestation with intensive farming of the area to grow sugar and coffee in the earlier decades, levels of rainfalls had declined, almost drying up the city. Replantation was carried out in the second half of the 19th century in a successful effort to protect Rio's water supply.

Our Coach stopped near the foot of the mountain. A train then spiralled around the hill to the top of a 710m granite peak.

At the top, in the centre over many steps, was the world-famous 38m statue of Christ the Redeemer, built 90 yrs back to celebrate Brazil's 100 yrs of independence from Portugal. From its surrounding platform, the panoramic view of Sugar Loaf, beautiful Rio with Copacabana and Ipanema beaches, Maracana Stadium and the colourful favela houses was breathtaking.

Amazon

I took a very early flight via Brasilia to Manaus.

Manaus   It was the 450 years old principal city for the Portuguese colonists and then a major rubber plantation area for the British. Rubber had made it the wealthiest city in South America during the late 1800s. Now it was a bustling city producing electronic and electrical goods; cars and motorcycles such as Honda and famous Harley Davidson; Brazil nuts; rubber; jute and rosewood oil. Its manufactures also included batteries, chemical products, and ship-building industries. As a premier site for offshore petrol drilling from Amazon basin, it contributed to the fifth of Brazil's economy.

This spiralling city, in the centre of Amazon rainforest, was now eating into the rainforest through deforestation and environmental degradation. As the economic powerhouse of Brazilian Amazon, Manaus attracted thousands of migrants each year. Failing to provide affordable housing for them had resulted in an extensive clearing of the forests around the city. Untreated waste and rubbish from these occupations also end up in little rivers across Manus before draining into and polluting the Amazon. Drilling for offshore oil, with oil spills and extensive mining around, had added to the severe impact on biodiversity in the upper Amazon basin.

It was also the key departure point for the surrounding Amazon Rainforest.

My boat left from a small fishing port at the east of Manaus. Amazon River was 14 km wide there. This great river accounted for about one-fifth of the world's total river flow. After sailing for 45 minutes, we came at the confluence where the dark Negro River converged with the brown, muddy Solimoes River. An incredible visual spectacle of a meeting of the Waters. Negra, old and slower, was dark with hardly any residue, while the young, almost white Solimoes flew rapidly carrying its load of sediments from the rainforest. A few river dolphins swam close by.

Amazon forest lodge   After going through many large and then smaller tributaries of the Amazon, we arrived at my resort on the bank of a muddy rivulet, for four nights stay in the Amazon. Manaus and modern civilisation were over 80km away. The guide said during the wet season Amazon River exceeded 190km in width, flooding these forests.

It was hot and extremely humid, but because of its higher acidity levels, not many mosquitoes. Even after a cold shower in this basic but comfortable place, I was sweating buckets. This floating lodge sitting on River Juma could accommodate a maximum of twenty people. But at the time there were only six of us. In colourful plants, amongst many insects on a large leaf rested a large tarantula.

After a buffet dinner, we left in the dark for a ride in a small paddle boat. The guide held a spotlight, trying to catch reflections from the eyes of any Cayman on muddy banks. An eerie yet exciting experience. After half an hour going through the narrow channels, occasionally having to push branches of trees from the water to get through, they stopped. I could see nothing, but one guide jumped in the water. By the bank, he caught a year old Cayman and brought to us. While it scared some to touch, I held the cute animal briefly. Afterwards, when I asked if there were any snakes, the guide nonchalantly replied there were many. Some were very poisonous and sometimes fell from the tree into the boat! From then on, we sat stiffly in the boat for the rest of the evening.

After dinner, holding my torch, I returned to my hut, looking out for the glistening eyes of any Jaguar, but no such luck.

Next morning with the guide, three of us walked in the rain forest. Others were too scared of snakes and insects. In this enchanted primary forest of ancient trees and bushes, we spotted spiders of many shapes and sizes. Sexual cannibalism in spiders, attack and consumption of males after copulation by females, were widespread. We saw a giant male spider nervously waiting on its web while an even larger female waited for him nearby. There were ants of various sizes and colour, each specialising in unique types of tree or plant. We kept an eye for the snakes and any lurking Jaguars but, in the two and half hours in the jungle, we did not see any. Not sure if they were watching us. We did not see many birds during this walk. The guide explained at this time of the day; it was almost impossible to spot them in their natural habitat.

After lunch, the plan was to go out on a boat, but within fifteen minutes, inky clouds came from nowhere, and the sky opened up. The rain cleared almost as soon as it came. We crossed through many rivulets looking for Anaconda and Sleuth, but no luck. We stopped by the river bank and walked to an indigenous village of about ten houses. Every house had more than one dinghy, with fishing nets drying nearby. Papaya, mangoes, lime, fig and avocados trees surrounded the houses.

In the evening, we left for another boat trip with a spotlight, only three of us, and this time saw some larger Caymans lying on the muddy banks.

Following morning we steered through another massive branch of Amazon before entering its narrow channels. I asked the guide about the large white nests on the upper branches of trees by the river. He explained they were ant's nest. Ants built their nests high on trees, as during wet season water level reached almost there. Nests were almost 6-7m above us now, impossible to imagine the wet season here. We spotted three sloths sleeping upside down, hanging from the branches. A mother slept with a baby clinging on to her. Sloths slept between 10-11 hours a day - so lucky! Trees were full of varieties of macaws, some deep blue; kingfishers of all sizes and colours; a few bright blue cotingas and sparkling crimson topazes.

Our boat entered a channel full of Piranhas, and the guide gave us rods and baits to catch them. A crafty lot of fishes nibbled away at the bait before I pulled. After a while, though, I caught a few.

The boat crossed the river to a small jetty. There, in a small hut, I gave the fish to a lady to fry for us. While she was doing this, I dived into the Amazon with two local fishermen, watching out for the Piranha family looking for revenge. It was an incredible swim on a hot, sweaty day. By the time I got ashore and had dried myself, Piranhas were fried and ready. Crunchy and mouth-watering!

We rode further to a dry bit of land on the inner section of the river. Our guides prepared a barbeque lunch of fish and crabs. While they were busy cooking, I walked carefully, looking out for snakes, through the forest amongst a group of chattering and scattering squirrel monkeys, disturbing the brightly coloured kingfishers. A harpy eagle circled above.

Before dawn, we left on a boat tour to see the sunrise over the river. Colours changed every second over the horizon, with its reflection over the river channels. Colours changing on the leaves was sensational. I wished I was an artist to capture this on a canvas.

Rest of the group left in the morning, and I was the only tourist in the lodge. They were expecting another ten the next day. Heaven opened up again for over an hour. Talking to the staff I learnt most of them, and all the women, came before 6 am by boat from surrounding localities. Most returned in the afternoon and a few more after dinner. Only a few men stayed overnight, taking turns. While most in their community lived off the jungle and through fishing, now eco-tourism provided a regular income for many families. Near Manus, many communities went to find work in mines or the township. Most of the staff left before lunch, as there was not much to do. I asked the remaining to join me for lunch and was grateful when they did so.

In the afternoon, I left again on a boat tour to spot any Anaconda, but again no luck. No sloths either, but we saw several groups of monkeys and many birds and beautiful views. Our lodge was serving every day lovely western-style food. For my dinner, I requested a traditional Amazonian dinner instead. We sat down together to dine on Tacaca, delicious shrimp soup and then Patarascha, fish grilled with onions, tomatoes, chillies and coriander all wrapped and cooked in large bijao leaf - gorgeous. I asked why they didn't serve these foods to the tourists regularly. They replied most tourists preferred western dishes.

I chatted with the remaining staff about their lives in Amazonia. I learnt loggings and mining in deeper Amazonia had displaced many indigenous communities. Manaus was not only a core city for international trade but also notorious for smuggling of illegal goods, including exotic animals such as monkeys, coloured parrots, and other birds. I returned to bed late but got up before dawn to watch another gorgeous sunrise from the river bank. Sadly, after breakfast, it was time to say goodbye. Ferry from Manaus brought another group of tourists, and I returned to the city to catch my flight to Rio.

Rio   I took a public bus to Leblon district and then went to its beach of the same name. Sitting at the foot of the towering Two Brothers Rock, Dois Irmaos, I just lazed for hours. In the afternoon, I walked to the charming Ipanema beach. Dotted by expensive houses and restaurants behind rows of palm trees, this beach looked exclusive. It was made famous by the popular Brazilian song 'Girl from Ipanema' written in honour of a local beauty who passed by the poet's bar every day. Rio's beaches were no doubt full of women of outstanding beauty. Before returning to my hotel, from a music shop cum cafe, I bought a CD of 'Girl from Ipanema'.

Samba show   After a quick shower, I took public transport to Plataforma on the other side of Rio. I was one of the first to enter the place for a barbeque dinner, followed by a dance show. Colourful dances with folklore themes from all the provinces of Brazil were mesmerising. Beautiful women and men in glamorous and dazzling outfits danced featuring this year's Carnival winning shows. During a brief break, there was an option of having photographs taken with the beautiful dancers, and I could not resist.

Then started Samba. Through music and dance it told stories of the slaves arriving in the country, their sorrows and joys over the century, then the marriage of Samba with jazz music. And finally started, it's re-emergence as pagode, a renewed samba in the last two decades with new instruments like a banjo; tan-tan, a cylindrical hand drum; bass and use of giria, slang languages spoken in the favelas - hypnotising three hours. By the time I got out of the place, it was after midnight. Next morning my last few hours in Rio was strolling on the Copacabana beach, where they were now getting ready for the Para Olympics games.

Argentina and voyage to Antarctica

December 2016   Back from South America, amongst hundreds of email was one from a tour company offering 30% discount for a voyage to Antarctica in mid-December. The continent I had dreamt for long. I booked immediately, adding a tour to Argentina beforehand.

Buenos Aires, Patagonia and Lands end Ushuaia Argentina

Buenos Aires   I fell in love with this city of relaxed atmosphere, easy-going and cafe-style life. Outside my hotel in a building, they were dowsing young men and women with paints, like in the Indian festival of Holi. Glowing parents said traditionally proud parents and families celebrate by throwing dye over the new graduates.

In Spanish, French Beaux-Arts, classic Italian and modernist diverse architectural styles, Buenos Aires looked inviting with fashionable shops, Parisian-style restaurants and cafes full of friends and families sharing Mate. With 250 beautiful parks, even with 2.8 million population, it did not appear crowded.

City tour next day started at the historic Plaza de Mayo. This place had been the focal point of political life in Buenos Aires for centuries. Its name commemorated the May Revolution of 1810, which led to Argentina's independence from Spain in 1816.

Inside the Metropolitan Cathedral along with statues of Virgin Mary and Christian saints was the mausoleum of General San Martin, guarded by statues of women figures representing Argentina, Peru and Chile. Not a saint, but San Martín was a national hero and liberator of these countries from the Spanish colonists. On one side of the plaza was the equestrian statue of General Manuel Belgrano, regarded as one of the liberators of the country, also, who created the Flag of Argentina. Argentina was the first country not only in South America but also in the world to break free from the shackles of colonial rules.

Mothers of Plaza de Mayo   Piramide de Mayo was the hub of the plaza - oldest national monument in the city to celebrate the first anniversary of May Revolution. White scarves of the Mothers painted on the pavement surrounded this monument.

'I am going out for a moment. Be right back.'
The last words Taty Uranga Almeida heard from her son, Alejandro, on June 17th, 1975. She never saw him again and never found out what happened to him. He was one of the thousands who 'disappeared' during political violence in Argentina between the 1970s and early 1980s. Mothers of Plaza de Mayo was a movement of Argentine mothers campaigning for their 'disappeared' children by marching in silence here against the military dictatorship. I stood in silence for several minutes.

Nearby treasury ministry building had bullet and bomb holes from attempts to kill democratic President Peron. Next was the Pink President's Palace, famous for its history with President Peron and his wife, Evita. To make the colour in its wall, they used animal blood, cheaper than producing any other colouring materials.

French quarters with its opulent buildings and mansions were at another part of the city. In contrast, not far from there was the old dock area of multi-coloured buildings of the poor Italian community, La Boca. Here was Caminito, a little path famous because it inspired the music for famous tango Caminito. In narrow streets and on pavements, painters and artists sold their crafts.

Plaza de las Naciones Unidas had the fascinating Floralis Generica, a beautiful enormous flower - 23m high, made of stainless steel and aluminium and weighing 18 tons. This mechanical flower opened and closed its petals depending on the time of day.

Vast and walled Recoleta cemetery was an expensive collection of the necropolis of city's wealthy departed, old and recent - not my cup of tea, unfortunately. Our tour finished there. After lunch in a side cafe of beef Milanesa, I returned through the beautiful Plaza San Martin Park.

Tango show in the evening was at El Querandi Tango Hall, a wood-panelled old theatre, once a meeting point for poets and students. In this cosy little place, I shared a table for my dinner before the show. We had asados, varieties of barbecued meat on a large grill, packed with steaks, ribs, chorizo, sweetbread and blood sausage. After this enormous meal, somehow I still managed some Helados, Argentinian ice cream.

The show started with a soulful folklore solo singing accompanied by charango, a tiny guitar. Musical arrangements smoothly charted the history of tango, Argentina's most authentic artistic expression, from its origins to modern-day. With three singers, six dancers and four musicians, passionate, sensuous partner dances followed - beautiful panpipes, guitar and drums accompanying. Tango originated in the 1880s near the Rio de la Plata, the natural border between Argentina and Uruguay in the impoverished port areas of enslaved Africans populations - a captivating two hours.

Before going for my boat trip on Tigre Delta, next day we made a brief stop at River Plate stadium where Argentina won the World Cup Football Final in 1978. The guide, also a football fan, and I recalled Argentina's football legend Diego Maradona of Boca Junior Club creating many football memories against River Plate on this ground.

Tigre Delta   We stopped at Tigre market, a bustling 19th-century bohemian market place on the riverfront, with many beautiful art galleries. We got into our boat on Tigre delta, only 30 minutes from Buenos Aires. Tigre Delta, a unique and extensive ecosystem of waterways, dissected lush green land into hundreds of islands. The name derived from 'tigres' or jaguars that once frequented but subsequently hunted down when the Europeans came. They farmed the land and developed a port to serve the Delta and to bring fruit and wood upstream on the Parana River. Its iron-rich, coffee-coloured waters finally emptied into the Rio de la Plata. Stilted wooden houses dotted the river banks. Islands on this delta were the most humanised of three large Delta islands I had seen so far, including Sundarban and Amazon basins. Every house had its boats, some more expensive than others.

There was no wildlife in this delta except humans and rare snakes. The river had many fishes, but no alligators. We stopped for lunch at Port of Fruits, an artisan and craftwork market, and once the fruits and woods market of Tigre. Nearby, Mate Museum showed the history of the traditional Argentinean drink and had a mate bar. Later we stopped by the old town of San Isidoro before heading back to the city.

Tango show again   I could not resist in the evening going out for another Tango show. Borges Cultural Centre was named after one of the country's best and most beloved authors, Jorge Luis Borges. Bien de Tango show started with men in suits and hats dancing without showing their faces. Slowly, with the play

of light, their faces became clear. They formed couples with women in colour and grace. An elegant and sensual orchestra followed dramatic choreography -sublime one and a half an hour.

Domestic airport for my flight to El Calafate was by the banks of Rio de la Plata. At 220 km wide, this was the widest river in the world, not a gulf of the sea. Parana River, carrying water with sediments, had travelled almost 5000km through Brazil, joining Paraguay River on its way and then proceeding south through Argentina, until it joined the Uruguay River. Then it drained into Rio de la Plata, ultimately ending in the Atlantic Ocean.

El Calafate Patagonia   El Calafate was a tiny town near the edge of the Southern Patagonian Ice Field - the gateway to Los Glaciares National Park, home to the massive Perito Moreno Glacier. My B&B was next to the Laguna Nimez Nature Reserve, by the enormous Lake Argentino. In the afternoon, I walked on the trail of the nature reserve with abundant birdlife. Against the backdrop of snow-capped Andes peaks, upland geese, silvery grebes, black-necked swans, black-faced ibis, red gartered coots and varieties of ducks rested by the lake. Not so far was a group of flamingo. About 70 species of birds, visited this lake.

Perito Merino Glacier

We drove for 80 km to the National Glacier Park. From the shores of the lake, I could see the massive Perito Merino glacier at a distance. We got into a catamaran on the south side of Lake Argentina. As we approached the glacier, the sheer scale of it rising 75m above the water level became stunning. Every so often there were cracking noises from of its section collapsing on to the lake. Ice burgs floated by us on a blue lake.

Almost 200m from the end of the glacier, we got off the boat to a hilly peninsula. Boardwalk through this jutting hill soon brought me within hundred metres of the south wall of Perito Merino.

This 20km long glacier had stopped here as if to catch a breath, dividing Lake Argentina in two. The southern part of the lake flew rapidly with pale blue coloured water, while the slower flowing main Argentina lake was turquoise blue from the sediments of the glacier. In the corner between the south and the east wall, 70-75m ice towers were almost touching the peninsula.

Glaciologists debate about the reason why Perito Merino maintained a state of equilibrium while numerous glaciers everywhere were retreating with global warming. End of the glacier was 5 km wide with a depth of 170m. Suddenly there was a low rumble followed by a loud cracking. The glacier was calving. A section of 30m ice wall broke free from its mother, and the massive iceberg floated in the blue lake - unbelievable. These calving or ruptures had no periodicity, and minor calving happened all the time. But significant breaks when the water level on the lake could rise to 30m occur every few years, but with no guarantee when. Lucky it did not happen when we were on the catamaran!

I woke from my reverie when a couple stood by me and asked 'hello, do you remember us?'
It was the French couple who had lent me a memory card for my camera in the Uyuni. We chatted for a while, sharing our memories of Bolivia. We stopped talking as there was another calving in another part of the glacier in front.
On the way to our car, a Condor flew majestically, not so high above us - what a fantastic day!

Next morning was lazy walking in the El Calafate streets. Name El Calafate came from Calafate plant, known for its barberry fruits, common in Patagonia. Before returning to my hotel, I bought a supply of high factor sun cream. A couple of dark freckles had already appeared on my face, even with my dark skin. UV light was intense in this part of the world because of the hole in the ozone layer and would get stronger closer to Antarctica.

Nibepo Aike Estancia   The 60 km drive on mountain gravel road took us first to a series of barren mountains until we reached close to the glacial lakes. Colour on the hills there changed to green with distant snow peaks of the Andes raising their heads for contrast. Covering an area of over 12,000 hectares, stretching to the border with Chile, Nibepo Aike retained the essence of original Patagonian estancias, ranches. Formerly devoted to sheep production, but now its main output was breeding prestigious herd of Hereford cattle. Only a handful of ranches stood 10-20km apart in this Patagonian wilderness.
From the ranch, after sampling some homemade cakes with coffee, I walked along the shores of the southern arm of Lake Argentino to the shores of Lake Roca with charming views of the snowy peaks. On the trail were many bushes of Calafate berries, not ripe yet. We returned through the woodlands of Lenga and Nire, a habitat of caracaras, eagles, woodpeckers, and hares. Back at the estancia, there was

a demonstration of horsemanship skills unique to Patagonia. Around the farm I saw many gladioli, spilling into the wilderness. The guide said these plants introduced a few decades back were now becoming part of native species.

At the 100-year-old farmhouse, a relic of Patagonian pioneer architecture, estancia's everyday life carried on with the men riding past herding the cattle and sheep. We had some hot chocolate, while on the other side of the room a man prepared over a large barbeque, cuts of fresh meat.

Soon we filled up our plates with all sorts of meat. By the time we said goodbye to our host, the sun had gone down behind the mountains.

After about 20kms on the gravel track, our minibus started spluttering and every so often came to a near stop. After driving slowly for another 2km like this, the car stopped. The Patagonian wind was howling outside. The driver got out of the vehicle with a manual and asked us to read it with a torch, probably enough sign we are in trouble. But somehow the car started again and continued at less than 5km per hour, spluttering all the way - you can only laugh. I was only hoping that I can get back in time for my early morning flight. About 10 km outside Calafate a rescue vehicle arrived for us, but could only take a few. I stayed loyal to my sick car and arrived at my hotel in time to have just two hours' nap before getting up to catch my flight for Ushuaia.

Ushuaia   Tierra del Fuego

Ushuaia, the last of the landmass of the world, was windy with rain and sleet. Tierra del Fuego group of islands were separated from the tip of South America. Only the eastern part of the main island, and a few small islands in the Beagle Channel, belonged to Argentina with Ushuaia as its principal town. From my bedroom, through the rain, was a view of the famous Beagle channel. There was no food in the hotel. I walked over 150m, down slippery steps to find one street where a few shops were open. After having my lunch in the shop, I bought some sandwich and drinks for my dinner. I did not fancy up and down these steps in the evening in the sleet. But the evening was difficult to define as the sun did not go down now until after 10-30pm.

Tierra del Fuego National Park   The weather cleared in the morning. Beagle channel and the bay looked most inviting. I left for a day tour to Tierra del Fuego National Park, 10km distance, a stunning national park as close to the end of the world as possible. We passed Mt Susana and arrived at the old prison, which once held the most notorious criminals of Argentina and was named 'Siberia of the South'. In the 19th century, the southern tip of Patagonia was a harsh frontier. First European settlers were Christian missionaries in the 1850s, followed by sheep ranchers and gold prospectors. Region's indigenous peoples were virtually wiped out. In 1896, the Europeans established a prison here. Inmates were forced to construct their own cells; municipal buildings and homes for Ushuaia, and a railway line to transport timber from the nearby forests.

Inside the prison museum now was a moving quote from an inmate: '*Labouring is the only way of defeating the prison. I'll go out in the wood. At least I can breathe some air and see the sun.*'

End of the World Train Tren del Fin del Mundo

End of the World Train, Tren del Fin del Mundo was like a toy train ride. The train left the station, a construction resembling an Alpine chalet, on a steam locomotive with panoramic coaches, through thickly forested Toro gorge.

We stopped at La Macarena station, manned by staff in yellow-and-blue-striped prisoner uniforms. Nearby, was a gently cascading waterfall and on another side a few rough wooden shelters, replicas of those used by the indigenous people.

Soon we crossed over Pipo River, named after a prisoner who escaped briefly before freezing to death on the riverbank. The landscape grew wilder as we moved past enchanting lakes and snowy peaks.

After 45 minutes we arrived at the deserted National Park station, gateway to a 630 sq.km national park, amongst peat bogs, sub-Antarctic tundra in the shadow of soaring Andean ranges. Southern Fuegian railway helped Ushuaia to flourish, but it finally ran out of steam in 1952 following the closure of the prison and a devastating earthquake. In 1994, a 7km section was restored and relaunched.

We drove afterwards from the station through dramatic forests, waterfalls, mountains and glaciers with a brief stop by Green lagoon and Black Lagoon. Then a hike on a rugged trail to the coastal path connecting Ensenada Bay to Lapataia Bay on Lake Roca. Lake Roca was 20% Argentinian and 80% Chilean, with a striking view of the Condor Hill on its shore. Tree branches had red-headed Magellan woodpeckers and green austral parakeets, world's southernmost parrot. This national park had a variety of wildlife including beavers, foxes and rabbits and some beautiful native flora. We continued through the valley towards Redonda and Estorbo Islands with a backdrop of snow-white Mountains of Sampaio chain on the other coast of Beagle Channel in Chile. Then down to the bay opening into Beagles Channel where the land ends for South America.

I was now at the end of the lands on this planet!

This dramatic landscape on the remotest corner of the world had been repeatedly under attacks from humans. Europeans introduced rabbits for meat in the late 19th century, which proved a menace for the region's many sheep farmers. To combat this, they brought grey Patagonian foxes, but unfortunately; the rabbits were not to their taste, and both species prospered. In the 1940s, the Argentine government introduced 50 North American beavers to create a profitable fur trade. The industry did not take off and the beavers, free of natural predators, spread throughout the archipelago. Now around 200,000, beavers damage Tierra del Fuego's forests and eradication programme were underway. Yet another lesson in dangers of unintended consequences of human interference with nature.

Next morning I walked down for a view of the Beagle Channel. This 240km long channel, 5km wide at its narrowest point, was one of three navigable passages between the Pacific and the Atlantic Oceans. Straits of Magellan is in the north between Tierra del Fuego and mainland South America. While the Drake Passage is the open-ocean passage between South America and the Antarctic. Beagle channel's eastern area forms part of the border between Argentina and Chile, and its western area is entirely within Chile. Beyond the channel are many islands. Humans had inhabited them for at least 10,000 years. Its name came after the ship HMS Beagle on its first survey of the coasts of the southern part of South America.

The second voyage of the ship famously carried Charles Darwin, an amateur naturalist.

Voyage to Antarctica

December 2016

I boarded Ocean Endeavour with a quiet air of excitement. At the safety briefings, there was a buzz amongst 118 passengers and 100 crews. Soon we were sailing through the Beagle Channel, leaving Ushuaia and Andes Mountains behind. On a small island on the channel, a group of sunbather sea lions completely ignored us. Then all the islands were behind us. We were on the Drake Passage. Next land will be the 7th continent!

The Drake Passage was named after the 16th-century English buccaneer Francis Drake. His only remaining ship was blown away south by a storm from the Magellan Strait, proving there was an ocean south of South America. First recorded voyage through the passage was by the Dutch navigator Willem Schouten in 1616, who had named Cape Horn earlier in the year. This gateway to wonders of Antarctica was indeed a rite of passage. Storms with colossal waves were frequent and unpredictable. I couldn't imagine how the sailors, with wooden crafts and sails made of cotton or flax, even dared to sail these waters.

After an elaborate dinner, we had some interesting lectures by the travelling scientists on ecology and eco safety. Outside was cloudy, but it was still daylight. Sun will not set for another hour, although it was nearly 10 pm. I explored the ship and was delighted to find they allowed us on the bridge to watch the ship's journey through the waves. For over 1100km cruise in about 48 hours, at first, we sailed at a speed of about 10 knots. Soon the waves in front got larger, at least 10-15m in heights. A storm was coming our way. The ship slowed down to 5 knots. Captain and his officers discussed whether they should change course or weather the storm out. They asked us to go back to our cabin or the seating areas inside.

I walked back as the ship started rocking. Rather than risking being sick, I returned to my cabin and tried to sleep. After a few hours, I woke up and sat by the window of the cafeteria with a cup of coffee and some croissants, available 24 hours a day. The sea was now sunny and calm. A few skuas and gulls flew by. I found a book on birds of Antarctica. Luckily, the lady sitting by the next window was a marine biologist and explained about ample birdlife around this part of the world. Plankton was abundant in these waters, allowing healthy populations of seabirds, dolphins and whales. She helped me identify types of petrels, cormorants and a few albatross flying by the boat.

Nothing but boundless sea all around, and almost 22 hours of daylight. With so much food available all day, I must watch out. More interesting lectures and time to get to know the fellow travellers and the crew. A sizeable group came from China, some from the same family and another group from Taiwan. I learnt for each of these groups they had a local travel agent who travelled for free with them. Agent's role was to smooth things over during the journey. I must seriously think of finding a job as a travel agent when I go back!

Most of my day, however, was at the bridge. The crew were from many parts of the world, mostly Southeast Asia and the Captain was from Ukraine. A dozen expedition team members were from Europe, USA and Australia. They worked throughout the Antarctic summer from early December to end of March. Then after only a few weeks holiday back home before returning to voyages around the arctic from June to September in summer months there.

The day was just between the viewing areas on the deck and the bridge. Sea again became choppy, and a few passengers got violently sick. More lectures on ecology, geology and the marine life of Antarctica. At almost 15 million sq.km, Antarctica was twice the size of Australia. 98% of the continent had ice coverage of average 1.9 km in thickness, which extended to all but the northernmost reaches of the Antarctic Peninsula where we were heading. Antarctica, on average, was the coldest, driest, and windiest continent, and had the highest average elevation of all the continents. Most of Antarctica had no rain for almost 2 million years, the largest desert in the world. But 80% of the freshwater reserve of the world was here, enough to raise global sea levels by 60m if all of it melted. The average winter temperature in Antarctica was -63°C although it had reached as low as -94.7°C.

Before breakfast the next day, there was excitement in the deck. Someone had spotted the first floating iceberg. We all rushed outside to find an iceberg at least five times the size of a football pitch floating by. Our crew pointed east to the foggy outline of Shetland Islands at a far distance.

Soon they called for an eco-safety check of bags and clothing items allowed to take onshore in Antarctica. They issued top quality warm jackets to keep and lend us snow boots. Everyone was excited by now. We will be in Antarctica in the next 10-12 hours!

A second iceberg floated by with many penguins using the place like a diving board. More and more icebergs of various sizes followed. With all the beautiful scenery around, I could not get away from the bridge to go to sleep till 11 pm. It was still bright in the sky. In mid-December here, the sun went out for less than an hour, but the sky remained bright. Because of its location, Antarctica was in all the time zones. The standard time zone used here was UTC, Universal Time Coordinate, the 24-hour time using precise atomic clocks combined with Earth's rotation.

The crew announced we would make our first landing next morning after breakfast. After tossing and turning in my bed, I was up at 3 am. I rushed to the deck. Large icebergs, one of them almost a kilometre long, floated past. We spotted a large Weddell seal lying next to a group of busy penguins on an iceberg. Nearby, some humpback whales did their flips.

On the 7th continent

The ship anchored with our first view of the continent - the Brown Bluff. We walked down long, narrow stairs to our zodiac. With 8-10 in each, an expedition team member motoring, within 20 minutes, we were ashore on the 7th Continent - lifetime dream! Brown Bluff was a flat-topped volcano of over million years old. We walked carefully on its long cobble and ash beach. Around us and on the slopes of the bluff was the colony of 60,000 pairs of Gentoo and Adele penguins who just had their chicks - extraordinary. A group of a maximum of 20 of us spent half an hour there before getting back on our craft. Then we cruised around icebergs and massive ice walls at the end of glaciers for another 45 minutes in wonder.

During lunch, between the main course and desserts, there was an announcement - Orcas around. We all rushed to the deck. About 20 Orcas gracefully swam and dived right by the ship, two mothers with their babies. A Minky whale had just swum by, but I had missed it.

Ship's officers in their full regalia came together and sat on a table by themselves, headed by the Captain. After their dinner, I introduced myself and got to talk to the only medical officer on board from

El Salvador. She said most of the time her job was prescribing anti seasickness tablets and some antacids for the overeaters. In the case of a major emergency, a rescue was difficult and hazardous. Luckily in her two years of working on the ship, she had not the misfortune of someone becoming so sick on board. When she learnt I was going to Guatemala for volunteering in a few months, she said hospitals in El Salvador were desperately looking for volunteer surgeons. I promised to look into this.

With us was travelling a man in his sixties with terminal cancer. His wish was to see Antarctica in his lifetime. He was on continuous oxygen, and his wife carried the oxygen cylinder for him. They did not get off the ship but enjoyed the magic of Antarctica.

A zodiac took us in the afternoon to Paulet Island. Near our landing site, a glacier cascaded its ice sheet into the sea. Around us were jagged, snow-capped peaks, results of uplift from volcanic activities. Antarctic Peninsula was an extension and continuation of the Andes Mountains of South America. In pure Antarctic air, we could smell a penguin rookery from a long way away before we landed! This place with a 300m high volcanic cone had a colony of over 100,000 pairs of Adelie penguins and their chicks. We carefully walked around penguin rookeries to the ruins of a stone hut built by the survivors of a wrecked Swedish vessel in 1903. A kelp gull, sitting on the wall, waiting to snatch a penguin chick for dinner, flew away. Weather, which was all day beautiful and sunny, suddenly turned windy with snow.

It was still incredible cruising around the icebergs for another 45 minutes. On our way back, we spotted two humpbacks, mother and a baby, doing their tricks.

Blizzard weather got worse as we sailed on. More lectures on penguins by the marine biologists. Of the total 17 species of penguin, only two, Emperor and Adelie, lived solely in the Antarctic. Chinstrap, Gentoo and Macaroni bred on the northern tip of Antarctic Peninsula, where conditions were less harsh. Penguins spent 75% of their time at sea and could descend to depths of over 250m. But most of their dives were in the top 10m. Penguins bred on exposed rocks known as rookeries, except for the Emperor, which bred on the sea-ice. Antarctica had about 20 million breeding pairs of penguins. They usually hatched two eggs except for the Emperor, which laid only one. Both parents shared incubation duties until the chicks hatched. Older chicks gather in a crèche, watched over by a few adults, allowing both parents to feed at sea.

Blizzard continued as we sailed on, but as we arrived at Cierva cove by lunchtime, the weather cleared. The beauty of this cove with icy mountains and massive icebergs of unimaginable shapes and sizes was indescribable. Small floating pack ice between the icebergs almost covered the sea.

After navigating through pack ice, our zodiac stopped as a whale flipped only 50m away. As we watched, another whale swam towards us. Soon a 12m southern Minke whale was in front. It swam straight towards us and then slowly dived under our boat and jumped out of the water on the other side.

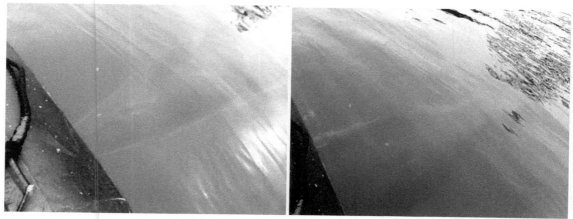

By now, all the other zodiacs gathered around. Stunned, **we** watched the Minke doing the same trick of going under our boat once again. Like it was our pet whale!

When it swam further away, we went around more gorgeous icebergs, our boat pushing away pack ice - ethereal beauty.

Back on the ship, they announced that Antarctic plunge would start in half an hour. I thought about it for a full minute, before deciding why not. Where would be a better place in the world to have a plunge in the sea than this? I lined up undressed and with the safety harness at a ground temperature of -8°C. Roped people, one at a time, jumped in front and then was pulled out of the water in less than a minute. My turn came, and I jumped. For a split second, my brain with everything else froze. Then I swam in the Antarctic for a full minute! Soon I got pulled out of the water.

Seawater temperature was only about -2°C. Danger to the swimmers, apart from freezing to death, was of being hit by the pack ice floating around. Two zodiacs continually cleared the pack ice away from the swimming area. Wow, I have done it!

Later, in the open deck with beautiful surrounds, we had a barbecue dinner with the expedition staff and the ship's crew doing some shows - a perfect end to a beautiful day.

Next day we arrived at the beautiful Orne harbour. On its icy slope, in the rookeries, were thousands of pairs of Chinstrap penguins with their twin chicks. We carefully walked through their rookeries to find a rock

cave where a Cormorant was feeding her chick. As I sat on the shore watching the penguin antics, many Chinstraps waddled by us in a line on the shore. Once there, no one wanted to dive in the water and hesitated for long. Soon one of them got almost pushed, and then everyone dived in the sea. Leopard seals were nearby, hence the hesitation.

My attention drew to the other end of the shore. A Chinese couple, the woman shivering in her white wedding dress and the man in his suit was getting married, presided by the expedition team leader. Both of their parents were on board, but this morning was still feeling seasick and not well enough to come by zodiac. Only a few of us watched this brief, memorable wedding ceremony, and as soon as it was over, the groom covered the shivering bride with her warm coat.

Back on our zodiac, we saw a leopard seal in the water with a half-eaten penguin. Now we could fully understand the poor penguins' hesitation to get into the water
We then cruised around and got onshore to a colony of Weddel seals. Not very far were few crabeater

seals resting on the ice and penguins were diving into the water from the icy shore. By a medium-sized iceberg, a Leopard seal was resting. Close by, this giant creature, even at rest, looked vicious.

Back on the ship during dinner, we all had a slice of the wedding cake.

Danco Island was 1.5km long with a 180m mountain. Danco, in the Errera Channel, was spectacular with deep crevasses in surrounding glaciers in the mountains. It had a colony of over 1600 pairs of Gentoo penguins who made their nests near the top. Only one hiking path to the top. We carefully trudged up from icy shore through knee-deep snow, avoiding the course of the Gentoo penguins to their rookeries. Going up penguins hobbled looking busy, while going down they just tobogganed on their belly. This had created a path up to the top of the mountain to their colony. Our guides called it the penguin highway!

Going up was tough, compounded by heavy winter gear. So-called Antarctic treaty of wildlife suggested we try to keep a distance from the animals. But some penguins just walked next to us, and we had to stop - they have been busy and had not yet read the treaty! At the top, sitting by the colony of Gentoos with their chicks, the 360° sweeping panoramic view of the mountains and our ship looking tiny surrounded by icebergs, was out of this world.

We cruised again on our zodiac through icebergs by an almost vertical ice wall. Warmer weather there had created a cave in shiny blue colour. The Antarctic was a beauty in black-and-white, with ice and snow against the crisp blue hues of the seawater and the sky. Even the fauna here was in black and white.

Only colours we had seen so far were red patches around the penguin nests and the lying seals from their coloured poop from a diet of krills. Antarctica flora consisted about 250 lichens, 100 mosses, two dozen liverworts and over seven hundred algae, an unknown number of microscopic fungi, and only two tiny flowering plants in its north-western peninsula.

Our zodiac stopped by a massive ice wall, parts of which looked as if someone was clumsily trying to paint the wall in light pink. The guide said this was Blood Falls, an outflow of an iron oxide-tainted plume of saltwater, flowing from the tongue of Taylor Glacier.

Soon we were on a bumpy ride through icepacks to a small island with about 20 Weddel seals sleeping on fast ice. As we got into unfrozen water, we could hear the noises made by the whales. We also spotted a Minke diving nearby, but this one was shy and did not come near us. We came across a lone crab eater seal lying still on a small iceberg surrounded by its red poop. As we wondered if it was dead or alive, it slowly turned around and yawned.

There were two optional extras for the tour: the first, the chance to sleep in the open overnight on Antarctic shore. The second was for paddle-boarding the next morning on the partly frozen sea. The first option tempted me, but it meant staying in the open with no toilet facilities for over 10 hours - my old bladder rejected it quickly. The second option looked colourful on the brochure, but I knew I had a problem with balance. Falling into the freezing water will not be at all pleasant. Instead, I stayed on the bridge.

We arrived by Goudier Island in the morning. Two other islands in Neumayer Channel sheltered this small island with more bare rocks than we had seen far - a nesting site of many hundred Gentoo penguins and Cormorants, both species were waiting for their chicks to hatch in the next few days. In this low-lying rocky island, in melting fast ice was the half-buried skeleton of a giant whale. We walked quietly and carefully by the attendant penguins and cormorants guarding their eggs against attacks by skuas and kelp gulls perched on the rocks. Several seals, Weddel and crabeater, rested on other stones. On the icy channel between Goudier and the Wiencke Island, our paddle boarders went by slowly. I took their photograph but was happy to be on the ground in this paradise amongst the wildlife.

Penguin Post Office   Our zodiac took us to another end of the island. There, carefully holding on to the pas
whalers' rusty chains on a tricky landing area, we walked up to the Penguin Post Office. Port Lockroy strangel
was the most southerly operational post office in the world. Discovered in 1904, they used the harbour on thi
bay for whaling until 1931. During World War II, it was a British military base and later a research station unt
the 60s.

Renovated in 1996, Port Lockroy is now a research station for Argentina and the UK. Also a British
post office with a museum of the history of naval expeditions to Antarctica. Surrounding the hut were many
penguins quietly sitting by their eggs. I got a postcard for my two granddaughters and then stamped it and
posted in a red letterbox for delivery in a few weeks. The young lady who was working there was one of
the four researchers, part of the Antarctic Heritage Trust from the UK. Apart from stamping and processing
thousands of letters, they also collected vital data on penguin colonies during their four-month stay.

We sailed then to an island with abandoned Argentinian whaling and observation post. Humans
have engaged in whaling since prehistoric times - part of daily lives in the Arctic Circle for centuries. In the
winter, Antarctic sea ice expanded around it to an area roughly equal to its size. Sea ice retreated almost
to its coastline during the summer months. Different species of whales migrated south to the waters of
Antarctica in summer for its krill and phytoplankton bloom.

From the earliest days of exploration, the human had plundered Antarctica for its natural resources,
seals and whales. By the time whaling started in Antarctica in the early 20th century, commercial whaling
had reached its industrial stage with explosive harpoons and small, fast catcher boats. After decades of
large- scale commercial whaling, stocks for most whale species in Antarctica are now only at a fraction of
their pre-whaling level. International Whaling Commission has been established, but even as of now,
exploiting loopholes, Japanese whalers kill over 50 whales every year in the Antarctic in the name of
science!

It became very windy and foggy by the time we got back to our ship. We sailed back across the
Drake Passage after an unforgettable week around Antarctica. Return passage in the first twenty-four hours
was choppy, but the weather cleared the next day. We arrived by the Beagles channel with the first sight of
land in the morning and soon docked in Ushuaia.

Aurora at last in Tromso Norway

2016/17

It was only 13,380km from Ushuaia when I arrived in the UK on 23rd December evening. I went to sleep straight away. After a quick grab of a microwave meal on the Christmas Eve, back to bed. Feeling fresh on the Christmas morning, I visited my granddaughters who were having more fun playing hide and seek in the cardboard boxes than with their Christmas presents.

'You are mad to be travelling again so soon,' said my son-in-law.

'But I have not seen the Northern Lights yet - the best place on earth to see the Aurora is from Tromso.'

Tromso was cold, dark and miserable when I arrived on the 29th December afternoon. In the sleet and thick cloud, I looked up to the sky for any sign of colour, but none. Next morning I strolled carefully on an icy path to the Tourist Office beyond an old Church and booked for a Northern light tour for the evening. Still, I had the entire day in Tromso. The helpful assistant suggested a whale watching tour, starting in an hour. I walked to the deserted icy dockside to find my boat.

Whale watching   Soon with twelve passengers, we sailed out of the harbour in arctic waters. Outside Tromso, we moved along the fjords and mountain. Everything looked grey and pale white, even at midday. The skipper said Orcas and Humpbacks come here in hundreds during winter months to feed on spawning herring in the fjords. Whales used to hang out closer to Tromso, but with overfishing, their behaviour had changed. Now came in enough numbers only away from Tromso.

After sailing by the mysterious-looking fjords for about 45 minutes, we stopped close to the shore where seagulls and cormorants were diving in. In an area close to the shore, thousands of herrings were jumping out of the water almost playfully. Then we spotted a group of five orcas diving towards them, swimming close to our boat. Not sure, but the orcas in arctic here were in black and white, but in Antarctica did they also have a bit of yellowish tinge?

Our boat stood still while we watched the eating frenzy. Rules were boats must stay at least 50m away from the whales, but another group of orca came from nowhere and swam right by us. We watched this display for about half an hour while other boats came to watch. We sailed away to give them space as only three vessels were allowed near the whales.

Northern Lights

Aurora forecast for the night was good. The Island of Tromso, at 350km north of the Arctic Circle, was right in the middle of Aurora Oval, which meant we could see Aurora even when the activity was low.

The company had advised us to bring our passports. We may go east into Finland or even Sweden, depending on the best sighting for the night. Our guide calculated the itinerary based on the last forecast update released every three hours as we drove through icy road for two hours towards the border. The minibus stopped in a field on the top of a hill just inside Finland border. The temperature outside was -15°C but felt colder in the dry air. Clear sky. The driver produced hot drinks.

Not before long, the show started from nowhere. Running away from the car for a better spot, I dropped my camera on the hard ice, and it stopped working. At first, a faint green arc of light appeared over the mountaintop at a distance. Soon the colour became darker, moving and changing shape and direction all the time, like a dream.

But Aurora was unpredictable. It disappeared after only ten minutes. Standing by our car, we had steaming soup and stamped our feet on the frozen ground. Lights came back without warning, exploding in the sky as if coming out of mountain tops like volcanic eruptions.

We stayed mesmerised until 2 am when the colours of Aurora faded. The guide said the company would have the professional photographs from the night available on their website.

Arctic University Museum Tromso had been home to Sami culture from around 200 AD. The museum showed how Sami people mastered the art of surviving in the arctic conditions - their transition to nomadic life, reindeer herding, migration, their dwellings and a multitude of Sami clothing and crafts. There were stories from ancient Sami mythology, with shamans and their magic drums.

'Aurora Explained' exhibition detailed the science behind the Lights. The word 'Aurora' came from the name of the Roman goddess of dawn and the princess in popular fairy tale Sleeping Beauty.

Northern Lights resulted from disturbances in the earth's magnetic field caused by solar storms which were potentially harmful particles. While stronger geomagnetic storms produced beautiful aurora, it could also wreak serious havoc on all our electronics and communication systems. KP index was one way of measuring the strength of a geomagnetic event. Ranging from 0 to 9, it respectively described quiet and extreme storm. Between 1 to 3, it predicted weak to moderate Aurora display, while 4 to 6 suggested an active show of colours but with increasing geomagnetic disturbances.

Solar cycle with maximum activity averaged 11 years. When the sunspot cycle was at a maximum, chances of seeing aurora even below the Arctic Circle went up. Most massive recorded geomagnetic storm in 1859, took down parts of the then recently created US telegraph network and started fires. In 1989, a solar storm disrupted electric power distribution throughout most of Quebec. Aurora was visible as far south as Texas.

The density of the atmosphere and altitude of geomagnetic collisions determined the colours. Most often it was striking green but occasionally ranged from red to pink or blue to purple. Oxygen at about 100km altitude gave off the familiar green-yellow colour, whereas at much higher altitudes it gave all-red auroras. Nitrogen at different heights produced blue and red-purple light.

Tromso was warmer than most other places on the same latitude. The warm-water current of Gulf Stream around allowed for a milder climate, even at 69°40'33"N 18°55'10"E. In the late 19th century, it was a major Arctic trade centre, and many Arctic expeditions such as by Roald Amundsen started here. With an average winter temperature of -4°C, rarely very windy, well-built roads allowing drive out to the islands in the west or on the mainland in the east, all the way to the Finnish border, an ideal place for Aurora hunting.

Next, I created my personal Northern Lights in the laboratory and thought of the Norwegian scientist Kristian Birkeland, who discovered their origin over 100 years ago.

Dog sledging Villmarksnter in Kvaloya, Whale Island, was half an hour from Tromso after crossing a bridge over the bay. In the gloomy afternoon, in the middle of nowhere, they welcomed us in the only hall with light. As they distributed thermal suits and explained the programme, someone asked where the huskies were? Lady in charge explained huskies were in a ground nearby. Dogs get very excited if they hear any noise or if the lights were on. They then wanted to run even before connecting to the sledges. Another reason was they fed the huskies only once a day, at the end of the run. And also the dogs just loved the fun of running in the wild.

As we got out of the place and they switched on the light, we could immediately hear howling of the dogs from a field. Eight huskies chained in two rows, very excited, wailing and trying to pull away two people to a sledge. One trainer joined me as I was on my own. With our headlamps on, huskies soon pulled us away through frozen beauty with the mountain landscape. With no sunlight, I could only see the sledge in front of me about 10m distance. I was glad the trainer was controlling the sledge as we bumped hard through ice and snow.

Some sledges got into trouble. As the riders had put their breaks on, the dogs had got all tangled up with their chains. While the trainer left to sort them out, I kept my foot hard on the brake. We came by a frozen river. The dogs pulled us over without care as some ice broke, and icy water splashed on us. Luckily, our gear was waterproof. As I got used to the bounces and used to the dark, in the flurry of snow, the surrounding became mythical - a thrilling and unforgettable 45 minutes.

Back at the farm, in the dog yard, once they were unchained, we cuddled and petted the dogs. We watched them fed a small diet of dried meat and fish. There were 300 Alaskan huskies, including their puppies. Dogs slept chained outdoors throughout the winter, except for the cute puppies who had small sheds next to their mothers.

In the old large Sami Gamme hut, we sat on a long wooden table by an open wood fire. Owner Tove Sorensen was next to me. Over a bowl of steaming Bacalao, a traditional Norwegian fish dish, I learnt she had competed 15 times in Europe's longest 1100km Finnmarkslopet dog sledging race, which lasted 5-7days. Tove was looking forward to her next race only five days later and was getting her favourite huskies ready. During the 11 stages of the race, she would be on her own with her dogs and couldn't wait. I was jealous of her adventurous spirit.

Before returning to Tromso, we said goodbye to the beautiful dogs, now curled up on snow ready to sleep after their dinner.

Northern Lights in the New Year   Another travel company picked me up around 9 pm for Aurora hunting. We drove to Kvaloya Island into the wilderness for 30km. On the way the guide told us owing to Tromso's high latitude, twilight was long, with no real night between March 27 and September 17. During the polar nights from 26th November to 15th January, the sun remained below the horizon. But because of the mountains, it was not visible from 21st November to 21st January. Return of the sun was an occasion for celebration. Teachers took school children for a picnic up a hill nearby to watch the sun appearing at horizon only for a few minutes for the first day on 21st January. Some years the sun was not visible because of the clouds and made the children cry!

Soon we stopped by a frozen river below a range of low hills. Out of nowhere, the magic started. Green lights started flowing upwards from the top of the mountain, like from the Indian Tubri fireworks. It then danced over us.

Humans have feeble night vision and could only see the green colour clearly in Aurora. But through my guide's lenses around the green were red, blue and purple. There was even a trace of pink with the KP

index for the night over 4.

Dancing aurora threw its reflection over the river- spellbinding. But the show, unfortunately, stopped as suddenly after only half an hour.

After waiting there for another twenty minutes, we returned by the Tromsdalen Church, separated from Tromso by the bay. Half an hour before the New Year, people arrived from all around to celebrate. We paid a brief visit inside the modern church, then watched from outside New Year's fireworks celebration. Tromso and Kvaloya coast line lighted up.

After a celebratory drink, the guide said the forecast was better for the next few hours. We drove for 45 minutes to the side of massive, partly frozen Lake Ersfjord, surrounded by the iced fjords and a small fishing community on one side. After twenty minutes, Aurora showed up. Against the enormous lake, it was a phenomenal display for over half an hour. Lights then started fading, and reluctantly we returned around 3 am.

I took my return flight in the afternoon while most of the city slept after celebrating the New Year.

Guatemala, Belize and Mexico Central America

January / February 2017

Guatemala – volunteering and volcano hike

A volunteering organisation, serving patients in the poorest and neglected areas of Guatemala, had invited me to join. I reconfirmed my travels plans soon after returning from Tromso.

At 1500m, Guatemala City was founded around 1500 BC and became capital of the country in 1776. Four volcanoes, two of them active, surrounded the city. In the Ring of Fire in mountainous highlands, earthquakes were frequent here - the last massive event registering 7.5 scales in 1976. Sinkholes often appeared in the middle of the city out of nowhere, emitting volcanic ash and limestone. Largest one recently, 100m deep, ended up with evacuation of one thousand people.

I explored on foot this cosmopolitan city and walked to Palacio Nacional de la Cultura, presidential office and a museum. Volcanoes about 40km away looked in their slumber. I was feeling sleepy too. As traffic got heavy, I returned to catch up on some sleep.

Next day I met up with the local volunteering team. In two days, a group of nine of us will travel to the western highlands area by car, spending eight days there. Almost half the population of the country were indigenous Mayan, over 80% of them living below the poverty level. Nearly 80% of doctors in the country resided around Guatemala City. Rural Mayan population suffered from the inadequate healthcare system, exorbitant medicine price added to their chronic malnutrition and ill health. Our team included a local doctor; three nurses; two health workers, whom we will pick up on our way; a coordinator and the driver. Dispersed mainly in the western highlands, Mayans had 22 indigenous languages, and only the two health workers in the team could understand some of them.

On the following free day, I visited Tikal, the largest archaeological sites in Mesoamerica of pre-Columbian Maya civilisation. After an hour's flight from Guatemala City, I arrived at Tikal National Park. From the entrance, it looked like a deep jungle with a few ancient structures sticking out their head through the trees in places.

Tikal The massive over 576 sq.km site was once the capital of powerful kingdoms of ancient Maya. Only its central city site of 16 sq.km had been excavated and included 3,000 structures. During the 400 BC to 900 AD, Tikal was the cradle of Maya civilization.

Grand Plaza, the main square of the city, had two great temple-pyramids on the east and west sides flanking the plaza. On its north lay a large acropolis dating back to 350 BC, a centre for funereal complex for the ruling dynasty. Over the centuries, royal burial chambers added new temples on top of the older structures. These buildings included a row of tall pyramids, each with stairways flanked by masks of the gods and hieroglyphic texts. On the opposite side, was the vast south Acropolis, ruins of royal residences.

'Lost world temple', Mundo Perdido, was an enormous pyramid, the largest ceremonial complex in the preclassical era. Nearby in a row were Seven Temples. By their side was a lengthy court with walls on each side for the Mesoamericana ball game. Some indigenous population still played this ritualistic sport from 650 BC. In the stone ball court, players struck the ball of 4 kg solid rubber, with their hips and tried to push them through the rings high on sidewalls. Some cultures in the past combined these competitions with religious human sacrifice.

Beautiful 55m tall temple of Great Jaguar was the last of great pyramids built at Tikal. Its outside stairs lead to the top of a steep temple. Across the way lay equally beautiful Temple of the Masks. The tallest temple-pyramid at Tikal, 70m high, Temple IV, close by was is the largest pyramid built anywhere in the Maya region in the 8th century and the tallest pre-Columbian structure in the Americas.

Most of the buildings were made of durable limestone and had endured. Pyramids, with their ruined steps, were still accessible for climbing. From the top, I could get a view of many other ancient structures dotted around in the middle of dense jungle. It was humid and boiling. We stopped briefly for iced drinks.

Ancient Mayans were mathematical geniuses, a gift which they used for religious purposes and to keep track of time. Mayans used a numeration system, based on the number 20, which included the concept of zero. They used a bar-dot system, similar to the binary system now used by computers. Mayans also devised calendars of great precision from complex astronomical calculations. Tikal's only water source was from the collected rainwaters stored in many reservoirs. In this area of moderate rainfall, they used their mathematical skills in hydraulic engineering in the construction of massive reservoirs that could hold several million gallons of rainwater collected by gravity through paved causeways, and an intricate series of canals. Mayans built the temples in an accurate spatial manner according to the sun's movement through the day, and the winter and summer solstice. Mayan astronomers had an in-depth knowledge of different constellations and had calculated the precise orbit of Venus around the sun.

At its height, Tikal's urban area had a population of over 50,000. But by the 9th century, with endemic war, the Mayan empire was collapsing across the region. Tikal's increasing population had speeded up intensive agriculture, resulting in extensive deforestation, erosion and nutrient loss in the surrounding area. This, in turn, led to recurrent crop failure. An influx of refugees from surrounding areas to the city following the wars stretched environmental resources further. People abandoned the city rather than starve.

In the modern world, are we not seeing the repeat versions of this in so many places?

Mayan Communities   Next morning, we had about 6 hours' drive west through beautiful highlands with many volcanoes in the background, to the town of Tejutla. We picked up one health workers on the way, and the other one joined us in Tejutla. I learnt several issues related to the healthcare of the indigenous population. Poor funding of infrastructure and outsourcing of secondary healthcare to private companies resulted in majority unable to afford the high cost. Although in theory, healthcare in the country was free for all. Most communities had strict cultural practices regarding birth, illness and death. When locals went to a health post or a hospital, often far away, their culture and beliefs were not respected, and the staff did not speak nor understand their languages. Chronic malnutrition with chronic diseases compounded this, leading to high maternal and child mortality.

Our role was to promote health education through culturally sensitive materials, cervical cancer screening, and breast cancer clinical screening. We would also screen and select surgical and gynaecological patients needing an operation, and list them for free surgery in Guatemala. Another team working with the same charity in a few weeks would operate. The charity offered free transport for patients with one of their relatives to the city and free accommodation. Local health promoters' roles were most important in organising and coordinating the entire process.

Our routine became arriving at the place early in the morning. Set up our clinic, work for two full days till the last patient and then move to another site in the evening or early morning depending on the distance.

In Tejutla 2500m, during my breakfast, around 6-30am, I noticed outside in light rain and sleet, there was already a lengthy queue. We soon started. None of the patients spoke Spanish. Even without understanding their language, I felt privileged to be with this community. A warm smile was the universal language of appreciation towards me. During dinner, I learnt some people had walked many kilometres to the clinic. The community had no working hospital. A nurse ran the only government clinic and came twice a week.

After two days, in the evening, we travelled through high mountain road for two hours to Takana 2500m, close to the Mexico border. It was freezing. In a clear night sky, massive Takana Volcano 4060m stood opposite the town. Healthcare provision was the same as in Tejutla. Women came to the clinic wearing skirts in bold colours held up by a woven faja, a sash. Men came with a chaqueta, an open jacket and a straw hat. In the chilly morning, most of them had a heavy woollen wrap, rodilllera.

After two days there, we left in the evening for San Marcos el Alto 2398m. It was known as Hippy town because of its drug trafficking history in the last decade. San Marcos el Alto had three small private hospitals. One of them provided us with space to use for our clinics. In the first evening, I went out by myself for some fresh air. In a tiny side shop, a lady was making empanada with her daughter. As I stood watching, she waved me to come inside in her cramped place from the cold and offered me a stool by her to sit on. Once she had made a sufficient amount, she fried them and gave me some. It tasted exquisite. She gave me a couple more. I had to insist on giving her money before I left.

Next evening we arrived at Coatepeque 500m, known as the Village of Gardenias. This town in the lowlands with its warm air was most welcome after the highlands. The nearest hospital was three hours through a mountain road, but the Pacific coast and the resorts only an hour's drive. Our free clinic was busier here than in the other two places. We stayed there for three nights. On the second night, we arranged in the local town hall, an evening session with about thirty local health and social workers, mostly women, on breast and cervical cancer awareness. After initial shyness, soon, the session became very interactive and productive.

Both health workers left the next day from here and took buses to their places.

We drove through a lovely road by low hills and forests, with an occasional view of the Pacific at a distance, to Antigua five hours away. As we got nearer to Antigua, I noticed larger brick-built houses by the roadside and at a distance. More than I had seen in the last few days. My colleagues said there was a saying in the country - 'anyone with a sizeable brick house in Guatemala must have someone working in the USA!'

Antigua Guatemala   I stayed three nights in Antigua. Chairman of the charity, an American, would host a dinner for us in his house on the second night. Antigua and Guatemala City at only 45 minutes' distance, both were favourite places for the US ex-pats to retire with a cheaper yet luxurious lifestyle and nearby good private healthcare facilities. And not very far in flying distances from their families.

Antigua with cobbled streets, beautifully restored colonial buildings sitting next to picturesque ruins and the backdrop of the imposing Volcan de Agua 3760m to the south and twin peaks of Volcan de Fuego 3763m and Acatenango 3880m to the west, looked charming. Antigua for over 200 years was the seat of Spanish military for a vast region that included almost all of present-day Central America and the southernmost part of Mexico. Following decades of earthquakes, and finally, after a massive quake in 1773, most of the city was destroyed and abandoned. The capital moved to a safer location in Guatemala City.

I stayed in a posada, a budget hostel, close to the centre. Streets of Antigua throbbed with tourists, most on foot like me and a few others on horse-drawn carriages. With its laid back vibe, a popular tourist destination. Cruise ships, both from Atlantic and Pacific, offered tours here for their passengers.

Next day, I visited the restored Church of Candelaria, San Jose Cathedral, Capuchin Covent and Santa Clara and many others. Museum of Colonial Art in its old building had a fantastic collection of 16th and 17th- century art. Artisan and craft market, a Co-operative displayed hundreds of most colourful wooden masks, vibrant textiles, sculptures and jewellery. By the streets, women in their embroidered huipiles (blouses) sold similar items to a crowd of wealthy tourists who bartered to get a few cents bargain. Next to the iconic arc, Arco de Santa Catalina, with the beautiful Volcano as its backdrop, a crowd gathered around a father and son singing to beautiful Guatemalan music. When they finished, I bought a CD from them for my music collection.

I had my lunch at Parque Central, with its walkways threading among flowering jacaranda trees and a fountain. On one side of the park, stood a cathedral. Shops and restaurants next to long corridors lined other sides. Vendors, women with their children, walked around trying to sell their crafts to the tourists.

Later I visited the sculpture park outside the city at the foot of a hill. Park dedicated to the work of Efrain Recinos, Guatemalan Picasso. Ten of his striking resin-mosaic tile murals were displayed in a lush garden. Park's highlight was El Triunfo de la Guatemala, the sculpture of a woman on top of a clapped out VW Beetle holding a torch in her right hand. The car once belonged to Recinos, and the piece represented the artist's search for justice.

Inside, the museum displayed collections from leading artists of the country and a room dedicated to Guatemalan Nobel laureate in literature, Miguel Angel Asturias Rosales.

From there, after an uphill walk to Cerro de la Cruz, Hill of the Cross, was a magnificent sweeping view over the city of Antigua with the immense Volcan de Agua, towering over the landscape. After spending a while there, I returned to the sculpture park to spend more time.

In the evening, we had an elaborate dinner in the mansion house of the charity president. Unfortunately, neither of the two health workers could attend.

Pacaya Volcano Hike

On my last full day in Guatemala, I wanted to get close to one of its many active volcanoes. Pacaya Volcano 2552m, only 1.5 hour's drive from Antigua, was the most accessible. Visitors' entrance sat in a tiny village near the top of a hill. While we chatted outside to our guide about the 500m intermediate plus grade hike through a steep hill, men and boys with horses stood by offering horseback rides. A young boy sold wooden walking sticks nearby. I bought one to give my damaged knee some respite, as it was playing up recently.

The first part of the hike was by many coffee plantations. Soon we entered a dense jungle and walked on a narrow unmarked route between the trees over loose lava rocks and stones of all sizes, the result of an eruption a few years back. The trail got steep and tricky. We needed to stop every fifteen minutes. Some in the group now took advantage of a horseback ride from the men walking along with us. We came out of the jungle after about an hour and forty-five minutes. Just above us was a plateau. Next to us on our left rose Pacaya, gently smoking away. In front, on the horizon on the other side, were many higher volcano peaks.

We trekked down to the side of Pacaya. Molten lava and rocks from a recent eruption had cooled to solidify, but through the cracks, steam was still coming out - hot enough to melt my bar of chocolate. It was already late afternoon. After spending a while amongst the molten lava, we came up to the plateau. Against the falling sunlight on the horizon peaks now looked gorgeous sticking out above the evening gathering of clouds, gently spewing out clouds of smoke. Smoke coming out of Pacaya looked denser.

As darkness swept below, most of us walked back. Our guide stayed with a small group, still taking pictures. Inside the jungle track, it was pitch black. Unfortunately, I did not have headlamps. Rest of my group, with their headlamps, trotted down quickly.

In complete darkness, I resorted to using my stick as a blind man does. Feeling with my stick the stone below me for every step, and then putting one foot at a time, carefully. It was painfully slow and precarious. As I thought I had got the hang of walking down like a blind, I toppled over loose rock and almost fell over. Luckily, not hurt. I sat down for a while to compose myself. While getting up, I saw behind me through the trees, an arc of bright red light coming out of the cone of Pacaya. Its eruption, which we could see only see as smoke in daylight, against a dark sky, now showed its magic. I watched in silence for a while. Then slowly and carefully started my descent again in the dark, stopping every few minutes to look at the spectacle behind.

After a while of walking and stumbling, the jungle cleared around me. I could see down below the lights in the houses on the opposite hill. Walking by the coffee plantations, I heard chattering above me. Soon the guide and three stragglers, with their headlamps on, came down and I joined them.

Back to Antigua just before 10 pm, I walked to Parque Central looking for some food. Hanging chain of colourful lights on the trees were still on, but most shops were closed except for a few noisy night clubs. Only one restaurant had its lights on. As I got closer, I noticed many women vendors sleeping in the long corridor fronting the closed shops. They slept next to their giant cloth bag of crafts, some with young children cuddling next to them.

While going inside the restaurant, I noted a woman with her 6-7-year-old son was still up and sitting close by. Once inside the empty restaurant, I asked the waiter to find out if the woman and her son had eaten. If not, would they be kind enough to join me for dinner? Soon the woman with her son joined, leaving her bag of crafts by the table.

Following the waiter's suggestion, I ordered Pepian, a Guatemalan national dish of meat and vegetable stew with rice for the three of us. With the waiter translating, I learnt that the women from surrounding villages, often as far as 20-30 km distance, came to sell their craft in the city for one week at a time every month except in the rainy seasons. They came as a group from their villages and looked after each other. Some of their crafts took many weeks to make. Husbands stayed at home, looking after the field and the animals. When I asked the boy about his school, he replied they had a school in another village. But he always looked forward to coming to town with his mother and did not mind skipping his classes.

Cay Caulker Belize

February 2017

From Guatemala City flight to Belize, then I flew to Caye Caulker in a single propeller twelve-seater plane over the azure Caribbean Sea with coral at a multitude of depth visible from above. The runway in Cay Caulker spanned the width of the island. The tiny airport had only one building, a hut with two compact rooms.

No car on this 8km x 0.8km island. Only local traffic sign on the island instructed bikers to 'slow down'.

A narrow water channel appropriately named 'the split' divided Caye Caulker. Only 1300 people inhabited the southern part. The northern part was a dense mangrove forest with diverse birdlife, a protected reserve. From the airport, most walked or took a bicycle. I walked with my rucksack.

On this small limestone coral island, entirely free of the hustle and bustle, from anywhere, a sandy beach on foot was within five minutes on the left or the right. Its one-story buildings all competed against each other for their vivid colours. An ideal place for me to do nothing for the next two days. Cay Caulker owed its laid back style to its Rastafarian culture, apparent in its many easy-going bars and restaurants. I spent the entire day swaying in a hammock on an empty sandy beachfront in the breeze drifting off azure Caribbean water, with occasional breaks to swim in the warm sea and drink coconut water.

In the evening, I forced myself to walk three minutes to a Caribbean restaurant and stuffed myself with lobster with jerk spices and coconut rice.

Next day for tour option, the famous Blue Hole tour caught my attention. But it was two hours boat ride each way, and one could only appreciate its beauty if you were a certified diver or looked at it from the sky. Instead, I took a boat ride around the island. We started going by the nature reserve, then by a sunken ship, with stops for snorkelling with the stingrays, while reef sharks swam around.

On the east, a shallow lagoon met the Barrier Reef, the second-longest barrier reef in the world. South part of the reef, known as a dry reef, was exposed at the surface. Windsurfers, snorkelers and divers were everywhere and some paddle-boarded in the calm water. The crew gave us a lunch of jerk chicken and rice. We finished near the small harbour after feeding hundreds of fishes of various sizes and shape, while pelicans flew around. At the dock, the crew helped us to spot many sea horses hanging around seaweeds, some male pregnant with a large belly.

After spending a while in a hammock, I walked to another tour shop and explained to the young man I wanted to try paddle-boarding. I explained my poor balance. He reassured I could only fall in the warm water and then I could swim. We got ready, and with him helping, I got standing on top of the board and paddled for at least full three minutes before falling over. Thanking him, I grinned. I had now 'done it', and glad I had not tried this in the Antarctic waters.

After swims in the warm water and spending a restful evening on this lovely island, reluctantly next day I left for Mexico via Belize. On my flight back from Caye Caulker I marvelled at many beautiful islands below, surrounded by extensive coral at different depths of the blue sea, showing contrasting colours.

Uxmal, Chichen Itza & swimming
with the whale shark Mexico

February 2017

From Cancun airport, I took an express bus to Merida at 290 km distance, the capital and largest city in Yucatan State in Mexico. This populous city looked dynamic in wide avenues amongst Mayan and colonial architecture.

Caste War   While walking in Merida, a small monument dedicated to the Caste War of Yucatan caught my attention. I had known of the caste system and struggle against it in India. But this was on the other side of the world! In Spanish colonial times, in Yucatan as in most of the colonial empire, the population operated under a strict legal caste system. Officials born in Spain were at the top. The criollos of Spanish descent in the next level; followed by mestizo of mixed European-Amerindian descent; next were the descendants of the natives who had collaborated with the Spanish and at the bottom were the other native Indios. Caste war of Yucatan in the late 19th century began with a revolt of native Maya people against the European- descended population. A lengthy war ensued, with regular raids and then was brutally ended by the Mexican army in 1901.

At Plaza de la Independencia, the bustling central square, I sat for a while surrounded by the colourful fortress-like Catedral de San Ildefonso, Church of Iglesia de la Tercera Orden and the mansion of Casa de Montejo. A ceremonial lowering of the Mexican flag in red, white and green colours, adopted by the country following independence from Spain, was taking place.

On my way back, in a restaurant, I ordered interesting sounding Los Mosqueteros, the Three Musketeers, a combination of black sauce made from burnt chilly over pork, an egg dish and pipian - a sauce made with pumpkin seeds over turkey. Exquisite, spicy hot and enormous, but I did not have any proper breakfast or lunch!

Uxmal

An hour's drive from Merida took us to Uxmal, an ancient Maya city, built on classic Mayan style, Puuc, with smooth low walls and ornate friezes. In its buildings, entwined snakes, some feathered and sometimes two-headed, were used for masks of the rain god, Chaac. In Maya mythology serpents were the vehicles by which celestial bodies, such as sun and stars, crossed the heavens. Shedding of their skin was a symbol of rebirth and renewal. A big nose represented the rays of the storms.

Governor's Palace, an extensive building on top of a large platform, had the longest facades in Pre-

Columbian Mesoamerica. It was oriented to the main pyramid of Cehtzuc within a forest at 5km distance. Observing from Cehtzuc, they could see Venus setting down behind the northern edge of the Governor's Palace. These events occurred every eight years, in late April or early May, forecasting the onset of the rainy season. In the building's facade were 400 Venus glyphs placed in the masks of the rain god Chaac, eight two-headed serpents and the numerals 8 in bar-and-dot notation.

Pyramid of Magician, strangely known as the Pyramid of Dwarf, was the tallest structure in Uxmal. Its lower walls were bare but very ornate at higher levels. From its top gave an engaging view of the whole site. Legend said a powerful dwarf magician, hatched from an egg by his mother, had built this pyramid within two weeks following a threat and order from the Uxmal King.

Nunnery Quadrangle, resembling a convent, comprised four palaces placed on different levels surrounding a vast courtyard with a formal entrance, very likely once was a royal palace. Outside was House of the Turtles and the Birds with ornate sculptures. A ball court for the ancient Mayan ballgame on this site lay in ruins.

Kabah

After a brief lunch, we drove to Kabah, connected to Uxmal by an 18 km long and 5m broad causeway with monumental arches at each end. Kabah had several step-pyramid temples, altars and stone buildings, some depicting scenes of warfare. Most interesting here was the Palace of Masks. In the stepped structure, over three hundred stone masks of the long-nosed rain god Chaac, protector of the harvest, decorated the walls.

With no rivers or sinkholes, in this part of northern Yucatan, Mayans had to depend for rain through their prayers to Chaac or predict through their astronomical knowledge.

Chichen Itza

After an hour's drive from Merida, we arrived at Chichen Itza, one of the largest Mayan cities, with a dense cluster of architecture. We started on this five sq. km complex on its east at Temples of the Jaguar. Staircases ascended on each of the four sides to the Platform of Eagles and Jaguars. Panels depicted eagles and jaguars consuming human hearts. In the entrance to the Lower Temple of the Jaguar stood a Jaguar throne next to the ball court.

Ballcourt   Chichen Itza had thirteen ball courts for the Mayan game. The well preserved Great Ball Court, 150m by 70m, looked as if ready for a game this weekend. A stone ring, 9m above the floor, on each wall, stood prepared to be tested.

At the base of sidewalls, were sculpted panels of ballplayers. It showed one player decapitated; blood streaming out in the form of wriggling snakes. Ultimate final in the country took place in this venue. They used the ball, wrapped up in wool set to fire, symbolising the movements of the stars in the sky.

At the end of the final, captain of the team sacrificed himself by cutting his throat, thus joining the gods of heaven.

Temple of Kukulkan   Temple of Kukulkan, the most well-known pyramid of the Mayan empire, dominated the area. Sides of the pyramid were 56m at the base. Protruding stairways in four faces of the pyramid ascended an angle of 45° to 30m high with a temple on its summit. The slanting steps from a certain angle looked as if a serpent was climbing up to the sky. Around spring and autumn equinoxes, in the late afternoon, northwest corner of the pyramid cast a series of triangular shadows against the western balustrade - evoking the appearance of a serpent wriggling down the staircase, a representation of the feathered serpent god Kukulkan. Inside its temple chamber stood a statue of Chaac on a Jaguar shaped throne.

On the opposite ground was Skull Platform, a wall of hundreds of vertically impaled skulls. Behind this, through several craft shops, we arrived at Cenote Sagrado, a natural sinkhole. Limestone plain here had no river or streams. Natural sinkholes pockmarked the region and exposed the water table to the surface. Impressive Cenote Sagrado, 60m in diameter, surrounded by sheer cliffs dropped to the water table some 27m below. It was a place of pilgrimage for the ancient Maya, who conducted sacrifices here during times of drought.

Massive **Temple of the Warriors complex** had a large stepped pyramid and was flanked by rows of carved columns depicting warriors. We sat on its steps for a while to take in the Mayan beauty around. On our south were thousand exposed columns, around temples on platforms with carved images of people, plants, birds and mythological scenes.

El Caracol Observatory

This building, on a large square platform, had its name from the stone spiral staircase inside. The structure stood on a platform and had a round shape, unlike the Maya practice of rectangular. This observatory had its doors and windows aligned to astronomical events around the path of Venus traversing the heavenly sky.

Casa Colorada nearby had one of the best-preserved buildings at Chichen Itza. One of its chambers had extensive carved hieroglyphs recordings. More temples, decorated with elaborate inscriptions and masks, surrounded the place.

Chichen Itza, the major focal point of Mayan civilization, was mind-blowing with its variety of architectural styles, a result of the most diverse population in the Maya world. I returned to the observatory for another look. All that my naked eyes could see was blue sky and a blazing sun. A small temple named Akab Dzib stood next to the observatory. Its name in Yucatan meant 'mysterious writing.'

Aren't we still wandering about mysteries of this universe?

Cabo San Lucas

I arrived at Cabo Sun Lucas, a resort city on the southern tip of Mexico's Baja California peninsula in the afternoon then walked its long wide beach till late.

Next day a whale watching tour on the Cortez Sea took us past Land's end promontory, Playa del amour (lovers' beach) and then by a beautiful natural archway in the sea cliffs, El Arco. We stopped by the arch where a few seals rested on the rock. Through the arch, we could see the great Pacific on the other side. After sailing another half an hour, we came across a group of humpbacks having fun blowing and then flipping their tails.

Tour Company offered a tour to Baza for swimming with the whale sharks in the open sea. I booked for the next day.

Only the driver as the guide and myself left early through a highway towards La Paz, the state capital of Baja California Sur, 160km distance. Stunning drive first through jutting mountain ranges, separating Cortez Sea from Pacific, then through a desert with a gorgeous view of the great ocean on our left. We stopped for coffee in an empty roadside restaurant. On its walls hung many pictures of Indie car racing. Soon I met the owner of the place, himself an Indie car driver only a few years back.

Swimming with the giant

In the laid back town of La Paz, at the northern end of Cortez Sea, we got into a small boat after putting on my dive suit, carrying my flippers and the snorkel. We sailed in open sea for a while before the crew spotted a whale shark 50m away. We sailed next to it. The guide warned not to get near its tail or its fins and not to touch it.

In the clear blue water, with hundreds of spots, it looked majestic and massive. Its giant mouth filtered plankton and tiny krill. At least 12m long, the size of a large school bus, it weighed around 20 tons. Bursting with excitement, I jumped right next to the giant, swimming gently. I swam right at its middle near the large pectoral fins.

I swam hard to keep up, so close to the giant that I could see the water coming out through its massive gills - a twenty minutes swim of my lifetime. Then the gentle giant dived to the depth, and I got back to the boat.

After sailing around for a while, we came across another whale shark, and I jumped out again. This time the giant swam slowly for a long time, testing and teasing my endurance to swim against the current in the open sea. Satisfied after about 200m, it dived. Bone tired, but exhilarated, I got back into the boat.

This time the giant swam slowly for a long time, testing and teasing my endurance to swim against the current in the open sea. Satisfied after about 200m, it dived. Bone tired, but exhilarated, I got back into the boat.

We returned to Cabo San Lucas in the evening. Tour included dinner. Guide asked what did I like to eat. I suggested something the locals ate. A large plate of Mexican chocolate Clam, shrimps and fish Tacos and smoked marlin arrived soon - a perfect meal to end the perfect day.

Mexico City

My hotel bedroom in Mexico City overlooked Centro Historico, the largest plaza in Latin America. In front stood the lavish National palace, on the left-hand side the Mexico City Cathedral and on the right the Supreme Court.

I paid a brief visit to the Cathedral built atop a former Aztec sacred precinct following the Spanish conquest. In 1552, the colonists enforced an agreement splitting the cost of building the new cathedral with the local indigenous groups. They invoked Encomienda, a Spanish labour system that rewarded conquerors with the labour of its subjects. Cathedral's exterior had bell towers, facades with reliefs inspired by the painter Rubens, a massive vault and opulent altars, including one named 'Altar of Forgiveness'. After a stroll around the main square, now full of people, I walked to the busy side street for my dinner, groups of musicians played on street corners.

Plaza de la Tres Culturas   Plaza de la Tres Culturas represented the three eras of Mexican history. Next to excavated pre-Hispanic Aztec ruins, stood a colonial church with a convent. Opposite both rose modern towers of a housing complex.

It was here in October 1968 the military committed the Tlatelolco massacre, part of Mexico's 'Dirty War', killing hundreds of student protesters. Ten days before the opening ceremony of 1968 Olympic Games, soldiers and rooftop snipers opened fire on the student protesters. Peruvian Nobel winner Mario Vargas Llosa described the brutal rule here as 'perfect dictatorship'.

Next door in the University Museum of the student revolution, I stood in silence opposite the pictures of the students killed for their youthful search of democracy. I remembered that as recently as in 2014, on an annual journey to commemorate this event, 43 students 'disappeared' after being rounded up by the authority.

Teotihuacan

Outside the city at Teotihuacan, the most known pre-Columbian site associated with the country's civilization and cultural complex, stood a giant six-level step-pyramid decorated with feathered serpent heads – Quetzalcoatl. From the top of Quetzalcoatl, the god of creation and a giver of life, I remembered that it became famous again in 1980 when they found over a hundred sacrificial victims buried under here.

I then walked the 40m wide, 2km long Avenida de Los Muertos, Avenue of the Dead, paved with tombs. Pyramid of the Moon and Pyramid of the Sun stood at opposite ends. Mayans oriented both these pyramids to summer and winter solstice.

Imposing 65m Pyramid of the Sun, the third-largest pyramid in the world, had on its top a massive pedestal for human sacrifice. History most definitely repeats cruelty against its fellow human in different disguises.

Teotihuacan was a multi-ethnic city, with the population reaching its peak around 5th -6th century AD to over 100,000. Even recently following heavy rain, when a sinkhole appeared, tunnels between the pyramids have been discovered, suggesting many unearthed monuments.

More recently Government permitted to build a supermarket in part of this archaeological site. No, the Conquistadors were not back; it was just the Walmart! During its construction, they found hundreds of fragments of ancient pottery in the soil from the site.

Now a Walmart stands in the place known as the 'bribery alley' in this archaeological complex.

With the young reef doctors in Madagascar

May 2017

There were two reasons for me to visit Madagascar, known as the 8th continent, because of its distinctive ecology. I wanted to have a glimpse of this biodiversity. More importantly, my oldest daughter had spent a few weeks there, working with a Reef Conservation charity. I wanted to be there on her birthday before going to Tanzania for volunteering.

I arrived in Antananarivo around midday. Antananarivo at 1,280m in the centre of the island, reminded me of rural towns in India, except most people here looked more of South-East Asian origin. The city skyline was a jumble of colourful houses and churches around the busy central area by the Royal Palace. Residential and commercial buildings stood next to rice fields in the lower terrain.

Despite its relative proximity to the African continent, Madagascar's 20 million population primarily descended from the Indonesian seafarers who settled here around 1500 years ago.
A domestic flight took me to the southern tip of Madagascar to Ivato airport in Tulear, by the St. Augustine's Bay.

Antsokay Arboretum was outside the town. This arboretum, set by a passionate amateur botanist around 1980, in an area of natural spiny forest and desert habitat, had 900 plant species, 90% of them endemic and 80% had medicinal value, still used for common ailments in the local families. I saw my first baobab tree, looking like a sapling, a youngster only sixty years old. Our guide in front looked back and asked us to be quiet. He had spotted something in a tree branch. We tiptoed to find a mouse lemur sleeping on a branch just above our head height. These nocturnal lemurs with a total length of less than 27cm were the smallest primate and had the smallest brain of any primate, at just 2 grams. 24 Mouse Lemur species had evolved from a common ancestor 10 million years ago. We left him to sleep.

In the arboretum museum, along with the display of local crafts, rocks and fossils, was an egg of the extinct Elephant bird. This giant egg, 25cm long and 20cm wide, weighing around 8kg, equated to 150 chicken eggs. Aepyornis, Elephant birds, stood over 3m and weighed over 600kg. They became extinct around the 11th-12th century, possibly because of human activities.

We drove next day through spiny forests with occasional baobab trees for Isalo National Park, 190km distance.

We stopped at Ilakaka, a shantytown. Since the first discovery of sapphires here in 1998, Madagascar had become number one sapphire exporter in the world. Miners from all over Madagascar and dealers from other countries, mostly Sri Lanka and Thailand had arrived in Ilakaka to seek their fortune in the big sapphire rush. Diggers, brokers, and dealers crowded dozens of shops. Rock-forming mineral corundum, if red, was ruby and sapphire if any other colour. Ilakaka was famous for the production of pink sapphires and of rare fine blue sapphires. On a good day, a digger made up to five dollars after hours of digging, while the dealers made thousands.

In the process, they uprooted trees and diverted streams in the surroundings. In open-cast mining, miners had to dig deeper and deeper in dangerous shafts. Now that they had mined the easier to find sapphires, they forayed further afield every month. Malagasy working the mines did not make their fortunes here, conspicuous by the derelict huts they lived in, compared to the grand buildings of the dealers in town.

Madagascar had one of the world's largest reserves of titanium ore and substantial reserves of chromite, zircon, coal, iron, cobalt, copper and nickel. Several major mining projects were underway along with onshore drilling for oil and gas. While boosting the Malagasy economy, these foreign-owned companies irreversibly destroyed the natural forests.

Just outside the gem shops, in an open area, they were making sugar cane rum in large drums. In the weekly market, women in colourful clothes sold fresh vegetables and fruits, while the men sat by roadside drinking cheap rum with their hard-earned money. 90% of Madagascar population lived on less than 2 dollars per day and 70% below 1 dollar a day.

Driving north, forests became denser before we came by the Zombitse National Park. We were lucky to spot a solitary Appert's tetraka, an endemic bird only discovered in 1972. It rested for a short time on a branch with its green plumage and pink bill, before flying away.

Isalo   Le Jardin du Roy resort was in the middle of a canyon on the edge of Isalo National Park. Built from granite against the sandstone rocks, it blended in with the landscape of rare beauty. Sun was still high in the sky. We left for a hike in the canyon on Isalo massif through endemic flora and fauna. On our return, we stopped by the resort's bio-farm, where local plants coexisted with a variety of European fruits and vegetables. Lovely to see pineapples and bananas growing next to cherries and plums, around decomposing cow manure.

Isalo National Park   We drove through vast rolling savannahs interspersed with natural rock formations, to Le Fenetre, a natural rock formation which beautifully framed the setting sun. Large rocks covered with lichens of various colours surrounded the place. The sun went down beyond an extensive plateau. Behind us, the fading and changing colours of the sunlight played magic on the layers of sandstone elevations ranging between 500 to 1200m. Soon the colours on low clouds started adding to the dramatic scenery. I sat in silence until it got dark.

After watching a dramatic sunrise from the top of a low hill behind the resort, we drove a few kilometres to Ranohira town for permits. Then we proceeded through the plains before crossing a river where village women gathered for washing clothes. By the canyon we hiked for half an hour up a steep massif wall, rewarded by breathtaking views from the rocky valleys of the vast plains below. Walking through the rocky plateau, in front were canyons as far as eyes could see.

Sitting on a rock ledge, I noticed on a high cliff what looked like a bird's nest. The guide said these were burial places of the Bara people. Baras buried the bodies after death at a lower height on the cliff. A year later, they brought the dead to their village, and all have a feast. Then, with the help of younger boys climbing, they left the remains finally in shelves of a higher cliff.

We walked through the canyon close to the edge of the massif with a view below of villages. I learnt of another traditional practice of the Bara people. The village in front had twenty houses. The guide said all these houses belonged to one man who had twenty wives, who all lived in their own homes with their children. The husband visited them one day and night at a time, taking regular turns - poor man!

A strange-looking plant was coming out of the bare rock. This bulbous plant, known as Elephant's foot (Aloe isaloensis), an endemic species, improbably clung to the rock. After walking in the canyon under a blazing sun for a while, below us was the forest. We passed by a shallow stream. Geckos hung around on the tree branches. A lizard with a spiky tail sunned on a rock. By the water's edge, my guide flipped over rocks to find a scorpion. Stinging by these scorpions in human did not cause death, just paralysis for a few hours! No, thank you - still a lot of hikes left for the day. We saw many stick insects and some beautiful rainbow coloured caterpillars on the leaves. Around us were 116 medicinal species of plants.

Canyon des Singes

We reached Canyon des Singes, Canyon of the Monkeys, place where the lemurs show up, but we were early. Lemurs visited the area only at a particular time of the day for an unknown reason. We hiked up following a stream to Piscine Naturelle, a crystalline blue pool fringed by pandanus trees. On the water edge, we spotted an endemic patterned Malagasy rainbow frog. But, we did not have time for a swim.

Back at Canyon des Singes, we waited for the lemurs. One by one Ring-tell lemur arrived, taking their positions on tree branches, picking fruits. Some Ring-tells jumped out of the trees and ambled with their tails curled up. Soon there were at least two dozens of them in the trees and on the ground. Occasionally there were mini scrambles between them.

The guide pointed to the trees behind us - three Sifakas were up in the branches, pale silky white fur with drab brown faces. Their long tails dangled straight down as they nibbled above me.

After making a bleating noise, one of them jumped out right next to me. It then crossed the open ground, sashaying on its hind leg, with arms flying around. Then, it jumped up into another tree before hopping 8m to another branch, settling down to eat. Not a dancing competition, but soon the second one and then the third one followed, dancing in their own style.

A group of Red-fronted lemurs came by, smaller and less photographed because none of them danced to entertain, even though one of them had a baby. Walking downhill from there, we spotted an endemic rock bill nearby. A group of school-age children sat hoping to sell coloured lemurs, crafted out of stones.

Then we drove by a river bed to an area of needle-shaped limestone formations. Locals called these sharp limestone formations of spiky hills 'tsingy', meaning a place where one cannot walk barefoot. The guide said in Melaky Region; there was an even larger area with these 'tsingy'.

From there we drove for a while before walking through thorny bushes. Next, we stood stunned by a few vertical cliffs. These coloured cliffs looked as if they were pages of an old book with different layers of compressed rocks with minerals over one another. Formed over millions of years in the Mesozoic era, eroded by wind and water, and covered by colourful lichens, these foliated rocks were a stunning example of geological history and wonder.

90% of wildlife in Madagascar were unique to the island, including many mammals, such as the cat-like fossa. The island had over 300 species of birds, over 60% endemic. Madagascar had lost over 90% of its original forests since human arrival, and 80% of it lost in the last 30 years. At least 17 species of lemur have become extinct. In Isalo, apart from the six species of lemur, three of them nocturnal, the scientists had documented over 100 species of bird, 24 amphibians and 47 reptiles. It had over 400 species of plants, and many types of lichens, some endemic. Wide-open savannahs of grassland interspersed with enormous rocky outcrops and deep canyons gave the place the impression of being from another world.

Ifaty

After driving west for 3 hours, first through canyons and forest, and then through desert landscapes with baobab trees, we reached Ifaty. This fishing village had only several huts built with dry bulrush. Fishing nets hung around for drying. Children played by the seashore while women washed clothes in the sea. Men repaired their pirogues and fishing nets.

I visited the Reniala Forest outside the village. Reniala was Malagasy name for baobab. This 60-hectare reserve of spiny bushes was home to over 2000 plants species, some endemic. Along with many birds in this reserve, including blue vanga and a red-capped coua, there were spider tortoises and some warty chameleons.

It was fascinating walking between so many types of the baobab tree in one place, often next to endemic Didieraceae plants with their spiny thickets. Iconic baobab trees, the upside-down tree, had their branches growing only at the top, more like roots than a canopy. Locals had named the baobabs here according to their appearances. Thus there was a lady with wide hips, twins and the giant one. The 1500-year-old 7m tall giant baobab had a 12.5m diameter trunk. The guide showed shells of its big fruit, a local delicacy. Logging of baobab was now prohibited.

A group of schoolchildren came on a tour with their teacher. Established only in 2001, while preserving the threatened ecosystem, this reserve did a marvellous job working together with the local communities and raising awareness in protecting the environment.

Reef Doctor

Next morning, I visited the Reef Doctor site on the outskirt of the village. My daughter had worked here as a volunteer a few years back and was passionate about their work. Only ten days before her sudden death, she had posted on social media about the lack of concern and acknowledgement by the western media about the devastating Cyclone Haruna here in February 2013. Typhoon had destroyed this area with the displacement of thousands from their home and livelihood. Following her death, we, family and her friends, had assisted Reef Doctor, a UK based charity, in introducing a scholarship programme for the local children in educating and championing conservation projects.

A reef here stretched over 450km along the southwestern coast of Madagascar in Mozambique Channel of Indian Ocean, the fifth-largest coral reef in the world. Overfishing by growing population had degraded much of the reef with loss of coral. Reef Doctor aimed to maintain and improve the ecosystem by working with and supporting the local fishing community with alternatives. I spent the entire day with the volunteers, sharing meals with them in their community kitchen. I learnt how overexploitation, climate change and deforestation-induced sedimentation from topsoil erosion had been destroying the island's coastal and marine habitats, including its coral reef.

Reef Doctor conducts long-term reef health monitoring and restores degraded coral reefs through the establishment of two marine reserves in the surrounding bay. They promote sustainable alternative marine-based livelihoods by implementing aquaculture projects such as seaweed and sea cucumber farming. These activities diversified income streams relieving pressure on over-exploited fisheries. Being in the intertidal zone and accessible to the women, they also promoted livelihood opportunities for women. By generating their income, in turn, women gained independence and were more respected in the social and cultural life of their communities.

I visited the local primary school with a volunteer. In Ifaty, and all across Madagascar, many parents could not afford to send their children to school. The cyclone had destroyed the local school, and now it had only two small size rooms for about 150 children of all ages. Children took turns to attend classes. The school desperately needed building one or two more classrooms.

Junior Reef Doctors' scheme was a new initiative to deliver a high standard of education and skill development training for the local children to become ambassadors and future leaders of their community. Reef Doctor School provided children with skills to understand broader social issues such as effects of climate change and declining fish stocks affecting everyday lives. Twenty-five children from the village, selected on their merits from the local schools, attended here. Four teachers worked with the children to offer a broader programme of education in science, mathematics, French, Malagasy, English, geography, history, sport and environmental studies. Reef Doctor School took students out for field trips to mangroves and older students for snorkelling to see the beautiful coral for the first time in their lives.

A memorial scholarship in my daughter's name had been supporting 15 children from the village, ages 8-12yrs, with all their needs to continue at school. I attended an English class and then learned geography together with a group of bubbly children. Later they sat around me while I showed them pictures and videos of wild animals on my iPad. Like everywhere else, the funny walks of the penguins were their favourite. Then I learnt some local children's game from them and played with them some Indian children's game - a wonderful day.

I returned to my hostel by the seashore and took a ride on a dinghy to the mangroves. Waves were crashing over the reef less than a kilometre from the shore. On my way back, I watched the sun going down in the Mozambique bay.

Next day was my daughter's birthday. She would have been 36 years old on this day. Children at the school welcomed me back with warm smiles as an old friend. Reef Doctor had arranged the day as a special celebration for my daughter's birthday. After morning classes, I had lunch with the students. Then some of them told the teacher and me their stories and about their ambition.

11-year-old Nambinintsoa was being raised solely by his mother, who sold shells and fish. He helped in the house with daily chores and took care of his younger sibling before doing his homework.

He wished one day to become a doctor. His favourite subject was French and English. As a Junior Reef Doctor, his solution to the problem of pollution and over-fishing was the restriction of access and reduction of the ecosystem abuse.

Lodafara was ten years old. She enjoyed French classes at school and wished to become a teacher with Reef Doctor one day. She was fond of drawing and looked forward to drinking juice after the class. At home, she helped by doing laundry, fetching water and taking care of her siblings.

Her father was a fisherman, and her mother sold fish. She was worried about over-fishing and people stepping on the corals as major reef threats. She wanted to teach the villagers about how to preserve the reef.

12-year-old Pascaline loved history and geography. She would like to be a teacher. Her father was a pousse- pousse driver while her mother sold shells. Outside of school, she helped with cooking and cleaning before doing her homework. She loved dancing.

She wanted to protect the reef, to provide future generations chance to see the beautiful coral and fishes she saw during a snorkelling trip.

Afterwards, the children did some special singing and dancing in my daughter's memory. Later on, I played with them for a while, and then they danced standing on a large flat rock in the sea. I agreed with Reef Doctor to continue to support the scholarship programme for the next few years and with the building of an extra classroom in the local school.

Before I left, the community leaders came to thank for the support. I returned to my hostel with tears streaming down.

I went to bed late as a full moon was rising. I could not sleep for a long time and woke up before dawn. Walking down the moonlit shore, I watched the moon, reflecting its shadow, going down slowly in the sea.

I was expecting my first moonset in the ocean. But behind me, the sky got lighter with the dawn, and soon the moon just faded away.

I returned to Antananarivo to catch my flight for Dar es Salaam.

Volunteering in Korogwe. At Bagamoyo, the old slave trade centre Tanzania

May 2017   In Dar es Salaam, the largest city in East Africa, open-air markets, mosques, churches, old colonial buildings and modern apartment blocks lined crowded streets near my hotel. Almost everyone was in a hurry. I returned to my hotel and waited for the rest of our UK volunteering team. Soon they arrived, and some went straight to bed after the long flight. Our team was of three surgeons, including me, two anaesthetists and a junior doctor.

Next morning with the ministry official, we left in a minibus for Korogwe, 300km journey. Korogwe was a transport junction station sitting on the outskirts of the densely forested Usambara Mountains.

Korogwe   It was raining by the time we stopped in the hospital courtyard. The only surgeon of the hospital, a catholic nun, welcomed us with her staff. Korogwe hospital served around a million people who came from far distances. Its old buildings with Nightingale wards had over 100 beds. They had chronic shortages of essential equipment and disposables. Patients listed and screened for us will arrive by lunchtime tomorrow. Several children were waiting for surgery. Because of the lack of expertise and equipment, Korogwe Hospital could not operate on children under the age of 12 yrs. As a result, many suffered complications, even deaths.

Next day, we checked the equipment and facilities in the operation theatre. None of the two anaesthetic machines worked. They had a reasonable number of instruments, and the autoclave worked. But their cupboard of sutures and disposables was bare. There was only one full oxygen cylinder, and the rest lay empty. We knew they had listed at least 15 children for surgery. For the adults, we could manage under spinal anaesthesia and heavy sedation - not possible with the children. Luckily, the senior anaesthetist in our team was also paediatric anaesthetist. As I was the surgeon who would operate on the children, between the two of us, we concocted a plan of action. And after a while, the anaesthetist also managed to get one of the anaesthetic machines partly working.

After this, we saw the patients, already screened by the local team. With them translating, we examined them and scheduled for surgery in the next few days. An anxious young mother brought her firstborn, a 10-month-old boy. After walking on foot for an hour, she had travelled by bus for three hours to get here. After examining him, through the translator, I explained the procedure and tried to reassure the young mum as best I could. She left, still looking worried.

People often ask me where I am from. I was born in India and had lived there for thirty years. Since then, I have lived for thirty-eight years in the UK. I had also lived in Australia for two years. During my many travels to Ethiopia over the seventeen years, I had spent over one year there. Ethiopians called me an Ethiopian. I have also been lucky to have travelled to many countries around the world. So who am I?

Next day the same mother brought her son. Outside the operation theatre, she handed her baby to me with an anxious and pleading look which said - please take care of the most precious gift of my life. After the operation, once the child had come round from anaesthesia, I went to hand over the baby to his mother. She took the baby in her arms and gave me the tiniest of a smile. And with that smile, she welcomed me to her world - a world without barriers of language, colour, race, religion or politics. I am privileged and proud to belong to that world.

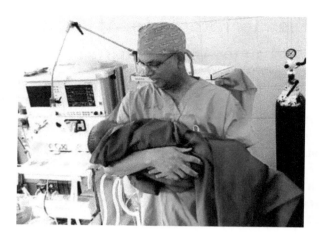

Local staff worked hard with us from early morning, often till the middle of the evenings. During lunch breaks, usually a mixture of ndizi-nyama (plantains with meat) or samaki (fish) with ugali (maize) and vegetables, I got to know them. Most lived with their families nearby, although some had come from other parts of the country leaving behind their families. Morale was low because of bureaucracies, lack of essential supplies, and low pay with increasing living costs. But they felt lucky that at least they had jobs unlike many in the country.

After work, I organised training sessions in emergency care skills and breast cancer awareness for the staff, well attended with a room full of people. On my way back to the hotel after this, one evening they asked me to see a patient they were worried. This 40yr man had surgery for a ruptured spleen the night before under only heavy sedation. They worried he might be internally bleeding again. I examined him and reassured that it did not look likely and advised them accordingly. While I was admiring them for doing such a major life-saving surgery under sedation only, they said there was no other choice. Anaesthetic machines have not been working for over a year, and despite repeated requests to authority, nothing happened. Many patients were not as lucky as this man and unfortunately died because of the lack of necessary equipment and supplies.

Next afternoon, the local surgeon asked me to come and help with a complicated operation she would do in her mission hospital outside Korogwe. The monsoon season had arrived early. We drove in her land rover through a muddy road, over flooding streams, through jungles for forty minutes. Catholic convent there in the middle of nowhere had a small hospital and a primary school. Facilities in this clean hospital were no better. Once we finished the operation, with sedation only, nuns brought us some coffee and snacks, and we talked. I learnt people from surrounding villages found it challenging to go to Korogwe on foot, especially in the rainy season. They came to the convent for help.

As we were talking, a lady came with her three-year-old son who needed surgery. She had heard we were in the convent and had walked in the rain for half an hour to get here. After examining the child, we asked her to come with her baby in our car to Korogwe for surgery in the next few days. She gave the nun surgeon and me the warmest of a smile before getting into the car.

Bagamoyo Slave trade

At the end of the week, we said goodbye to the staff and headed back. We stayed for one night in Bagamoyo town on the coast of the Indian Ocean, 75km from Dar es Salaam airport. I walked the shores and watched against falling light, boys playing football in the sand, while a group of women standing in knee-deep water tried to catch fishes with their handheld nets and a solitary fishing boat anchored for the night in the background.

Founded at the end of the 18th century, Bagamoyo was an extension of the 8th-century Arab settlement, Kaole. It was the capital of colonial German East Africa until 1891 when Dar es Salaam became the new capital. With its proximity to the major trading port of Zanzibar, 20 nautical miles away, this town was a terminus of a trade route over the centuries. Initially, Arabs traded ivory and slaves bringing from many parts of eastern and central African hinterlands over 1200km, as far as and beyond Lake Tanganyika and Lake Victoria. Captured by the slave hunters, chained together, the slaves were forced to walk hundreds of kilometres. Traders sold the slaves to Arabic countries, India, and Persia and later to the European market. Slave trade continued here under the European Colonists until the end of the 19th century, but only entirely abolished in 1922.

Next morning, I walked to the town. By the shore, small fishing boats had moored with their first catch and were busy negotiating the best price with the dealers. A group of women sat in a circle on the sand to get the cheaper remains from the fishermen. Away from the shop in a smoky market, many shops cooked fish in massive pots on open fires. I could not resist getting myself a portion of freshly cooked sardines.

Opposite stood the old customs house used for a last count of the slaves before they were crammed into the ships for Zanzibar. Kaole, about 1 km away had ruins and monuments of churches, mosques and several German tombs. For millions of individuals after walking hundreds of kilometres in shackles and chains, seeing Bagamoyo was the end of a terrible journey. But only the beginning of a worse one.

Roman Catholic Church here, first in East Africa, played an important role in the abolition of slavery in the 19th century. They bought slaves from the traders to set them free and allow them to live in the freedom villages they had created. They taught the freed slaves new skills in workshops and organised farming projects for them. The church also established an orphanage and a school for the slave children.

It was apparent walking by the site and in the town that unlike in Korogwe, the population here was of mixed ethnicity. Because of the slave trade and freeing of them later, around here was a fusion of different ethnic groups from the hinterland and the coastal area, even with some of the Arab descent.

Bagamoyo was also a starting point for renowned European explorers, moving inland from here to find the source of River Nile and exploring the African inner lakes. Famous explorer Dr Livingstone had never set foot here in his lifetime. But after his death, his body lay overnight in the Old Church's tower, to wait for the high tide to ship his body to Zanzibar and finally to London. Now there was a memorial here for him.

In the church museum, I watched with horror black and white photographs of the slaves arriving in chains and then sold in the slave market to elegantly dressed European men standing with their ladies. After seeing the collection of shackles, chains and other torture items in the museum, silently I shed a tear at the inhumanity.

In search of tigers Bandhavgarh, India

June 2017

In Sundarban, I have felt the tiger's eerie presence, but I did not see one.

Nearly half of almost 3000 tiger population in India lives in the 17 national parks of Central Indian Highlands. Bandhavgarh had the highest density of tiger population in India, one tiger per every five sq.km.

From Jabalpur airport, a 200km drive to Bandhavgarh. Bandhavgarh had 105 sq.km core, and a 400 sq.km buffer area spread between the steep ridges, undulating forest and open meadows. It had three zones - Tala, Magdi and Khitauli camps with villages dotted around its buffer zone. My eco-friendly accommodation was near the Tala gate.

Open Jeep Safari was the best way to explore the national park. Morning safari started before the sunrise and the afternoon one at 3 pm until after the sunset. They permitted a limited number of Jeeps in the national park in each session to avoid overcrowding. A maximum of twenty jeeps with only six passengers could go at any session in each of the three camps. To avoid disappointment, I had pre-booked five safaris for three days.

Royal Bengal tiger ranks among the biggest wild cats alive. Males have an average length of 3.1m, head to tail, while females measure 2.6m. Their tails are typically around 1 meter long. Tigers stand about 1 meter in height at the shoulders. Males weighed up to 325 kg. Their canines are 10cm long, the longest among all cats. These feline icons of power and beauty have a coat of yellow to light orange, with dark brown to black stripes, individual to each tiger.

My guide and I arrived at the ranger office in the dark. We waited for our permit and an assigned park ranger, a must for a safari here. We reached outside the Tala zone as the sky was getting lighter. Soon other cars piled up behind us. I understood why our guide was rushing to get here. Gate opened just before 6 am.

We drove in a thick sal and bamboo forest interspersed with open grassland. Within 10 minutes, the ranger in front motioned the driver to slow down and pointed on the ground - fresh tiger footprints.

We slowly turned a corner. Right in front was the most magnificent animal without a care in the world. We stopped. A majestic female tiger walked for about 20m before slowly going inside the thicket. Other cars piled up behind. Then we heard the cries of an animal from inside the jungle. The ranger said it was a gaur, an Indian bison, the tiger was killing. As the cry weakened, three other gaurs ran out of the forest between our cars. After several minutes, the anguished cry of the animal stopped. We moved on — the tiger has got her kill, and unlikely

to come out.

Bandhavgarh had over 200 species of birds and two dozen species of mammals including tiger, leopard, sambar, spotted and barking deer, nilgai (blue-tinted antelope), wild boar, gaur, jackal, fox, sloth bear, mongoose, striped hyena and jungle cat.

We heard loud monkey noises in the forest. Our guide explained the monkeys were warning other animals about leopards. They made another distinct noise for the tigers. We looked in the trees but could spot nothing. He said it was unlikely to see a leopard in this thick forest unless it came out on the road. We moved on and came behind a line of cars stationed by a water pool. There in the water was a large male tiger in all its glory. We waited transfixed, cameras clicking, as the giant beast lazily had its bath. After almost twenty minutes, it slowly got out of the water, shook its body and then disappeared in the bushes.

We drove to a place around a few wooden sheds where the villagers sold freshly fried pakoras. Our guide took out a flask of coffee and snacks for our breakfast. Afterwards, we only saw hundreds of deer and monkeys. We returned in time before the gate closed at 10-30.

After lunch and a brief rest, in the scorching heat, we left at 3 pm for afternoon safari, this time to Magdi camp. We drove with no sighting of tigers but many langurs and rhesus monkeys sitting by the road. Peacocks wandered around, showing their full plumage. Our car ran near the high walls. On the other side stood villages. The guide said these 3m high barriers did not stop the tigers from jumping over and killing cows in the villages. To prevent the villagers trapping and killing the tigers, the government compensated them with a decent sum of money for each domestic animal destroyed by a tiger.

As evening drew to a close, we heard a distinct sound of monkeys at a distance. 50m from the road, over a rocky area, a tigress lay on the ground with two cubs playing around. The cubs were only 3-4 months old. It grew darker. Before the gate, we had to wait as two female nilgais with their cubs grazed on the road. The mothers, largest of antelopes, stood almost 1.5m high. After a while, they moved away, and we drove back.

At the lodge, I chatted with the night security guard, a man in his late sixties from a nearby village. He spent the night in a small shed inside the gate, even in the winter. He had learnt from the owner that I was a doctor and asked if I would see his son and give advice. The 30yr old had suffered a paralysis of his left leg many years back. They had been to the local health centre over the years and had also seen many traditional practitioners and spent a lot of money with no improvement. Some have suggested to take him to Jabalpur, which was far and will cost a lot of money. I asked him to bring his son the next day during lunch with all his reports.

Next morning, back to Tala camp. I was the only one in the Jeep on this tour. Soon after we entered the park, there were loud monkey calls. By now, I was almost an expert to know that a tiger was nearby. We drove around to find another large male tiger in a pool.

We watched him for a while until other cars piled up behind.

According to legends, Lord Rama gifted the ancient fort here to his younger brother Lakshmana. 'Bandhav' meant brother and 'Garh' meant fort, hence the name, Bandhavgarh. Its history dated back to 2000 yrs. Through a rocky outcrop, we reached the top of a flat hill at over 800m. Next to a stepped pond full of algae, lay a giant statue of reclining Lord Vishnu. This area, the ranger said, was a favourite jaunt for leopards, but recently a tiger with her two cubs had moved nearby. We did not see any. Down below the pond was a human-made three cave point with ancient carvings and inscriptions on its wall. Further down the track lay larger Badi Gufa, another cave, for the soldiers 1000 year back. From this high plateau, we enjoyed in silence the gorgeous view down below of the national park.

We returned to the same place for our late morning breakfast. Sitting by the car, the only place they allowed you to get off the car, we shared fresh pakoras with coffee. Bandhavgarh had about 110 park rangers and the same number of guides. But only sixty-five drivers, as they allowed only 60 cars in its three zones at any time. The rangers and the guides took turns for their assignment and did not have work every day. As they all came from the surrounding villages, in the rainy season, they were busy in their fields with the crops. This park provided a reasonable income for almost five hundred people.

After lunch, the night guard brought his son walking with a wooden stick. I examined him with all his reports. It appeared he had suffered paralysis of his leg after an attack of polio in his teenage years. I explained to them that there was no medicine to cure this. But he would benefit from physiotherapy exercises, which I showed him. They thanked me profusely, glad and reassured at least they wouldn't waste more money to find a cure.

For the afternoon tour was a choice to go to Khitauli, known for its birdlife but less chance to see the tigers. I returned to Magdi. Glad that I did. No sooner than we had gone through the gate, there were monkey calls. Our female ranger explained to the new tourists the difference between warning calls for the tiger and the leopard. As we came by an area with many tall sal trees, three tigers crossed majestically in front. Soon two of them chose to take a nap right next to the road. Third one walked to a tree, rubbed his nose on it, raised its tail and urinated. Then, like the other two, curled up to sleep. We watched them for about 40 minutes. They showed no sign of moving from the place. The ranger said with their bellies full; they may stay there for some time. We moved on.

During our coffee break, we spotted some jungle babblers camouflaging their dusty coloured feathers against dry leaves. Nearby was a group of langurs. Babies hung on to their mothers. Our ranger explained there were 20 female rangers there. She had always wanted to be a ranger, despite suffering a partial loss of sight in her one eye from a childhood injury. Her husband was also a ranger who worked in the park. Rangers working in the forest here looked out for poachers and loggers. They also helped with spotting and counting the tigers. They carried with them a book of all the tigers identified by their individual stripes and made a note of their daily sightings and reported to the park office. Walking in pairs, mostly on foot in the park, they knew the tigers by their given names. On our way back, we saw a crested serpent eagle circling over. The guide explained it must have spotted a tiger kill below.

On my last morning in Bandhavgarh, I returned to Tala and was lucky to see two more tigers walking over the track. Soon they both walked to the side and lied down. Then the guide spotted some colourful Indian roller bird with various shades of blue on the wings, tails, and its belly. As it flew away, it looked even more colourful. One of my fellow tourists, a keen birdwatcher then spotted with his binocular an oriental honey buzzard sitting on a fallen tree. He also then somehow found an Indian pitta, a tiny bird with a bright green feather. We saw many peacocks on the way, but no more tigers.

But I had seen almost a dozen tigers in the last few days, more than I ever imagined.

After volunteering, the team stuck in a balcony for the night Kerala

June 2017 Kerala India

It was after 9 pm when I arrived in Cochin from Jabalpur. After my overnight stay, I got picked up and headed towards Thiruvalla, 110km distance. A group of friends, who now lived in Texas, USA and UAE, had between them organised this programme to provide free surgery for one hundred patients from the villages where they grew up as a child. All of them had businesses abroad. The medical team comprised me; two anaesthetists and a theatre nurse from my previous hospital in the UK; another surgeon and a gynaecologist from Delhi - husband and wife, and two local junior doctors.

Two local doctors had already screened the patients. The Non-Resident Indians (NRI) had arranged with a local Catholic mission hospital, free operation theatre time and overnight stay for the patients. The medical team arrived at their own expenses, but our NRI friends took care of all local costs, including accommodation and meals.

Thiruvalla was known as the 'Land of the NRIs'. It was also famous for Kathakali, the famous south Indian dramatic classical dance, played daily as an offering in its Sreevallabhan temple of over thousand years of history. The city was full of high-rise buildings, malls, and shops - also, many large private hospitals, private schools and colleges in elaborate gated buildings. Hotel by the river outside the town where we stayed, had in its grounds a large hall for wedding receptions.

In present-day India, the healthcare system had a distinct two-tier system. While its modern private hospitals offered state-of-the-art treatment, they were beyond the means of ordinary people. They went to the Government facilities, with poor infrastructure, inadequate workforce and supplies. Routine but necessary operations rarely took place there. As a result, a vast population suffered disability and often serious complications. A hundred patients screened by our team had all been waiting between one to five years for their surgery, which they could not afford. Charitable hospitals of various religious affiliations did not offer free care and were only slightly less expensive than the private hospitals - beyond the reach of ordinary people for any inpatient care.

In the following days, we worked with the local nurses in the hospital with modern facilities. Some senior nurses were nuns. I loved the unique present NRI team arranged for each patient's family to take home upon their discharge - a tree sapling. Families were requested to plant these near their places and look after them - a lovely gesture in a country with rapid deforestation.

One day in-between the operations, nurses called me back to the ward to see a patient I had discharged in the morning. The patient was all ready to go. Her husband and teenage daughter were waiting with her. Her daughter wanted to sing a song for me to thank for her mother's surgery - most touching and beautiful.

Matron and dean of the nursing college, a nun, requested me for a teaching session for the nursing students and staff. I learnt that for the three-year course in this missionary college; students paid an entrance fee and annual fees, which totalled to more than their three full years of earning in the hospital after qualification. I asked one of the nuns if there were any free scholarship scheme for the students. She smiled and said no.

At the hospital, I gathered from the nurses their pay was poor. Most looked for opportunities to go to the Middle East for a few years to save enough money for their families. For now, they felt lucky they had a job they loved and had some money, unlike many in the country.

One evening, the NRI group took us to an orphanage they supported in the town. Over three hundred children welcomed us with a show of songs and dances. Then we sat down together to have a simple dinner - it was amazing and heartbreaking.

Next evening in our hotel, a wedding reception was going on in the vast hall with over three hundred guests. Cost for every ten guest's dinner was equal to a month's pay of a nurse at the hospital.

On our last day at the hospital, they arranged a big thank you ceremony with beautiful Kathakali dancesperformed by the nursing students. After speeches by the local dignitaries, they asked me to say a few words. After thanking the staff and the hospital for their friendliness and support, I asked them if they would consider in future giving one patient free treatment for every hundred they treated. The nuns only smiled.

Three of the UK team and the couple from Delhi left, while I travelled with the NRI group to their village 40 km outside Thiruvalla. We drove past beautiful backwaters lined with coconut trees and then hills green with coffee plantations. At their place, I had never seen so many grand palaces in any village in my lifetime- no wonder this village held a record for the number of banks in one village!

After a delicious lunch of rice and vegetable curry with coconut at the home of one NRI friend, we drove to a small church at the foot of a hill. The hillslope was full of huts where many labourers lived, most at the poverty level. Men came down the hill every morning and waited by the road, hoping to be picked by the contractors coming with trucks for working at building sites, agricultural fields or at the rubber plantations. Women came later after finishing their housework, some carrying their babies, and got into buses to go to rich people's houses for cleaning and cooking.

The team had arranged a general free clinic for the locals. Two local junior doctors and I saw several patients from the community. The NRI group paid for any medicine we prescribed. One of the patients was too unwell to walk down from the hill. I walked up to his cottage. He had lost his job as a daily labourer since he became ill. Luckily, his illness was possible to treat with medicines at home. I prescribed, and my NRI friends gave the family some money for sustenance and agreed to deliver his drugs later on the same day. His wife was in tears and insisted we stayed for coffee. As we sipped our coffee, heavy rain started falling, making our return path like streams of a river. The rain stopped as quickly as it had started and we walked down with a trickle of water still flowing over the track.

In the early evening, they took me to an orphanage with about 30 children near their village. Wife of one of the NRI was giving her husband a special 40th birthday treat by having a special dinner with the children and some neighbours from the village where he grew up. Children gave him a garland of flowers from their garden and then sang happy birthday before we had dinner- a memorable birthdaycelebration.

For the night I stayed at a newly built six-story apartment block belonging to one of the NRI. In the entire building with a security guard, so far there was only another family who lived on the second floor. Four bedrooms were luxurious. From the 5th floor balcony, one could see other buildings at a distance - all very peaceful. As I stood watching outside, the automatic door closed behind me. I had to knock for someone to come and open from inside.

After we showered, my friends asked me to join them at a bar in the locality. I declined and wished them fun for the rest of the night with their local friends. I soon fell to sleep in my room at the far end of the apartment. Next morning at breakfast, I asked them how their night went. They had come back around midnight and had chatted outside my room quietly, hoping they had not disturbed me. I said I had not heard a single thing and had slept through.

In the morning, we visited a church-run health post where the two local junior doctors worked. It was a clinic where patients had to pay, and it had a few beds for terminally ill patients for which the families had to pay. These two bright junior doctors had recently qualified from one of the prestigious medical colleges in the country. This college was of a religious denomination. Entrance to it was highly competitive. Local church groups of the province had a small quota to nominate a few students, the college accepted without entrance exam. These two doctors were the lucky ones. They still had to pay college fees etc. like anyone else. But once graduated, it bonded them to work for two years at these local church 'charity hospitals' for a small salary with no training.

In contrast, their friends received proper practical training in hospitals under supervision. These two doctors like a few others worked in shifts of twelve hours most days without any training - waiting for the bond period to be over so they can join proper training. I was disgusted.

The afternoon was at the same clinic by the hill. Not a hint of a cloud in the sky and more people came down for free consultation and medicine.

It was my last night in the country and same for the NRI friends. They ordered a takeaway dinner. We chatted over cups of coffee, and then the dinner arrived around 9-30pm. After we finished dinner, I retired to bed, leaving them to talk. Later from my bed, I heard some noises outside and thought the boys were having fun. Soon I was fast asleep. I woke up from a deep sleep when the calling bell of the flat kept ringing. I checked my watch - only 5 am!

It was the security guard at the door. Rooms of my friends were open. No one was there. Then I heard loud noises and banging from the balcony. I opened the door to find six of them stranded in that cramped place. One of them rushed to use the toilet.

Then I heard what had happened in the night. After I had gone to my room, so they did not make noise to disturb me, they had gone to the balcony with their bottles of beer. Last person coming out there had forgotten to hold the door, and it had closed behind them. They had made noises for a while, to wake me, but with no luck. They had spent the night, last night of their holiday in their birthplace, in the balcony. Drinking so much beer earlier had not helped. They had to relieve themselves from the height. Once a gust of wind had swept in suddenly, and one of them had got wet with his own urine. Only when the morning security guard walked below to relieve the night guard, they had shouted to him to come up and ring the bell at the flat.

I made coffee for them soon, and we all laughed.

Denali and Katmai Singing to a grizzly Alaska

September 2017

Documentaries showing Brown bears waiting by the mini-falls to catch salmon in Alaska was a favourite of mine. Salmon runs in Alaska between June and September. I wanted to be there and also added the Denali National Park in my itinerary.

In early September I left via Reykjavik for Anchorage in Alaska, a small airport.

Train to Denali   In the early morning, I arrived at the Anchorage train station. Travellers waited for the scenic train ride, many on their fishing trips. Soon we walked over the train line to our coaches for Denali. The panoramic train offered unimpeded views.

The train crossed Eklutna River. Eklutna village local cemetery had brightly painted spirit houses, first settled over 800 years ago, oldest inhabited location near Anchorage. Several long bridges took us over Knik and Matanuska Rivers. Mighty Matanuska River divided the Chugach Mountain Range on the right and the Talkeetna Mountains to the north.

Fall colours, patches of bright yellow, gold, red and purple breaking through the backdrop of evergreens, grounds covered with blankets of crunchy golden leaves, took my breath away. Glacial rivers, lakes and snowy peaked mountains in the background compounded the scenery.

The train stopped briefly at Wasilla where many on their fishing trips got off to the nearby Big Lake, Nancy Lake and fishing streams on the creeks. We passed by the Nancy Lake to Willow. Soon there was a gorgeous view of Mt. Denali on our left. As we travelled along the Susitna River, the train slowed. An announcement came - moose near the track. I rushed to the viewing platform. By the track in the bush were two massive moose, a mother with her calf.

Our train stopped for longer at Talkeetna. Many people got off there. Talkeetna was famous for boat rides, scenic flights over Denali and staging post for the climbers preparing for Mt. Denali expeditions. Then the train crossed over the Talkeetna River at its confluence with Susitna and Chulitna. We chugged along the Susitna River with an even better photo opportunity of Mt. Denali. Now we were following the eastern boundary of Denali State Park, sharing its western border with its big brother, Denali National Park. Fall colours became even more dramatic.

The train crossed the Susitna River and then through Broad Pass, with blueberry bushes against the mountains. The train stopped and pulled to a siding. A train coming from Fairbanks via Denali to Anchorage crossed us. As customary, passengers for both trains gave each other a 'moose antler' wave. After passing the Summit Lake 720m, the highest point on the Alaska Railroad, we moved along the Nenana River bordering Denali National Park.

In another twenty minutes, we were at Denali. Eight-hour train journey had gone so fast, as if in a trance. We got off the train through steps, no platform here as in my village station when I was eight years old. We crossed the railway lines to the buses waiting to take guests to their respective hotels.

It was still daylight and only around 0°C. Later, after dinner back in my hotel, as I looked through the window in the dark, there was a surprise. A beautiful Aurora was chasing me here in Denali. I rushed outside and watched for about 45 minutes the magical light show.

Denali National Park

I left for a 14 hours bus tour of 6 million acres Denali National Park, larger than Wales. On a bright morning against the snowy mountains, the autumnal colour show got better, if that was possible. We stopped briefly to see on a rocky cliff a herd of nimble Dall sheep. Then we went over the Polychrome pass with overlooking multi-coloured volcanic rocks. Only after we had crossed, the driver/guide told us it was a site of frequent landslides!

Rest stop by the Toklat River, a place of merging glacial rivers and towering cliffs. While we were taking pictures of more Dall sheep on the steep rocky hillsides, and a few marmots next to the road, the driver, pointed below to the bushes of soapberries by the river bed - a grizzly!

Soon we continued to the Stony Hill overlook. From the edge of this mountain pass, with alpine tundra all around, we had the full view of Mt Denali 6190m from base to summit, the highest peak in North America. Strangely, I heard a few of my fellow US tourists telling each other they were watching the highest peak in the world. Obviously, for some, there was no world outside the US! Politely I reminded them there were fourteen over 8000m mountains in the world, Everest being the highest. I tried to imagine and envied the climbers up on Mt Denali at present.

After going through another high pass, we stopped to see in the bush below, a massive bull moose with its impressive antlers. The road then dropped down to the Eielson visitor centre, named after the bush pilot Carl Eielson. After coffee and some snacks, I visited its gallery of art inspired by Denali's wilderness and wildlife.

With moose antlers left all around, I watched from here the glorious mountain in front only 45km away. Many went for a hike down towards the mountain, and I returned to the bus to continue our tour.

Colours of the bushes on our left, leading to the McKinley River against Mt Denali, became unbelievable. The driver slowed and pointed in front, right next to the road, a she-wolf. Without a care, she walked next to our bus as we clicked, and then casually disappeared into the bush.

We drove on and saw some arctic land squirrels, snowshoe hares, many cow moose and another bull moose. On the rocky hill on our right, more Dall sheep grazed precariously. Further down was a caribou with its impressive antlers. I have now seen all the five Alaska's stars - grizzly bears, bull and cow moose, caribou and Dall sheep!

Next, we stopped near a camping site by the Wonder Lake and walked through rocks towards the Reflection Lake. This small pool perfectly reflected Mt Denali in its clear blue waters. It was a bit windy, but on a cloudless day, a dazzling view.

We then arrived at Kantishna Roadhouse, the end of our 148km road. This backcountry lodge was built when miners rushed to find gold in the early 20th century. Lunch was in the restored log cabin. Grounds here had cosy cabins, some with large caribou antlers above their doors. Common ravens, grey jay, willow ptarmigan and blue bill magpie rested in trees in full fall colours. A harrier hawk flew over.

In Moose River, we had a go at panning for gold. I rolled up my trousers, and standing in the icy water tried panning with no luck. But two from our group found tiny flakes of the shiny precious metal. The driver put these in a small plastic container for them to take home. Not rich, but lucky fellows.

On our return, before the Eielson visitor centre, our driver stopped and pointed towards the river. There was another caribou with its massive antler, about 50m from us. Near the glacial plains at Tolkat, we spotted another grizzly. But we were not sure if this dark brown bear was the same one we had seen earlier or not.

We arrived at Denali after dark. But only clear sky with stars tonight, no Aurora.

Nenana River rafting   Next morning I went for rafting in the Nenana River, just outside Denali National Park. In this icy cold glacially fed waters, now at the end of summer, rapids were less dramatic. The first half of the trip ran parallel to the forests with Dall sheep and moose grazing with their new babies. A Golden eagle flew over us towards the canyon. In the trees, harrier hawks and spruce grouse perched.

Our crew warned us before we dipped into a canyon - white-water ahead. Now it was real white-water rafting. We hung on to the ropes as the river entered a steep-walled gorge. Our boat moved through Class 3-4 rapids appropriately named as Cable Car, The Royal Flush, Coffee Grinder and Train Wreck, with the river churning into a maelstrom of foam.

After lunch, I visited the Denali Visitor's centre. An excellent twenty-minute documentary, 'Heartbeats of Denali', showed the landscape and the wildlife in its full glory through various seasons.

Denali National park will close in two days, and all the hotels and shops will close the day after. Almost a holiday mood for the seasonal workers who have come from many parts of the US. The people who lived around here were preparing for the harsh winter months. Their nearest supply will be in Fairbanks, 195 km distance. The train would then run only once a week each way!

A lovely train journey back to Anchorage with a grand view all the way. During lunch on the train, I met a group of very friendly women, mothers, daughters, with their children and grandchildren returning to Washington State. Their older sons, husbands and fathers were still fishing around the park until it closed and will rejoin them the day after tomorrow in Anchorage.

Katmai National Park Brook Falls

From Anchorage, I caught an early morning flight to King Salmon, in the Alaska Peninsula on the west. From there, a six-seater seaplane, my first time, took us to the Katmai National Park. The plane landed on the river. The guide warned us a bear was resting on the shore only 50m away. We took a detour to the park ranger's office, skirting around a sleeping large brown bear.

The ranger explained about bears and gave us a safety briefing. Katmai had over 2200 brown bears, grizzlies, highest population in the world, and we would see many of them. Females weighed up to 180 kg, while males ranged between 180–360 kg. Their standing heights were up to 2.4m, and their sharp claws were 8cm long, 75% of their diet comprised berries, leaves and nuts. But here, in this season, they mostly ate fish.

Rules were:

1) Stay at least 45m from any bear at all times. 2) Never run from any bear. They can run over 56km/hr. Usain Bolt's fastest run 44.72km/hr. There is no chance you will overrun them. 3) Try to travel in groups. Talk to each other loudly. Avoid surprising the bears and make your presence known by making noise to alert them to your presence, not to scare them. 4) During a close encounter, speak to the bear in a calm voice. 5) Do not carry any food item with you.

Six of us followed a ranger to the side of the bridge on Brooks River. It was closed because two bears were catching salmon in the river underneath. After a while, the bears moved on. We walked over the bridge to a viewing platform on the other side. From there we could see many bears busy feeding in the river.

Soon we walked behind our guide on a narrow path through an ancient forest, for about 1km. Then we entered a track between the bushes. The guide showed us fresh bear scratch marks on the trees. Within another 100m we were on the famous viewing platform overlooking Brooks Falls. Sockeye salmons flooded the shallow river, resting to recoup energy before leaping over the 2m falls.

Eight bears were by the falls. One of them stood right at the edge of the plunge, waiting for the salmon to leap into its mouth. A big brown bear, oldest here, was called Otis. He just stayed on a rock below the falls and waited for any fish to come in its way.

On the other side of the water, two bears wrestled standing on their hind legs, almost playfully - spellbinding.

After 40 minutes, we had to leave the viewing platform for another group to come. We walked through the jungle path for another 1km to the massive Brooks Lake, spawning grounds of the salmons. The most magical place to come to die after swimming hundreds of miles from the sea. Bears crowded the narrow channel of the Brooks River from the lake.

Almost 400,000 salmon successfully leap Brooks Falls each year. Each female salmon swells with about 4000 eggs. Once they spawn in the lake, they die. When in the winter, ice and snow cover much of this landscape, newly hatched Salmon bide their time. Once the snow melts they return to the ocean. From late June, schools of the silvery and energetic fishes pulse through the river. By August and September, coloured sockeyes dot the Brooks River on their way to their birthplace in the Brook Lake. Best time for the grizzlies to fatten up with the oily fish before going to hibernate in the hills for the winter.

During our return, we saw several more bears on the river by the bridge. The enormous crocodile earlier we had spotted on a cay, was now joined by two others for sunbathing. Today bears here bears there and bears everywhere. I had seen about 30 bears in the last few hours – staggering!

Our seaplane left before dark for King Salmon. We flew over the moon-like landscape of the Valley of 10,000 Smokes, a post-volcanic landscape created after the eruption of Novarupta in 1912, the most massive volcanic eruption of the 20th century. Now snow partly covered the top of these volcanic hills.

Overnight in King Salmon, by the beautiful Naknek River. This community of about 300 people had no road connection to the rest of Alaska, only by flights. Apart from the visit to Brooks Falls, it was a favourite place on the way to Katmai or other areas for fly-fishing. There was only one place to eat -Eddie's restaurant pub. Great food and atmosphere with few hardened but friendly locals and fly-fishers from all over the US. It was like being in one of those backwater American meeting places; I had seen in the films. I talked with some locals. Life was hard here, not only in the harsh winter months without the tourists but throughout the year for most. But they loved the area and would live nowhere else in the world.

Next morning, I was back at Brooks Camp under a cloudy sky. From the visitor centre, we took a tour to a prehistoric site nearby. Natural choke point for salmon runs with 2km long Brooks River connecting Brooks Lake, and Naknek Lake had made it an attractive location for the prehistoric Alaskans. The oldest sites found around here dated 3000 BC. Finds included the remains of pit houses, stone tools, and the evidence of toolmaking.

With usual safety warnings, they allowed us to go to the visiting platforms on our own if we wanted. Today there were bears near the visitor centre. After they moved on, I walked by myself over the bridge to the platform next to the river. As I got up on it for a view, rangers closed the gate. A mother with her cub swam from the water and then lied down right below us. Soon we spotted another cub, still playing in the water. Mother slept cuddling her baby. The second cub, feeling left out, soon came up with a fish in its mouth and started crunching next to his mum. This woke up the other two, but their bellies were full. They yawned and went back to sleep. The second cub, a bit disappointed, finished his fish and returned for another swim.

Carefully I got down through the stairs on the other side of the platform. Avoiding the bears' purple coloured poos, from their blueberry diet, I walked with two other people to the viewing platform by Brooks Falls.

Otis was there in his usual spot. More bears there today having their feast. In a day, in the season, they ate about 15-20 salmon, each weighing 3-4kg. We saw Fiffy, a cuddly cub born only a few months back, nervously walking on the edge of the river with mum. Soon it spotted the swimming fishes and started chasing them and splashed everywhere.

I walked by myself, talking nonsense loudly, through the jungle path to Brook Lake. There I sat and watched the bears on the Brook River for a while. Back to Brooks Falls for my last viewing. Otis was still there, but Fiffy and its mum had moved on. As I was walking back by myself over the boardwalk from the platform, three bears came from nowhere in the jungle below me. Two of them walked under us towards the falls. Third one stood upright and started having a good scratch against an Antarctic beech tree. I could not stop chuckling.

Then, slowly, I walked back by myself through the forest path, happy that I had come to this famous place. Suddenly in front, less than 15m away, a bear came out of nowhere. It stopped, looked towards me and started walking in front.

I followed the ranger's advice by talking loudly. Singing a song was not on, as I cannot sing to save my life! And even a grizzly will find me out of tune. I sang loudly, Bengali nursery rhymes. Hoping, unless the bear was multilingual, it would not understand anyway. The grizzly stopped and looked back at me for a few seconds and then walked on. After walking about 200m together, the bear moved to the other side of the jungle and then to the river.

I walked to the safety of the viewing post by the river.

Elmina slave castle Ghana

October 2017

It was my first time in West Africa. Local volunteering coordinators picked me up at Accra airport. On our way to Mampong Akuapem, we stopped briefly near a marketplace by the flyover in the central area of the city. Physical features of the West African, compared to the East African, was at once visible. Unlike the East Africans with a pointed chin, pointed ears, thinner nose and longer face, in the west, they had broad noses and fuller lips and were broad-shouldered. Women and men wore more colourful clothes here.

Densely populated Accra was like any other city in the continent. Busy, with signs of poverty side by side with areas of affluence. Massive billboards of different preachers and god channels caught my attention, unlike I had seen so far in my travels. We drove up the side of a hill to our accommodation with a view of Accra city below.

I met my US colleagues there. Tetteh Quarshie Memorial Hospital, a Govt. hospital, served a population of a 35km radius of semi-urban and rural areas. It had good facilities, but because of inadequate staffing and lack of supplies, routine but essential procedures did not get done.

On our 15 minutes' drive to the hospital, there were at least ten churches of various denomination and many more enormous posters of the preachers. TV in the room blared dozens of God channels. Must be a very god-fearing place! In the next six days, we carried out over sixty procedures and did many training sessions.

In one evening, they treated us with a dinner in the local tribal leader's house. Amongst a village with abject poverty, the mansion house reeked of opulence.

Elmina

After the week, I took a trip to Elmina. After two hours drive from Accra, we stopped at Cape Coast, a coastal town.

An enormous quantity of gold dust found on this coastline attracted the Europeans. Local tribal kings using this to their advantage bartered for gold, mahogany, ivory and their people against textiles, silk, woollen items, spices and sugar.

Cape Coast Castle, built-in 1667 by the Swedes and later taken over by the British was a holding station for the slaves - one of about forty slave castles built on the Gold Coast.

Its underground dungeon was a space of blackness, terror and death, in sharp contrast to the commanding heights of whiteness above, where the Europeans lived in luxury. The basement of this imposing fortress was the last memory slaves had of their homeland before being shipped off across the Atlantic. The Museum of West African History was a grim reminder of the horror inflicted upon fellow human by another. Next to its slave quarters was Negotiation Hill. There, traders displayed and bargained for their captives in chains before selling them for the best price - shocking.

After 15km drive through a beautiful coastal road, we arrived in the town next to Elmina Castle. Against the coast, lined with coconut and palm trees, this monumental white building looked impressive. After the vast grounds with gardens, we walked over moats around the castle. Cannons looked upon us from all corners.

Elmina was the first trading post built by the Portuguese in 1482, the oldest European building in existence south of the Sahara. Established as a trade settlement, this castle soon became one of the most critical stops on the Atlantic slave trade route. Dutch seized the fort from the Portuguese in 1637 and soon took over all the Portuguese Gold Coast by 1642. Until 1814, the slave trade continued here under the Dutch in competition with the British running their slave trade from Cape Castle. Gold Coast, now Ghana, finally gained its independence from Britain in 1957.

By the 18th century, annually, 30,000 slaves on their way to the Americas passed through Elmina. Deportation through outposts like Elmina had continued for nearly three hundred years in this part of the world. At least twelve million Africans were sent as slaves. Millions died during the process. The grandeur of Elmina, its picturesque surroundings with blue skies, sandy beaches, and tropical palms, disguised its dark history. Horrors transpired within the walls of the fortress would never be erased with time.

By the 18th century, annually, 30,000 slaves on their way to the Americas passed through Elmina. Deportation through outposts like Elmina had continued for nearly three hundred years in this part of the world. At least twelve million Africans were sent as slaves. Millions died during the process. The grandeur of Elmina, its picturesque surroundings with blue skies, sandy beaches, and tropical palms, disguised its dark history. Horrors transpired within the walls of the fortress would never be erased with time.

Inside Elmina, opposite a large forecourt, stood a church. Above its doorway was an inscription 'This is the Lord's everlasting resting place'. Next to it stood the female dungeon. On one side of the courtyard was a three-storied building. European officers' and the priests' quarters on the second floor were spacious with parquet floors and gorgeous sea views, comparable to a modern five-star hotel. Rest of the surrounding buildings were two stories. On the first floor, in less luxurious but spacious rooms, lived the soldiers.

We then visited the dungeons on the ground floor. At any time, up to 1,000 male and 500 female slaves were shackled and crammed in the rooms with only one small hole near the top for ventilation. We stood inside one. The guide closed the door behind us. We were only ten people in the group, and within five minutes in the darkness, we were gasping for air. In a room such as these, they kept about 50 slaves with no space to lie down. Men and women were held in separate chambers. There were no toilets, resulting in the dungeon floors littered with human waste. Outbreaks of malaria and yellow fever were rampant.

Revolts by slaves at Elmina were met with intense oppression. Some were murdered outright. Others were placed in solitary confinement in an airtight dark cell next to the church, where they starved to death. Only to show who was in charge, slaves, both men and women, were chained outside and forced to stay in the blazing sun for days.

Next, we came by the stairway of horror. This narrow staircase connected the top floor to the courtyard in front of the female dungeons. Officers standing on top floor chose slave women. Soldiers then washed them naked in the open and took them through these stairs for the officers to rape and satisfy their lust. Then they were left with the soldiers. In the courtyard, chains dangled from a stone block. There, any women showing slightest of dissent were kept chained under the sun for days and nights, sometimes until death, as an example to others.

In the male dungeon, they chained the stronger slaves to the floor throughout their stay in Elmina. Two nights before we visited, a group of African Americans on their pilgrim to trace their roots, had spent one night in the dungeon by chaining themselves to the floor - to experience what their forefathers had faced.

European traders in the slave market wanted healthy captives for the long voyage. For this, they used metal instrument to force the slaves to open their mouth to count the number of teeth. More teeth meant in better shape. They also whipped the captives to make them jump. Higher they jumped, stronger they were. That was the first phase. Buyers then branded their new property, in the most inhumane way, with their personal metallic stamps burnt on an open fire. On average, slaves spent three months in the dungeons before being shipped.

We moved to a room with a narrow portal at one end – the infamous 'Door of No Return'. Through this, slaves boarded the ships on the treacherous journey across the Atlantic known as the Middle Passage, to the New World. We crawled through this ingress to the side of the harbour. Male prisoners had handcuffs chained close to the shackles on their ankles, making them bend over like we were doing.

On the roof of the first floor, on one side, was glorious sea view with palm trees. Towards the town above a hill stood Fort St Jago, built by the Dutch to protect Elmina castle. On our left was Benya lagoon, a busy fishing harbour, full of colourful traditional fishing boats, pirogues. Elmina's roof was lined with cannons, heavier ones against assault from the sea from the other European empires. Only a few lighter guns faced towards the inland for unlikely attacks by local Africans.

Days of slave trade may have long gone, but the walls of Elmina and Cape Coast was a haunting reminder of the most tragic and brutal periods in the history of humanity. In the forecourt opposite the church in Elmina now stood a plaque.

Numbed, I went outside the castle area in the town where now women in their colourful dresses, sold everyday goods. On the bay, fishermen were busy selling their fresh catch in the bustling fish market.

Back in my hotel in the evening, the TV was showing a CNN report. In a marketplace in Tripoli, only this week they were selling human as slaves for only 20 dollars! As of now, about 40 million men, women and children all over the world stay victims of modern slavery!

My brain hurts – stop; it's a bleed.

November / December 2017

Today, 1st December 2017, I would have been in Costa Rican tropical jungle with a view of the beautiful Arenal volcano - if I flew to Cuba on the way there last Sunday. If I flew last Sunday, I would have most likely died in the air soon as the plane took off from London and the cabin pressure changed. With so much blood pressing on my brain already, a most likely outcome. It would have made international news.

But I did not fly last Sunday.

For over a week leading to that, I had an increasingly intense headache. Full doses of painkillers were no match. The last couple of times I played badminton, my shots were all over the place. My friends said I looked tired and needed a holiday.

As my balance got worse, the evening before my holiday, my daughter insisted on taking me to the hospital. A CT scan showed 150ml of blood. More than the tenth of my brain size, sitting inside my skull and competing for space against my brain. Emergency surgery followed with three holes in my head.

Forty-eight hours later, I realised I have full control of my four limbs, I could read and use my computer, albeit with a sore head. The surgeon advised after four weeks; I can start local volunteering again and play badminton a few weeks after that. But no flying for at least three months. First thing I did was to email the Charity hospital in Rajasthan to postpone my trip agreed there at the end of January. Then I booked a trip to the North Pole in the summer.

I can get back to travelling/volunteering etc. again after about three months. Probably no more mountains, I am getting old for that now anyway, but who knows - I am over 70!

Patient in the next bed was a 43-year-old man, 1.9m tall, athletically built. Could easily have been a great fast bowler, but he was a keen cyclist, regular swimmer and loved football. Ten days back, he took his wife and their young children to town in the evening to show them the Christmas light decorations. Probably to do some early Christmas shopping as well. Not the Santa presents, that will be without the children around.

While the lights mesmerised the children, he had an epileptic fit and became unconscious. An ambulance brought him to the hospital. A CT scan showed a brain tumour, and he had surgery the same day as me. Like me, he would go home on the 2nd day of Christmas month.

With their Daddy back, children would happily talk about Christmas decorations in the house. They will keep reminding him they have been very good this year. They hoped Santa would bring them all the presents they have asked. They will chatter about fun things they were doing at school, and he will definitely go to their Christmas play. They will have their best Christmas ever in their life with their dad. He will make sure of that. Because even with the best treatment available for his brain tumour, he will start going downhill soon. He had already lost vision in one of his eyes! At best, his family and children will have him for three to four years.

This is life.

Part 4

Volunteering, adventure and travel 2017 - 2020

Volunteering in Rajasthan India

April 2018

I took a flight to Jodhpur, via Delhi, four months after they cut holes in my skull. A friend of mine, an NRI from Rajasthan, got a request from her friend In Phalodi. They wanted help with surgical volunteering in their charity hospital.

Jodhpur airport to Phalodi was 50km. I arrived in the late afternoon to a 45°C temperature. A family, most living in Jodhpur, had built a charity hospital in Phalodi where their father was born. Two unmarried sisters looked after the project. The hospital was one km outside the desert village of Khichan and 4km from Phalodi in the buffer zone of the Thar Desert.

The team included me, the surgeon and a gynaecologist couple I had worked with last year in Kerala, an anaesthetist and a trainee surgeon, all from Delhi. One of my brothers from West Bengal had sent a large supply of surgical instruments.

The hospital provided free treatment for the locals. They also helped with free renal dialysis. In this desert area, renal failure was common. Most could not afford the recurring costs of dialysis. Until a few years back, a surgeon from Phalodi came once a week doing free surgery. But since his practice in the town got busier, he does not have the time.

There were decent facilities in this spacious hospital. One anaesthetist from the town also kindly agreed to work with us for the week. The family running the hospital provided free accommodation and meal for its staff along with a regular salary.

Beautiful peacocks wandered around hospital grounds without care. During our dinner together with the two sisters, I got to know the benefactor family. They belonged to the Jain religion. Jina Vardhamana Mahavira founded this non-theistic 6th century BC religion, as a reaction against the teachings of orthodox Brahmins. Jain religion teaches salvation by perfection through successive lives, non-injury to living creatures, and known for its ascetics.

We had only fifty patients for the week, less than expected. We heard this was because of a very recent state government health scheme. This scheme promised to help low-income families needing operation with a decent sum of money. Because of this, many private hospitals were now sending out touts in the villages searching for patients, sometimes also doing unnecessary procedures. We witnessed a tragic example of this later in the week.

In the evening, we visited the 15th-century Phalodi town with many Jain temples. Ruins of a fort lay outside. We waited outside a temple with our Muslim driver while prayer was going on inside. Once the prayer finished, they allowed us in. I looked at the driver. He quietly got into his car. The 19th-century Parasnath Glass temple, made from stone with no girders, beautifully decorated with Belgium glass, was a marvellous architecture. In Phalodi, many havelis - mansion houses, lay deserted. Owners of these houses had left after setting up businesses in Jodhpur.

We worked for the next few days with friendly theatre and nursing staff. One afternoon, one of the benefactor sisters took me to the secondary school the family had set up within the same compound which educated children from nearby villages at no cost. Teachers there proudly told me in the last two years in state-level exams; their students had gained the highest marks in the state - extraordinary achievement.

Nearby Khichan village was well known in the National Geographic circle because of migratory Demoiselle cranes arriving there between January and the end of March. Locals fed bird seeds, an average of 3000kg every day. In season, about 20,000 of these smallest species of crane with beautiful plumage migrated from central Siberia. They told me unfortunately last of the three pairs had left the area only two days back.

One evening after work they took us again to Phalodi. In a hall, the Jain community shared food with the town's impoverished families. In the area, 2% were Jains, over 80% were Hindus, and of the rest, some were Christians and other Muslims. I noticed our Muslim driver again stayed outside. Later, I spoke to him alone. I asked why he didn't come in. He hesitated and then said they gave the Muslims food outside the hall. I asked about how the rising communal sentiment against the Muslims in India affected his community. He said in the charity hospital, there were many Muslim workers and were treated equally. In the township it was different. He gave an example. Their small community, mostly Shia, used to have a procession in town during their annual Muharram festival. In the last two years, because of the increasing dissent by the town's Hindu community, they had to curtail the procession around their houses only.

On our penultimate evening at the hospital, after finishing our work, we were waiting by the reception area. A distraught father holding a newborn baby came rushing through the door, desperately asking for help. The baby looked blue. We took them quickly to the room with oxygen. Our anaesthetist colleague did her best, but the hospital was not equipped to deal with neonates. The baby needed ventilating. She advised taking the baby to the nearest neonatal unit in Jodhpur, 50km away. The hospital arranged an ambulance immediately. We knew it was unlikely the baby would survive. Tears ran down our faces.

We then heard the story behind this tragedy. The husband had taken his wife, nine months pregnant with their first child, for a routine antenatal check-up at a private nursing home in the town. She had been well and had no complaints. The gynaecologist there had decided she needed an immediate caesarean section. They had done this within two hours. When the baby was delivered, the doctor said he was not breathing well and had a low score. He had advised to take him to a neonatal unit which they did not have in their nursing home. The father, in desperation, had brought his child to this hospital by a taxi. The mother was still recovering from her spinal anaesthesia in the nursing home. Friends at the hospital told us these situations were frequently happening now. With the new Government scheme, scrupulous doctors were doing many unnecessary operations, only to make money.

After saying goodbye at the hospital in the morning, we dropped our colleagues from Delhi at the railway station. One of the brothers was returning to Jodhpur and had kindly arranged for my overnight stay with them.

During my travel in Rajasthan in the late 60s, I did not visit Jodhpur. Founded in 1459, Jodhpur was the capital of Marwar kingdom. Set in the stark landscape of Thar Desert, it featured many palaces, temples and forts. Mehrangarh Fort stood high and could be seen from anywhere in the city. I only had the afternoon before my return flight the next morning and visited the Mehrangarh Fort.

We drove through a windy road to the fort at 125m above the city, enclosed by imposing thick walls. Then I walked up a wide twisty road through its seven commanding gates, each with its history. The last gate, before the main fort complex, had some handprints on its wall. Known as the marks of Sati, these were a tragic reminder of a barbaric Hindu religious practice of the past. Women who in 1843 immolated themselves on the funeral pyre of their husband, Maharaja Man Singh, had left their handprints on the wall before the ritual.

Inside, surrounding its expansive courtyard, were several palaces with intricate carvings. Its opulent palaces included Moti Mahal (Pearl Palace), Phool Mahal (Flower Palace) and Sheesh Mahal (Mirror Palace). The fort had a well-stocked museum with a collection of royal palanquins, howdahs, musical instruments, costumes, elaborate furniture and an excellent collection of Rajasthani art. From its roof, was a glorious view of the city below and the desert at a distance. I tried to imagine unjust of the way the royals living in such luxury - at the expense of millions in the country.

I returned to the family for dinner together. If you have to choose vegetarian food from anywhere in the world, I would recommend going to Rajasthan. Home-cooked dal baati choorma, ker sangri pickle, gatte ki sabji, besan ke ladoo, dal kachori, with lahsun ki chatni was most delicious I had ever tasted. I was full and waited an hour chatting before indulging in the desserts of ras malai and moong dal halwa.

Russia

July 2018 Moscow

My taxi driver Ivan was a friendly, chatty Ukrainian. We drove two and a half hours from the Domodedovo airport in outer Moscow in heavy traffic by Kremlin and Bolshoi Theatre. Then through Lenin Avenue with the only remaining statue of Lenin in the city. Ivan had been living in Moscow for ten years. His wife, a language teacher, lived in Ukraine. Their son worked in Dublin for Google, and their daughter was a business administrator in Holland. He earned more money as a driver than his teacher wife in Ukraine and visited Ukraine every three months to keep his immigration status. I asked him directly about being Ukrainian living in Moscow. Did he face any problem since the trouble between the two countries?
Without hesitation, he answered 'no'.

I asked him about the current border trouble between the two countries. He replied TV in both countries multiplies everything. He said most ordinary people felt life was more comfortable, both in Russia and Ukraine during the Soviet era than now, especially with health care, education and social care.

I walked in the evening in a broad avenue full of people strolling with families - a pleasant atmosphere all around. At the restaurant, I met an usher from Sudan - a 4th-year medical student in Moscow, doing a part-time job for his upkeep.

Red Square

Next morning I walked by heavy but orderly traffic before arriving at the famous Red Square. Inside the massive place, was a festival-like atmosphere. People from all over the world and Russians from its many provinces mulled together. A high red-brick facade separated the brightly domed Kremlin. At the far end stood the picturesque Saint Basil Cathedral, next to an elegant tall clock tower with the famous red star at its top. The red, blue and white Russian flag and flags from all 32 countries taking part in the world cup adorned the square.

Except for a massive departmental store, most buildings were red. Red Square name derived from the word Krasnyi, 'beautiful'. The Red Square, the symbolic centre of Russia, dating back to 1490, began its ife as a slum outside the Kremlin walls. For a while, it was known as 'Fire Square', reflecting the number of imes medieval Moscow burned.

St Basil's Cathedral stood at one end shaped like colourful flames rising into the sky. Its bright domes bloomed like an elaborate stone flower planted in the 16th century. While its western facade facing Kremlin was symmetrical and monolithic, north and south presented deliberate, subtle asymmetry of multi-axial shape. A construction of immense beauty.

I left Red Square and walked by the beautiful Alexander Garden to reach the Tomb of an unknown soldier killed in the battle of Moscow in 1941. Easy to forget that in WWII, over 20 million people died in the Soviet Republic. For every single American soldier killed fighting the Germans, 80 Soviet soldiers died doing the same. Soldiers stood in silence by an eternal flame with a five-pointed star illuminating a bronze inscription 'Your name is unknown, your deed is immortal.'

Further down the wall was the public entrance to Kremlin. A lengthy queue there. Instead, I walked a short distance to the bridge over the Moskva River. A panoramic view from there of Kremlin and the Cathedral against the wide river. Afterwards, I returned to the carnival atmosphere of Red Square.

I stood on steps of the only sculptured monument on the square - bronze statues of Kuzma Minin and Dmitry Pozharsky. In the early 17th century, they gathered an all-Russian volunteer army and expelled the Polish invaders.

Some young Russian boys and girl came up to me and asked to take their photograph together - all college students. One of them spoke good English. Then two of them wanted a picture of me with them, holding a Russian flag. They had come from a provincial town for a holiday, their first time in Moscow. I asked if they were here for the football. They said no, the tickets were too expensive. But they were all going to the fan zone tomorrow to watch Russia win the quarterfinal.

Later, I took a tour of the famous Bolshoi Theatre. Opened in 1856, Bolshoi was a symbol of Russia for all time. Inside this grand building, renovated recently to its old glory, circles of seats on four floors and balconies surrounded large stalls on the ground floor. I did not have enough money and time to spend to watch a proper show. Outside, in the evening, the building decorated with lights looked sumptuous.

By then, the avenue towards my place was busy with easy-going pedestrians. Opposite a playground and next to another theatre building, I found a lovely place for a buffet dinner the locals favoured. Great choice of food and very cheap. Decent lunch or dinner for around 4 dollars. People all around were friendly and easy to talk as many of the younger generations spoke English.

In my bedsit, I met a German tourist. Over a cup of tea, I heard he was a retired engineer and was travelling alone like me. He had tickets for all the group stage games Germany had played. He had also purchased tickets for the quarterfinal, the semi-final and the final, hoping to see Germany play in the final. I asked him now Germany was out of the competition after the group stage, what was his plan. He said he would go on to the games hoping to see good football. Great to see football-mad people.

Next day I went by an underground train to Vorob'yovy Gory station in outer Moscow. I walked a bridge there over to Sparrow Hills, a great outdoor place and nature reserve, popular with joggers, bikers and tourists like me. People were going on boat tours, cable car riding and roller skating or just strolling its steep path. In the winter people come for skiing, snowboarding and ski jumping around this place.

After walking up the steep hill, opposite stood the enormous complex of the Moscow State University. Cheerful football fans with banners crowded the path, going to the football fan zone park. Opposite the carnival-like atmosphere of the fan-zone entrance was a high observation platform. A lovely panoramic view of Moscow from there. On the other side of Moskva River stood Luzhniki Olympic Complex, Novodevichy Convent, Red gates along with Kremlin's domes at a distance.

Back in town, was very much a family atmosphere with children running around everywhere, parents just relaxing. Wonderful and surely this was not a put up show for the rest of the world during the world cup games! In a crowded eatery with an enormous screen, I watched England beat Sweden easily. Russia game was later in the night, and I had to leave by 4 am, so back to my bedsit. I watched the game from my bed. Russia, unfortunately, lost in the penalty shootout!

Murmansk   After 3 hour's sleep, I got up and took a pre-booked taxi to Sheremetyevo Airport in Moscow's north for a flight to Murmansk by the Barents Sea. After the carnival atmosphere of Moscow, it was quieter in Murmansk, and decidedly colder. The city had a jaded appearance with many apartment blocks. My hotel was by the Five Corners Square, the main square of Murmansk.

Murmansk was the largest city in the Arctic and an important Russian naval base and commercial port. I walked to the grand building of Central railway station and then to Alyosha monument, 35m statue of a soldier in a greatcoat with a rifle, dedicated to the soldiers of WWII.

North Pole Expedition

July 2018

You could travel to the North Pole in three ways. Helicopter ride from Svalbard directly to the North Pole or a helicopter ride to 50 miles south of the North Pole and ski from there to the pole. I chose the third way, sailing 2341 km by a nuclear-powered icebreaker ship. Only between July and August, a maximum of five tours like these took place starting from Murmansk.

Murmansk Seaport, on the eastern shore of Kola Bay of Barents Sea, was the northernmost port city in Arctic Europe. As the largest year-round ice-free port, it formed the backbone of Russian marine economy. It was also, a strategic site for the Russian Naval base, including its nuclear-powered ships and submarines.

In the evening, most of the North Pole expedition team arrived at the hotel. Some will join tomorrow on the ship after flying from Helsinki. People were from various parts of the world, many Chinese. From now on, I would share a cabin with a travel agent from Taiwan, starting tonight with a twin bedroom in the hotel.

I did not get much sleep in the night with the 24-hour daylight and the loud snoring of my roommate. First thing in the morning, I bought earplugs from a shop.

Bus for 3km took us to the naval base and then very minimal security check there. We got on board the enormous nuclear-powered ice-breaker, 50 Let Pobedy, 50years of Victory.

The voyage

In the winter months this ice-breaker, along with 30 others, nine nuclear powered, carved through sea-ice to make way for the cargo and military ships. Ships carrying oil, natural gas, minerals, and grain, regularly used this northern sea route travelling between Asia, North America, and Europe, thus saving hundreds of thousands of dollars by avoiding the lengthy trip to and through the Panama Canal.

The 160 tons steel ship, 160m long, 30m wide, stood 30m tall. Above the hull were two bow decks for the crew, then four decks of passenger cabins, one above for the ship's officers and an extensive bridge at the top. On one end, it had a helipad with a helicopter and an enormous hot-air balloon for a ride. In its brick red colour, massive **50 Let Pobedy** looked impressive.

Every year only around six hundred people reached the North Pole, less than the number who successfully climbed Mt Everest in 2017!

Soon, with the 124 passengers including 16 expedition team members, and 140 crew, we sailed through Kola Bay towards the Barents Sea. We took pictures freely of the Russian Navy submarine base. Channels of Kola Bay, ice-free throughout the year, was popular for fishing sport. On the ship, we had many interesting lectures on geography, history and ecology about the North Pole and the Arctic Circle. After dinner, my cabin mate and I talked for a while before he drifted off to sleep and snore. I put on my earplugs and retired to catch up on sleep too.

By the time I woke up, we had reached the Barents Sea. From the bridge, I tried to spot any whales with no luck. At breakfast, I met up and talked with a young man and his fiance from Thailand on their dream holiday. An Iranian couple joined us. Neither of them spoke English, and I did not know Farsi. Soon their two daughters joined. The elder girl was in college and could speak English. The younger girl in her last year at school understood English but could only say a few words. In the next few days, we became friends, and I learned a lot from them about Iran.

We sailed through the fog on the open waters of the Barents Sea. I explored the ship. It had a library, a gym, and a sauna. But what caught my eyes was a badminton court where the Russian crews were playing. After watching them for a while, I asked if I could join. They motioned me in, and we played doubles. This became my place for the rest of the tour if there was nothing to watch outside - good fun.

In the evening, with a few members of the expedition team, one from France, I watched the France Belgium semi-final game. At half time, all the expedition crew left. I thought they had gone for an urgent briefing. Soon they came back with many of the passengers carrying a birthday cake and candles and sang Happy Birthday to me!

In the next few hours, we sailed through sea ice. Not compact enough for our ship to crush, but gently to push aside. Sea-ice got more compact, and we just trampled through. We had so far sailed over 1200km from Murmansk. Our expedition team colleagues said we would arrive Franz Josef Land archipelago in the next hour. Ice permitting, we would try to make a landing in one of its islands.

Franz Josef Land   This group of 192 islands, formed the northernmost archipelago in Eurasia. Glaciers covered its 85% and were the largest frozen areas of land in the Russian Arctic. We got into zodiacs in groups, heading for the Hooker Island. We paddled by a smaller island; shore crowded with giant walruses with their sabre teeth. While we watched, a few of them slumbering down from the ice to swim between the pack ice. The ranger pointed above. There, on the glacier cliff, walked an arctic fox. We got off at Hooker Island, site of previous staging post for the exploration of Arctic region. One of the national park rangers who had travelled with us got off here to relieve his colleague who would return to Murmansk with us. Two park rangers spent the summer months here in a wooden hut, protecting and exploring flora and fauna.

We walked up the slippery ice to an area of grassy turf, covered with mosses, colourful lichens and liverworts. Instead of seeds, liverworts produced spores for reproduction. Next to them were rare blossoming yellow Arctic poppies, most northerly plant highlighted by the Mountain Pinks around them. Papaver Dahlianum stood at 30cm, the tallest plant on these islands. On exposed rocks nested thousands of Fulmar, Kittiwake, Guillemots and Little Auks.

We then sailed between the islands. Soon a cruise ship from Svalbard, going to Franz Josef Land, ame by and we all waved to each other from the deck. We continued before stopping in front of an land with a massive cliff. Seabirds in their nests covered every inch of the elevation. About 5 million eabirds nest on the archipelago every year, one million of them thick-billed guillemot. There were also ommon Eider, Purple Sandpiper, Arctic Skua, Gulls and Arctic Terns. Medium-sized 30cm Arctic terns spent s spring and summer in the Arctic. It then flies 30,000km south, to the Antarctic Circle, doing an Arctic-ntarctic round- trip migration every year. Moving continually between Arctic summer and Antarctic immer, Arctic terns saw more daylight than any other animal on Earth.

We sailed on North; now the North Pole was only another 900km away. Sea ice was now getting icker, but it surprised me to see in places pools of clear blue water between the icepacks. Suddenly there as an announcement on the tannoy - polar bear on the port side in front. We all rushed to the deck and nly at 40m distance a majestic giant male bear hopped from one ice pack to other. Soon he left the area nd was out of our sight. I watched our icebreaker crunching bigger chunks of ice for a while before it was me for dinner.

At dinner, the Thai couple joined me. As I came back, filling my plate with the deserts after the main ourse, the girl timidly asked if they could ask me for a favour. They said they were getting married on the

North Pole. Then she surprised me by saying none of their families was with them, and would I mind giving her away at the ceremony. I replied at once it would be an honour.

Back at the badminton court, I played more doubles with the crew. There I learnt my partner for the last few days was the chief engineer of this nuclear-powered ship. He and his team would give us a tour of the engine and the nuclear reactor on our way back. I retired to bed, sun still up, with so many exciting events in one day.

Only after two hours, an announcement came of a polar bear sighting. I rushed out. Our ship had slowed down and on the starboard side was a Polar bear mother with her cub, only 20m from the boat.

The cute cub tried to jump between the ice packs, following its mother. Once it almost fell into a pool. Mother looked back as the cub balanced itself clumsily and followed - sumptuous. They hung around for some time as if giving everybody a chance to take photos. Hopefully, their agent will not ask for any commission!

Unfortunately, there was no satellite connection now, and no chance of watching the semi-final between England and Croatia, and not the final in a few days! I returned to my bed but could not sleep.

The North Pole did not belong to any country. But with the melting of sea ice from the climate changes, the possibility of an ice-free trade route in future between the continents made it an economically valuable territory. Oil and gas exploration in other parts of the Arctic had also proved lucrative. Many nations had been interested in claiming the North Pole as its territory. But at present, an Arctic Council, composed of Canada, Denmark, Finland, Iceland, Norway, Russia, Sweden, and the USA jointly addressed the ecological issues faced around here.

I played a game of chess with one of the Russian crew after lunch and lost badly. In the afternoon, I waited for my turn, six at a time, for a helicopter ride. Soon my turn came. From above, an unbelievable scenery of pack ice as far as I could see up to the horizon. And alone within the panorama of white ice field was our red ship. A red speck, looking like a toy, deserted in an otherwise white wilderness of nothing else for hundreds of kilometres in all directions. We flew around for twenty minutes enjoying the incredible vista.

Onboard, we had an interesting lecture on sea ice and land ice. They asked for volunteers to join a group for ground research of the sea ice conditions around us on the way and at the North Pole. Satellites regularly collected data to monitor the polar condition, but only during these few voyages in summer months, they could corroborate its data with the findings on the ground. Twelve of us joined.

The North Pole is covered by floating pack-ice continually shifting over the Arctic Ocean. Portions of the ice that do not melt seasonally can get very thick, up to 3–4m over large areas, with ridges up to 20m. Annual sea ice at the North Pole is usually only about 1m thick. Two to three meters of thick sea ice covered the Arctic. Drifting ice over the area is an unpredictable habitat and did not allow for migration routes or establishment of dens for fauna to raise its young. Still, polar bears sometimes wander into the area in search of food. The undersea ecosystem of the North Pole was more varied than the ice above. Shrimps, sea anemones, and tiny crustaceans are abundant which often invited a few ringed seals.

In the afternoon I played Table Tennis, then Badminton, followed by Volleyball with the Russian crews. Then a lovely barbecue on the rooftop. The outside temperature was -3°C and with wind chill probably a few degrees further down. But it was terrific, we all laughed and shivered at the same time.

Over at the bridge after breakfast, I checked on the screen we were at 88.3 degrees north. The officers said we would reach the North Pole in the late evening today, in about 11-12 hours. There was no time at the Poles, as time is calculated using longitude and all lines of longitude meet at the poles. Scientists and explorers at the poles record time-related data of their country.

As I was talking to the Iranian family over a cup of coffee, an announcement came of more bear sighting. We rushed outside. There was a grand male Polar bear right next to our vessel. He was looking up and growling at the ship. As if to challenge - this is my territory, what do you think you are doing here? Awesome. We moved on, leaving his kingdom.

North Pole

Entire ship now buzzed with excitement. We would reach the North Pole in less than two hours. The pack-ice around us was not much different. Anticipation was reaching its climax. There was no site marking or anything to point to the location of the North Pole. By calculating with onboard navigation equipment and computer with help from the satellite, they announced another ten minutes to go. We all rushed out to the open deck.

The temperature outside was below -2°C, but no one cared. Anticipation reached a climax as the counting started - ten, nine, down to three, two - one. At 9-55pm Russian time, we were at the North Pole. Under a clear blue sky, the sun high up, we all shouted, hugged and kissed. Some waved flags. Champagne was served, and music played. We danced and celebrated on top of the world!

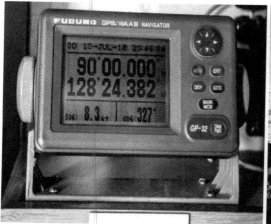

After countless photos, they announced it would be advisable to get some sleep for a few hours now. As tomorrow we will have a big day on the grounds of the North Pole.

Next day, 14th July Saturday was cloudy outside. The expedition team had put a large flag to mark the site of the North Pole. We were standing on 2-3m thick ice above a 4000m deep ocean. Any direction I looked from here was south!

We took pictures and then we stood in a circle around the North Pole flag for one minute of silence in memory of anybody or anything we wanted. I thought about my daughter and how she would have reacted to this geographical and ecological marvel site. Then, still holding hands, we danced around the top of the globe celebrating anything we wanted! I remembered all the amazing memory she had left for me in her brief life.

Soon I joined for field observations on the ice conditions on the Pole. We measured with tape thicknesses of annual sea ice at different sites, depth and width of the pools of various sizes. The geologist said, unfortunately, the ice covering was getting thinner every year because of the climate change. At this rate in another 2-3 decades, there would be no sea ice here. The ecosystem at the North Pole was an important indicator of Arctic shrinkage and global temperature. It also predicted medium and long-term weather around the world, including major events such as cyclones.

Russia sent drifting stations every year through ships like ours. They recorded important data about ice conditions, temperature, current and weather around here throughout the year, before moving with the drifting icepack in the Arctic Ocean. These usually lasted 2-3 years before the warmer climate of Greenland Sea broke up the ice-floe.

There was a choice of going for a plunge in a pool or going for a hike. I chose the latter. Fifteen of us sloshed through the sea ice for about 2km from the Pole. Two rangers joined with guns, one at the front and other at the back. Although uncommon, stray Polar bears came around here searching for seals. As usual, I walked at the back of the line. I spoke to the female ranger behind me. She lived in Granitnyy, a small fishing port on the Barents Sea at the end of Koba Bay and was married with a teenage daughter. Her husband was also a ranger. She loved her job. In the winter months, they helped to monitor the unfrozen channels around Kola Bay looking out for illegal fishing. After a while, the ranger in front asked everyone to stop and be quiet. With her binocular, she had spotted a Polar bear at about 1km distance. Polar bears could run at a top speed of almost 40km per hour, only slightly slower than Usain Bolt. We cut short our hike and returned to the safety of our vessel.

The first person to claim to reach the North Pole was an American explorer Cook in 1908 without providing navigational records of his achievement. Rest of his team later reported they did not quite arrive at the pole. Norwegian explorer Roald Amundsen in 1926 flew over the North Pole on airship Norge. First verified persons to have set foot on the North Pole was a Soviet research team of geologists and oceanographers in 1948.

Now, was the time for the wedding. I, the proxy father, escorted my 'daughter' Nan(cy) from the ship in her wedding dress, covered with red Polar jacket in -1°C temp. Groom with a few more passengers and the expedition leader was waiting at the flag-marked site of the North Pole. Nearer the place, she threw off her jacket. I handed Nan over to her future husband. After a brief ceremony presided by the expedition leader and customary photographs, we returned to the ship.

The crew and the cooks had already set up chairs and tables on sea-ice for a barbeque. While all the waiters and waitresses were Russian, most college students earning money in the summer holiday, all the cooks were from the Philippines. We had a lovely dinner and also raised our glasses to wish future happiness to my 'daughter' and her husband.

During our meal, we heard stories from the few who had taken the plunge challenge. They had waited on one end of the 10m pool of water. As soon as the first person had plunged, a ringed seal had come out of nowhere and swam in front to the other end. It had waited there on the ice before disappearing soon in the water. It became cloudy and windy. The promised hot-air balloon ride was cancelled. After spending almost 24 hours on the North Pole, we started our return journey. Still, in a jubilant mood, we learnt the exact location of the North Pole varied by up to 9m over seven years, because of the slight wobbling of the Earth's axis. The precise location of the intersection at any given moment was known as the 'instantaneous pole.'

The North Pole was much warmer than the South Pole, as its at a lower sea level in the middle of an ocean, warmer than the ice-covered continent of Antarctica. Summer temperature here ranged close to 0°C. From the North Pole, the sun was always above the horizon in the summer and below the horizon in the winter. This meant the region had up to 24 hours of sunlight in the summer and 24 hours of darkness in the winter.

In the morning, while we were still babbling at breakfast about the North Pole, an announcement came of more bear sightings. We rushed outside, some leisurely now. Three Polar bears walked about 500m from us. Soon we sailed on. There was a charity auction in the ship in the evening. Chinese women were the big spenders. One Chinese man won the Captain's cap and an opportunity of 10 minutes to steer one of the most powerful ships in the world.

Plan for a helicopter landing to the northernmost island on the Franz Joseph land was cancelled at the last minute as the weather had a sudden turn with high winds. We cruised further down south to another island, hoping for better weather to make a zodiac landing. We saw several walruses on the ice and swimming in the sea. Then a polar bear appeared on the rock face. But the weather remained awful. I waited until just before midnight for a zodiac tour. At 12-30am, as I had got into bed, there was a call to get ready for a zodiac tour. The weather had turned for the better. We landed on a small island. On a rock face, a Polar bear walked by the birds' nest. Many birds were flying in and pecking him to chase him away from stealing their eggs.

In the morning we saw another polar bear on the green moss over a rock in an island about 400m away. After a while, our ship somehow got right next to the magnificent glacier shelf of Chap Island.

We were less than 100m from the ice shelf of incredible beauty. And to add to the show, a polar bear turned up right on top of the glacier.

During our badminton game, my partner, Igor said soon he would take us for a tour of the ship's engine rooms. After lunch, we had a fantastic tour of this nuclear-powered ship. This Arktika Class nuclear- powered icebreaker was commissioned in 2007, although the building was completed in 1995, hence the name 50 years of Victory. Igor had been working on these types of ships for 44 years. This, one of the most powerful icebreakers ever built, generated 75,000 horsepower and crushes multi-year ice layers over 3-4m thick. Two OK-900A nuclear-powered propulsion system had a power output of 27.6MW. There were also three 17.6MW electric propulsion motors. They provided a maximum speed of 21.4kt (40km) in the open water. A double hull, coated with polymer paint to reduce friction and spoon-shaped bow of the vessel increased its ice-breaking capabilities.

A fascinating piece of engineering! Then we played more badminton later.

After sailing for a few more hours in the late evening, the sun still shining overhead, we made another zodiac landing, this time at Tikhaya Bukhta Bay of Hooker Island. Since the early 20th century, this site had been a major base for polar expeditions, and location of a meteorological station. We saw more arctic summer flowers there, including the Arctic Poppies. On the bay were many mosquitoes. The ranger said there were also many mites, all of them vegetarian, and survived frozen in the ice for over four years. On the ledges above us, were more nesting birds.

We sailed back over the Barents Sea, after early lightning and thunderstorms, the sea was calm with clear blue sky. We saw a whale close to the ship, probably a fin whale. I played the last games of badminton with my Russian friends. Our ship was expected to dock 2 am tonight at Murmansk.

We arrived back in Murmansk in the early hours of the morning. It took time to say goodbye to my friends from 18 countries and then a hug to my 'daughter' Nan and her husband.

St Petersburg / Leningrad   Russia

July 201

Still buzzing from the excitement of the voyage to the North Pole, I arrived in St Petersburg from Murmansk in the late afternoon. From the airport, going to my accommodation by Neva River, the city looked beautiful. After walking by the river for a while, I found a restaurant for a hearty meal of beef stroganoff with sour cream.

Next day, I took a tour of the city with 28yrs old guide Tataniya and Alexander, the 64yrs old driver. Beautiful wide roads, palatial buildings and churches stood on either side of the River Neva. St Petersburg was now the largest economic, cultural and scientific centre of Russia.

First, we went to the Kazan Cathedral, the foremost Russian Orthodox Church. A massive cathedral reminiscent of a palatial hall dedicated to the Russian military glory in 1812. It contained a copy of the miracle working icon of Our Lady of Kazan, one of the most venerated icons in Russia. In 1876 Kazan demonstration the first political demonstration in Russia took place in front of this church. After the 1917 Russian Revolution the authorities closed the cathedral. In 1932 it reopened as 'Museum of the History of Religion and Atheism. Church services resumed only in 1992. Tataniya was a devout Christian, like most in the country. She said only about 5-10% of Russians did not believe in religion. There were also about 10-20% Muslim.

Ostentatious palaces stood on the banks of River Neva. Many cruise boats and ships sailed leisurely. This city's proximity to the Gulf of Finland, and connecting riverways through inland Russia to Moscow, made it popular with cruise boat lovers from Europe and other parts of the world. Peter the 'Great' in 1703 founded this as a naval base and trading post, 'window to Europe.' His only 'greatness' was to strengthen the military expand borders, centralise royal power, and westernise Russia. These were all at the expense of over 99% of the people living in destitution. Peter even instituted a tax on beards, to make Russians look and act more like the Western Europeans. He had his eldest son tortured to death for not following his way.

Winter Palace   We walked to the colossal Winter Palace, the residence of the Tsars. In between this building and the 580m long bow-shaped facade of General Staff Building, was the Palace Square, an important

landmark in Russia's history. This was where the infamous 'Bloody Sunday' massacre of 1905 took place.

St Petersburg had witnessed both the apogee of the Russian Empire and the beginnings of its collapse. Over the centuries, Tsarist Russia oppressed and exploited its citizens through serfdom. Serfs living conditions here were like those of black slaves in the United States, only worse because of the harsh Russian winter. Serfdom survived in Russia longer than in any other major European country and not abolished until 1861. It was in this place where started the crucible of a revolution, the single most important event of the ensuing twentieth century.

Bloody Sunday massacre   Most Russian workers kept their traditional conservative values of Orthodoxy, faith in the autocracy, and indifference to political life. Led by Father Gabon, workers of St. Petersburg decided to petition the tsar in the hope of fair treatment and better working conditions. On Sunday,   22 January 1905, over 3000 workers and their families, holding religious icons and singing hymns and patriotic songs, 'God save the Tsar' proceeded without police interference towards the Winter Palace, Tsar's residence. Women, children and elderly workers lead to emphasise their united nature. Tsar's military opened fire and killed at least 1,000; many more died trampled during the panic.

Tataniya was a student of history before doing her degree in tourism. During a cup of coffee together, we talked more about the Russian Revolution.

First Russian Revolution of 1905, was a wave of mass political and social unrest that spread through vast areas of the Russian Empire. Already suffering from centuries of oppression and Russian defeat in the Russo-Japanese war spurred the 1905 revolution. It led to worker strikes, peasant unrest, and military mutinies and resulted in some constitutional reform and forming of the Russian Constitution of 1906.

By the end of 1914, only five months into the WWI war, around 390,000 Russian men had lost their lives and nearly 1,000,000 injured. Staggering losses continued. Centuries of oppression of lower classes by the Tsarist regime, and Nicholas's failures in WWI, now burst into a revolution.

Monarchist forces, organised into the White Army, fought Bolsheviks' Red Army, in a series of battle known as the Russian Civil War starting in October 1917. Allies from the prime Western countries sent troops and weapons to support the White Army. Though Lenin led the Bolshevik Party, initially from abroad, he was not present during the takeover of the Winter Palace. Interestingly, the US bankers, including those from the Federal Reserve, provided the Bolshevik revolutionaries much-needed capital and office space in downtown Manhattan - to keep their both options open. Following several incursions into the Winter Palace, the Bolsheviks under Yakov Yurovsky, executed Tsar Nicholas II, his wife and five children in July 1918.

We returned by the river near the Faberge Museum. I was not interested. Tataniya said there were 50 palaces and 250 museums in this city. And the magnificent summer palace was just a few kilometres away by boat. It was not possible to see all in one day. What did I want to see? I explained I was not keen on how the royals lived in luxury but would be interested in the city's modern and political history and talking about it with them.

We drove to the battleship Aurora anchored by the river, now a museum. One of the first incidents of October Revolution took place on this battle cruiser. It fired the first blank shot, signalling the beginning of the attack on the Winter Palace. At 9.40 pm, on 25 October 1917, started the October Revolution.

Museum of Political History   From there, we drove to a quiet location of mansion houses. There, in an attractive building, built initially for the prima ballerina and Emperor Nicholas II's mistress, was now the Museum of Political History. Seized in 1917 when the ballerina escaped to Europe, it was initially the headquarters of the Bolsheviks. Lenin made his famous speech from its balcony after he arrived in the city. In 1957, it became the Museum of the Revolution, renamed recently as the Museum of Political History.

Its collection embraced a broad time spectrum, from the reign of the emperors to the political climate in contemporary Russia, dispassionately revealing the secret history of the Soviet Union. Its nearly 500,000 exhibits included a rich collection of original documents; a signed decree from Napoleon and the correspondences of Mikhail Gorbachev. It housed artefacts owned by key figures in Russian history, including Nicholas II, Vladimir Lenin, Mikhail Gorbachev and the first man in space - Yuri Gagarin.

So far, I had seen no statue of Lenin in this city until recently known as Leningrad. I asked Tataniya. She said there were still some. She took us to a medium-sized garden with statues of the fallen soldiers during the world wars and of Lenin. We walked to Smolny in the centre of the city. It was here on November 7, 1917 (October 25 on Julian calendar) Vladimir Lenin declared Bolshevik victory. Outside stood the statues of Lenin, Marx and Engels.

We sat for lunch. Following Alexander's suggestion, we had Golubtsy, delicious meat-stuffed cabbage leaves. During the tour, Tataniya had been speaking enthusiastically about Tsars and their palaces and the orthodox churches. She said this was what most tourists now wanted to see and hear. I asked why the name Leningrad disappeared. She replied because it was of the Soviet era. I asked what was wrong with that period.

Tataniya was only seven in 1991 when the Soviet Union collapsed. She remembered the shops were always empty, even for essential goods. Alexander agreed but added that education, healthcare, was then free for all. They guaranteed a job and housing. Now everyone had to pay to get treatment in time. And even a small flat in the city was beyond most. Tataniya was lucky to have inherited a flat in the middle of the city. The Soviet state had provided it free to her mother when she became widowed. During frank discussions, they said most hated Gorbachev because he gave away parts of the Soviet Union to the Americans. Then both made jokes - now Putin, born in St Petersburg, was their new tsar. Majority admired him in the country, including Tataniya, Alexander remained silent.

I asked what was better now than before 1991. Both said it was freedom and more consumable oods, including food, were available. Both then complained about rising prices and the billionaire friends of Putin, most in the oil and natural gas industry. Very interesting! Seventy-four years of the Soviet history of the liberation of millions was deliberately erased and the oppressive regime of the Tsars now glorified! We then walked by the river, but it started raining heavily, putting an end to our tour.

In the evening, the rain cleared. I walked to the bridge and standing over it reflected upon my brief experience in Russia. Like most countries, it had its share of a horrible past and now faced many challenges. Contrary to what I had heard, the Russians had been friendly and open everywhere on this trip. I enjoyed the country.

Kruger Game reserve, Cape Town & whale watching in Hermanus South Africa

September 2018

In my youth in the 60s, and over the decades after, my blood had boiled at the horrible apartheid regime of the white settlers in South Africa. I had watched with admiration the country's struggle under Nelson Mandela to break its shackles. I had revered President Mandela more for his leadership in avoiding a major bloodbath in the country following its independence in 1994, finally breaking its chain from centuries of brutal colonialism.

After an overnight stay in Johannesburg, the next morning I took an hour's flight to Hoidespruit and then a 40 minutes drive to the game reserve of Thornybush within the greater Kruger National Park.

Game park   Chapungu game lodge created and supported the Thornybush Community Projects, a non-profit organisation established to nurture and uplift the surrounding local community. Most of its staff came from the local areas. After lunch and a decent shower, I rested in my tented lodge, hiding from the boiling midday heat.

In the afternoon and into the evening, we left for a game drive. We came across many giraffes, a herd of buffalos and varieties of deers including Thomson's gazelles. By a large lily pond, two hippos just

yawned at us, while a leopard nervously walked there to drink.

Then we saw another leopard on a tree - finishing his dinner. Once it got dark, the guide with his powerful torch spotted a porcupine which disappeared quickly under the bush.

After dinner, one guard accompanied us to our lodges in between the bushes. They gave us a foghorn to blow in case of any animal popped into our place in the dark! We all laughed.

I woke up to 5 am call and after a cup of tea, left for an early morning game drive. We saw many giraffes Then we came by a narrow dry riverbed. Two lionesses rested languidly on a bank, while six cubs played on the sand next to us. Three of the cubs were less than three months old and were playing happily with the three older cubs about nine months old. After playing their tricks, one cub came next to us and watched for a while. Then it ran to its mother and suckled. After spending over half an hour, we left them.

Further away, we stopped as a baby elephant with its mother was crossing the road in front. Soon a big herd of about 20 elephants came out of the bushes and followed them. On our way back, we stopped next to a hyena's den. Three spotted adults slept on while their darker coloured babies ranaround.

Back at the lodge, several warthogs wandered around while a few tree squirrels busied themselves collecting nuts.

After a pleasant lunch and a nap, it was time for the afternoon game drive. I was on my own this time with Jock, a white South African ranger and Oscar, our spotter. Oscar had fled from Mozambique in the 80s during the war. We followed an old female leopard on the road for about 200m. It then moved down to the water for a drink and afterwards lied down on the sand. A group of hippos popped their head from the water a few times, just to check out. We carried on further, and just before it was getting dark, we were fortunate to see a pack of eight wild dogs resting.

On the next morning's game drive almost outside our lodge we spotted a honey badger. Then we passed a group of about fifty guinea fowls busily pecking on the ground. We continued to a dried riverbed and came across a pack of three lionesses and two young females resting on the bank after their night's killing feast. We moved on and about 1km from there we stopped on the same river bed. A beautiful male leopard strolled by the riverside. It stopped to mark one bush with his urine and then without care ambled

by our car to the other side of the river. We saw more giraffes, before coming near a white (although dark coloured) two-horned rhino. This magnificent creature was shy and moved on once it had spotted us. We followed it at a distance for a while before it disappeared. On our way back, the spotter showed us an aardvark.

So far, the lodge was providing excellent western-style dinner. During lunch, I learnt that the chefs, from the local villages, had gone through two years of professional training in Hoedspruit. I asked them if they would like to prepare South African dishes for the night. They kindly agreed.

In the afternoon drive, we came across beautiful looking male nyalas with their females. The males of these large antelopes had lovely spiral-horns. A few wildebeests scattered around before we found another herd of elephants. We then came across the same pack of wild dogs who have travelled further south overnight. One of them came right across to our car and sniffed.

My head suddenly started reeling, and I needed to lie down on the back seat of the moving car. In the dusk, soon we came across a big herd of Elephants by the watering hole with many cute baby elephants, but I could not get up. By now, I was sweating and got sick. Behind me, luckily, one of the tourists from the USA was an ICU nurse. She kept an eye on me, and soon we got back to the lodge. They called a doctor from Hoedspruit, who came after an hour. He checked me, but by then, I was feeling better. I skipped my dinner missing the South African cuisine they had prepared and retired to my bed. I told them I had decided not to join the 5 am drive the next morning.

Next morning I was almost back to normal. After a lazy breakfast with about ten warthogs hanging around,

I sat on the verandah of my tent lodge. Soon a large herd of impalas moved by within 30m.

Then two enormous elephants came and munched from the branches near my place before moving on, raising their trunks as if to say goodbye.

Cape Town   My flight arrived in the early evening in a rainy and windy Cape Town. It was still cloudy and very windy the next morning when I arrived at the waterfront for my Robben Island tour. Robben Island was one of the places I wanted to visit in South Africa where Nelson Mandela had spent in a cell eighteen of his twenty-seven years of imprisonment. I waited with a large group of people. Soon they announced that because of the high wind and swells, the tours were cancelled for the entire day - very very disappointing. I took a taxi to the cable car entrance of the Table Mountain covered with cloud. That too was cancelled for the day!

District Six Museum   Instead, I visited the District Six Museum. This museum in an old Methodist church was in the former inner-city residential area, District Six. On February 11, 1966, the apartheid government declared Cape Town's District Six a white-only area under the Group Areas Act of 1950. The racist government forcibly removed over 60,000 of inhabitants of here to 25 km away outside the city. They

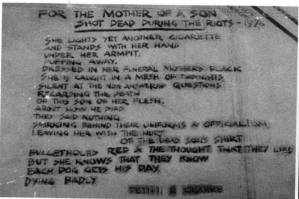

bulldozed houses to make this area white only. Similar things happened in 42 other areas of the city. A 73yrs old former resident who had suffered through this told us the story of this atrocity in this powerful museum. Over the last two decades, former residents of this area had come over to write their stories in large drawing papers which were now displayed on the wall. It told powerful stories of how the rich fabric of an mpoverished but vibrant community was torn to shreds by the apartheid regime.

From there, I walked to the old Slave Lodge, now a museum about slavery. The Slave Lodge built-in 1679 was one of the oldest buildings in Cape Town which were used to confine men, women and children transported by the VOC, Dutch East India Company as slaves to the Cape during the 17th and 18th centuries.

Drawing of a slave ship

Under the umbrella theme, 'From human wrongs to human rights', this museum now explored the long history of slavery in South Africa and around the world. It also depicted how these slaves, the unwilling immigrants, had since contributed to the richness and diversity of South African history, heritage and culture.

Later I walked around the waterfront. Cape Town somehow reminded me of Rio, albeit smaller. During my day in Cape Town, I was lucky to talk with many local people, including taxi drivers and restaurant waiters. Most thought that South Africa was probably going in the right direction, although very slowly. Crime and corruption remained a big problem. Still, the whites were the richest people in the country, and more importantly, they were the landowners. Many of them had moved abroad but still owned vast areas of land, whereas black South African who over the centuries had nothing, still had nothing. The country urgently needed land reform. There was also unease about the non-black people of colour of Indian origin who had businesses. The new apartheid by the black South African was slowly turning against them. I also met several people who had moved from Zambia, Zimbabwe and Mozambique, looking for a better future in South Africa. Their stories were like the stories of immigrants all over the world.

It rained heavily again in the night. In the morning I left for Hermanus 125 km away. It was still cloudy and windy. I heard that the Robben Island ferries were cancelled for today as well. The beautiful Table Mountain never took the veil off her face during my stay in Cape Town.

Set on the hills rising above the Atlantic Ocean, with its sweep of apartments, business buildings, restaurants and beautiful beaches with men, women and their children - black, white and Asian, scampering through, was a scene unthinkable during apartheid. Spruced up before the 2010 World Cup football, no wonder Cape Town won the World Design Capital in 2014.

But after driving east outside Cape Town was the Khayelitsha township ghetto, like many more surrounding the city. Only twenty minutes from the opulent cliff-top villas with infinity pools was this sprawling township of crammed unhygienic makeshift tin-roofed shacks where nearly a million people lived. With a high level of poverty, and well over 50% unemployment for any kind of job, no wonder Khayelitsha had one of the highest crime rates in the country.

Soon we crossed this area to large factories and outlets, with modern townships built around them, before driving through scenic mountain road with massive wineries dotted around on the hills.

Hermanus Whale watchers' bliss   I arrived at Hermanus in bright sunshine. My B&B was across a road on a cliff above the sea-shore. I rushed to the shore to see a whale pod floating by to say Hello. Hermanus lied along the Walker Bay on the south coast of the Western Cape - one of the best places in the world for whale watching. Between June and December every year, thousands of the Southern Right whales arrived here to give birth and care for their newborn calves, the reason I had chosen this month to come here.

Later I walked on the shores of this small town of only a few thousand people, watching many whales with their young babies, just playing around. I went to check at the tour company office for the schedule of my next day's shark cage diving. They told me because of the weather forecast of high wind tomorrow; they had now cancelled it! Well, what can I do? I went back to the shore, watching the whales with their calves.

Heavy rain and wind continued overnight into the morning. In warm rain, I watched whales floating by in the bay in front of my B&B. By about midday, the sun started appearing. In the afternoon, I took a taxi through the beautiful coastal road for the penguin colony.

Outside the quaint coastal town of Betty's Bay was the Stony Point nature reserve. About 1000 pairs of African penguins, also known as Cape penguins, nested there. These 60–70cm birds were smaller than I came across in the Antarctic. Some walked busily to their nests by low bushes, while a few parents regurgitated food to their hungry chicks. Breeding on the rocks by the shore were four varieties of Cormorants in their hundreds. Hartlaub's Gulls and Kelp Gulls flew in to forage in the colony for the unhatched eggs. And everywhere on the rocks were resting cute looking Dassies. These short-tailed furry mammals looked like marmots, but the guide told me they were more closely related to elephants and manatees.

My driver cum guide and I had lunch together in a roadside place near Bettys Bay. He suggested pap and vleis, which was a maize meal with grilled meat - wonderful. He was originally from Zimbabwe. Like his two brothers, he had moved here about 10 years back during the violence of the Mugabe regime. He worked there in the Ministry of Information, doing propaganda work with very little pay. He was very enthusiastic talking about the politics in Zimbabwe and South Africa. I learnt a lot from him about this part of this world during our journey.

Back in Hermanus, I spent the rest of the afternoon by the shore watching the whales play.

Next morning, under a clear blue sky, I took a 45 minutes trip to the fishing village of Gansbaai. There we got into a boat for a whale-watching with 5-6m high waves. We saw many Southern Right whale mothers with their calves. Adult females were 15-16m long and weighed up to 47 tonnes. Their 3-month-old babies were 5m long and were learning tricks from their mothers. Southern Rights were so named because they moved slowly and did not dive for a long period, making them the 'right whales' to hunt by the whalers. Once close to extinction by commercial whaling, now its population was about 10,000 along this coastline.

We sailed to see a South African seal colony. In a tiny island, there were about 60,000 seals. We anchored there briefly, and many adults and their babies swam next to us doing their tricks in the clear blue water.

These brown fur seals were also known as Cape seals. Like the whales, they were once close to extinction, killed for their furs. But the population have now been restored. Marine pollution, however, now is causing a threat to their survival.

On our way, we saw where shark cage diving was taking place. I told the crew about my disappointment of yesterday not being close to a Great White. They said that for the last few weeks there were no Great Whites around here, but only a few catsharks and weasel sharks - I felt better. After watching more Southern Rights and a few Bryde's whales, doing their tail flips, we returned to Gansbaai. The wave near the coast was now almost 8m, and our boat was rolling. A couple in our boat got sick.

Next morning was cloudy and windy again. Before breakfast, across the road, I watched a few whales tail flipping nearby.

For my transport back to Cape Town airport, the driver was born in Seychelles, but for many years he had settled here. His father died when he was two. His mother was a naval officer and travelled a lot, and he was in boarding school growing up. Then his mother had a stroke and died shortly after. He just wanted to get out of the country. He went to France for a year but did not feel very welcome there. Back in Seychelles, he was lucky to listen to Nelson Mandela, who visited there following his release from the prison. He felt inspired. I told him that I envied him. He then moved to South Africa and trained for four years as a tour guide. During this time, he met his wife, who had a white father and a black mother, both died early in her young days. She was a midwife and adored everything Indian and was especially fond of the Indian movies. He spoke eloquently about the grim history of South Africa and the current political situation and progress.

He said that the end of apartheid was supposed to be a beginning. In the aftermath of apartheid, the government had left land and other assets including the precious mines in the hands of a predominantly white elite. He pointed to the wineries we passed by and said that they all belonged to the white South Africans, and the workers were all black. The government's resistance to large-scale land transfers reflected its reluctance to rattle its international investors. Today, millions of black South African were chronically short of capital needed to start businesses. Less than half of the working-age population was in employment. Land reform and redistribution of wealth were urgently required.

South Africa was now in crossroads, almost a quarter of a century since its independence, appeared stuck behind heavy traffic and moving very slowly

Two Gambia   The Gambia

November 2018
I agreed to join a UK charity for volunteering in The Gambia in early November.

My flight via Casablanca to Banjul arrived late in Casablanca, missing the connecting once-daily flight to Banjul. I had an entire day before my night flight.

Casablanca Morocco I took a taxi for a trip around Casablanca, the largest city in Morocco. Unfortunately, with heavy traffic, it took us two hours to reach the city centre. Casablanca was a modern city, but very crowded. I visited its famous grand mosque, with the tallest minaret in the world at 210m. Then, I strolled in the colourful local Bazar. I wanted to return to the airport before the afternoon traffic. I asked the driver his suggestion for a place where I may try the country's famous Tajine dish. He brought me to a place midway to the airport. Next to another mosque, in a restaurant, we had a beautiful lunch of tajine chicken and pita bread with a trio of dips.

Banjul The Gambia I got out of Banjul airport at 1-30am. Samuel, a driver from the hotel, picked me up. I had found on most occasion to open up the barrier, best to start talking football. On every part of the continent, men loved football and supported a team in the English Premier League and the Spanish league. Samuel was a Liverpool supporter. We laughed as they had not done so well in the last season. He played football himself until he married. They had five children and all but the little one, six months old, loved football. After a while, he asked me if I would like to meet his family. I agreed at once and promised to see them at the end of my trip.

The hotel was in the luxury resort area on the Atlantic shore. Next morning, I walked the neighbourhood. Only 5 minutes outside the popular resort was poverty-stricken Banjul, a poor neighbourhood with shanty houses. I ended up in a small protected pool with many crocodiles. Close by was an interesting museum with traditional musical instruments and costumes of the Gambian people over the last few centuries. In the evening, the rest of the team arrived.

We left the next morning for Farafenni. Outside Banjul at the busy ferry port, women vendors with babies on their back went around selling items. Our bus got onto a ferry to cross the enormous Gambia River. Then, through almost 110km road through green, sparsely populated country to Farafenni, a border town next to Senegal. The hospital was a massive place with 250 beds but poorly designed. It served the town population of around 30,000 people. It was the only hospital north of the river for the 110km we travelled and for another 100km to the east. Also, for many from Senegal, this was the only hospital nearby.

The hospital director welcomed us in a vast room. To our surprise, we found so far they had not registered any patient, although we would start from next morning. They made a radio announcement later in the day. In the hospital, we found most of the buildings were not in use. The hospital had only one Cuban Anaesthetist and a Cuban Surgeon for surgery and gynaecology and only two junior Gambian doctors for the whole hospital.

We stayed in a clean, very basic guest house with no water. In a store nearby, we bought bottles of water for drinking and cleaning ourselves.

Next morning we screened only twenty-five patients and between the three surgeons had twenty of them operated by the end of the day. Following day we finished operating on the remaining five patients by mid-morning. No more patients!

Before lunch, a few of us visited the only secondary high school in the area. The headteacher showed us around the classrooms crammed with well-behaved children in their uniform. He said his school had only thirty teachers for over two thousand students. Teacher's salaries were low and often not paid for months. We thanked him for showing us around.

After lunch, we drove for an hour before reaching the site of Wassu ancient stone circles. Between the villages, the place stood empty except a guard. Inside were eleven concentration of circles, 1200 years old. Each ring had between 10-20 stones of 4-6m in sizes. In this central river region astonishingly there were thousand stone circles with over twenty-five thousand monoliths between River Gambia and River Senegal, dating to 300BC.

As we were coming out, a group of children from the villages gathered around us. I taught them a game of touch with hop and scotch. They loved it.

In another hour, we reached by River Gambia and took a boat ride by the Monkey Islands, site of a chimpanzee rehabilitation project. Luckily we spotted a few chimps on the trees by the river. Our local friends said not to touch the water because of crocs and hippos. We saw only one hippo at a distance.

From there we boarded up on the south side of the river to an old fort. Next to it stood the House of Slaves. Its dungeon kept slaves captured from the inner parts of Africa before selling them in a market on another side of the fort. It was initially owned by the Dutch and then taken over by the British. Over the three centuries, millions of human were taken from this region in the transatlantic slave trade and many more by the Arab traders.

We returned late in the evening, everyone heat exhausted, no water in the rooms, only the litre bottles of drinking water we had with us!

Next day only one patient turned up. I talked to the Cuban Surgeon and the anaesthetist. They had been working in Farafenni for the last two years. Many Cuban doctors took the opportunity of the UN scheme of supplying trained doctors to underdeveloped countries, mostly in Africa. It gave them a decent salary, although both of them were now looking forward to going back home.

Two Gambia

There were two Gambia. One for the tourists - mainly from Europe, staying in the lofty standard Atlantic bay resorts, excellent food and bar in an 'exotic' African country. Glimpses of poverty from a safe distance for them.

The second one was for most of the Gambians who lived here.

Back in Banjul, Samuel took me to his family the next day. In one small bedroom and a sitting cum kitchen area, they had five children between the ages of 11 years to six months. Four boys and a girl. I talked to the children about their favourite subjects at school. One by one, they brought out their school books. The oldest one liked science, the girl loved maths and the fourth one, the five-year-old, loved drawing. Their third child, a seven-year-old, remained quiet. Samuel and his wife explained they don't have enough money to send all four of their older children to school - so he was missing out. Education was not free and expensive! I could not even imagine how heartbreaking it was for the parents to choose which of their children must miss out on the opportunities in life to allow others. I played with the children, a fun drawing game for a while before returning to my luxury resort, feeling guilty.

Coming from Samuel's house, I met our security guard waiting for a bus after working a twelve hours shift. Through Samuel, I learnt he had four children and they just about afforded to send only two of them to school. A tour guide, knowing I was a surgeon, showed me his badly united broken right wrist, bone sticking out under the skin. He could not grasp anything with his right wrist and could not afford treatment in the private facilities after the accident. I felt sorry that I could not help him.

By the streets near the resort, many vendors sold souvenirs. A young pregnant mother sat outside her stall. It did not look like she had made any sale today. But she was trying to stay happy for the moment by nodding with the tune of Taylor Swift coming from a nearby coffee shop. In the next shop, wealthy tourists were bartering for a bargain. These vendors at best made a profit of 1000-1500 Dalasi, per month, equivalent to 18-25 dollars, the same price as a single buffet dinner at the resort hotel opposite. That too, during the 6-7 months of the tourist season only. For the rest of the six months, they had no earnings.

Volunteering in Sierra Leone

December 2018

The same US group I worked with in Ghana, invited me to Sierra Leone at the end of November. My daughter and friends asked me to be extra careful.

Most still associated Sierra Leone with its history of brutal 1991-2002 civil war - instigated and supported by the outside forces interested in its reserve of diamond and precious metals. Over 50,000 people had died, and hundreds of thousands were displaced in the country of 7.6 million. Then, just as the country was recovering, in 2014, it faced the deadly Ebola virus epidemic. In two years, 3500 people died and only in 2016, WHO declared Sierra Leone Ebola-free. As if these were not enough, in August 2017, following torrential rainfall, a massive mudflow around its capital city Freetown killed 1100 and made 3000 homeless.

At Lungi Airport, I met the US team. Next day was for recuperating. In the afternoon we heard from a local lady championing against Female Genital Mutilation, FGM. After dinner, we heard from Sierra Leone born volunteers in our team, about their experiences growing up during the 'civil war'. It then led to a lively discussion about FGM still prevalent in the country of the majority Muslim population.

Next day we left for Kabala, 6 hour's journey to the north-east. It was surprising to find roads were empty of traffic and people everywhere were cleaning out rubbish from the roadside and from around their huts. Dumpster trucks moved around collecting. Local colleagues explained on 1st Saturday of the month, until noon, was cleaning day in the country. Everyone took part voluntarily. No vehicles except emergency vehicles allowed. Then we realised why we were on a police bus. What an excellent initiative!

The young man who was taking us to his hospital was Alpha. Talking to him made me thrilled. Unknown to me, a Norwegian charity had introduced a training programme of non-doctor Emergency Surgeons in the last few years in Sierra Leone. The programme we started in Ethiopia in 2009 had now spread to other parts of Africa - brilliant! Alpha was one of the twenty trained so far. He was the only trained surgeon in Kabala.

Between low hills, Kabala was colder than the rest of the country. Near Guinea border, it was once the site of British colonial administration because of its climate. The hospital had similar issues as I had seen in my early days in Ethiopia in 2000.

Another surgeon in the team and I screened and listed about seventy patients, a third of them children, for the following week. When I talked to the mothers who had brought their children for surgery, sadly, I found most of them had lost a few of their children before they were five. Some said they had lost two of their four children; others said only one out of three. They were stoic about it, the way of life here. Apart from the very high infant mortality rate, one in twenty mothers here died giving birth. Current life expectancy in Sierra Leone was only 53.9yrs!

In the evening, I taught Alpha and another non-doctor surgeon on various aspects of emergency surgical management. They were very keen and grateful for the teaching. This became our routine for the next few evenings after our day's work at the hospital.

In the next few days, we operated on over seventy patients, including a few more who turned up during the week. Staff in the hospital, from cleaners to nurses and the anaesthetic team, were terrific and most friendly. A wonderful working atmosphere, despite the lack of facilities.

One evening, the local peacemaker, an elderly man given this title because of his role during the civil war, came to me. He asked if I could give a talk on the local radio on breast and cervical cancer awareness, a rising problem in the country. I knew the country had no mammography machine nor any radiotherapy treatment available. Most patients presented in the late stages and died without treatment. Next evening, with one of the non-doctor surgeon translating, I held a talk show to raise breast and cervical cancer awareness. Many phoned and asked for a check. In the next few days, in between and after work, I saw all of them. Fortunately, none had breast cancer. It surprised me to hear that the hospital director was upset. He thought raising awareness would result in more people coming to his hospital asking for advice. I stressed the purpose was to present early for advice from the healthcare professionals.

One day after work, the local team took us to a village as many of our US colleagues had not seen any. As we arrived, the children gathered around our car. While others walked to see the village houses, I showed the children a game of dropping a handkerchief, an Indian game. Children sat in a circle and sang while one of them ran behind them, hiding a hankie in hand and quietly dropping it behind one of the sitting ones. He/she went round and if he/she could come back to the person with the hankie still lying behind, gave a slap on the back. It did not take long for the children to get the hang of it.

Soon all the children from the village, ages 2-13yrs, about forty of them, joined. Soon the place was reverberating with the sound of the children singing and having fun.

On our way back, we stopped at a residential school for the blind children of age 3-16yrs. Of the 56 residents, most had treatable trachoma or congenital cataract. Unfortunately, the local hospital had no facility for eye treatment, and no international eye charity was working here. But these residents were the lucky ones, as at least they were getting any form of education from their blind headteacher. I heard in the surrounding villages were hundreds of children with visual impairment with no access to treatment or education. A couple from our US team, who had visited before, donated a few mattresses for the school's dormitory.

Truly memorable few days for many reasons.

Cuba

January 2019

This travel should have happened over a year back, except for my brain thinggy. I had admired Cuba since my youth for its spirit and resilience against pressures from its big neighbour. I wanted to see the country and meet its people.

Havana   Forty minutes before arrival time in Havana, the Captain asked us to put our seatbelts on - there was turbulence. Soon it was a more than mild turbulence. We flew through a storm cloud and arrived at Havana in a blackout and flood.

The taxi arranged by the travel company, however, was waiting. We braved through a blackout, amidst flooded streets and torrents of water, for 25 km to Old Havana. I hoped we don't have a breakdown or get swept away in flood.

I arrived at my homestay in a dark street in the pouring rain after 9 pm. Even in the darkness inside the house looked charming and welcoming. With no chance of going out to find dinner, the family kindly offered me their food - very tasty. Next morning the radio said a mini-tornado had hit Havana yesterday, killing three people and two hundred injured.

After a lovely breakfast, I walked leisurely through narrow cobblestoned streets of Old Havana, Habana Vieja. Children ran around, men and women stood by their doors or on balconies, chatting. Narrow roads and

the atmosphere reminded me of old Calcutta, except here was no sign of extremes of wealth, side by side with poverty. It's beautiful, shabby colonial buildings had a certain appeal, although some were badly in need of repair and others deserted.

By Refugio, Avenida de las Misiones and Zulueta streets stood the Museum of Revolution - the past palace of the Cuban presidents till Batista's dictatorship. The revolutionaries threw him out in 1959. Few of its halls were about pre-revolutionary Cuba, the 1895-1898 period of the war of independence against Spain. But I was more interested in the revolutionary period in the 1950s and the post-1959 history.

Horrors of the ousted dictatorship were gruesome. Then, a section about Bay of Pigs invasion in 1961, orchestrated under US President Kennedy, showed how Cuban forces countered it in only three days. One section showed how over the decades until recently, the CIA had tried to subvert Cuba. I had read in my youth about economic blockades by the US and the Bay of Pigs incident. This had led to the 1962 Cuban Missile crisis which brought the entire world at the brink of a nuclear holocaust.

But I had not known about other horrific attempts by one powerful country against its neighbour, to subvert a small island of only seven million people. International reports depicted outrageous acts by the US, including several attempts to murder Castro and his associates. Covert CIA attempts included Operation Mongoose to sabotage railway bridges, petroleum refineries, power plants, sugar refineries and sawmills. They even sent a floating crane to one of its busy harbours to damage other ships. Horrific accounts of the next four decades of biological warfare against Cuba's tobacco and potato plantations, the possible introduction of the haemorrhagic fever to the population, were documented. A chilling reminder of human atrocity against another nation, it's neighbour!

Fidel Castro and Che Guevara's photographs and their items used during the war of the revolution were on display. In another section was a fascinating chronology of the development of the Cuban healthcare, social care and education system in the last five decades, even under the economic blockade.

After a few hours inside, I visited outside Granma, the famous boat in which Fidel Castro and his comrades sailed to Cuba from Mexico in November 1956. Also on display, there were planes and vehicles used both in Revolution itself and in subsequent repelling of Bay of Pigs invasion. Next to this area, I stood in silence by the eternal flame in tribute to the heroes of the motherland.

Next to the museum by an enormous park, a souvenirs shop had an unusual statue of a giant open pair of scissors covered with hundreds of scissors of various shapes and sizes. As I watched, several classic cars were passing by. American cars were imported into Cuba until the 1950s, and today its cities were a living museum for classic cars. Instead of a drive in one of them, I took a rickshaw tour. First, we drove past the house where Che lived and then through old Havana - a cheerful atmosphere everywhere. Finally, I ended up in the Moyalla square with side street cafes and restaurants reverberating with live music and great food.

After a shower in my homestead, I returned in the late afternoon to the same square as it started filling up. I sat there, just enjoying the relaxed atmosphere until dark. Then in one of its side streets, I had dinner of arroz con pollo - rice and black beans with chicken and shrimps in coconut sauce. I was hungry, and it was delicious. Then, I sat listening to the beautiful singing and acoustic guitar while many danced.

Next day, was a walking tour by myself with a local guide. We explored Old Havana through its World Heritage colonial architecture on cobblestoned streets, walking by Plaza de Armas, Plaza de San Francisco de Asis, Plaza Vieja and Plaza de la Catedral. Then we arrived by the harbourside where massive American luxury cruise ships had anchored. Opposite the harbour, across the water, stood the old fort. We stopped by a shop, he said, served the best coffee in the city. With a cup of coffee, we shared a plate of yuca chips and talked.

I asked him about his growing up and the last few decades of living in Cuba. His parents had different experiences growing up in the revolutionary period. His father was an orphan with very little education, and after the revolution with free education, he got into the University and became an architect. He could not have done this before. He retired in his mid-sixties. Whereas his mother's family were well to do, although not rich, and lost out slightly with the revolution. She was not a fervent supporter of the revolution. She also became an architect and continues to work in her early seventies. His father's pension was only 40 dollars, but hers will be higher as she was still working.

The guide's wife worked in a Catholic Church. In the country, 50% were Catholics, 30% Yoruba - an African religion brought by the slaves centuries back, now becoming popular, 10% agnostics or atheists. Remaining were Jews, Muslims and other faiths.

Their only daughter was studying Psychology. Education was free at all levels, but the teachers were paid poorly and lacked motivation. Now, parents who could afford are arranging private tuitions for their children. There was no private education system in the country, but teachers in state schools could have a licence to offer private tutoring to earn extra money.

In the local fresh food market, a co-operative, we met a young lady at the counter. She worked 8 hours a day, six days a week, earning about 12 dollars per week, about the same she was getting in two weeks in her previous job as a nursery school teacher.

The market had only bananas, pineapples, guavas and three or four types of vegetables, apparently cheap as it came directly from the villages. The only kind of meat available was pork, beef and chicken were not easily available. There was still a rationing system in Cuba for essential food items. For example, ten eggs, one chicken, half a litre of cooking oil per month for a relatively low price. Children up to the age of 12 additionally had 1 litre of milk per day. As a result, no one was left hungry in the country.

At the end of the four hours interesting tour, I sat on a bench under the tree shed opposite an old building where renovation work was going on. Two electricians came and sat next to me. Through my limited Spanish,

enhanced by the translating app on my iPad, we talked for a while as they were on a break, waiting for supplie
to arrive.

Both were in their early fifty and earned about 24 dollars a week. They had their apartments, inherite
from parents by one and other from his unmarried uncle. Their wives worked, one as a secretary and the othe
in the social services. Both had only one daughter. Restricted families were by choice because of a tight budget
In Cuba, all the buildings belonged to the state, but people could rent or own apartments. There was no rea
maintenance on these old buildings. As a result, approximately 150 buildings in Havana were collapsing eac
year, many lie empty and in ruins.

They asked me about my job. When I said, I was a doctor, one of them said his daughter was a first-
year medic. Healthcare was free for all. There was no private healthcare system. But nurses and doctors
had low salaries, and morale was low. Many immigrated to other countries. Doctors earned about 50-60
dollars a month and for a Specialist only 80 dollars/month! It was common to see teachers or doctors taking
up driving taxis, which paid more. Also, second only to tourism, the export of trained doctors by Cuba to
the developing countries in Africa and South America was one of the leading foreign revenue for the
government. These doctors earned between 800- 1000 dollars per month, which was way above they made
in Cuba. The government also got about 2000 dollars for each doctor's assignment abroad. There were now
nearly 30,000 Cuban doctors working in 87 countries, earning Cuba billions of dollars in revenue!

Because of low morale, often there were long waiting in the hospitals. Only in recent years, mini
corruptions of jumping the queue by paying a small backhander were occasionally happening. Both said
major corruption, however, was not common in the country, even amongst the party leaders. There were
rich people, but no one was superior. Wealthy people mostly were those who ran big hotel chains and
restaurants. There were no areas in Havana where the rich lived exclusively. All levels of education were
free, but after qualification, male university graduates had to do two years' social service plus one-year
military training. Female graduates did three years of social services.

Their supply truck arrived, and we said goodbye to each other. I then walked back through a row of
vintage cars near the dockside, hoping to attract cruise tourists hiring to hire. If you loved vintage cars, there
was probably nowhere else in the world more collection of these which worked.

Refreshed after a cold shower, I sat with the lady owner and her son in my homestead. I learnt it was
common for adults to stay in their parent's house. When people got married, they had to decide whose
parents' house they will live, the boy's or the girl's. In turn, they took care of their parents, including
economic support for as much as they could. Although there were many state-run elderly care home, it
was difficult to find places there. Most tried their best not to send their elderly parents there. Pension in
old age depended on the job and its length and was not index-linked. It was about half of their basic salary
during employment, and with time, the value of the pension became low. Even the proudest parents
needed support from their children. Disability care was basic.

In the evening, I returned to Moyalla square and stayed until late, enjoying with the crowd salsa
music and dancing in a great ambience. Dinner again was with arroz con pollo, and I also had agua fresca,
a non-alcoholic beverage with varieties of fruits, seeds and hibiscus flowers. Later I wandered through now
deserted narrow streets back to my place.

A very early bus ride from Havana towards Trinidad, 288km distance. Agricultural fields of rice and sugarcane in the countryside looked well organised as in any European country. Houses dotted in villages on the way were in good shape and were all brick-built. We stopped briefly at the beautiful bayside city of Cienfuegos. French had built this city in the early 19th century. This European style holiday town with its Caribbean vibe, lingering Spanish influence, with the backdrop of Sierra del Escambray Mountain, looked unique.

Trinidad   Trinidad, a 500yr old city, was the first place colonised by the Spanish in Cuba. I stayed in another homestay there. Soon I left for a walk in the early evening to the small square where a group of young musicians played the guitar. A young man and a woman sang beautifully to the music, while many passers-by, young and old, stopped and danced with their partners, a superb atmosphere. Dinner included for my stay was gorgeous, but Western style. I requested for Cuban home food for the next night instead.

Next morning I took a guided walking tour of Trinidad. This beautifully preserved Spanish colonial settlement was built on the back of the sugar and slave trade. At the peak of the sugar industry, there were 56 sugar mills in the region. Trinidad was full of old colonial buildings. A private company recently renovated one of them and now charged 530 dollars per night for a double room for the wealthy tourists!

We wandered the cobble-stoned streets, by mansions adorned with Italian frescoes, with troubadours strumming their guitars in most street corners. We visited the opulent mansion of a former sugar Baron and then the nearby church. We stopped in its colourful market for a while. In the old part of the town was a lovely architectural garden next to a slave market, active until the 1880s! Nearby on the side street, a man sang to his guitar - Guantanamera, guajira Guantanamera, Yo soy un hombre sincero - my favourite tune of all time.

My guide took me to a church hall. Within the building, was a kindergarten. Children had gone home at the end of the morning, and a teacher was tidying up. I talked to her and found she earned about 20 dollars a month. Women got one year of maternity leave with pay in Cuba. Places for pre-school child care were scarce. Private nurseries like these cost about 12 dollars a month and beyond most. But luckily many had retired grandparents at home to look after their preschool-age children. Because of this, most couples chose to have only one child, at most two.

In the afternoon, I took a taxi to the seaside 15km away. The taxi driver was a qualified engineer, but because of poor pay had taken up taxi driving, which paid a lot more. The seaside was beautiful, and I could not resist the temptation of a quick swim in the warm water. But it was a typical resort. In the bay nearby in luxury yachts, foreign tourists were having fun and drinking expensive alcohol.

On the way back, I learnt from my taxi driver friend that unfortunately, his wife recently had been diagnosed with uterine cancer. Despite surgery, radiotherapy and chemotherapy, she was not doing well. She was only 28yrs old! I gave him my best wishes and consolation.

In the late afternoon, near the church square, I saw two men of my age playing chess. I sat down to watch. Soon one of them had his daughter dropping off two of his grandchildren, a boy and girl about 6-7yr olds. He asked me if I wanted to play with the other guy while he gave tuition for his grandchildren. I played two games and lost badly!

At the homestead, I had a wonderful Cuban dinner, traditional ropa vieja - slow-cooked shredded beef, with fresh tomatoes, onions, peppers, garlic and wine. With rice, black beans and sweet plantains - mouth-watering.

After a hearty breakfast, I thanked and said goodbye to my hosts before the return journey to Havana. Luckily I was staying in a hostal next to the same Moyalla square. I spent most of the evening there in its great atmosphere with vibrant music, children running around, playing hide and seek and adults dancing to music in between food and drinks.

Just before 2 am, there was a knock on my door. The taxi to take me to the airport had arrived. In the square, there were still last of the partygoers enjoying themselves. Within 200m from my place, the car started sputtering and stopped. The young driver switched off the engine, calmly got out and opened the bonnet - no oil. With no panic, he opened the boot to find a bottle of oil and filled. The engine started. We drove off as if nothing had happened. On the street, women were walking alone, going home after their late-night party.

This was Cuba - a day after a tornado, everything back to normal by the afternoon as if nothing had happened. In late-night in a deserted street, a car would not start with a tight schedule to take me to catch my flight 25km away - what's the problem? Women were going home alone late in the night in an empty city street with no worries. Resilience under difficulty, enjoy life to the full despite any hardship. I learnt a lot.

Costa Rica

February 2019

At 5 am, my flight from Havana went to Panama. After the Caribbean Sea, we flew over a jungle with a view of the Panama Canal at a distance. There, breakfast at Tocumen Airport before my connecting flight to San Jose in Costa Rica. Then a two-and-a-half hours' drive through the rain forests to La Fortuna.

This small tourist town was almost under the shadow of majestic Arenal Volcano 1680m, only a few kilometres away. Clouds covered the top of Arenal. Hotels closer to volcano all have their hot springs and thermal pools.

I took a guided hike around the volcano through its lava trail of 1968. A 4 km trek through lava rocks and ow bushes to about 800m was reasonably straightforward.

But unfortunately, they did not allow us to go up any higher as it was an active volcano. By now the cloud ad lifted, and in the late afternoon, we could see at a distance of less than a kilometre smoke and cinder blocks illowing from its top. As we were coming down through lava trail, it got dark and reminded me of doing the ame in the complete darkness in Guatemala. But luckily here, the guide had head torches, and we could follow. Ve stopped to look behind us and now in the dark, fiery-red lava was pouring down Arenal's sides.

Then we drove to Ecotermales Hot Springs. In a thermal pool within an exotic tropical garden, we soaked urselves for a long time. Soon they called us for a meal at a posh restaurant - all included in the tour. So what lse could I do but enjoy!

Next morning was rafting for two hours in the slow-flowing Penas Blancas River. Trogons, toucans, white-hroated magpies and many other birds flew in and out of overhanging branches by the river. Loud howling from he trees and then several howler monkeys jumped over branches. Further down, on a tree, a sloth was catching ip on its fourteen hours a day of sleep. It did not bother to wake up and say hello. On the mud bank, we saw a aiman resting with its jaws open.

On both sides of the river were large plantations of pineapple, banana and coffee. Extensive sections of he tropical forest were cleared for these plantations. We got off our boat to visit Don Pedro's farm. Costa Rican armers made a delicious homemade snack and grounded recently harvested and dried coca for us. We had a drink of it. Two capuchin monkey watched us with interest from nearby trees; an iguana sat nearby, and macaws winged their way over our head. The guide gave us a few coca leaves to chew, a plant, intricate part of the Andean culture. It boosted energy and was without the crash effect of caffeine, popular with the people working ong hours. They also used this as a painkiller and for altitude sickness. The guide added it was also an aphrodisiac. A few of my fellow tourists stuffed their pockets with more leaves.

We then drove by many plantations and learnt, since 2017 the country's second-largest export was pineapple, banana, coffee and cocoa, in that order. To my surprise, its biggest export was medical devices. Costa Rica was a relatively affluent country with a life expectancy of 79yrs, and the literacy rate was in the high 90s - both higher than in the US. But about 20% live in poverty, mostly farm helpers and helpers in the city. They were mostly the people who had legally or illegally arrived from neighbouring Nicaragua and lately from Venezuela. The guide said with a smile, the wealthiest person in the country was a Colombian. Although healthcare and education were free, people who could afford opted for private education for their children. Emergency healthcare was trusted, but for routine treatments, often, there was a lengthy delay, and most chose private care.

In the afternoon we took a 4km hike in the hills with many hanging bridges to the Mystic forest - a primary rainforest, relatively unaffected by human activities. With a high canopy and layers of the understory, it indeed looked mystic. The ground was mostly clear of dense vegetation. The canopy above allowed very little sunlight. We walked silently and saw many birds, including toucans, blue-crowned motmots and blue-grey tanagers.

Black howler monkeys made their presence known with their vocal practices. We saw many wide wake sloths here and one sleeping mother with her baby clinging on to her. Brown spider monkeys did their acrobatics by dangerously hanging on minor branches with their spidery hands and tails. Our guide asked us to stop and pointed next to the path. Next to us was lying a curled up poisonous viper. From then on, we kept one eye on the dark path and another for the wildlife in the trees.

Nearby on a tree, the guide spotted us for the sleeping long-nosed bats. These tiny creatures, weighing only 4-5 grams easily camouflaged like the bark of the tree trunk.

After an enchanted four hours in the heart of nature, we returned to La Fortuna. Arenal had again covered itself with a veil of cloud.

Early the next morning, we arrived by bus to Arenal Lake. Created in the 70s, it was the largest human-made lake in Central and South America. It supplied the country with 75% of its electricity and also provided its neighbour Nicaragua. Then, a beautiful boat ride on the lake with the gorgeous view of Arenal with a lower chain of mountains next to it, known as its daughters. We got off at the other end of the lake and got into a bus for Monteverde.

Monteverde   The bus drove for three hours through fabulous mountain road with small settlements and coffee plantations dotted around the hills to the petite hilly town of Monteverde at 1440m. I stayed at a lodge in the town's edge with the forest with a beautiful open view of the cloud forest from my 1st-floor room with a balcony.

History of Monteverde dated to the late 1940s. After four young Quakers, peaceful, anti-war people in the US, were imprisoned for a year as conscientious objectors to Korean War draft, a group of 44 Quakers from Alabama arrived in Costa Rica for a better and peaceful life. They chose Costa Rica as it had recently in 1949, disbanded its military entirely, offering the Quakers an opportunity to start fresh and live peacefully. They found a 3500-acre of land straddling the Continental Divide in the Cordillera de Tilaran Mountain range, near Puntarenas, and named it Monteverde, meaning Green Mountain.

In the afternoon, I visited the Quaker Meeting House. Over homemade ice cream, I learnt more about the area. In the late 1960s, following a visit by a conservation scientist, the Quakers set aside 1300 acres as Watershed Property, which ultimately became the first private nature reserve in Costa Rica. In 1972, a doctoral research student, George Powell, from the US, visited here to study birds of the area. The damage to Monteverde by the hunters and the land squatters alarmed him. Soon, with the help of the Quakers and with his own money, he purchased 810 acres of land in 1973 to set up a reserve.

Now, 45 years later, Monteverde Cloud Forest Reserve encompasses over 46,000 acres of a cloud forest, protecting a diverse array of flora and fauna. But it might never have happened if it weren't for a small group of peace lovers from Alabama and the admirable young naturalist. Quakers were also influential in sponsoring community and development, which continues. Eco Bambu, a women's cooperative, now made recycled paper products such as the bags used by the local coffee farmers.

During night tour of the rainforest, we saw a giant sloth, sleeping upside down, completely ignoring the tourists below. Toucans and jays slept right at the end of the branches, to avoid the snakes. Smaller branches made more vibrations by the predators and woke them up so they could fly away. A few green viper snakes slept by the bush. The guide pointed spotlight to a large hairy tarantula resting in his silken tube tent. Nearby, many beautiful moths flew around, attracted by our flashlight. Varieties of stick insects lay still on other branches.

Cloud forest   Next day, I toured the unique cloud forest in its fascinating biodiversity. These rare forests occurred within tropical or subtropical mountainous environments, where the atmospheric conditions allowed for a consistent cover of clouds. Monteverde, with its altitude and location within 100 km on either side of the two great oceans, was one of the best.

We entered through a mist between ferns and orchids and hanging bridges. Low-hanging clouds like fog hovered around the upper canopy of the dense forest. Some of it condensed onto the leaves and then dripped onto the plants below and upon us. On the suspension bridges, we walked through the clouds, made mysterious by the call of rare birds and monkeys.

We heard a patter of rain above us, but none of it reached us on the ground. The greedy trees had them all in their leaves. This moisture promoted a tremendous amount of biodiversity, especially within the plants known as epiphytes. These plants grow on other plants, non-parasitically, collecting their water and nutrients from the air, rain, and debris that surround them. Lichens, orchids, and bromeliads, examples of this, were abundant – a botanist's paradise.

This cloud forest encompassed eight life zones atop the Continental Divide. Over 100 species of mammals, 400 species of birds, and 1,200 species of amphibians and reptiles flourished within its bounds. It was one of the few remaining habitats that supported all six species of the cat family of Central America - jaguars, ocelots, pumas, oncillas, margays, and jaguarundis. Unfortunately, we did not see any. But our young guide was excited when he spotted for us an endangered resplendent quetzal sitting on a nearby branch. This parrot-like bird, with

411

s colourful plumage and long tail, in the mist, looked magical.

We returned to a coffee place. Outside in a flowering tree came many hummingbirds. Tiny birds with long arrow beaks hovered in mid-air, rapidly flapping their wings. I tried to see their wings but flapping at a rate of bout 30 beats per second; they were only a blur. I was lucky to see four varieties, one purple throated with lue wings, an endemic copper headed emerald, colourful, fiery- throated birds, and a few sabre wing ones. nchanting creatures. Forest here had nearly fifty varieties of hummingbirds.

Over a cup of coffee, I talked to our guide. He was from an Indigenous population which was well upported by the Government. His parents ran a grocery shop in their village. Both his brothers and two isters, like him, had tertiary education. He had done a four-year degree in tourism and recently joined his lder brother as a tour guide.

The climate change we are creating will alter this incredible biodiversity forever. Models suggest low-evel cloud coverage will go down, and as a result, temperatures will go up and in turn will destroy this nique part of the world!

Back at my lodge after lunch on its open veranda, I watched more colourful birds and monkeys in nearby trees. Some cleaners were finishing work. Through the receptionist, I talked with them. Most of the cleaners and other support workers in this and other lodges were from Nicaragua. They earned between 2-3 dollars per day. Lodge receptionist herself, after her four years of university education, made about 100 dollars a month.

I took another night tour in the jungle. We saw this time several green vipers, many sleeping birds, moths and insects. A sloth had just got up after a 15 hrs nap and was actively moving around and eating leaves.

Next day was a five-hour car trip to San Jose. After going briefly through a coastal area, we stopped for lunch at the port town of Punta in a roadside cafe. Outside, the local artists painted sloths and resplendent quetzal next to our table.

I arrived in San Jose 1150m, a crowded modern city in the evening. San Jose had a majestic view of Poas, Barva and Irazu volcanoes rising gracefully over the city to the north and the rugged Talamanca Mountains to the south. I walked to the site of the National Theatre and then to the monument of Pepe.

It was here, Jose Pepe Figueres Ferrer in 1949, abolished the army after the country's war-prone past. For the last 70 years, Costa Rica has done well with no military. In 1983, when many Central American countries were riven with war, Costa Rica declared its permanent neutrality.

A lesson for the rest of the world embroiled in unnecessary and savage warfare? Nature's biodiversity saved by a young scientist with the help of a few peace lovers.

An example for us to follow?

Jamaica

February 2019   At last, I was flying to the islands of my West Indian cricket heroes. I chose Jamaica for three go
reasons. Birthplace of all-time cricket greats like batsmen George Headley, Lawrence Rowe and Chris Gayle. B
more important for me, the two best bowlers of all time in the world, Michael Holding and Courtney Wals
Second, the birthplace of Bob Marley and last but as important, the place of the modern great Usain Bolt.

Kingston   To my surprise, after arrival at Kingston airport, all the Jamaican immigration officers, withou
exception, were stone-faced and less than welcoming. Something I was not expecting and had not come acros
as bad as anywhere else in my travel. I had thought this was 'easy come easy go' place!

My taxi from the airport located on a narrow island moved through a bank, before turning towards the cit
We drove through dilapidated housing estates and poorly maintained streets to come to the centre area. On th
hills stood many grand mansions of the rich. The driver called it the Beverly Hills. My homestay was at th
northern outskirt of town at Stony Hills. The host lady, a retired schoolteacher, was very welcoming, but the sit
was very much out of the way. Even for my dinner, I needed to call for a taxi. The nearest place, a tiny supermarke
with only two burgers and fries shops, was 10 minutes by car. I did not venture on foot as most of it was withou
street lighting.

Next morning on my day tour, first was to Fort Royal at the end of the same narrow island of the airpor
opposite Kingston Harbour. Founded in 1494 by the Spanish, it was once the largest city in the Caribbean. As
port city, it was then a popular homeport for the English and the Dutch privateers. By the 17th century, Englan
had successfully set up a system of defence for Port Royal for its sugar and slave trade. In 1692 an earthquak
followed by a tsunami destroyed this place.

As I was watching its small museum displaying the records of slavery, a group of local schoolchildren cam
in. While their teacher wanted to show them history, their forefathers had endured, children were just happ
for an outing. On the grounds was the Giddy House. Another severe earthquake in 1907 had tilted an artiller
storage room. Standing inside on its tilted floor, it made me feel giddy.

Back in town, at the National tracks and fields stadium of Usain Bolt fame - maintenance was going o
- not allowed inside. Outside stood the statues of famous Jamaican athletes by renowned sculptor Alvin
Mariott. Shelly Ann Fraser-Pryce, Merlene Ottey, a sculpture of an unknown runner, and of course, Usain
Bolt. Next door at National swimming pool, an island's school competition was taking place. Enthusiastic
boys and girls competed to make their mark in the world of swimming.

At last, I was at the famous Sabina Park. In this ground, Gary Sobers scored 365 not out, which stood as a Test record for over 36 years. Inside its pavilion, on the beams, were plaques of many cricket greats. I checked and found the next day there was a regional cricket match and I decided to come back.

Bob Marley museum was in the house he had lived. Inside was a colourful depiction of his musical journey and his belongings. As we moved from room to room his famous songs played loudly. Fellow tourists danced to 'One love. One heart. Let's get together and feel all right,' while I only listened.

The last place on tour was Devon House, house of the first Afro-Caribbean millionaire. I was not interested and only looked at the ostentatious buildings from outside. But I loved their famous ice cream - one of the best I have tasted.

In the evening I took a taxi to the recently opened Usain Bolt restaurant, hoping to catch sight of the great man. A posh restaurant with lovely music and food, but the waitress said Usain was there last night and not expected until the next evening.

Next morning, on Saturday, my homestead host Michelle invited me to go with her to their breakfast club. A lovely gathering of the mostly old. A few came in their wheelchairs. Many young people also came to have breakfast and chat together. This gathering had been now going on in the same venue over the last two decades. Our host, a disabled man, was in his late 70s. Everyone attending brought whatever food they could, to share.

There were talks, music, poetry reading and comedy. They invited me to say something about my travels and healthcare. I shared my thoughts about what being a global citizen meant. Well-received, it appeared. Then I learnt from the discussions, in Jamaica, primary education was free, but from then on the parents had to pay for most things. College education was expensive. Primary healthcare was free, but in the hospital, one had to pay for most items. A better option was private if you could afford it.

Afterwards, I took a taxi to Sabina Park to watch a game of regional cricket. I sat there for a while in the Courtney Walsh stand and later in the Michael Holding stand, both empty. Sitting between the two teams, I had the same lunch as them.

Next day I took a tour to the Blue Mountains. We drove on a hilly road with shacks by the side, to a small coffee plantation. A young man gave me a tour of the place, before bringing in a lunch of tasty chicken curry with roasted and fried Breadfruit, cooked by his mother. There was a table tennis board in a room. I asked for a game, but neither my guide nor the driver knew how to play. I gave a quick lesson to both. A young girl, there for cleaning the place, was watching with interest. I asked her if she wanted to play. She nodded. After a brief lesson, she easily outclassed the other two.

In the evening, my host Michelle cooked fish with national fruit Ackee. Gorgeous. We talked about Jamaica's current situation for a while.

Long drive next day across the country through a hilly road to North shore, a popular tourist spot. A few swam in the warm Caribbean Sea, and others moved to Dunn's fall. Between the rocks, this lovely fall came down for 500m before ending up on a secluded beach. I rolled up my trousers and trudged upstream, while many walked in groups, some holding hands - great fun and a mini family adventure.

During lunch, I met a couple from Germany who had come on a cruise ship, anchored nearby. They had only three hours on this island before moving on to another. They regretted they couldn't stay longer.

We returned to Kingston Airport was via a different but scenic route, traversing the country. It gave me a chance to speak to my driver friend. He used to play cricket regularly, but now with his job, only managed occasional games. We talked about the state of current West Indies cricket. He lived close to the place where Chris Gayle grew up.

I was glad that I went to Kingston rather than to other tourist beach resort sites in Jamaica. Inequality between the super poor, poor and the very few super-rich who lived in their large gated palatial buildings in 'Beverly Hills', was stark and open to see. People, however, were friendly everywhere, loved their music and sports, especially cricket.

Brunei

March 2019

runei was going to be only a quick stop on my way to Tasmania after a few days in the world's most wildlife-ich equatorial rainforests in Borneo.

From Bandar Seri Begawan airport, I took a taxi to the city centre. Brunei of less than half a million had ultan as the ruler. The taxi driver said there were only about 50 taxis in the country. Most owned cars and rinking was not allowed. Very few tourists came, and it was easy to walk in this compact city. Brunei's massive il and natural gas wealth made its ruler, Sultan, one of the richest men in the world. He flaunted his wealth hamelessly, like buying a gold Rolls Royce. The government paid for education, healthcare, and most other living xpenses of its citizens, financed through Brunei's natural reserves.

I got off by the waterfront overlooking impressive Omar Ali Saifuddien Mosque. A few men were hanging round to take people for a ride on their foot-pedalled rickshaws. Near the mosque stood the grand building of stana Nurul Iman Palace, with curved roofs, golden domes and minarets oozing wealth.

I wandered by the waterfront where people strolled around open food stalls. On the other side of the bay vere the fishermen's houses on stilt. It took less than two hours to see this city's important landmarks. In the evening I went for dinner at Tarindak restaurant, recommended by the taxi driver. A sumptuous buffet dinner :ost only 12 dollars. Fresh fish cooked with okra looked interesting. The same taxi driver with his wife and Jaughter came for their dinner and asked me to join them.

The daughter had recently returned after finishing business studies in Singapore. She missed the freedom of Singapore and wanted to return there, although she already had an offer of a high-paid job in Brunei. I said Brunei appeared a well-to-do place, and I was not talking about the Sultan. And I also praised the comprehensive support for health and education, social care here.

She said, her parents agreed, there was another side of Brunei people from outside did not know. Although only 5% lived in poverty, another face of poverty in this small nation was the poverty of freedom and opportunity. She added Brunei was a destination, and to a lesser extent, a source and transit country for human trafficking and prostitution.

Men and women from Indonesia, Malaysia, Philippines, Pakistan, India, Bangladesh and Thailand migrated to Brunei for domestic or other low-skilled labour. Many faced involuntary servitude upon arrival. There were over 88,000 migrant workers in Brunei. Most faced debt bondage, non-payment of wages, passport confiscation, and confinement to home - all of which were contributing to trafficking. Some 25,000 female domestic workers in Brunei worked exceptionally long hours without being granted a day for rest, in involuntary servitude. She felt ashamed that Brunei was a transit country for trafficking victims in South East Asia.

I thanked her and then praised the parents for bringing up such a spirited woman. They gave me a lift to my hotel for my one-night stay in the country.

Borneo Malaysia

March 2019

A short flight from Bandar Seri to Sandakan via Kota Kinabalu. Then a 20-minute car journey from the airport to Sepilok Nature Resort. I am now in Malaysian Borneo. Borneo Island is shared between three nations- Malaysia, Indonesia and Brunei, home of the world's oldest rainforest.

On the drive to Sepilok, I could see many palm oil plantations destroying the rainforests and its habitat. I remembered how passionately my daughter spoke about this after she visited here in her college days. She also climbed Mt Kinabalu 4095m, the highest mountain in South East Asia - I would not attempt.

My eco-resort was in the middle of a jungle with a stream flowing through it. Birds, monkeys, and butterflies were everywhere. In guided night walk to Sepilok Forest trails, we spotted sleeping hornbills, kingfishers and Taylor birds, varieties of stick insects and spiders, being careful all the time of the leeches and the angry jungle ants.

Orangutans and Sun Bear   Next day, I visited the Sepilok Orangutan Sanctuary. Here they cared for about 40 orphan or injured orangutans. About ten young orangs were doing their tricks on the ropes in the primary feeding station. Only occasionally they came down to feed between their playtimes. In the nursery nearby were another 15 orphan babies, cared for by the volunteers. Some very young ones came holding hands with their buddy volunteers. Young apes were paired with an older one to help them develop the skills they needed in the wild. Enchanting to see older ones coming, holding hands with the babies. One large female sat with her suckling baby and monitored the boisterous group of young ones. After having their food, they played on the ropes, the first step in learning to climb trees - just like in a children's playground.

From there, I went to the secondary feeding station during their daily feeding time. Set in the middle of the jungle, a sanctuary volunteer brought food there by a tree. Soon older orangs arrived from nowhere, swinging on the ropes. About 70% of the orangs from here were rehabilitated to the wild. In this protected 43 sq.km forest, there were about 70 orangutans. Unfortunately, beyond the reserve, the forest was increasingly cleared for palm plantations.

The Bornean orangutan is the second-largest ape after the gorilla. Watching these critically endangered apes, I remembered they shared 97% of their DNA with humans. I hoped that we would do everything to stop their path to extinction.

Nearby was the Sun Bear sanctuary. Another species under threat from deforestations and poaching. Malayan sun bears are the smallest bears in the world and endemic to Southeast Asia. These small black bear with a golden crest on their chest barked exactly like dogs.

There were 40 bears rescued from captivity here. They were more people shy than orangs. But I was lucky to see two babies by their mothers and many adults.

Following a car journey to Sandakan, I boarded a boat on the Kinabatangan River, the second-longest river in Malaysia. After about half an hour, we entered one of its large tributaries. Then, sailing through the forest, we reached a jungle lodge between the forest and the riverbank.

In the afternoon, we had a boat ride on the Menanggul River and was lucky to see many Macao monkeys and then an orangutan on a tree. Orangs built their nests high in the tree. From a distance, it looked like a large bird's nest! Further down the river, we found several leaf monkeys, looking like the squirrel monkeys in Costa Rica. Later we came across several groups of the proboscis monkey. These endemic monkeys in their reddish-brown skin with an enormous nose; males with their bright red erect penis and long tails looked comical. They jumped carelessly from one tree to another just to show off.

Soon the changing colours of the clouds in the setting sun reflected on the river water. It was like an artist's canvas, which updated itself every few minutes. As darkness fell, thousands of fireflies glittered in the trees. Many of my fellow tourists had never seen one. But I remembered growing up in our village where we used to see them so often! But not in recent years, unfortunately.

After dinner, on a night tour, we spotted a green viper precariously curled up on a branch above us. We came across many sleeping butterflies, including a lovely black wing one. The guide pointed his flashlight on a Huntsman spider, also known as giant crab spider because of their leg span of 30cm. Then we saw one dwarf kingfisher, sleeping on a terminal branch.

I took a boat ride before the sunrise. A single orangutan was waking up by the river in a low branch. On the mud bank were many crocodiles, including a few babies, waiting for the sun to rise. Our boat followed a small channel through mangroves into a beautiful lake, full of flowering lilies and a few lotuses. The still water shined gloriously in the soft morning sun rays. We stopped there for our morning coffee. Large and small fishes jumped out of surrounding still water. The guide said not to touch the water, large crocks were around here - not surprising because the place was full of fishes. We did not see any.

We moved on through a tight channel, pushing away overhanging branches, many with Macao monkeys. The guide brought out packed breakfast and coffee. We ate with one eye open for the monkeys jumping in to steal our food. A wild pig wandered by in the mud, just in case there were any scraps! The guide said around this spot pygmy elephants often came in the early morning. We waited for a while, but no sign of any - late sleepers!

Later we got off at a tiny village of seven houses. Fishing nets hung around the huts, all with beautiful ower gardens around them. Our guide took us to a home where they cooked lunch for us. The lady said in recent ears, more and more people were leaving these villages. The fishing stock had gone down, and they were ruggling to cope. Children took a boat ride every day for their primary education. Only secondary school was r away, and most children boarded there. Later once the young arrived in Sandakan city, they wanted to settle ere for its facilities.

I played with three children aged between 2-10 years and showed them animal videos. One teenager slept the way through on the floor next to us. Food with freshly cooked fish, shrimps and rice was gorgeous. As we id goodbye, the two-year-old boy would not leave me. He wanted to come with me!

Late afternoon, we got into the boat for another ride. Very quiet on the river bank. We found only a few oboscis monkeys and then a solitary short-tailed Macao monkey - a lot bigger than its other cousin!

In the evening, I went for a boardwalk in the jungle by myself - nothing much to see this time except a few eeping butterflies. Moths were flying around them, wondering why these creatures were still sleeping o sign of the pygmy elephants. Same dwarf tail kingfisher was sleeping on the same branch, but facing the her way this evening. Next to the river I heard hooting sound. A fish owl was sitting on a tree, keeping its wide e open, monitoring the water.

We returned to Sandakan by the river. This busy town looked relatively tidy. In the marketplace, vendors ld all kinds of vegetables, halal meats and dried fish and shrimp.

Later I took a flight from Sandakan to Kota Kinabalu, the capital city of Sabah province on the northwest ast of Borneo, facing the South China Sea. Famous Tunku Abdul Rahman National Park lied on its west and at east was Mount Kinabalu, which gave the city its name. A clean and friendly town.

The receptionist at my hotel had been working for ten years and had no formal qualification. She earned out 70 dollars a month, and her husband was a taxi driver. They had three children - the 7yr old was in a overnment school. They only had to pay for his uniform and books. But for their 6yr old in primary school, erything had to be paid, a bit strange. The 2yr old was a toddler.

I took a boat ride from the busy Star Marina jetty next morning to Mamutik Island, the smallest island in nku Abdul Rahman Marine Park. I was there for one particular reason. I wanted to scuba dive again. I plained to my instructor Jonathan that it was almost five years since I had done diving. Then I also told him out my brain thinggy only over a year back. We agreed to start with a gentle dive walking from the rocky

beach. Under the water, at only 5m, was inviting with coral of all shapes and sizes and colourful fishes. Back o
the shore, I told Jonathan I felt good and wanted to dive deeper.

After lunch, we walked to a small motorboat moored by the north-east side of the island. Jonathan kindly carried my heavy cylinder along with his own. We sailed north from there. Soon we jumped in the sea and dived - Jonathan next to me. We swam by mesmerising colourful coral, including gorgeous purple ones with swarms of bright-coloured Damselfish, Parrot Fish, Nemo and others. Even a shoal of barracuda came around and checked us over. Jonathan pointed downwards, and we dived deeper to about 15m. Coral became magnificent. After a hypnotizing thirty minutes, we had to go up. Once onboard, I thanked Jonathan profusely for his help and patience.

In the evening, I strolled to the local street food area. I followed the heady smell of famous Durian fruits, King of Fruits in South East Asia. Vast open-air food stalls were nearby. People crowded the place for lovely fresh seafood and other Bornean delicacies, cooked to order at a cheap price. No wonder when I had asked one taxi driver what their favourite home food was, he had told me they did not cook at home anymore because street food was excellent with many varieties, freshly cooked and yet so cheap!

Stuffed after a gorgeous dinner as I walked by the shops selling Durian, its intoxicating smell forced me to try some. From outside it looked like Jack fruit, common in India, but the fruit inside tasted sweeter.

Next day, I took a boat ride to Bunga Raya, known as the Gaya Island, largest in Tunku Abdul Rahman National Park. This 15 sq. km island had 300m elevation covered with dense virgin tropical forest. There were long hiking trails for people who stayed overnight in one of its two expensive resorts. Rest of the island was uninhabited.

At Police Bay, a 400m stretch of white sand gently sloped into a crystal clear sea. Ideal place for swimming or snorkelling. On the day there was no swimming or snorkelling allowed because of jellyfishes. Instead, I went kayaking with a resort attendant. From the kayak, my friend doing most of the rowing, I watched several jellyfishes in the water above the coral.

He said most of the attendants in the two resorts came in the first boat and left by the last boat to Sandakan. Only a handful stayed overnight serving the resort overnighters. Our kayak went on the other side of the island by a large stilted village. He said illegal immigrant fishermen from the Philippines occupied the area, a high crime area and best avoided. Kayaking back towards the shore, he let me do most of the work. Rowing against the high waves breaking against the beach was tiring but exciting.

After lunch in a resort restaurant, I wandered. Soon I came across a 1m dragon having a snooze by a stream. Later, in another area, I walked close to a larger dragon, at least 1.5m in size. It ran as soon as it spotted me. I followed and saw him once more by a tree, but then it disappeared.

On our way back to Kota Kinabalu, I noticed one of the crew was holding a long stick with a net, picking up any plastic bottles from the water. I had also seen this in the last few rides. The crew said unfortunately plastic pollutions in the sea was now a significant problem. Surrounding villages had no drinking water and often used plastic bottles. Even from the township plastic ended up in sea through its sewers. They added, to their shame, Malaysia was the fifth largest plastic polluter of the ocean in the world. These were now destroying the coral and marine life, and they worried about the future of tourism here. At present, there were only a few minor projects to address this issue, but it needed a major effort on all sides.

We stopped by Manukan Island, the second largest island in the park. With its good beaches, snorkelling and diving, a popular tourist area. It had many less expensive chalets and restaurants. We picked up the workers from the resort on their way home after a day's work.

In the evening, I was drawn to the food market again. I could not resist picking the largest lobster and crab. They cooked these with noodles and vegetable for me. When the food arrived, I found by mistake they had cooked two lobsters. I did not complain. Sipping a fresh coconut drink, I took time over my dinner, watching families and friends turning up for their dinner. I slowly walked back; my belly stretched to the limit. No durian tasting tonight.

Borneo had been a superb place to come. People were always very polite and friendly. Food was gorgeous and so many beautiful places in nature to visit. Hope they last for future generations.

Australia

March 2019   Arriving in Melbourne from Borneo on my way to Tasmania, I spent a lovely few days with my daughter, her husband and two adorable grandchildren. I had been to Melbourne before. They were there for only six months. We drove through the scenic Great Ocean Road and stayed in an Airbnb by a forest with resident koalas in the trees by the house. Kangaroos came in the early morning and the evening to say hello.

Kookaburra birds arrived during dinner on the balcony. Before our drive to see more koalas, colourful parrots came down from the branches and ate from our hands, thrilling the children. Swimming in the sea, we spotted dolphins at a distance checking us out—wonderful few days.

Tasmania

During my previous stay in Australia, I did not get time to visit Tasmania. By far the largest island of Australia, it was almost the size of England. Over 40% of its land was protected as national parks and world heritage sites. Evidence shows indigenous people occupied this island at least 30,000yrs before the British colonisation. Following the ice age, the sea rose to form the Bass Strait, separating it from the Australian mainland.

In 1803 the British established a penal settlement here. At the time of colonisation, about 7,000 Aboriginal population lived here. Over the next decades, up to 75,000 convicts were sent to Tasmania. At the same time, systematically through the infamous 'Black War', the indigenous population was ethnically cleansed from this island.

Now, the elusive Tasmanian devil, platypuses and its beautiful Cradle Mountain were what attracted me. I arrived at Launceston, known as 'Lonnie'. In the late afternoon, I walked to Cataract gorge. There was a more leisurely walk by the bank of the canyon. But instinctively I took the 1.5km steep uphill trek to the top of the hill for a view. Some of its section was tricky. It got dark at the top. I went downhill carefully in the darkness.

Next day, we drove towards the Cradle Mountain, three and a half hour distance. We passed rough hills and forests, with occasional villages, wineries, agricultural fields and large cattle herds. A brief op for ice cream in Sheffield, a tiny settlement. Amazingly, outside walls of almost all the shops and houses ere had beautiful murals depicting the history of settlements in Cradle Valley.

adle Mountain   Then drive by the bluffs of the Great Western Tiers before arriving at the Dove Lake. its clear water, Cradle Mountain reflected beautifully from the background.

After walking the shores of the lake for a while, we drove to the Waldheim Cottage. It belonged to e Austrian naturalist Gustav Weindorfer, the first person who tried a century back to save this area of tural beauty from deforestation and create a national park. Behind the cottage, we walked into an ancient ol temperate rainforest. It had millions of years of history and ancient King Billy Pine trees, conifers, not nes. Many trees were almost 2000 years old. A few dead tree trunks, still solid logs, over 1000 years old, on the ground covered with moss. Unbelievable to be around something so ancient.

Later, in the evening, I went out on an animal spotting tour. Several wombats, wallabies, ddymelons and bush tail opossums busily munched grass. We came across a few carnivorous spotted olls, but unfortunately no Tasmanian devil. The driver said it was rare to spot them in the wild. Soon we pped in an open field and got out to silently watch the vast expanse of the clear Cradle night sky with untless stars, planets and the milky ways.

The driver with his girlfriend collected me the next morning for a hike. She left for a hike up the adle Mountain by herself. I envied her. We took a breathtaking 8km hike up on the side of Cradle Mountain, e Cradle Lake circuit walk. Leaving Dove lake below, we walked by Lake Lila.

Further up, we stopped at Wombat Pool, a small lake between the rugged hills and the Pencil pines. any trekkers with their rucksacks of tents and sleeping bags passed us by. They would spend a few nights these mountains, reminding me of my younger days.

424

Then we trekked up a steep path. There, high cliffs surrounded another beautiful glacial lake. After spending a while on its hilly shore, we walked downwards by many Crater falls, and then through the Pandani Forest. In fresh mountain air, Grade 2 hiking after a long time, it felt good. We stopped at a mountain hut for our lunch the driver brought with him.

As soon as we were inside, rain poured in. It stopped as abruptly as it came. Outside a few wet wombats were still munching grass.

On our way back, I stopped to see the Devils, an iconic symbol of Tasmania, in a sanctuary. Size of a small dog, devils, were stocky and muscular with black fur and smelly. In their pens, they made loud, screeching noises. I watched them eat their meal ferociously. When another came nearby, it chased him away, furiously,

making loud noises. Cute baby devils stayed at a distance. These creatures, once found in mainland Australia, were now endemic in Tasmania. Hunted to near extinction, they became officially protected in 1941. Since the 90s, devil facial tumour disease had been threatening the survival of this species. In 2008, it was declared endangered.

Many eastern quolls and larger spotted quolls were also in the sanctuary. These primarily nocturnal carnivorous marsupials, native to Australia and New Guinea, were 65cm long with hairy tails - also vicious looking. Significant threats to the survival of devil and the quoll species included introduced cane toad, feral cats and foxes, poisoning and urban development.

From there, I walked to a museum with a history of the area. It had the reconstruction of Thylacine, Tasmanian tiger. Newspaper cuttings showed the last picture of this beautiful species in a zoo in 1936. Sadly, it has since become extinct.

In the late afternoon, I walked 3km to a creek, a popular site for spotting another iconic animal, platypuses. I wandered around the stream until it got dark, but no luck seeing this mysterious creature. But overall, a good day.

Next morning another walk by the creek to find platypus, but still no luck. Around midday, we drove back to Launceston.

Next day I took a 50km car ride following the Tamar River to the Beauty Point - a lovely small town by the river. On the riverfront, was the Platypus house. Finally, I witnessed the elusive platypuses, in real life, swimming. With duckbill, beavertail and otter feet, they looked a funny creature put together in a hurry by drunken nature. These animals were semiaquatic and endemic to eastern Australia and Tasmania.

The same place had a few Echidnas, spiny animals looking like hedgehogs, only mammals along with platypuses which laid eggs. These two monotremes, highly specialised egg-laying predatory mammals, sensed their prey through electrolocation. They were one of the few species of venomous mammals.

Back to Sierra Leone

April 2019 Freetown   I knew I had a busy schedule this year. But when a call came to join another trip to Sierra Leone, I immediately agreed. Some Sierra Leone born US volunteers, I had worked with during my last visit, now with a separate charity had organised this trip. From Lungi airport it took me an exciting 20 minutes water taxi on more than gentle Atlantic waves to Freetown. Two other surgeons in our team, one of them, an Orthopaedic surgeon, would work in Freetown's premier teaching hospital, while I would work at the newly built Police Hospital. Police hospital had been for a while serving the general population and also the police families. But this would be the first time; however, the hospital will offer surgical procedures.

I visited the place - keen staff, but with no operating theatre experience. Of the only two doctors in the hospital, one was eager to learn surgery, and our role was to teach and train the staff and offer free surgery. The hospital had a reasonable infrastructure but as usual no disposables. Luckily, our team had brought enough supplies. It would be fun.

Next day was the 58th Independence Day of Sierra Leone. In 1462 a Portuguese explorer, because of the shape of the hills surrounding the harbour, called it Serra da Leoa, Portuguese for Lioness Mountains.   In the late 18th century, the British had founded a settlement in Sierra Leone and called the 'Province of Freedom.' The intention was to resettle some 'Black poor' of London, some of whom were African- Americans freed by the British during the American war of independence. About 400 blacks and 60 whites had reached Sierra Leone in 1787. Many of these former slaves, although African and black, were not from this part of Africa. Most of these first settlers died of diseases and war with the indigenous peoples, who did not want them here.

Later, more freed slaves from Nova Scotia crossed Atlantic to build the second and only permanent colony of Sierra Leone and established Freetown. At about the same time, following the formal abolition of the slave trade in 1807, British crews delivered thousands of formerly enslaved Africans to Freetown. These returned Africans were from many parts of Africa, but principally the west coast. During the 19th century, freed black Americans from West Indies also immigrated and settled in Freetown. Together these peoples created a new ethnicity called Creoles and a trading language, Krio, which became the language here.

We visited the town's square for the Independence Day festival. A low key affair. Some local bands played around a few stalls selling souvenirs. Later in the evening, a local pop star would be here to sing, and people were already gathering for it. I talked to four youthful girls in hijab, running a stall on the ground.

All of them were near graduation but said there was absolutely no prospect of finding any job after. They were running the tiny stall to make some money. Afterwards, they wanted a picture with me on their mobile.

Later I visited the famous 500yr old cotton tree of Freetown. Freed slaves from Nova Scotia after landing on the shoreline here, had walked up to this giant tree above the bay. They had then held a thanksgiving service, praying and singing to thank God for their deliverance to free land. Nowadays, African Americans tracing their roots, came and tied white flags on its branches.

Next day all day, we screened patients at Police Hospital for surgery in the next few days. A large number of cases with a multitude of surgical conditions, all waiting long for any hope of surgery.

Following morning we started the first-ever operation in the hospital's history. I let the local doctor make the first cut and assisted him in doing the first operation to make it memorable for him and the staff. After initial hiccough, we got all the cases done - very appreciative staff. Everyone cheered at the end of a long day.

In the evening, I found the orthopaedic surgeon looking distraught. In his first time abroad volunteering, his first case was shocking. A six-year-old girl was brought from the villages in a moribund condition. She had suffered an open fracture of her forearm after a fall while playing a few days back. Traditional healers had wrapped her with a tight poultice which had resulted in gangrene below her elbow. She was in septic shock. Our colleague, after resuscitating her, had performed an amputation above the elbow.

In the next few days, including on a local holiday, we did about 40 procedures, all the way training the local staff. Because of the usual logistical issues, often we finished late in the evening. Staff were most cooperative and did not mind staying late. By the end of the week, we operated on all the patients we had screened. On Friday evening, our team invited the hospital staff for dinner, and we had a great time.

Our Orthopaedic colleague was also happy that the child after amputation was doing very well. A few months later, the girls' mother sent us a video of her dancing, which made everyone smile.

Next morning, I visited the hospital to see all the patients and then thanked all the staff. It had been great week. I then travelled to Masanga.

Masanga   Between my visits to Sierra Leone, I had contacted the Norwegian charity, which was runnir the programme of training nurses to become non-doctor Emergency Surgeon similar in many ways to th programme in Ethiopia we had initiated. They were delighted with my offer to give these essential healthca specialists additional skills training. They invited me to run a two-day skills course in Masanga Hospital, whei the programme was based.

After four hour's drive to the east from Freetown, I arrived in Masanga. In the middle of agricultur villages and mining sites, the hospital was basic, like in Kabala. There were signs of extreme poverty all aroun

Ironically, this place was also next to a gold mine! Like many African countries, Sierra Leone had courte foreign companies, which paid governments some fees for mining rights. But locals benefited very little. Apa from its diamonds, the country was among the biggest producers of titanium, bauxite, gold and had the world largest deposits of rutile quartz.

One newly trained non-doctor surgeon and a handful of voluntary doctors, most from Europe worked Masanga. Tin hut accommodation next to the river was rudimentary, and for the duration of my stay, there wa no electricity. But to our relief, in this oppressive heat, at least we had a shower. A lady came from the villag to cook food for us on an open fire. After a brief tour of the facilities, in the evening with candlelight, I had long chat with the coordinator of the programme Dr Wouter, a 32yr old medic from Holland. He had been hei for the last few years and was the only medically qualified surgeon for the hospital. His passion for improvir the quality of surgical care in the country impressed me. There were also a few newly qualified medics from th UK volunteering for a few months.

It was raining, and soon we retired to bed. They reminded me to tuck my mosquito nets properly. Apart from the mosquitos, there were occasional stray rats! In the night I woke up with intermittent loud banging noises above. Next morning, I realised they were from mangoes falling on the roof from overhanging trees! As I collected some, a few local children came to gather some, and we had some laugh.

Gold mine

Ten attended the next two days' skills training, six of them non-doctor surgeons and four doctors from hospitals all around the country. Some had travelled for one and half day by public transport changing bus two or three times. At the end of the session, I gave each of them a USB loaded with current textbooks and training material I had downloaded. They were all grateful for the training and the mobile library in their pocket.

When I came back to the accommodation by early evening, the children brought me some ripe mangoes, and I shared with them pictures of animals from all over the world. In the evening I talked again to Wouter and other medics. Wouter talked passionately about the friendliness of people despite abject poverty and also about corruption of the higher officials in the country.

In the night, I woke up with a lot of mechanical noise and singing from across the river. I learnt later this was from excavators digging for gold by the river bank. They preferred to work in the nights rather than in the day's oppressive heat. Villagers who worked there earned slightly better than working in the fields or at the nearby palm oil farms.

At the end of another day's training, and thanking everyone, I left for Freetown.

Following morning I returned to the Police Hospital and did a teaching on postoperative care and breast cancer awareness to the staff. All the staff, about forty of them, attended. Soon it was time to say goodbye and a promise to return in a few months.

Uzbekistan, Kyrgyzstan &

volunteering in Mongolia

June/July 2019   In my school days, names like Bukhara, Samarkand and Silk Road intrigued me, and Mongolia had always been a land of mystery. A UK charity asked me to volunteer in Mongolia for two weeks. I combined that with a visit to Uzbekistan and Kyrgyzstan beforehand.

Uzbekistan

Tashkent   After miles and miles of desert, Tashkent by a river looked like an oasis from the sky. Tashkent on the Silk Road was the largest city in Central Asia with a history dating back to 4th century B.C. In 1966 an earthquake had devastated the place. Now it was a modern city with restored Islamic and Soviet architecture.

On my guided tour, the first stop was by the Hazrat Imam Complex. They constructed this mosque in 2007 in a record-breaking four months. Empty prayer hall here could hold over two thousand people. But they allowed only men to pray. Women were not allowed inside. Expensive construction here involved bringing sandalwood from India, green marble from Turkey, and blue tiles from Iran.

Next to it under construction was an even more massive complex. My male guide proudly said this would be the main cultural and administrative centre of official Islam in the Republic, a new bastion of Islam in the world.

Nearby stood the Muyi Mubarak Library. In a small building, it displayed the world's oldest Quran, over 600 years old, written over animal skin. The library also had the world's tiniest Quran, only six sq.cm in size.

From there, I went to the Kukeldash Madrasa. This 16th century Quran School, built of yellow brick, had an inner yard with hujras, student accommodation. Here boys from 4-16yrs of age stayed and learned. Girls learned elsewhere. Only at the University for Islamic studies, boys and girls could study together, and there were also a few women teachers there. School-level education and healthcare were free.

Within walking distance was the beautiful Chorsu Bazaar, biggest and oldest in Central Asia, operating on the same spot for 2000 years. Under this huge blue-coloured domed building and in the adjacent areas, they sold all daily necessities-spices, grain, dairy products and fruits. The bread stall caught my attention. A baker,

aking traditional bread in the oven, let us try some freshly baked bread - delicious. I saw some large round atbread, which they said could last up to six months and once popular with caravans crossing vast deserts. nder small domes, artisans made and sold jewellery, gold embroidery, tapestries, lace and quilted caftans. ther stalls sold knives next to musical instruments and beautiful carpets.

We stopped briefly at an art museum with beautiful carpets, woodworks and sculptures. I watched ith intrigue women sitting with concentration weaving magic, making beautiful carpets.

The guide got for us famous peanuts boiled in honey, covered with sesame seeds. We enjoyed this runchy and yummy snack getting back to our car.

Vast Friendship Square had statues of an Uzbek family. During WWII, Shomahmudov family dopted 15 children of Russian, Kazakh, Belarusian, Moldovan, Latvian, Jewish, and Tatar origin. This statue, rected during the Soviet era, was removed after the collapse of the union. Only recently this has been einstated to celebrate a symbol of unity and friendship of all ethnic groups living as one family in the city.

Next stop was at the Mustakillik maydoni, the Independence Square, the largest square in Tashkent and a showcase of modern Uzbekistan. Glory and Memory Alley stood in honour of soldiers who died in WWII. Opposite the alley lay a statue depicting a mourning mother, sadly looking down onto an eternal lame in memory of her children who fell defending the country. We passed under an arch with figures of torks to a fountain. There stood the Independence Monument, a high pedestal with a golden globe erected on the top with a map of Uzbekistan. Opposite the Ankhor channel was a memorial square remembering killing of many Uzbeks by Stalin Govt.

The Earthquake Memorial remembered the 1966 disaster and support from the Soviet countries in

rebuilding the city. Statues of soviet workers and soldiers stood next to a fissure on the ground from the earthquake. Known as Monument to Courage, they dedicated it to the men and women who rebuilt the flattened city following the quake. Its bronze reliefs depicted builders from all Soviet republics taking part in reconstruction, who in only three and a half years had fully restored Tashkent.

We then walked to the massive Amir Timur Square in the centre of the city with a festival-like atmosphere around. Two men were playing table tennis. I asked, and they let me play. I beat the first one but lost badly against the second.

Amir Timur, the 14th century Turco -Mongol warlord, founded Timurid Empire. As an undefeated military commander, he was regarded as the greatest military leader and tactician. In the middle of the square stood Timur's statue on a horse. At the other end were the famous twin towers of Tashkent chimes. They called it Tashkent's Big Ben.

I sat on a bench by the park with the guide where two gardener ladies were resting. I talked to them through my guide. One of them, unfortunately, had lost her husband suddenly at 39 years of age. She looked after four young children with no state support. They earned about 150 dollars a month, but house rent and food took up most of it. The guide said breaking up of Soviet Union had helped country's economy, but only big companies have got rich, not the ordinary people. Islamic culture oppressed during the Soviet era, was now flourishing. Although I saw most women without headscarves and few girls riding bikes in the park, he said attitude towards women had gone backwards.

Khiva My evening flight to Urgench arrived late. I came out of the small airport after 10 pm to find no one waiting, as arranged by the travel company. Outside there were only 5-6 taxis and only a few people. I got into a cab for Khiva, over 40 minutes' journey through the desert. After leaving Urgench, we drove through an empty dark road. On the side of the road, women in groups, occasionally solitary, were waiting in the dark. The driver said they were waiting for the last bus going home after working in nearby establishments. I immediately knew where women could wait by the roadside in late night for their transport, was a safe place.

We arrived in the old town of Khiva. My driver was from Urgench and did not know Khiva well. After asking a man by the road, we arrived at the hotel only to find we were in the wrong place. Khiva had three hotels of the same name with a slight difference. Finally, before midnight, I got to the right hotel, inside the inner city walls.

Following day was a guided tour of Khiva. With 2000yrs history, Khiva was one of the important stops of Silk Road and once a rival to Bukhara. A massive wall, Dichan Kala, with 11 gates protected the outer town. Inside, another wall encircled the inner town, Itchan Kala. Within it stood the city palace. In inner town, a heritage site, only 250 families had lived for centuries. But they could not build their houses higher than 10m and had to cover outside walls and the roof with mud. One could not buy property here, only handed over a heritage.

This small town had 79 mosques, many palatial buildings, minarets, towers and domes. In the impressive 10th-century Djuma mosque, oldest in Uzbekistan, 213 carved wooden pillars supported its roof. Every pillar was carved to an individual pattern, like being in a forest of exquisitely carved trees. Three centuries ago, a fire had destroyed most of the pillars, but 16 of them, over 1000 years old, remained, the rest was rebuilt. These wooden pillars had in their base a camel skin to prevent damp from the ground.

One pillar came from India, showing the close relations between the countries.

We walked to the tombstone of Pahlavan, a wrestler and a poet. Pahlavan Mahmud Mausoleum had six

hundred years of history. Under the largest dome in Khiva, people came here for their blessings before a wedding or after childbirth. While we were visiting, an Uzbek bride and groom, surprisingly in a western-style wedding dress, came for a blessing. My guide, a Muslim mother of two, said, traditionally, wedding around here used to go on for at least seven days, like in India. The bride had 40 new dresses, and there were hundreds of guests. Families usually saved for weddings and special feast after childbirth. The government tried to reduce wedding days to a maximum of 3 days and a maximum of 100 guests, but that had not worked.

Over 50,000 years ago, this area was part of the Aral Sea. But since the sea disappeared, as the place was at the bottom of a depression, water level here was very close to the surface. Because of this, although surrounded by deserts, this area produced a lot of cotton and rice. Germans introduced vegetables in the country only in the last century.

Over a cup of coffee, my guide eloquently took me through the history of the country. In the early 20th century, abandoned by the other Europeans, Uzbekistan had turned to USSR for support. This resulted in access to secular education. As USSR prospered, so did Uzbekistan. But now, in mosques, women could not pray, at least not with the men. I asked her how she felt about this. She said it was not right, but most women were happy to be away from the mass gatherings of men. At least they could gossip!

Kalta Minor, the large colourful blue tower, stood by one of the inner-city gates. 29m tall, it was supposed to be a minaret, but only one-third complete. The story was Khan wanted to build a minaret higher than any in Bukhara. The architect, considering it against the rule of the country, escaped, leaving his work unfinished.

The Royal Palace, Kunya Ark, dated back to 5th century. Inside a fortress, were mosque, arsenal and royal residence. This palace had a harem right until the 1920s, guarded by eunuchs. View of the old city from its roof, especially of the inner city wall, was sumptuous. City walls protected from occasional incursions by tribal raiders but also ensured keeping the slaves. In medieval times, this city flourished in the slave trade.

In sweltering heat, we sat under a tin shed for our lunch. A school bus came with children in their uniform on their history tour. They queued in an orderly manner for ice creams before sitting on the same table with me. I asked them their names. After replying, they asked my name, and where was I from? When   I said from India, their lady school teacher said 'Oh, the place of Raj Kapoor'. My guide said Bollywood cinemas were most popular in the country.

In front, next to the stalls, several women danced to traditional music. Soon a few passerby men joined them. Hardly any women, except the older ones, wore head covers and many had only knee-length dresses. Dancing on the street to Uzbek music were common. Marrying more than one woman was forbidden by law since the last century. Women here had four months of maternity leaves, and after 3yrs of age, children had a free daycare.

We walked under an arch to the city's tallest minaret, Islam Hoja Minaret, built in the old style but only a century old. The guide suggested I should try to go to the top when I had time for the view. I decided to come back early in the morning as it was closing for the evening.

She said although communist ideology forbade religion, Soviets respected artistic and scientific legacy of Islam. After WWII, they restored much of the country's Silk Road sites. Mosques and mausoleums were rebuilt, and madrasas were reopened. I asked what happened since the breakdown of the Soviet.

Then she added - 'life became hard. State support has gone for ordinary people. If you wanted to prosper, you need to have a private business. It's easier for younger people to adapt, but the older generation is struggling'.

Near one of the four city gates, named Darvaza, Bachtscha, Palawan and Dascht, I saw a craftsman working inside his small shop. I walked down to his work area with the guide. He came and sat next to us, mopping his brow. He offered us coffee from his flask while he took a break. Same age as me, he was doing metal work on an open fire to make souvenirs. It took about two weeks' labour to make a large piece, which, if he was lucky, sold for only 70 dollars. Like others, he asked me where I was from. And after hearing e answer, the same comment - 'Oh Raj Kapoor was from there'. My guide smiled and then told me in Soviet mes, he would have retired with a state pension by this age.

Next day I returned to Islam Hoja Minaret as it opened. I carefully climbed up its very narrow, steep orkscrew spiral stairs, mostly in the dark except for occasional sunlight coming through small openings on very floor. It was tricky, but once I was up the 56m, view of Khiva town itself was not as good as from the palace oof. It was too high. I could only see the roofs of the buildings. But beyond the outer city wall, the desert spread s far as I could see - magnificent. Coming down, bordered on dangerous, as people were now coming up. There vas hardly any place to wait and let them pass by. Luckily, no obese people had ventured up!

Smiling, I came out of the minaret and walked around the beautiful city by myself.

Next day a car journey of 450 km through the Kyzyl Kum desert to Bukhara. A beautiful wide road between he dunes. Air conditioning inside makes you forget that outside temp was in the mid 40°C. River Amu Darya ame close by a few times. This 2400km river, coming from Afghanistan and Tajikistan, separated Uzbekistan rom Turkmenistan. Previously it used to end up in the Aral Sea, but in the last few decades with irrigation canals nd dams, it does not reach the sea anymore. We stopped for a brief lunch break. Taking the lead from my driver, I ordered for both of us traditional Uzbek bread and shish kebab with salads.

Bukhara We arrived in Bukhara, the city of good fortune, after eight hours. My B&B was in the old town. In the evening, I strolled its cobbled streets to the centre before arriving at Lyab-i-Hauz, a pond with the architectural ensemble of Kukeldash madrasa, Mosques, a lodging-house for itinerant Sufis stood around this pond within a park. Hauz meant pond, and this was the only pond that survived in Bukhara. Before the Soviet era, there were many such ponds and the city's principal source of water. But they were notorious for spreading diseases. Most were filled in during the 1930s. Lyab-i-Hauz survived because of its surroundings.

At one end of the park, I came across a statue of Khoja Nasreddin. Born in present-day Turkey 1000yrs back, he was renowned all around Central Asia and beyond for his wit, ready tongue and stories. While growing up, I had read the translation of his tales in Bengali. One of those riotously lovable characters, able to tickle the ribs of the world.

Once Nasreddin was invited to deliver a sermon.

When he got on the pulpit, he asked, '*Do you know what I am going to say?*' The audience replied '*no*'. He announced, '*I have no desire to speak to people who don't even know what I will be talking about!*' and left. People felt embarrassed and called him back. This time, when he asked the same question, they replied *'yes'*. Nasreddin said, *'Well, since you already know what I am going to say, I won't waste any more of your time!'* and left. Now the audience was perplexed. They decided to try one more time and called him back. Once again, he asked the same question—*'Do you know what I am going to say?'* Now the audience was prepared, and so half of them answered 'yes' while the other half replied 'no'. Nasreddin said, *'Let the half who know what I am going to say, tell it to the half who don't,'* and left.

I explored Bukhara next day in a guided tour. We started at Chashma-Ayub, or Job's spring near a mausoleum. Its name was from a legend that Job (Ayub) visited this place and brought out a spring of water by blowing his staff on the ground. The water of this was now revered for its 'healing qualities'.

Nearby was the 9th century Ismail Samani Mausoleum, an esteemed Central Asian architectural piece combining Zoroastrian and Islamic motifs, the oldest monuments in Bukhara region. Intricately decorated brickworks, had circular patterns of the sun, a common image in Zoroastrian art. The cuboid shape of the building was like Kaaba in Makkah, and its domed roof had typical mosque architecture. At the time of Genghis Khan's invasion, it was buried in mud from flooding, thus spared from destruction. It remained unknown to the world until rediscovery, excavation and restoration by the Soviet researchers in the early 20th century. Now, it was known as a 'Jewel Box' owing to its elegant yet compact size and mathematical proportions.

In a large empty square was the 9th-century Magok-i-Attari mosque, on the remains of an older Zoroastrian temple. The mosque itself was destroyed and rebuilt more than once, only its south facade survived with an exquisite underground level, excavated in 1935.

We walked under massive walls of a fortress, The Ark of Bukhara. Then we entered the place, on a hill, through an impressive gate. Built in the 5th century AD, this was more than a fortress and included a town of various royal courts. While we were by the Royal Pavilion where the Khans met his commanders and ordinary people, on the stage a rehearsal was going on. Men and women in colourful clothes sang and danced. President of Bangladesh was expected later!

After watching the rehearsal, we walked to 19th-century Chor Minor, a building with four marble towers, for ritual and shelter.

Nearby stood Bukhara's grand minaret, Kalyan Minaret, known as the Tower of Death. According to legend, they executed criminals by throwing them off from its top. But the role of this minaret for centuries had been for the muezzin to call out people to prayer. Architect, Bako, designed the minaret in the form of a circular-pillar brick tower, narrowing upwards. This beautiful 45.6m tall minaret could be seen from well outside the city over the flat desert plains.

Next to it stood grand the 16th century Kalyan Mosque. It could hold twelve thousand people. Two hundred eighty-eight beautifully curved pylons supported multi-domed roofing of the galleries encircling its courtyard. The courtyard ended up in a portal to maksura, the main chamber with a massive blue cupola on a mosaic drum.

Opposite the square was the Trading domes (Taqi), under which was a bustling market. Next to it stood two 16th century madrasas, each competing with others for beauty. At the square, as I was taking photographs of the minaret with the grand mosque, about two dozen of tourist police turned up for a change of duty. I asked their officer, a lady if they would mind if I had photographs with them. She looked at me and said- 'Amitav Bacchan country'. And then she nodded with a smile - obviously from the younger generation of Bollywood fans!

People inhabited the region around Bukhara for at least 5000 years, and the city has existed for half that time. On the Silk Road, it had long been a centre of trade, culture, and religion. History of Babur connected this city to Indian Mughal dynasty. Al Qumari, a 10th-century physician and scholar from here, taught Avicenna, the father of modern medicine - so much history.

At the end of the tour of this fairy-tale city, in an alleyway, I came across Synagogue of Bukhara. According to ancient texts, Israelites had travelled here as traders during the reign of King David in 10th century BC. Their number had gone down gradually since the establishment of Israel. And recently most of the remaining Jews had left for the USA after the dissolution of the Soviet Union.

My travel agent wanted to treat me with a dinner in Bukhara, to compensate for transport not picking me up in Urgench. The choice was in a restaurant or with a family. I chose the latter. In the evening, I arrived for a lovely home-cooked dinner with an Uzbek family. The wife was a GP. Medical care was free for all at all levels. But for sophisticated treatment like organ replacement, wealthy people often went to India. Her husband brought out their family album, and in exchange, I showed them photos of my grandchildren on my iPad. At dinnertime varieties of lovely salads, fruits and pastries arrived. I was full. I thought the family was vegetarian. As I prepared to leave, they brought delicious meat and potato soup, followed by kebabs! I was bursting at the end.

After breakfast the next day, I strolled in the old city, arriving at an art centre. There, a man and woman in a very relaxed manner were teaching painting and drawings to young children, now on their three months summer holiday. I saw an old man, turned out later to be two years younger than me, playing chess. I was never good at chess, but I loved it. I asked if I could play. He had me checkmate in five moves. Then he asked his eleven years old granddaughter to play against me. She also beat me, although I showed more fight this time. For her victory reward, I showed her and the other children animal photos and videos from my travels. Later I saw the old man teaching the children intricate chess moves too advanced for me!

Later we drove 15km from the city to brand new Bukhara railway station, only two years old. While waiting for my first bullet train journey to Samarkand, to most people's surprise, a few women fully clothed in black burkas and with a full face covering turned up. I had not seen women dressed like this in my last few days anywhere in Uzbekistan. The train whizzed through at 220km per hour. Opposite and next to me were three women in full burka. Soon another woman came and asked me, in English, if I minded seating with the family of three Uzbeks on the other side so she could sit with her friends. I obliged and asked her where they were from. I learnt they were from Pakistan on tour. Men were in the next compartment. Now the men were not there; she was happy to talk to me - a man. She asked me if I had seen the recent Bollywood film 'Three idiots' by Amir Khan, and what I thought about it.

The Uzbek family of parents, with their teenage son, was also surprised at the full burkas. Like most young people here, the boy could speak English and wanted to chat. Learning I was born in India, he said his grandfather told him his forefathers worked together with architects from India. I had also heard from the guides that many Uzbek monuments were built with the help of Indian masters from 6th century onwards. They brought marbles here from India on the back of elephants. By the time it took to chat with the family, the train had sped through 260km and in an hour and twenty minutes we reached Samarkand.

Samarkand   Along with Bukhara, this is one of the oldest continuously inhabited cities in Central Asia. Excavations unearthed 40,000yrs of human activity dating back to Upper Palaeolithic age. Founded in 7th century BC, Samarkand was conquered by Alexander the Great in 329 BC, at that time known by its Sanskrit name, Markanda. Samarkand was the centre of Islamic studies and birthplace of Timurid renaissance. The secret of papermaking was obtained here from the Chinese prisoners, leading to the foundation of the first paper mill here, then spreading to rest of the Islamic world and soon to Europe.

Samarkand, a modern city at 705m, surrounded by mountains on all sides except the south, had a lovely breeze most of the time. This made the mid 30°C heat here bearable.

We drove towards Mausoleums of Amir Timur. On the way, in a junction of boulevards, was a massive statue of Timur. A century after Genghis Khan had conquered Samarkand, following a revolt in 1370, Timur made the city capital of his Timurid Empire.

The architecture of the mausoleum of Amir Timur was the precursor and model of many future Mughal
mbs, including Taj Mahal in India. Inside a one-cupola azure fluted dome, this octahedral building had a lofty
amber with intricate decorations. Onyx slabs with refined paintings covered the lower part of its wall. Arches
d the dome above were decorated with gilded and painted marble stalactite cornice. Ornately carved
adstones inside the mausoleum indicated location of the actual tombs in a crypt directly underneath the main
amber. There along with Timur's families, was his teacher's tomb.

mur earned a reputation as a patron of arts. In contrast with cruelty, he showed his enemies; he showed mercy
ward those with special artistic abilities. He spared the lives of artists, artisans and architects to help him
autify his capital.

Ulughbek Observatory in Samarkhand, built in the 1420s by astronomer Ulugh Beg was one of the
est observatories in the Islamic world. It was destroyed in 1449 and rediscovered in 1908 by the Russians.
ilt on a hill, it was a cylindrical-shaped and 30m high with a sextant in the middle of the building. Ulugh
g's Zij-I Sultan, published in 1437, listed around 1,000 stars. Ulugh Beg determined the length of the year
365d 5h 49m 15s, only an error of +25 seconds, making it more accurate than Nicolaus Copernicus's. He
o determined the Earth's axial tilt, still considered accurate – a genius.

Next, we went to the Bibi Khanym Mosque. Timur wanted this place to be the largest mosque in his
npire. During its building period, he led an invasion of India. There he plundered many cities, including
lhi. In Delhi alone, in two weeks, he massacred over 100,000 people. During a fight there, he was
punded in one leg and limped the rest of his life. He became the Timur, the Lame. By the time he returned
om India, the mosque was almost complete. But Timur was not happy and wanted it to be larger where all
e male residents of Samarkand could pray together. He died before it was finished. After destruction over
e centuries, in 1974, the Uzbek Soviet Government started its complex reconstruction.

Now four minarets stood at outer corners, with four more majestic minarets flanking portal arch
the entrance. The main domed building of the mosque was not yet completed. In the middle of the
urtyard stood a marble stone pedestal, a huge Quran stand.

Next to it was the Siyob bazaar, the largest in the city. I wandered around its stalls. A lady gave me a
mple of the famous fresh-baked Samarkand naan bread - most delicious. While waiting under the shade
a tree for our driver, I had time to talk to a few men waiting for their bus. Soon, two women tourist police
ined in. I asked about Uzbek society's attitude toward women. One lady said in the Soviet-era women
d more freedom. In Freedom Square in Tashkent in the 1960s, on one day, over three thousand women

took out their hijabs and burnt them publicly. Since 1991, following 'Independence' from Soviet, however, attitudes have gone backwards for women.

She said now in the country women can be doctors, engineers, but only work as secretaries in the Government offices. They were not allowed to hold Government offices or stand as a member of the parliament. One man said it was Islamic tradition. Other lady replied it was a Muslim country, not an Islamic country. Then she challenged the men – you talk about the Islamic tradition. Our religion forbids drinking alcohol. Why, then, drinking is so common around by men? I asked one man if he had any daughters. He said they had a son aged seven, and a daughter aged 5yrs. I asked - do you think your daughter could one day become president of this country? He said the way things were going; we are running backwards. It was lovely to be able, as a visitor, to discuss the social issues openly with people, including the women. Soon their bus came, and we thanked each other and left.

Next, we visited the ancient city of Afrasiab. Russians carried out the first archaeological excavations here in the late 19th century and more actively during the 1960-70s. This site was occupied from 500 BC to 1220 AD before the Mongol invasion. After walking around the ruins of the ancient place on a hilly grass mound, I visited its museum. It contained many retrieved glazed pottery and other artefacts. But most interesting were the uncovered frescoes. Famous Ambassador's painting was discovered in 1965 when local authorities were constructing a road near the site. Now preserved in the museum, this 7th-century art showed a Chinese festival and pictures of Samarkand, India, Iran and Turkey of the time.

From there, we drove to the famous Registan Square. Regarded as the hub of Timurid renaissance, th[is] was where people gathered to hear royal proclamations, heralded by blasts on enormous copper pipes calle[d] dzharchis. This was also a place of public executions. Three madrasas of distinctive architecture surrounded th[e] square, the 15th century Ulugh Beg Madrasa, the 17th-century Tilya-Kori Madrasah and the Sher-Do[r] Madrasah. In the wall of the Sher-Dor Madrasa, known as the resident of the lions, symbolizing power, illustrated leopards with the sun on their back with a large swastika. Indian master architects had left the[ir] marks in many buildings around the city.

As in some other places, while visiting some stalls nearby, I ended up with medical consultation with a lady sta[ll] owner. My guide must have told I was a doctor. She was worried about her 14-year-old son's growth. After talkin[g] to her, I found nothing worrying and reassured her. The lovely lady gave me an Uzbek hat, and even though [I] insisted, she refused money from me.

Next, we visited the marvellous site of Shah-i-Zinda ensemble. Over twenty mausoleums and other ritual buildings of 9th-19th century, competing for magnificence, outside and inside.

Name Shah-i-Zinda, meaning 'The living king', was connected to a legend that a cousin of Prophet Muhammed was buried here. He came to Samarkand in the 7th century to preach Islam. According to legend, he was beheaded for his faith but didn't die. He took his head and went into the deep well in the garden of Paradise, where he was still living.

Outside the complex, I sat on a bench with ice cream with my guide. A man came from the nearby souvenir shop and spoke to me in Bengali and had a chat. Soon, I realised he was a personal security guard of the Bangladeshi President who was due to arrive shortly – the President was following me!

On our way back, the guide said although the majority of the population of Samarkand were Muslims, there were Russians, Ukrainians, Poles and Germans who were mostly orthodox Christians. Russians conquered Samarkand in the mid-19th century. Over the year they had rebuilt most of the city and populated it with the artisans and craftsmen from across its empire.

We sat with the driver for a cup of coffee. I learnt while plundering Genghis Khan was hated, Amir Timur, who built the architecture in Samarkand, was seen as a national hero. The guide added, between the 14th and the 17th century there was huge interest in the various aspects of science, more so of astronomy in the country. These stopped from the 17th century with more conservative Islamic empires.

The driver was in his sixties. He added, translated by the guide - older generation regretted breakdown of Soviet republic when ordinary people were better off. But he admitted in the last few years of Soviet-era, supplies in the stores were pitiful. The younger generation was now happy to be independent. But both agreed life for the rich had become easier, and ordinary people were struggling harder. By the end of the tour, I thanked them profusely. Next day on my bullet train to Tashkent 310km distance, they served free coffee and pastry. By the time I finished, we were reaching Tashkent.

I truly enjoyed Uzbekistan and its people. Everywhere was spotlessly clean. When you see in a small town like Khiva, a toddler walking to put a wrapper in a bin several meters away from his mother, who was chatting to someone else, you can see the source of civic sense. People were very friendly, welcoming, and easy and open to talk. But the rise of conservative religion and gradual suppression of civil liberty such as of equality of women in the society worried me for its future.

Kyrgyzstan

June 2019   Bishkek   From Tashkent, we flew over low green hills with the views of distant snow-capped peaks and then over the vast plains to Manas airport, 30 minutes outside Bishkek.

The guide drove through vast agricultural fields and said the main economy of Kyrgyzstan was agriculture, which they exported to Russia and China. There were gold mines, but because of a treaty signed in the past with the Canadian and Chinese companies, foreigners made 67% profit and the country only 33%. Education was free at the school level, but the classes were crammed. Teachers earned only around 150 dollars a month, same as doctors in the hospitals. House rent in the city cost almost twice that per month. Health care now, apart from minor things, had to be paid for and was expensive. Relatives begged in market places for their near one's treatment, especially for cancers and heart diseases. Doctors either moved to private work or left for Russia, for better pay. Since 1991, unemployment in the country was over 20%.

Kyrgyzstan's history before the Russian empire was of swamps with many nomadic tribes. Russian emperors wanted to have a barrier outside of Russia, against the advancing British Empire north through Afghanistan.

443

Bishkek looked a run-down city. Tired Soviet-style houses crammed the places. For an unknown ason, the young guide wanted to show me the local market. It looked in a sorry street, especially coming om Uzbekistan. He warned me several times about the risk of pickpocketing. In the fruit stall, I met a lady ho ran the booth with her 24-year-old daughter. The daughter trained as a nurse, but because of low pay, ow worked as a shop assistant. Outside the busy market were boxes for donation for people needing eatment, with members of the family standing by. Beggars crowded the market entrance. From there, alking by the street next, I noticed several seedy-looking massage parlours with lurid posters. The guide id, unfortunately, like begging, prostitution was now common.

I walked up the steps of the Museum of Modern Art in a massive park. Inside was mostly empty. There ere many paintings of the Soviet era. In one hall were interesting photographs of Lenin with school ildren and young girls in their uniform walking through school gates. Free education, including those for e girls, was introduced in the country under the Soviet Republic as early as 1920.

In front of the building, in a flower garden, facing the Ala-Too square, now stood a statue of Manas. A rgyz national hero of the 10th century, like Amir Timur in Uzbekistan. Airport, streets and monuments were med after him. Now warlords seemed to be the flavour around this part of the world! Lenin's statue, which ed to stand there, has been moved to the back of the building. Across the city, a new mega-mosque funded Turkey was almost complete. Now the country had more mosques than schools. Fundamental Islam replacing mmunism?

We stopped by the Victory square. An eternal flame and statues remembered victory over Germany WWII. On my way to the hotel, a massive presidential palace stood behind high walls and barbed wire. med guards patrolled outside. There have been already three 'revolutions' since 1991 against the corrupt d nepotistic presidents.

Beyond the palace, a busy mall and a cinema with an enormous billboard were showing scenes from ar Wars. Next to the pavement were rough sleepers.

After checking in, I walked to a busy square opposite Grand National Opera and Ballet hall. Children n around the fountains while adults openly drank alcohol. Later I returned to the park by a volleyball court. layed for a while with six teenage boys and three girls, one of them in burka but without face cover. One the girls was the best amongst all of us.

In the evening, I found a restaurant serving traditional Kyrgyz food. The place was busy with families. I dered Beshbarmak, a national dish of horse meat boiled in its broth and served over homemade noodles with rsley - different. Some women came here wearing burkas while others wore skirts. Most of them drank cohol - strange.

Next day I took a drive to Ala Archa National Park, for trekking. On the way to the mountain, I talked the same guide. His father was a professor of physics. Their grandparents lived with them. They had a larg agricultural farm outside the city. He added his grandparents regretted the breakup of the Soviet Union whe everybody had a job, a house, healthcare and free education. His parents were not sure. They thought the was now more freedom, though life was more challenging if you were are not a businessman with hig connections. Usually, the youngest in the family looked after elderly parents and lived with them after marriag Older ones left, a few months after getting married. The guide himself was looking for an opportunity to find job in Europe or the US.

Ala Archa National Park Through gorgeous mountains and rivers, we arrived at Ala Archa. Then we trekke through coloured junipers, archa, above the gorge of the Ala Archa River. Ala Archa had 20 glaciers and ! mountain peaks, highest at just under 5000m. We first walked through a wooded valley, then up a challengir rocky outcrop for about 200m.

Soon we were walking by beautiful flowering meadows with gorgeous views all around. Then trek furth up through another tricky rock face and from there down to the site of two smaller rivers, Adygene and Ak-Sa originating from the glacier's melting waters and then joining Ala Archa. So far, we have trekked for 4 hours. Son trekkers went higher to establish camp before attempting to summit a peak.

It was wonderful to be back in the mountains again, only if I had more time and was younger! On the wa back, we sat in a beautiful meadow and had snacks and drinks. The guide said only last winter, in the opposi mountain, park's camera had photographed snow leopard.

At Manas airport the next day in the departure lounge, I saw a sizeable group of young Indian men and women. They were going back to India on summer vacation from their medical college studies in Bishkek. I learnt Bishkek had six medical colleges. Kyrgyzstan was among the top choices for medical studies abroad by international students because of the low cost. The entrance was non-competitive, and the price was much less than in private colleges in India. Currently, Bishkek had over 2000 Indian medical students. Interesting - not a bad way to help repair Kyrgyzstan's economy!

Volunteering in Ulaanbaatar and Northern Mongolia
Adventure travel near the Siberian Border

June / July 2019

Flight from Bishkek to Ulaanbaatar took only four hours. On the plane were several Mongolian primary school children. The teacher said they have been to Bishkek for a talent contest. One of them had won a cup!

Ulaanbaatar The local co-ordinator met me at the airport. Two other members of our team, both female surgeons from the US would arrive later. On the 17 km drive, Ulaanbaatar (UB) looked a busy post- Soviet city, with many apartment blocks, tired buildings next to brand new glass-fronted buildings, wide roads. We would work for one week in UB and another week in northern Mongolia.

Mongolia was six times larger than the UK but with only 3.17 million people. A country of herding people, now half of the population lived in UB. After checking in, I left for a stroll. Streets choked with traffic, with packed buses and trams. Very few litters, but many cigarette stubs scattered the streets. Later in the evening, the two US surgeons arrived.

Next morning, Sunday, we visited the hospital. Despite unimpressive gates and outside, the hospital interior was spacious and clean, but old. It was one of the country's leading teaching hospitals. After screening the patients for operations for the coming week, we talked to the local team in their coffee room.

Doctors and teachers earned here only around 300- 400 dollars a month. Our host, a surgeon with 15 years' experience, made only 700 dollars/month, including night and weekend on-call payment. Mongolia had a basic health insurance system for all, but it excluded many conditions. Most people tried hard to get private care, which was expensive. School education was free in public schools, but they were crammed with students. People who had money sent their children to private schools. A two-bedroom house costs between 300-600 dollars per month according to the location and state of the building. Men retired at 60, but women at 55 and had their pension earlier if they had over four children.

Following morning at a formal reception, the hospital director, all the surgical and theatre staff lined up to welcome us. A man in traditional costume played a Mongolian string instrument.

In the next few days, we worked with the local team, mostly training and teaching residents. All doctors, trainees and consultants, worked here around 100 hours/week, reminding me of my NHS days in the 70s and 80s. Specialists on top of their 100 hours/week worked in private sectors and could make an additional 200-300 dollars/ month.

Operating staff coffee room had a free to use massage chair - excellent, especially for the doctors working 100 hours per week! I made use of that every day. Lunch break was always fun. A trolley came with an enormous pot of boiling soup, and everyone lined up. Then there was meat and other stuff -all free for the operating team.

In midweek, one afternoon, they invited me to give a talk at the National Cancer Centre. I talked about the current status of Breast Cancer management to about 30 surgeons, oncologists and residents. Walking back, I learnt from one resident escorting me that residents did not get any salary, only free meals and basic accommodation. It reminded me of Bolivia.

In the evening they took us to the National Theatre, a beautiful building in the city centre. We watched a fantastic performance of dancing, music, contortionists and then a concert. An excellent combination of national and regional traditional music and dances in colourful costumes. Interesting to see so much vibrancy in their music and dance from its remote corners.

From the theatre, they took us to a Mongolian restaurant. Rest of the surgical team also arrived. We had a fantastic spread of meat of all kinds. And drinks and lots of drinks. I learnt Mongolians loved their meat in as many forms as possible. And they loved their alcohol even more. Mostly vodka, but anything would do. Some got drunk at the end of the evening. At least a chance to relax after a 100 hrs/week of work!

After work, on other evenings, I did teaching for the residents. Whole surgical team, including the consultants, attended.

At the end of the week, a short thank you ceremony. Then we were on our way to Murun in the country's north, about 800km distance.

Travel through Mongolia   We drove in two cars. A team of seven from UB surgical team was coming to Murun with us, three on a well-deserved annual holiday and others to work with us including two ladies, one a senior surgeon and other a resident. We went through UB traffic for about an hour before getting on the road to Murun.

We drove through beautiful countryside with rolling green hills with vast green pasture with occasional Gher (Yurts) in the meadows. Herds of cows, sheep, yaks and horses grazed on the green.

After driving for nearly 8 hours and 370 km, we stopped at a campsite. Two previous herd owner brothers had sold their herd to start this campsite. We sat together for our dinner of boiled or roasted meat with fat on bones of sheep, cows and horses, with bread. There was toasting with vodka every few minutes. After the first toast with vodka, I toasted with my bottle of water for the next hour. By midnight we slept four people to a room on bunk beds. The toilet, a hole in the ground, was across an enormous field, 100m away. Fortunately, it did not rain in the night!

Next morning we got up early to walk to a nearby collection of springs. Clear water came out of the soggy ground on the slope of a hill, forming the springs down below. All of our team drank the spring water and filled up their bottles. Apparently, this spring water cured diabetes! About fifty horses in the pasture next to the spring checked us out.

After a breakfast of last night's leftover meat, we drove for over 400 km through stunning mountain road before arriving in Murun at 1750m by lunchtime. This small provincial town had a population of only 40,000 people and was the only hospital with surgical facilities for 170,000 people of Khovsgol Province.

ovsgol bordered Russia and was just less than half of the UK in size. Mountainous terrain here had over 4
illion livestock.

We had a brief coffee break in Murun in a small coffeehouse, with books on shelves and playing
aditional music - a lovely place to stop. The shop assistant worked in a primary school on weekdays and
as keen to practice her English on us.

Soon we drove another 100km to Lake Khovsgol for sightseeing. This freshwater glacial lake was
8x38 km in size and 262m deep. It contained 2% of all freshwater in the world. Famous Lake Baikal in
beria was only 200km from here. They nicknamed Lake Khovsgol its younger sister.

An adventure trip in the Mongolian mountain

next to the Siberian border

As we arrived by the lake, our Mongolian colleagues asked if we wanted to go for an adventure trip to a
ve site. My US colleagues and the coordinator stayed by the lake. As it was only Saturday and we were not
arting until Monday, I said 'sure'. My rucksack with the winter clothes remained with my US colleagues as I
ought we should be back in the night.

I could not get out any more details of the adventure as we rushed to a junkyard of cars. There we changed
o a 1970s Russian minibus. On the mountain road, this would be apparently more suitable than their four by
urs.

Like its driver, the bus looked old, with broken door handles and so on. None in the team had been to the
ve before. One guessed it was at least 140km each way by car. Then a 5km walk up and down to the cave in the
buntain. We should be back by Sunday late afternoon. Too late to change my mind as we were already on the
ad!

Soon the Russian car drove, making groaning sounds all the way. We left the asphalt road for a mountain
ack, full of puddles and bumps because of the last night's rain. After about an hour of driving, we could see
e beautiful Khovsgol Lake down below our route on the left. My colleagues said in the winter, the lake froze,
d it was easier to drive over it than through the mountain.

After driving with a view of the lake for a while, we went through narrow dirt tracks and swamps. Several
all stream crossings were on the way. At a distance stood Ghers, separated from each other by hills. Each
er had large herds of sheep, cows, goats, horses and yaks. We slowed down before a group of yaks crossing the
ack with their cute spring babies.

448

After driving for about four hours, we reached a village of about ten houses. We stopped here, and from its only store, I bought biscuits, nuts and water. Our city adventurer colleagues had not realised we might need to eat in this long journey! We have not had anything apart from snacks in Murun since our breakfast.

We drove again. By now the sun was going down and in the mountain the night came early. The team had not thought about what we would do in the night! Driving through mountain terrain was now getting dangerous. The driver was a lovely 77yr man, travelling with his 72yr old wife for their 50th anniversary to the famous Shaman cave for the first time. He stopped by a small hut by the track and walked inside.

He came back and said they had given him the direction of a village where one of his relatives lived. He might provide us with shelter for the night. It was in the next village, about 3 hours away. Now driving through pitch-black darkness was getting perilous.

Night shelter in the rain with a Mongolian family   After a few hours, we reached the tiny village. The driver took us next to his relative's house. As soon as we got inside, it started pouring down with rain. It was 11-30pm. The family had only two rooms. They kindly gave us their places to stay for the night and some Mongolian tea and butter, which we had with our biscuits. It was almost midnight by now. In the larger bedroom, the wife slept on a small bed with her 7-year-old daughter, and the two women of our team slept on the other bed. Rest of us slept on the floor in the other tiny room on mattresses and blankets provided by the family. Man of the house slept by the porch!

This was Mongolian hospitality, opening their home to an unknown bunch of people to take shelter for the night. There was no question of any payment.

We got up before 5 am, and after tea and biscuit left for the road again. After last night's rain, the journey was now more difficult with the track full of soft mud. Streams we crossed were now more like torrents. Our driver stopped by isolated houses and Ghers on the way to find someone to guide us rest of the way. From one place, a 15yr old boy, on his school holiday, joined us as our guide. We drove through wet meadows, forests and muddy swamps. The minibus was now getting stuck in deep mud almost every 100m. We needed to get out and break a few sturdy tree branches to put in front of the wheels. Then, as the driver started the engine, we pushed the bus over the deep mud.

449

After about 5 hours on the road since this morning like this, the car finally refused to go any further. The Russian car was strong and sturdy, and I don't think any other car would have made this far on this road! We were now in a swamp of thick mud.

Some guessed it was 5km to the cave from there. But our young guide said it was probably 2km each way. We walked through ankle-deep mud, then through a jungle. After crossing a few streams, we were in the middle of a beautiful flowering meadow by a small forest.

The young guide was walking with me. I learnt that his secondary school was only 40 minutes' walk each way from his house beyond a hill. Some days he took a horseback ride, which was quicker. The school had about 60 students. Primary schools for every two or three villages had about 15-20 students. I asked him what he wanted to do when he grew up. He wanted to be a singer. I asked him to sing, but he was shy.

Dayan Degereki Shaman cave   Entering the forest we could see through the tall trees, traditional ceremonial scarves, khatta coving a hill opposite. Out of the forest, we could see Dayan Degereki cave almost halfway up a hill. After about 500m of a steep climb, through loose rocks in the last section, I reached the cave entrance. The forest between the mountains, with meadows on either side, looked enchanting.

I looked down and saw our driver and his wife were slowly coming up too. Through a narrow entrance, I dropped down inside the cave on a wooden ladder. I was now by the famous Shamanic religious site, believed to be the oldest in the country, from about 7th or 8th century.

From there, through slippery rocks, I crawled through a small hole into the adjacent smaller cave. It was dark and cold. Some of my colleagues crawled through narrow tunnels to another cave higher up. They had head torches, but I didn't. It was slippery and pitch-black dark. With no head torch and planning to operate the next day, I decided against going any further. The driver and his wife joined after a while. It was their first time to this site, as was for the rest of our team.

Shamanism was practised in Mongolia and its surrounding countries, at least since the age of recorded history. Shamanism was an all-encompassing spiritual and social system of belief that included medicine, religion, reverence of nature and ancestor worship. Central to the theme were activities of the intercessors between the human world and the spiritual world. Along the way, it was influenced by and mingled with Buddhism. During the socialist years of the 20th century, it was repressed, but now was coming back.

Dayan Degereki cave on the Mongolia Siberia border, even during the communist regime, was continuously worshipped. Interestingly, shamanism shared the same symbol of a swastika as in Indian Hindu religion.

After spending a while there, we returned to our car around midday. Our guide boy sang beautifully on the way back. After a few pushes and prod, we moved the car from the mud. But after about 200m, it gave up. The driver opened the engine and asked our team to get water from a stream down the gorge. Luckily with water refreshment, the car started. We reached the house of our young guide and dropped him back there with a big thank you.

Most houses and Ghers I noticed on this journey had a solar panel and usually a satellite dish. After a few hours, we reached the village where we rested the night before. We had lovely Mongolian soup and snacks made in the same family's coffee shop. First proper food after almost 28hrs! We loved it.

Soon drive again way back. Going through the same route, drier now with the sunshine, we came across a Gher about 500m from our track. I asked if it was possible to visit and see the inside of a Gher. Our minibus left our route, and we arrived by the Gher. But the driver pulled away quickly. He said there was a sign outside the house showing they have a newborn baby - and visitors should not come.

Now we were driving through near darkness. All the passengers at the back, including the driver's wife, were fast asleep. From the front passenger street, I kept talking to the driver as best I could with my sparse Mongolian words- if only to keep him awake. This man had been driving for over 24 hours! I did not want him to doze off on this tricky mountain path. After about another three hours' drive, the car again started showing its age and needed a push from the back a few times. After a while, its headlight then started going off and on. One of our colleague, a thin one, had to sit by the driver holding a torchlight when the headlight went off.

By one am we reached back in Khovsgol. I could not have enough words to praise and thanks for the 77yr old driver. He had driven for about 27 hours on the dangerous mountain with only a few hours' sleep on the floor. He had then walked and climbed to the cave - all to celebrate their 50th anniversary! Always with a smile, such a lovely man. And the old Russian junk too had served us well.

After changing back to our cars, we returned to Murun and checked in our hotel by 3 am!

Murun   After an early breakfast at 7 am, we left for the hospital, in time for the usual welcome meeting with the local hospital team and management.

Three of us, with the help of the UB and the Murun team, screened and then operated for the next few days. There were many children who came for surgery. As usual for discharge planning, I asked their parents, all nomads, how far had they travelled. Nonchalantly some said 300km and others said only 100km. Our medical colleagues said in the next few months in the winter, when the temperature dropped below -40°C, these places were inaccessible.

One late afternoon, after work, they took us to ancient Deer stones site outside the town. This Bronze Age gravesite had megaliths carved with symbols -many of the stones dated between 2500-4000 yrs. The name came from their carved depictions of flying deer.

Carved on granite or greenstone, some of them looked fresh in colours. A few of the stones were 2-3m high while most were of 1-2m. Several had fallen and lay on the ground. Only recently, the site was protected.

For some reasons amongst many children I operated in Mongolia, there were many girls, unlike in other places. As my usual routine, while I saw the children in the clinic, I let them draw some pictures for me while I talked to their parents. In Murun, one mother brought two of her daughters, seven years and three years old. The seven years old had drawn a flower for me and given to me in the clinic. Two days after their operation, I saw both sisters in the morning ward rounds and said to the mother she could take them home when she wanted. She was happy as they lived only 100km away. In between my cases, the operation theatre nurse asked if I could go back to see the family before they left. I arrived at the ward to find the 3yrs old had a drawn a picture for me with her handprint and wanted to give it to me. I gave her a hug.

In the middle of the week, our 77yrs old driver came for his operation and had his surgery!
In one afternoon, I arranged a symposium on Breast Cancer Awareness for the community health workers of the province. About 50 attended, some coming from far distances and we had a lively interactive session.

An evening in a Gher

On our last day in Murun, the hospital director invited us to his brother's home for dinner. We drove for about 15km in the late afternoon amongst hills through a dirt track. In the middle of nowhere, between the mountains, was a Gher and some small sheds. His elder brother, the same age as me, was head of the family who was disabled after a stroke and was in a rusty wheelchair. He welcomed us inside the Gher and offered us homemade yoghurt, butter, snacks, and various kinds of meats and meat soups with bread. With plenty of alcohol to go around.

Two old men, him and me, had a lovely chat about life in Gher in the middle of nowhere in the mountain in the winter months. A traditional Gher was a portable, round tent covered with animal skins. For at least 3000 yrs. Gher has been a distinctive feature of nomad life in Central Asia. Inside their Gher, eight of us and their family of seven fitted comfortably. In the centre, by a large pole holding up the roof, was a heater fuelled by dried animal dung. They used it for cooking and for keeping the place warm when the temperature dropped around -45°C in the winter.

There were four young children in the family: a one-year-old and three other between 4-9yrs of age. The older ones were interested in my iPad, and I showed them animal photos. While others continued toasting with

vodka every ten minutes, they dragged me outside to play. The baby wanted to come too. I carried him on my lap. Outside we played hide and seek between the Gher and the animal sheds used for the calves.

Soon the lady of the house called us to join her to watch their animals coming back from the hills. The family had over 1000 animals, including yaks, cows, sheep and horses. As they came down and passed us, the lady, with the help from others and us, herded the milking cows in a large pen. They had about 60 milking animals, and they did it all by hand. As they milked the animals in buckets, older children carried them down to the Gher.

Later we sat outside the Gher and spent a lovely hour talking, drinking warmed fresh milk and vodka, of course. Children dragged me again to play hide and seek around the Gher. Soon it was time to return - a memorable evening with the nomad family and experiencing the famous Mongolian hospitality.

Ulaanbaatar Next morning three of us we took a flight to UB as the rest of the UB team would spend a few more days around Murun. I had a few more days in UB.

I enjoyed walking its busy street and arrived at the vast Sukhbaatar Square in the centre of the city. It was named after the Mongolian's revolutionary hero Damdin Sukhbaatar shortly after his death in 1923, fighting the occupying Chinese army. This square's name was changed to Genghis Square in 2013 in honour of

Genghis Khan, considered the national hero of Mongolia. Genghis Khan was the founder of Mongolia after uniting many of the nomadic tribes of northeast Asia. Due to his exceptional military successes, he was considered the greatest conqueror of all time, and with his brutality, which left millions dead, a genocidal ruler.

In 2016, the original name of the square was restored. In the middle of the square, now stood a large statue of Sukhbaatar. A large colonnade monument had a colossal statue of Genghis Khan at one end. Mongolia had also created a giant monument in honour of Genghis Khan outside UB to celebrate his 800th anniversary of the coronation.

Mongolia's famous Naadam festival, a national holiday lasting five days, would start in a few days. This festival, celebrated across Mongolia, focussed on three traditional games: horseracing, wrestling and archery. Naadam was inseparable from the nomadic culture of the Mongols. All the finals of these games were held in UB. Sukhbaatar square, and other parts of the city now buzzed with people in colourful costumes who had travelled from the countryside for the week. Many of our UB colleagues left the city during this holiday for the countryside with their families.

From there I took a taxi to Gandan monastery a few kilometres away. A tall statue of Avalokiteswara in this 200yr old monastery was the largest in Mongolia. In this monastery, about Buddhist 200 monks lived. Like many other religious sites, this place was destroyed during the Stalin era and rebuilt in the early 1990s.

Walking back, I found a few trams going towards my hotel. Just to experience the local trams, I got up into one. But I did not have the right currency notes. The driver waved me in. One local in the tram took out his wallet and wanted to pay for me. But after thanking him, I got off at the next stop and walked.

In the evening, the UB hospital friends arranged a goodbye evening of barbecue and more drinks in a garden restaurant. We chatted like old friends and had a wonderful time.

Przewalski horses   Next day, I took a drive to Hustai National Park, 104 km distance. This self-financing ecology park and conservation area were in the Khentii Mountains on the western edge of the Mongolian steppe. At the visitor entrance in the hills, we took a guide, a 17yr old boy on his summer holiday. After driving several kilometres through the mountain track, the guide asked to stop. We walked through hills for a while before he pointed on the hill above at a distance - wild Przewalski horses. This endangered breed was the only breed of 'wild' horse in the world never domesticated. Only 400 horses remained in the world in the wild, in three national parks, including here.

Back at the visitor centre after having a delicious Guriltai shul, a meat and vegetable soup with fried noodles, I came outside to find an archery place on its grounds. I had to try, after all, I was in Mongolia! To

my luck, the second shot hit the bull! Rest of them hit the ground in front. My young guide was embarrassed as he could not hit the board after three attempts.

Intellectual (puzzle) Museum   On my last morning in UB, I visited the fantastic Intellectual (puzzle)Museum. On four floors were mind-bending collections of puzzles and woodworks, all made by the founder since 1990. It was an institution dedicated to curiosity, logic, riddles, and Mongolia's long history of puzzles. Tumen Ulzii, the museum's creator, was born to nomadic herders and would have followed that path had he not fallen in love with logic puzzles at an early age.

In this museum, over 5,000 puzzles and games were on view. They allowed visitors to fiddle with most of them. One turtle-shaped puzzle offered a prize of 100,000 US dollars if solved within a specific timeframe. In the museum's three decades of operation, no one has ever solved it.

Mongolia definitely grew upon me in the two-and-a-half weeks I spent there. Its countryside w picturesque in its vast emptiness. The country had such a rich history of art and music. People in rural are lived happily despite the harsh conditions they faced for most of the year. Most touching hospitality an friendliness, more so in the countryside.

Europe again A whistlestop tour

August 2019   During my hitchhiking Europe tour in 1977, I could not travel to northern Europe. I had run out of money. This tour would, I hoped, fill some of that gap.

Berlin Germany   I wanted to visit Berlin, now that it was one Berlin, to see what might have changed since my last visit.

I walked all day to its famous sites. The infamous Berlin Wall I saw dividing the city 42 years back, now was mostly gone. Only a section of the Wall remained as a visitor site. Underneath the wall was an exhibition about the destruction of Warsaw during WWII. It reminded me of the recent TV images from Iraq, Libya and Syria - history surely keeps repeating itself.

From there, it was only a short walk to Check Point Charlie. What a difference in four decades! In 1977, I had gone through this military checkpoint on a gloomy grey chilly afternoon with no smile on the faces of the American soldiers.

2019   1977

Now the place is used to take souvenir photos by the tourists. For a sum of money, locals dressed up as soldiers posing for effect. Next to the site now stood a massive McDonalds!

Brandenburg Gate, originally named as Peace Gate, was busy with tourists on both sides. Now I could walk through it to the other side.

From there I walked to the nearby Reichstag building, now Bundestag. Now it had an enormous dome built on its roof for the visitors. Last time, I was not allowed to go inside, this time I chose not to. Instead, I sat on the benches in the beautiful garden for a while, watching the flow of tourists. Then I ambled to the banks of River Elbe to sit on its concrete steps, the same place I had sat all those years back.

Through the city, I then walked by the State Opera house and Humboldt University. In vast Bebelplatz Square was a plaque remembering Nazi book burning here in 1933. Close by was a touching memorial of the dark episode. Under the ground covered by the glass, was a symbolic room of many bookcases - all empty.

By the riverbank, the new DDR museum showed through photographs and artefacts of life in East Germany, like what most of the west had in the 60s. From there, I walked by the Berlin Cathedral to Alexanderplatz, now a thriving shopping area.

In the evening I chatted with the usher, a young German. He was born in what was then East Germany, near the eastern border. He was only five before the reunification and had no memory of East Germany. His parents and families still lived there. According to him, since unification, the economy of the entire country had improved drastically. But rural areas of the eastern part were finding it difficult to compete with the larger corporations. All Germans now had a good health insurance scheme. But in areas such as where his parents lived, there were no doctors for many, many kilometres. Most doctors wanted to move to the prosperous cities in the west. He worried about them as they were getting older. His family felt the healthcare system was readily available and better in East Germany than now. But everyone hated the system for many other reasons. This confirmed what I had heard not so long ago from my German colleagues in global conferences.

After a brief visit to the small and compact Natural History Museum, I arrived at the fascinating Museum of Medical History, on the grounds of 19th century Rudolf Virchow's pathological museum. Virchow was well known for his contribution to medicine, including the first description of leukaemia, a triad of thrombosis, and many others. Showing three centuries of history of medicine, the most interesting place there was the hall with 750 pathologic-anatomical wet and dry preparations on display.

I learnt there another side of Virchow. He suffered from authorities because he had joined the German Revolution of the mid-19th century against the rules of the empires. He actively worked for social change to ht poverty and diseases. I read with interest one of his quotes - *'Physicians are the natural attorneys of e poor, and the social problems should largely be solved by them.'* I left the place inspired.

Above the stairs of the Pergamon Museum was a lengthy queue. I had visited its galleries in my uth, so I left. Potsdam Place near my hotel was only a busy shopping district.

Wide Berlin footpaths easily accommodated walkers and many many bicycles. But also there were any e- scooters. In the excellent underground system, there were no ticket barriers going in or out. But eryone purchased tickets - honesty pays.

People in Berlin were friendly and easy to talk. In an almost empty coffee shop, I spoke to the wner cum waiter, originally from Tunisia. I asked him how it had been for him settling in Germany coming om Africa. He said in Berlin, there were no issues, but a number of his native friends who had settled in e smaller cities are recently facing racial hatred.

In 1977 West Berlin, still under the Allied forces, was a great city, but you could feel the tension as u neared East Berlin. Then, I thought East Berliner was more welcoming than in the West. All these years ter, I found Berliners confident, friendly and easy to get on with. Not so much as to say -'Ich bin Berliner'- at would be fake, but I liked the city and its people.

openhagen Denmark   After only one hour flight from Berlin, I arrived by train to the central station on rainy evening in Copenhagen.

Next morning luckily the rain stopped. I walked by Tivoli Gardens, quiet in the morning, and then rough the cobbled streets of the charming medieval section of the city, Middelalderbyen. In a few kilometres, was by the waterfront, empty and quiet. Giant Gefion fountain stood by depicting the Norse goddess. I asked jogger if I was in the right direction for the Little Mermaid. He asked me to carry on for another kilometre. I alked by Kastellet, a star-shaped 17th-century fortress with a cute windmill in its garden. After a dockyard and offee shop, I arrived by a narrow island. From a distance, I could see the city's famous landmark.

ittle Mermaid   It was now drizzling with rain. The place was deserted. Shortly, I was by the statue. Based n Hans Christian Andersen's fairy tale of the same name, this bronze statue since 1913 had symbolised Copenhagen.

The weather, the beautiful mermaid and the choppy water, all made this fairy tale almost come true.

Standing alone on the rocks by the shore in the rain, I tried to imagine the stories I would make up for m granddaughters when I see them next. As the rain got heavier, I left her and jogged, time to time glancing ba to see if she had disappeared under the water. I dried myself with paper towels and warmed with coffee ar hot snacks in the coffee shop. The rain stopped soon. I returned to Little Mermaid. By now, the sun had con out. Two tourist buses had arrived, and the place was full of people. Little Mermaid now looked more like statue than a fairy tale.

I walked from there to Amalienborg, an 18th-century complex of palaces, with a museum. In its squar by a large statue of the royals, people gathered for display by the royal guards. I carried on and arrived a Kongens Nytorv. Sun was shining now, and in this cobble-stoned square, locals were setting up stalls. Close b in a narrow street stood the Guinness World Records Museum in an old building, the only one in Europe. Book of the same name were favourite presents for my nephews, and I had always checked them out befor wrapping up. The museum was filled with exciting records in sport, art, music, nature and science - fastes highest, strongest and many bizarre records. And that of the animal kingdom, too. I had a customary phot taken against the cardboard statue of the world's tallest man at 272 cm - good one hour of fun.

Then I wandered Copenhagen streets, a prosperous city and came across Stroget, the longest pedestrian shopping streets in Europe. Almost 80% of Denmark's economy was in the service industry, rest in exports of oil, technology and food. With excellent Government-funded health and social care for all, all citizens here had a high minimum standard of living. I learnt that the famous Pride festival was taking place this week. Around the entire city were posters, banners and flags, and many smaller events were taking place everywhere.

Soon I came by the old port near the beautifully renovated contrasting coloured houses in Nyhavn. The place was filled with people enjoying a relaxed atmosphere by the canal. Jaz music played, and people danced next to many small restaurants and cafe. I found a wok food shop and sat inside for my lunch. The place was full. A man came and asked if he could sit with me. Soon I found he was from Ghana. I talked to him about my visit to Ghana the year before. He had been living in Denmark for the last eight years and was a cleaner. His wife had come over five years back, and now they had two children. I found him eating his noodles with a fork and spoon. I showed him how to use chopsticks. Soon he mastered the skills, and we laughed. Two young girls joined us at our table. They were travelling from Bucharest and were here for the Pride week. We talked about my time in Bucharest in 1977, well before they were born. I told them about my memorable Easter egg experience at Brancusi Sculpture Park. They said although Bucharest had changed a lot since; the park had remained as before. After about half an hour of lovely lunchtime, we left each in our way.

From the canal by Gammel Strand, I boarded for a boat tour. We cruised through the city's many canals across important landmarks under ornate bridges. Some bridges were so low it just about allowed our boat to pass. The guide warned not to stand. He talked about the history of beautiful churches, castles, old listed houses and style of architecture of the city we passed. We cruised by newly built Royal Danish Opera House on the riverbank. Several modern Danish artists working together designed this fourteen-story building. Guide highly recommended a visit. Hundred thousand sheets of 24-carat gold leaf adorned its ceiling in the main auditorium. Sounded interesting, but I would not have the time. Soon we were by Little Mermaid. From the water, with hundreds of people on the shore behind the statue, in bright sunshine, it looked less mystique. We then cruised past the majestic Christiansborg Palace before boarding off.

Later, I walked back by Tivoli Gardens; the vast amusement park was now full of people. I have walked around 13-14 km today in Copenhagen, but it had been an enjoyable day.

Copenhagen Pride March   Next day, a Saturday, it rained for most of the morning. Late morning I walked to the city centre. By then, the streets were filling up with people in their colourful outfits holding banners. Copenhagen Pride festival was one of Europe's largest human rights and LGBTQ festival. Denmark was the first country in the world to recognize same-sex unions as far back as 1989. I arrived at a square by Stroget. Already full of people waiting for the Pride march to start. There, I had lunch in a buffet restaurant, the cashier and the staff all wearing clothes in various shades of the rainbow. On my table were young parents with their children who had travelled from neighbouring Sweden just for the festival. I bought from a stall, a pride bracelet, and put on my wrist.

Soon the excitement outside reached its peak, and the pavements filled up. Pride march from Frederiksberg Town Hall arrived. Over 70 floats and carriages, with colourful tableau and over 20,000 people dressed in rainbow colours on foot, many carrying giant rainbow flag over their heads, followed, singing and dancing. Crowds from the packed footpaths and balconies cheered and clapped.

I joined the march to express my respect and support for all people, irrespective of their sexual orientation, race or religion. We marched through the city's charming streets in an outrageous party atmosphere. After walking with pride for a while, I stepped out from the parade before it arrived at the City Hall Square. Named as Pride Square, the place was decorated with flags of all colours and filled to the brim with people. Music from various groups blared out. Later there would be concerts, dancing, and quirky fun events to follow late into the evening. The famous official Copenhagen parade after-party was free to all.

I was probably old for that and had an early morning train to catch for Sweden. I returned to my hotel.

Sweden   I left before 6 AM to catch a train from Copenhagen central station for Stockholm. Within a few kilometres, the train entered a long tunnel before going over Oresund Bridge, the longest combined road and rail bridge in Europe, opened in 2000. This 8km bridge connected Copenhagen with Malmo in Sweden. After reaching Malmo, I learnt rail service was not working on Sunday. In a replacement bus, we drove for Lund 40km distance.

The bus stand was near Lund's 17th-century university, one of the oldest and largest institutions for education and research in Sweden. University buildings dominated the area. There were only twenty minutes before getting into my connecting bus for the 620km distance. I quickly bought sandwiches and a cup of coffee.

I was glad in making this journey by bus traversing the whole of Sweden instead of a five-hour train journey. Although this would take double the time, it would allow me to see Sweden's countryside. Our bus moved through towns and villages stopping at near-empty railway stations, dropping and collecting a handful of passengers. A cloudy day, but I loved the beautiful view. Village houses were all neatly laid out, but surprisingly in a midsummer morning, hardly any people anywhere. Even in the backyards of the homes or nearby playgrounds, not a single child was playing.

We stopped after about three hours for a forty minutes break. This tiny town also was empty. Next to the stop was the town's swimming pool, the only place to get something to eat nearby. On a Sunday during summer school break, there were only a couple of children and two adults swimming in the pool. I asked the lady at the cafe why there were not many people around? She said it was like this. When I asked, it was in the middle of summer, so what was like in the bleak winter? She replied it was the same in the winter.

We drove again through Nordic forests interspersed with serene lakes and large agricultural fields. After 14 hours since I left Copenhagen, by the time we arrived in Stockholm, it was raining.

Stockholm   Next day I explored Stockholm on foot. I walked to a small island, the city's core 13th century Gamla Stan, one of the largest and best-preserved medieval city centre in Europe. Walking its cobbled streets in medieval alleyways was like venturing in a giant museum. The place was full of facades with cellar vaults and middle age frescos, restaurants, cafes, and handicraft shops in quaint buildings. Its narrow winding streets, with centuries-old buildings in many shades of gold, felt almost unreal.

After a while, I reached Stortorget square in the centre of Gamla Stan, the site of Stockholm bloodbath in 1520 when a Danish King massacred many Swedish noblemen. Following revolt and civil war after this, the Kalmar Union was dissolved and was the beginning of an independent Sweden. Around the place were picturesque Stockholm Cathedral and Riddarholm Church. But what interested me was the Nobel Prize Museum next to it.

Nobel Prize Museum   Inside, the museum was filled with pictures, donated artefacts, telling stories of people who all contributed to the greatest benefit to humankind. Alfred Nobel of Sweden, a chemist, invented smokeless military explosives and was a major arms manufacturer. It shocked him to read his obituary in a French newspaper - *The merchant of death is dead*. It was Alfred's brother Ludvig who had died! Alfred lived for eight more years. The article shook Alfred about how people would remember him, motivating him to change his will, allocating 94% of his assets, to award the Nobel Peace Prize.

There were joint winners of the first Nobel Peace Prize. Swiss Jean Henri Dunant for founding the International Red Cross and starting the Geneva Convention, jointly with the French pacifist Frederic Passy, founder of the Peace League. Wilhelm Rontgen received the first Physics Nobel Prize for his discovery of X-rays.

A fifteen minutes slide show and then twenty minutes guided tour took us through history and interesting articles donated by the Nobel winners or by their families posthumously. In the main hall, from the ceiling on a conveyer moved large cards detailing every winner, but not in any chronological order. In one room, there was an exhibition going on about Martin Luther King Jr, awarded the peace prize in 1964. After the tour, I explored the place again by myself.

There had been so far nine Indian Nobel winners over the years, mostly in science. Nobel peace prize had sometimes been controversial and criticised. No better example of this was than the one awarded to Henry Kissinger, US Secretary of State, for negotiating a ceasefire in Vietnam in 1973. Two Nobel committee members

d resigned in protest as he had played a prominent role in the Vietnam War since 1969. He was also behind
e policies of a military coup and giving the green light to dictatorships in many South American countries. He
d pushed for US support for the Pakistan army during its genocide in Bangladesh war of independence in
71. Le Duc Tho of Vietnam, the joint winner with him, had refused the award. He had stated that there was
real peace in Vietnam.

Only another person who voluntarily declined the Nobel Prize was Jean Paul Sartre in 1964. Awarded the
terature Prize, he had stated, '*A writer must refuse to allow himself to be transformed into an institution, even
it takes place in the most honourable form.*'

There had also been significant gender disparity in awarding this prestigious award. Of over eight hundred
inners since 1901, only less than two dozen were women. Despite these, Marie Curie was to date the only
erson awarded Nobel Prizes in two different sciences, Physics in 1903 and Chemistry in 1911. Linus Pauling
as so far the only person to have won two unshared prizes in separate areas. He won the Chemistry Prize in
954 and the Peace Prize in 1962 for his activism against nuclear weapons.

After a fascinating couple of hours at the museum, I sat in its coffee shop and indulged in traditional
wedish Princess cake with coffee.

From there I walked past a crowded narrow alley, only 90 cm wide at its narrowest, to reach the Royal
alace. I watched from outside and was not interested in exploring its over 600 royal rooms of the armoury, royal
ostumes and decor. Soon I was by the Riddarfijarden Bay. I sat there on the steps by a monument, watching
he flow of people on this beautiful bay.

After grabbing a Toast Skagen, a delicious spread of prawns on sauteed bread and fries, I took a boat
rip in the afternoon. Stockholm was on Sweden's east coast, where freshwater Lake Malaren flows into
Baltic Sea. Stockholm spread over an archipelago of fourteen islands. People had settled here since 6000BC.
Vikings built Stockholm around 1000AD. We cruised upon Lake Malaren, now busy with water sports,
wimming and fishing. I couldn't imagine that being a freshwater lake, in the winter, it froze completely and
became the favourite site for winter sports.

In the evening, before going out for my dinner, I chatted with the young receptionist. I found Swedish
people loved their sports, mostly outdoor and winter sports. Healthcare model here was like Denmark.
Education, including up to PhD level was free, and students at the university also received a bursary. An
Indian student arrived at the reception from Delhi. On his first day out of India, the young man looked
overwhelmed. He sought me out because of my look. I went with him to dinner at a nearby place. We
talked. He would start a postgraduate course in two days. He loved trekking in the Himalayas and always

wanted to ski. I told him in a few months from now; he would have ample opportunities for that in Sweden.

Next morning, I walked via the bay area to Djurgarden Island, a few kilometres distance. On the way, there were options for E-scooters or E-bikes. I did not want to risk testing my balance, instead leisurely walked by the bay in its festive atmosphere.

Even before reaching the island over a bridge, I could see the large copper roof building with the stylized masts of the Vasa Museum. Inside, the Vasa Ship stood from the keel to its top, on six levels. Vasa sank on her maiden voyage in 1628 and was salvaged from the seabed in 1961. The fully restored ship, 69m long and 52m tall, ornamented on its outer walls with its colourful sculptures, looked mighty impressive.

Great King Gustaf of Sweden in 1600 was one of the most feared rulers in Europe. He wanted to build a navy ship that would be the strongest and best ever. When the building was almost complete, Gustaf visited the boat. He told the builders it was not good enough yet. He wanted it to be even stronger, with more cannons and more decks for more soldiers. Builders and the architect, scared of the King, did not dare to tell him it would make the ship top-heavy and may sink.

A few months later, with thousands of people gathered around the shoreline, King waved a flag, and the ship sailed amongst cheers. But only after 1000m, a mild wind tilted the boat slightly. It corrected itself and continued sailing. Within another 100m, with another gust of wind, the ship tilted completely. It sunk to the bottom of the ocean with all aboard, and it's valuable bronze cannons.

From there, I visited the ABBA Museum site. I did not go inside, instead had my coffee and snacks sitting out. Then I had my fun photo taken with the Swedish music icons before moving on.

Opposite on a hilltop was Skansen, the world's oldest open-air museum. With old-style wooden Swedish village houses, mills and stores, it showcased Sweden. It showed how Swedes lived in changing seasons, through their customs and traditions and, celebrations. From there, I strolled by the beautiful shoreline of the island. Many grey herons monitored the water from branches, while a few colobus monkeys kept an eye from a distance.

Sweden had been lovely, and its people were free-spirited, sport-loving and easy. But why smoking is so common in this modern country?

Helsinki Finland   Next day was a short flight to Helsinki, and then half an hour on a train to Central Station in the city. From there, a tram across the city to my Airbnb flat.

Later, I walked around Helsinki. Most of the streets were empty except around Central Station. Helsinki was a modern city with new skyscrapers and many tired old neoclassical buildings - probably B grade compared to Berlin or Copenhagen. I visited the 19th century Helsinki Cathedral. In this distinctive landmark of Helsinki cityscape, four smaller domes surrounded a tall green dome in the shape of a cross. From there, I walked down to the busy Market square by the waterfront.

On one side of the square stood Helsinki City Hall. Interestingly, they allowed visitors to attend council meetings here. Opposite this was a domed market with food stalls. But the open market next to the waterfront was where everybody gathered. The place was busy with vendors selling fresh fish, meat pastries, other food and souvenirs. I bought pea soup and freshly fried herrings. Nearby, a seagull swooped from nowhere and took the fish away from another customer. I sat under the safety of a tarpaulin roof by the shop and finished my lunch. I learnt the height of the season in this market was in October when the annual Herring market began. On the first Friday of every month, there were also displays of old American cars in this square.

From there, I took a boat trip around Helsinki archipelago. Called 'Daughter of the Baltic', Helsinki was on the tip of a peninsula and 315 islands. Gustav I of Sweden established this relatively modern city as a trading town in the mid-16th century. We sailed next to ornate red-brick Uspenski Cathedral and then between many small islands, most inhabited with modern buildings and then by National Museum and the imposing Parliament House.

Back at the harbour, I could not resist a bowl of lovely Salmon soup from the shop at the waterfront. Then I wandered across the streets of Helsinki. I was sitting on the steps of a church building where two construction workers came and sat nearby to have coffee. I spoke to them about their work. Young apprentice construction workers here made about 30,000 Euros a year. The five years trained manager with Masters made around 100,000 Euros/ year. Healthcare and education system was like Sweden and Denmark.

By the time I got back to my flat after dinner in a nearby restaurant, it was raining. I checked the weather forecast for the next day - heavy rain all day in Helsinki tomorrow. I looked upon the internet for options. Weather forecast for Tallinn, Estonia only 80km south over the Baltic Sea, was sunny all day tomorrow.

Tallinn Estonia   It was raining heavily in the morning in Helsinki. By taxi, I got to the ferry port and then into a crowded Viking Line Ferry for 2.5 hours sail on the Baltic Sea. Well before we reached Tallinn, the clouds were gone and a perfect sunny day lay ahead.

From the ferry port, I walked a lovely garden path to the medieval city passing through Viru gate, two towers on the impressive city fortification wall into Old Town. Tallinn's Old Town was one of the best-preserved medieval towns in Europe.

In its narrow cobbled street with many churches and spires, I came across the former KGB headquarters in Tallinn. In Pagari Street, this place, now a museum, had long been a symbol of former Soviet oppression in Estonia. Until 1950, in its basement, KGB imprisoned and interrogated suspected 'enemies of the state' before they were shot or sent to the Siberian labour camps. Basement windows were bricked up to mute the sounds of interrogations and torturing. Its prison cells now stood as silent witnesses of atrocious violations of human rights by an inhumane regime.

I then walked up through St Catherine's passage. On the stone walls, local artists displayed their paintings for sale. Top of the town at Toompea, also known as Cathedral Hill, was the residence of aristocracy until late 19th century. Nearby stood the impressive 9th-century Toompea Castle, now the seat of Estonian Parliament. Opposite a small square there stood Alexander Nevsky Cathedral, an orthodox church.

From there, I walked by Lutheran St Mary's Cathedral with an enormous dome to Kohtuotsa viewing platform. This crowded hilltop area offered a magnificent sweeping panorama of Old Town's rooftops and towers against the backdrop of Tallinn's modern city skyline. Tall medieval St Nicholas Church, dedicated to Saint Nicholas, patron of fishermen and sailors, stood proudly above all other buildings.

Back near the Orthodox Church, I found a small restaurant for lunch. I ordered Tallinn's famous seafood dish Vurtsikilu - spicy sprats, pickled with black pepper, allspice and cloves. While they prepared, I sat on a table outside, watching the flow of tourists. Soon the dish arrived, and it was fantastic.

Then I walked down to its lively market square. After a stroll, I walked up the steps to the oldest Apothecary, now a pharmacy, continuously running since 1422. While it sold modern medicine from the counter, its rooms exhibited ancient machines and instruments for making potions and pills. The old town had about 60 museums and galleries, not enough time for me to explore on a day trip.

At the square in a coffee shop, I talked to two Estonians who spoke English. Most people spoke Russian as their first or second language. Health care was free until 18yrs of age and then only for emergencies. Most people were self-employed and depended on the short tourist season for their income from homemade merchandise. People usually did not buy health insurance to cover routine medical care and hoped for the best.

Interestingly, they told me Tallinn had the highest number of start-ups per person in European countries. Known as Silicon Valley on the Baltic Sea, Tallinn was the birthplace of many international high-tech companies including Skype. It was also the headquarters of the European Union's IT agency and provided cybersecurity as NATO Cyber Defence Centre of Excellence.

From the square, I walked by the round and large Fat Margaret tower then to the intact section of the
d City defence wall. From the top section of the wall, was a beautiful view of the Old town with its churches
d other monuments. After spending a bit more time around Oldtown, it was time to return to port to
ch my return ferry.

On the ferry, I sat to drink my coffee. A few men joined me. I noticed they had bought flowers, alcohol
d many other everyday items, not something I expected tourists to buy. They said many from Helsinki
velled for shopping in Tallinn. It was cheaper there, even when the price of the return ferry was included,
d there was no tax in the port!

It was still raining in Helsinki in the evening. After a lengthy wait, I found a taxi. I heard from the chatty
y driver there was flooding in parts of the city, including in the metro today. Traffic was bad. She was
ppy to talk when I asked her about Finland. She gave me a brief account of the current social and political
up and history of Finland while she negotiated the flooded streets to my place.

Early the next morning, still raining, I took a taxi to the central station for going to the airport. The
ver was from Somalia and had come to Finland ten years back with his wife, fleeing from war. He said in
beginning, when a group of them as immigrants arrived from Africa; there were many incidences of overt
ism they faced. But it was now only subtle. He added, however, life was definitely better than in his war-
n homeland, and prospect for their children was a lot better.

During my brief visit to Denmark, Sweden, Finland, and in Estonia, I found the Nordic people were
s complicated, on the whole very polite and helpful and easy-going. I thoroughly enjoyed my time here.

akow Poland   Arriving in Krakow, I soon left for a stroll around the main square in Old Town, the
h century Stare Miasto, the largest medieval town square in Europe. Renaissance Cloth Hall, Sukiennice,
y remaining part of old Krakow Town Hall, stood as its centrepiece, once a major centre of international
de. Now inside its arched hall, were hundreds of gift shops and merchant stalls and on the upper floor,
Sukiennice Museum held a permanent display of 19th-century Polish painting and sculpture. Its cellars
ce housed a city prison with a medieval torture chamber.

At the end of the square stood gothic 13th century St Mary's Basilica. As I walked across, a trumpet
nalled on the hour from the top of the taller of its two towers. The tune broke off in mid-stream to
nmemorate a famous 13th-century trumpeter shot in the throat while sounding the alarm before a
ngol attack on the city.

I sat by the fountain in the square and watched people from all around the world strolling, while a fe travelled on decorated horse-drawn carriages. Soon I found a food stall and had a refreshing beetroot sou with vegetables and sour cream, Barszcz czerwony and sourdough rye bread. I reflected during the Na occupation of Poland; they renamed this square Adolf Hitler-Platz. Nazis also destroyed and stole man historical items from the buildings here.

A Royal Road once traversed the square centre, from Wawel Cathedral in the south to Krakow Barbica on the north. I wandered towards Barbican, a fortified outpost which once connected to the city walls. Barbica was now one of the few remaining relics of the complex network of fortifications and defensive barriers tha once encircled the Royal city.

Next morning, I walked through the main square to the south end of the Royal road by the Wawel Castl for my tour bus to the salt mine. Wawel Castle, the first UNESCO World Heritage site in the world stood atop limestone hill on the bank of Vistula River. My tour bus was due in 45 minutes. I found a coffee shop by the roa instead.

Not everyone spoke English in Poland, unlike in Germany or the Nordic countries, but always very helpful The waitress, a nineteen-year-old, was a first-year medical student and spoke English. She told me she loved neuroanatomy. Both her parents were engineers. She was doing a summer holiday work at the shop. Education including at the university in Poland was free, as were all aspects of health care.

Outside came a colourful procession of men, women and children singing and dancing, dressed in traditional costumes. I went out to watch. The waitress said they were from the mountain regions. This was the smaller version of annual Highlander's Folk Festival, held in Zakopane, oldest and biggest folk events in Poland.

Wieliczka Salt Mine   Soon it was time to get into my bus for the salt mines, 15km outside the city. I knew little about Wieliczka Salt Mine and had a three hour guided tour of the heritage site. It was beyond any expectation.

At its deepest point, it was down to 327m in 9 levels with 245 galleries. Now only 2% of the site was opened for tours. In Neolithic times, they boiled salt water drawn from nearby springs in clay vessels. In the following centuries, the secret of evaporated salt production was passed from generation to generation and evolved into a specialised professional group. Used as a preservative for meat and fish, salt became a means of payment in trade in the early 13th century. During the digging of the saline well, they accidentally found the first lumps of rock salt which soon led to the mining here.

In the early 20th century interwar period, salt production here became a profitable enterprise, with an annual output of 203,000 tonnes at peak times. Hundreds of people worked hard underground. The place was also used as a tourist attraction and a prime site for holding political rallies, conventions, anniversaries and social events. In 1996, industrial salt production ended here, and it became a tourist attraction solely.

We descended by 380 steep spiral stairs to the first level of the mine, 64m underground. Through tunnels carved into rock salt, we could only go down to its third level out of the nine. This 700 years old site was a wonderful example of human ingenuity and hard labour. Salt was brought up by pulleys run by horses kept underground and human.

The underground landscapes were unimaginable with saline lakes, beautiful underground chambers, commemorative statues and massive and unique St Kinga's Chapel. Saint Kinga lived in the 13th century and became a patron of salt miners. This chapel, 101m underground, 465 sq.metres in size, 11m to its ceiling, could hold 400 people.

Salt sculptures and carving of saints on its wall were everywhere. I stood in silence by a beautiful carving of Last Supper on one of its walls, with details beyond belief. Overhanging chandeliers and beautifully decorated salt floors adored the place. This chapel had been used for centuries till date for holding Holy Mass, and Christian family celebrations such as baptism and weddings. Anyone coming to Poland must visit this place.

After the tour, I sat outside for an iced drink under the shades of a tree with a guide. She was doing a summer job as a guide and was a primary school teacher. Her average class sizes varied from 15 to 30. The tour bus driver joined us. He was a Physics teacher in a high school. Both said pay for the teachers was poor in public sectors. He earned about 500 euros a month. His wife earned more working for HSBC Bank as a clerk. Both said although healthcare was free, waiting time for routine operations were long. He had been waiting three years for his sinus operation in the Government hospital. But a private operation for the same would cost him about four months of his salary, which he could not afford.

Back in Krakow, I was drawn to the city square in the evening, now throbbing with people. Food bars at the square were full. In a restaurant behind the church, I chose bigos, sauerkraut stewed with chopped sausage, cabbage leaves, mushrooms and onion with rye bread - delightful.

Auschwitz

Next day, we arrived in over one hour from Krakow to the busy car park outside Oswiecim town. By the entry office counters and its souvenir shops, people talked excitedly, just as in any other tourist destination.

Under a tree, the guides separated us into groups of ten. We walked under a bright sun towards a railway line and barracks with a barbed-wire fence.

Auschwitz I

Suddenly, everyone stopped. Pin drop silence from then on for the next three hours. In front was the infamous wrought-iron gate. Boldly carved above it - 'Arbeit Macht Frei' - Work Shall Set You Free. We were entering the Auschwitz I concentration camp.

This place was synonymous with the worst things human beings can do to a fellow human, on an ustrial scale. Nazis killed almost 1.5 million people, only because they belonged to a different race. st killed were Jews, but also included Poles, Hungarians, gipsies and anyone else Nazis wanted.

We walked silently inside some of its 28 two-storey blocks. Evidence of evil systematic deception at various ges, so that there was no panic until they entered the gas chambers, was clear. In early days, new arrivals at camp were photographed and recorded, until the numbers got too big to continue. Along the walls in the cks were lines of photographs of real human looking down at us, many children among them. Their faces wed apprehension about being in prison, but no real fear as they did not know what the heinous Nazis had nned for them soon after.

It was heartbreaking to see piles of people's last belongings. Huge stacks of suitcases, shoes, cups and wls and everyday items were now laid behind glass. Prisoners had thought they were just being sent away work, and one day they would return home soon. In another place were piles of spectacles, wooden legs and nan hair. Prisoners were told they kept these, for health reasons, until they had a proper shower and a anup. But to the Nazis taking away people's belongings and shaving their hair were another way of umanising them before mass execution.

The Soviet army entered to liberate Auschwitz on January 27, 1945. They found approximately 7,600 sick aciated detainees, left behind. They also discovered mounds of corpses, hundreds of thousands of pieces of thing and pairs of shoes, and seven tons of human hair shaved from detainees before their liquidation.

Block 10 was known as the Krankenbau or the hospital barrack. Inside its blacked-out windows, Josef ngele and Carl Clauberg carried out experiments on prisoners in the name of medical science. Mengele's eriments often involved twins. If one twin died, he at once killed the other to carry out comparative opsies - I shivered.

Block 11 was the camp prison within the prison. Here, guards came up with new and more horrific ways to ture prisoners who dared to rebel. Its basement contained the first experimental gas chamber, which they d earlier tested on the Soviet prisoners of war.

On the closed courtyard between Blocks 10 and 11, was an execution wall, the Black Wall, where prisoners re shot in early days. In walls of many blocks were George Santayana quotes - *'Those who do not remember past are condemned to repeat it.'*

Outside the blocks stood the single gas chamber of Auschwitz I and the crematorium. SS men to avoid panic t the prisoners unaware of what awaited them. Nazis lied they were going to another camp, but first had to undergo disinfection and bathe. After the victims undressed, they were directed into the gas chamber, locked in, and killed with Zyklon B, prussic acid gas.

After they were killed, other prisoners, forced to work on the threat of deaths, dragged the corpses out of the gas chambers and then brought them to burn in one of the three furnaces in the crematorium. Tears flowed down our faces.

Nazi guards and the officers lived within 100m of the gas chamber. To them, Auschwitz camp was like a small town, with their staff canteen, cinema, theatre and grocery store. Guards had their own sports teams! In a stone throw distance was a two-storey luxurious bungalow, occupied by Rudolph Hess and his wife with three children. While gas blew out 24 hours a day of the crematorium's chimney, Hess's wife, in a letter to her relatives in Germany, described the place as 'paradise'.

It was almost a relief of retribution I felt when the guide showed us the site of a gallow, halfway between the bungalow and the gas chamber where they hanged Rudolf Hess after Nuremberg trial.

Birkenau

We walked silently to the bus for Auschwitz II, Birkenau 3.5 km away. Birkenau stretched over 425 acres of a bleak, barren landscape, with lines of barbed-wire fences and watchtowers stretching off into the distance in each direction.

Nazis had realised soon that Auschwitz I was in a way experimental place. They wanted a more efficient way of killing Jews fast enough in terms of time taken and numbers. In Birkenau's vast extermination camp, Nazis industrialised killing. They built four gas chambers to dispose of as many Jews as they could quickly.

Most of Birkenau's buildings were destroyed in 1945 before the Soviet Army had arrived. Nazis had tried to hide the evidence. We walked by empty locomotives used to bring human for mass extermination. Then we walked around piles of brick and twisted metal where the gas chambers once stood. Each of its four gas chambers killed up to 6,000 human every day in Birkenau. About 1.1 million passed through Birkenau's gates during its three-year existence. Prisoners were sorted in a regimented process. They kept alive the healthy adults suitable for work while taking the remaining elderly, children and ill were taken directly to the gas chambers. chambers.

We came out of the place numb. Auschwitz was not, by any means, a museum but a nightmare journey through the worst horrors of human history, only 75 years back.

Zakopane   Tour to Zakopane next day in the south was by 2 hours bus journey from Krakow. After a 1.5 hour's drive, we stopped in a small charming village. All parts of the houses there, including the roofs, were made of natural, untreated timber sourced from a nearby hill forest. With gardens around the houses, the village looked like one out of a storybook.

In another half an hour, we arrived at the tourist town of Zakopane. A popular highland tourist destination, near the Carpathian Mountains and close to borders with the Czech Republic and Hungary. 90% of the tourists, here were Polish. In summer months, it was a loved family destination for hiking and relaxing, and by winter months, when the temperature dropped below -25°C, an ideal place for winter sports.

Outside Zakopane, we visited a small most unusual graveyard. Instead of the usual gravestones, here, artists expressed their art, mostly in wood, in memory of their beloved. Even the place of mourning was a site of beauty.

The famous International Highland Folklore festival in Zakopane had finished only yesterday. The hilly town was still buzzing with fun, dancing and music. During a coffee break, I chatted with our bus driver. He was born in a village nearby. His father was a postman and mother, a teacher. He was one of three brothers and one younger sister. Traditionally here, the youngest, his sister, will look after their parents and stay with them once they retire.

Soon we took a funicular to the top of the hill with a beautiful view of the Tatra Mountain 2655m, highest in the Carpathian Range. We walked on the mountain, busy with tourists. The guide stopped us by a tiny shop. A man was selling Oscypek. We waited while he roasted a lump of smoked cheese on a flat iron pan on an open fire. We tasted some. This salted, smoked and roasted cheese made from Tatra Mountain sheep's milk was exclusive to this region. Known as 'baca', it was a traditional holiday cheese in Poland - wonderful.

We took a chair lift back to the town. During lunch, an American couple from my bus, travelling from Florida, joined me. They had been to Auschwitz two days ago. His grandfather had escaped death camp and immigrated to the US. Our discussion moved on to the ongoing systematic separation and death of children in detention at the American border with Mexico. To my surprise, they were a firm supporter of Trump in this action – a strange world!

After a while, I sat outside on a bench with my coffee, watching the flow of joyful people. Soon it was time to get back to the bus. Just as I was getting on the bus, I remembered I had left my bag where I sat earlier. I hurried back there. It was still in the same place.

From there we drove by the ski jumping sites on the hill. Poland had won a few gold medals in the Winter Olympics. Next, we stopped by a small, beautiful wooden church in the forest outside the town. This early 19th-century church, first in Zakopane, was made purely from wood. With its single-aisle, wooden sculptures, ornaments and folk glass paintings, it was quaint and beautiful.

On our way back to Krakow, when most snoozed, I spoke to the guide about Poland. She had a degree in history and spoke eloquently about the political and social history of the country. I learnt 98% of the population was Catholic. She agonised that the ruling rightist political party supported the church, and in lieu, the church told people to vote for them. She felt strongly against the church policy of trying to ban abortion, and of the law here that did not allow sexual orientation of homosexuality. She added, on the whole Poland was making steady progress economically, but there were many worries.

Back in Krakow, I returned for my last stroll in the evening at the main square. I did not know what to expect in Poland. I found it a wonderful country, with friendly, relaxed and outgoing people. Cities and even the small towns were spotless. Krakow had been one of the best cities I have travelled in a long while. Evidence of the influence of Catholic Churches was everywhere, but after all Pope John Paul II was born around here!

Slovakia

I found the bus I had arranged online for my 400 km travel to Budapest from Krakow, involved three changes, with only a brief time gap in between. At the bus station, I learned an express bus to Budapest took 4 hours less time and cost only 20 dollars. I booked on the express bus.

We travelled south, first towards Zakopane, and then entered Slovakia. The bus would traverse the width of Slovakia. We drove through mountain roads in Carpathian range with a view of High Tatra. This small country, with nine national parks and fourteen protected landscapes with steep slopes and narrow valleys, attracted adventurous skier from all over Europe.

We crossed many meadows, and several narrow streams and a few rivers, but not a single bit of plastic or any other rubbish anywhere. Our bus stopped at a long and wide valley by Hron River, encircled by a mountain chain. Banska Bystrica, in central Slovakia, a 13th-century small copper mining town looked picturesque. The driver said we had forty minutes. I walked to the main square and bought Oblozene Chlebicky. These open sandwiches with ham, salami, sausage, sliced hard-boiled egg, cheeses, cucumber and tomato looked delicious. But no way I could eat them in the moving bus without spilling. I sat in a beautiful garden to eat. I recalled in this place in 1944 the Slovak National Uprising took place against the German invaders.

Back at our mostly empty bus, I noticed two middle-aged ladies were now occupying the seats on my posite side, chatting and laughing. They looked like sisters or could just be friends. Soon they took out from ·eir bag a packet of round paper thin thing, the size of a chapatti. Then they happily munched through it and ·k selfies. It intrigued me. A while later, after they had finished eating, I asked them politely what was this ·ng they were eating. We did not understand each other's language, but somehow we communicated. One of · ladies took out an unopened packet and gave it to me. It read Oravsky hrad. She indicated I take it as a gift ·m them. I tried to say I only wanted to know what they were, but she insisted.

The crackers in the packet were paper-thin, slightly sweetened and delicious, a local delicacy. I ·ared the packet of eight crackers with fellow passengers. I made sure I had two myself. We all thanked ·em. After traversing through beautiful villages in Slovakia, we entered Hungary.

Budapest Hungary

After coming out of the metro in Budapest, I was looking at my papers for the hotel address. A lady ·me over to me and asked if she could help. When I showed her the documents, she said I was on the ·ght road, but the hotel was across the other side. As I waited to cross the heavy traffic, she came back. ·he apologised, saying she had made a mistake. My hotel was on the same side of the road, only a few blocks ·way. I thanked her.

Beautiful pictures of Buda and Pest on either side of the River Danube had fascinated me for a long ·me. Soon I took a tram and arrived by a busy three-way bridge on the river. Margit Bridge, longest of all ·he eight bridges between Buda and Pest, also connected to a narrow island on the Danube. As the sun set ·ehind the Buda monuments, and the lights came on, the cityscape on the riverbanks was most ·icturesque. Lights of the parliament building on the Pest side competed with the churches and castle on ·uda hills. River Danube was full of cruises, jolly with people singing and dancing on the decks.

I walked to the Margaret Island in the middle of the river, full of joggers. This small island was ·riginally known as the Island of Rabbits, later renamed after Saint Margaret in the 13th century. It had a ·elightful compact Japanese Garden. Nearby was a Centennial Memorial of 1973, commemorating the ·00th anniversary of the city's unification. But my eyes soon caught sight of beach volleyball next to an ·athletic track. I sat beside the court and at the end of a game asked if I could join. They were happy with it, and I played a game with them.

Returning to my place, I found a place for a decent dinner of famous Hungarian goulash. It was out-of-th worldly delicious, or maybe just I had a long day! In this busy restaurant, two guys from Holland joined me my table. One of them in his 50s and the other in his 60s. The older guy had also hitchhiked across Europe, li me, but in the early 80s. We shared stories of our travels of those times. Now, they were in Hungary after visiti Berlin, Poland and now Hungary in their caravan, before heading home. We had a lovely conversation before turned to world politics. I was pleased they too were appalled at the rise of right-wing politics in Europe a around the world.

Next morning I took a tram to the Parliament building. Opened in 1902, this gothic revival style building h been the largest in Hungary since its completion. Its 96m central dome referred to the nation's millennium 1896, celebrating the founding of this nation in 896. With its main facade facing the Danube, the place look majestic

Behind the building was Lajos Kossuth square. This reformist in 1836 had demanded a legal declarati of freedom of the press and speech. He had led Hungarians to rise against the Austrian Empire. In front of statue, there had been many massive anti-government demonstrations. In 1956, Hungarian Uprising agai

the Soviet-imposed policies here was one of the first major demonstrations against the Soviet control of t country. More recently, in 2006, the place had seen continuous protest against the Government for lying to w the election.

I took another tram to the famous Chain Bridge. Of the eight bridges in the city, opened in 1849, this w the oldest. Each of the bridges in Budapest had a different character and style. I walked over the bridge to Bu From there a funicular took me up to Buda Castle, on the southern tip of Castle Hill. Once a Royal pala the castle now housed the Hungarian National Gallery and Budapest History Museum. The museum, along w Hungarian masters' paintings of the country's battle against Turkish and Austrian occupation, held works Cezanne, Pissarro and Monet.

Baroque style houses, churches, and monuments surrounded its massive square and the quarters. View from here of the Danube and Pest on its bank was spectacular.

From there I walked to the scenic 11th century Matthias Church with an ornate 80m spire in Holy Trinity square. Inside the church, its ornamental galleries contained many sacred relics, medieval stone carvings and replicas of royal coronation jewels.

Spectacular Fishermen's Bastion stood next to the church. Its seven tall stone towers represented seven Hungarian chieftains who founded Hungary in the 9th century. This monument, built in the late 19th century to celebrate the millennium of the Hungarian state, offered the best view of the Budapest along the Danube. Unfortunately, the best spot here now belonged to a restaurant and was not open to the public. But there were enough stone steps in its 140m facade, to enjoy the glorious view with the magnificent Parliament Building on the opposite shore.

In the cellar, under one of its tower, was a small museum. As I came up its spiral staircase, a lady came asking for donations for feeding homeless people in Budapest. I had come across many scammers looking for money during my travels. But soon I realised she was genuine and we talked. She worked as a teacher in the local college. I learnt from her there were around 50,000 homeless people in and around Budapest. Although the unemployment rate was low overall, youth unemployment was high. Some of these homeless had previous decent jobs as teachers, etc. or worked in private companies. But because of ill health or other reasons, once they had lost their jobs, they could not get any pension until they reached retirement age. Government support was non-existent. Current Government policy only encouraged and supported who made money, not the poor. Her charity cooked food every morning and then used 26 feeding stations all across Budapest to help homeless people. I shared with her my experience of working for Food Bank in the UK.

At the end of the conversation, she asked me where I was from. When she learnt I was born near Calcutta, she greeted me in Bengali! She invited me to join their feeding station the next day, but unfortunately, I would not have any time during my short trip.

Later I spent the rest of the day walking in Buda before taking a tram to return to Pest. Like the night before, I saw many rough sleepers on the pavement or near the railway station. Now I had a better understanding of the issue.

Next morning a tram took me to the far end of Pest to the enormous City Park which was once a swamp and a favourite hunting ground. In the 18-19th century, it was transformed into a National Garden and was among the first public parks in the world. During millennium celebrations at the end of the 19th century, the spacious Heroes' Square was created with a 40m tall column statue of Archangel Gabriel holding the St Stephen's crown.

At the other end of the park, a big palace had a public bath. One hundred-year-old Szechenyi Bath was one of the biggest natural hot spring spa baths in Europe. Across the park stood the massive Vajdahunyad Castle with the City Lake at its foot. In the winter months, they used most of this 300-acre park for ice skating and other winter sports.

I could not resist taking an evening dinner and cruise on the Danube. I boarded just before sunset. After having dinner inside the deck, like most, I stood on the open deck. By now the lights had come on and the city buildings and the bridges shined. Next two hours was the fairy tale riverfront panorama with the lights on Buda Castle, Matthias Church, Fishermen's Bastion, Hungarian Parliament and the beautiful bridges. Most definitely a genuine treat for the eyes.

Volunteering in Kigali & with the Gorillas in the mist Rwanda

ptember/October 2019

nocide in Rwanda in 1994 had shocked me to the core. Fifty years after the holocaust atrocity by the zis, I had hoped the world had learnt a lesson. In Rwanda, Hutus, in only four months, massacred nearly e million Tutsis, 70% of the country's Tutsi population. The outside world failed to intervene.

I readily accepted an invitation to volunteer in Rwanda. A UK based charity, Legacy of Hope, set up the Rwandan ex-pats worked there on many projects. They wanted me to help the surgical team in Kigali h an increasing number of breast cancers in the country.

Arriving in Kigali, cleanliness of the city and orderly traffic was far better than I had seen in my ent travel in northern Europe. Later I met up with the only local surgeon dealing with breast cancer in ali University hospital. The large hospital spread across different levels on a hill was spotless, with decent ilities and welcoming staff.

My colleague surgeon was only 15yrs old during the 1994 Genocide. Hutu neighbours killed his ner, only because he was Tutsi. They spared his mother and the children because they were of a mixed e. The coordinator of the charity witnessed his mother butchered by the Hutus. He escaped death at the second himself. The Hutus had lined him up with a few others to kill with a machete. Some were already ed next to him. He was next in line when searchlights from a flying helicopter of the Tutsi's army fell on m. The attackers had dispersed, sparing him. Earlier his young son had gone out to play with friends and s lost. They did not find him for several years until a chance meeting far from their place. The boy was ying with some stray children. The father had spotted him from a distance. The man who butchered his ther was recently given a job in the firm of the coordinator.

nocide Memorial Museum   Next day I paid my visit to the Genocide Memorial Museum. It was heart-enching to watch the archives which included human remains, smashed skulls and bones and the weapons d. The museum featured video testimonies from the genocide survivors and the rescuers, documents and otographs of this atrocity. There were also photographs from the Gacaca courts. This traditional system of ice was adapted to fit the needs of Rwanda after the Genocide.

Along with a million butchered, hundred thousand women were raped, and Rwanda's new governme struggled to pursue justice on such a massive scale. Over 130,000 people were accused of genocide, war crim and crimes against humanity. The museum contained over one hundred perpetrator testimonies from Gaca court proceedings.

One hall had pictures of the children before their massacre. I could not stop tears flowing down on i cheeks watching these innocent faces photographed by their families, only a few months before they we butchered.

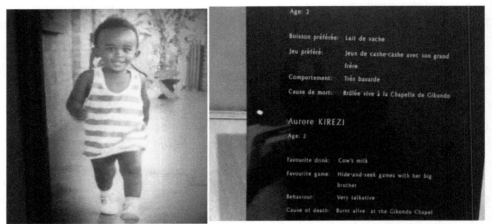

But the motto here was *'Remember, forgive but not forget and renew'*. The museum devoted a secti to education programmes, both on-site and in the communities to prevent future mass atrocities. In its groun were buried over 250,000 victims as a memorial for the nation. Impossible to believe how Rwanda had con through this genocide to become one of the most stable countries in Africa in only 25 years. One cannot b praise the nation for its achievement coming up from the bottom of the hell. Even after this genocide, promotes 'Ubumuntu Heart' - a single heart formed by two people embracing, connected to the Woi reflecting the concept of our shared humanity, expressed through empathy and caring for others.

Kigali   In the next two weeks, I worked with the surgeon at the hospital, offering the best support I could. Life expectancy at birth in Rwanda was 67 years, one of the highest in Africa. Remarkable on any account, considering where the country was only 25 years ago. Reduction of communicable diseases through clean water, vaccination and other preventive measures was the primary reason behind this.

But this also meant non-communicable diseases such as cancers were on the rise. Cancer awareness alone was not good enough, without an easily accessible pathway for cancer management. Even more critical in a country such as Rwanda, where the majority live in rural areas. People were not only afraid of 'Cancer' but also of prohibitive costs involved in its diagnosis and treatment.

For a population of 12 million, only two surgeons were carrying out breast surgery in Rwanda, one in Kigali and the other in the north in Butare. The whole country had its only mammography unit in Kigali, only oncology unit in Butare and a radiotherapy unit in Kigali.

Rwandan health insurance system offered mostly free health care for the poor. But it involved upfront payment at all stages except in cases of emergency or basic primary care. A working village woman, after finding a painless lump in her breast, tries to ignore it for as long as possible. She carries on with her daily work, without which her family would suffer. If she went for medical care, at all stages, starting from her local hospital, consultation, tests, biopsy, all involved upfront payment - something her family could hardly afford. Then she is referred to one of the two surgeons in the country depending upon where she lived. Again, more costs added to the cost of her and her family's transport and accommodation in those places.

Once seen by the specialists, they would put her on a waiting list. I found this was often over a year. All this time, her cancer progressed, and by the time she had surgery, it had advanced to an incurable stage. No surprise in Rwanda, like in many African countries, over 60% of patients with breast cancer presented in an advanced stage. Now in developed countries, 90% of patients with breast cancer, survived beyond 5-10yrs compared to less than 40% in low and middle-income countries.

In Rwanda, almost 39% of the population lived in poverty and 16% in extreme poverty. Majority of these were in the rural areas but also in and around Kigali.

In between working at the clinic and operating, I did some teaching for the young surgical residents. I found that only 10% of medical students in Rwanda were women, and only 1% in surgical training. This was in sharp contrast to women in the Rwandan Society now. Over 60% of members of the parliament, now were women. In one morning, before starting work, the matron of the hospital arranged for me to give a breast awareness talk to the nurses at the hospital. On the same day after work, jointly with the local surgeon, I did a national TV interview regarding breast cancer awareness.

Unfortunately, apart from raising awareness, what was needed was a patient-friendly, and a joined-up pathway for breast cancer care in the country. Following requests from my charity and the Rwandan Government, I sent my detailed recommendation following my return.

During my stay at the hotel, I often spoke to the security guards. Two of them, one female, walked over two hours from their homes to come to work every day. The other two guards were luckier, having to walk only one hour each way to work! I found they admiringly looked at some construction workers at a building site nearby. I learnt construction workers earned here about 5 dollars a day, although seasonal. Security guards made only 1.5 dollars per day and had no food from the hotel. One of them had two children, 10yrs and 7yrs old. He could not send his older children to school anymore as they could not find the extra money each term they needed to pay for his school. The driver from the hospital, who was taking me to the hospital every day, said with over ten years' experience, he earned only over 4 dollars per day. Half of it was spent towards his only child's school expenses. Luckily, he got free health cover through the hospital.

In one evening, I was invited to Dining in the Dark - a unique evening organised by a local charity for the Blind Children. After arriving there before going into the dining hall, they blindfolded us. Then a volunteer held our hands, guiding us to our table. They served food, and we ate blindfolded. We talked to each other at the table without knowing who they were - a brief insight into the world of the blind. The charity organiser, Vanessa's fourth child, was born without eyes. Later I talked to her and mentioned there were a few UK based eye charities which she might like to contact. She came back to my hotel one evening, and we talked in detail.

At the end of the first week on Saturday, I got up before 4 am for over 2 hour's drive to Akagera National Park in the south-eastern part of Rwanda. A physiotherapist from Switzerland, on her first volunteering trip abroad, joined me. The driver explained we needed to leave early before the traffic closed. On last Saturday of each month, roads were closed in the country for traffic from 6-12 in the morning, for national cleaning day. Every citizen, including the president, cleaned the streets. This meant not only the cleaning got done but was also an incentive not to trash the places.

On the eastern side of the park, Akagera River bordered with Tanzania. The park had many beautiful lakes and swamps. We saw several Nile crocodiles and hippos in the Lake Ihema. The park had all big 5s, but we saw only many buffalos, a few giraffes and only three elephants. But there were other animals like baboons, impalas, bushbuck, etope, zebras and many birds.

From the park, the driver took us to a village pasture with Inyambo cows. These domestic animals with their long white horns, curved in the shape of a lyre, looked majestic. As we were watching them with the farmer, a young boy, about 10yrs old came over. He was very interested in my iPad. I let him take some pictures of his father with the cows and then showed them back to him. He was thrilled.

Then we walked through the villages. All the houses in the villages were brick built with a tin roof and built toilets outside. There was also brick-built Primary and Secondary schools nearby and Primary Health Centres. Everywhere around the village was spotlessly clean -very impressive.

On Sunday morning, we visited the Legacy of Hope's centre, outside Kigali. There they supported over 100 children of all ages. The charity looked after their feeding, clothing, education, sports and everything else. Most of the children were orphans and were housed with local families with the charity's support. Following the genocide in 1994, there were over 100,000 orphan children in the country. A resettlement programme of these orphans with the local families had reduced this number now to only around three thousand. Rwanda hoped to close all the orphanages in the next 2-3 years. It was beautiful to see the smiling faces of the children enjoying.

Later I went to the Campaign Against Genocide Museum in the Parliament buildings. It showed the campaign against genocide plan and told the story of the courageous men and women of the Rwandan Patriotic Force army, RPF. Finding that the international community and the rest of the world had abandoned Rwanda, leaving Tutsis to die at the hands of the Hutu genocide regime, bravely RPF launched the campaign to stop the 94 genocide. On rooftop was a monument of two soldiers with a machine gun who stopped the advancing genocidal forces. On its ground was a large monument narrating the story of rescue missions carried out by the RPF during the liberation war.

Kigali as a city, set within many hills, with its spotless clean wide boulevards, greenery and modern facilities could be the envy of any modern city anywhere in the world. One evening after work, I asked my hospital driver to drop me at the market. I walked around there before stopping for a cup of African Coffee and chapati, like a chapatti made of maze grain. In Kigali I had seen, over the last few days, hundreds of motorcycle taxis going all around its steep hilly roads. I wanted to try. I sat on the back seat of one. The helmet was loose as I had no Afro hair! It kept bobbing up and down, covering my eyes. But I absolutely loved the 8km ride back to my hotel. Hilly roads of Kigali were mountain biker's paradise. On the national cleaning day, young skateboarders frequented the place after the cleaning was over.

Following Saturday, I left for Ruhengeri. A spectacular two hours' drive through many hills, no wonder Rwanda was known as the country of thousand hills.

Everywhere, small towns or villages were spotless and with decent housing. Farmers worked on mountain slopes with no modern machinery in view. Many, including children, carried loads up the steep hills. Some pushed bicycles heavily loaded with goods. After a brief stop in Ruhengeri at 1860m, also known as Musanze, we left for Lake Kivu 50km away.

Lake Kivu Kivu Lake, one of the largest and deepest in Africa, lies between Rwanda and Democratic Republic of Congo, DRC. This 2700 sq.km lake with an average depth of 240m sits upon a rift valley which being slowly pulled apart, causing volcanic activity in and around it. It contained over 55 billion cubic metres of dissolved biogas at a depth of 300m. Recently Rwanda had started a large scale extraction process of the gas.

Lake Kivu along with the smaller lakes of Monoun and Nyos are subject to limnic eruptions, a catastrophic release of suffocating carbon dioxide triggered by volcanic activities underneath. This phenomenon, known as 'mazuku', recently killed over two thousand people around Lake Nyos. Kivu is 2,000 times bigger than Lake Nyos! Kivu was without Bilharziasis and as a result, popular for swimming and boating. We next drove through the spotless border town of Gisenyi and stopped by the border check post with Goma town on the other side in DRC.

The shantytown of Goma, recently infamous for Ebola, looked from another world. In another part of Gisenyi, people from DRC came in hundreds on foot with loads on their heads through a single busy checkpoint - only for a few hours to sell mostly fruits, vegetables and maize flour, into the local market next to the border.

I stood by a barbed fence separating Goma from Rwanda for a while. Goma with its collapsing shacks, dirty roads looked in stark contrast to Gisenyi on the Rwandan side. I wondered what these people who crossed the border daily from DRC to Rwanda, felt about their country with its ongoing violent history, and of still shielding many perpetrators of the Rwandan Genocide.

On our return journey, we stopped by a small market place by the roadside. Women walked from villages down the valley, carrying loads on their heads. There, women from spotless stalls sold onions, cabbage, tomatoes, avocados, carrots, pineapples, passion fruits and maize. I bought a few passion fruits and shared with my driver before setting off towards Musanze.

Gorillas in the mist

My visit to northern Rwanda was for the rare chance to see mountain Gorillas in the famous Volcanoes National Park. A chain of dormant volcanoes in Virunga Massif, including Karisimbi 4507m, the highest; Bisoke; Sabinyo; Gahinga and Muhabura in Rwanda, with others in DRC and Uganda, made up this national park. In the setting sun, with floating clouds above them, the mountains looked majestic.

We left at 5 am in heavy rain for the Volcanoes National Park. Even in this pouring rain, farmers wer walking to go to their place of work to start on time. We gave a ride to some of them in our car. We arrived at th visitors' site of the national park in Kinigi 2249m, as it was opening. Cold and wet, we were glad when a guide came and started the coffee machine. Soon other people began arriving. After cups of coffee and some snacks we had an orientation talk by a ranger.

Of only 1000 mountain Gorillas in the world, over 600 lived in the Virunga massif. On the Rwandan side twelve family groups of this endangered species lived. Family groups ranged from twelve to over thirty. The allowed only twelve groups of tourists, per day, to visit the gorillas. I was glad I had booked my permit a few months back as soon as I accepted the invitation to Rwanda. Each group of only eight tourists could visit one gorilla family for a strict maximum of one hour. No gorilla family came into contact with people for over one hour a day.

The ranger explained the protocol of keeping a minimum 2m distance from the gorillas and looking down if they approached us, never to run.

We left the park office in another car, one ranger and eight tourists in each. This morning there were only four groups. After half an hour, we stopped by the last village on the slope of the mountain. It was still drizzling. A single villager to each group joined us as the ranger's assistant, learning the tricks from him. With a bamboo stick in hand, we started our trek towards the jungle of the Mt Bisoke 3711m. I was glad that they had given us mud boots, as we struggled in ankle-deep mud, through potato fields between the eucalyptus trees.

On these lava slopes, vegetables thrived. Because of the slopes, all farming was done manually and separating the lava rocks from the soil must be hard work. After about 1 km journey upwards through the fields, we reached the outer part of the jungle, separated by a thick stone wall to prevent buffaloes charging inside the jungle. Here we waited. The ranger said the tracker inside the forest had not found any sign of the Gorillas. Heavy rain had wiped out all the marks from the day before.

We waited over half an hour to hear from the tracker. The ranger looking at the disappointed faces assured that a chance of sighting was almost 99%. Although two days back a group, however, left without seeing any gorilla.

The rain got lighter. Our mood also lightened when we heard the tracker had found something, but on the other side of the mountain. We walked for another half an hour through a thick bush of bamboos and trees in the mist. Soon the ranger heard from the tracker he had spotted the gorillas, but they were down in the volcano's crater. We laboured up to the crest, toehold to toehold, frequently slipping as our mud boots had no grip. But luckily the bamboo sticks stopped any dangerous falls. Helpful ranger assistants were always there to lend a hand. Going down to the crater was trickier. Soon we heard the gorillas had moved to another part of the crater. We carried on gingerly through the dense thicket of bamboos. Luckily the rain was now only a slight drizzle. Mist covered the entire place.

I was the last in our group behind the ranger's assistant. Although we were moving in a tight group, I could see no one else apart from him because of the dense bush and the mist. He suddenly stopped and then pointed to the ground - a big fresh gorilla poo with a pungent smell. He motioned I was near them. I had to give up my bamboo sticks so that the gorillas did not feel threatened. I followed him through a slight gap in the bush. Suddenly I was next to a massive Silverback resting only at less than 3-metre distance - it was uncanny!

Great David Attenborough, in his 1978 Life on Earth series, described his first meeting with a Rwandan mountain Gorilla family, as 'one of the most exciting encounters of my life.' In silence, we watched, and all snapped while the 208kg Silverback rested, occasionally yawning. On the other side of the bush, a mother sat cuddling her very young baby, protecting it from the light rain. Soon the rain stopped. She decided to have a lie-down, still holding on to her newborn baby.

A 2yr old baby came from nowhere and cautiously went to the Silverback and gently started scratching his daddy's back. Soon another mother, cradling her baby, came from the bush and sat right next to us - then she relieved herself before leaving us with her smelly poo.

In this Muhazo group were 14 gorillas including the single Silverback, eight mothers and five babies. Soon others in the group came to check us over. Teenagers showed their tricks on the branches of the bushy trees. One moment the gorillas appeared not to notice us and continue to play and eat the leaves, the next, they stared at us, checking us out. They walked right by us, brushing our legs with their black fur.

After a while, the Silverback sat up, yawned, ignored the baby next to him, and stood up. He then walked right between us to another clearing. He did not care for the 2 metres rule. He was the boss, after all! We watched these magnificent creatures in silence, but soon our allotted maximum one hour time with the gorillas was over. Reluctantly, we left them.

We returned through the muddy bushes, first up to the crater rim and then down towards the
ato fields. By now, the sun was up. I talked to a mother with a baby on her back collecting potatoes from
soggy field with her husband. Luckily they had harvested most of the potatoes a few days ago. But the
last night had ruined the chance of salvaging the rest. They were trying to get as many as out possible.

We returned through the muddy bushes, first up to the crater rim and then down towards the
ato fields. By now, the sun was up. I talked to a mother with a baby on her back collecting potatoes from
soggy field with her husband. Luckily they had harvested most of the potatoes a few days ago. But the
last night had ruined the chance of salvaging the rest. They were trying to get as many as out possible.

We walked to another village where our cars were waiting. In souvenir shops there, I bought two
illas for my twin granddaughters. Some tourists, who were staying overnight in the nearby lodges, were
ng to visit the Dian Fossey Research centre she had set up during her years in this area.

I left for Kigali after lunch. Coming back to Kigali after spending two memorable days in the
ntryside, and on the mountain, the city looked congested.

My impression of Rwanda was mixed after spending only two weeks there. The country had ma remarkable progress in its infrastructure, economy and health care compared to any other countries I had visit in Sub-Saharan Africa. And this was even without considering the destruction genocide caused only 25 years ba People were wonderful and friendly everywhere. I enjoyed talking to people of all ranks. It looked and felt s everywhere for men and women, even at night.

But there was vast inequality, not only between the countryside and the city but also within society. The was an open embracement of capitalism. Some are getting very rich quickly and enjoying all the luxuries. contrast, many others struggled to cope in about one dollar a day wage if they were lucky. There was arou 15% unemployment rate with no Government support, and almost 40% lived below the poverty level.

It was apparent there was considerable respect and fear for the authority, such as police, the army a the Government officials. I fear that this might sow the seeds of dictatorship in decades to come, if challenged. With the free promotion of alcohol and betting, lack of affordable education and complicated acc to healthcare, the situation was likely to get worse, unless challenged and changed.

Fall colours in Canada

October 2019 Toronto

I had just over a week between my trips to Rwanda and Sierra Leone. My daughter had recently moved w her family to Toronto for a year. Apart from seeing my granddaughters, I wanted to see the famous fall colo there.

I had been to Toronto a while back and found this modern city a concrete jungle. Strangely, having j returned from Kigali in Rwanda, I found the city not as clean.

Next day we walked through downtown to catch a short ferry to Toronto Islands, also known as Island. The Island was a group of 15 islands inter-connected by pathways and bridges. One could easily walk t place, only 5km long, no cars allowed - an excellent place for children to run around.

In mid-October, trees glowed with leaves in orange, red and yellow colours against a clear blue s Their images on the small lakes quivered in a gentle, cool breeze. Children ran around crunching colourful car of fallen leaves under their feet - a lovely day out.

On one evening we visited the Toronto Tower for our dinner. I had been there previously, but it their first time. We all marvelled at the view of Toronto below from the revolving restaurant at 355m. Ther walked down to the glass floor. After only a moment's hesitation, my grandchildren were lying on it, looking d 342m at the buildings and grounds underneath. They had no fear! I dared my son-in-law for an 'edge walk', a ha free walk on the 1.5m ledge outside the central pod at 365m, attached to a safety harness and rope. He grinned.

Next day another family outing to the quaint Black Creek Pioneer Village in the Toronto suburb. With restored 19th-century timber frame houses, an old printing press and mills within a forest, trees bursting out in fall colours, it was enchanting. The children loved running around until they came by the Border Leicester sheep beyond the fences, who did not look that friendly. Soon their attention was drawn to the stout Clydesdale horses and wanted a ride on the wagons pulled by them.

After spending a lovely few hours there, we walked towards the subway through the football fields. Hundreds of Canada geese were picking insects and eating grass. They completely ignored us until the children walked towards them when they moved only a meter or two. It became a chasing game for the kids.

Following day we drove north for about 2 hours to Peterborough. From there we went to Burleigh Falls. Boating was now closed for the season. But its forest had that sumptuous beauty of autumn, I had read and heard so much. Trees with leaves in green, orange, red and yellow looked as if drawn from a talented painter's pallet. I watched mesmerised as the breeze lifted and spun coloured leaves, then after letting them float for a while, dropped them gently on the ground, already a magical, colourful carpet of fallen leaves.

Burleigh Falls was a narrowing of the flow of water between the Lovesick Lake and the Stoney Lake, more of a cascade than a fall. The children loved the adventure of jumping between the large rocks by the falls.

We drove a few kilometres from there to the shore of the Stoney Lake in the Trent Severn waterway. Against the backdrop of blue waters of the beautiful lake, fall colours on the trees looked out of this world.

With the wind blowing from the lake, a myriad of shapes and sized leaves fell from the trees like multi-coloured rain in gold, red and brown - spellbinding.

We then walked on a forest path, some bushes full of ripe berries. I could not resist picking a few of them and put in my mouth. One of my five-year-old granddaughters immediately chastised me for picking wild fruits. She would not talk to me until I said sorry.

Next day, sadly. I had to return to the UK.

Death of a young humanitarian

October / November 2019 Sierra Leone

Arriving at Lungi airport, I stayed overnight in a hotel nearby. This area of over 30,000 people had no hospital. The nearest hospital was across an expensive ferry or 4 hrs by road to Freetown. Only one medic served this area, but only a few could afford the fee. I talked to the waitresses. They trained for three years in the college in an expensive course and then did a year of unpaid internship. After that, they earned about 2 dollars per day, more than many people around. Most lived with their families 15-20 km away in the villages and took a dangerous ride on the back of a motorcycle every day for their work.

With the former US team, we drove to Kabala. It was heartbreaking to see 4-5-year-olds nonchalantly carrying loads on their heads by the side of the street.

In Kabala in the late afternoon, all the staff came out to welcome us. Back to the same guest house, 2km distance, we had stayed last year.

After the usual triage on Sunday, we worked for the rest of the week at the hospital. From our accommodation, it was our daily routine to walk to the hospital and back. During our morning walk, we passed by children, collecting water from deep tube wells before going to school, while older girls washed pots and pan. But the older boys were mostly going for a run to improve fitness for their football in the afternoon! Everyone said 'Hello', and some came to shake our hands.

In the hospital, there was no electricity. With no light in the operating room, we managed with our headlamps. All the local staff were like old friends now, and always with a smile. Between the two surgeons, including myself, we carried out ninety procedures. Patients and their relatives were eternally grateful.

On the final evening was a thank you and goodbye dinner to all the staff from the hospital. Great evening and ended up with dancing till midnight.

Next day in Freetown, most of the US team left. With one of Sierra Leone born US ex-pat anaesthetist, I returned to the Police Hospital. All the staff welcomed me back as if a close family member had returned. I was delighted to see that slowly they had started doing some emergency and minor procedures in the hospital. In the next few days, this time mostly supervising the local two doctors, we managed twenty cases between us.

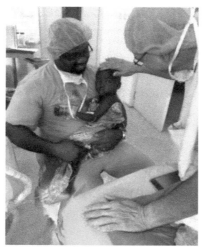

Sierra Leone recognised the contribution of the UN peacekeeping force during the civil war in many ws. In honour of the Bangladeshi troop who came, Bengali was an official language in the country, ough no one spoke the lingo! In gratitude for the corps from Somalia, every year they sent a Sierra Leone m of doctors and nurses there for several months to work. They had already assigned one doctor and a nurses from the Police Hospital to go there in April next year. They were worried.

At the end of the week, I ran hands-on 'Training the Trainers' and a 'Leadership skills' course for the f. They all appreciated it and thought would be valuable in making progress at their new institution and en they go to Somalia.

I left Sierra Leone on 11th November. Two weeks later, I had a shocking email to find that Dr Wouter, I t in Masanga a few months back, had passed away. On 11th November night, a lady with obstructed delivery come to Masanga Hospital from a long distance. By the time she arrived, she was bleeding from rywhere. Wouter had done a caesarean section. Unfortunately, the mother died later, although the baby survived.

Next day Wouter was running a course in another town. In the evening, he had a high fever. Initially, he thought he had contracted malaria again. But the fever had persisted, and he had worsened. From etown, in the next few days, they had transferred him by an air ambulance to his home country Holland. er eleven days in the ICU, sadly he had passed away from Lhasa fever. The other medic lady assistant, the :-year doctor from another country, had also contracted Lhasa fever but after two weeks in the ICU in her ntry, had recovered.

I was numb for days with the news of this young man's death who had truly devoted his life to helping others in a desperate situation.

Dubai   United Arab Emirates

January 2020

I had no intention to visit Dubai, known for its luxury six-star hotels, multinational businesses, convention cent
and skyscrapers, an artificially created place supposed to be a heaven for the 'haves' served by the 'have no

I was visiting my family in India. My niece, who I had not seen for ages, lived now in Dubai, with th
seven-year-old daughter. I had not seen her yet. I arranged a stopover for two nights in Dubai on my return journ
from India.

I was glad to be soon outside and away from the glitzy shops of the vast airport.

My taxi driver was from Pakistan, working in Dubai for the last eight years. We got talking, ignoring t
skyscrapers in the city, we passed by. He earned a lot more than he did in his country as a teacher. He share
room with seven others in downtown Dubai. His company provided basic medical care. But if he ended
needing hospital admission, he would need to find the money by himself, which was not cheap. He said in su
case he would have to go back to Pakistan. I learnt he was a cricketer and soon got into an in-depth discussi
about his swing bowling. We got so involved that he passed my destination without realising it. But we we
happy talking about something we both loved.

My niece worked as a teacher in a special school, and her husband in a software company. They had t
most loving seven-year-old daughter. In their apartment, both security guards I met there were from Pakist
earning less than the taxi driver.

In the evening we walked to a children's park by a lake. Here we met a father with his child with ADHD.
My niece got talking to him. He worked in a low-paid job as an immigrant worker and was yet to find any
help with their son's schooling. My niece gave him some advice about how to go around it.

Dubai had over 8 million immigrant workers, over 88% of the country's population. Most worked in
low- paid jobs, living alone in cramped accommodations, trying to save money to send to their families in
their country. UAE government did not release official poverty level data. UAE was one of the top ten
wealthiest countries in the world, and yet 20% of the population here lived in poverty.

Next day we went to drop off my grand-niece at her school. Later, in the supermarket, I met with
workers from the Philippines and in the coffee shop with workers from Bangladesh, all sharing similar stories.
Low paid immigrant workers did not have to worry about the schooling of their children. They could not
afford to bring over their families to UAE from their native countries. Visiting them every couple of years was
the best they could do.

Speaking to them, I found not only they were treated as a second-class citizen but almost as dirt. A
local man got away with anything, but immigrants needed to watch every step. The authority always held
their passports. A worker at the coffee shop told us recently his mother was seriously ill in Bangladesh. But
he did not get his passport back for over a week from them to go to visit her. By the time he got his passport,
his mother had passed away!

After spending two wonderful days with my most loving grand-niece and niece, it was time to leave.
On the way back, surprise, surprise, the taxi driver was also from Pakistan, an opening batsman this time!
We had a pleasant journey talking cricket back to the airport.

Sleeping in an igloo under the Aurora Greenland

February / March 2020

Five days before travelling to Greenland, I broke my left wrist after slipping while playing badminton. As I went down, trying to protect my already damaged skull, I fell on my wrist and passed out. When I came around, they had called an ambulance. In agony, I checked myself and knew I had broken my wrist (confirmed by an x-ray following return from Greenland). The ambulance crew wanted to take me to the hospital for x-ray, etc. But I refused and signed some papers. I knew if they put a plaster on my wrist, there was no way I could survive the winter temperature of -40°C in Greenland. I dosed myself with painkillers plus anti-inflammatory drugs and bought some wrist support.

I had wanted to visit Greenland in the winter. Travel Company said, before the end of February flight disruptions was frequent and not guaranteed because of weather. Although next to Canada, there were no flights from there. My plan to visit my daughter working there, after my Greenland tour, had to be via Copenhagen.

My Bristol flight was delayed, so for the connecting flight to Copenhagen, I ran the length of massive Amsterdam Schiphol. Not fun with heavy Sorrel winter boots on and the North Pole jacket plus my rook sac on my back! I just made the last flight to Copenhagen in time.

The Greenland flight was in the morning, so I spent the night on a bench at Copenhagen Airport - the only airport open 24 hours a day. Nearby, a man was reading an Israeli Newspapers headlining Netanyahu's corruption. Over coffee, we talked. He was an Israeli journalist and like many, hated right-wing politics going on there. Three Gambians were going back home. They worked for NATO. I talked about my last year's visit to Banjul and Farafenni - they were delighted.

Greenland, the world's largest island, was nine times larger than the UK with a population of only 56,000. One third lived in Nuuk; it's capital on the south-west coast. Permanent ice sheet covered 81% of the country. All the towns and smaller settlements were along its ice-free coast, concentrated along the west coast. Arctic people, from what was now Canada, at intervals have inhabited Greenland for at least 4,500 years.

Kangerlussuaq

Four and a half hour's flight to Kangerlussuaq arrived in the middle of an ice field just before midday. The pilot announced weather outside was bright and sunny with a ground temperature of only -30°C. It was the only international airport in Greenland, built during the 1941 US occupation. Kangerlussuaq had a population of about 500, most working for the airport or in the tourist trade.

Our arctic truck, with wire netting, took me to Old Camp hotel, 2km outside the airport, originally a shelter for the workers building the airport and was the regular first-time settlement of Kangerlussuaq. In the middle of an ice field, with a meter of ice and snow on the ground, this old-fashioned lodge, with narrow beds, shared toilet and kitchen was charming and intimate.

Old camp hotel

Immediately after check-in, I left for a five-hour tour to Inner Icecap. Kangerlussuaq, in Arctic Circle, has very little annual rainfall and was always dry with bright sunshine. We drove through frozen Watson River, and many frozen lakes until we stopped briefly by the frozen Long Lake. In this icy wonderland, impossible to imagine, herds of reindeer gathered by this lake in the summer.

We stopped next with a view of Russell Glacier. Because of climate change, this glacier in the last few years had widespread surface melt, worst on record for the past 125 years. The guide said even in the last five years the glacier has receded by almost 1 km. Receding of the glacier was also exposing the subglacial methane sink, releasing a high concentration of methane, a potent greenhouse gas, in the atmosphere.

Russell Glacier

Nearby on the ice slopes were several reindeer, only females with thin antlers in the winter. Soon we came across a few massive Musk-Oxes. Standing 1.5m tall with curved horns, they dug with their hooves for mosses and lichens beneath the ice.

Inland Icecap Soon we were by the spectacular Inland Ice Cap. Inland Ice Cap comprised thousands of years of ice. Measuring 600km from East to West and 1800km from north to south, in its central part the Inland Ice Cap was 3.5km deep. It held about 1/10th of all freshwater in the world, and if this ice sheet melted, as threatened by climate change, sea level around the world would rise by about 6 metres.

Inland Icecap

Our guides allowed a maximum of half an hour trek on the Icecap. I had to contain myself against the more
llenging section of the trek on slippery ice without crampons. I stopped after 100m and immersed myself in
vista. I could not risk further damaging my broken, painful wrist.

We stopped briefly on our return journey, at the wreckage of three of US military jet planes that crashed
968 in poor weather. Surprisingly, all the pilots had survived by parachute and then sheltering in the ice till
t day before being rescued.

We drove in the evening to the only restaurant outside the town and had a lovely dish of musk-ox and
deer meat. I learnt from a Danish couple I was sitting with, their daughter, a newly qualified doctor, was
king in Nuuk where they were going next. For any major problem, from Nuuk, they sent patients to
enhagen via Kangerlussuaq by flight.

Later a group left for a Northern Lights tour. I stayed in to catch some decent sleep after almost 48hrs. As I
tched off the light, through the window was the Northern Lights, dancing lazily. One Australian, I met here,
been to Iceland twice without seeing the Aurora. I knocked on his door and asked him to pull the curtain. Not
he brightest colour, but I watched the magic of lights well after midnight.

g Sledging (in minus mid-forties) As the sun was coming out at 7-30am while waiting at the small
eption area for my transport, the receptionist said the outside temperature was -43°C. I left by an arctic
k for a dog sledge ride. Even with all layers of clothing I had, I was shivering. Luckily they kitted us out with
fur outer clothing and a pair of sealskin gloves, perfect splint for my broken wrist. Walking towards the dogs'
area, we could hear them, excited with the prospect of a run soon.

In Greenland, 12-13 dogs pulled the sledge on long leashes in a formation like sun rays. Unlike in
and, where they pulled from two lines of chains. Dogs ran, pulling the sledge with three of us, a touring couple
myself, and the sledge driver sitting in front. The temperature on the icefield was in the minus mid-forties,
with the wind chill probably around minus fifty. After an hour of sledging, we stopped briefly
hot chocolate.

Our sledge driver was a 66-year-old lady. She had been doing this job for 35 years and loved it. She
d near the coast, about 80km away, and came by herself with the dogs and sledge for 3-4 months every
ter. Her husband ran a small tour company at home. They have two daughters in their 40s and have
grandchildren aged 4 to 20 years. I learnt from her there was no hospital in Kangerlussuaq, only one
se. Seriously ill were transferred by helicopter to Nuuk over a 300km distance.

She said that the Greenland dogs were pure breeds, introduced by the Inuits. They fed the dogs once
ay after the day's tours. Dogs lived outside in all weathers, and only the puppies and their young mothers

had a hut shelter for the night. She loved her animals. These working dogs lived only 5-6 years!

She was wearing a lovely fur coat. The couple from our group came back after talking to fellow tourists and asked her about what was that lovely fur that she was wearing which did not look like seal fur. She answered, with no emotion, it was from one of her old dogs! Nothing left to waste.

After another hour of the dog sledge, my toes, fingers and nose tip were in serious risk of frostbite. Soon I said goodbye to the lady. She gave me a warm hug.

In the late afternoon, I left for a Tundra tour to see the landscape and possibly some animals. Near the airport, the guide pointed to the only orphanage on the west coast of Greenland, with around 100 children.

Next, we drove to the top of a mountain by an unmanned weather station. Greenland weather

station was one of the most important in the world. What happened with the weather here predicted the weather patterns and ocean currents in the Atlantic and then for the rest of the world.

We drove further before stopping by a site with a beautiful panorama of the magical ice world. Frozen mountains and rivers lay below and all around us. In the north, at a distance, the view of Inland Ice Cap was breathtaking. Soon came the gorgeous sunset and coloured the icy mountains like a dream world.

In the restaurant in the evening, this time they served a lovely buffet with varieties of meat including musk-ox and reindeers cooked different ways and also many types of fish and prawns. Most interestingly, they offered a small portion of raw blubber of a whale which frequented the gorge around here in the summer!

Again the Northern Lights were in the sky, but not strong enough to keep me awake. Next morning, my last morning in Kangerlussuaq, there was no water in the hostel and no chance of any hot drink.

After a cup of coffee at the airport, I boarded the Air Greenland plane. A pilot and one air hostess welcomed us on board. The pilot could easily have been a stand-up comedian. Before anything else, he gave us a five- minute comedy sketch inside the 28 seater plane!

Ilulissat

Only forty minutes' flight to Ilulissat. In the sunshine, it was only -25°C here but felt much colder. The air was moist on the coast and wind from the sea added to that. My hotel was on the shore of a frozen sea, now with a narrow channel of broken ice through which only a few boats sailed.

From the hotel balcony

We left for a brief tour of this town of only 4600 people. Nearby on the coastline was Ilulissat Hospital with the best outside view in the world. Patients came from all along the west coast. Healthcare, like in Denmark, was free for all, including prescription costs and travel costs. Ilulissat hospital however treated only intermediate cases, others were referred to Nuuk Hospital. I decided to go there in the next couple of days to find out more.

Zion Church, built in the 18th century, stood nearby. Christianity was first brought to Greenland in 1000AD by the Norse settlers. But they disappeared from the country after a while because of the harsh climate. Originally named Jakobshavn, Ilulissat was established about 300yrs back. In early 18th century, Norse returned to start a new Danish colony, with the prime purpose of converting the country's residents to Christianity. We sat outside for a while, watching the huge icebergs in the ice fjord. Ilulissat was unique in its location at the mouth of the World Heritage site of Disco Bay and Ilulissat Ice Fjord.

At this point, for some reason, my broken wrist became agonisingly painful. My layers of arctic gloves were not good enough for the cold. I left the group and slowly walked to the only store selling warm clothing and bought myself a pair of sealskin gloves. They were perfect - warm and excellent replacement for a plaster cast.

Sermermiut point

Next morning I went for a hike to Sermermiut point, a 5 km return. Ilulissat with its picturesque coloured houses shined in the morning sunlight against the icy background. The tradition of brightly coloured houses began here, a practical way of indicating the function of each building.

After crossing several sledge dog pens, we left the town and walked across an icefield. Below us lay the Disco Bay with breathtaking views of giant icebergs.

Further down, close to the bay, were the remnants of an Inuit settlement, inhabited from as early as 600BC. Last remaining residents abandoned this place in 1850 and moved to Ilulissat. Nearby was a warning sign for a tsunami. Calving of massive icebergs, because of expansion and shrinking of the ice cap, can and cause a tsunami. The guide said mini tsunamis were frequent, but an enormous iceberg toppling over could cause a wave of 20m high with no warning. We kept an eye on the fjord from then on!

Walking down towards the shore, we came to a small gap between two large rocks. We came up through there to an unimaginable viewing point for glaciers and icebergs. Known as Nakkaavik, this place was out of this world. Combination of the ice sheet and fast-moving glacier calving into a fjord is a phenomenon that only occurred in Greenland and Antarctica. Flowing from Jakobshavn Glacier, 35 billion tonnes of icebergs calved here into the surrounding Disco Bay every year!

We sat there watching in disbelief as icebergs, more enormous than several houses, broke off from the glacier edge into the bay, known as calving. Some of us were getting too close to the cliff edge to take pictures when the guide reminded us Nakkaavik translated as 'the place to fall'. This was the spot where in the past, the elderly would throw themselves off the cliff during times of hardship to make way for the younger members of the village.

Unfortunately, after an hour surrounded by nature's most magical landscape, we had to return.

sco Bay

on I got picked up for a boat ride in the frozen Disco Bay. From the port, our boat followed a narrow annel of broken ice in the icy sea with a fantastic view of Ilulissat above. It was -35°C but, with the wind owing, at least five degrees lower, however, I had my sealskin gloves on.

The best view was from the open area of this tiny fishing boat. The problem was, I could not take ctures with those gloves on without the risk of dropping the camera or my mobile phone. Fortunately, the at's assistant captain Andreas took many pictures for me. We sailed surrounded by icebergs of many es, some like a tiny hill, others only the size of a house. We spent a wonderful two hours in the frozen y, only seeing rare boats here were catching halibuts with lines. Seagulls rested on the floating ice after eir meals. How did they survive this cold with only their feathers!

Andreas had never pictures taken of him on his boat, neither had he taken any photographs of the rea. He snapped away, and I promised to send some of his pictures to him by email.

Back at the port, the usual jetty was not available because a large ship had anchored there on its daily oyage. We anchored next to a site with the walkway high above us. It was tricky climbing up the 3m rail fixed o a vertical wall with only one working hand. But with help from Andreas and others, I managed without alling in the frozen sea - a most wonderful day.

In the evening, the hotel had its weekly Greenlandic buffet. People from the town regularly came for his. I was hungry after having no time for lunch with all the hikes and the boat tour. There was a fantastic

assortment of halibut, salmon and other small fish, prawns, lobster claws and mussels with caviar and a
delicious suaasat, meat soup with vegetables. Then there was whale blubber, smoked whale, reindeer meat a
musk-ox meat chowder. And finally some strawberries out of nowhere. I gorged myself. It was my kind
heaven. Afterwards, came the Greenlandic 'flaming' dessert coffee, set alight before serving, made with coff
whiskey, Kahlua, Grand Marnier, and whipped cream. I only sipped a little for taste and then to bed.

Sleeping in the Igloo under the Northern Lights

Next morning, I got ready for my lifetime dream - to sleep in an igloo.

The first task, however, was to get properly kitted out for the snowmobile ride to 15 km outside the to
The temperature was only around -30°C, but with the wind against us, it would be another 5-8 degrees bel
On top of my five layers of warm clothes and North Pole jacket, they fitted us with another outfit of wa
insulated overall, large boots, and a crash helmet. It was difficult to move with that extra 7-8 kg gear. By car,
arrived in an ice field on the outer part of the town. Looking like a spaceman, I walked to our snowmobile. D
in the pens nearby looked with no interest - they had seen many like this before.

I had so far walked carefully on the ice. There was no way I could sit on the pillion seat behind the dri
as I could hold nothing with my left hand. The compromise was for me to sit in the open cart used for bags pul
behind the snowmobile - no problem. But trying to get into the cart, unable to use my left hand, I slipped a
fell again on the same wrist. My sealskin protected the fall somehow, but I was in agony. I could have easily
out a cry, but I didn't. Only a few drops of tears flowed out and froze immediately against my cheek. Holding
to the side of the cart with my right hand, both my legs stretched against its wall, to stop me toppling over,
moved on.

Drive through beautiful mountain gorges, fully choked with ice and going sharply up and then down ag
on the snowmobile through the ravines was hair-raising and electrifying at the same time. But I was in too m
pain to appreciate the beauty of the surroundings. We arrived at a solitary wooden hut next to a frozen I
by midday. The charming views of six Igloos about 50m outside the shelter were the best analgesics for me
a while, but still, I dosed myself to a maximum amount of pain killers. Soon another two snowmobiles brou
more people. One of the snowmobiles dropped off its passengers and quickly drove back to rescue anot
snowmobile on the road a few kilometres back. Later I learnt it had overturned on the icy road and
passengers had fallen off. No one got hurt, but they needed help in restarting the engine.

After a quick cup of hot drink, they told us to check out our igloos in the warm sunlight.

I walked to my igloo and then crawled on my knees through a 3m tunnel in the ice. A seal fur hung
like a sort of curtain at the end of the tunnel. Beyond the seal fur, I stood up and sat on the ice block base of
the igloo, about one metre above the tunnel. The tunnel was below the level of the base to keep the icy air
out! With a dome of ice blocks about two metres from its base, a seal fur spread on the ice and a warm
sleeping bag, inside the igloo looked cosy although cramped. Even in the bright sunshine outside, it was
freezing.

After a brief lunch, the rest of the group left for a short hike towards the frozen mountain. I went with one guide for another ride on a snowmobile through a breathtaking and riveting drive for another 15 m through iced and narrow gorges.

We arrived by a single hut used by the fishermen at the fjord next to the mouth of the mighty ermeq Kujalleq glacier. From this glacier, the majority of Greenland's and all of Ilulissat's massive icebergs merge. A major international report on Greenland released last December concluded that because of limate change it was losing ice seven times faster than it was during the 1990s. In 2019 Greenland lost 532 igatonnes of ice - the equivalent of adding 1.5mm to global mean sea levels, approximately 40% of the verage rise in one year. The guide said in recent years because of climate change height of the glacier had educed significantly. Massive calving rarely occurred now.

This deserted part of the world was beyond belief in its allure. By the single tiny hut were several packs of ledge dogs. Fishermen came here on dog sledges from Ilulissat over 30km distance. They made holes in the ce and left a lengthy fishing line with multiple hooks overnight. Next morning when they came back they pulled ut several 150-200kg halibuts to sell in the town.

Soon we returned to our hut as the evening closed in. Of the nine visitors in the group, most were couples. Ve sat in the compact room chatting over a dinner of bread, rice and hearty reindeer stew. I learnt from the ireenlandic guide lady sitting next to me that she played volleyball for the town's team. She added popular ports in Greenland was football, handball, volleyball and skiing.

Our guides had already let us chose our bunk beds in the hut if we needed to come back from the igloo. But it was too early to go to bed. I talked to a Danish man from Copenhagen who had brought his father for his lifetime dream of sleeping in an Igloo. Suddenly the Northern light appeared in the sky. We put on our overalls and boots to rush outside.

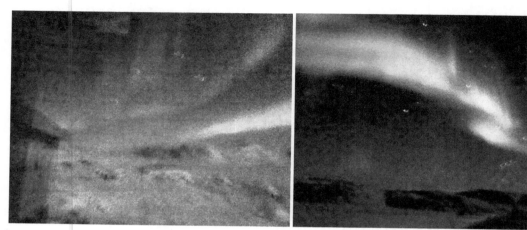

Over the massive frozen lake and the mountains in the background, Aurora danced for us, changing colour all the time. But it was too cold, -40°C, to stay outside for more than a few minutes. Not for the first time I wished had a better camera. For the next three hours, we alternated between going out and rushing back inside to watch through the window. The magic in the sky lighting up the icy world was beyond my description.

By now it was after 11 pm, and everyone so far has been delaying getting into their igloos. Now one by one, couples picked up courage and left for their igloos with headlamps on. It was only me, and the father and the son left in the hut, chatting. The son was a bit drunk by now and kept saying what a wonderful father he was lucky to have. Soon one couple returned from the igloo - too cold and cramped!

All evening I have been avoiding drinking coffee/tea or water and visited the toilet before going inside my igloo. Inside, one wrist out of action, getting into the sleeping bag in that cramped space was more than difficult. But once I got in the sleeping bag, there was no way I could pull the zip up with one hand, so I left it open.

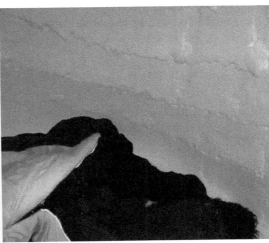

Surprisingly, inside the igloo was warmer by at least 10°C than outside and got even warmer with my body
at. I fell asleep briefly. But only after an hour or so, I woke up with a desperate need to go to the toilet! I held
 for another hour but could wait no longer. Intense cold and old aged bladder does not go well together! I
d to go back to the hut. The father and the son were still talking, and the father had decided not to sleep in
 e igloo after all! All the others had already come back from their igloos; I was the last one. I did not find
ough enthusiasm to go back to the igloo and slept in a bunk bed in the warm hut. Aurora was still there but
ly faint now.

After breakfast, we waited for our snowmobile to come and pick us up. Soon there was a message there
ll be a delay. The ground temperature was below -40°C. The engine oil had partly frozen, and the engine was
t starting. Better to have the problem before the start than in the middle on our way back through the icy
ountain!

An hour later, our snowmobiles arrived. We returned through breathtaking scenery, and by now, I had
me practice on the cart. With the sun behind, I thoroughly enjoyed the tableau in ice and the adventurous
de. Back in the hotel after a welcome hot shower, I slept all afternoon in my warm bed under a blanket.

At dinner, I sat with two Inuit gentlemen, both government inspectors for fisheries of all the towns and
ettlements on the west coast, maintaining EEC standards. Fishing accounted for over 90% of Greenland's
xports. Greenland was an independent country and a protectorate of Denmark. The USA had been interested

in Greenland for a long time, initially, for its strategic location in the Arctic Circle. The United States had bui
secret nuclear-powered base on the Greenland ice sheet. In 1968, a B-52G, with four nuclear bombs aboa
crashed into the North Star bay here attempting an emergency landing. The resulting fire caused extens
radioactive contamination, and one of the Hydrogen bombs remains lost.

More recently the US had shown interest in tapping hydrocarbons off the Greenlandic coast and
proposed to buy Greenland. As recently as six months back, Trump had restated the same interest. My frie
at the table proudly stated with a smile, Greenland had refused such offers.

Next morning the plan was to go by snowmobile to a remote fishing community of about 60 people, 20
outside Ilulissat on the coast. Unfortunately, the tour was cancelled as the ground temperature was -43°C an
was not possible to travel safely. Instead, I walked to the hospital to find out more about the health care

Hospital with the best view in the world

facilities. A nurse brought me to the chief of staff. But he was in a hurry to go to an urgent meeting with
Government officials regarding the emerging problem of Corona Virus. The nurse showed me around.
hospital had seven doctors, 24 beds, half of them were for psychiatric patients. She said Greenland had a h
rate of alcoholism and related health issues. It had a patient hotel facility as many came from far away
helicopter or plane. They did intermediate procedures, dealt with simple fractures and caesarean sectic
Doctors, nurses and other staff all came from Denmark for a period of between 8 weeks to 2 years, if they las
that long.

Afterwards, I walked by the fjord, enjoying the beauty of the frozen world. Back at the hotel, the TV
screen was full of Covid-19 news. My original plan was to visit my daughter and grandchildren in Canadian
winter via Copenhagen. But with the spread of Corona Virus and the cancellation of many flights, I talked
to my daughter and agreed to get back to the UK instead.

After my flight from Ilulissat to Kangerlussuaq, we had had a few hours before the Copenhagen
flight. At the coffee and restaurant place, I sat by the window. Opposite me was a lady working on her
laptop, but she shut her computer and wanted to talk to me.

She was a Danish social and cultural science researcher, returning after spending a few weeks in a
rural community. Her special area was teenage children. She described how imposing the Danish way of life
and culture had affected the local Inuit population. Inuits traditionally had powerful family bonds, but the
colonist's way had been to promote the growth of individuals. Depression, often leading to suicides, were

common amongst teenagers. The suicide rate [in] Greenland was one of the highest in the world. Introduction of alcohol to the indigenous populati[on] had a devastating effect over the last two centuries. I shared with her stories of the same issues I had co[me] across with the 'Aboriginal' community in Australia.

After a while, I walked to the only empty sm[all] souvenir shop outside the airport building to buy an Inuit children's storybook for my grandchildren. They d[id] not have any. I talked to the Inuit shopkeeper about what [I] learnt earlier from the Danish lady. She added i[n the] country, 88% were Greenlandic Inuit, including Danish-Inuit mixed, and the remaining 12% were mainly D[an]es. Over 95% of the population were Protestant Christians; [t]he nomadic Inuits were traditionally Shamanistic [pe]ople used to believe in Shamanism before Christianity was [f]orcefully introduced 200 years back. But most In[ui]ts still believed in some Shaman ideas. She openly added [o]pportunities for Inuits always came second to an[y D]anish people who came over.

She proudly announced that her daughter w[as] expecting, and soon she would be a grandmother. I told her [a]bout my joy of making up stories for my grandchi[ldr]en. She recalled an Inuit story she had grown up with.

'Sea Mother was the patron of all sea crea[tu]res and provider of food for the Inuit people. At one time, [fi]shermen became greedy and were unneces[sari]ly killing animals more than they needed. Sea Mother [b]ecame angry and sheltered all the creatures [in h]er wild curly hair and dived under the sea to punish the [In]uits. With no catch, everyone was starving. [A]fter a few days, all of them came by the seashore and [p]romised Sea Mother not to be cruel to anim[al]s and kill unnecessarily except for what they needed to [s]urvive. Sea Mother released the creatures fro[m] her hair into the sea.'

A lesson for all [of] us in today's world?

Then Covid-19 came and [s]tarted exploring the world,

stopping m[e] from doing so.

Acknowledgement

I have been fortunate not only to travel all the seven continents but was also able to come close to many wonderful people who had kindly let me in their daily lives during my lifetime of travels.

Mostly being a solo traveller, I was also lucky to interact with my guides, drivers and their friends about their personal lives and hear about their opinion of their country and society.

I am deeply indebted to my colleagues in many countries for their unforgettable support and friendship during my volunteering around the world.

In my earlier days, I did not have a camera most of the time and am grateful for some of the freely available web photos. Later, to supplement my inexpensive camera photos, I was lucky to receive specialised images of the day from my tour companies such as of the scuba diving pictures, some of the Antarctic and North Pole photos and the Aurora in Tromso.

I must thank Laura and Andrew Tillotson for reminding me to check my English grammar.

I have tried my best to reduce the print cost (myself taking less than a dollar in royalty), I had to edit out many of the photos and chapters to minimise the page counts of the book. Hopefully, it still gives a glimpse of our beautiful world.

I am grateful for Rudi Hartono and 99Designs for their patience and a great help with the cover design.

Finally, I would like to acknowledge IngramSpark and Amazon Kindle service for their help in publishing this book and open to the public for reading my travel memoir.

'We looked for workers. We got people instead.' - Max Frisch

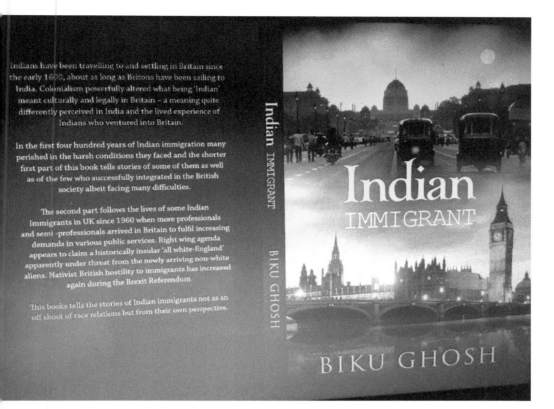

Indians have been travelling to and settling in Britain since the early 1600, about as long as Britons have been sailing to India. Colonialism powerfully altered what being 'Indian' meant culturally and legally in Britain – a meaning quite differently perceived in India and the lived experience of Indians who ventured into Britain.

In the first four hundred years of Indian immigration many perished in the harsh conditions they faced and the shorter first part of this book tells stories of some of them as well as of the few who successfully integrated in the British society albeit facing many difficulties.

The second part follows the lives of some Indian Immigrants in UK since 1960 when more professionals and semi-professionals arrived in Britain to fulfil increasing demands in various public services. Right wing agenda appears to claim a historically insular 'all white-England' apparently under threat from the newly arriving non-white aliens. Nativist British hostility to immigrants has increased again during the Brexit Referendum.

This books tells the stories of Indian immigrants not as an off shoot of race relations but from their own perspective.

Indian
IMMIGRANT

BIKU GHOSH

Indian
IMMIGRANT

BIKU GHOSH

Reviews :

- **Not Just for History Buffs--Shedding Light on Discrimination Against Immigrants! Ghosh skillfully intertwines stories within the collection through the use of close family relationships while shedding light on the harsh injustices and racial discrimination the immigrants faced.**
- **This is a fascinating read.**
- **Must read.**
- **Well written, really good read.**

Lightning Source UK Ltd.
Milton Keynes UK
UKHW051426251120
374034UK00004B/41

9 781838 1917